W9-CIJ-033

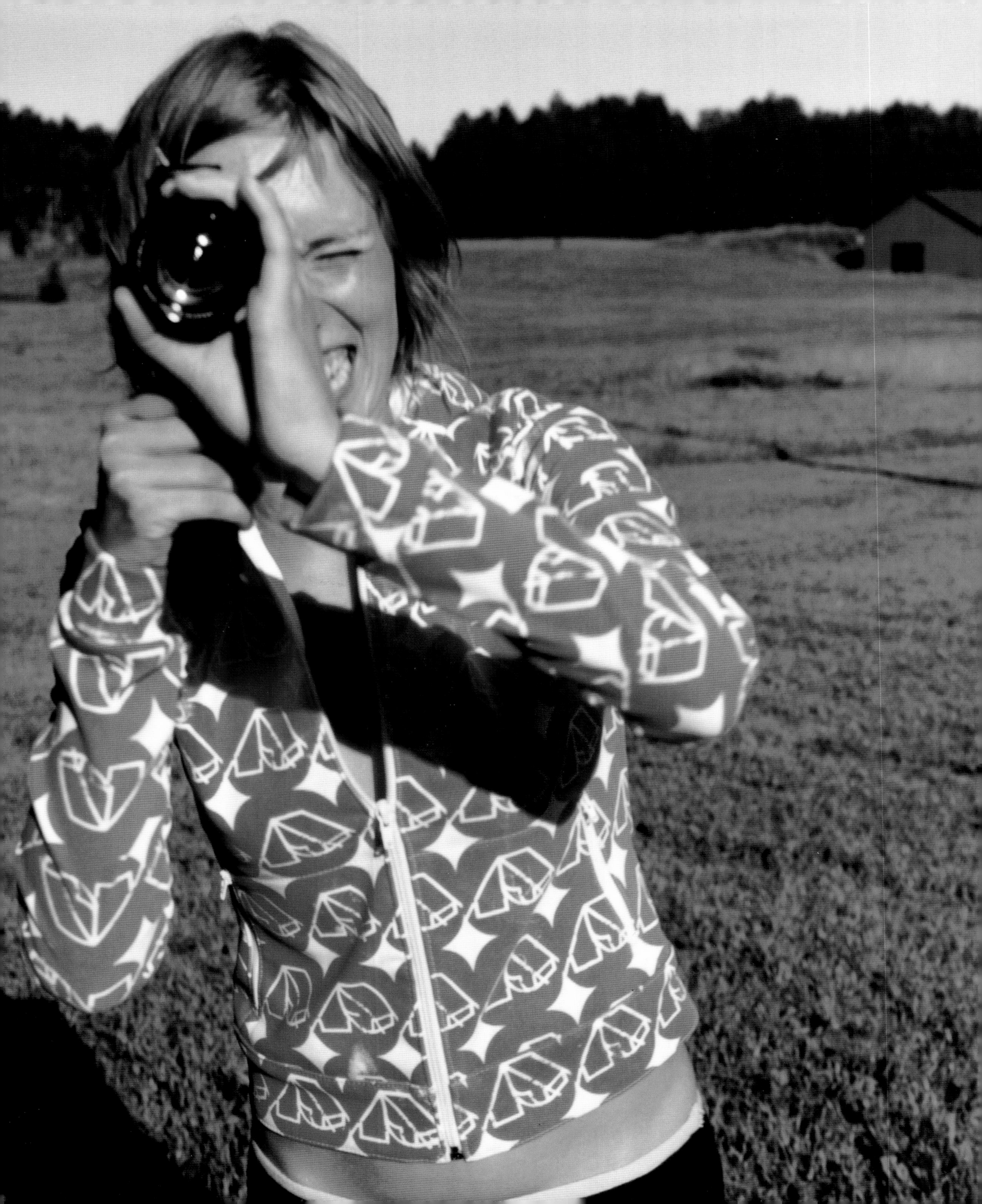

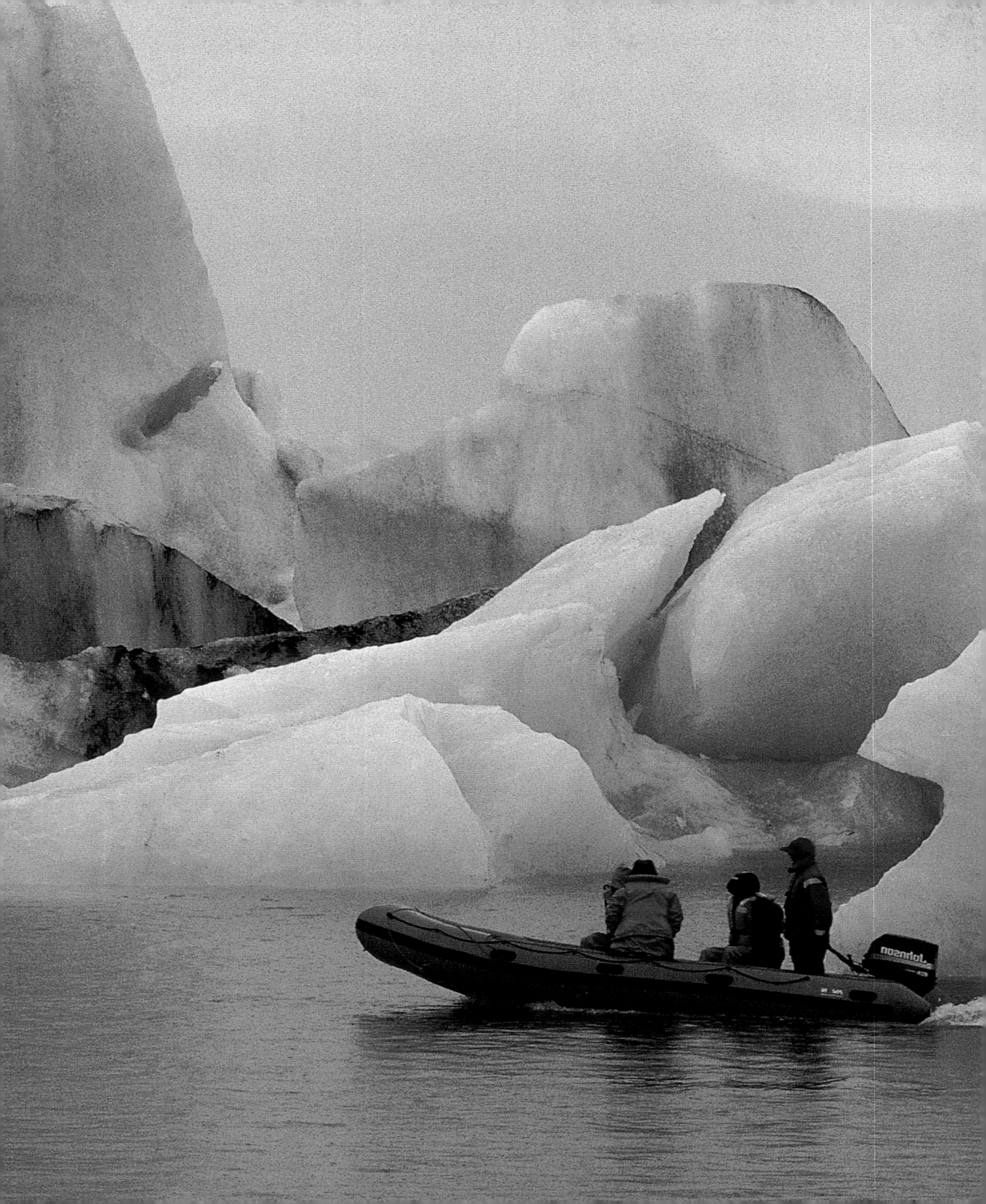

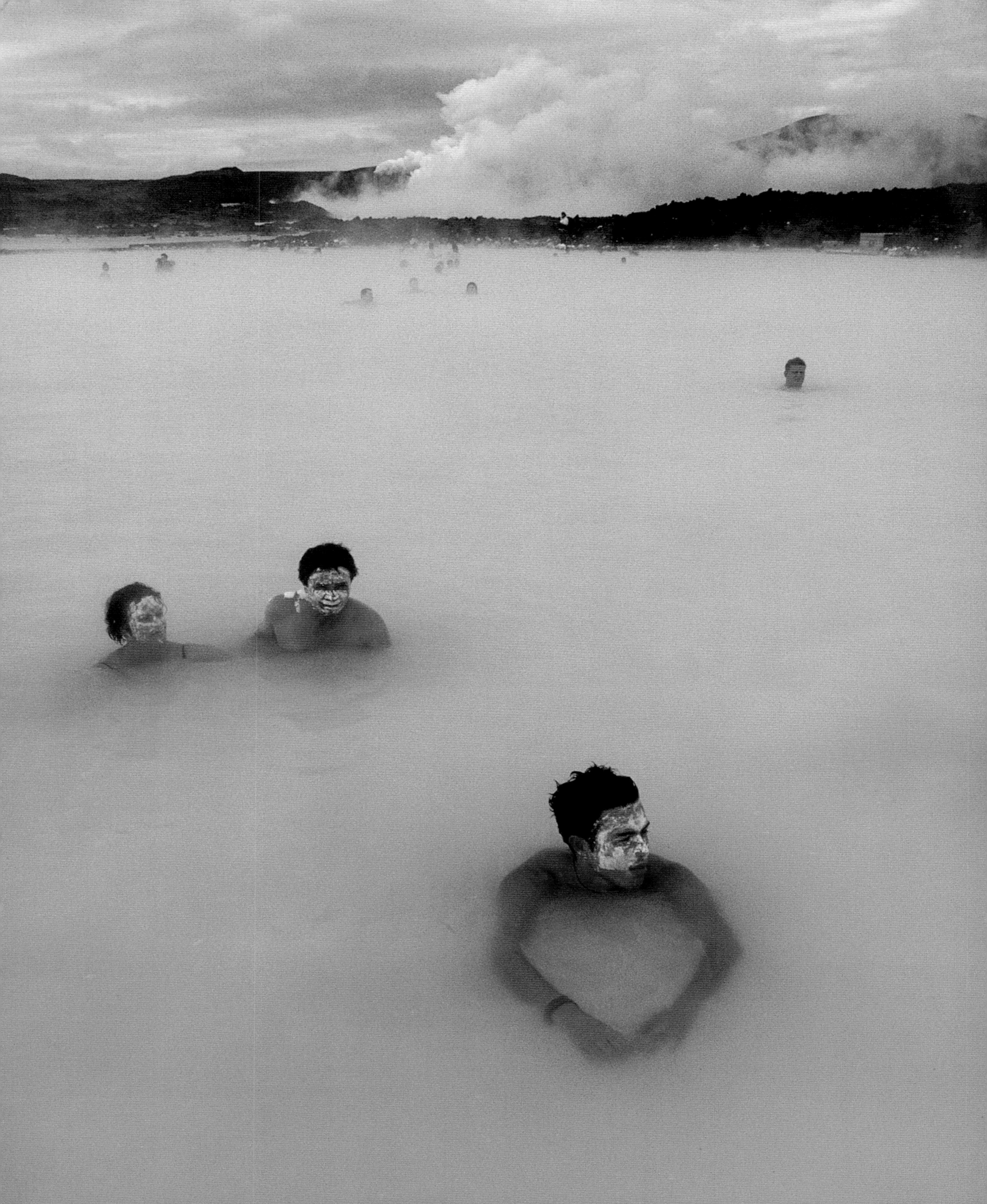

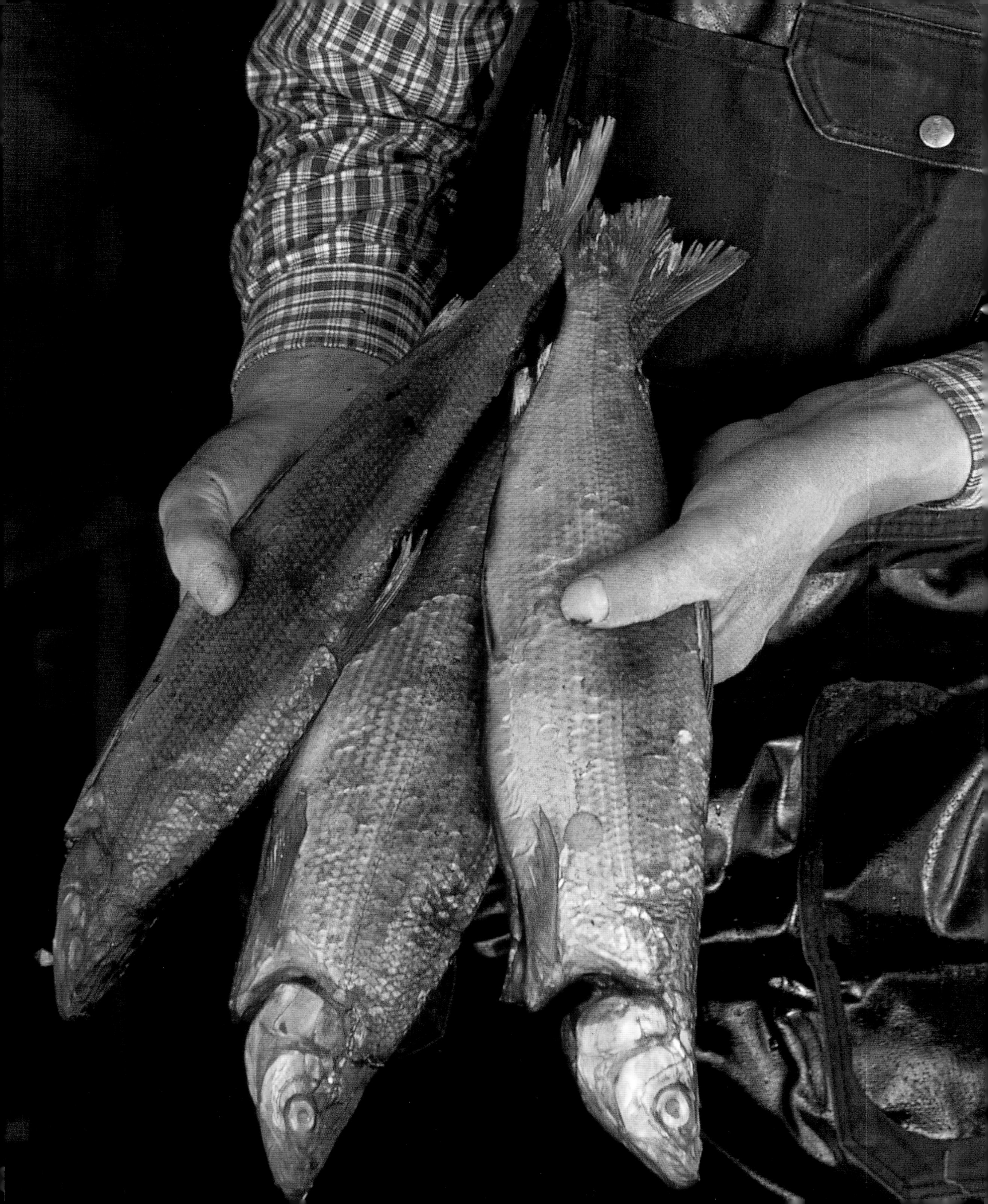

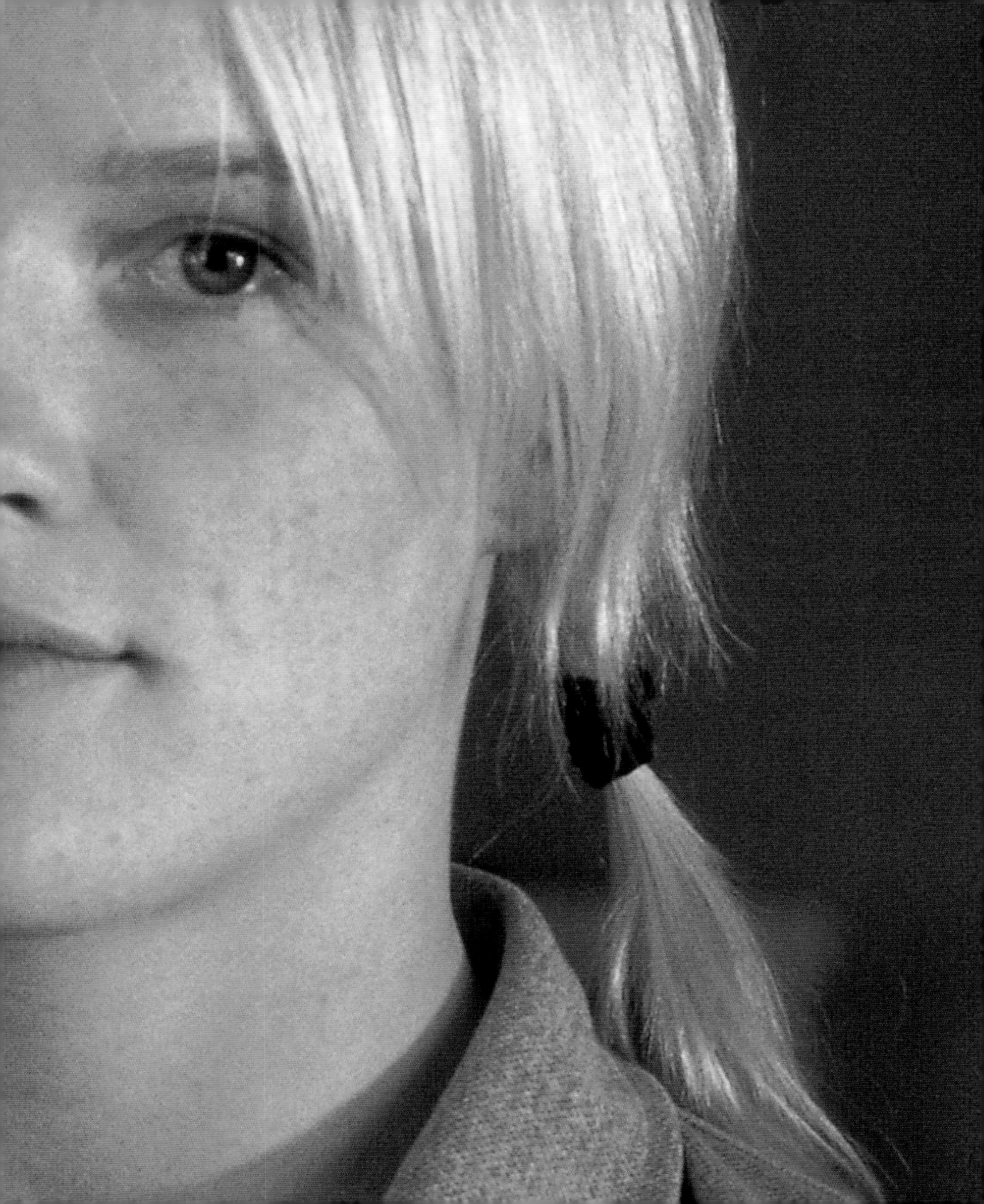

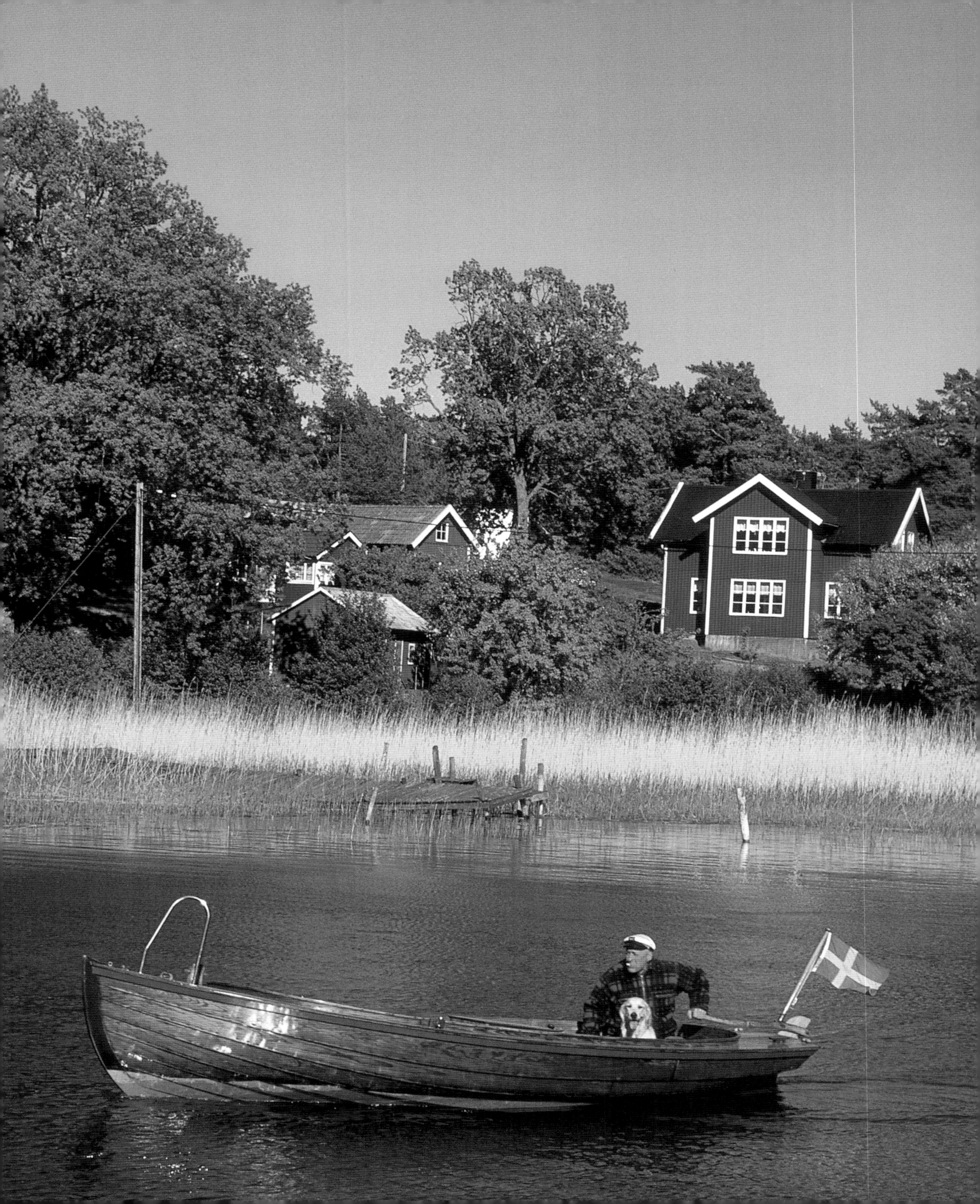

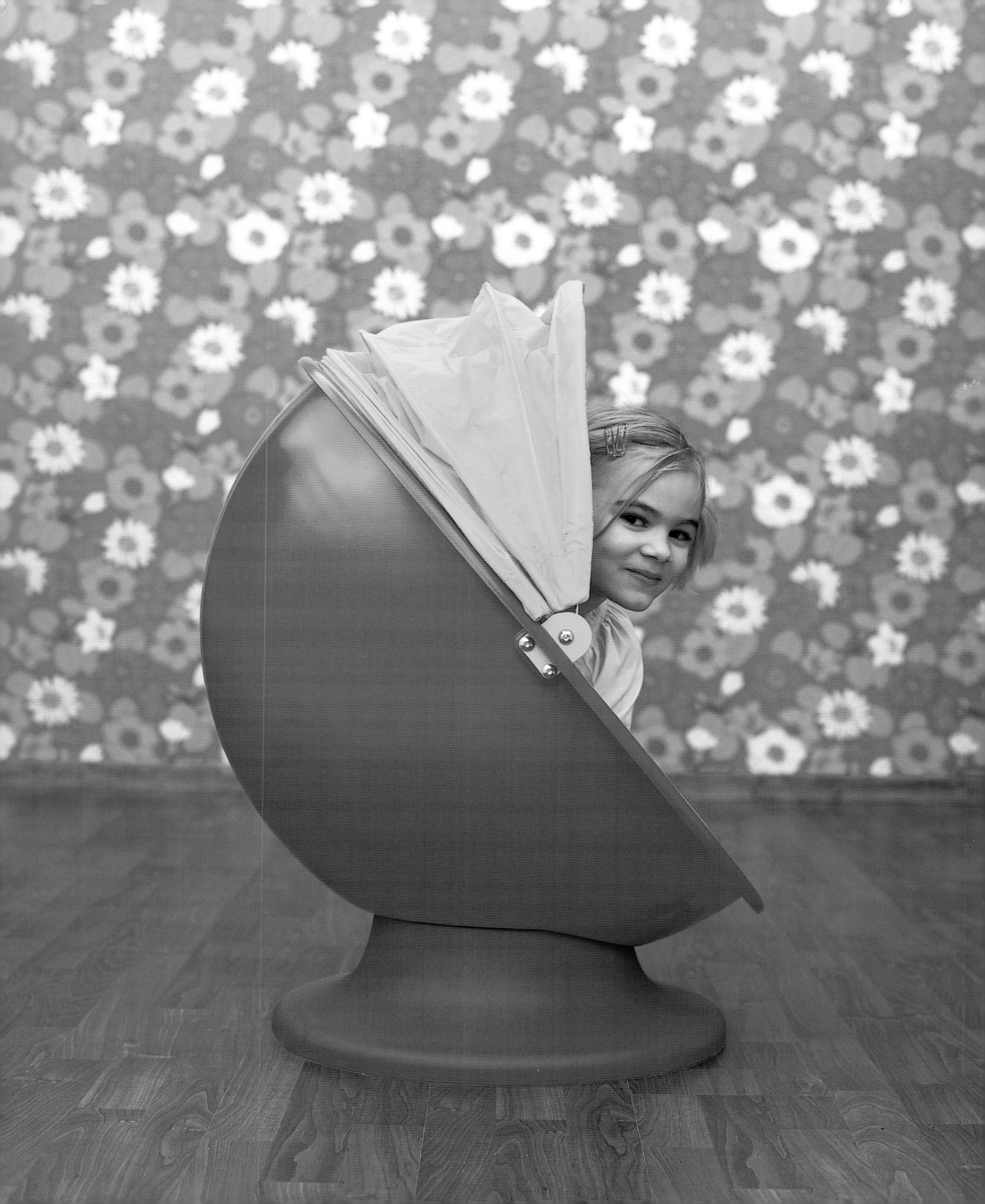

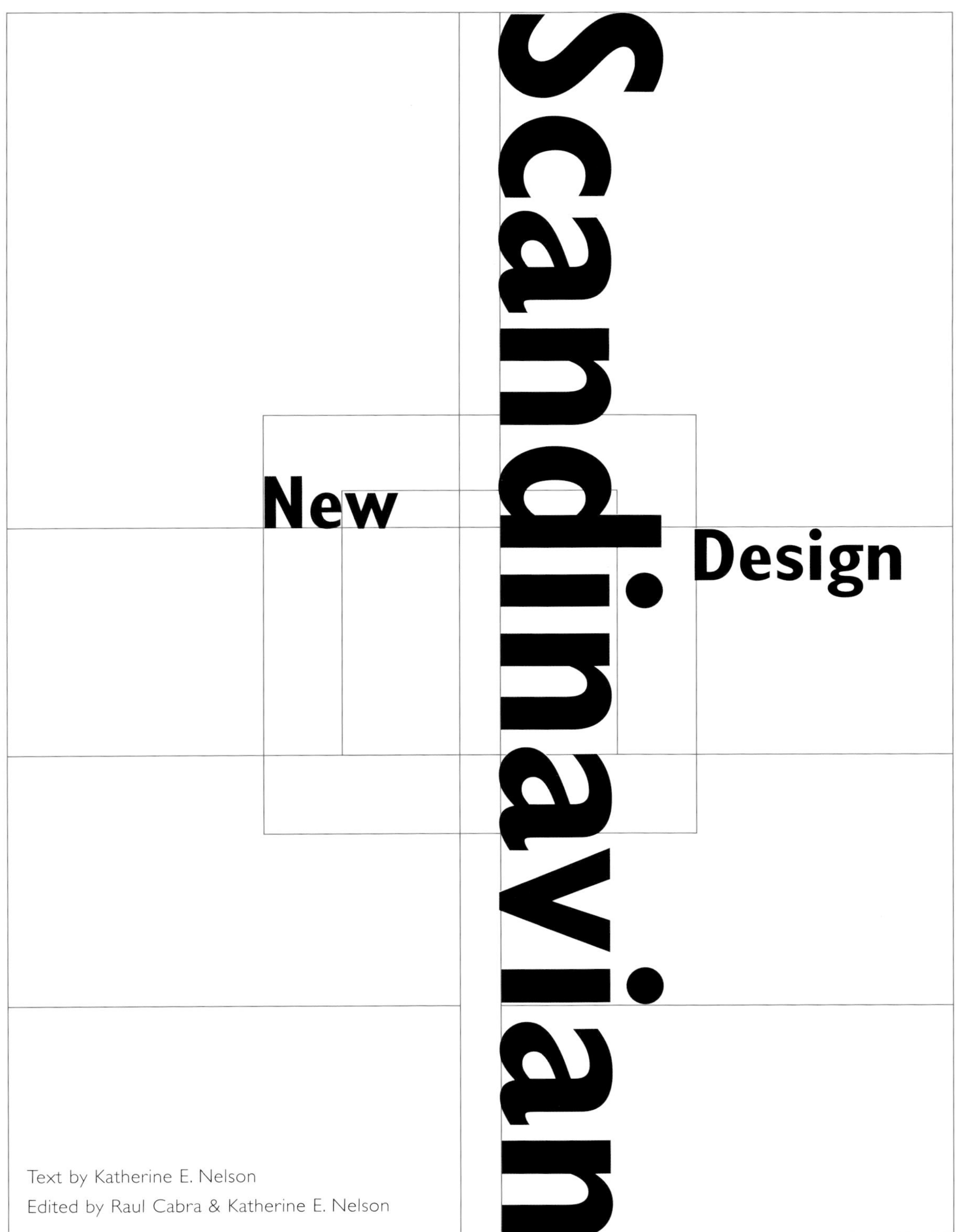

New Scandinavian Design

Text by Katherine E. Nelson

Edited by Raul Cabra & Katherine E. Nelson

CHRONICLE BOOKS

SAN FRANCISCO

EDITORS:
Raul Cabra
and Katherine E. Nelson

TEXT BY :
Katherine E. Nelson

CHRONICLE EDITOR:
Alan Rapp

COPY EDITOR:
Karen O'Donnell Stein

DESIGN:
Raul Cabra,
Jillian Moffett,
Piper Grimsrud,
Wesley Ito,
for Cabra Diseño,
San Francisco

PRODUCTION:
Piper Grimsrud,
Jillian Moffett

Text copyright
© 2004 Katherine E. Nelson.
All rights reserved. No part of this book may be reproduced in any form without written permission from the publisher.
Pages 262–265 and 271constitute a continuation of the copyright page.

Library of Congress Cataloging-in-Publication Data available.
ISBN 0-8118-4040-9

Manufactured in Hong Kong

Designed by Cabra Diseño, San Francisco

Distributed in Canada by Raincoast Books
9050 Shaughnessy Street
Vancouver, British Columbia V6P 6E5

10 9 8 7 6 5 4 3 2 1

Chronicle Books LLC
85 Second Street
San Francisco, California 94105
www.chroniclebooks.com

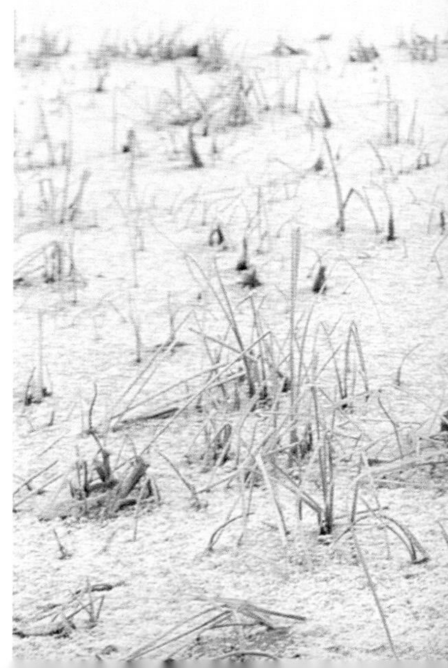

VISUAL ESSAY:
Ivana Helsinki, Telttatakki ("Tent Jacket"), Finland, (p. 1)
SAS Royal Hotel lobby in Copenhagen, Denmark (p. 2)
Jokulsarlon, Lagoon of Icebergs, Iceland, (p. 3)
The Blue Lagoon, Naturally heated water from geothermal power plant, near Reykjavik, Iceland, (p. 4)
Rune Wikstrom, legendary fisherman with smoked whitefish, Island of Moja, Sweden, (p. 5)
Staff, Grinda Wardshus historic hotel, Island of Grinda, Sweden, (p. 6)
Kjell Karlsson, retired fisherman with dog in Sodermoja, Sweden (p. 7)
IKEA/PS LÖMSK, Swivel chair, Sweden,(p. 8)

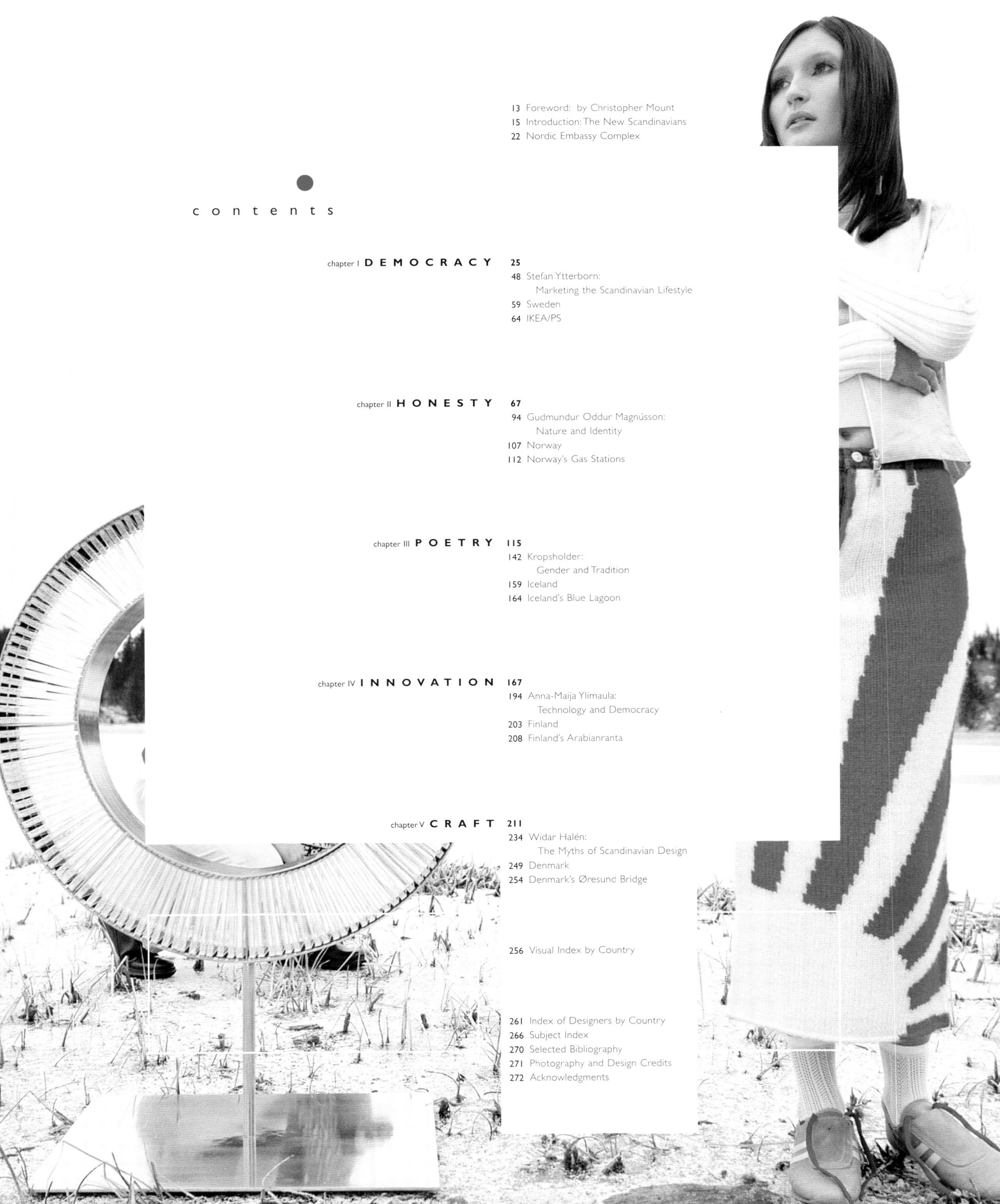

contents

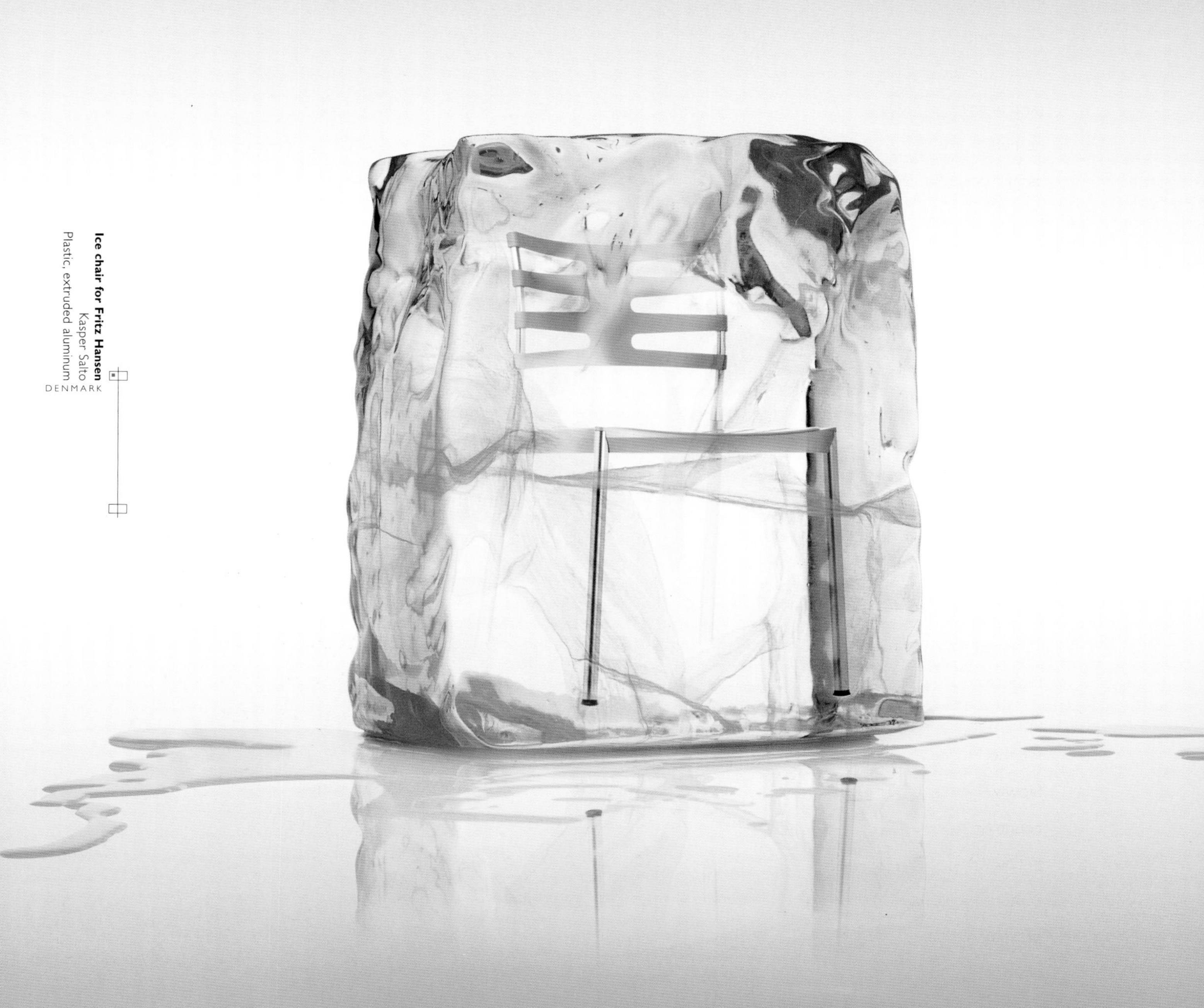

Ice chair for Fritz Hansen
Kasper Salto
Plastic, extruded aluminum
DENMARK

Foreword

By Christopher Mount

Perhaps surprisingly, many of the ideals that are so often associated with Scandinavian design even today were established in the work of seminal pre–World War II designers and propagandists such as Ellen Key, Gregor Paulsson, Alvar Aalto, and Kaare Klint. Among them the most significant (and ironically the least well known outside of her homeland, Sweden) is arguably Key. In her series of essays entitled "Beauty for All," she matures many of the themes of William Morris and adapts them to an industrial, more forward-looking and ultimately more realistic perspective. She stresses the importance of the domestic environment, individual taste, and beauty in our surroundings. But she also encourages the use of "bright colors," emphasizing affordability and underscoring that most Scandinavian of concepts: truthfulness in the use of materials.

The humanism that characterized Key's ideas of pre-war Scandinanian design soon grew to define Scandinavian design's outward identity after World War II. The succeeding period of the late 1970s and 1980s was a nadir for most industrial design—not just in Scandinavia but internationally—and this lull seems to have created a necessary and healthy gestation period for the Scandinavian nations and their young designers. Slowly, but notably since the early 1990s, the Nordic countries have begun to reestablish themselves as competitors in the international marketplace and as creative centers for all sorts of design. The wonderful new work presented in this book illustrates a much greater globalism and technological savvy on the part of the designers, as well as a greater propensity for experimentation with new materials, than seen in earlier generations. In addition, a new sort of pluralism has taken hold, which allows the designers greater freedom to express themselves and, in some cases, to test the boundaries of what was thought to be "Scandinavian good taste." In many respects, contemporary design in this region is once again ahead of its time. Fifty years ago we got our first look at what would become Scandinavian Modern; now we are again taking a peek at the future of the domestic interior.

This handsome book celebrates this important changing of the guard, a new kind of Scandinavian design, which is less insular and perhaps even less conscious of its own history. It illustrates new vibrant work from nations less well known for their products, such as Iceland and Norway. It also records an important period, when the great generations of designers of the 1950s and 1960s have for the most part passed and the younger generation can feel a weight lifted from their shoulders, freeing them from an often-intimidating past. Variety and inventiveness seem to be operative words. However, this is a book filled with thoughtful, clever, humorous, and, most important, intelligent design. Thankfully for us, humanism remains a strong consideration in modern global design; this is certainly Scandinavian design's most endearing quality and something that is still as robust today as it was fifty years ago.

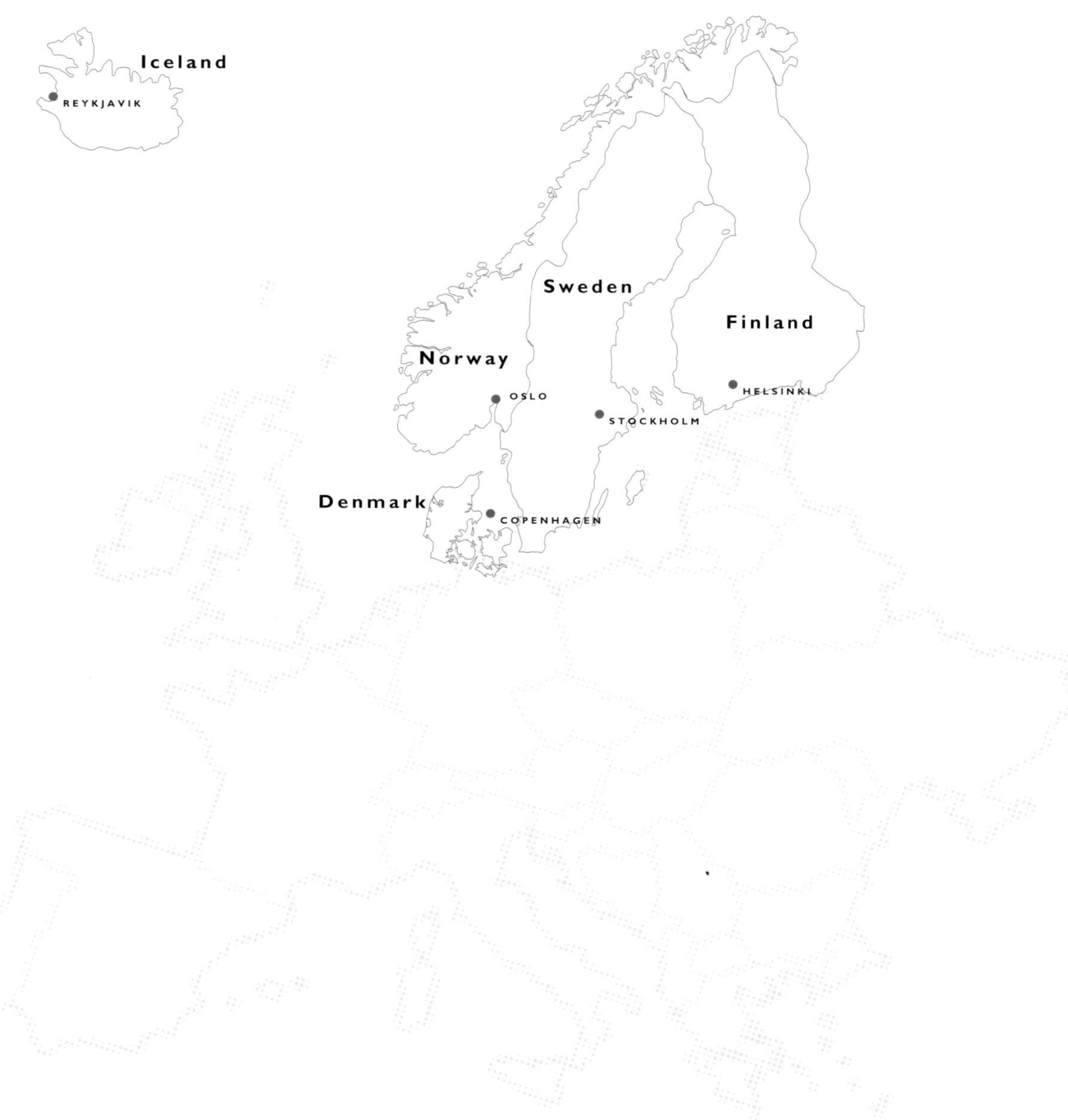
Iceland
REYKJAVIK
Sweden
Finland
Norway
OSLO
STOCKHOLM
HELSINKI
Denmark
COPENHAGEN

Introduction:

The New Scandinavians

With a combined population of only twenty four million, the Scandinavian countries have exerted amazing influence on the field of international design for more than sixty years. An astounding array of products with a Scandinavian imprint have engaged people around the globe who find these products not only desirable in themselves but also reflective of a philosophy of comfortable living and social equality. During the mid-twentieth century, when Scandinavian design first gained international renown, products such as high-quality wooden furniture and fine porcelain and glass blended affordability and elegance, gracing homes worldwide. But is there still such a thing as Scandinavian design? During the process of assembling this volume, this was by far the most common question that arose during conversations with hundreds of contemporary Scandinavian designers, curators, policy makers, and entrepreneurs. Even in an increasingly global marketplace, the core values of a regional design style with a history of widespread influence don't just disappear. Rather, the work of young Scandinavian designers today demonstrates that they are, in fact, mining their Modernist heritage to offer a culturally distinct vision of design for the twenty-first century.

During the "Golden Age" of the 1950s, Scandinavia produced a huge number of international design icons, and this unparalleled creative outpouring resulted in designs that combined a receptive attitude toward new technology with a realistic view of human needs. With its focus on Functionalism, Scandinavian design took the strict industrial aesthetic of the Bauhaus a step further, offering Modern goods that were accessible and humane. In their designs for the home, Scandinavians employed organic forms and natural materials, pursuing truthful expression in wood and glass. For example, Finnish architect Alvar Aalto refined the bentwood process for furniture production, and Finnish designer Timo Sarpaneva applied his poetic view of nature—evident in works like his Orkidea ("Orchid") vase (1953)—equally to utilitarian objects, such as his i-Glass range line (mid-1950s).

An appreciation of tasteful design, an ideal promoted by Scandinavian social reformers beginning in the late nineteenth century, as well as a relatively isolated market encouraged these Modern designers' democratic vision. It meant they would seek to marry craftsmanship with mass production to make high-quality goods available to people from all walks of

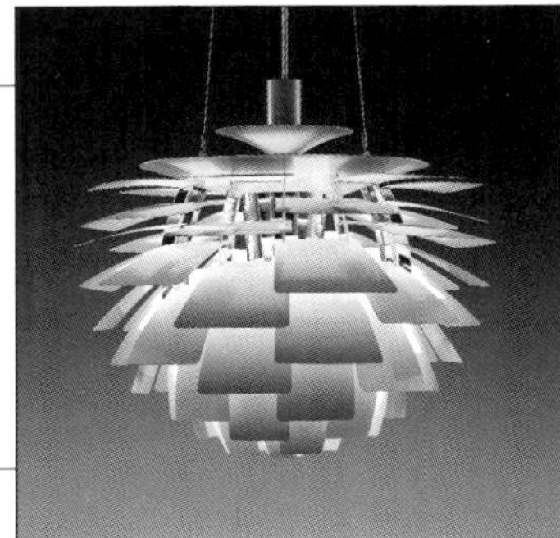

life. A case in point is Danish architect Arne Jacobsen's Myran ("The Ant") chair (1952), the Danish furniture industry's biggest commercial success to date, which combined new innovations in pressed plywood with meticulous handicraft. (Although the chair is a prized example of design simplicity and efficiency, the assembly process requires twenty pairs of hands for sorting of the inner and outer wooden veneers, sanding, molding, gluing, and other tasks.)

Expanding on the fundamental humanism of this period were an unprecedented number of Scandinavian masters including Swedes Bruno Mathsson and Sixten Sason; Danes Hans Wegner, Poul Kjaerholm, Finn Juhl, and Børge Mogensen; Finns Kaj Franck and Tapio Wirkkala; and Norwegians Tias Eckhoff and Willy Johansson.

The philosophies of this Golden Age—functionality, modesty, equality, beauty—eventually gave way to new concerns, though they never quite lost their grip on the Scandinavian imagination. By the late 1960s and early 1970s, the new pop-culture ethos beckoned designers such as Dane Verner Panton, who produced the first-ever single-form, injection-molded plastic chair, called Panton, with the manufacturer Vitra in 1967, and Finn Eero Aarnio, who emphasized bold colors and youthful, graphic forms in his furniture design.

By the early 1970s, design production had turned its focus from the home toward the public sectors, as commissions from the various Nordic government bureaucracies became engines for the design community. Envisioning a more comfortable working environment, Norwegian Peter Opsvik tempered strict Functionalism with ergonomics—a human-centered design methodology—in his office furniture designs for the manufacturer Håg. Although design innovations continued into the 1970s, shifting global trends—including rising labor costs, increased international competition, and a flood of corporate mergers and acquisitions—remade the landscape of Scandinavian consumer-product manufacturing. In turn, these changes undermined many of the factors, such as the isolated market and emphasis on manual labor, that had initially come together to establish the Scandinavian Modern movement.

Today in Scandinavia, though its legacy is steadfast, Modernism is only one of many influences shaping the design field. A new generation of Scandinavian designers views its heritage, not as a creative burden, but as fuel for innovation. Designing with a pace and ingenuity that may soon rival that of the earlier Golden Age, these Scandinavians update Modern conventions to fit the current mood. While

PH Artichoke lamp (previous spread)
Poul Henningsen
1958
DENMARK

Ant chair
Arne Jacobsen
1952
DENMARK

Miranda with footstool Mifot
Bruno Mathsson
1942
SWEDEN

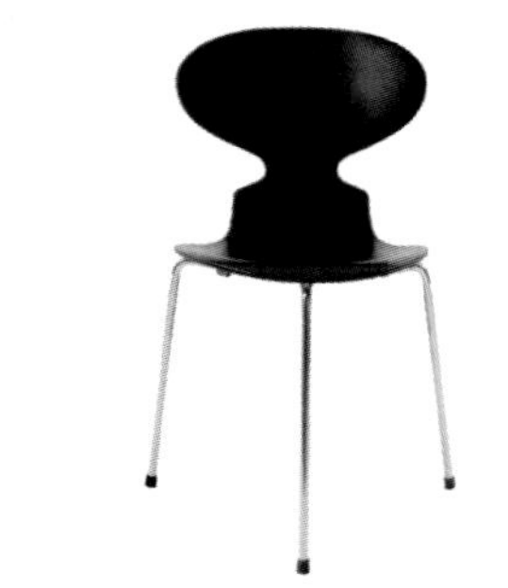

some renew traditional principles such as Functionalism, enlivening the notion with humor and irony, others seek to broaden the concept of Scandinavian design altogether by using their medium to make artistic statements. *New Scandinavian Design* documents some of these prolific and diverse contributions.

To further understand what comprises new Scandinavian design, we should define the word *Scandinavia* itself. A debatable term, it usually connotes the countries of Norway, Sweden, and Denmark, and sometimes Finland and Iceland. This book employs the word in its broadest sense, and it uses *Scandinavian* interchangeably with a term increasingly popular since the end of the Cold War, *Nordic*, which always includes the five countries listed above. The phrase *Scandinavian design*, rather than underscoring geographic proximity or national identity, underlines a common design history and intuitive understanding of shared values. The phrase is only about fifty years old—the various Nordic governments, responding to the region's economic and political challenges of the postwar period, promoted some of its earliest uses during the 1950s in a series of exhibitions, notably "Design in Scandinavia" (1954–1957), which traveled in North America, and "Formes Scandinave" (1958), shown in France.

To explore Scandinavian cultural and artistic ideals more pointedly, this book focuses primarily on 3-D design—housewares, furniture, and consumer products—the field that has been of primary interest to many Scandinavian creatives throughout the last century and typically comes to mind when people think of Scandinavian design. Narrowing the focus in this way makes it easier to assess the current state of the design culture. (Other design fields, like architecture, vehicle design, graphic design, illustration, and fashion, are obviously active and innovative enough to warrant their own volumes.) Most of the designs shown here have been produced since the early 1990s, and the word *new* in the title emphasizes this contemporary quality of the works in this book—a snapshot of current production.

But the word also implies something else: a crucial change in the direction of Scandinavian design throughout the Nordic countries entailing a serious and extensive reevaluation of Modern ideals. Interestingly, countries responsible for the fewest contributions to the Scandinavian Modern movement—Norway and Iceland—today are home to some of the region's most active design communities. In Norway, the chief curator of Oslo's Museum of Decorative Arts and Design, Widar Halén, calls the

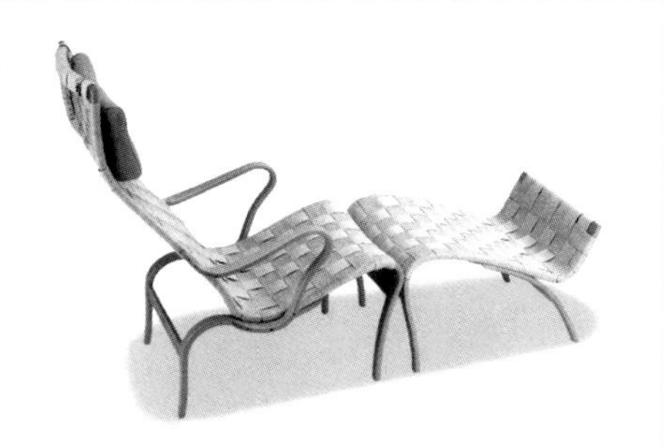

current Norwegian scene "quite powerful" and says that young Norwegians may feel more free because they "do not have the burden of the great golden designers of the 1950s and 1960s to such a degree as in Denmark and Sweden." But even in a city like Copenhagen, Denmark, a mecca of the Modern style, the weight of the past has inspired new thinking. From the fiber-optic textiles of Astrid Krogh to the unnervingly surreal works of Aleksej Iskos, the Danish furniture and product design scene is one of the liveliest in Scandinavia today.

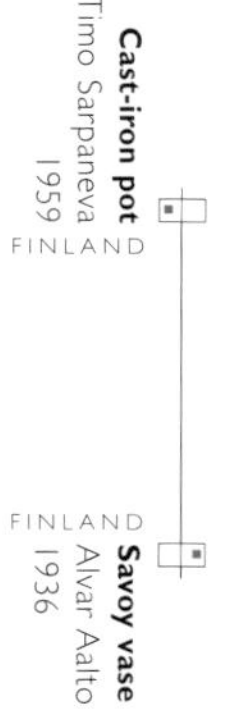

Clearly, contemporary designers are responding to concerns that are different from those of their predecessors. *Globalization*, the buzzword of the day, has had a major impact on much new work. Some Scandinavians, inspired by digital technology, readily appreciate the closer connection to the rest of the world provided by globalization; others view the trend with skepticism and revisit conventions of craft—such as making items by hand and limiting production runs—to provide a sense of intimacy, a quality they see as lost in the shuffle of global industry. Still other designers choose to address globalization head-on with self-aware irony. They play with notions of corporate communication such as branding and advertising, presenting cultural identity as a kind of commodity. A variety of design groups (Finland's Snowcrash, Norway's Permafrost, and Finland's Ocean North, among others) self-consciously allude to stereotypes of the region as cold and remote as they build Nordic design "brands."

These geographically isolated countries are undergoing other powerful sociopolitical transitions, such as increasing diversity of their relatively small and historically homogenous populations. The various Scandinavian political systems, which have become known as models of social democracy, employ some of the world's highest rates of taxation to redistribute wealth and fund extensive social programs—such as medical treatment, retirement, insurance coverage, and maternity and paternity leaves—that perpetuate ideals of equality and middle-class living among the various populations. However, growing multiculturalism has forced designers to reevaluate the traditional emphasis on community needs and consensus ideas that have been so integral to the success of these political systems. In particular, Scandinavian designers are increasingly uncomfortable with the early-twentieth-century reformers' message of tasteful design, which they have begun to see as moralistic. One way young creatives debate the relevance of this traditional social value is to look beyond democratic

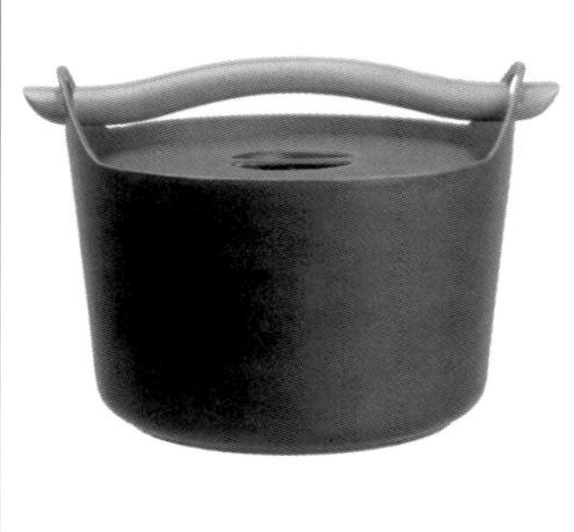

tradition for inspiration, exploring more personal and idiosyncratic directions. Engaging Scandinavia's lesser-known tradition of artistic and limited-edition objects, these young practitioners make expressive statements rather than accessible, utilitarian works. From the fragile furniture of Danish designer Cecilie Manz to the fantasized pop motifs of Icelandic designer Katrín Pétursdóttir, this work offers a strong reply to Scandinavia's golden democratic ideal.

Although Scandinavian design is undergoing a major transition in the face of global trends like multiculturalism, the Nordic countries continue to make design a cultural priority. Unlike in the United States, the general populaces and governments of Scandinavia regard the practice with great esteem, and famous Scandinavian designers often become household names. (It is commonly understood that design has brought these countries valuable economic resources and international media attention.) In turn, the various Scandinavian social systems also support the economic viability of vibrant design communities. Nordic governments offer free education for all citizens, even through the university level, and encourage designers by providing support and funding with a minimum of red tape. In all of the Nordic countries, governments have made solid commitments to support design with legislation at the national level that sets specific goals for consumer product export; offers job retraining; and, in most cases, provides monies for design research, innovation, and entrepreneurship. As the activity of Scandinavian designers has increased since the late twentieth century, so have Scandinavian governments become more willing to invest in and promote design efforts.

To illustrate the developments cited above, the work shown in *New Scandinavian Design* is presented not country by country, but rather is grouped into five themes, addressing traditional qualities that designers engage and update today. This organizational structure moves beyond the conventional national groupings and alphabetically arranged artist profiles to explore the concept of shared cultural values more critically.

The first theme, Democracy, examines the social and political roots of Scandinavian design. Throughout the twentieth century, Scandinavians viewed design as a tool to provide a better life for all members of society rather than to produce luxurious goods for the wealthy few. Today, this democratic tradition faces new demands from international corporations and globalization.

Honesty, the second theme, looks at the early influences of European Modernism on

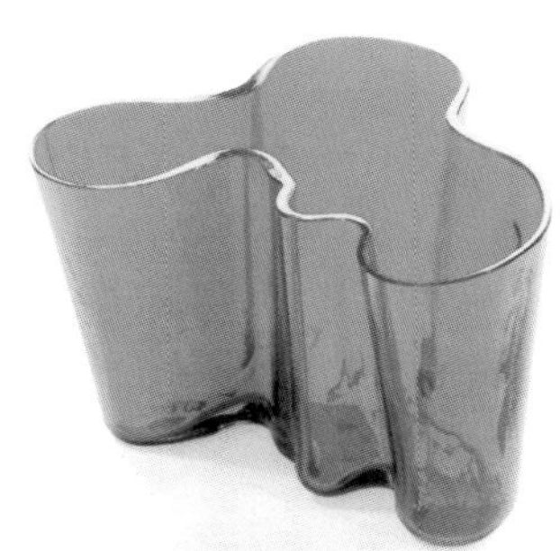

Scandinavian design. In response to the historicist and Neoclassical styles of the early twentieth century, Scandinavians saw in Modernism truthful expression and a rational method for addressing social ills resulting from industrialization. Though a focus on Functionalism continues to inform much of Scandinavian design today, young designers use humor and irony to bring new relevance to this traditional value.

The work in Poetry, the third theme, shows many designers making artful statements that question accepted wisdoms of comfort and functionality. These poetic designers reject democratic dogma by drawing inspiration from Scandinavia's alternative tradition of creating artistic objects, and their explorations broaden the notion of Scandinavian design.

Innovation, the fourth theme, suggests that Scandinavia, one of the most wired regions in the world, is combining its traditional strength in engineering with an optimistic view of new technology, welcoming its continuing influence on design.

The final theme, Craft, brings us back to the beginning. It explores how designers revisit this most traditional cultural expression, so crucial in the creation of the Scandinavian Modern style, to update local values in response to the perceived perils of globalization.

Ongoing local and regional dialogues on all these subjects are also taking place within the different Scandinavian countries themselves. Short essays and interviews with major national design figures in each of the five countries introduce a few of the historic, economic, and creative factors that play into each of these contemporary local scenes.

As we (the editors) discovered while compiling this book, yes, there is such a thing as Scandinavian design. Rather than a fixed idea or the repetition of a historical style, however, this concept should be understood as a dynamic, actively debated set of shared values. *New Scandinavian Design* celebrates the next generation of Nordic designers who are eagerly evolving these cultural ideals, reinterpreting the fundamental humanism of Scandinavian tradition for a new century.

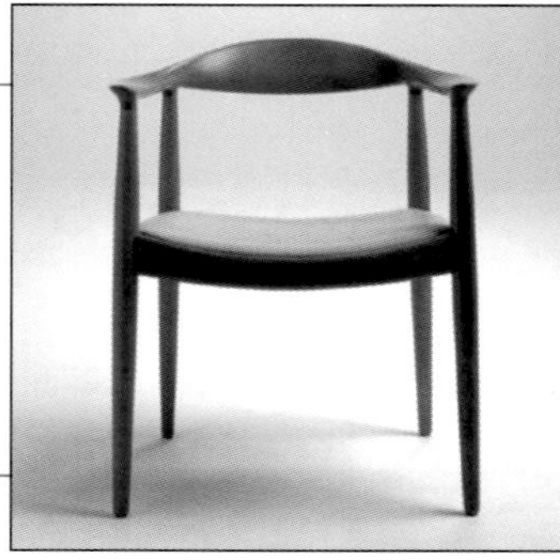

The Chair no. 501
Hans J. Wegner
1949
DENMARK

SWEDEN
Peoples Delite backpack for Boblbee
Jonas Blanking
1999

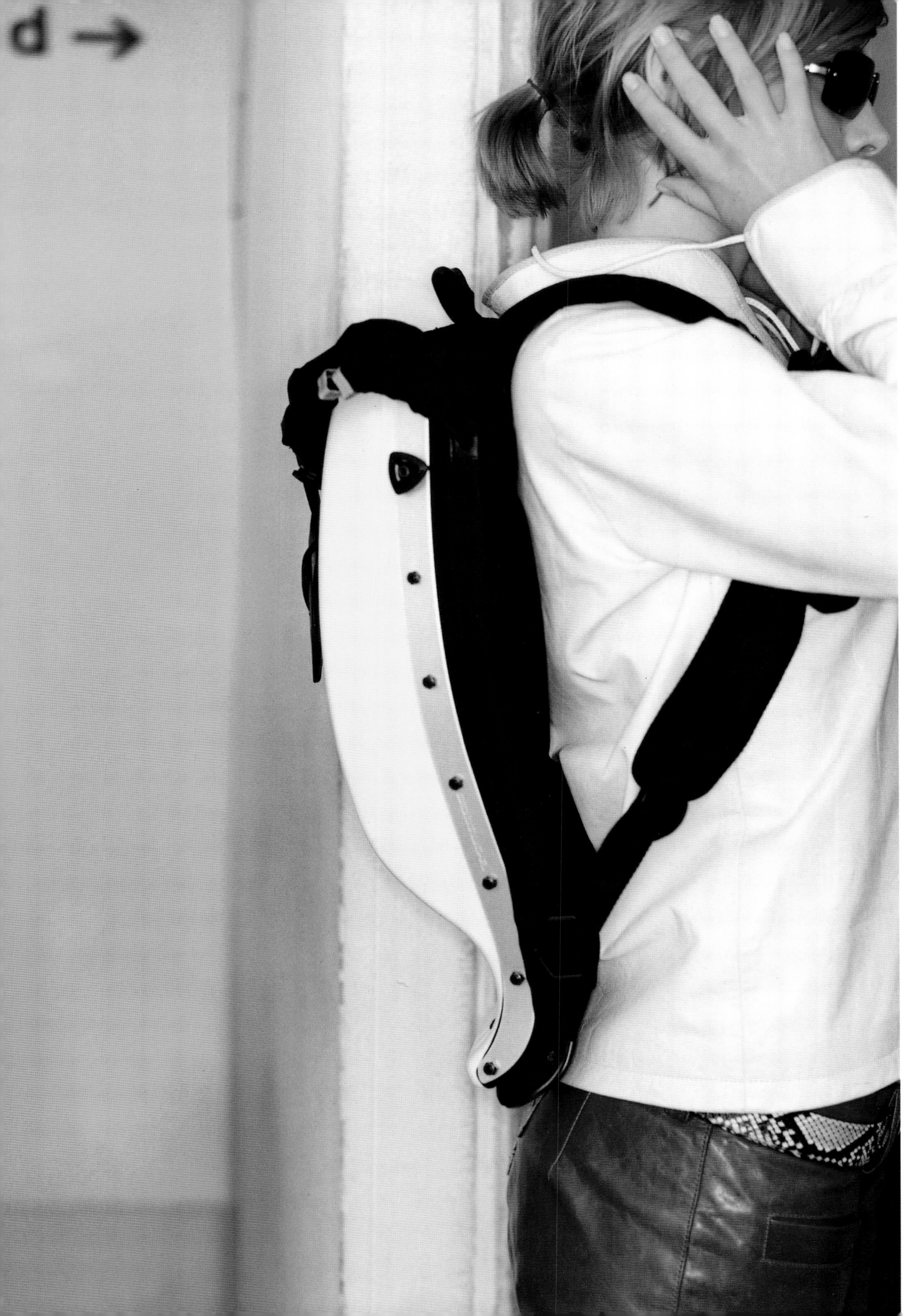

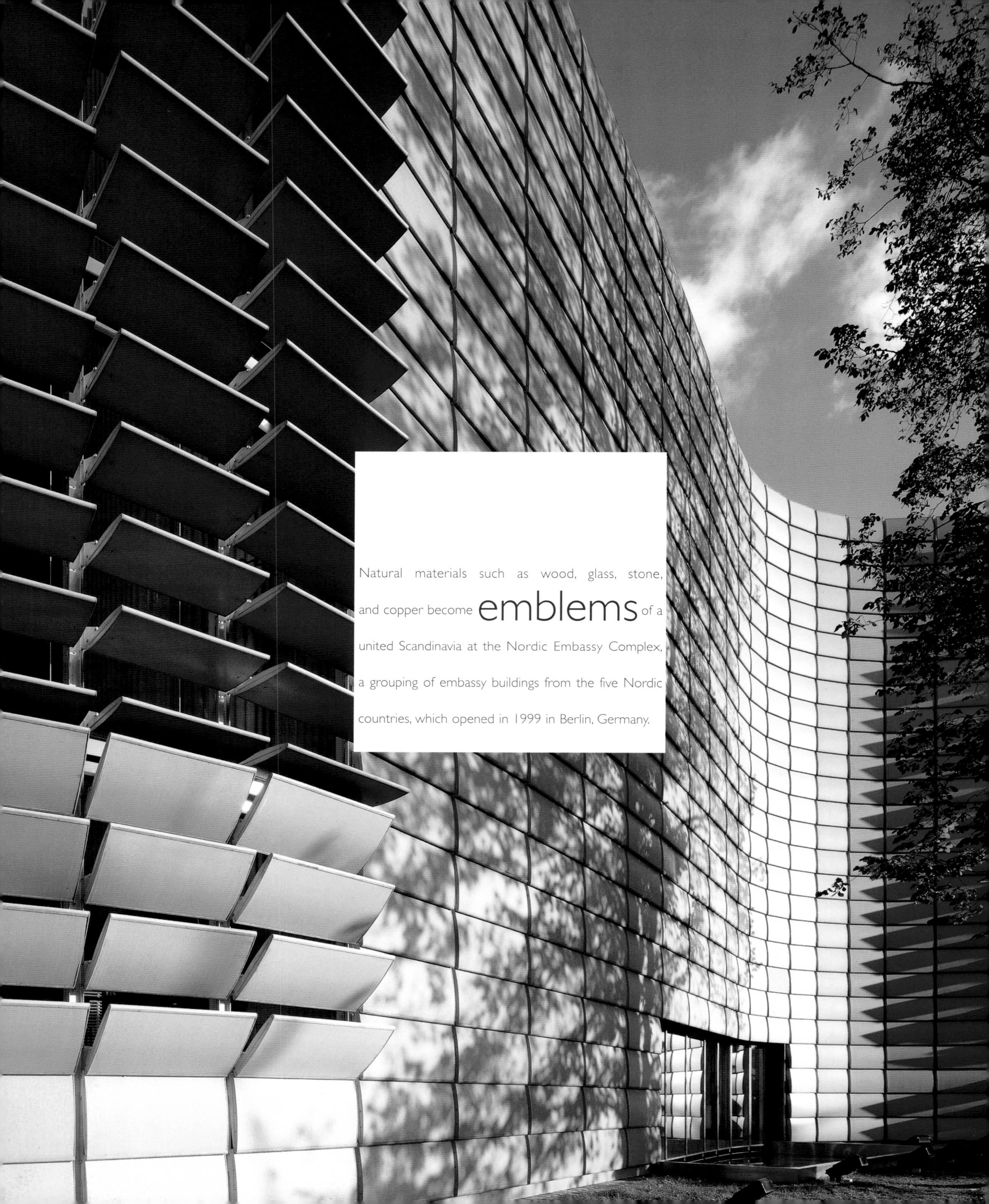

Natural materials such as wood, glass, stone, and copper become **emblems** of a united Scandinavia at the Nordic Embassy Complex, a grouping of embassy buildings from the five Nordic countries, which opened in 1999 in Berlin, Germany.

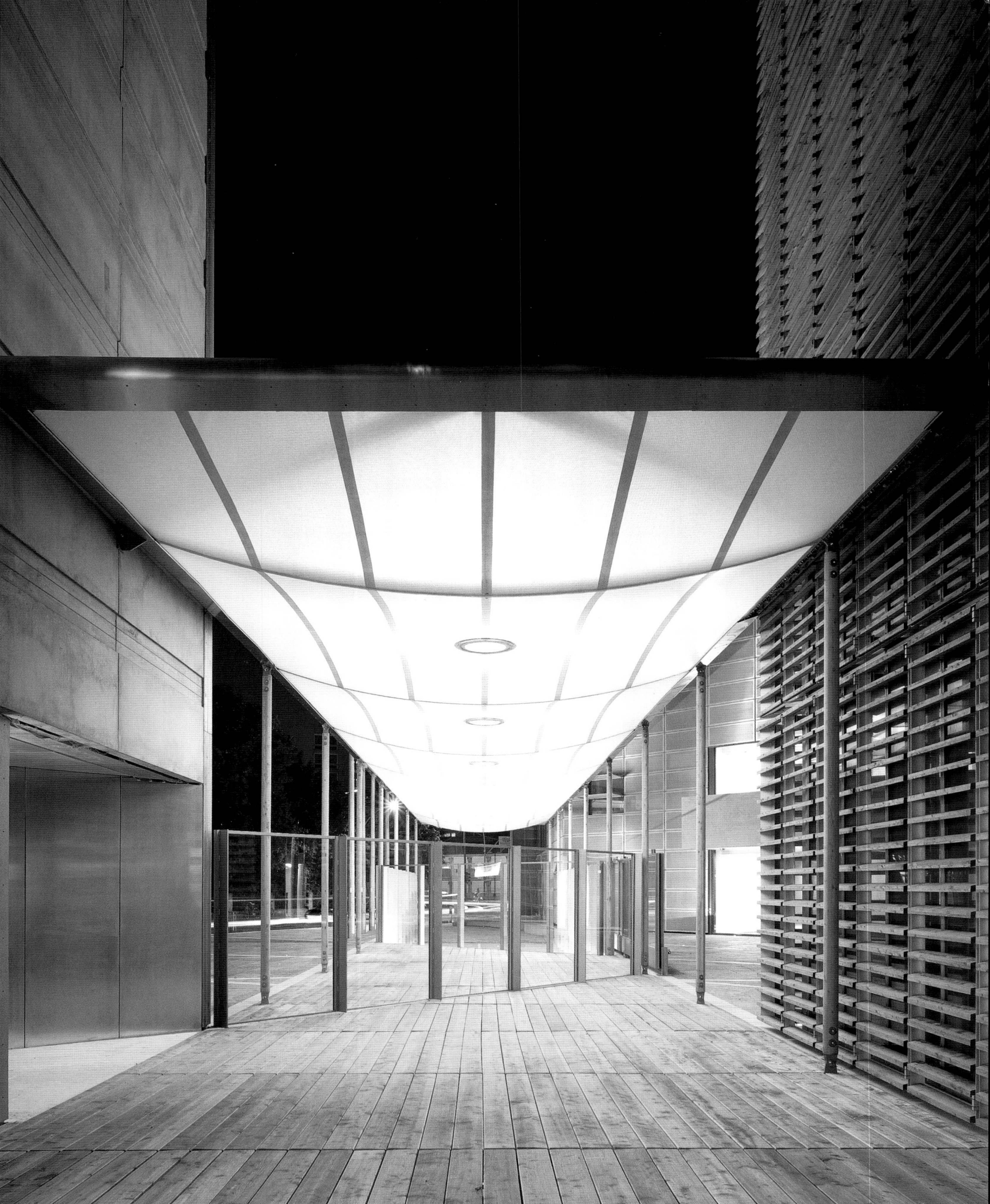

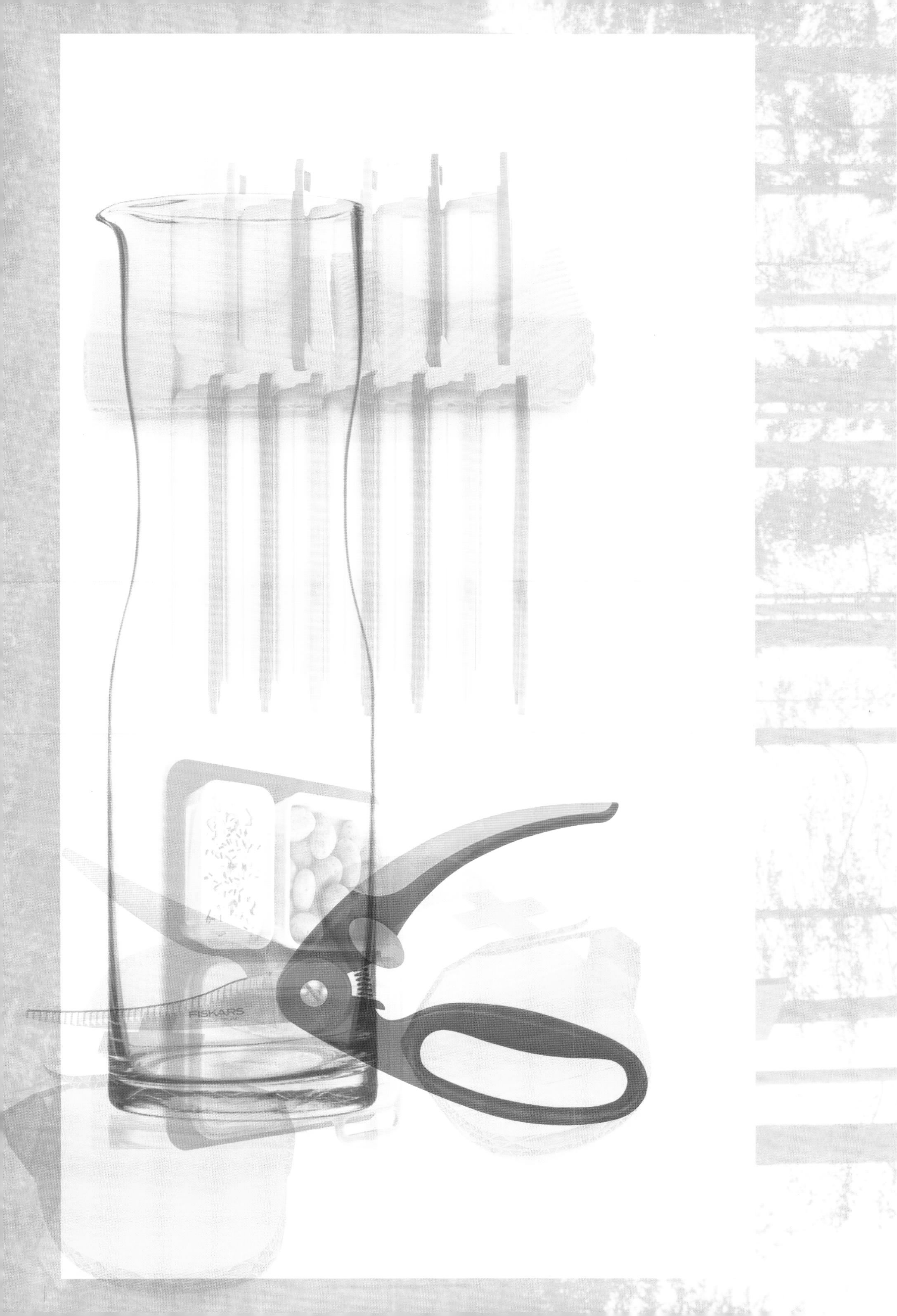

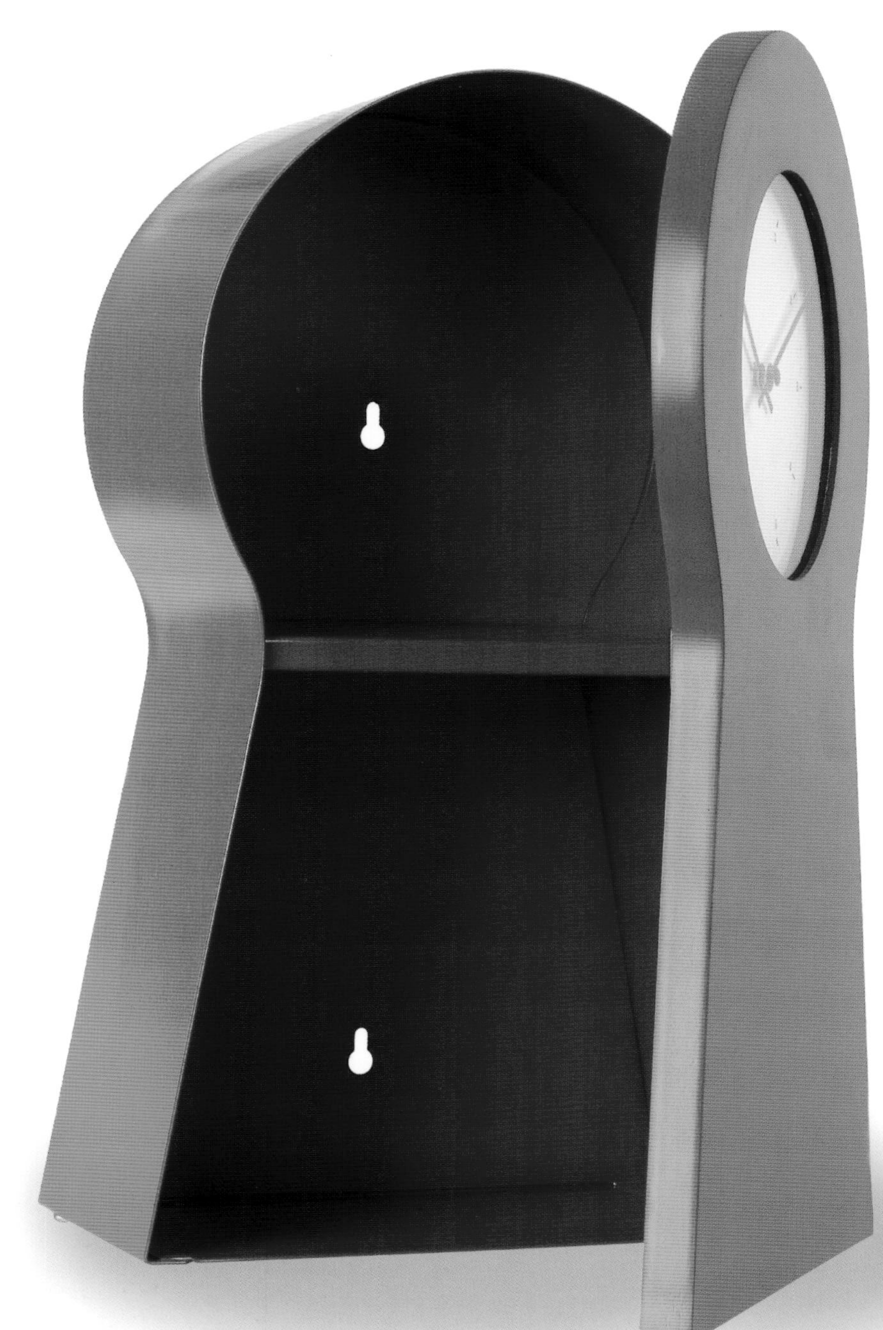

Clock for IKEA/PS
Thomas Eriksson
Lacquered steel, particleboard, glass
SWEDEN

DEMOCRACY

"Democratic design is all about making well-designed functional furniture that everyone can afford," reads an IKEA catalog from 1999. "It's one of IKEA's founding principles and its application can be found in every item we sell." Behind a banner of blue and yellow, the national colors of Sweden, the furniture superstore IKEA has established a recognizable design language—a friendly twist on Modern design. Producing practical products at an affordable price for everyone from kids to the most design-conscious consumer, IKEA has found enormous success with its assemble-at-home vision of stylish domesticity.

The notion of democratic design, however, is hardly IKEA's invention. The company's catalog copy speaks to a Scandinavian commitment almost one hundred years old. Early in the twentieth century, designers shared a common goal of enhancing quality of life by creating *vackrare vardagsvara* ("more beautiful things for everyday use"). IKEA's current version of democratic design may be commercially inclined, but it springs from this Scandinavian tradition. Indeed, Scandinavian tradition encourages capitalism, but always in the context of social and political consequences. Here, design becomes a tool to question elitism, break down social barriers, and empower individuals, not to mention producing high-quality objects on a large scale. Increasingly, the challenge for Scandinavian designers will be to balance the needs of the individual with corporate demands and globalization.

One early proponent of democratic design, Swedish art historian Gregor Paulsson, proposed an antibourgeois view of materialism, in which possessions act as social equalizers to lift people from poverty. Prompted by wretched living conditions resulting from industrialization, Paulsson wrote, nearly a century ago, "A unified taste gives a unified form to all of society. This is the deeper meaning of the slogan 'more beautiful things for everyday use.'" His phrase became the motto of progressive thinkers, and his notion of "unified taste" (frequently referred to as "good taste") inspired many of his contemporaries. New technology, in particular mass production, offered a means to make high-quality products available to all. "Not until nothing ugly can be bought," wrote another influential Swedish social reformer, Ellen Key, in 1899, "when the beautiful is as cheap as the ugly, only then can beauty for all become a reality." One such effort at affordable, ethical beauty included a modest dinner service by Wilhelm Kåge for the company Gustavsberg, called "the Workers' Service," which was shown in Stockholm at the seminal Hemutställning ("Home Exhibition") in 1917. Created to appeal to the working classes, Kåge's design wasn't cost effective in mass production at the time; not until the postwar period, after advances in technology and the introduction of the welfare state, would these ideas finally reach the broader public.

By the 1940s and '50s, the functional language of the Bauhaus had eclipsed the folk-arts sensibility of the Workers' Service. Innovations such as Finnish designer Kaj Franck's Kilta (1953), a modular dinnerware set for the company Iittala, met the demand for affordable domestic products, though an interest in the

"The furniture, textiles, silver, glass, and china; the utensils and ornaments . . . all possess a rare beauty and charm. Racially unified, geographically isolated, politically agreed, numerically small, the peoples of Norway, Sweden, Denmark, and Finland have created a surrounding for present-day living which other nations can envy."

SWEDEN
Carafe for IKEA/PS
Sofia Uddén
Glass

improvement of workers' lives was gradually giving way to a focus on the burgeoning middle class. A strong commercial aspect pervaded this period, evident in a series of traveling exhibitions, including the groundbreaking "Design in Scandinavia" (1954–57), which promoted the display and the sale of Scandinavian Modern goods in North America. Incorporating one of the earliest uses of the phrase "Scandinavian design," the exhibition purposefully blurred cultural differences between the Nordic countries to underline associations with allied democracies, positioning "democratic design" against communism. This promotional strategy came out of need, not simply a desire for commerce—in particular, Norway and Finland had been hard hit by World War II and were desperate for economic renewal—but the exhibition created the first international buzz for Scandinavian products on a large scale. At its first stop, the Virginia Museum of Fine Arts, the members' bulletin read, "The furniture, textiles, silver, glass, and china; the utensils and ornaments . . . all possess a rare beauty and charm. Racially unified, geographically isolated, politically agreed, numerically small, the peoples of Norway, Sweden, Denmark, and Finland have created a surrounding for present-day living which other nations can envy."

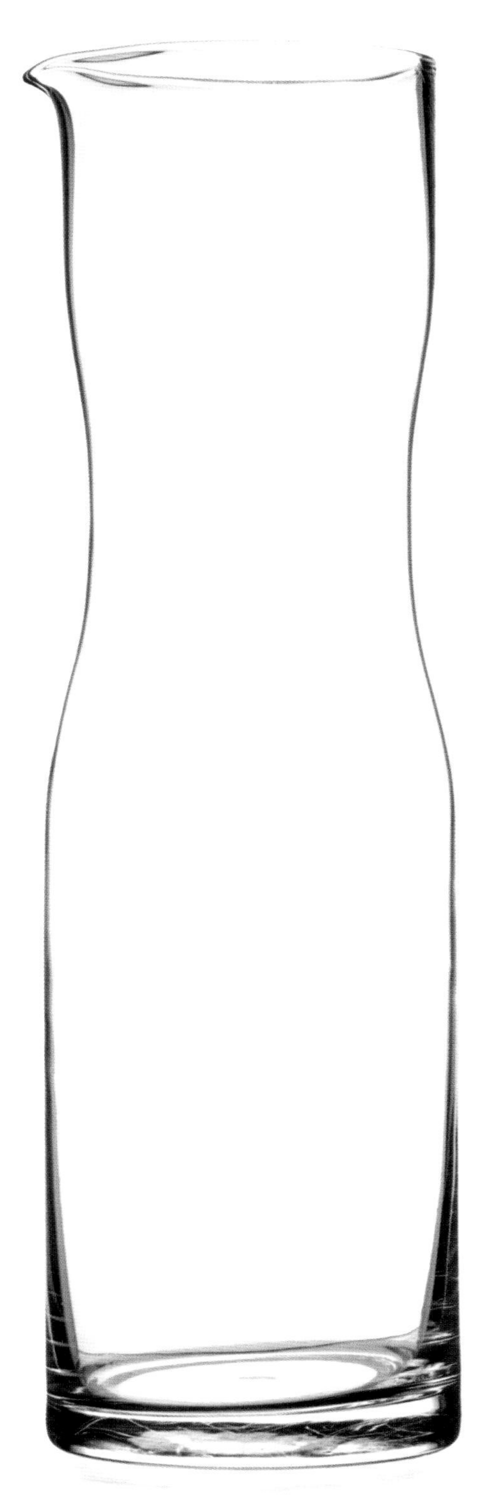

In the following decades, the understanding of democratic design changed with the times. In the face of the conflict in Vietnam and the economic crisis of the 1970s, designers reaffirmed their reformist roots. Young designers shunned what they saw as the bourgeois tendencies of the previous generation—its polished housewares, refined glass, and elegant wooden furniture. Instead, these new designers sought success in the public sector, vehicle safety, and the environment. While the notion of democratic design was still vital in the 1970s, designers no longer sought to create a comfortable, middle-class lifestyle. Democratic design became a method of social justice, particularly in the embrace of previously marginalized members of society—children, the elderly, and the disabled. In the growing field of industrial design, the Swedish groups Ergonomidesign and A&E Design and the Finnish tool company Fiskars used ergonomics and consumer research to accommodate a wide range of age and ability in the design of products as varied as bread slicers, poultry shears **(C)**, mushroom brushes **(A)** see **p 63**, diaper bags, and double-handed screwdrivers. The Finnish clothing company Marimekko rebelled against the elitism of the fashion industry with pop patterns **(B)** and unconventional unisex designs. And Ergonomidesign, Fiskars, Marimekko, the Danish toy company

Poultry shears for Fiskars (C)
Olavi Lindén
Stainless steel, plastic, thermoplastic rubber
FINLAND

Kaktus Pattern for Marimekko (B)
Erja Hirvi
Cotton
FINLAND

Barbecue utensils for Hackman (E)
Harri Koskinen
Stainless steel, plastic brush
FINLAND

Motor oil canisters for Neste (D)
Stefan Lindfors
Plastic
FINLAND

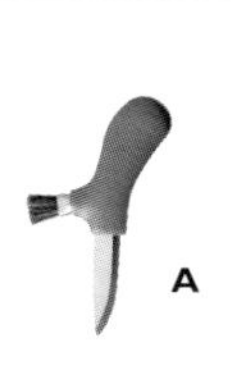
A

B

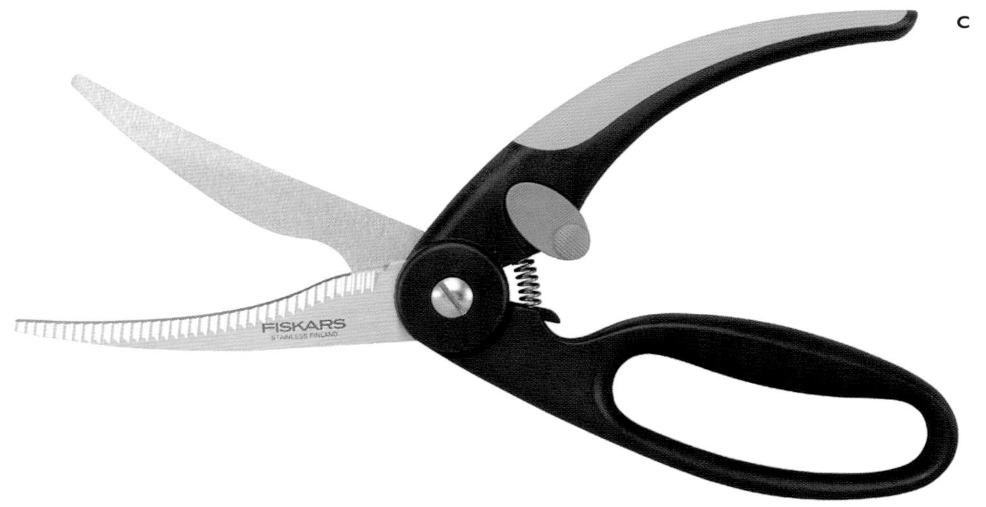

C

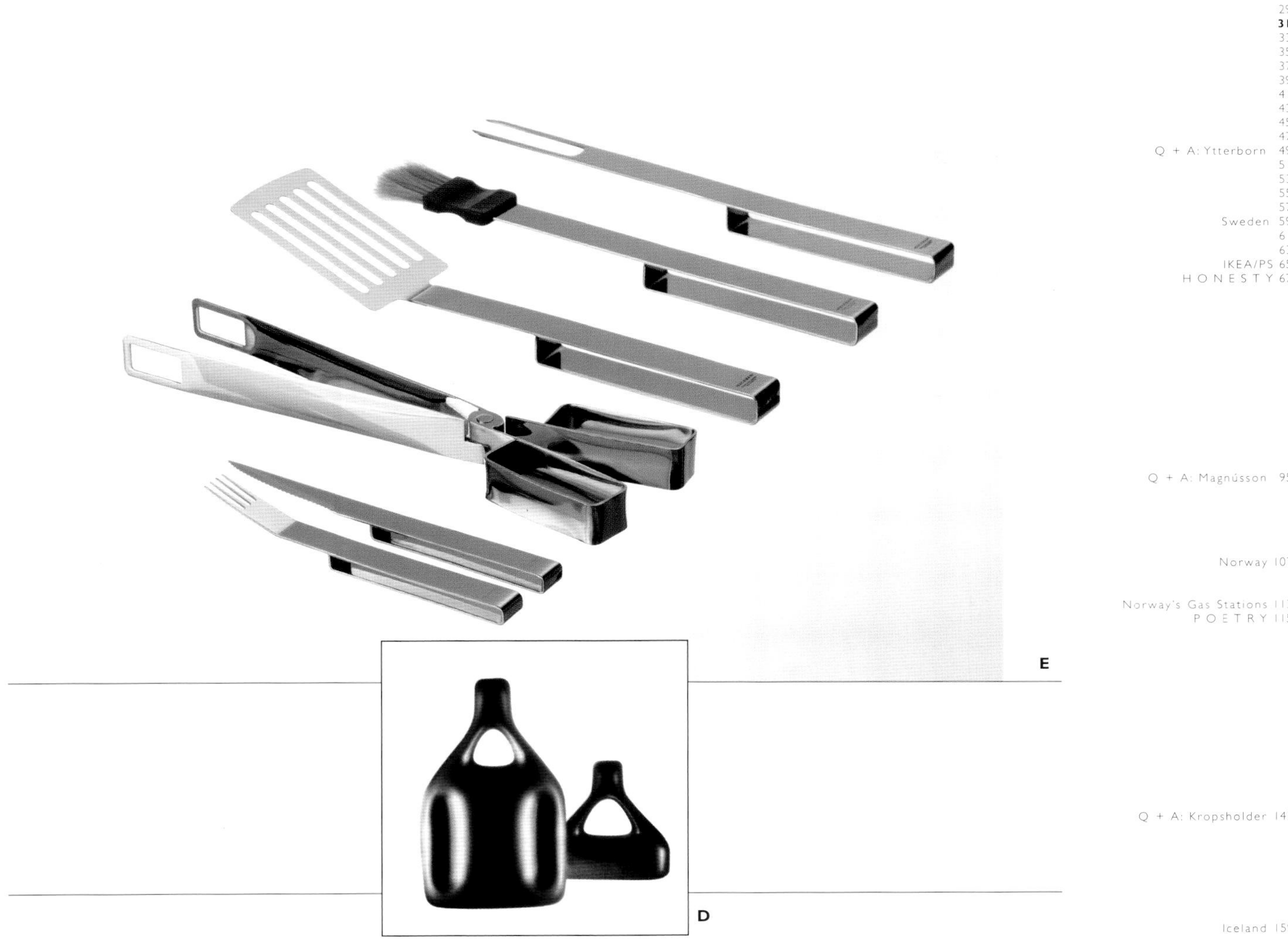

E

D

LEGO, and other companies that hit their stride during the 1960s and 1970s continue to make active contributions to today's scene. The work of these groups reinforces the notion that good design should be human-centric, that it should subvert, rather than support, class and gender distinctions, and that design should welcome all abilities, ages, and tastes.

Today in Scandinavia, as the reformist Paulsson once predicted, design is the stuff of everyday life. From mailboxes to doorknobs, from cars to watering cans, Scandinavian designers celebrate beauty in mundane objects. Finnish designer and filmmaker Stefan Lindfors tackled the common motor oil canister **(D)**, crafting a gorgeous design for the chemical company Neste. Exemplifying Paulsson's ideal of everyday elegance, these blue-black blow-mold containers unite aesthetics with utility: a sculptural hole in each bottleneck seems a dramatic gesture, but it also makes the canister easy to grab and the pouring process more efficient. The outdoor grill is the site of Finnish designer Harri Koskinen's efforts: he dresses up the backyard barbecue with his sleek, stainless-steel cooking utensil set **(E)** for Hackman. Even ubiquitous snack foods don't escape reinterpretation. With a

DEMOCRACY 25
27
29
31
33
35
37
39
41
43
45
47
Q + A: Ytterborn 49
51
53
55
57
Sweden 59
61
63
IKEA/PS 65
HONESTY 67
Q + A: Magnússon 95
Norway 107
Norway's Gas Stations 113
POETRY 115
Q + A: Kropsholder 143
Iceland 159
Iceland's Blue Lagoon 165
INNOVATION 167
Q + A: Ylimaula 195
Finland 203
Finland's Arabianranta 209
CRAFT 211
Q + A: Halén 235
Denmark 249
Denmark's Øresund Bridge 255

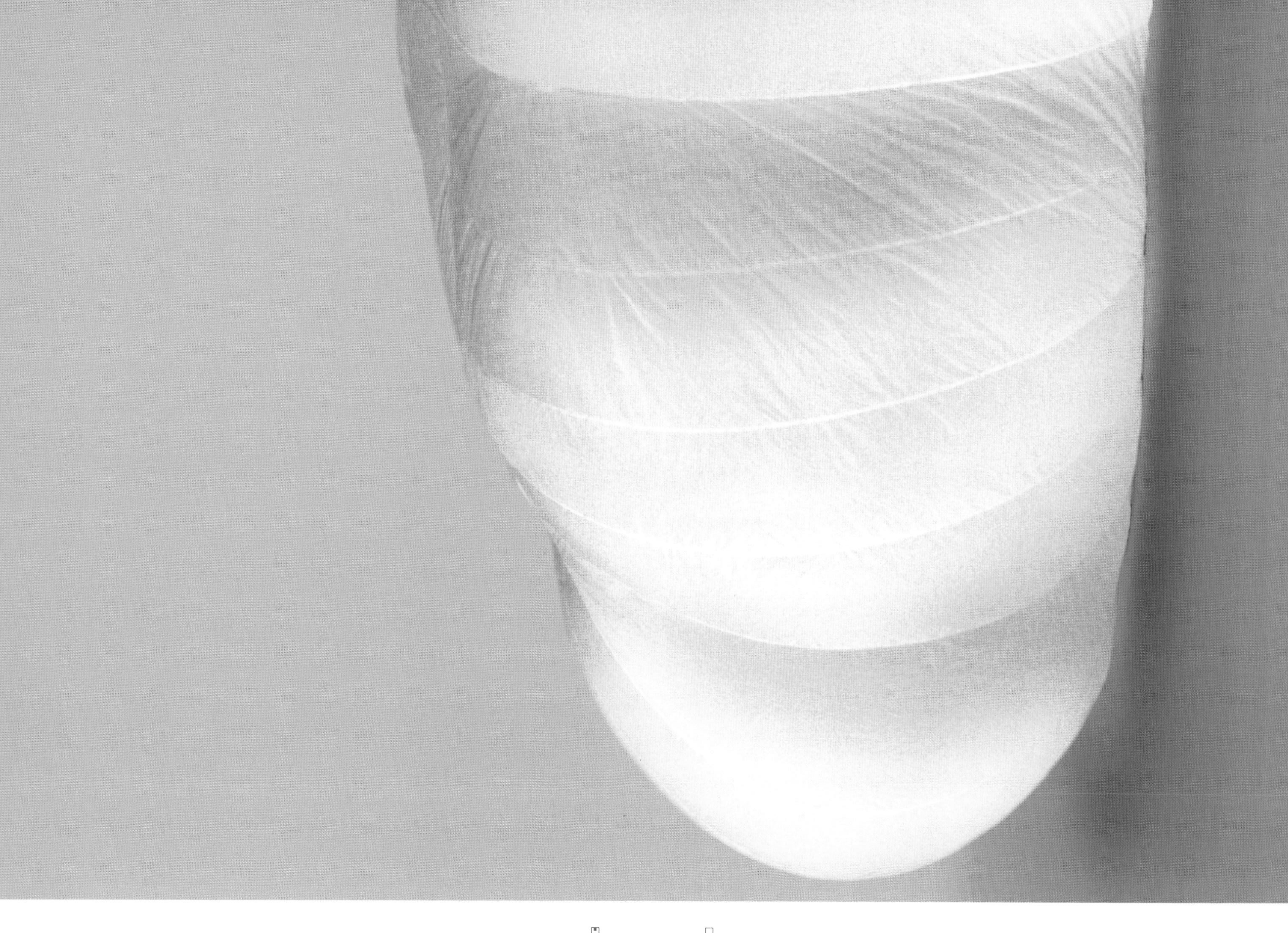

Cloud, an inflatable meeting room
Monica Förster
Coated ripstop nylon, sound-absorbent textile
SWEDEN

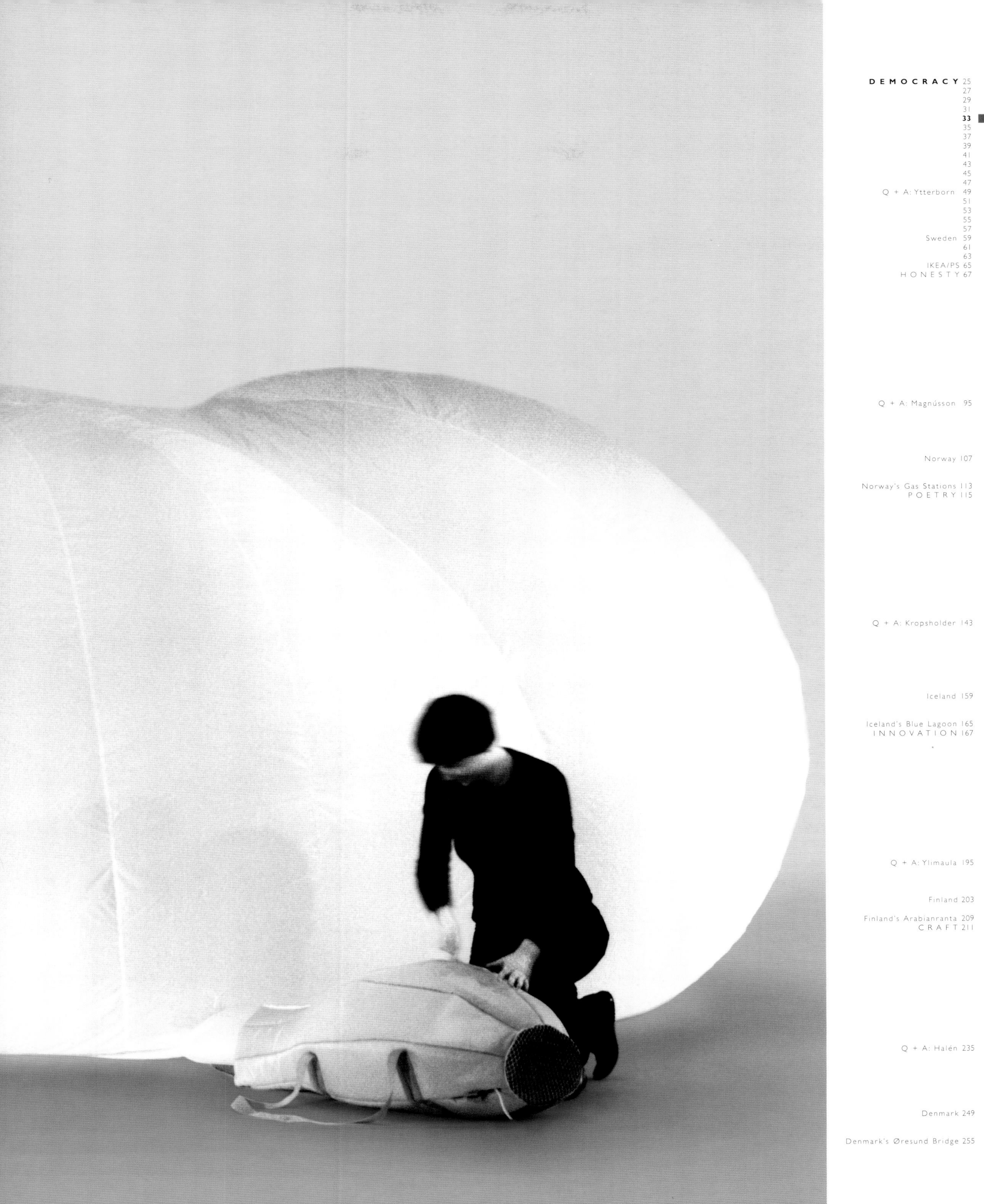

stylized swash of chocolate, Norwegian designer Johan Verde creates a minimalistic, two-tone cream bar **(H)** for Diplom-Is. For another client, candy maker Nidar, Verde shapes little chocolates like precious gems.

Democratic designers are open to a diversity of projects, and they seem to believe that all materials are created equal. They unite high-end luxury materials, like porcelain and crystal, with utilitarian ones, like stainless steel and rubber. Monica Förster combined clear crystal with colorful plastic in her elegant bowls **(F)** see **p 52** for the Swedish glass producer Skruf. "Perhaps there is a little socialist in all of us Scandinavians," says Förster.

To encourage the use of previously overlooked materials, many Nordic designers are rethinking notions of waste and recycling. With the improvement of sustainable technology, designers find the use of recycled substances increasingly viable and often promote awareness of this issue in their own work. To ease end-of-life disassembly for her in her award-winning Kiss chair **(G)**, developed in collaboration with the Finnish furniture company Piiroinen, Finn Sari Anttonen created a system of modular seats and backrests that also improves her product's longevity (damaged parts can be easily replaced and recycled without having to discard the entire chair).

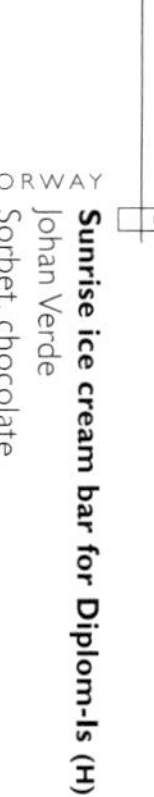

Kiss chair for Piiroinen (G)
Sari Anttonen
Polyurethane, tubular steel
FINLAND

NORWAY
Sunrise ice cream bar for Diplom-Is (H)
Johan Verde
Sorbet, chocolate

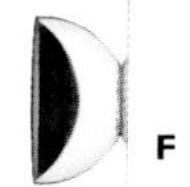

F

H ➤

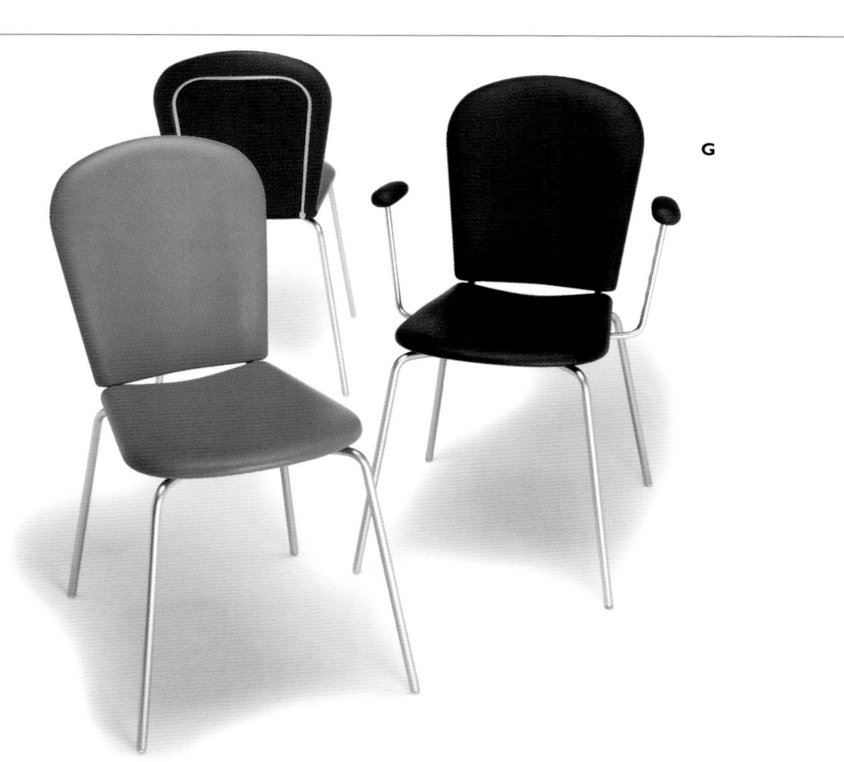

G

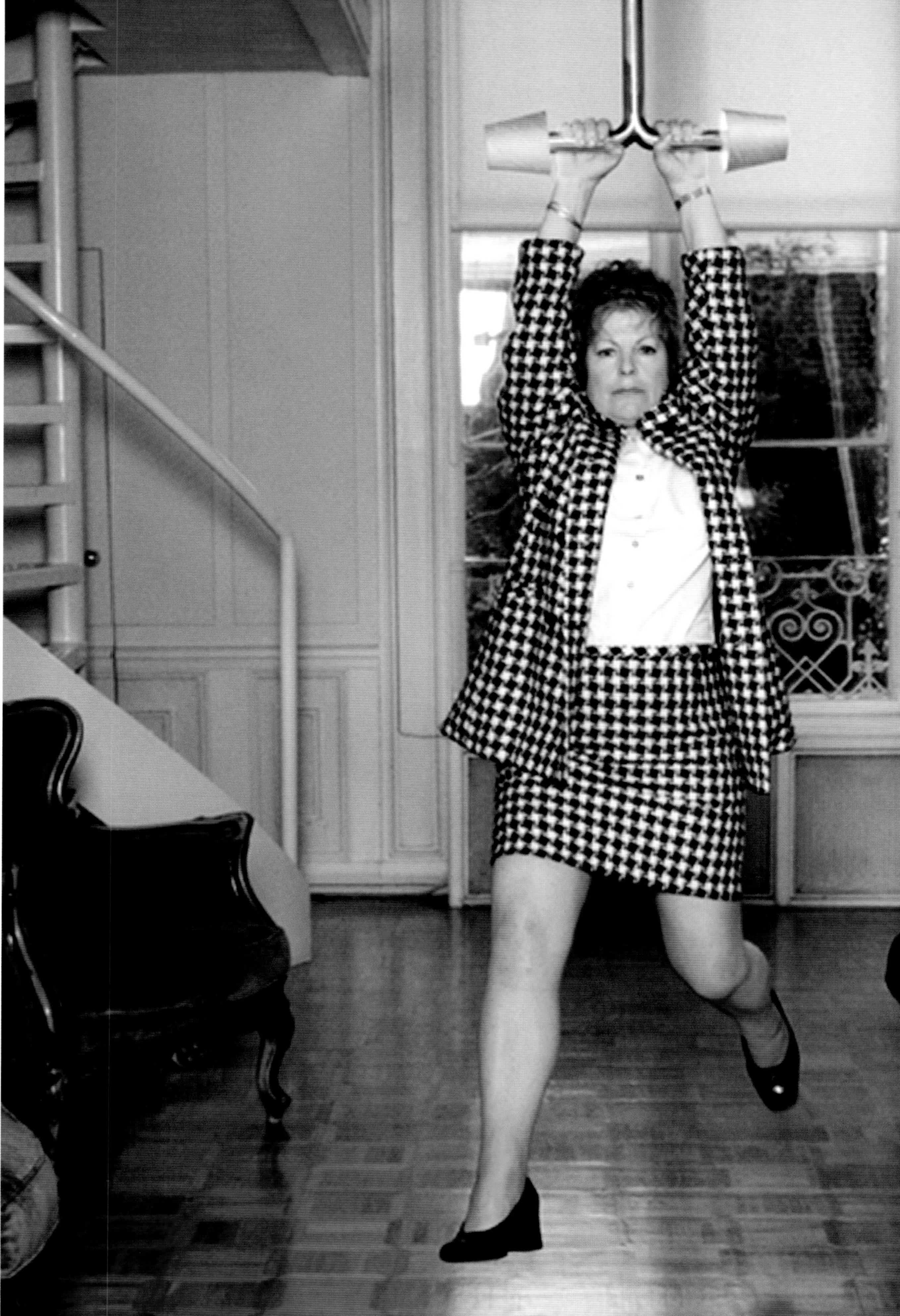

Do Swing for KesselsKramer, Droog Design (l)
Thomas Bernstrand
Metal chassis, used lampshades
SWEDEN

Solidarity chair (L)
Peter Andersson
Laminated wood steel tubes, upholstery
SWEDEN

While contemporary Scandinavian designers often bring patrician and work-horse materials together, they also reexamine social order by uniting traditionally hierarchical tasks. Danish designer Ole Jensen's friendly yellow colander **(J)** see **p 57** for Royal Copenhagen raises food preparation to the level of fine dining. Jensen's faience colander has two conjoined bowls, one perforated to wash salad and the other smooth to present it on the dining room table. Harri Koskinen's Air service **(K)** see **p 46** suggests a similar idea: elegant china serving dishes can be topped with colorful plastic lids, and leftovers can go right into the refrigerator.

Democratic design also rejects formality by dismantling social barriers. Thomas Bernstrand, a member of the Swedish collective Our, created the Do Swing light for Droog Design. With Do Swing **(I)**, Bernstrand invites the young at heart to hang from his trapezelike chandelier, encouraging people to break the rules. "I guess I got tired of my mother telling me to take my feet off of the coffee table," the designer explains. With his Solidarity chair **(L)**, Peter Andersson provides room for a friend with a ledge on the side of the seat. His chair functions not only practically but also emotionally as a space for whispered intimacies.

◄ **I**

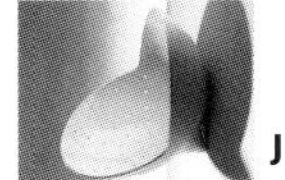

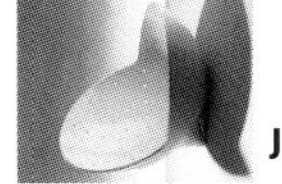

J

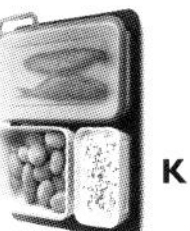

K

L

Spreads from Designer for a Day brochure (M,O)
Iceland Academy of the Arts
Newsprint
ICELAND

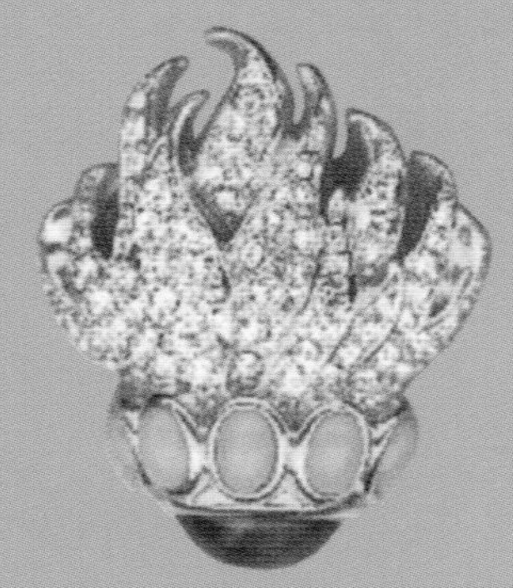
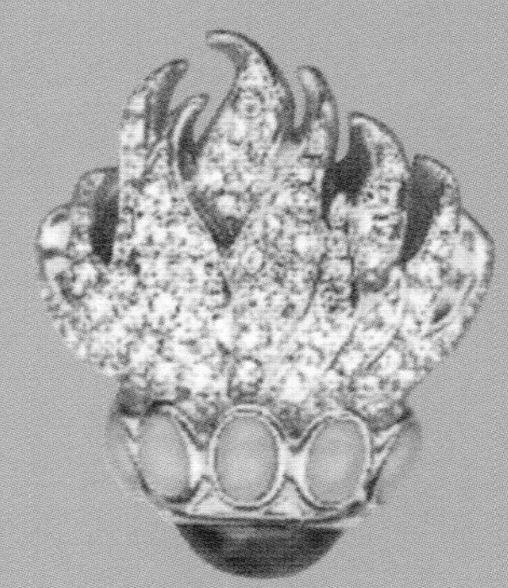

do you dream of jewelry?

try on these Elizabeth Taylor earings
by cutting them out and
putting clips on them.

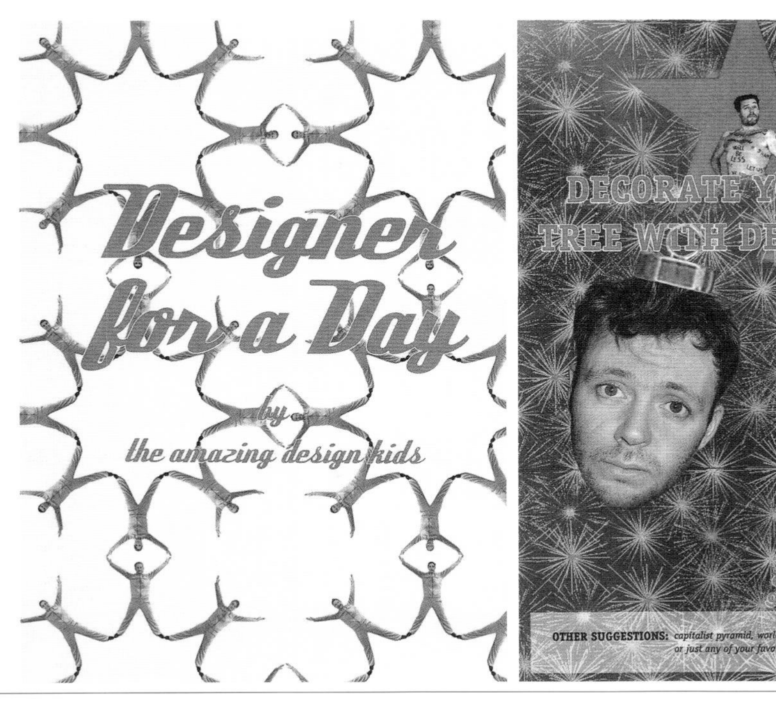

O

◄ M

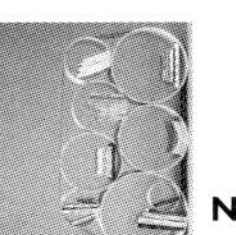

N

In democratic design today, those who use products are themselves increasingly invited to participate in the design process. Granted, this isn't a new idea—it has its roots in the 1960s when the literary critic Roland Barthes proclaimed the "death of the author," arguing that meaning is created by readers as much as by writers. Today's democratic designers endeavor to break down the barriers between the two entities, designer and user. When assembling a tubular shelf system called 1 to 100 **(N)** see **p 45**, designed by Dane Pil Bredahl, the consumer decides on the arrangement of the various circular compartments, which can be easily organized and reorganized. With an ironic wink, students at the Iceland Academy of the Arts authored an iconoclastic *Designer for a Day* **(O)** handbook suggesting that anyone can be a designer. The handbook encourages readers to follow step-by-step instructions for a number of ad hoc designs. With proposed activities such as recreating a tabletop version of the Pearl, an Icelandic landmark, with whiskey glasses, and cutting out and wearing a pair of paper "Elizabeth Taylor earrings" **(M)**, the handbook gives a good ribbing to the ivory-tower environment of design education.

Today, corporate clients and globalization place new demands on Scandinavian designers to create marketable objects. Yet unlike in the United States, where design is first and foremost a commodity, Scandinavians instinctively consider the social and political ramifications of their work (one possible reason: the taxation rates in Scandinavia—some of the highest in the world—reaffirm the shared values of a middle class society). The collective Claesson Koivisto Rune carefully balances a respect for the individual with the needs of a corporation in its interior of a McDonald's **(P)** see **p 58** in downtown Stockholm. Awash in warm blond wood, the store features minimally decorated surfaces and straightforward furniture. The store's interior and the mission of McDonald's meld surprisingly seamlessly: McDonald's is affordable and ubiquitous, and has always been a predictable purveyor of sameness, aside from occasional minor menu adjustments. So, too, has Scandinavian democratic design perpetuated unified taste. However, while the quiet minimalism of the franchise reinforces the democratic aspects of McDonald's, it also undermines corporate hegemony. The only eye-catching corporate mark is a single set of softly glowing golden arches, stripped of its namesake, at the ordering station. In this sense, the McDonald's interior leverages the power of democratic design to mitigate blatant consumerism.

Nen table for Pintade (Q)
Sari Anttonen
Recycled metal sheets, tubular steel
FINLAND

Glow-in-the-dark toilet seat
Monica Förster
Injection-molded plastic, photoluminescent color
SWEDEN

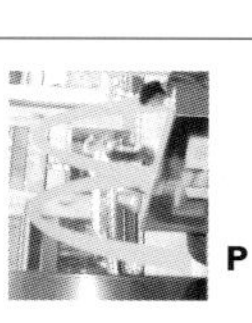

P

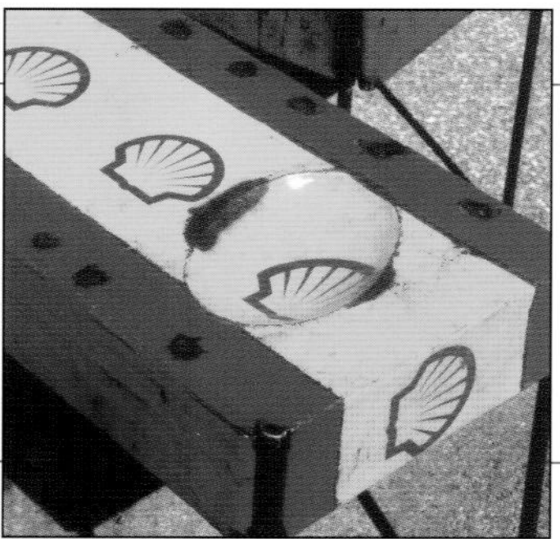

Q

Above all, contemporary Scandinavian designers remain sensitive to the social impact of their work, especially in the global arena. They regard design as a powerful tool to unite people and create international community. In 1996, in the Senegalese city of Rufisque, Africa, Sari Anttonen worked with metal and wood craftsmen to design a contemporary furniture series called Tubab **(Q)** for the Villa Roche, a cultural institute. Employing previously used metal sheets and steel, the Finnish-Senegalese team produced a variety of unique pieces including chairs, clothing racks, shelves, and tables. Demand for the furniture, now sold in Europe, opened new markets to the Senegalese craftsmen, and the new revenue stream has encouraged education and development within the local Senegalese community.

Beginning in the early twentieth century, Scandinavians viewed design not as an accessory of luxurious living but as a method of political critique. Although they are capitalists at heart, Scandinavians consider design in its social, political, and commercial contexts. In a world of blatant consumerism, the vision of democratic design is modest and humane. Today, young designers carefully balance their region's prosperity with social responsibility. Responding to both the opportunities and the perils of globalization, democratic design will evolve, its political underpinnings and social commitment influencing the future of Scandinavian design.

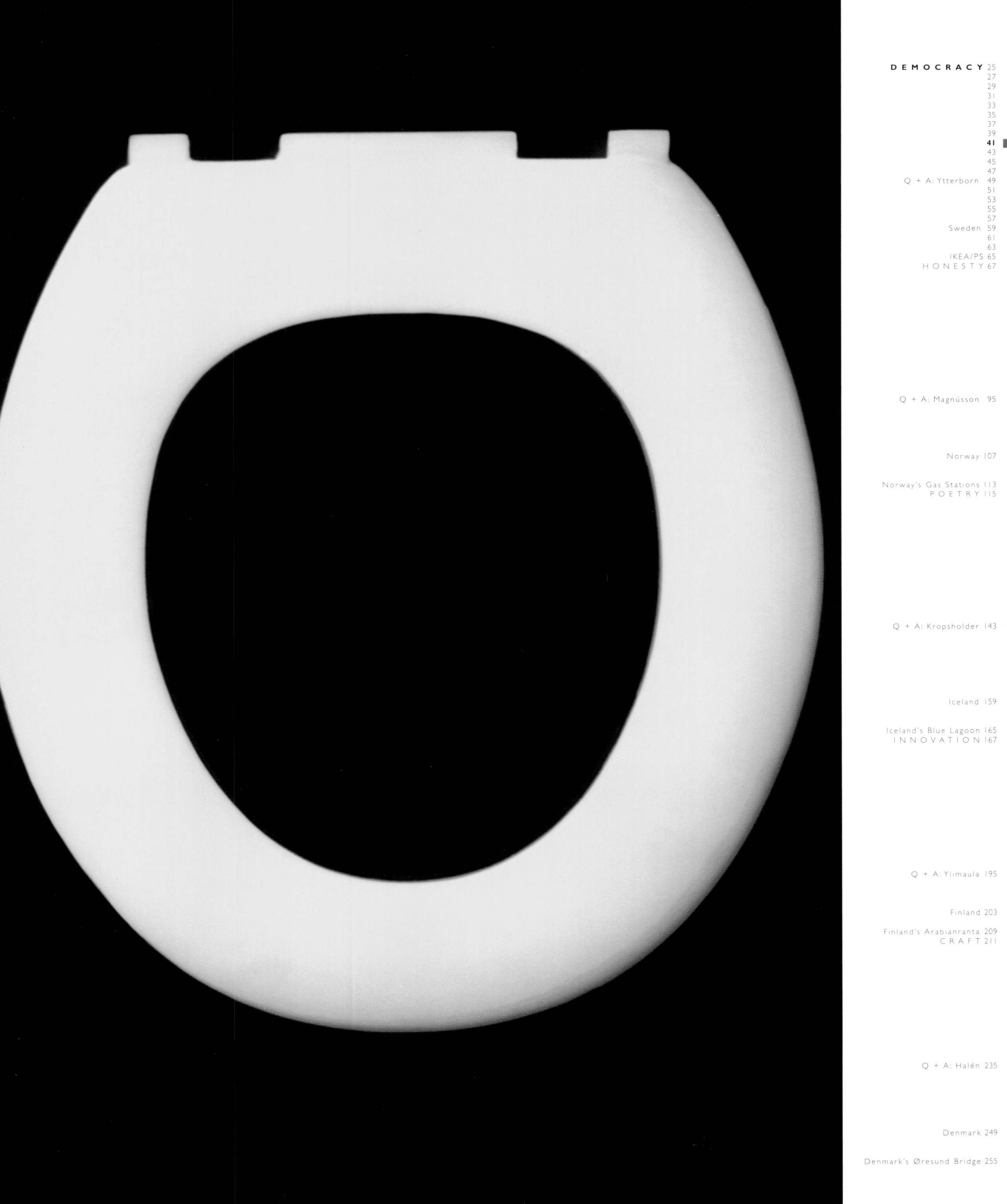

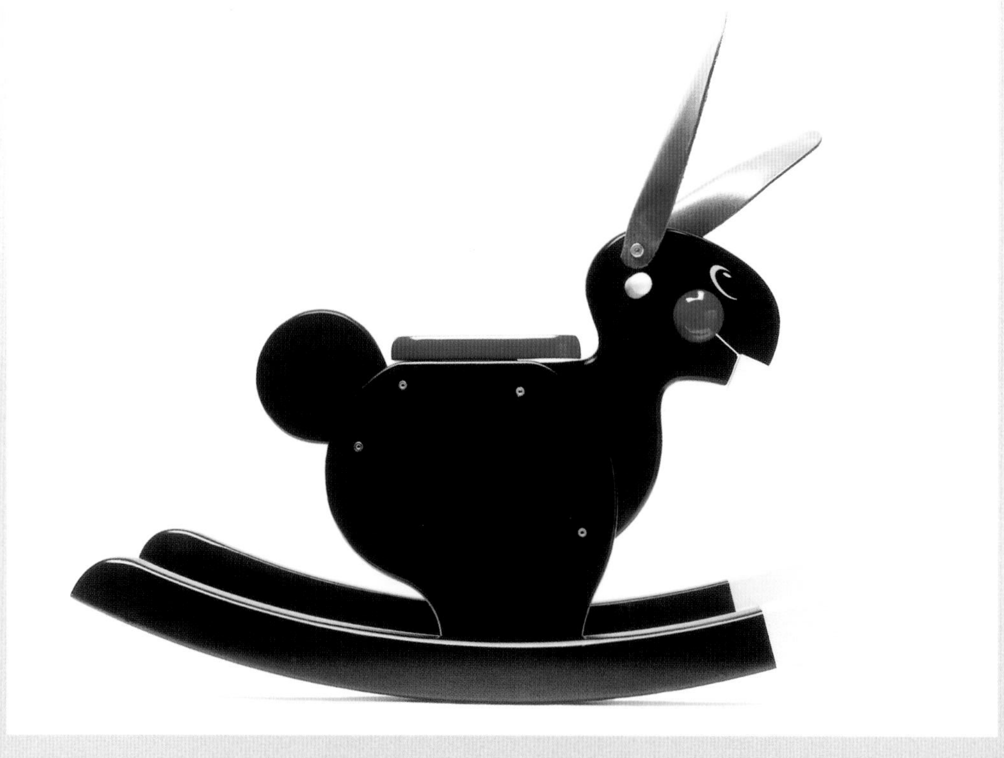

Rocking Rabbit for Playsam
Björn Dahlström
Wood, leather, high-density board
SWEDEN

Wool wine cooler for David Design
Erika Mörn
Knitted wool
SWEDEN

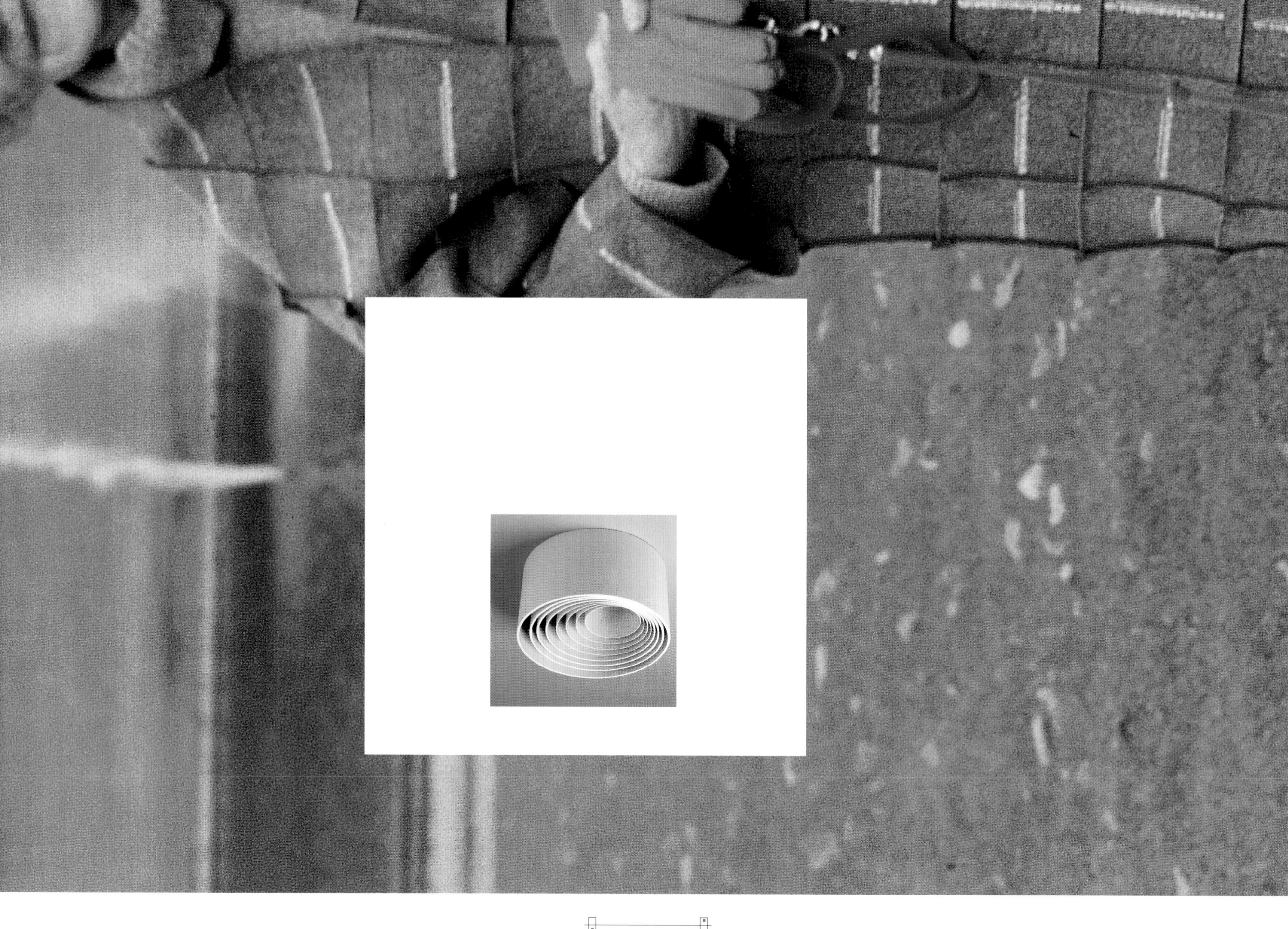

Fortunecookies, a modular clothing system
Jacob Ravn Jürgensen, Christina Widholm, Jonas Larsen, Stine Andersen
Felt, velcro
DENMARK

DENMARK
1 to 100 shelf system
Pil Bredahl
Painted paper, rubber bands

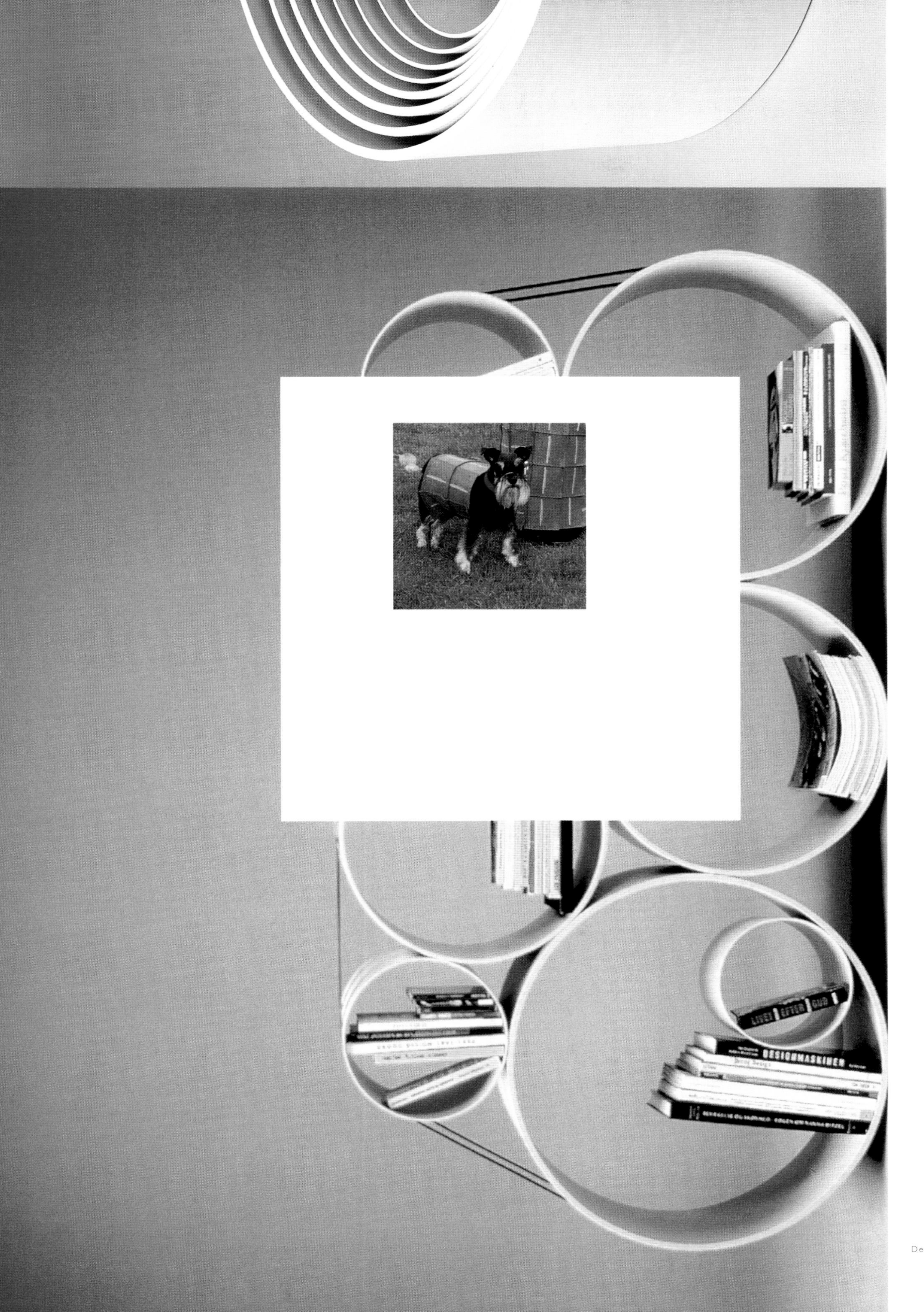
LIVET EFTER GUD
DESIGNMASKINER

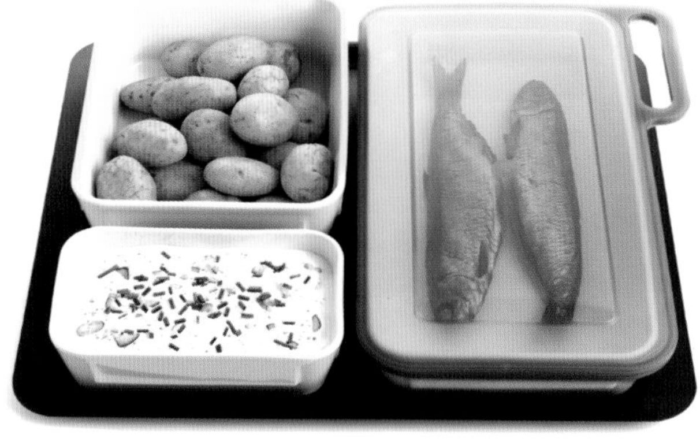

Air service for Arabia
Harri Koskinen
Vitreous china, plastic lids, aluminum tray
FINLAND

Summer Container, a portable plywood holiday cabin, for Schauman Wood
Markku Hedman
FINLAND

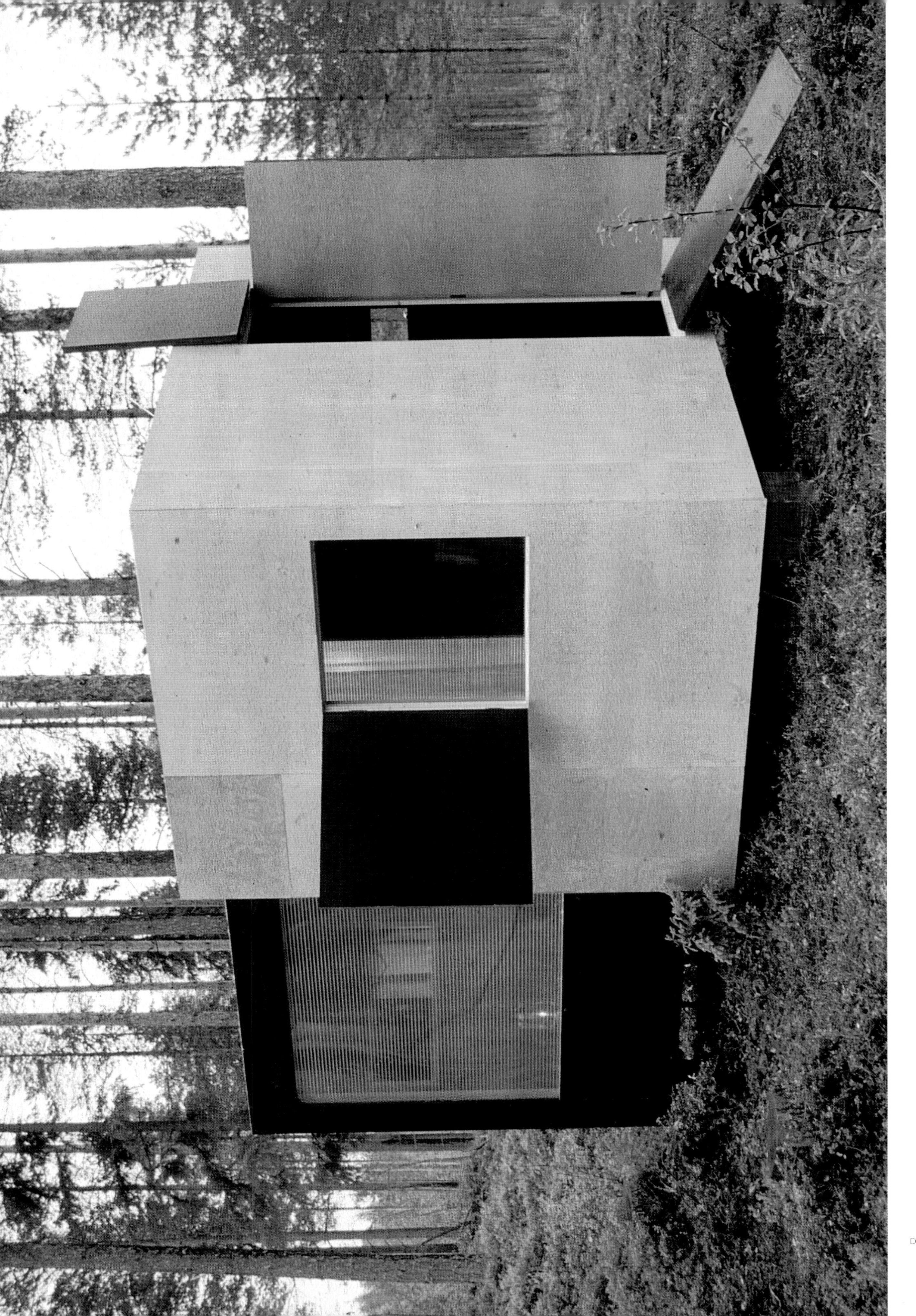

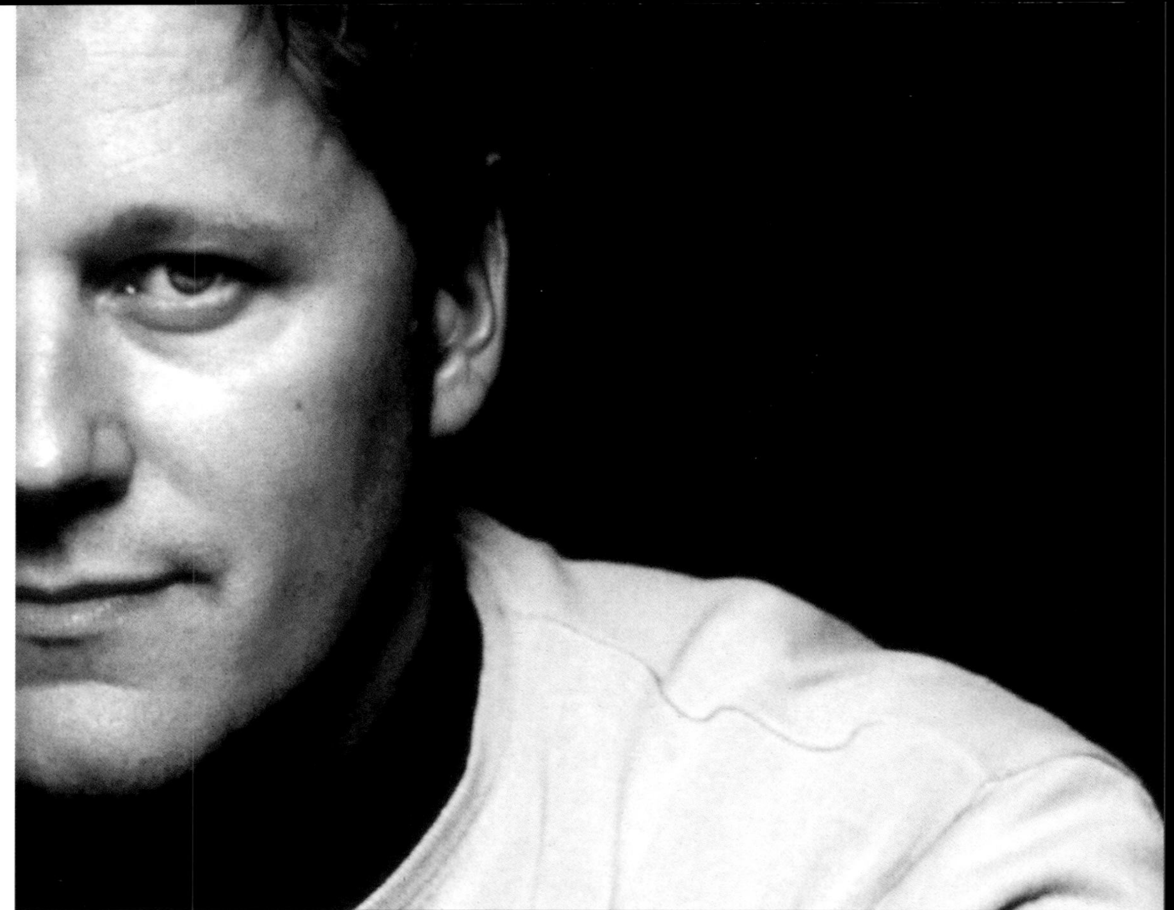

Stefan Ytterborn

Marketing the Scandinavian Lifestyle

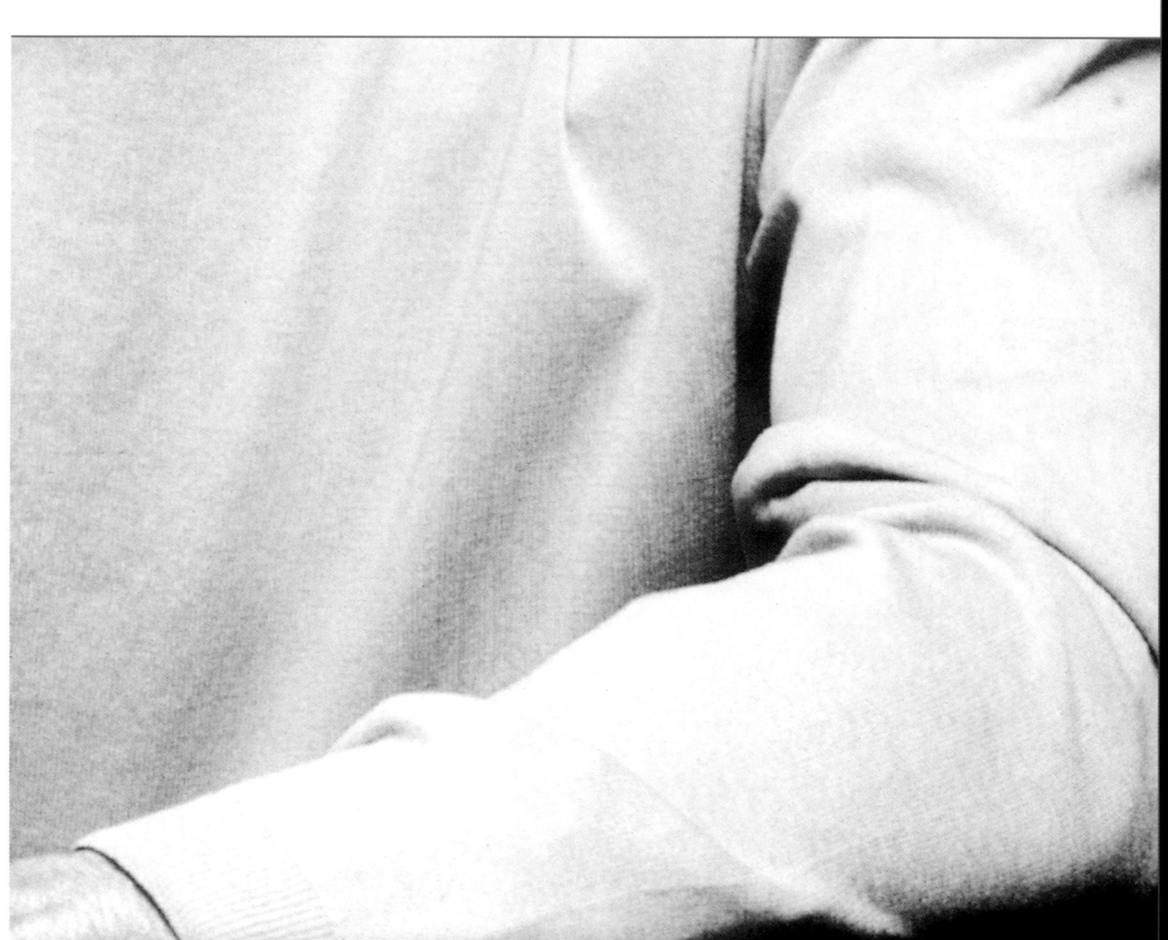

Stefan Ytterborn, entrepreneur, marketer, and principal of the design strategy consultancy Ytterborn & Fuentes, has been a major force in the contemporary design scene in Sweden. In the early 1990s, he launched the successful Swedish furniture companies Klara and cbi and was the originator of IKEA's influential, popular PS (Post Scriptum) line. In the mid-1990s, Ytterborn united a group of young, design-conscious Swedish producers including David Design and Asplund under the label Swecode (Swedish Contemporary Design). The group shared promotion costs and attended international exhibitions together, bringing international media attention to Swedish design. In 1996, Ytterborn established Ytterborn & Fuentes, which has relaunched classics by the Finnish designer Kaj Franck and persuaded McDonald's to turn two of its Stockholm franchises into Swedish design showcases. Ytterborn & Fuentes continues to tackle identity, design strategy, and branding projects for clients such as Hackman Group and Sony Ericsson.

Q: WHAT ARE SOME OF THE FACTORS THAT SET THE STAGE FOR THE REBIRTH OF DESIGN IN SWEDEN IN THE EARLY '90S? A: Design was increasingly hyped in the late '80s and the international economy was booming. At that time, Swedish designers didn't have much to contribute. It was an era of excess. But suddenly the recession hit, and there was a whole new situation. A weak global economy combined with a general international interest in the environment and ecology put the spotlight on the traditional values of Scandinavian design, such as long-lasting aesthetics, functionality, simplicity, and respect for materials, as well as concern for the environment. All that set a stage to communicate something new. I think that allowed Swedish designers to come up with designs that had validity to a large international audience. Suddenly, everything came together. That was the platform from which we have moved forward.

Of course, values are developed through what is happening in society in general; the design community didn't invent them. Scandinavian and Swedish design wouldn't have become this attractive if it hadn't been for those reasons I mention, with the economy collapsing and the increasing ecological awareness, and so forth. The world will change and new values will become important. This will encourage other expressions and eventually new designs. **Q: HOW WAS THE SCANDINAVIAN LIFESTYLE INFUSED IN THE NEW DESIGN MOVEMENT? A:** In general, I would say there is a strong anthropological aspect to it, and that gets back to our geography. We live in a harsh climate. For much of our history, Swedish people have been poor. If we compare ourselves to our Nordic neighbors, our situation was probably better in some ways, but it's been tough. People needed to depend on each other. Because of this history of poverty, we couldn't view things as temporary. Everything that was produced—a chair, a house, or whatever—needed to incorporate a long-lasting strategy. This involved how to process the material, how it was treated, that it would work for as many people as possible, and so forth. Also, in Scandinavia, there is a great respect for nature and what it provides. Whether it is wood or stone, [natural materials] have certain qualities. You could even say we look at the materials as having a soul to them. They are treated almost as though they were organisms rather than dead materials. Q: WHAT ARE EXAMPLES OF THE SCANDINAVIAN LIFESTYLE BEING REFLECTED IN ADVERTISING? A: Anything from a Volvo to an IKEA would be an example of this. Promoting a sound attitude and what you could call a definition of obviousness: things should be natural in a clear and apparent way, whether it be about how you use or consume the products, how they function, or whatever. Saab, Volvo, and IKEA materialize that whole culture. Q: IN 1998, SCANDINAVIAN AIRLINES (SAS) INITIATED A COMPREHENSIVE CORPORATE-IDENTITY AND AIRPORT-LOUNGE DESIGN PROGRAM WITH THE AGENCY STOCKHOLM DESIGN LAB, WHOSE FOUNDERS INCLUDE THOMAS ERIKSSON AND BJÖRN KUSOFFSKY. DOES THE SAS CAMPAIGN LEVERAGE TRADITIONAL SCANDINAVIAN VALUES? A: I would say so. I have great respect for what they did. It has a lot of integrity. In Scandinavia, there is a very specific cultural history. We are brought up with trying to bring meaning to things, relevance, transparency, honesty. In that context, there is a strong honesty to the whole SAS campaign. It has an ambition to share something that has relevance and integrity. Q: IS IT POSSIBLE TO HAVE HONESTY IN ADVERTISING AND MARKETING? A: I'm a bit of a romantic when it comes to that. I believe in a market economy from a consumer's perspective. If a company falls short on its product or promises, then consumers won't believe in the company anymore and will leave it for another company. Today, consumers as groups and collectives are more and more informed and picky about details. I do believe that there is force enough [in consumer choices] to actually make the world better. This is my romantic vision.

I think Sweden has something to share. There are loads of values that we need to import and learn about to become better in a sense. But from our perspective, we have a limited contribution in making the world a better one. Q: HOW DO YOU WALK THE LINE BETWEEN PRESENTING AN AUTHENTIC VISION OF SCANDINAVIAN LIFESTYLE AND PRESENTING A STEREOTYPE? A: There is a risk that as we discuss these notions of Scandinavian and Swedish style that they have already become stereotypes. In my work with the Finnish company Iittala, we didn't want to promote the definition or expression of Scandinavian design, but we wanted to promote the values. We didn't want to use the notion of Scandinavian design as a criterion or excuse for people to accept the products. That would be what we say in Sweden as "slamming into open doors." Therefore we tried to embrace everything from philosophical to conceptual and functional aspects of the products in the text that we wrote and the visual language we chose. We used the palette of Scandinavian values basically. Otherwise, it would have been too much of a cosmetic treatment. But I think, unfortunately, there are many companies just capitalizing on a stereotypical attitude or appearance. This is a big risk because if there is nothing behind it—if it is just hype—we will dissolve the relevance of Scandinavian design pretty quickly. Q: WHAT ROLE HAS THE INTERNATIONAL MEDIA PLAYED IN DEVELOPING THE CONCEPT OF THE "SCANDINAVIAN LIFESTYLE"? A: Everything. When we started off in the early 1990s, there was nothing to it. CBI, David Design, and the others were small companies with no industrial relevance at all. We were just showing prototypes to see if there was interest, and if there was, we struggled like hell trying to solve the production issues and distribute the stuff. Mainly, we were just promoting contemporary design ideas coming from Sweden. The image of Swedish design created by media at the time reflects a false reality. Even today, except for perhaps IKEA, we aren't exporting that much. But that image, from a business and industrial perspective, has had a lot of positive effects. It's not what the media has been writing about that has been selling, but it has opened a door to general interest in Swedish designers and companies.

In the early '90s, the Scandinavian lifestyle was something that the British press, and *Wallpaper** in particular, leveraged to create brands and sell its magazines. At the time, it was a part of *Wallpaper**'s luxury attitude. Not that Scandinavian design would be a traditionally luxury item, defined by high price and exclusive materials. The luxury part of it is in the exoticness. This has to do again with nature: on the archipelago, perhaps it is winter and people are going skating, or it's summer and they go sailing. There is a liberal kind of freshness to that image that makes it exotic. I'm not saying that it is a true reflection. It is easy to create a story around this image that has an exclusivity to it and therefore it promotes the idea of luxury. This is a new type of luxury that has attracted people. This isn't the traditional diamonds-and-gold kind of thing. It's quality-time luxury and quality-activity luxury. Q: DO YOU THINK THE RECENT INTEREST IN THE SCANDINAVIAN LIFESTYLE WILL HAVE ANY LASTING IMPACT ON INTERNATIONAL DESIGN? A: One of the reasons that Swedish and Scandinavian design have reestablished themselves is due to a global interest in different cultures that is much broader than ever before. There are loads of design scenes happening everywhere from South America to Portugal and being accepted simultaneously. The best thing that we have been able to do over the last ten years, when Swedish design interested the world in general, has been that we were able to share a couple of ideas that were imported by other countries in a positive way. That's probably the most important part of it if you have a holistic point of view.

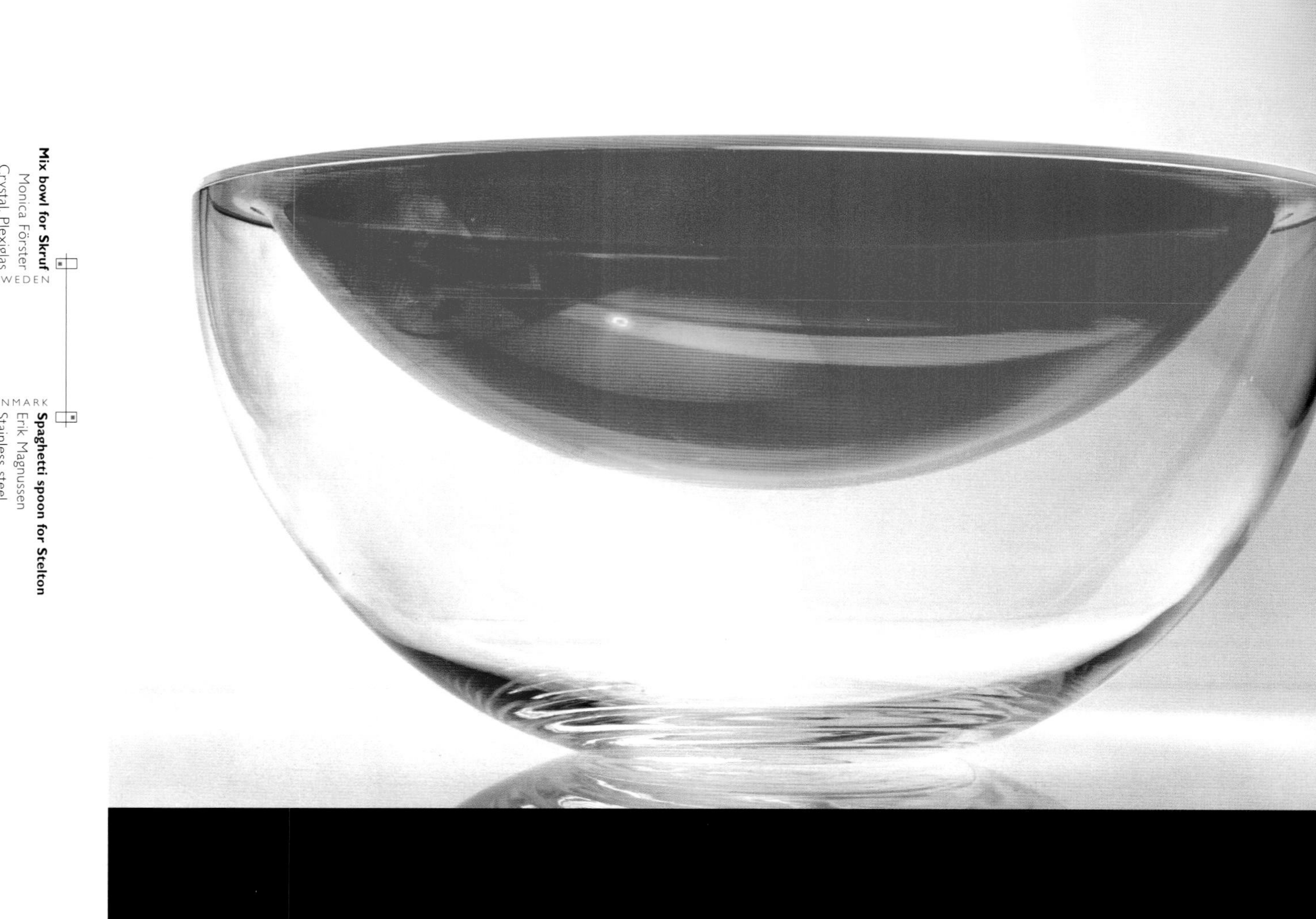

Mix bowl for Skruf
Monica Förster
Crystal, Plexiglas
SWEDEN

DENMARK
Spaghetti spoon for Stelton
Erik Magnussen
Stainless steel

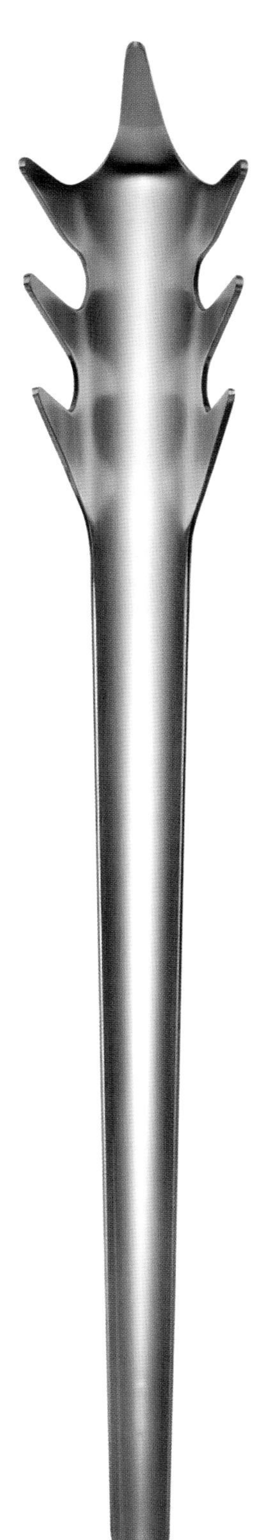

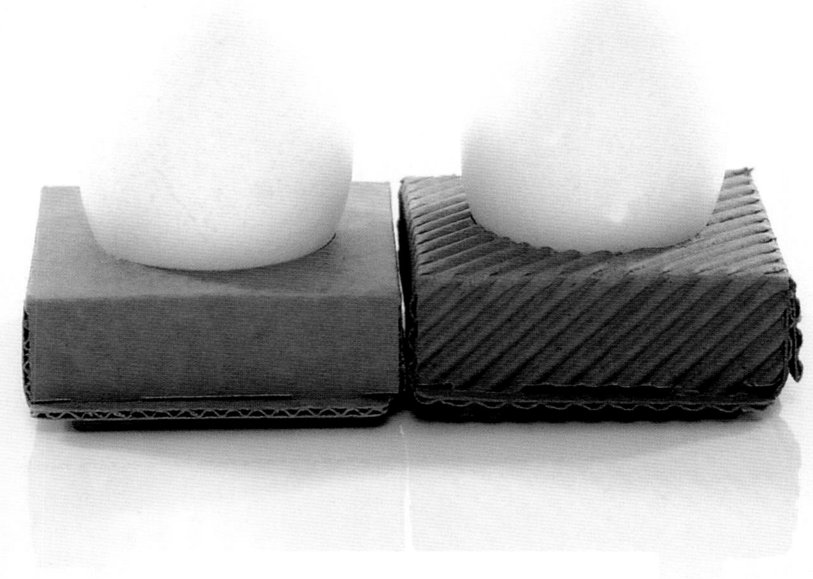

SWEDEN
Omtanke bowl
Jessica Signell
Glass, rubber stoppers

Democratic designers are open to diverse projects, and they seem to believe that all materials are created equal.

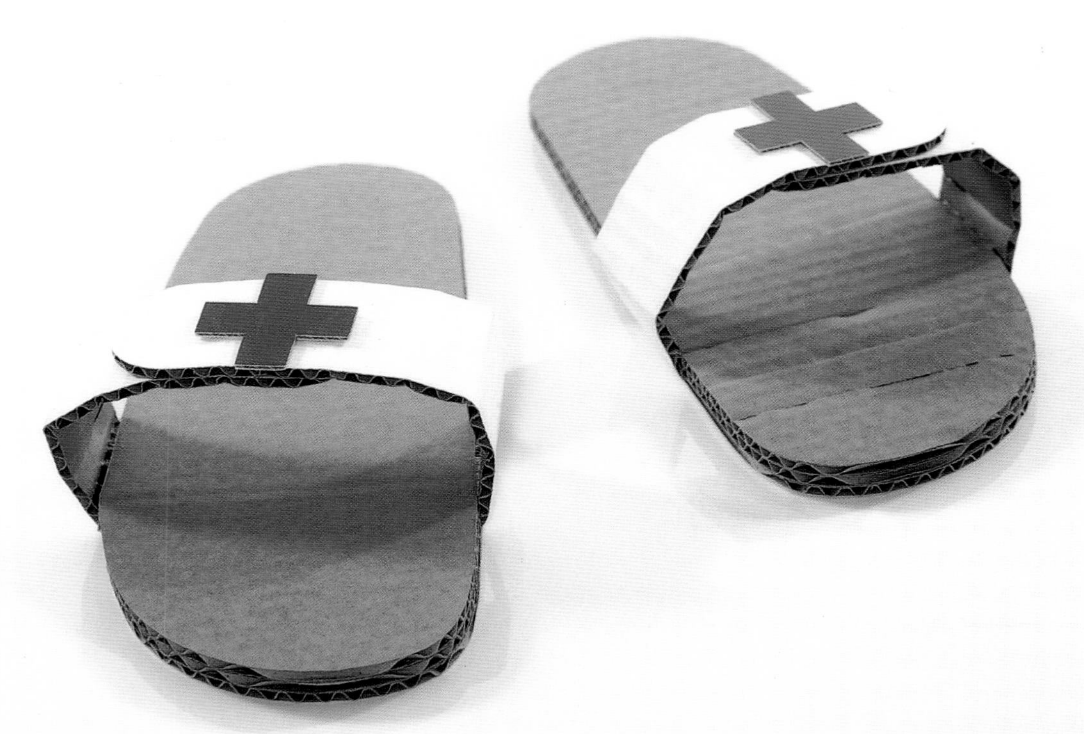

Papp Fiction, a design exhibition that explored new uses for cardboard
K8 Industridesign
NORWAY

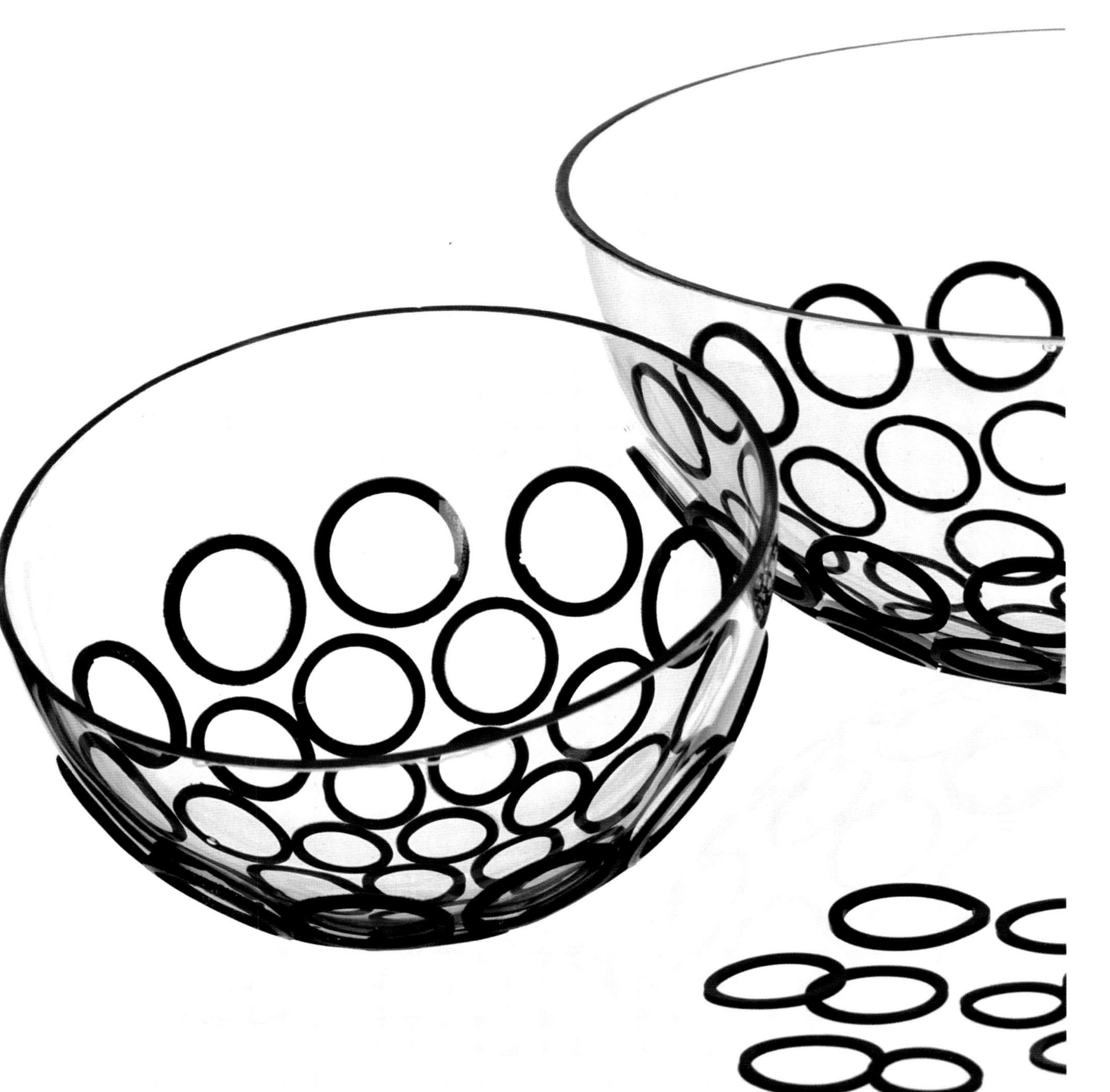

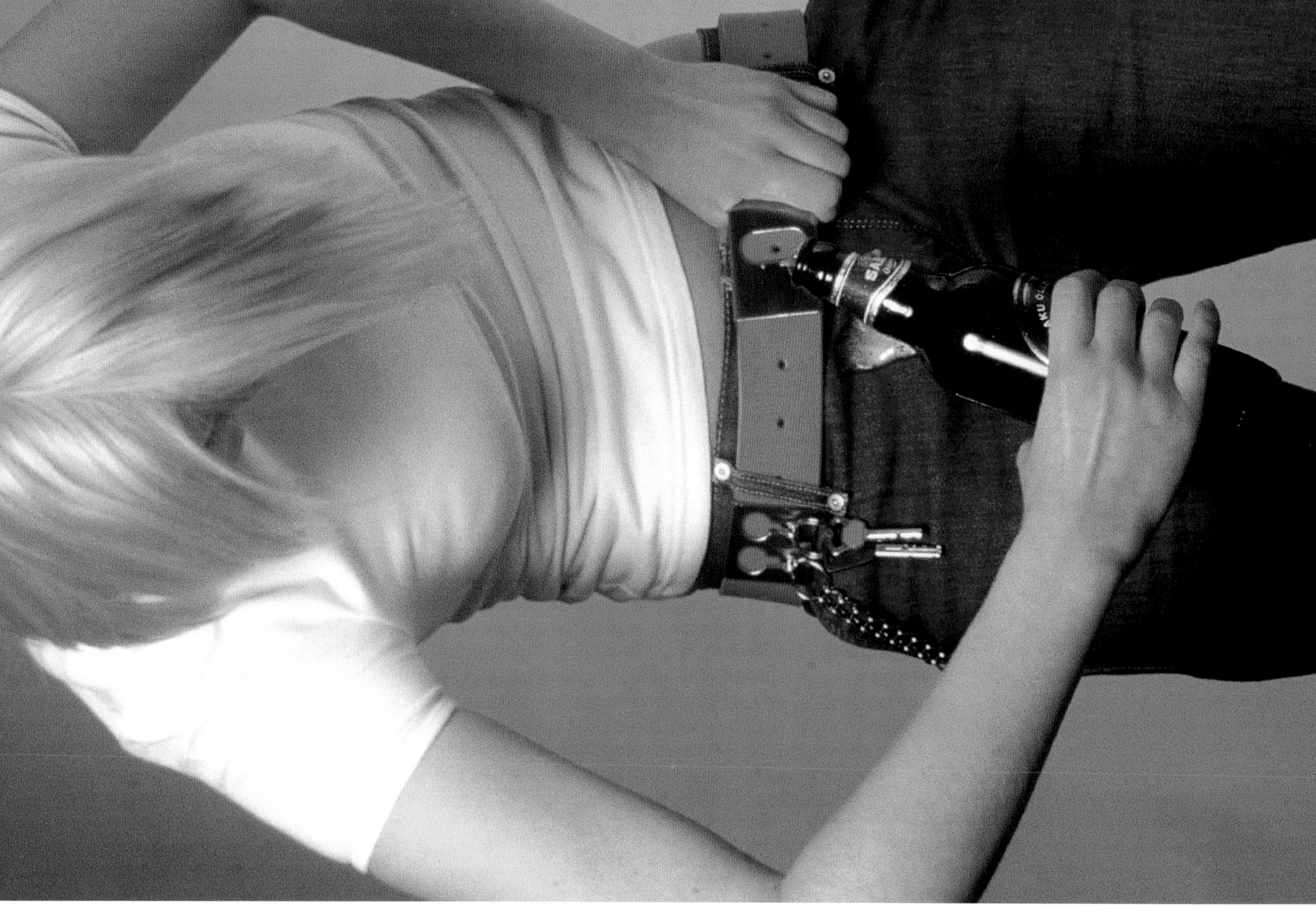

Belt
Mikko Paakkanen FINLAND
Brushed stainless steel, leather

➤ Ole colander for Royal Copenhagen
Ole Jensen DENMARK
Faience

➤ Tea light for IKEA/PS
Pelikan Copenhagen DENMARK
Porcelain

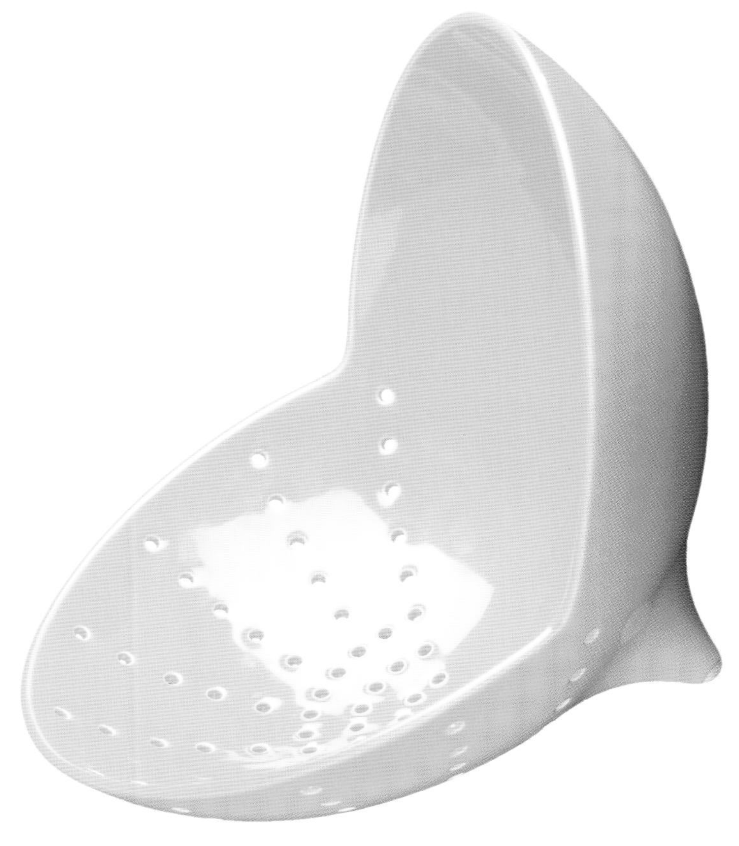

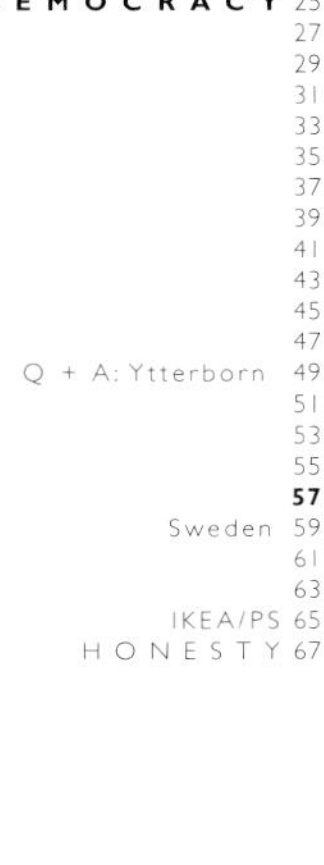

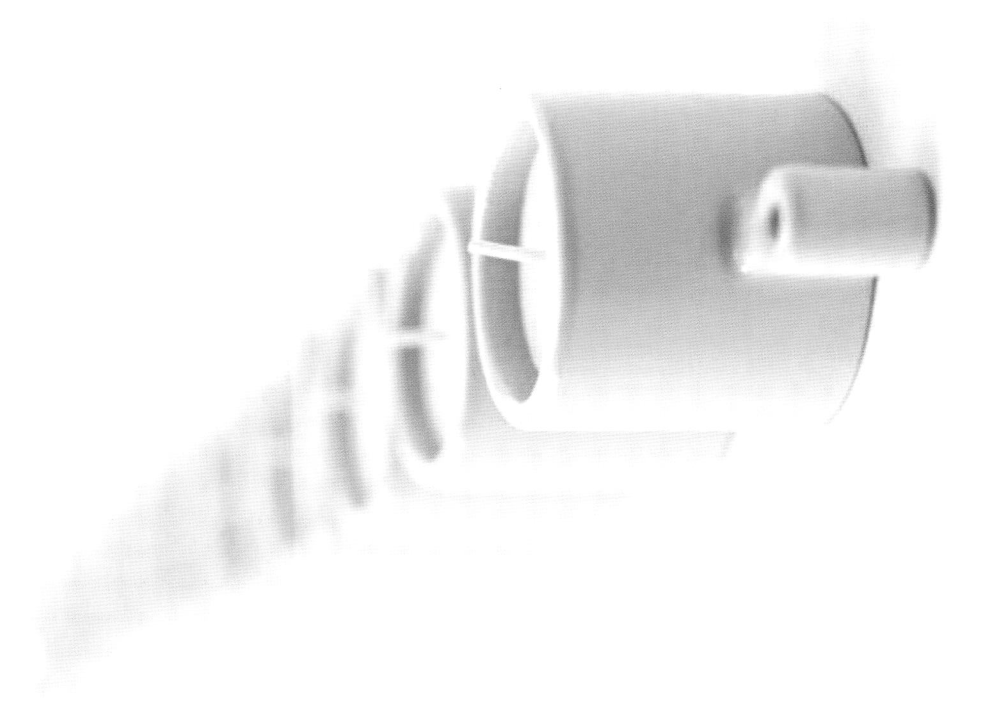

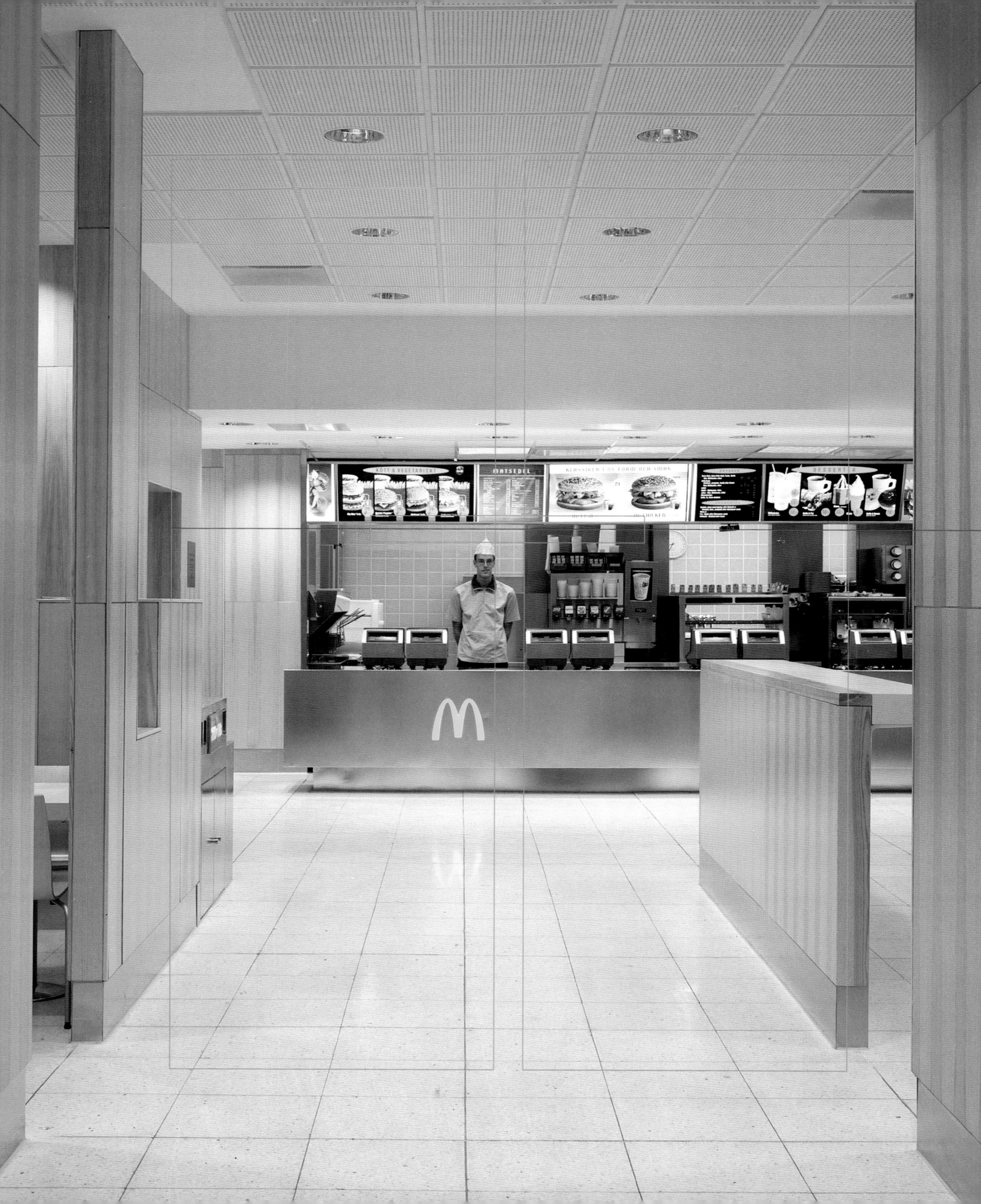
KÖTT & VEGETARISKT
MATSEDEL
KLASSIKER I NY FORM OCH SMAK

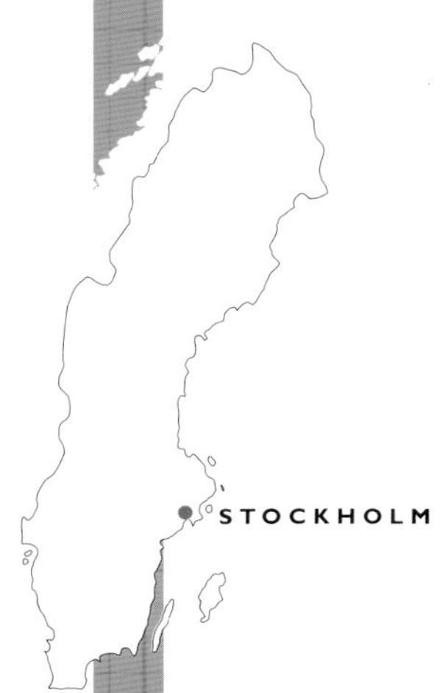

Sweden

The Swedish word *lagom* can't be translated easily into English. It means something like "not too much, and not too little." Swedes often use this word to describe their way of life in a country where there are few rich people and even fewer poor people, and where there are high taxes and solid social supports. But while Sweden has a reputation for being as safe and insulated as a brand-new Volvo, it is also home to market-savvy brands like Absolut vodka, trend-setting rock bands like the Hives, and innovative technology from companies like Sony Ericsson.

So, too, the best of Swedish design balances between two extremes. Swedish designers are experts at producing down-to-earth, domestic products that convey great sophistication. As early as the late 1980s, Swedish designers took inspiration as much from their heritage as from their global outlook, single-handedly putting the Nordic region back on the map as a center for design and innovation. Today, though a focus on functionality still defines much of the Swedish scene, young designers tweak tradition by imbuing their work with humor, irony, and lighthearted references to pop culture.

The recent renaissance of design in Scandinavia first gained momentum in Sweden in the early 1990s with the coming-of-age of a new generation of designers. Entrepreneur Stefan Ytterborn founded two successful venues for new Swedish design during that period, the retail store Klara and the furniture and design label cbi. "Not to be bigheaded," says Ytterborn, now principal of the design strategy consultancy Ytterborn & Fuentes, "but this generation of Swedish designers had been around quite a bit. We were the first group to travel a lot internationally. We were familiar with the media and could communicate well. We had learned English well enough to become a

Official name: The Kingdom of Sweden • Population: Almost 9 million • Area: 174,000 square miles (449,964 square kilometers) (the third-largest

Interior of McDonald's restaurant in downtown Stockholm (previous spread)
Claesson Koivisto Rune

SWEDEN

part of something larger than the local culture." The group boasted a broad spectrum of talent. One of the most prominent designers, architect Thomas Sandell, fashioned minimal designs that ranged from practical furniture for the Swedish company IKEA to sensual, style-conscious pieces for the Italian producer Cappellini. Sandell's schoolmate, Thomas Eriksson, opted for strong, specific gestures such as his iconic 1992 Red Cross cabinet for Cappellini. Other major talents included the industrial designer Björn Dahlström, fashion designer Pia Wallén, and furniture designer Jonas Bohlin. By the mid-1990s, the collective Claesson Koivisto Rune had refined Swedish simplicity to the extreme, crafting their Spartan designs for producers in far-flung countries including Italy and Japan.

While this new generation showed great promise, one of the keys to its future success lay in the breadth of its members' expertise. Not only did the community possess solid design skill but it also had means to curate exhibitions and produce, distribute, and promote work. In addition to designers, the group included entrepreneurs such as Ytterborn; retailers such as David Carlson of David Design and the Asplund brothers, Michael and Thomas, of Asplund; and publishers such as Claes Britton, who founded the magazine *Stockholm New* with his wife, Christina Sollenberg Britton, in 1991.

Before this new group appeared in the early 1990s, innovation in Swedish design was flagging. Its golden age had come just after World War II. Unlike its Nordic neighbors, Sweden remained neutral in the war. "We had no physical damages and there had been many technical achievements during the war, industrially and artistically," says Cilla Robach, curator of applied art at the National Museum of Fine Arts in Stockholm. However, by the 1960s and '70s, a dramatic increase in consumer-product imports was putting financial pressure on Swedish companies. "Our salaries were so high that there was no way we could compete with goods from Eastern Europe and Asia." says Robach. The influx of affordable goods caused a wave of mergers and acquisitions that changed the dynamic of design production. The furniture and consumer products sectors came to depend on commissions from the growing bureaucracy of the Swedish welfare state rather than on consumer demand, according to Claes Britton, who says that design companies focused on "quantity instead of quality. The 1960s and 1970s was a time when we lost a lot of important industries like textiles. When that happened, a respect for beauty was lost as well." But by the 1980s, says Britton, "the pendulum was swinging back to design."

During the economic decline of the late 1980s, the Swedish design community found renewal by returning to its roots—folk arts and crafts—which became popular subjects in several art schools. Folk tradition has occupied an important place in Swedish design since the late nineteenth century, in the work of the influential painter Carl Larsson and the writings of social reformer Ellen Key, who was inspired by the British Arts and Crafts movement. For designer Pia Wallén, a student project at Anders Beckman School of Design in Stockholm inspired a lifelong fascination with felt, an ancient Scandinavian wool textile. With a poetic sense of geometry and color, Wallén

country in Europe, behind Spain and France but ahead of Germany) • Capital: Stockholm • Longest annual period of daylight in Stockholm: 18 hours • Shortest annual peri-

sculpts delicate felt items such as slippers, dresses, bags, bowls, and blankets. "It is interesting that the process of making felt is the oldest way to make a textile fabric," she says. "The fabric has inspired me for twenty years." After receiving his architecture degree from Stockholm's Royal Institute of Technology in 1985, Thomas Sandell bisected a traditional Swedish folk symbol, a Dalarna horse (a hand-painted wooden horse figurine), and used the pieces for handles on the doors of a new cabinet design. The work caused a sensation. "The Dalarna horse is a national symbol, so cutting it in half and putting it on a door was a bit like burning the flag," says Sandell, who claims that he was attracted to the object more for its decorative and historical value than for its power to outrage. "It got a lot of attention, and, suddenly, it became an art piece."

Folk tradition was only one of the many influences on this young group of designers. The concept of treating furniture as art, which had made a dramatic impact in southern Europe, particularly in the work of the Italian design group Memphis, worked its way north. In 1981, Jonas Bohlin designed a chair called Concrete that created a stir at his graduation from Stockholm's Konstfack, University College of Arts, Crafts and Design. Constructed from concrete and tubular steel, the heavy, brooding piece violated all established norms of ergonomics and ease of use, turning upside down the fundamental principles of Scandinavian design—utility, functionality, modesty, and affordability. Though perhaps the chair could have been mass-produced, the furniture company Källemo made Concrete in limited editions numbered from one to one hundred.

As the Swedish scene slowly gained momentum, production of contemporary design remained limited and expensive. This all changed in 1995 when IKEA introduced its original PS (Post Scriptum) line, the brainchild of Stefan Ytterborn. Long before Target enlisted the help of Michael Graves, the IKEA/PS collection brought together the work of nineteen well-known designers, including Thomas Sandell and Thomas Eriksson, proving that good design could be affordable. "That's why the PS line was so talked about," says Robach. "These designers had created very expensive and exclusive things, but then, for the first time, their work was mass-produced and suddenly accessible to new consumer groups." The collection featured clean lines, minimal ornament, and a predominant use of birch with technologically advanced and cost-effective materials such as particleboard. A perfect response to the economic belt-tightening of the early 1990s, the new line fascinated members of the press and public at that year's Milan Furniture Fair. At home and abroad, a wave of interest in Swedish design followed.

Today, the national government is capitalizing on the enthusiasm for Swedish design by transforming media attention into economic growth. The government has sponsored a national program that aims to make Sweden a world leader in design exports by 2005, called the "Year of Design." And there has definitely been movement in that direction. Furniture production has reached around $2 billion (19 billion kronor), almost doubling since 1995, according to Dag Klockby, managing director of the furniture company Galleri Stolen and former vice-chairman of the Swedish Furniture Industry Association. Furniture

od of daylight in Stockholm: 6 hours • Official language: Swedish (minority languages include the Lapp language Sami, Finnish, Tornedalen Finnish, Yiddish, and the gypsy

exports are also up from $550 million (5 billion Swedish kronor) in 1995 to more than $1 billion (11.5 billion Swedish kronor) today.

While this generation of Swedish designers is still active, the new millennium witnessed the entrance of the next class of talent, educated in the 1990s. In many ways, the international attention that Sweden garnered in that decade has provided the newcomers with direction. "In school, we were supposed to do our courses and then go straight to a big architectural studio after graduation," says Peter Andersson, a member of the furniture design collective Our. "But today, like in the early '90s, there aren't many ordinary jobs to be found. Those earlier designers created their own market by starting their own studios, and this built up our confidence: if they could do it, so could we."

To carve out their own identity, young Swedish designers fine-tune Swedish Functionalism by adding touches of play and irony. Blatantly untraditional colors and materials, as in the day-glow mohair wool pillows hand-knitted by textile designer Nina Jobs, have worked their way into a number of new designs. Patterns on textiles and furniture, as opposed to the solid colors that were so ubiquitous in the original IKEA/PS line, are more pronounced today. And storytelling, a popular concept, provides the genesis for some new designs, such as Eva Schildt's double-decker, decanter-inspired café table, where water runoff creates a birdbath.

Emerging from the previous decade's emphasis on functionality and laconic form, some designers are now feeling restless. They shake free from what they view as the restrictive notions of "good design" by engaging kitsch, as in Per B. Sundberg's Moose Radio. This over-the-top art piece functions as a radio and is sculpted from ceramic tourist trinkets. It holds a spot in the permanent design collection at the National Museum of Fine Arts in Stockholm. Awkward, craft-inspired elements also pervade some new pieces. Uglycute, a collective of four artists and designers, critiques minimalism with sentimental, tacky shapes and materials such as glittering particleboard and spongy foam rubber—the group's designs would make any Swedish neo-Modernist cringe. "In the late '90s everyone was talking about design," says artist and Uglycute member Markus Degerman. "The problem was that it all looked the same. I didn't see much beneath the surface." Another member, interior architect Andreas Nobel, adds, "A sleek minimal design is a closed argument. We like to think of our designs as messy and leaking."

Over the last decade, Sweden, a country of only nine million, has achieved impressive international success in design. Yet the active dialogue among Swedish creatives shows that they are hardly intent on perpetuating the achievements of the past. "We have been lucky enough to be able to contribute a few ideas to the international design community and to establish a strong position for Swedish design," says Ytterborn. "At the same time, there are many ideas out there that we still need to import and learn about if we are to look to the future." With characteristic dexterity, Swedish designers are sure to take inspiration from global trends and local traditions, all the while maintaining their keen sense of *lagom*.

SWEDEN
Mushroom knife for K J Eriksson AB, Mora
Ergonomidesign
Steel, Polypropylene

language Romani Chib.) • Percentage of births outside marriages: 55 • Most famous contributions to the English language: Moped; smorgasbord

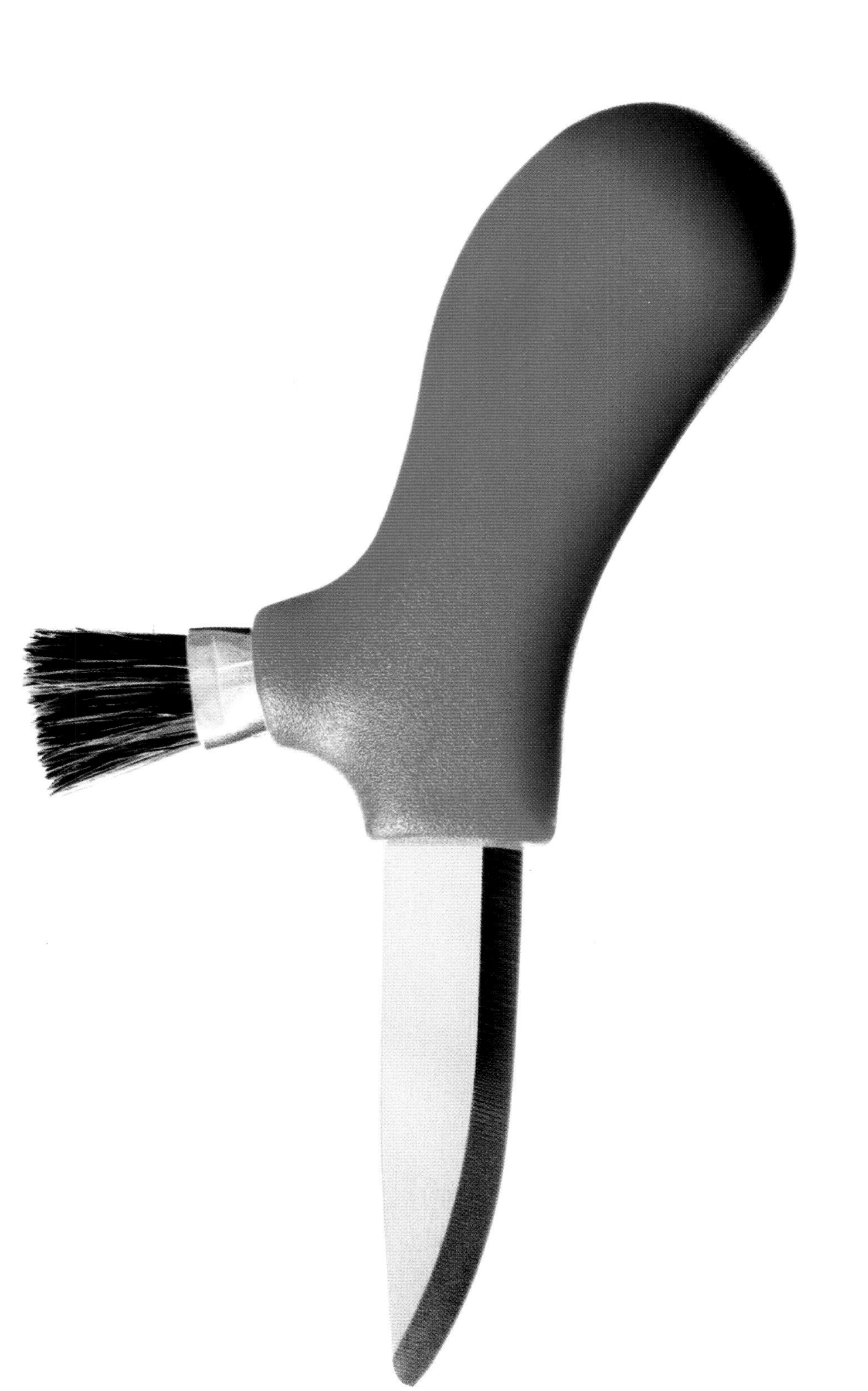

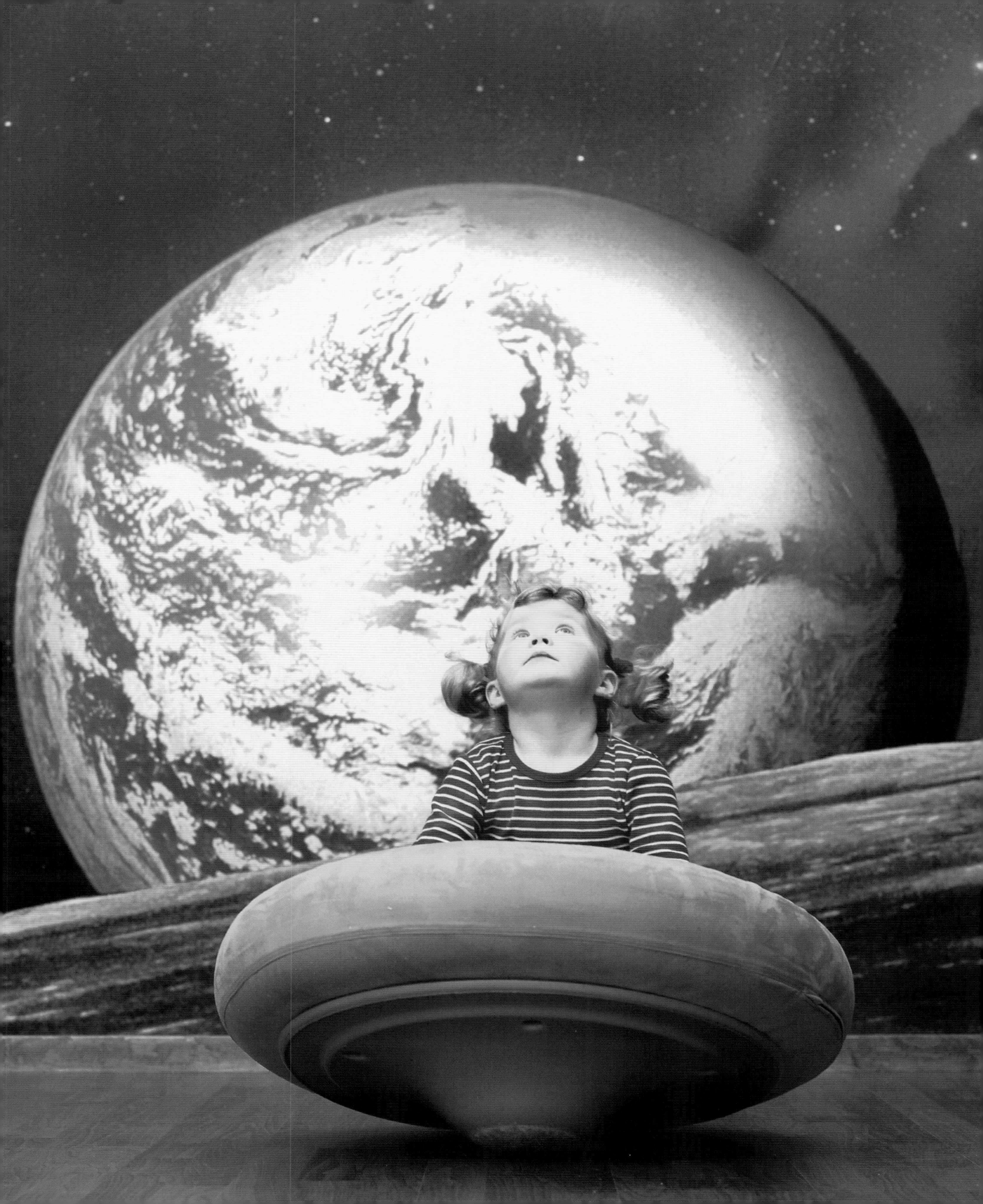

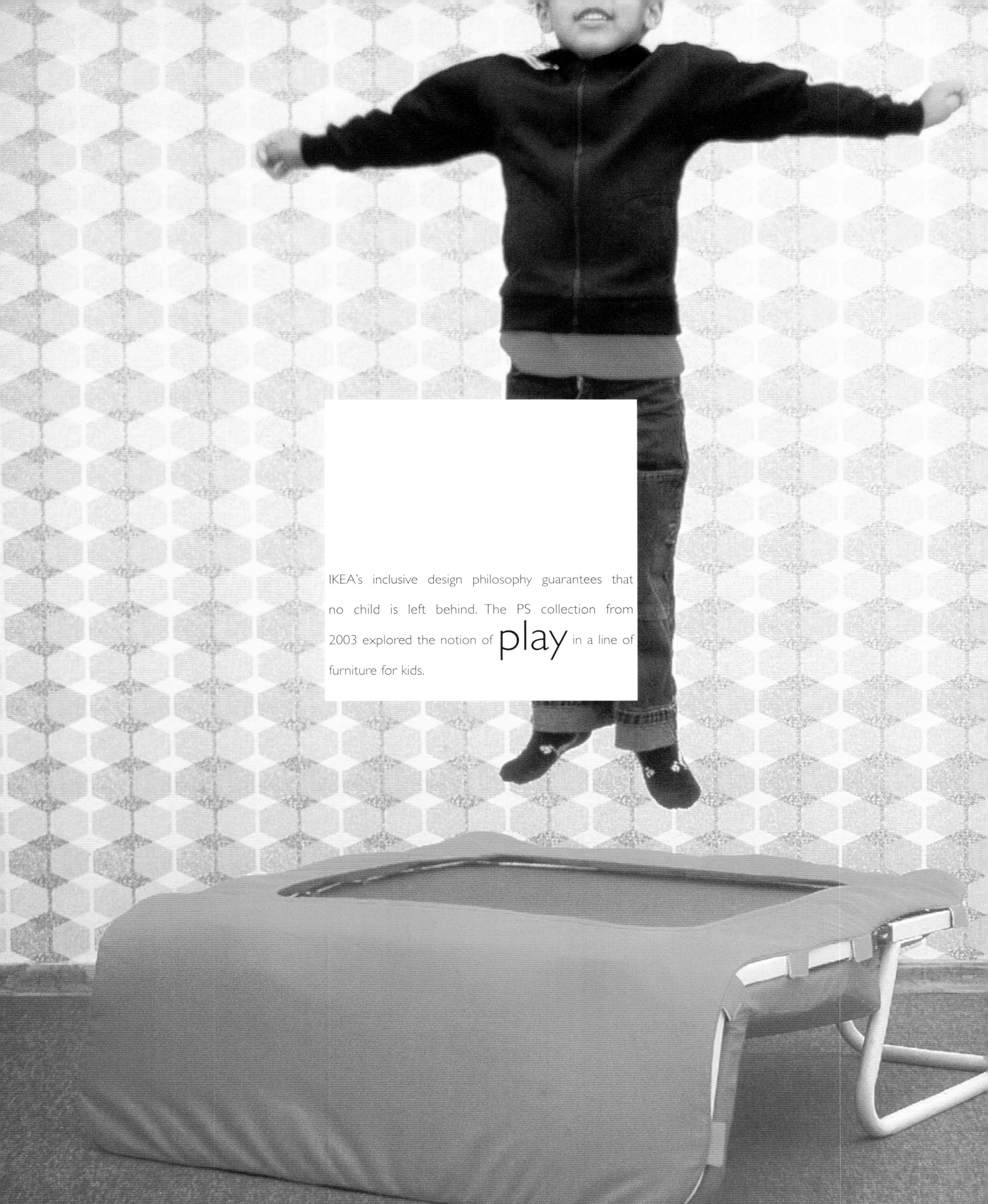

IKEA's inclusive design philosophy guarantees that no child is left behind. The PS collection from 2003 explored the notion of play in a line of furniture for kids.

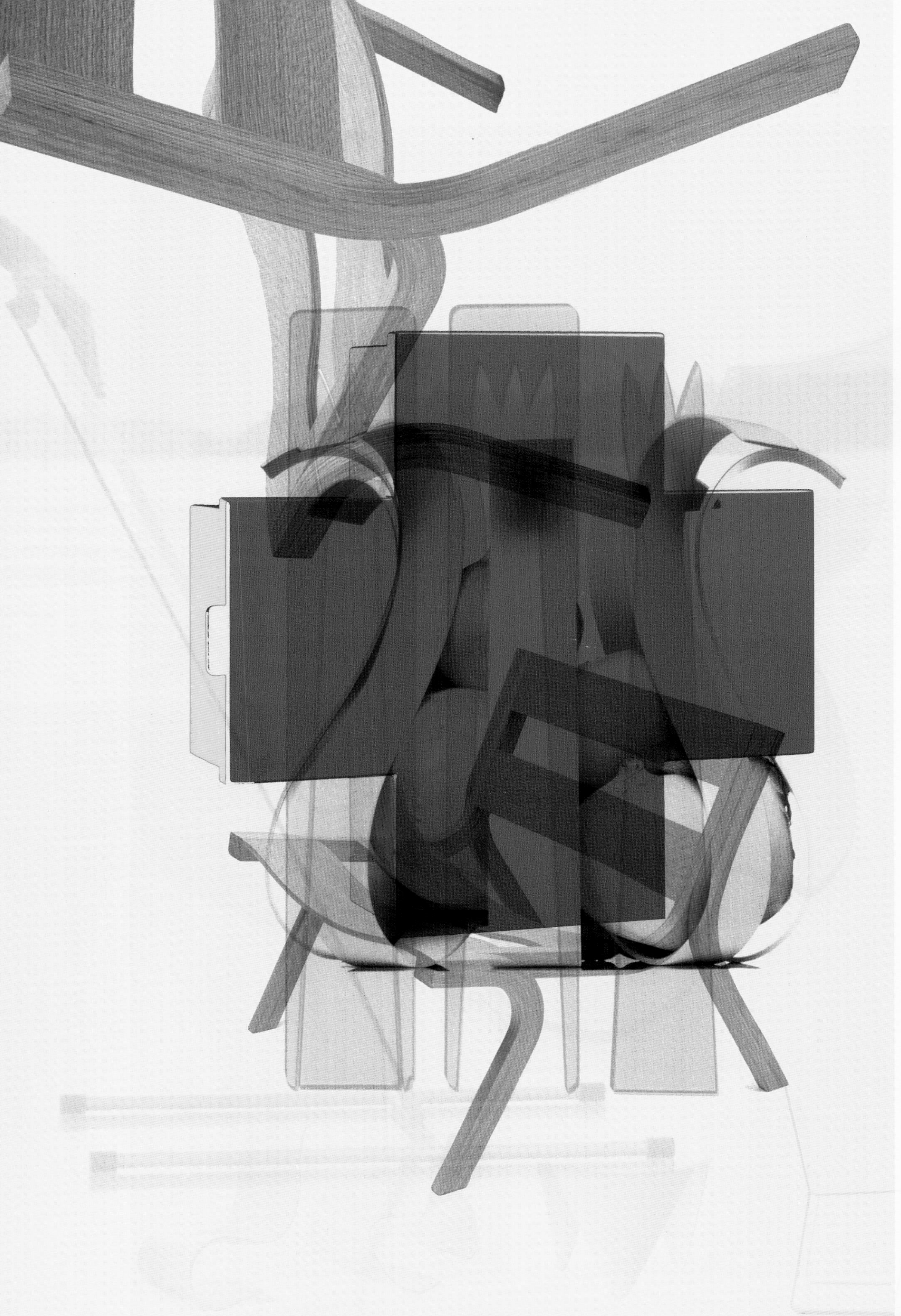

CHAPTER II

HONESTY

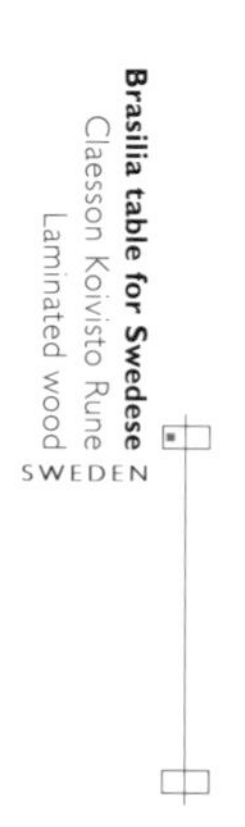

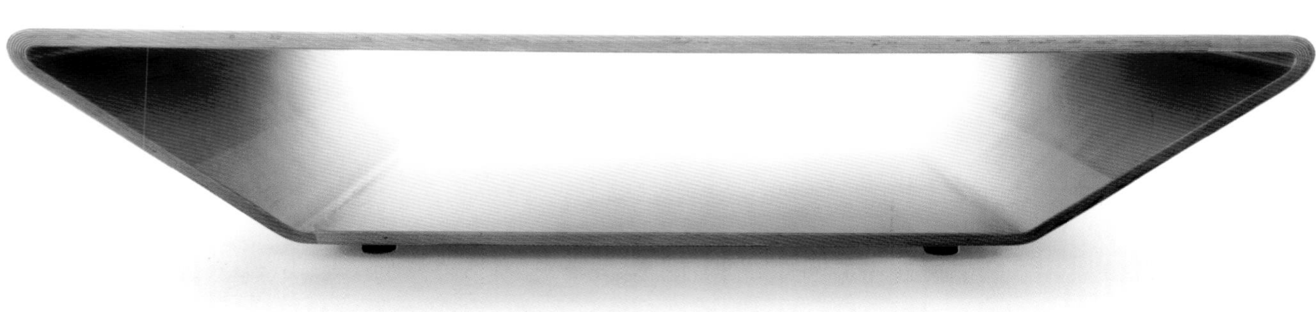

Brasilia table for Swedese
Claesson Koivisto Rune
Laminated wood
SWEDEN

HONESTY

Heralding a new age of functional design, the 1930 Stockholmsutställningen ("Stockholm Exhibition") introduced Modernism to the Scandinavian countries. Inspired by the new movement—which was established by the Bauhaus school, the architect Le Corbusier, and other designers in central and western Europe—the exhibition's chief architect, Erik Gunnar Asplund, celebrated rationality with a city of gleaming white pavilions. Built on a picturesque waterfront, the exhibition united nature and architecture, proposing new concepts for urban housing and living. While detractors felt that the imported Modern style would erase national characteristics, the exhibition defined a new language of orderly beauty that would transform the future of Scandinavian design. The critic Gotthard Johansson, a supporter of the exhibition, wrote, "[Asplund] has shown that pure cubes and clear spaces can be built up into a shining architectural poem of festivities."

A watershed event, the Stockholm Exhibition inspired Scandinavian architects and designers to embrace the new Modern style, which they viewed as rational and honest. As the twentieth century went on, Scandinavians would evolve their own brand of Modernism, not as an industrial aesthetic or theoretical truth but as a response to human need. This unpretentious ideology, emphasizing beauty in utility, still exerts a strong influence on Scandinavian design. While young designers expand the medium's practical demands to include humor, emotion, and the concept of leisure time, a focus on function still pervades much of their design.

At the Stockholm Exhibition, the International Style crossed paths with what was quickly becoming an established human-centered design practice within Scandinavia. As early as 1917, Kaare Klint, a professor at the Royal Academy of Fine Art in Denmark (and now considered the father of Modern Danish furniture design), was pioneering the field of "anthropometrics," the then-revolutionary study of the relationship between empirical human measurements and furniture. The tradition was reinforced by the work of the young Finnish designer Alvar Aalto, who created humane designs with natural materials in the late 1920s and early 1930s. In his early architectural masterpiece, the Paimio Sanitarium, Aalto tempered the industrial aesthetic championed by his continental colleagues designing bentwood chairs for hospital patients. Aalto preferred wood to the tubular steel embraced by Bauhaus designers, believing that the material's giving nature and soft aesthetic made it more comfortable for the patients physically and comforting psychologically.

During the 1920s, European innovations such as Le Corbusier's 1925 Pavillon de l'Esprit Nouveau informed many of the ideas later present in the Stockholm Exhibition. (After viewing Le Corbusier's work, the Swedish architect Uno Åhrén wrote, "'Functionality' is in the process of becoming a value to

In Scandinavia, the new Modern style—termed "Functionalism"—eventually brought together traditional humanistic values and utilitarian form.

NORWAY
Chopsticks for the restaurant Palmehaven
Cathrine Maske, Espen Voll
Plexiglas

be considered in its own right.") In Scandinavia, the new Modern style—termed "Functionalism"—eventually brought together traditional humanistic values and utilitarian form. In Sweden in the 1930s, Functionalism provided the newly elected Social Democrats, who came to power on a platform promoting the creation of new housing, with a rational methodology for addressing rampant overcrowding, poverty, and other problems resulting from modernization. Functionalism flourished during the 1950s, known as the "Golden Age" of Scandinavian Modern, and designers in every Nordic country evolved compelling solutions based on need. The Nordic Council of Ministers encouraged the pan-Scandinavian aesthetic—notably in exhibitions such as "Design in Scandinavia" (1954–57), which traveled in North America, and "Formes Scandinave" (1958), shown in France. Classic examples of Scandinavian Functionalism during this period include a 1954 shelf system by the Danish designers Grethe Meyer and Børge Mogensen (a student of Kaare Klint) that, depending on the requirements of the household, could be installed in any room. The Finnish designer Kaj Franck also championed convenience and utility in his mix-and-match 1953 dinnerware set Kilta, the pieces of which could be purchased separately.

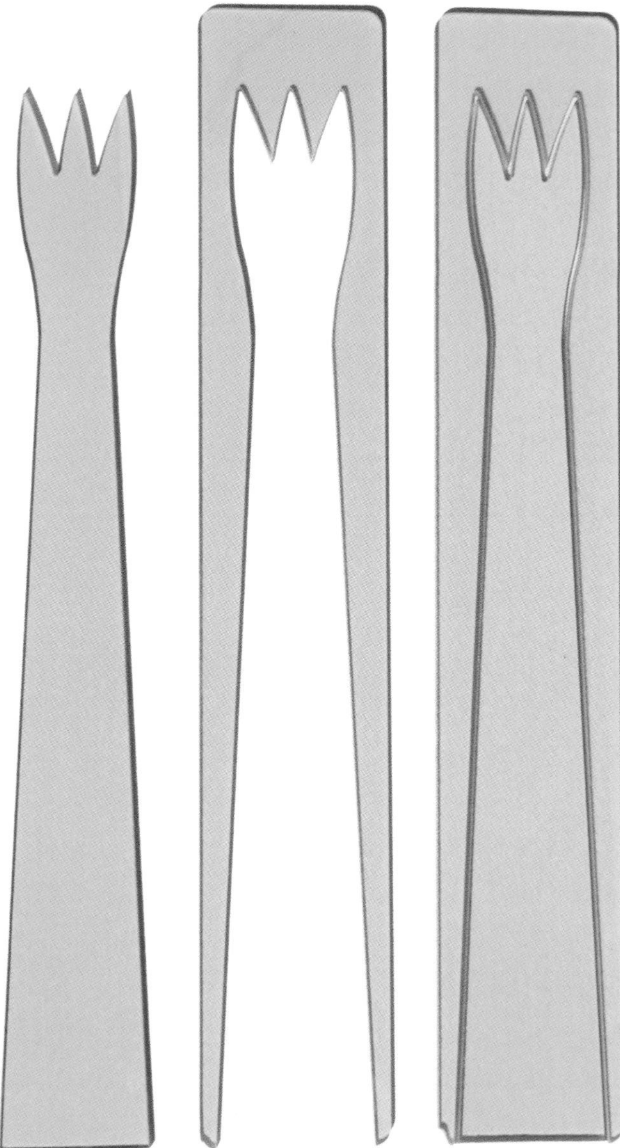

While the rational qualities of Scandinavian design were overrun by plastic and pop in the 1960s, and mass production overtook craftsmanship in the 1970s, the heritage of honest, efficient design remained steadfast. And Scandinavian designers continued to reinterpret the vision of the creation of practical, beautiful objects to fit the times. In the 1970s and early 1980s, industrial design groups such as Sweden's Ergonomidesign and A&E Design and Finland's Fiskars and Creadesign established international reputations with noteworthy studies of usability. In the furniture field, designers were inspired by the human-centric design methodology first practiced by Klint. One of the most active proponents of this approach today is the innovative Norwegian designer Peter Opsvik, who made his name in 1972 with a child's chair called Tripp Trapp. Opsvik bases his approach on observation and rejects single, static solutions by creating ergonomic designs that take into account a range of motion.

By the late 1980s and early 1990s, a new generation of Scandinavian designers, particularly a group of young Swedes, including Thomas Sandell and Thomas Eriksson, rediscovered the Golden Age of Scandinavian Modern. Exposed to media and travel, these young designers updated the message of Functionalism, taking inspiration from its matter-of-fact approach and international outlook. "In the late 1980s, a

B ➤

SWEDEN
Red Cross cabinet for Cappellini (B)
Thomas Eriksson
Steel plate

weak global economy combined with a general interest in the environment and ecology put the spotlight on traditional values of Scandinavian design, such as long-lasting aesthetics, functionality, simplicity, and respect for materials," says design consultant Stefan Ytterborn, who helped launch the careers of several designers during this period. "I think that allowed Scandinavian designers to come up with designs that had validity to a large international audience." This neo-Modernist design joined beauty and utility. For example, Eriksson designed a medicine cabinet **(B)** (1992) for Cappellini in the shape of a red cross; the piece works on an iconic as well as practical level. A stylish economy of materials and simplified forms also characterizes the work, as exemplified by Sandell's elegant aluminum Lucia candlesticks **(A)** see **p 100** (1995). Pragmatic solutions were paramount to these designers: wheels attached for mobility and convenience distinguish Eriksson's television table and Sandell's chest of drawers, both for IKEA/PS (1995).

Although the new style engaged aspects of Functionalism, the social agenda of earlier times felt less urgent. Contemporary designers were reacting to a different set of problems, which they viewed as the consumer product industry's creative malaise. "We were the victims of an isolated market situation," says Ytterborn. Government commissions from the growing bureaucracy of the Scandinavian governments, booming

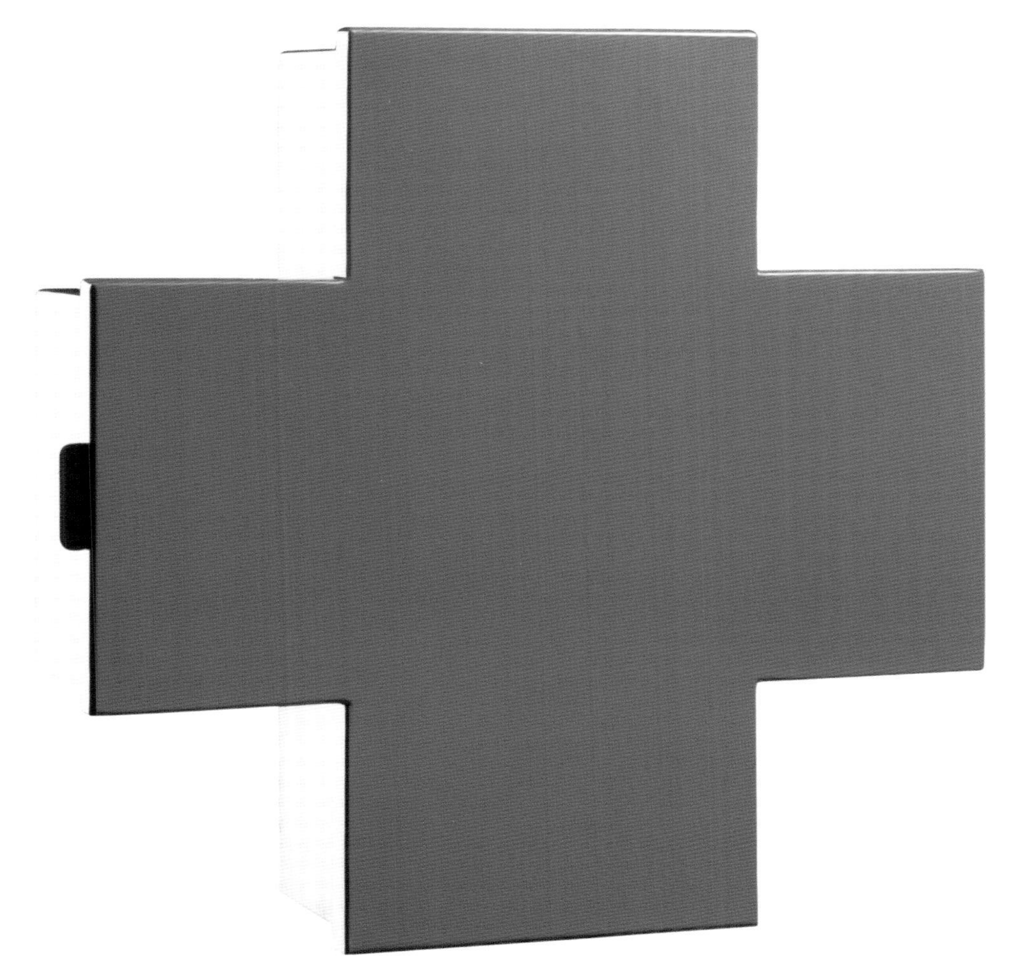

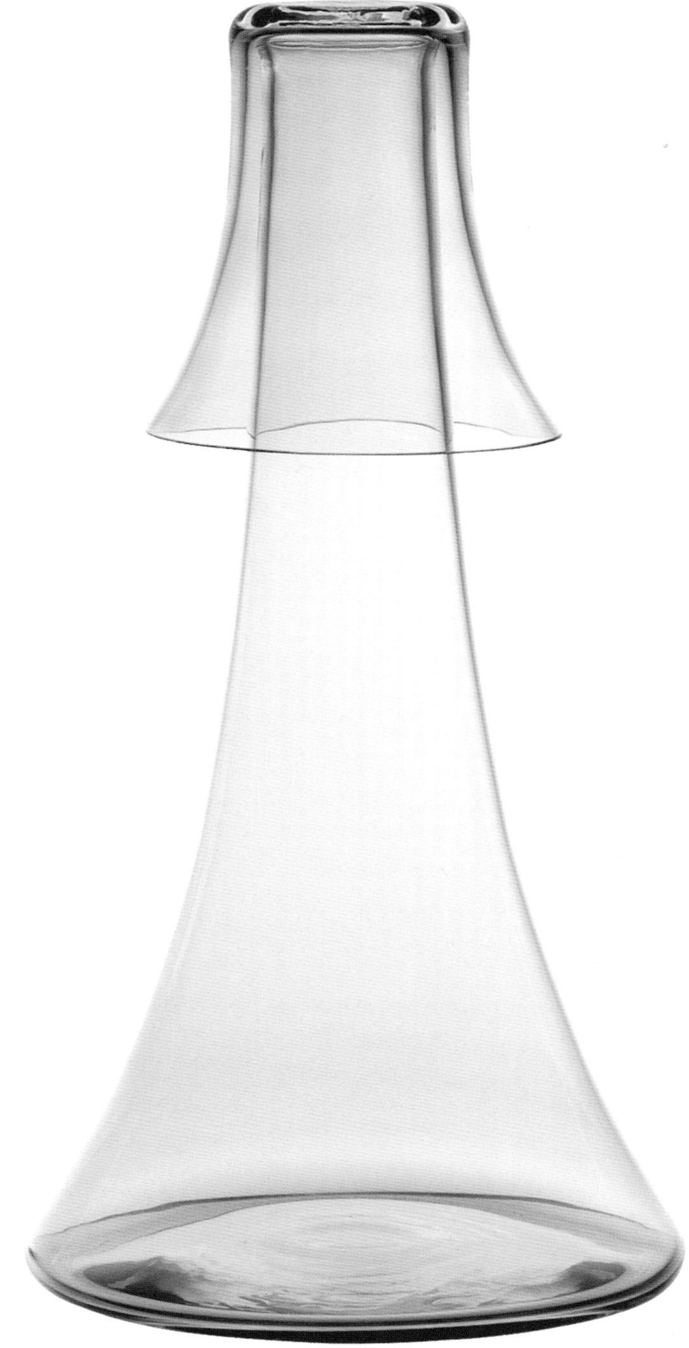

Tanteralla decanter for Orrefors (C)
Ingegerd Råman
Hand-blown glass
SWEDEN

in the 1960s and 1970s, had subsided by the '80s, and the region's industry was hit hard by international competition. Turning their attention to the largely ignored export and consumer markets, these young designers revived a traditional Scandinavian value: design for the home. New domestic objects blended style and practicality. With their muted colors and Shakerlike sparseness, Sandell's modular Wedding Stools have seats that link conveniently together. The Swede Ingegerd Råman, one of Scandinavia's leading glass designers, demonstrates nonchalant elegance with her series of translucent water carafes and decanters, notably Tanteralla **(C)**. These pieces, remarkable for their pure lines, clarity, and lack of ornament, are also multifunctional; the lids serve as drinking glasses, and the basic shape often lends itself to other roles—a vase, for example.

Today, function remains a critical factor in a design process that reduces objects to their essential elements. The challenge for contemporary Scandinavian designers is to create original, dynamic solutions using this method. The Swedish designer Thomas Bernstrand strips away unessential ingredients to discover the basic recipe for the American La-Z-Boy. Bernstrand rids his version, called Boxer **(E)** see **p 82**. of

C

D

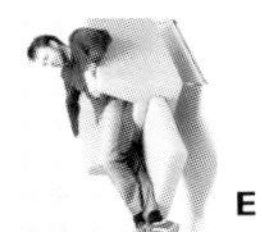

E

extra gadgetry, simplifies its shape, and chooses monochromatic upholstery. This solution derives not from a search for truth but from a reexamination of necessity.

Ironically, the essential forms of functional designs can be extremely difficult to produce, as in the case of Swedish trio Claesson Koivisto Rune's Brasilia coffee table **(D)** see **p 68**. The process of constructing the table's deceptively simple geometries required a highly complex solution. The seamless bentwood table actually consists of four parts—two sides, a top, and a bottom—that are glued together. During the process of refining the table's tight curves, "the pressure [on the corners] created uneven tension on the glue joints," explains Eero Koivisto. The result was a sagging tabletop. The answer, which "took a very long time to develop and involved many, many prototypes," required placing a core of composite material in the top panel to give needed resilience. Adding to the table's seamless appearance, all visible surface veneers are taken from one wood source. "This is all, of course, quite a time-consuming operation that has to be done by hand," says Koivisto.

An honest approach hardly rules out aesthetic appeal. Many Scandinavian designers continue to draw upon the "less is more" tenet of Modernism, and decoration often goes hand in hand with a masterly grasp of negative space. An elegant bowl, called Po 0018 **(J)**, designed by Claesson Koivisto Rune for Cappellini, alternates between emptiness and curving strips of laminated white wood. The deep grooves in the Seza sofa **(I)**, by the Norwegian team Norway Says, mirror its legs, resulting in a pleasant symmetry. Some of these subtle touches also have practical functions. The single round hole in the backrest of Åke Axelsson's minimal wooden Anselm chair **(G)** also makes it easier to carry or move.

Scandinavian designers often reject material excess in favor of sculpting fundamental form. The Danish designer Peter Karpf is a master of this approach, particularly evident in his furniture line VOXIA for Iform. One of the pieces, his sinuous OTO chair **(F)** see **p 86** is shaped from a single sheet of laminate beech. The work of the Swede Björn Dahlström, a contemporary of Thomas Sandell and Thomas Eriksson, also engages in this kind of stylization. In particular, his much-admired BD 5 easy chair **(H)** see **p 93**, part of his BD furniture series for

Anselm chair for Galleri Stolen (G)
Åke Axelsson
Clear lacquered birch
SWEDEN

Seza sofa (I)
Norway Says
Steel rod, foam, fabric
NORWAY

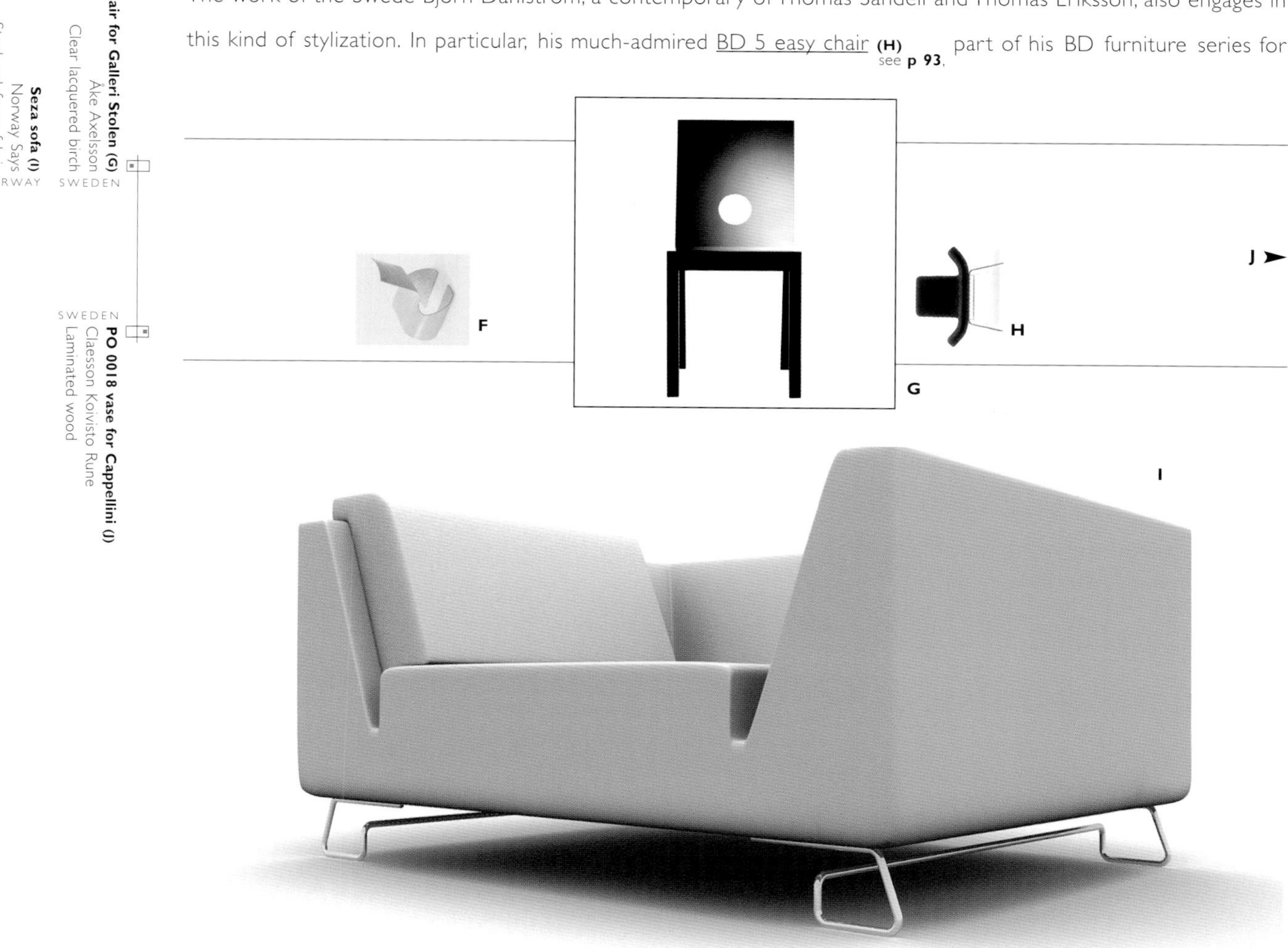

PO 0018 vase for Cappellini (J)
Claesson Koivisto Rune
Laminated wood
SWEDEN

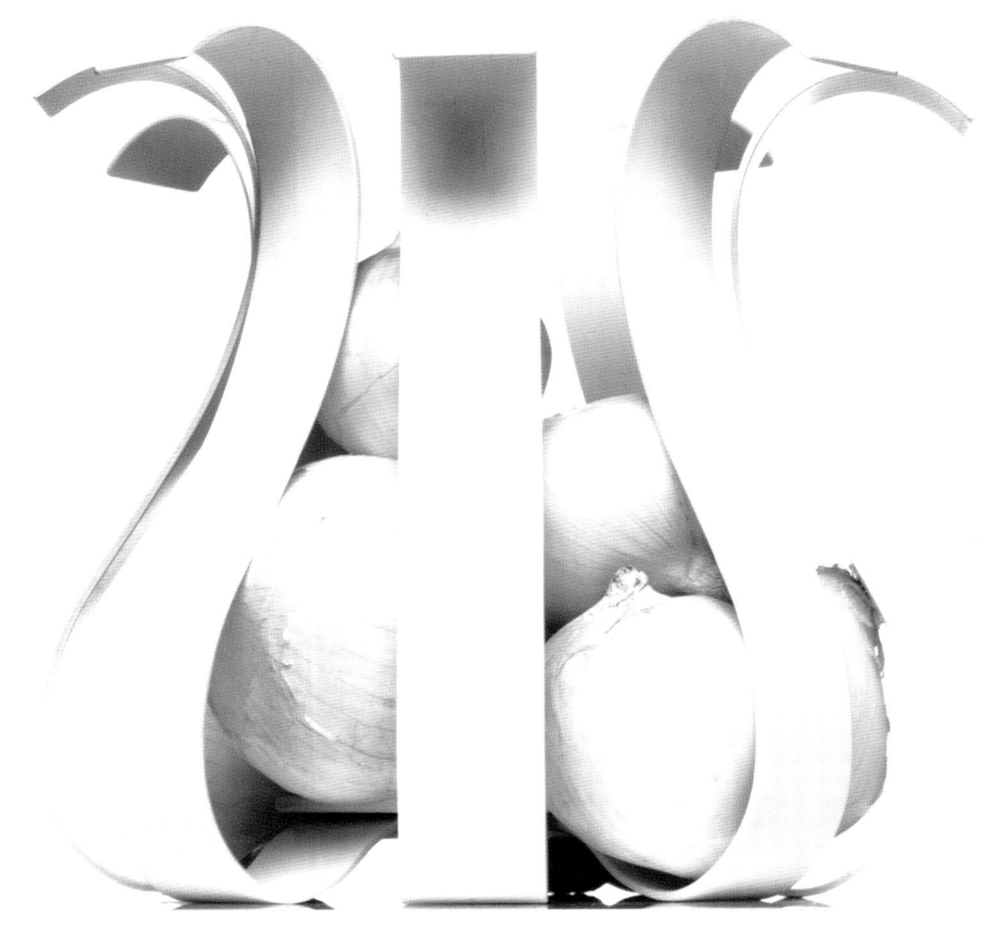

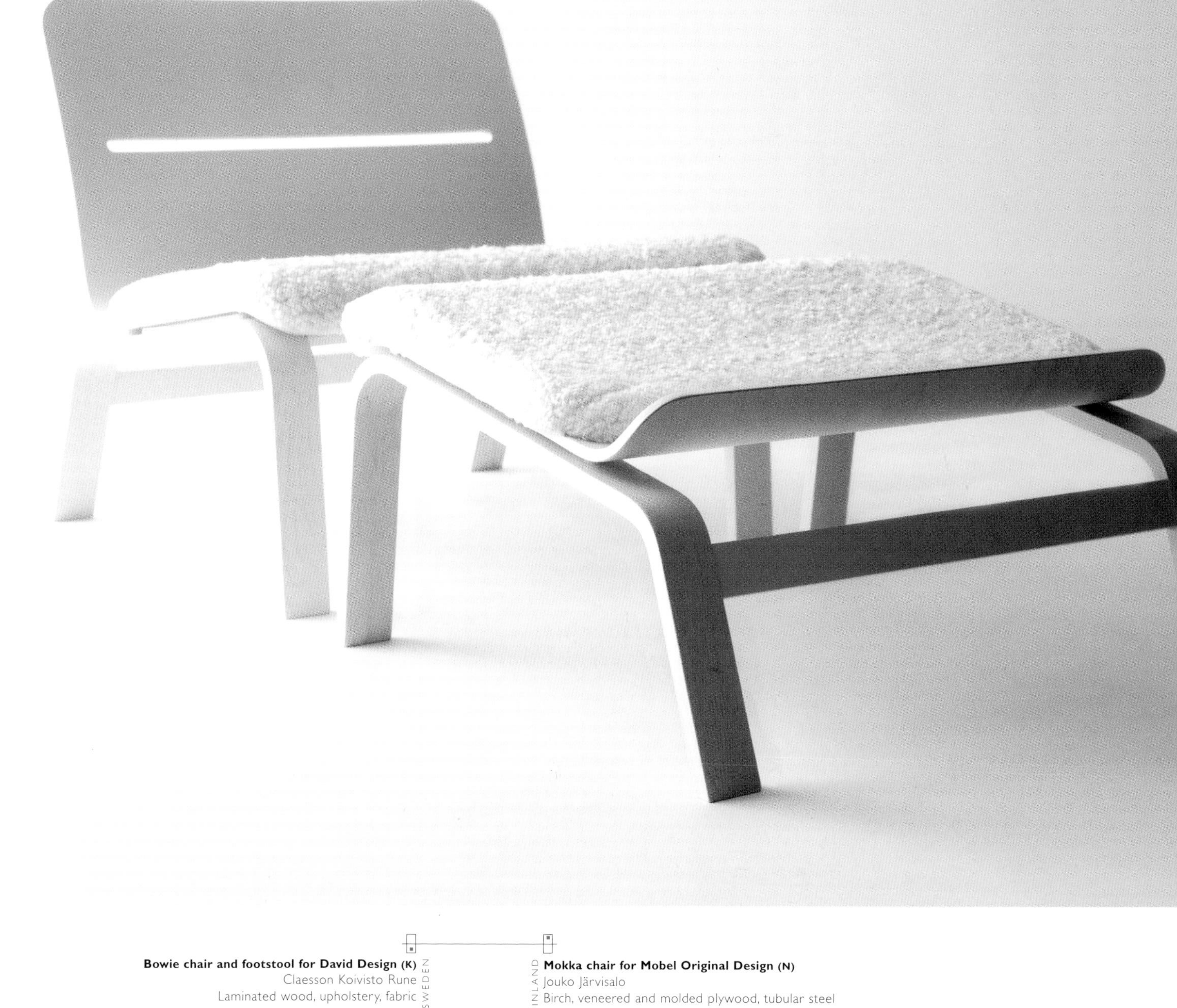

Bowie chair and footstool for David Design (K)
Claesson Koivisto Rune
Laminated wood, upholstery, fabric
SWEDEN

FINLAND
Mokka chair for Mobel Original Design (N)
Jouko Järvisalo
Birch, veneered and molded plywood, tubular steel

cbi, preserves a powerful graphic silhouette with minimal black upholstery and a simple shape influenced by Dahlström's early work in animation.

Like Alvar Aalto did early in the century, Scandinavians warm the cool lines of their designs with natural materials, suggesting authenticity through an intimate connection to the natural world. However, the formal references to nature in many significant mid-twentieth-century designs, such as the leaf-shaped platter (1951) by Finnish designer Tapio Wirkkala or the Poppy textile pattern (1960) by Finnish designer Maija Isola for Marimekko, are less prevalent today. Light, an element prized in wintry Scandinavia, still plays a key role, particularly in glass and ceramics. The Swedish ceramic artist Pia Törnell uses thin matte porcelain to suggest sensuality and softness, particularly in her stoneware tiles **(M)** see **p 101** for the Swedish Museum of Architecture. While wood has gone in and out of fashion, it is currently extremely popular, enlivening quiet forms, as in Claesson Koivisto Rune's Bowie chair **(K)** and Norway Says's Konrad chair **(L)** see **p 91**. and displaying high-quality craftsmanship as in the meticulous work of Finnish designer Jouko Järvisalo **(N)**.

K

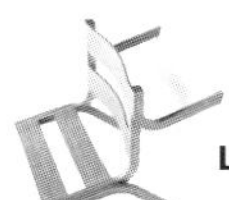
L

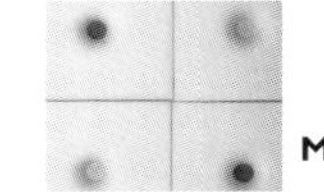
M

N

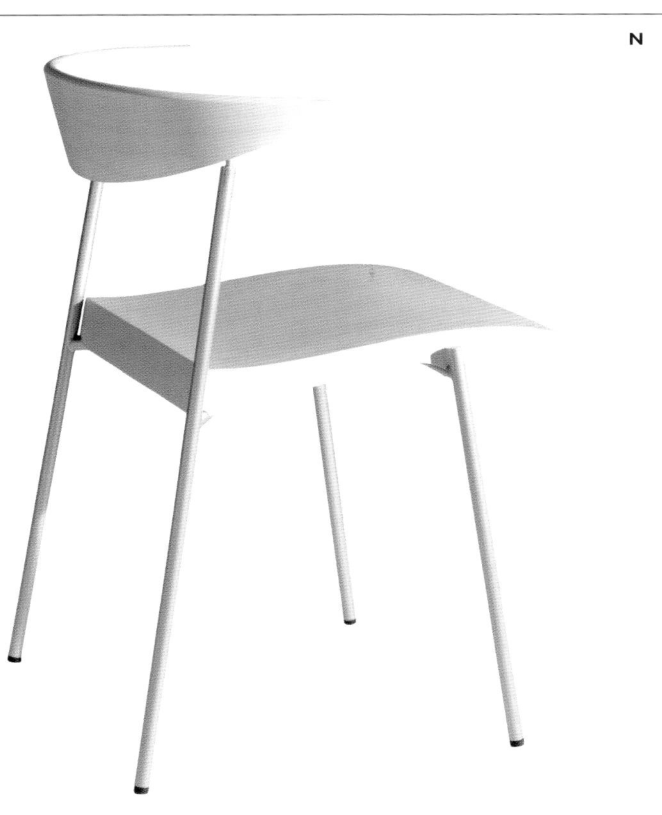

Employing natural materials perpetuates another tenet of Modernism close to the heart of many Scandinavian designers—"truth in materials." As they did during the Golden Age, Scandinavians continue to use a minimum of processing and production in their treatment of materials, looking to illuminate the beauty of innate properties. This respectful relationship to their medium manifests itself in designs such as Råman's glass carafes, Törnell's stoneware tiles, and Swedish designer Pia Wallén's felt clothing, which present these natural substances as pure and uncorrupted.

Even though they self-consciously engage many traditional forms and values, contemporary Scandinavian designers are not satisfied with straightforward usability. Their work incorporates humor and irony in a playful take on Functionalism. Claesson Koivisto Rune's Beckham coatrack **(Q)** see **p 84** named after the British soccer star David Beckham, bears a subtle resemblance to a goalpost. A lamp by another Swedish designer, Matti Klenell, combines the functions of both reading light and bookend, in an amusing design called Enlightenment **(R)** see **p 90**. Today, play and leisure are often presented on the same level as basic function. To open the 1789/Cupboard **(P)** created by Arihiro Miyake, a Japanese-

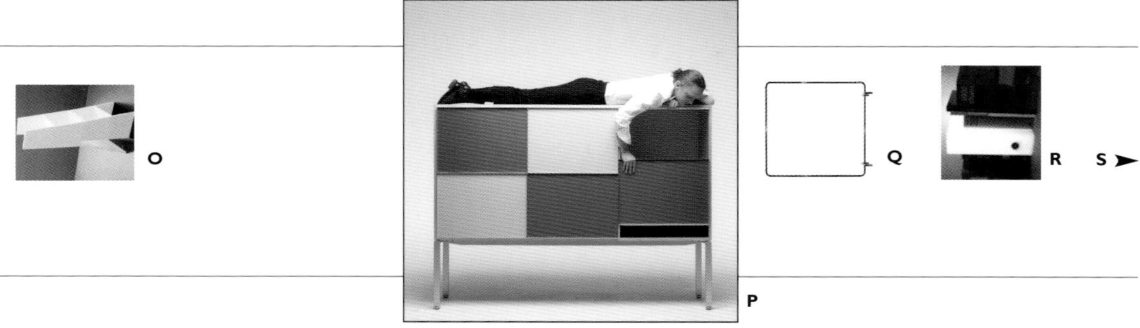

1789/Cupboard (P)
Arihiro Miyake
Aluminum, MDF nel, polyester, steel
FINLAND

Lantern for Iittala (S)
Harri Koskinen
Hand-blown glass
FINLAND

born designer living in Finland, the user must shift doors like puzzle pieces. These doors also allow the owner to choose one shelf for display and keep others private.

There are several theories explaining why Scandinavians have responded so positively to the strict tenets of Functionalism. Many credit Scandinavia's history of rural, agrarian living, which made efficient use of limited resources, with a matter-of-fact outlook. Others indicate that the austere Lutheran tradition may have facilitated the ready acceptance of Spartan dogma. When considering these theories, one can certainly sense an ascetic strain in Scandinavian design, which Michael Asplund (of the retailer Asplund) calls "farmer minimalism." Products such as Finn Harri Koskinen's reserved glass lantern **(S)** for Iittala and the modest ReachUp chair **(O)** see **p 83** by Norwegian designers Linda Lien and Camilla Songe-Møller convey a sense of a simple country living.

But an honest approach to design, based on practical solutions and basic needs, is not necessarily a naive one, as some critics have suggested. Tempering an industrial aesthetic with human concerns, honest solutions are always appropriate in their exploration of fundamental function and form. Mid-twentieth-century Scandinavian designers perpetuated a human-centric understanding of Modernist principles, nurturing a unique Nordic style. While today's young designers evolve their understanding of human needs to fit the times, their work displays a genuine effort to enhance quality of life—a shared goal of Scandinavians throughout the last century.

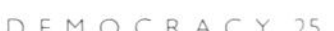

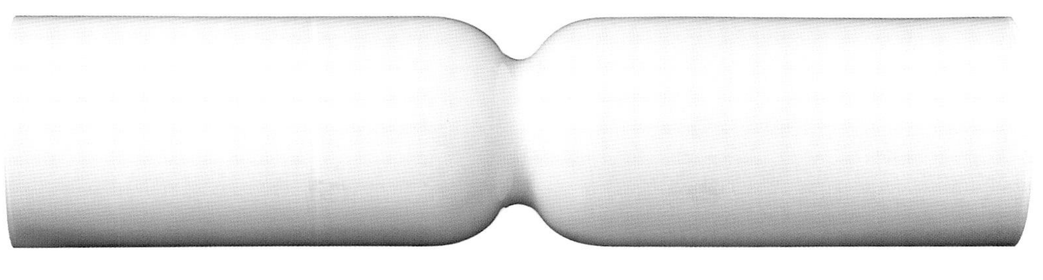

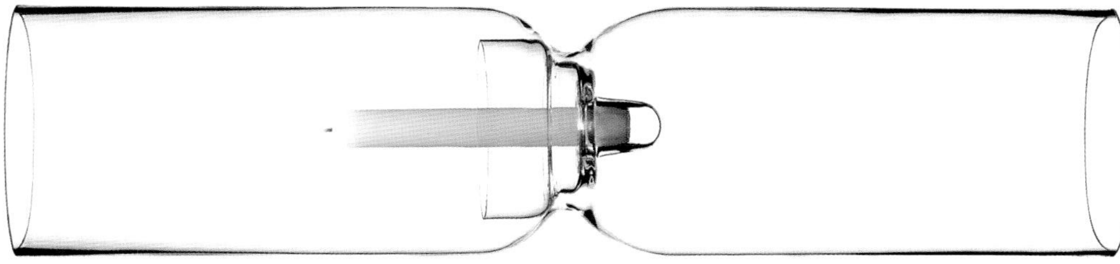

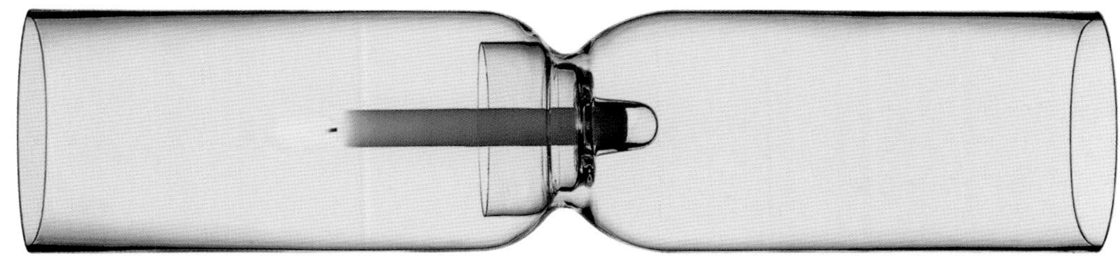

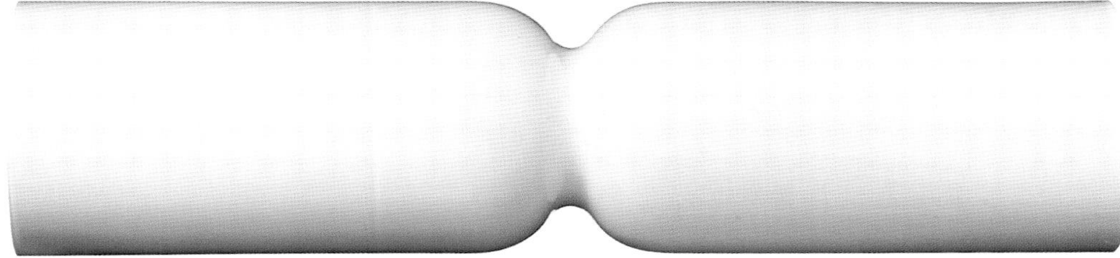

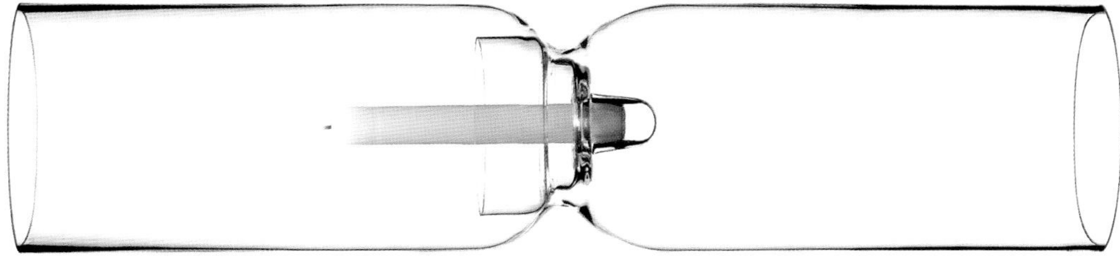

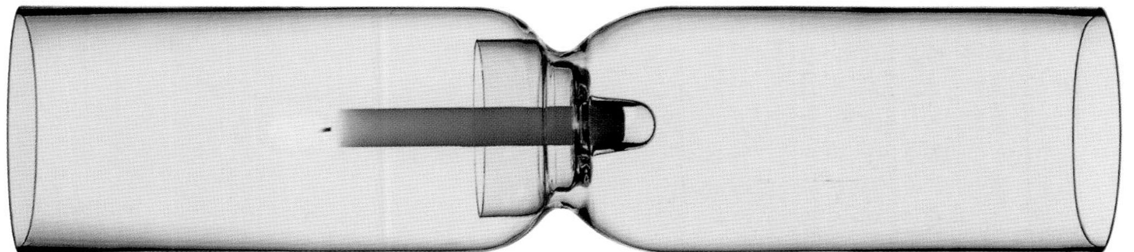

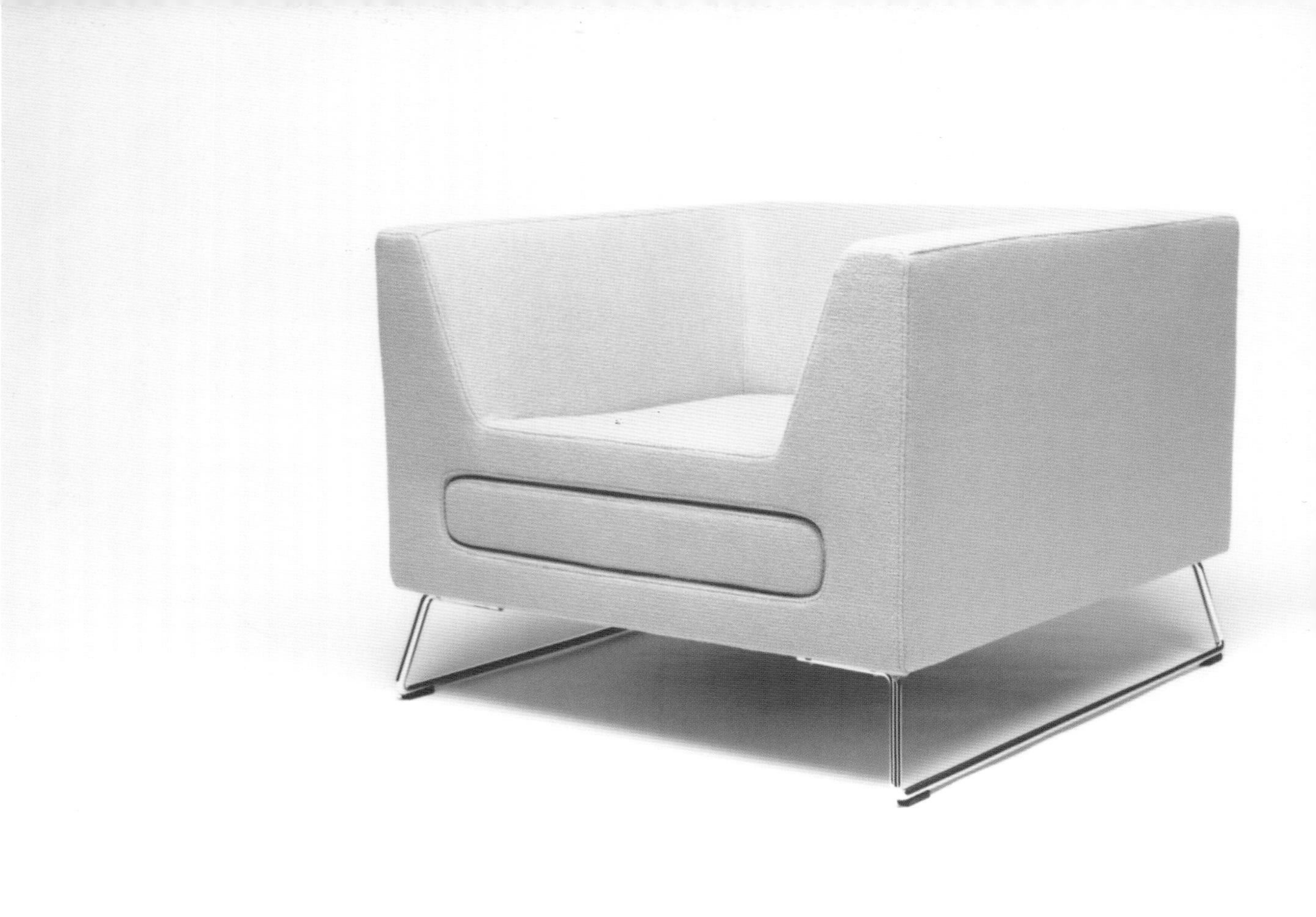

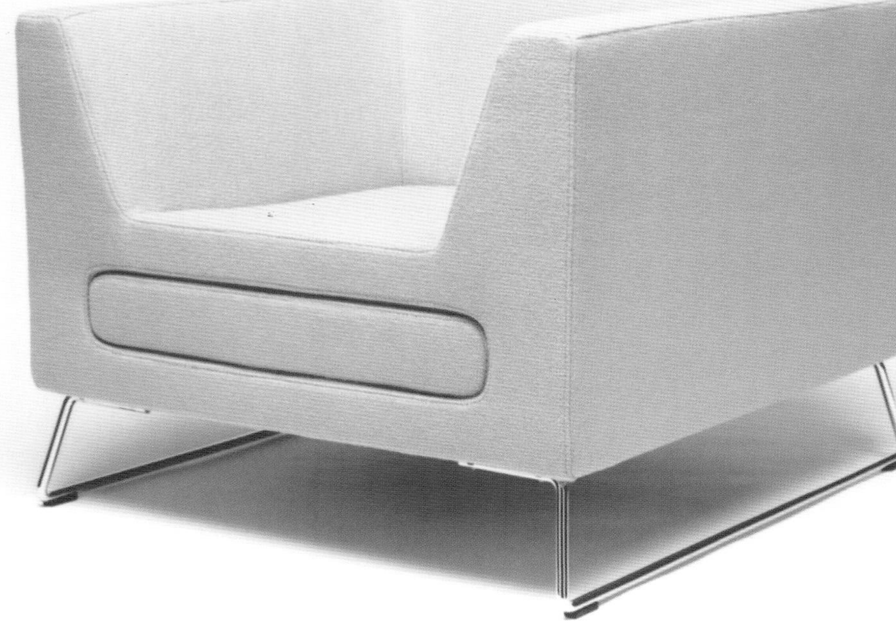

Boxer armchair for Söderbergs Möbler
Thomas Bernstrand
Wooden frame, textile, metal chassis
SWEDEN

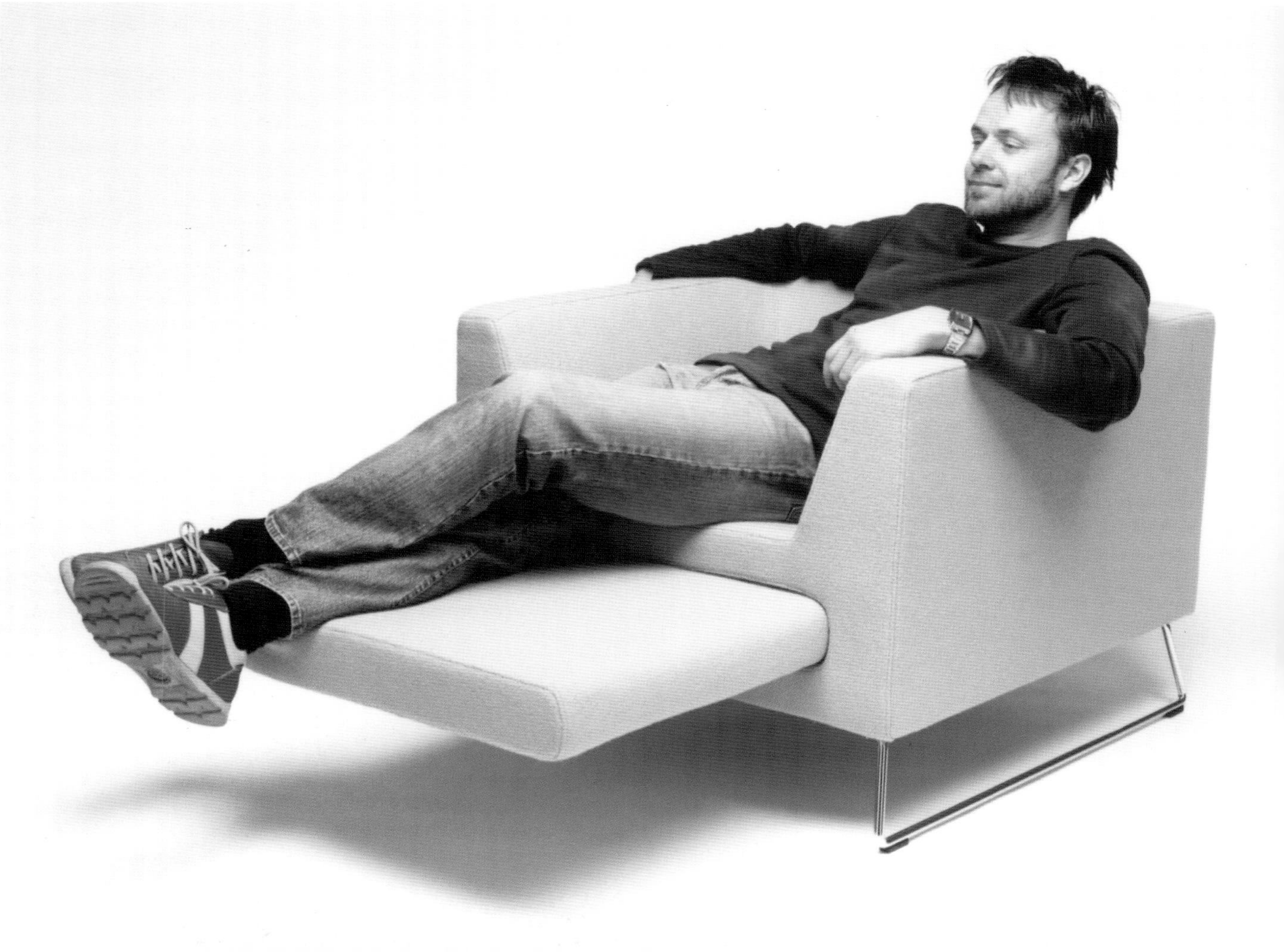

NORWAY
ReachUp chair for Bygge & Gjertsen
Linda Lien, Camilla Songe-Møller
Enameled plywood

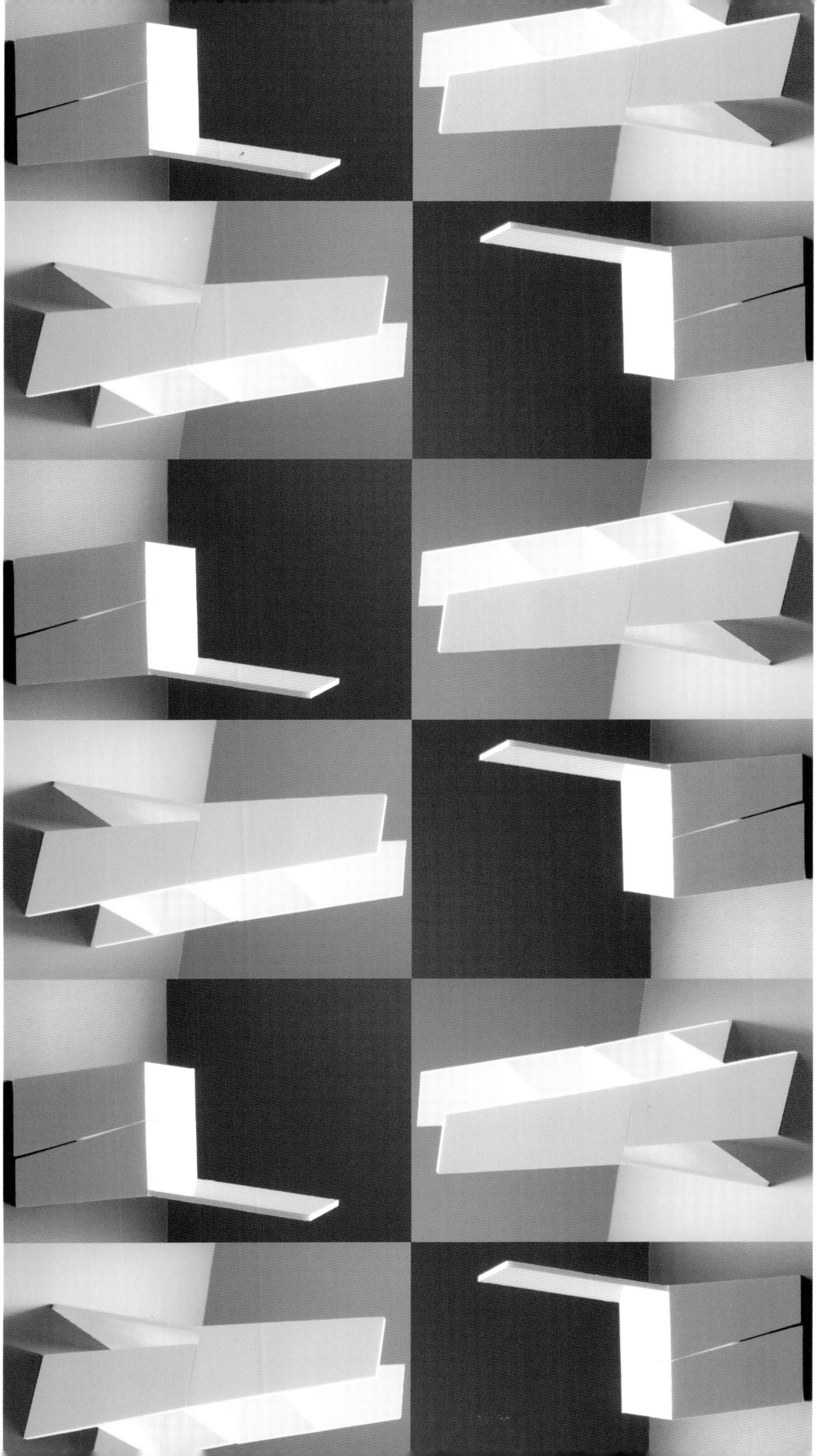

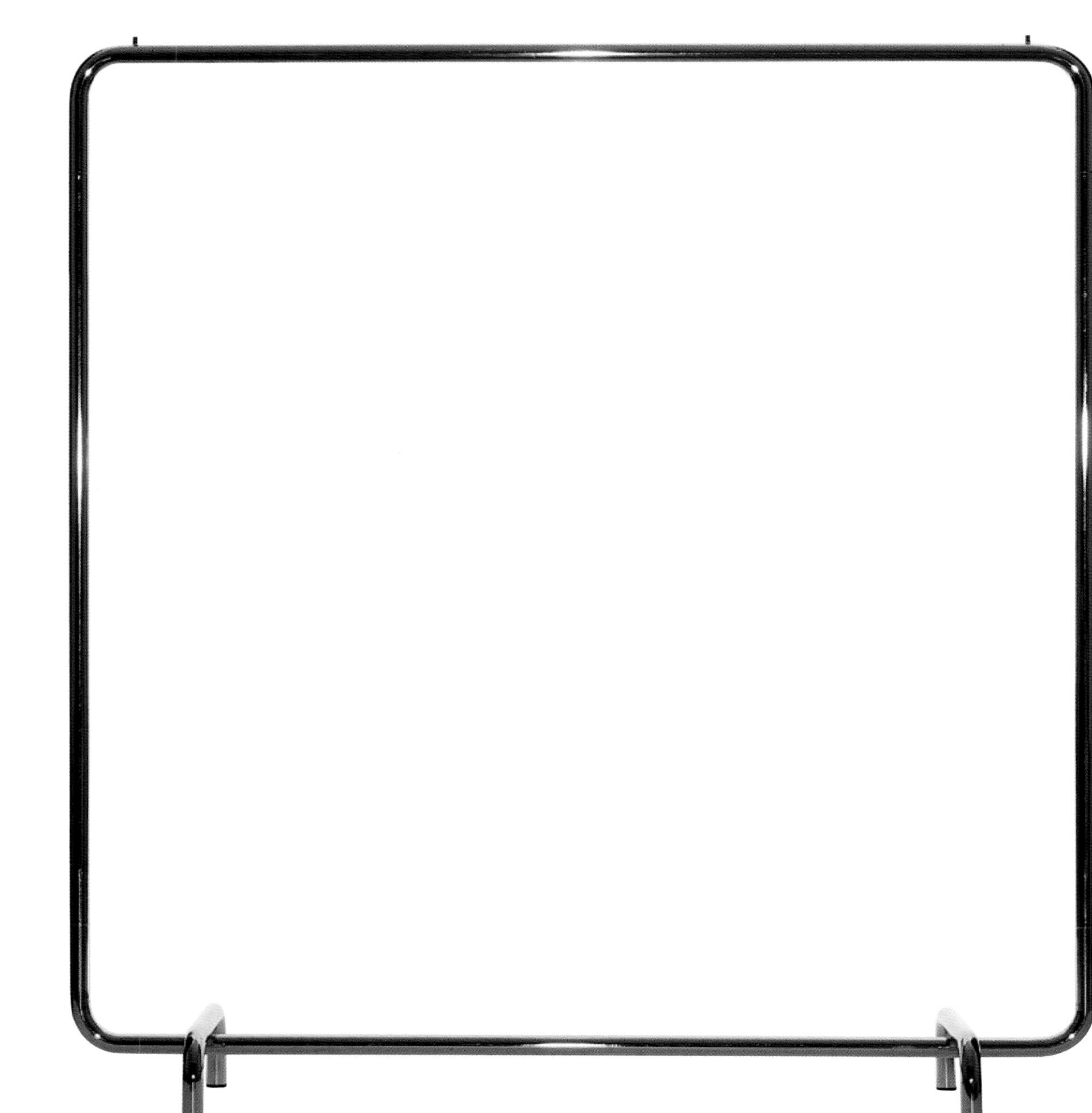

Beckham coatrack for David Design
Claesson Koivisto Rune
Steel
SWEDEN

Omni chair and footstool for Swedese
Claesson Koivisto Rune
Laminated wood, upholstery, net fabric
SWEDEN

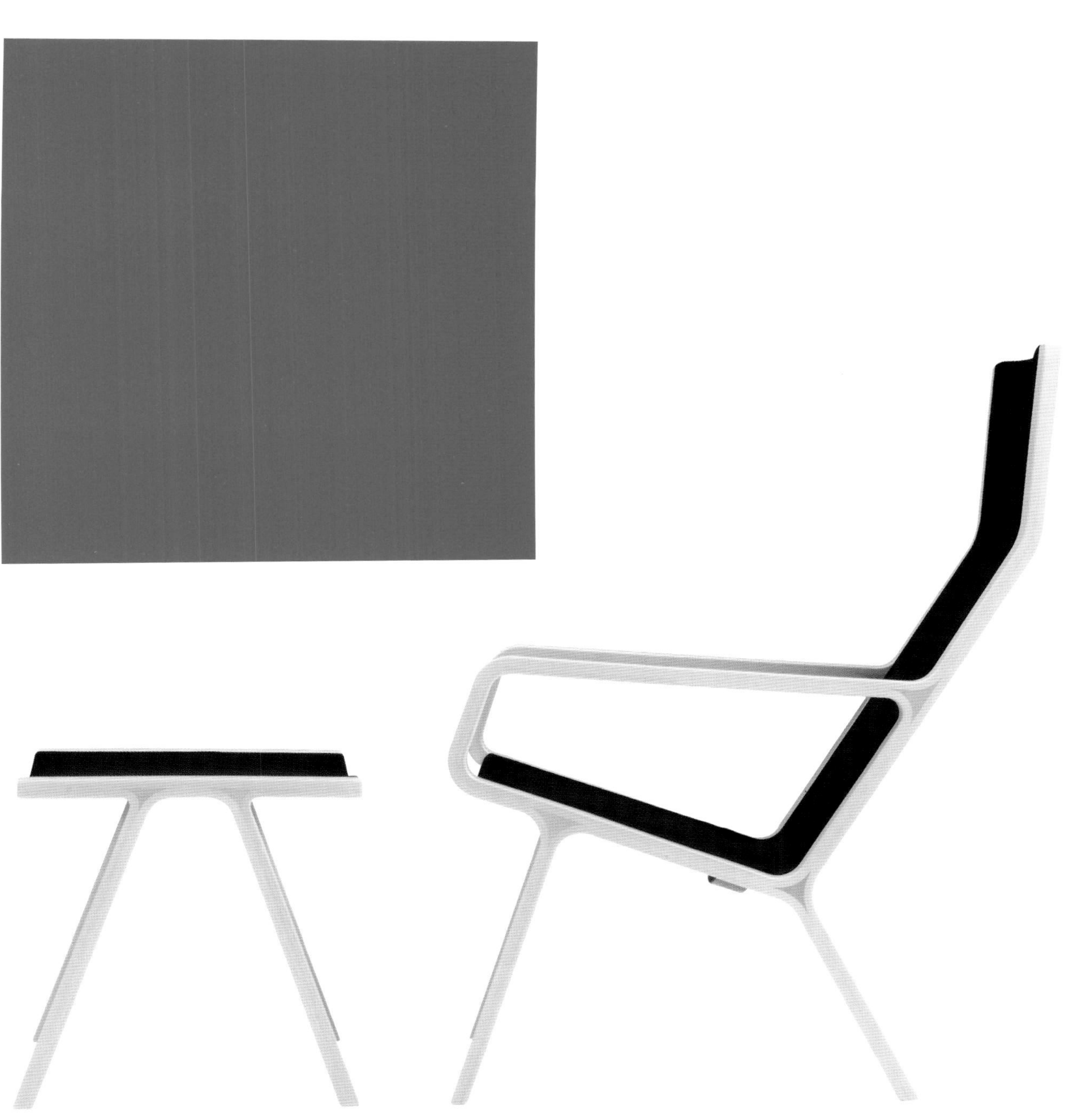

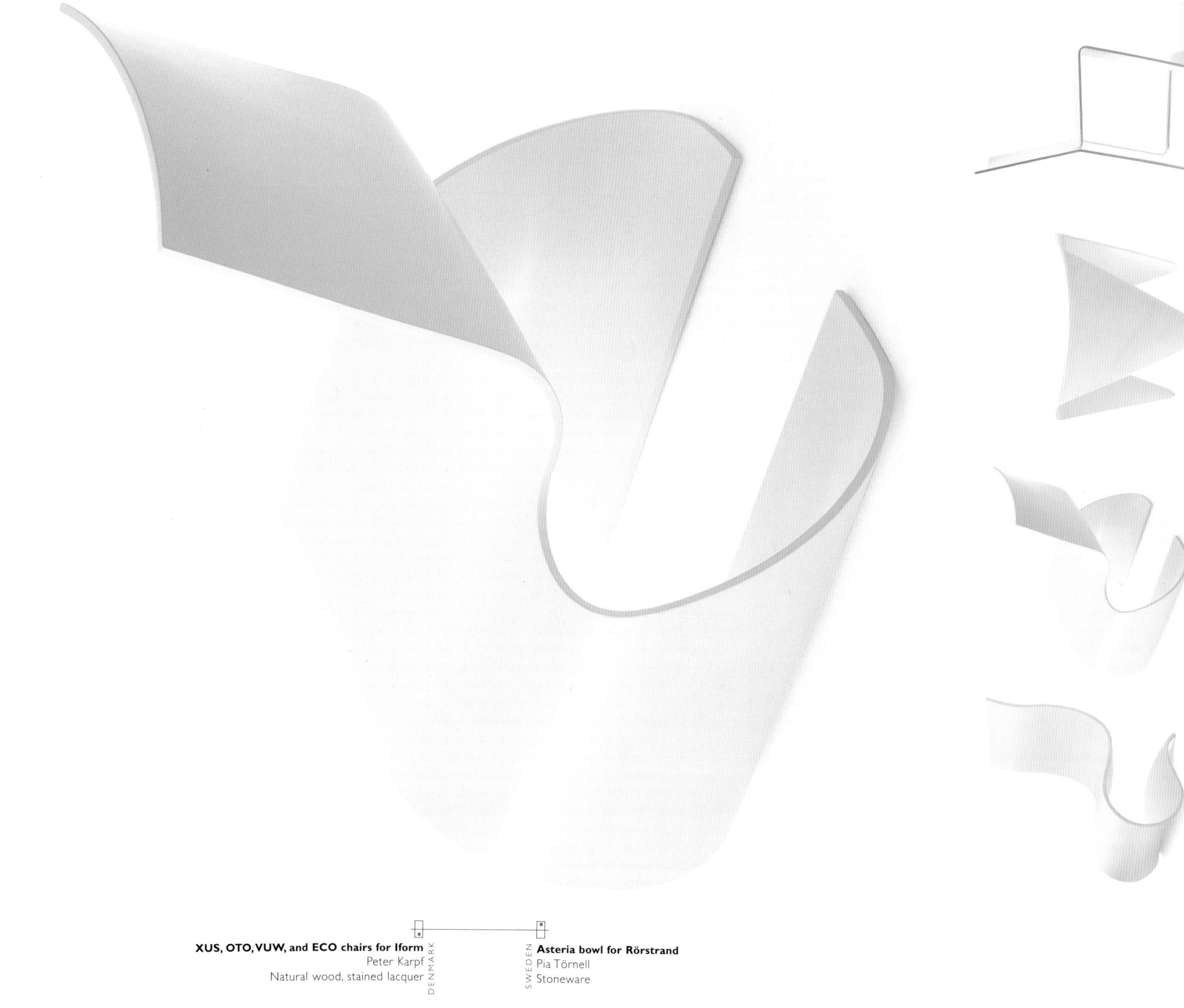

XUS, OTO, VUW, and ECO chairs for Iform
Peter Karpf
Natural wood, stained lacquer
DENMARK

SWEDEN
Asteria bowl for Rörstrand
Pia Törnell
Stoneware

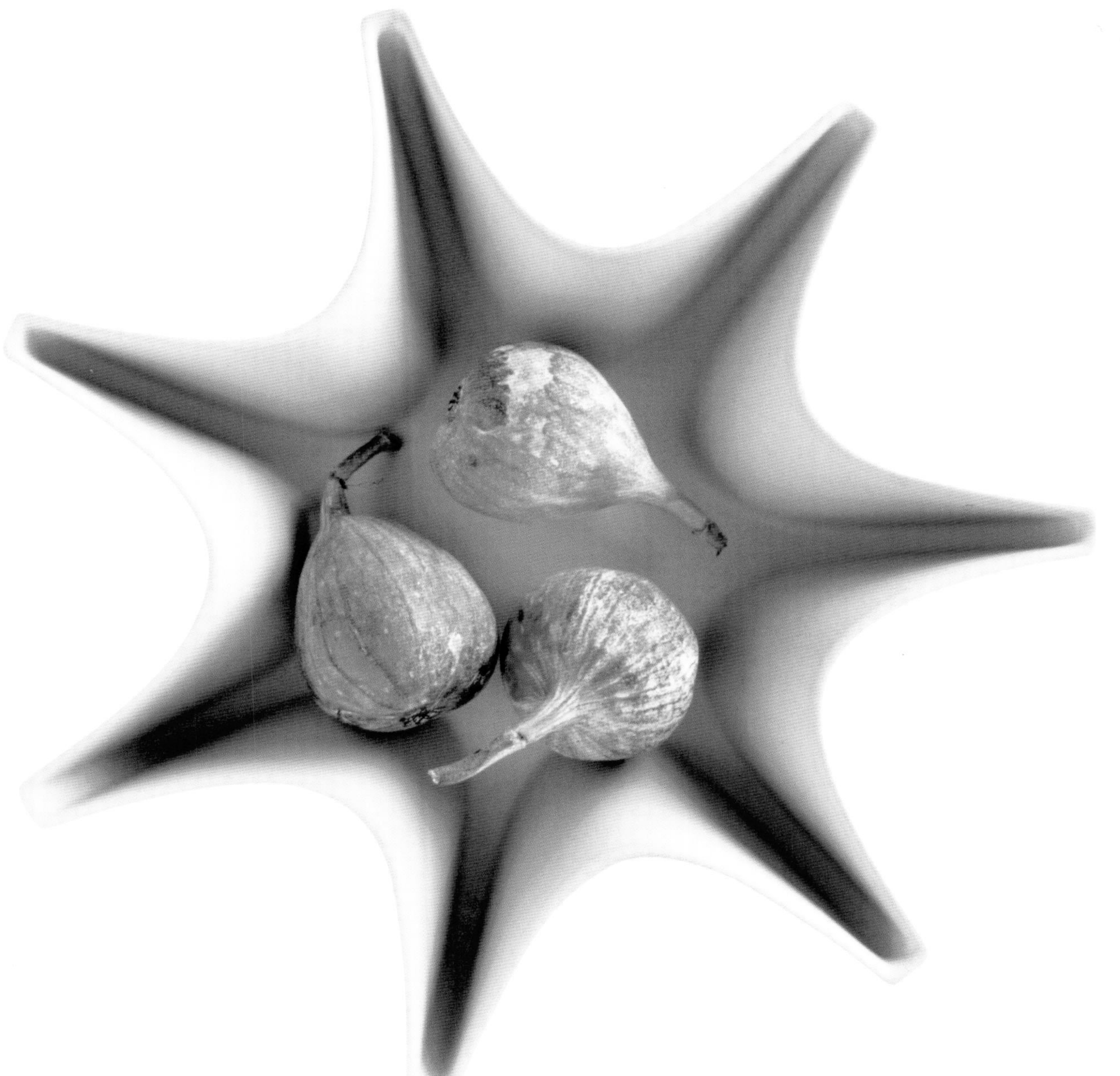

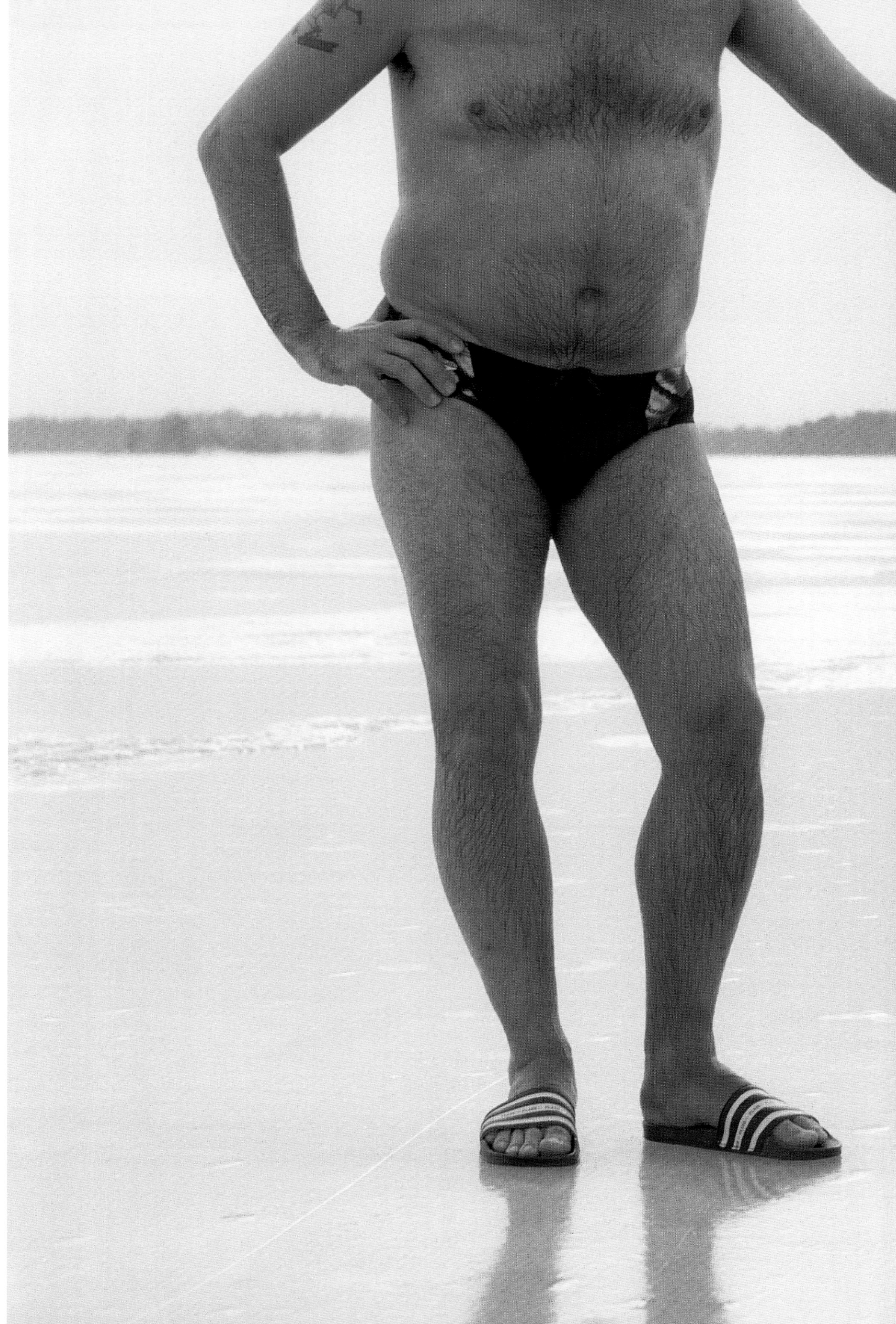

Rocking Chair
Anna Katriina Tilli
Fiberglass stick, plywood, steel
FINLAND

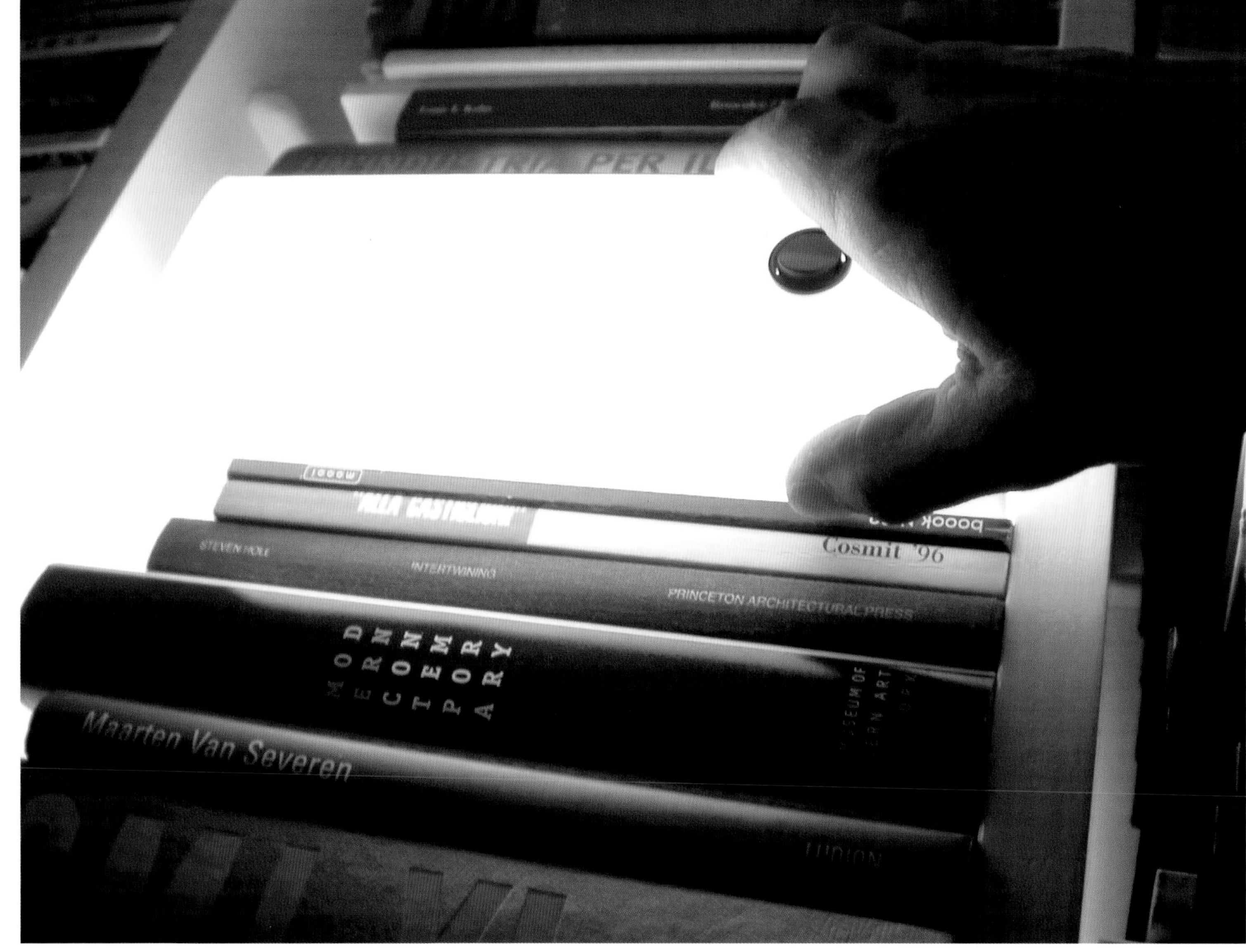

Enlightenment lamp for Agata
Matti Klenell
ABS plastic, fluorescent light source
SWEDEN

Konrad chair
Norways Says
Laminated oak
NORWAY

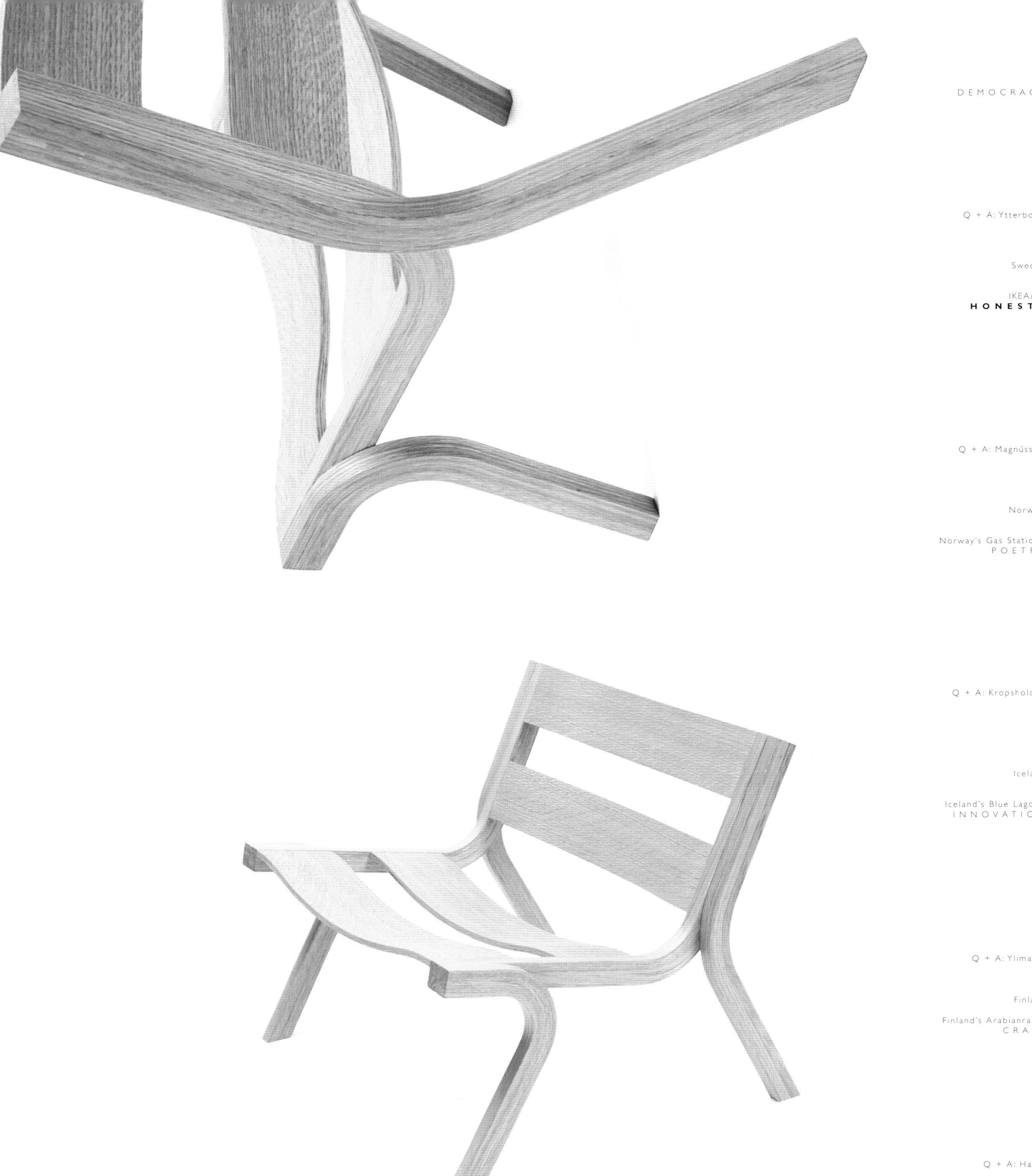

PlussMinus salt and pepper shakers for Magnor Glassverk
Cathrine Maske
Glass
NORWAY

SWEDEN
BD 5 Easy Chair for cbi
Björn Dahlström
Molded plywood, steel, high-density foam, upholstery

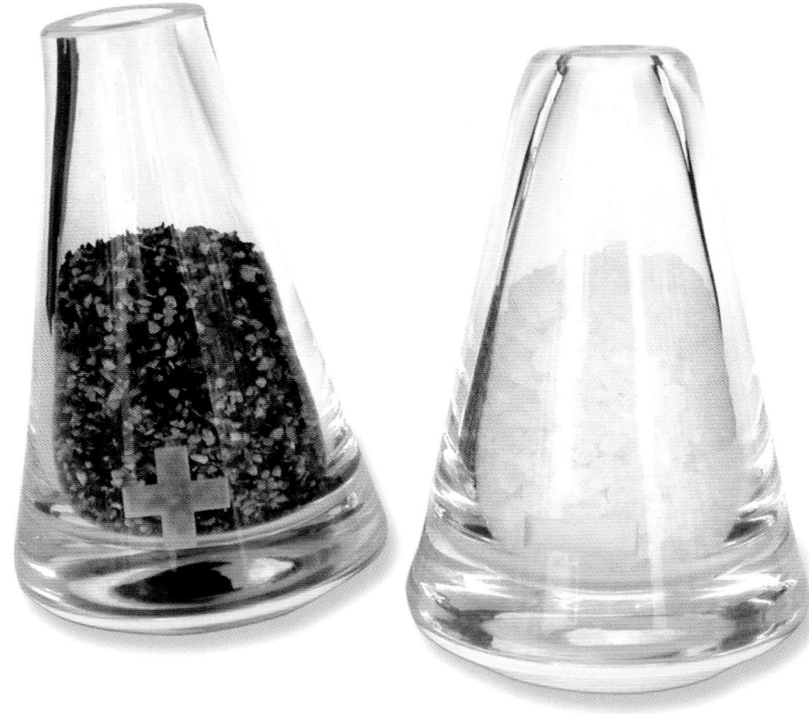

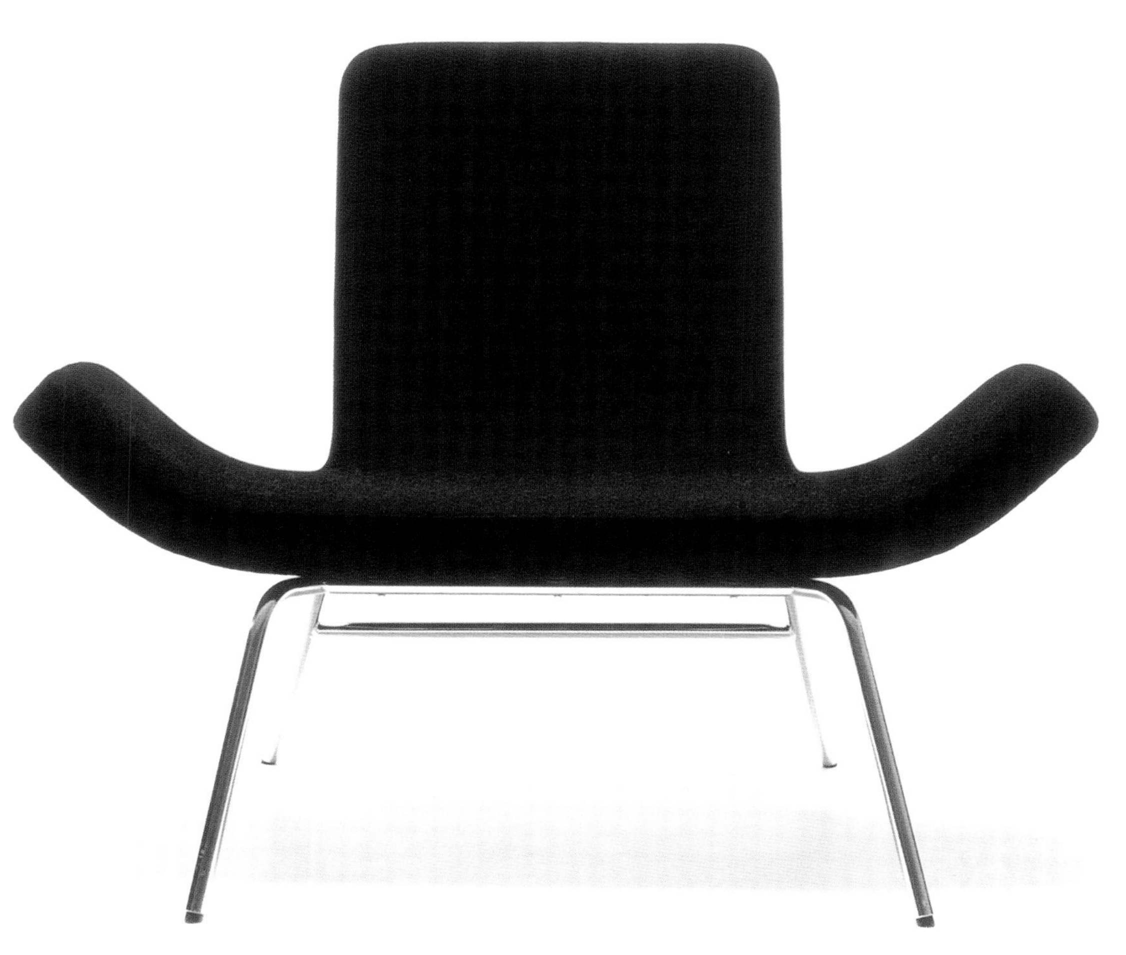

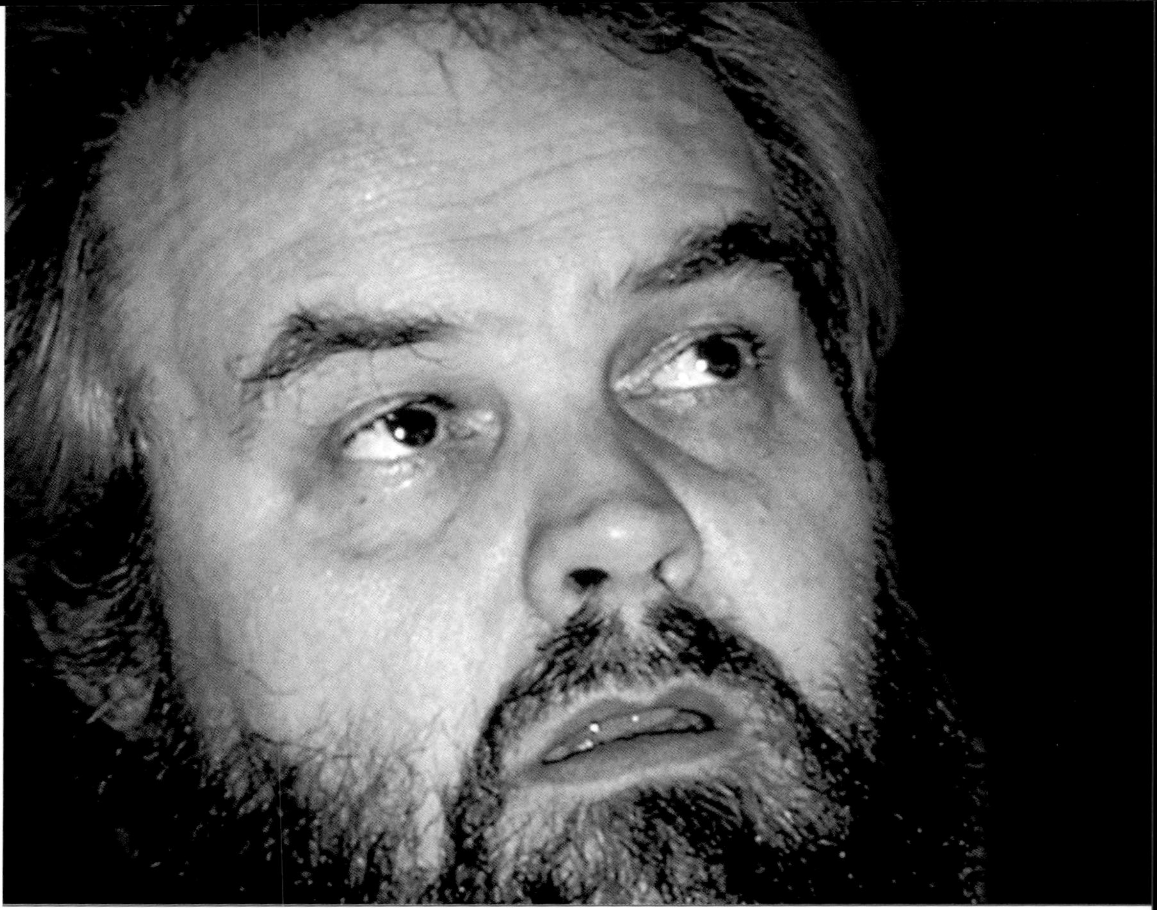

Gudmundur Oddur Magnússon

Nature and Identity

GUDMUNDUR ODDUR MAGNÚSSON ("GODDUR") IS DIRECTOR OF STUDIES FOR GRAPHIC ESIGN AT THE ICELAND ACADEMY OF THE ARTS. BORN IN AKUREYRI ON THE NORTHERN COAST OF ICELAND IN 1955, HE RECEIVED HIS AINING IN ICELAND AND IN VANCOUVER, BRITISH COLUMBIA, AT THE EMILY CARR COLLEGE OF ART AND DESIGN. AFTER WORKING AS A DE- GNER AT THE VANCOUVER STUDIO ION, MAGNÚSSON RETURNED TO ICELAND IN 1991. AS THE HEAD OF GRAPHIC DESIGN AT THE ICELANDIC OLLEGE OF ARTS AND CRAFTS (NOW THE ICELAND ACADEMY OF THE ARTS), MAGNÚSSON PLAYED A VITAL ROLE IN BRINGING UNIVERSITY-LEVEL ESIGN EDUCATION TO ICELAND. PART PHILOSOPHER, PART ARTIST, AND PART TEACHER, MAGNÚSSON HAS INSPIRED A SURGE OF INTEREST IN ESIGN IN ICELAND WITH HIS COMMITMENT TO THE FIELD AND HIS DEPTH OF UNDERSTANDING OF ICELANDIC CULTURE.

Q: FROM ACTIVE VOLCANOES TO GEYSERS AND GLACIERS, THE CELANDIC LANDSCAPE IS UNIQUE. HOW WOULD YOU DESCRIBE CELANDERS' RELATIONSHIP TO THEIR SURROUNDINGS? A: There is ne key factor many people forget that really influences people's mind and behavior—the weather. It is so unstable. here is never time to finish outdoor activities properly because the next storm is always coming. Some people y that there is only one kind of management in Iceland, crisis management. It goes something like this: Dear friend Uncle, I'm in trouble. Can you help me out? There is some truth to this since traditionally farmers have only ree months or so for haying, and summers can be both windy and rainy. If it rains for weeks there can be trouble. he storms also mean you can't expect the fish to stay in the same place all year round. And sometimes you catch ore than you thought you would, which again involves crisis management—Hey! Can you help me out here? Also, e fact that Icelanders have traditionally been scattered around the island and didn't form villages until the twen- eth century really influences the way people think. **Q: LIGHT IS AN IMPORTANT LEMENT OF SCANDINAVIAN DESIGN. DOES THE DESIGNER'S RELATIONSHIP TO LIGHT IN ICELAND DIFFER FROM THAT IN OTHER NORDIC COUNTRIES? A:** There is no question that light in Iceland is different from e other Nordic countries. It has to do with our climate. The light that plays across an island surrounded by heavy eas and cloudy storms is very different from the light on the Scandinavian peninsula. In general, I have the feeling e dramatize light more than the Scandinavians do and have a tendency toward stronger contrasts—softness is ot an Icelandic quality for sure! I became aware of this when I was studying in Canada with students who came om many different parts of the world. There was no question that there were differences in the scale of contrast epending on whether you came from the south, west, east, or north. **Q: NATURE HAS HISTOR- CALLY PLAYED AN IMPORTANT ROLE IN SCANDINAVIAN DESIGN. HAS IT HAD THE SAME INFLUENCE IN ICELANDIC DESIGN? A:** The nature here in Iceland influenced designers differently than in the other Scandinavian countries. We did not apply Modernism to nature the same way the Scandinavians did. There are no trees here to work with, and we never developed the same kind of craftsmanship or industrial techniques [involving wood and natural materials that they did. Q: CAN YOU DESCRIBE THE INTIMATE RELATIONSHIP BETWEEN THE ICELANDIC LANDSCAPE AND ITS LANGUAGE? A: First, the Icelandic language is very transparent—you can see a word's origin very clearly—and the root of a word very often comes from shapes or motifs in the landscape. Likewise, names tell you a lot about the look or the ambiance of a place. Second, in Iceland you have a rich tradition of literature, which is about eight hundred or so years old, and the literature relates specifically to locations on an island that isn't that big. Icelanders are very aware of their past. We all come from the countryside since the formation of villages began very late. We often describe the character of a place by telling our own stories about that place. Q: IS THIS TENDENCY TOWARD NARRATIVE MANIFESTED IN ICELANDIC DESIGN? A: Icelandic product design is so young that there has been a problem identifying what it is really about. There is no question that there is storytelling in some of it, but it isn't the main characteristic. You find good storytelling in the lyrics of musicians Björk and in the works of many graphic designers, but I don't necessarily detect this quality in 3-D design. I have the feeling that it is more about the way we do things—it's not about forms that tell a story, but stories that produce forms. Q: YOU HAVE USED THE TERM "VERNACULAR WONDERS" TO DESCRIBE ICELANDIC ARCHITECTURE. HOW DID THIS PHRASE COME ABOUT? A: This comes from my instructor, Dieter Roth, a graphic artist and member of the international art group Fluxus. Dieter lived here, and he was constantly amazed at the individual way of doing things in Iceland: Icelanders always prefer to do things themselves, like build their own house, etc. In general, they don't like the idea of hiring an architect or a designer. Q: WHY DO YOU THINK ICELAND AND THE ICELANDIC COUNTRYSIDE HAVE BECOME SO APPEALING TO FOREIGNERS RECENTLY? A: As strange as it may seem for us Icelanders, many tourists are city people who come from overdesigned environments to see what they regard as "the untouched." Some of them have only experienced the man-made environment first-hand—meaning that even their countryside is planned out for them. This is reality for many Europeans and North Americans—they have never been out of the "designed" environment. Q: IN 1999, *THE NEW YORK TIMES* PUBLISHED AN ARTICLE STATING THAT MANY ICELANDERS STILL BELIEVE IN ELVES. WHERE DID THIS STORY COME FROM? A: There have been some surveys made by University of Iceland's department of psychology, which state that, unbelievably, many Icelanders still believe in elves and trolls. True, there are many examples in Iceland of highway planners being made to re-route roads around supposed elf dwellings. And when Iceland's first shopping mall was built, the electrical cables and similar underground installations were laid well away from suspected locations of gnomes and fairies. When planning a new house, people will sometimes hire an "elf spotter" to ensure the site is free of spirit folk. This does happen, yes, but it is not that common. **Q: YOU HAVE CALLED THE RECENT WAVE OF INTERNATIONAL INTEREST IN ICELAND A PROCESS OF "FETISHIZING THE NORTH" WHY? A:** Iceland has a strong mystical appeal, partially because our language is the oldest form of all Germanic languages. Icelanders can still read the original manuscripts that keep the mythology in the *Völuspá* as the vision of how the medieval man placed himself in the world. These are the stories of Askur, Yggdrasil, Thor, and Odin, etc. This fact has influenced Germanic artists throughout history—for instance, Richard Wagner based some of his most famous operas on this mythology. And it continues to happen. In 1980, Hermann Nitsch, the Vienna actionist, composed and conducted a symphony in ten movements called *Iceland*. One of the movements is called "Aurora Borealis" and another is named after Iceland's biggest glacier, Vatnajökull. What I'm saying is that these artists are not simply inspired by the Icelandic sagas, but they really feel that the sagas connect them to Icelanders at their deepest roots.

For many European artists—and especially designers—it is often important to have national undertones. There is an increasing emphasis on national identity due to globalization. It isn't difficult to differentiate Italian design from Danish design or Swedish. You really can see the difference.

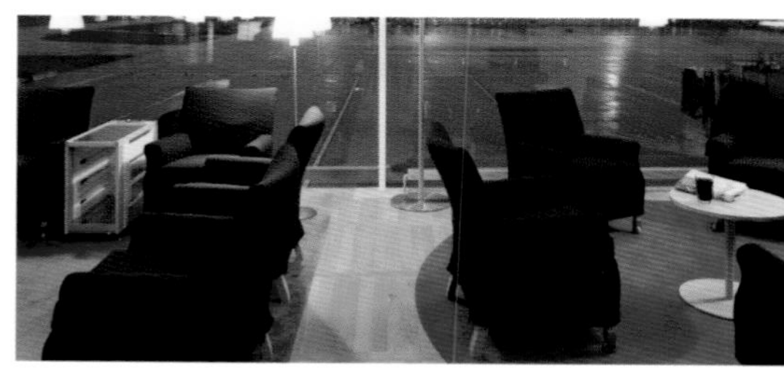

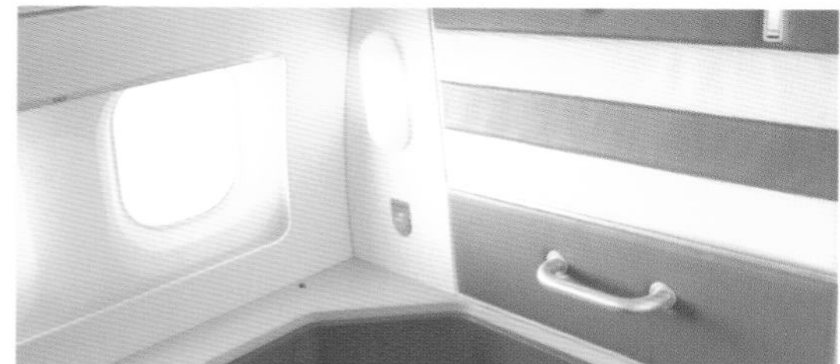

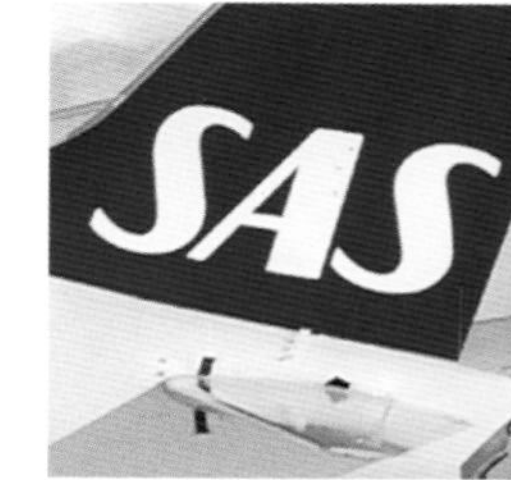

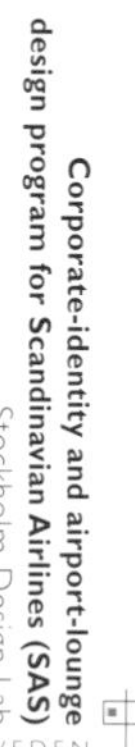

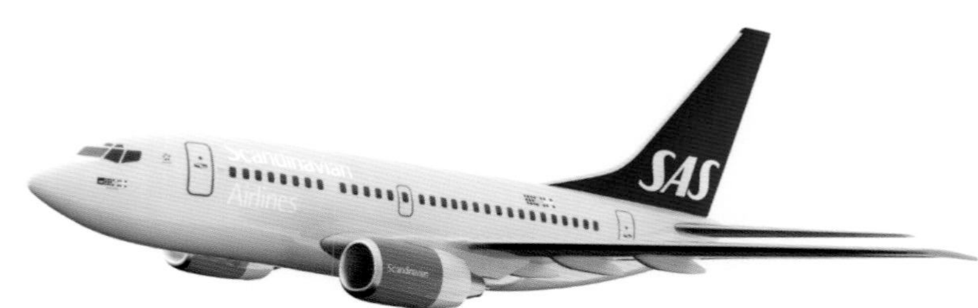

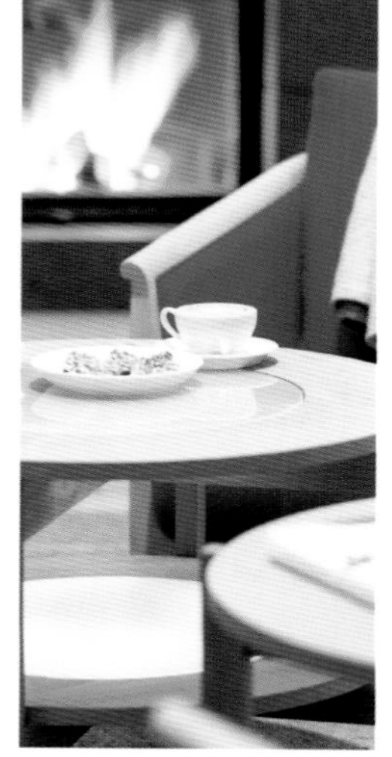

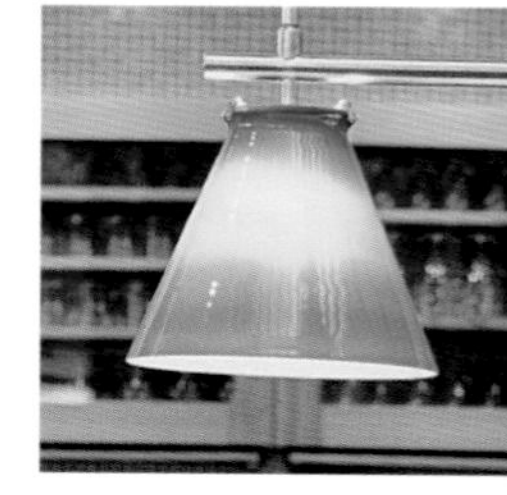

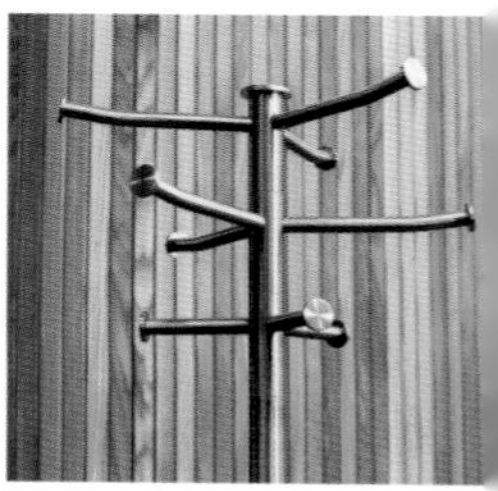

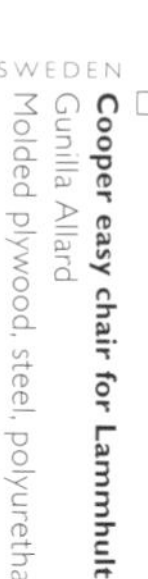

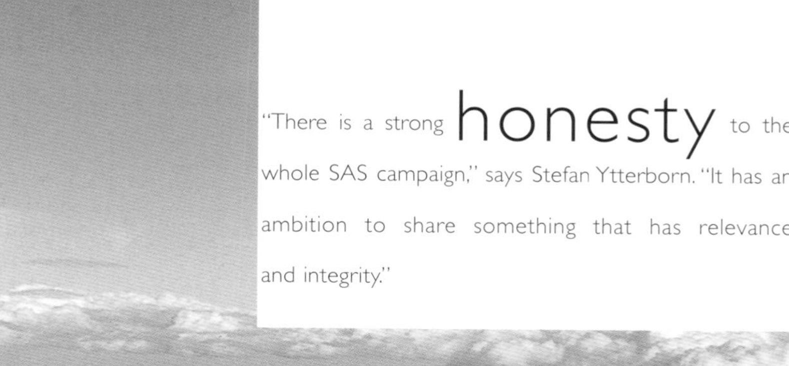

"There is a strong **honesty** to the whole SAS campaign," says Stefan Ytterborn. "It has an ambition to share something that has relevance and integrity."

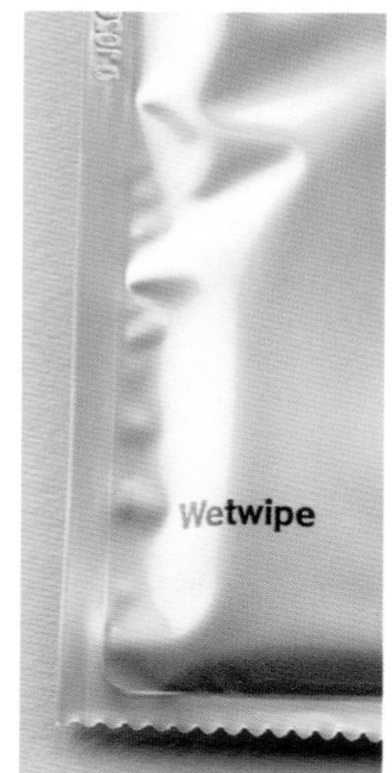

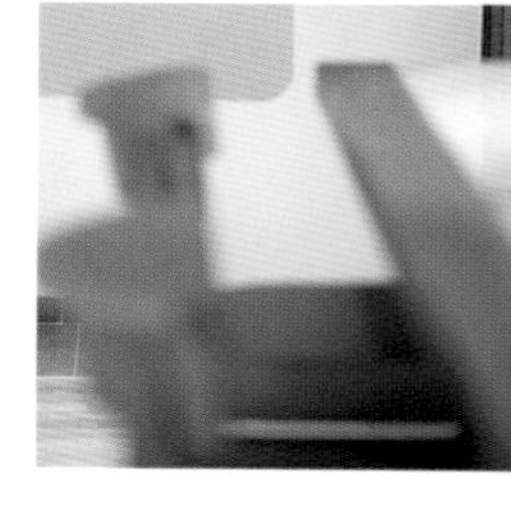

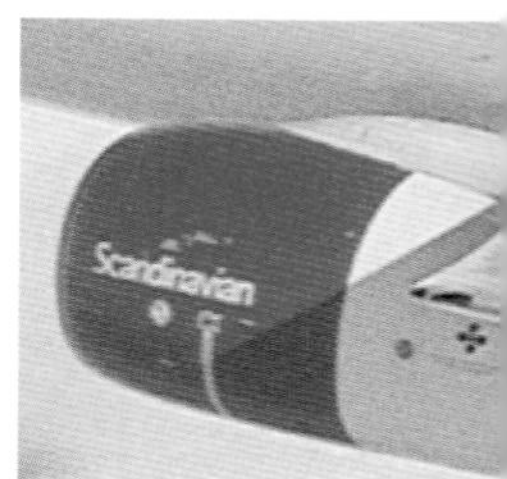

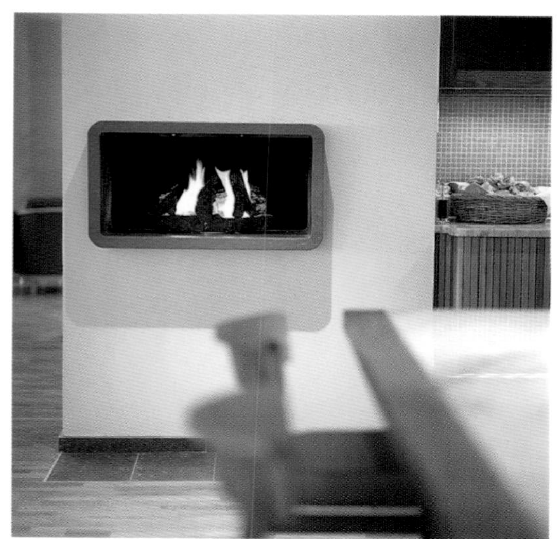

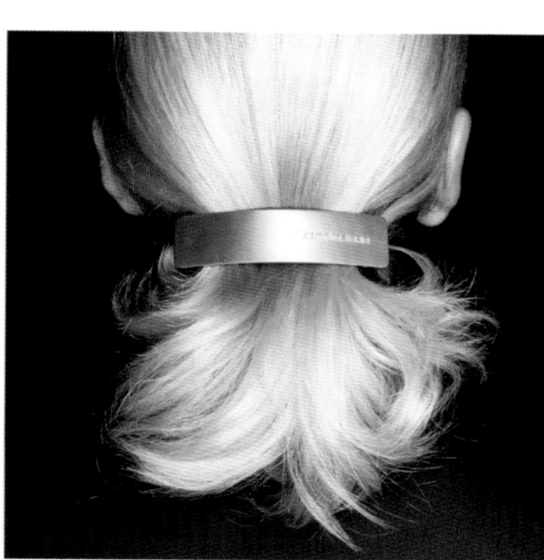

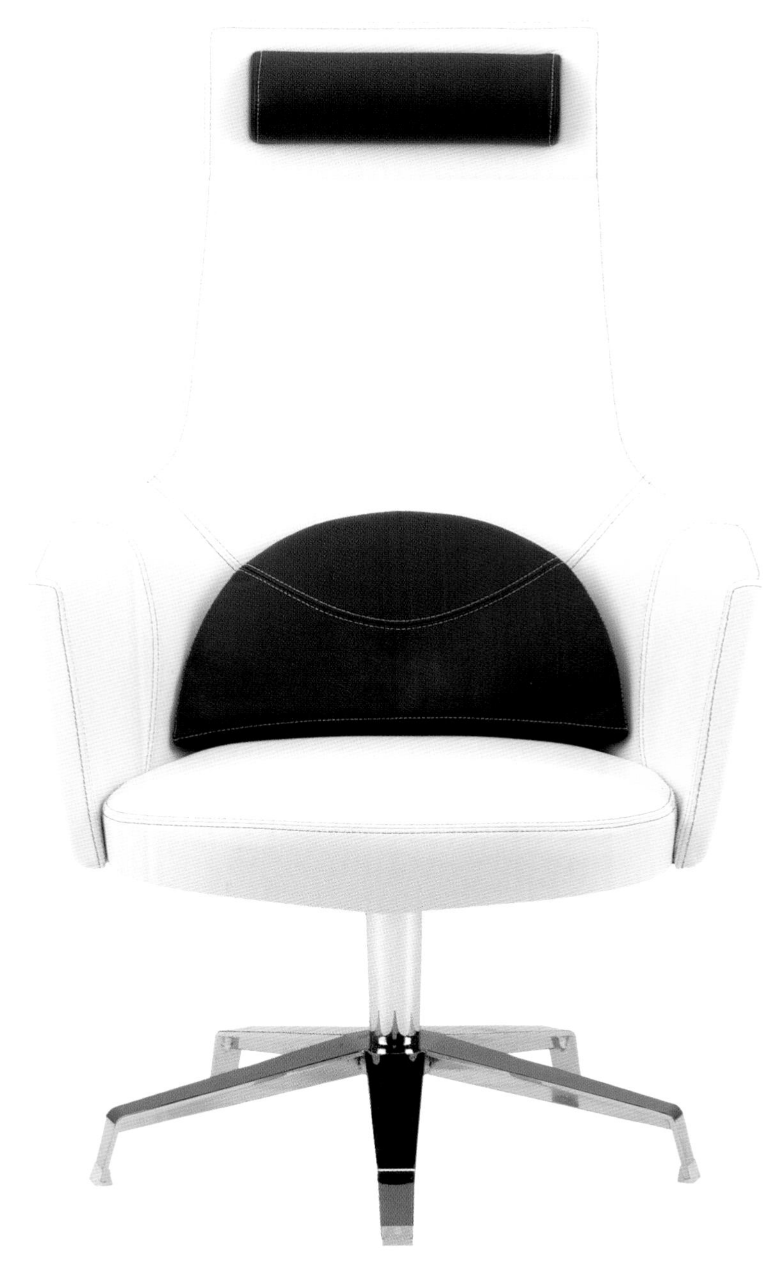

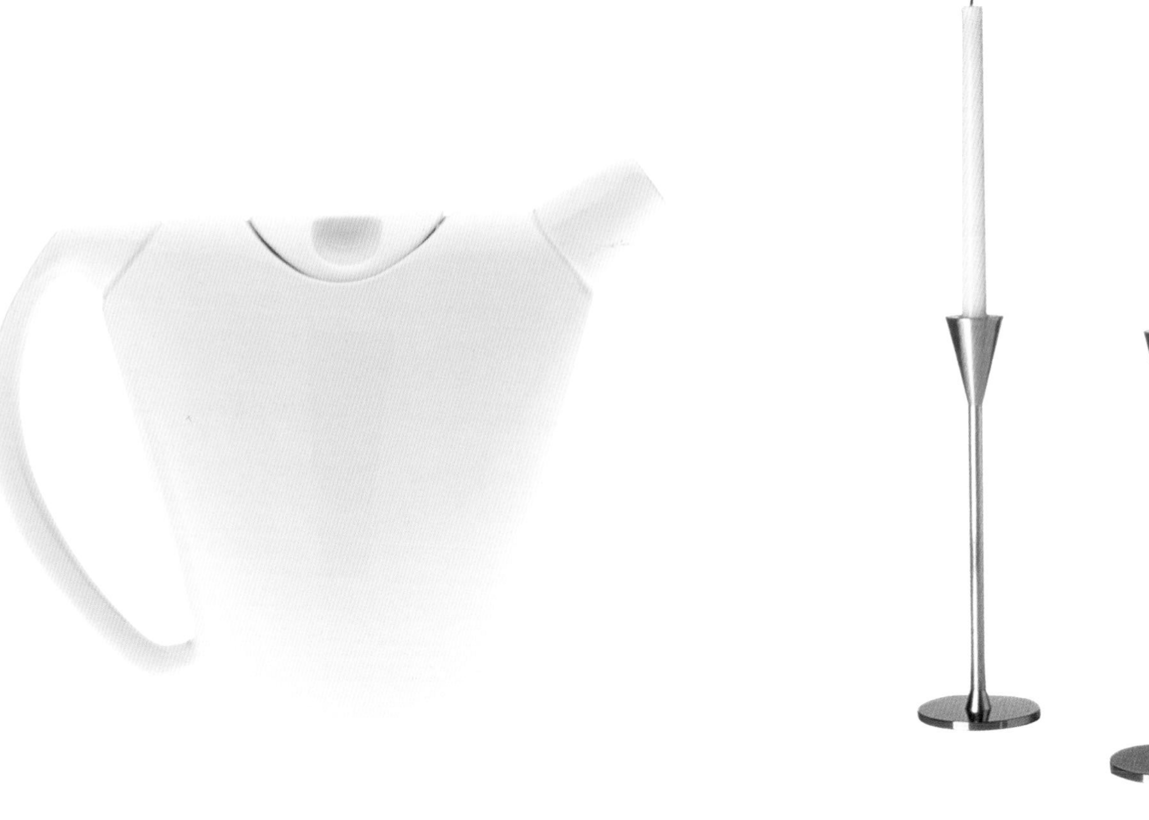

Spir teapot for Figgjo ◄
Johan Verde
China
NORWAY

Lucia candlestick for Asplund ►
Thomas Sandell
Aluminum, painted aluminum
SWEDEN

Tiles for the Swedish Museum of Architecture
Pia Törnell
Stoneware
SWEDEN

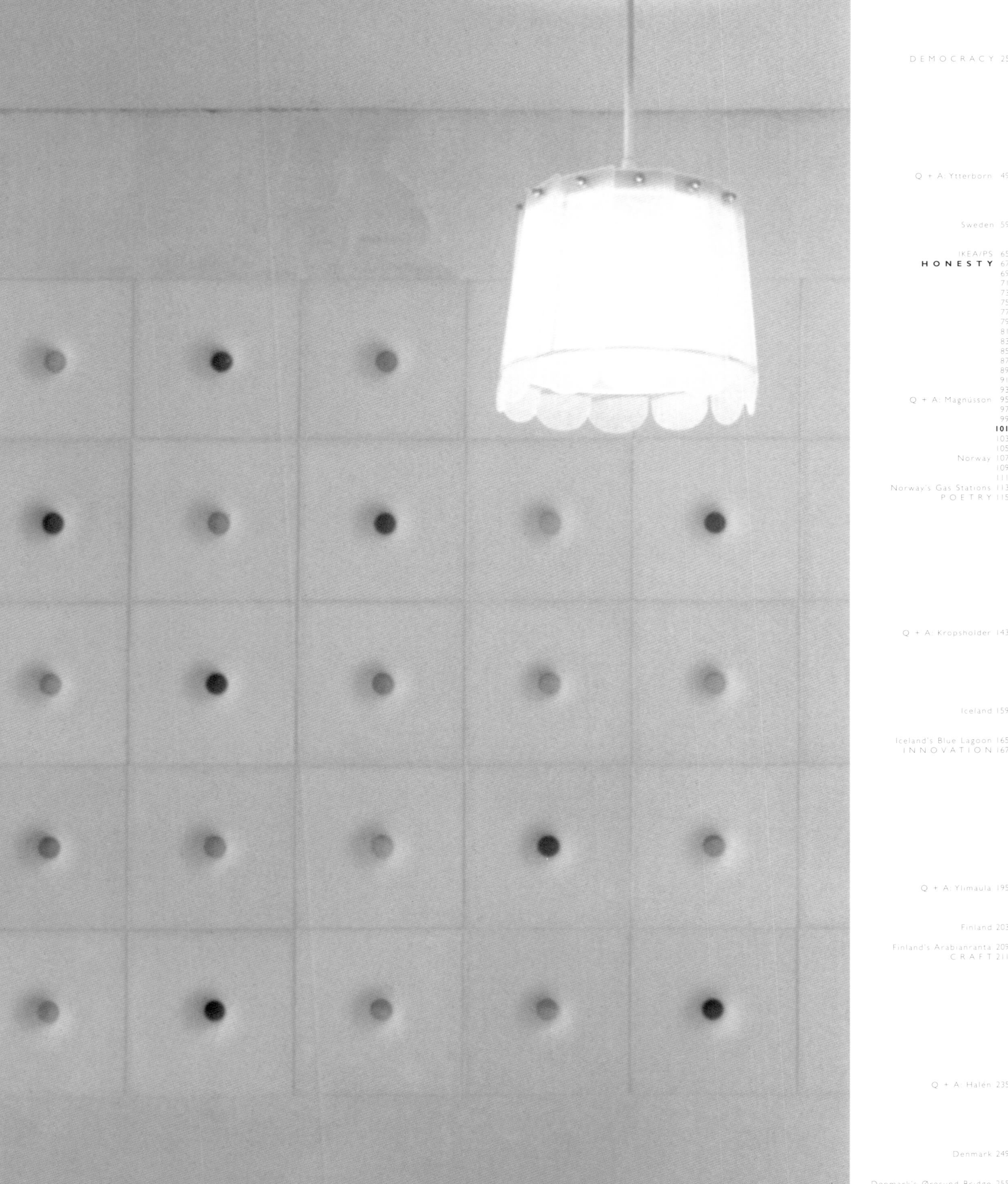

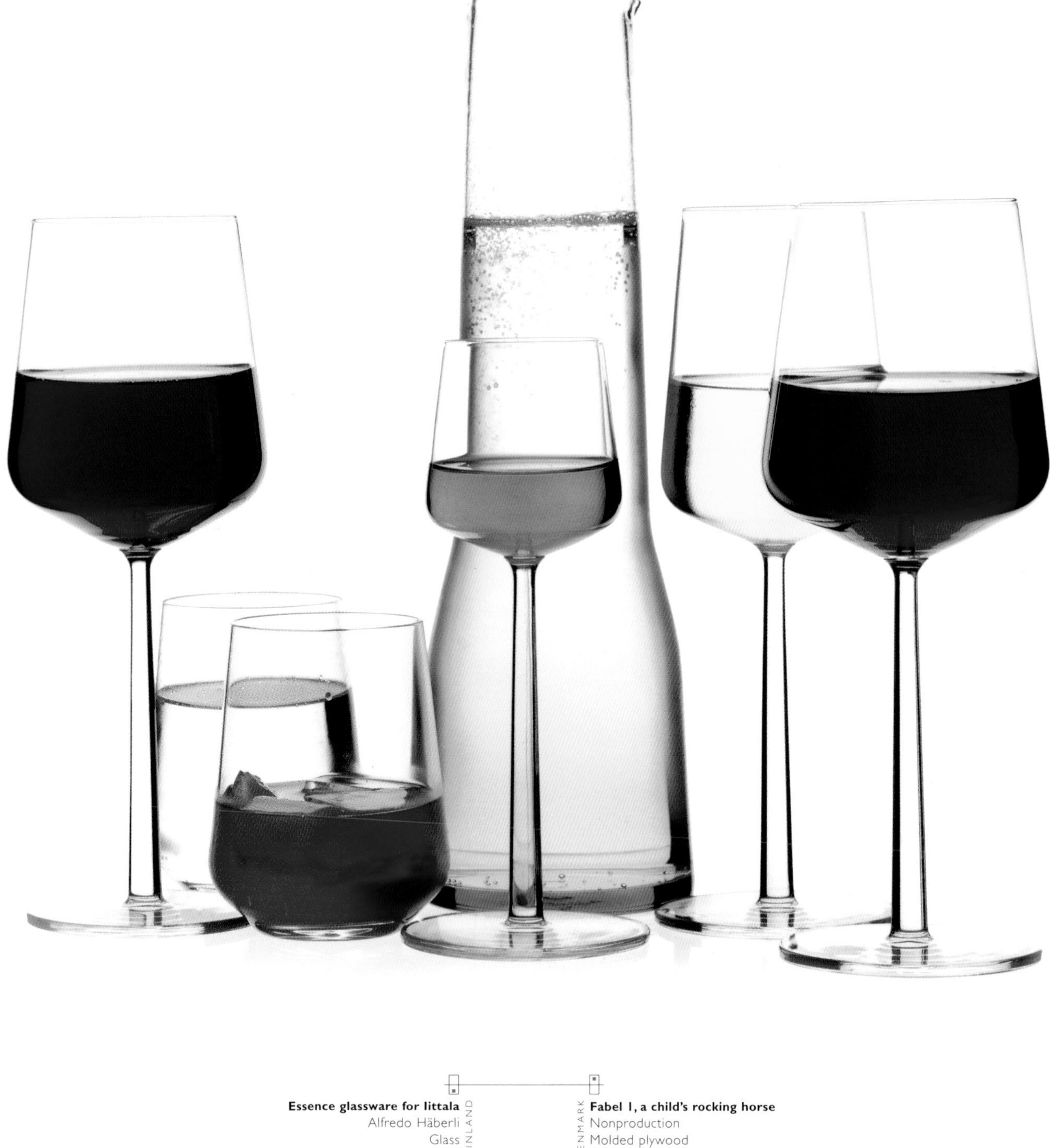

Essence glassware for Iittala
Alfredo Häberli
Glass
FINLAND

DENMARK
Fabel 1, a child's rocking horse
Nonproduction
Molded plywood

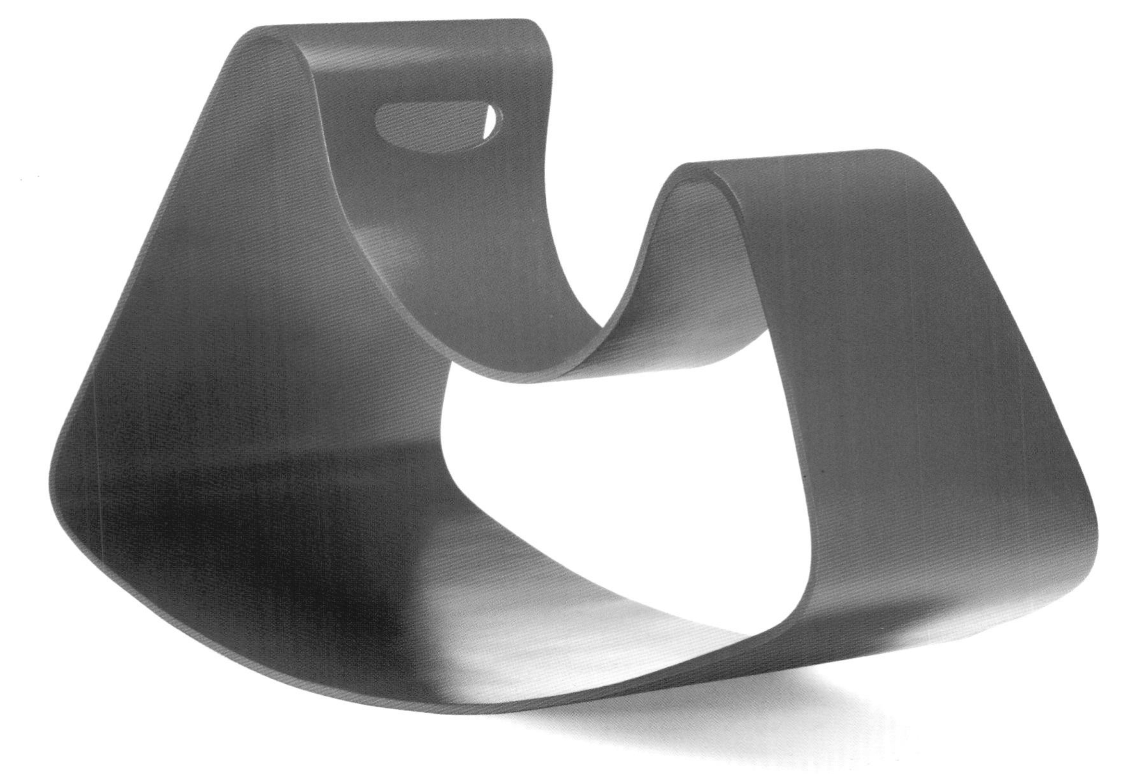

Egg carpet for Asplund
Mats Bigert, Lars Bergström
Wool
SWEDEN

FINLAND
Orgio mugs and bowls for Iittala
Alfredo Häberli
Porcelain

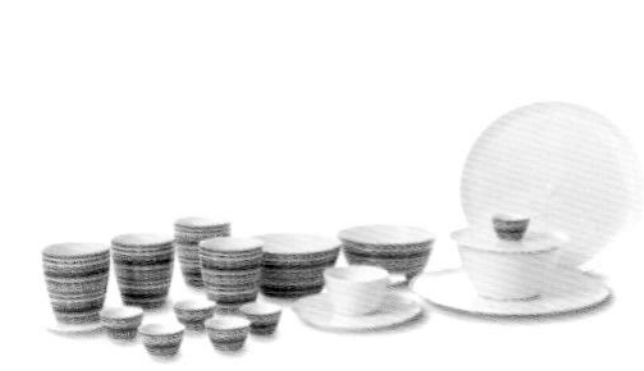

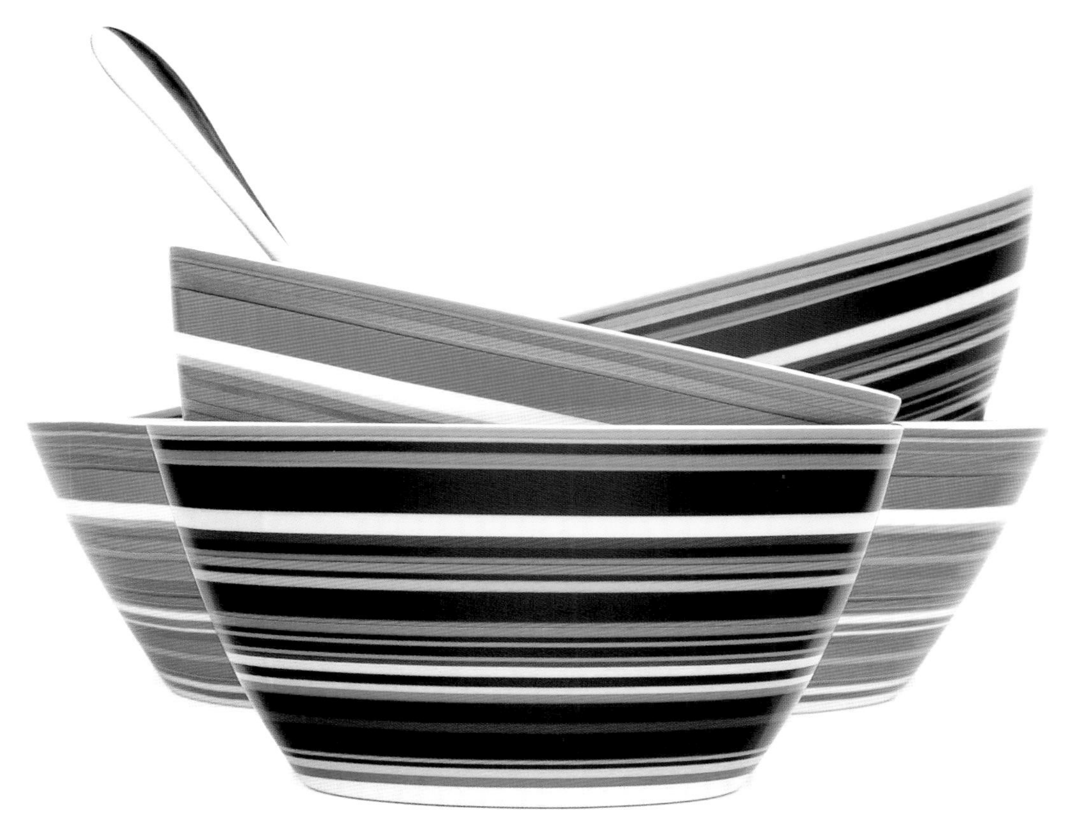

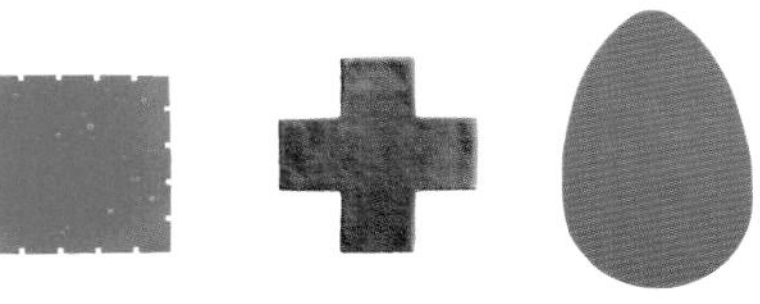

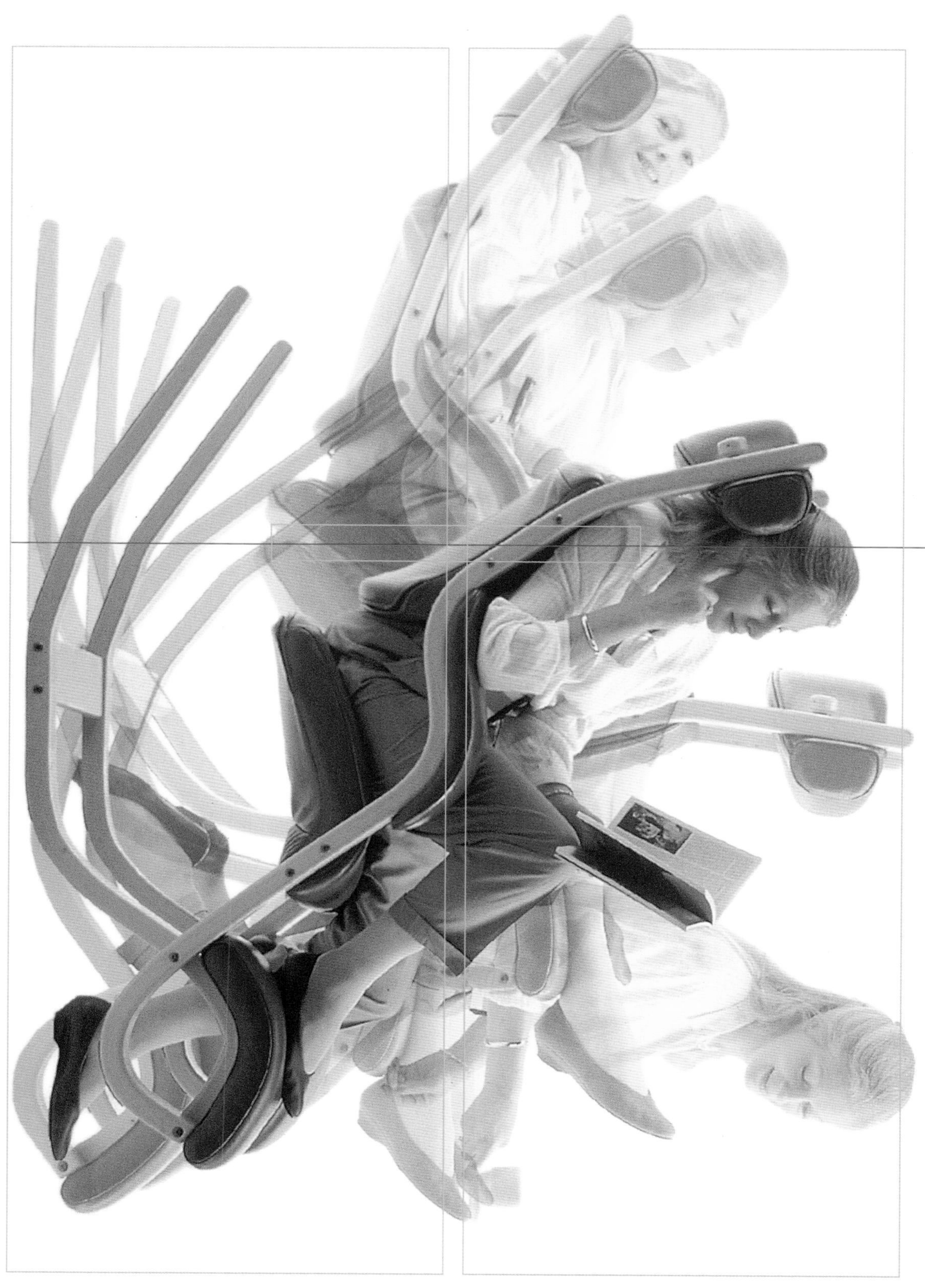

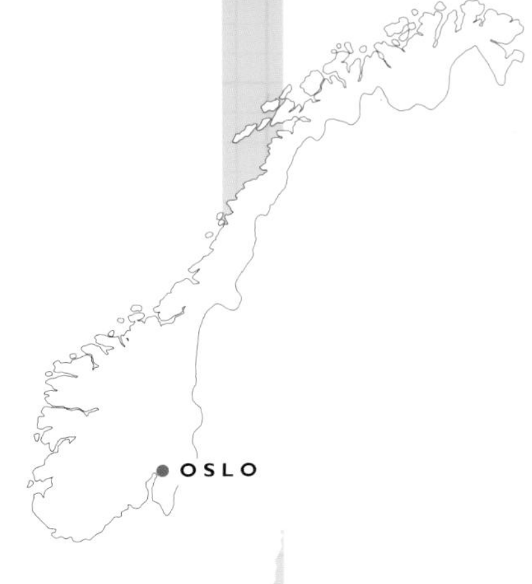

Norway

Think of Norway, and what comes to mind? Oil, illustrious polar explorers, Olympic skiers, the Nobel Peace Prize. But one thing this rugged land of forests and fjords has never been celebrated for is design. Although Norwegian designers made many contributions to the Modern Movement, they never achieved the international recognition of their Scandinavian colleagues. But Norway, often called the "little brother" of Scandinavia, may finally be growing up. An ambitious new group of practitioners is reaching beyond Norway's borders to develop a healthy export market for contemporary design. Little brother isn't simply heading off to college—he may soon take over the family business.

Long colonized by its more powerful Scandinavian neighbors, the relatively new nation of Norway, which gained independence in 1905, acquired a reputation as an introverted society. But today, while shy Norway still refuses to join the European Union, globalization beckons. A new generation of Norwegian designers longs for connection to the international design community. These artists view their efforts as a way to renew Norway's aging infrastructure and decrease the country's dependence on oil reserves, which are predicted to be severely depleted by around 2023. In particular, the globe-trotting tendencies of the design collective Norway Says, whose moniker pokes fun at Norway's perceived status as a follower in the field, have set the pace for the current crop of young designers. In 2000, while several of its members were still students, the group loaded up a rental van and drove south to the Milan Furniture Fair. The first Norwegian design group to exhibit at the fair in more than thirty years, Norway Says garnered commissions from companies in Sweden, Denmark, Italy, and

Official name: The Kingdom of Norway • Year Norway gained independence from Sweden: 1905 • Population: Approximately 4,500,000 • Area:

Germany as a result. Its work, a cool update of Scandinavian minimalism, features playful but functional details, sensual surfaces, and the technical finesse exemplified by a piece like Torbjørn Anderssen's magazine rack, Papermaster, now in the collection of the Victoria and Albert Museum in London.

Norway Says is only one member of a growing community still finding its footing, and this new design scene incorporates a happy jumble of approaches. More traditional Modern styling pervades much new work, such as that of Lars Ernst Hole, whose refined wooden furniture contains hints of retro. "Most of my inspiration comes from Modern Scandinavian designers such as Arne Jacobsen and Poul Kjaerholm and also the American designers Charles and Ray Eames," says Hole. The edgy industrial design firm Permafrost lies at the other end of the spectrum, creating ironic pop pieces such as its Room with a View pillow, which is stuffed with sadly deflated teddy bears. "Our work is not Scandinavian design," says Permafrost founder Tore Vinje Brustad. "That is something old-fashioned that our teachers practiced—not us." Although a range of disparate inspirations and philosophies informs this community's work, its members share a sense of making up for lost time. Only three years after Norway Says headed to Milan, nine design groups attended the 2003 furniture fair. This crowd included promising artists such as furniture designer Andreas Aas, glass designer Cathrine Maske, textile and product design duo Liminal, and the industrial design firm K8.

Although the enthusiasm of these young designers accounts for much of the flurry of activity in Norway, several other factors have contributed to their momentum. Many designers view the 1994 Winter Olympics in Lillehammer as a defining moment for the field. "The Olympic Games at Lillehammer were a unique chance to present Norway abroad," says Per Farstad, designer and educator, who says the high visibility of the Olympic graphic design program underscored the importance of design to those unfamiliar with the field. "The design program was a great success. The significance of design was made apparent to ordinary people and to Norwegian industry, and a new attitude toward design evolved." To further promote design literacy, the Norwegian Foreign Ministry today assists young designers by funding trips to exhibitions in Milan as well as Stockholm and New York. Other important pieces of the puzzle are falling into place: a growing network of Norwegian design magazines, distributors, and retailers provides new ways for designers and potential producers and consumers to connect. Also, after many years of operating independently, the two main design organizations, Norsk Form, the design community's public face, and the Norwegian Design Council, which promotes design within industry and manufacturing, are not only collaborating but actually moving in together as well. A new joint office space will serve as a high-profile location for exhibitions, promotions, and public educational programs.

Although success now seems just around the corner for Norway, the country played

Balans Gravity rocker for Stokke Gruppen (previous spread)
Peter Opsvik
Beech
NORWAY

118,467 square miles (324,220 square kilometers) • Capital: Oslo • Highest annual temperature in Oslo: 84 degrees F (29 degrees C) • Lowest annual temperature in

catch-up with the other Scandinavian states during most of the twentieth century, and it suffered for decades as one of Europe's poorest nations. Even so, says industrial designer Johan Verde, "we actually have a tradition of good designers, though it isn't very well known." Modern Norwegian furniture masters include Adolf Relling, Ingmar Relling (whose 1965 laminated wood Siesta chair is in the Victoria and Albert Museum), Sven Ivar Dysthe, and Bjørn Engø. Arguably, designer Tias Eckhoff, winner of the Lunning prize (a prestigious award given annually to Nordic designers and craftsmen between 1951 and 1970 that recognized outstanding contributions to the Scandinavian Modern movement), is the biggest "name" in Norwegian Modern design. His coffee and tea service Det Riflede ("The Fluted Ones"), designed in 1952 for Danish producer Georg Jensen, exemplifies an important transition from Bauhaus-inspired Functionalism to the more organic form of Modernism that came to define the Scandinavian movement during the 1950s.

In the 1960s, struggling Norway struck oil in the North Sea. Unfortunately, the success of the nation's oil ventures seemed to sidetrack efforts to promote consumer product exports. Even with increased wealth from oil production, innovation in design faltered. Norwegian companies, like their counterparts in other Scandinavian countries, labored under the weight of international imports and corporate mergers and acquisitions. "We were part of the original Scandinavian movement, and Norwegian designers were prominent in the 1950s and 1960s," says Permafrost's Vinje Brustad. "Sadly, Norwegian manufacturers made the mistake of sticking to their winners and got left behind in the 1970s and 1980s."

There were notable exceptions, however. Updating Scandinavian Functionalism with a mindful observation of human movement, furniture designer Peter Opsvik created a child's chair called Tripp Trapp (1972) for the Norwegian manufacturer Stokke and achieved massive export success. Tripp Trapp established Stokke's export business almost single-handedly; at least three million units have sold. Opsvik's social consciousness still informs many new pieces, including the ergonomically groundbreaking Balans collection and his chair Capisco ("the Saddle chair") for the manufacturer Håg, which is one of the most ubiquitous office chairs in Scandinavia today; his products remain big export successes.

Today, the Norwegian government and design organizations are focusing on increasing consumer product exports, though members of the design community report that Norway must surmount a few remaining hurdles in order to compete efficiently in the global marketplace. "Since the Norwegian economy remains oriented toward raw materials and semi-finished goods, the country lacks the international brands that you see in other Scandinavian countries," says Jan Stavik, managing director of the Norwegian Design Council. And, Stavik suggests, with so much wealth within the country, consumer product manufacturers generally haven't felt the pressure to start global trends. "One of the major obstacles is the consumer product industry's insufficient ambition for innovation," he says. Even so, change is in the air: more flexible

Oslo: -5.26 degrees F (-20.7 degrees C) • Number of Norwegian kings born in Norway since 1300: 1 (King Harald V) • Rank in world's oil exports: Second (Saudi Arabia

business models, such as Fjord Fiesta, a new manufacturer, may help Norway gain a competitive edge. Headed by design manager and entrepreneur Pål Lunder, Fjord Fiesta produces contemporary furniture designs and relaunches Modern classics. "I like to use subcontractors as much as possible," says Lunder. "Traditional factories have invested large amounts of money in expensive machines that set limits for their designs. This way, I choose a good design first, and then I find someone suitable to do the work."

Although challenges still lie ahead, the promising new direction of Norwegian design could mean that the little brother of Scandinavia may soon outgrow his older siblings. "The current scene is quite powerful," says the Museum of Decorative Arts and Design's chief curator, Widar Halén. Luckily for contemporary Norwegian designers, the lack of a well-known design tradition allows them the freedom to head off in new directions unfettered. "We do not have the burden of the great golden designers of the 1950s and 1960s to such a degree as in Denmark and Sweden," says Halén. Permafrost's Vinje Brustad agrees. "It's really hard for young Danish designers to compete with Arne Jacobsen and the like."

Perhaps most surprising, Norwegian citizens themselves are proving active supporters and consumers of contemporary design—whether because of their high level of disposable income, the value they place on home life, or, more simply, the contagious wave of enthusiasm for design all over the world. "A low price is still just about the only aspect of a design that marketers find worth mentioning," says Vinje Brustad. "But I do think Norwegians themselves are finally gaining enough confidence to recognize values in design other than purely economic ones."

For its part, Norway Says recently joined forces with its first Norwegian manufacturer, L.K. Hjelle, maker of high-quality, traditional, upholstered furniture. "This year in Milan, we challenged them to be the first Norwegian company to give us an assignment," says Espen Voll, a member of Norway Says. "Our enthusiasm and their own ambition came together. We started to discuss a possible collaboration and now things are moving fast."

NORWAY
Boat dish from Figgjo
Olav Joa
Vitreous china

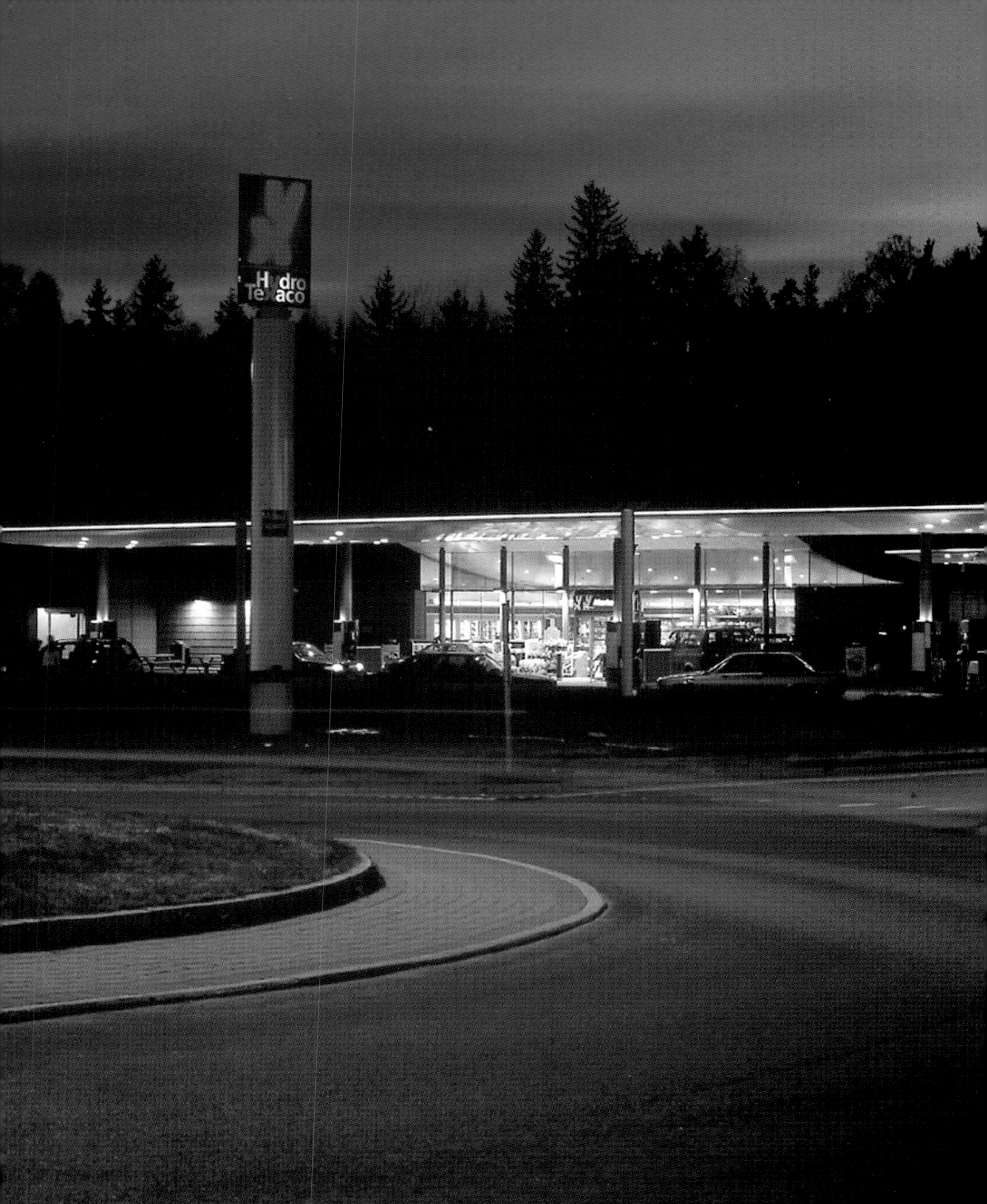
Hydro
Texaco

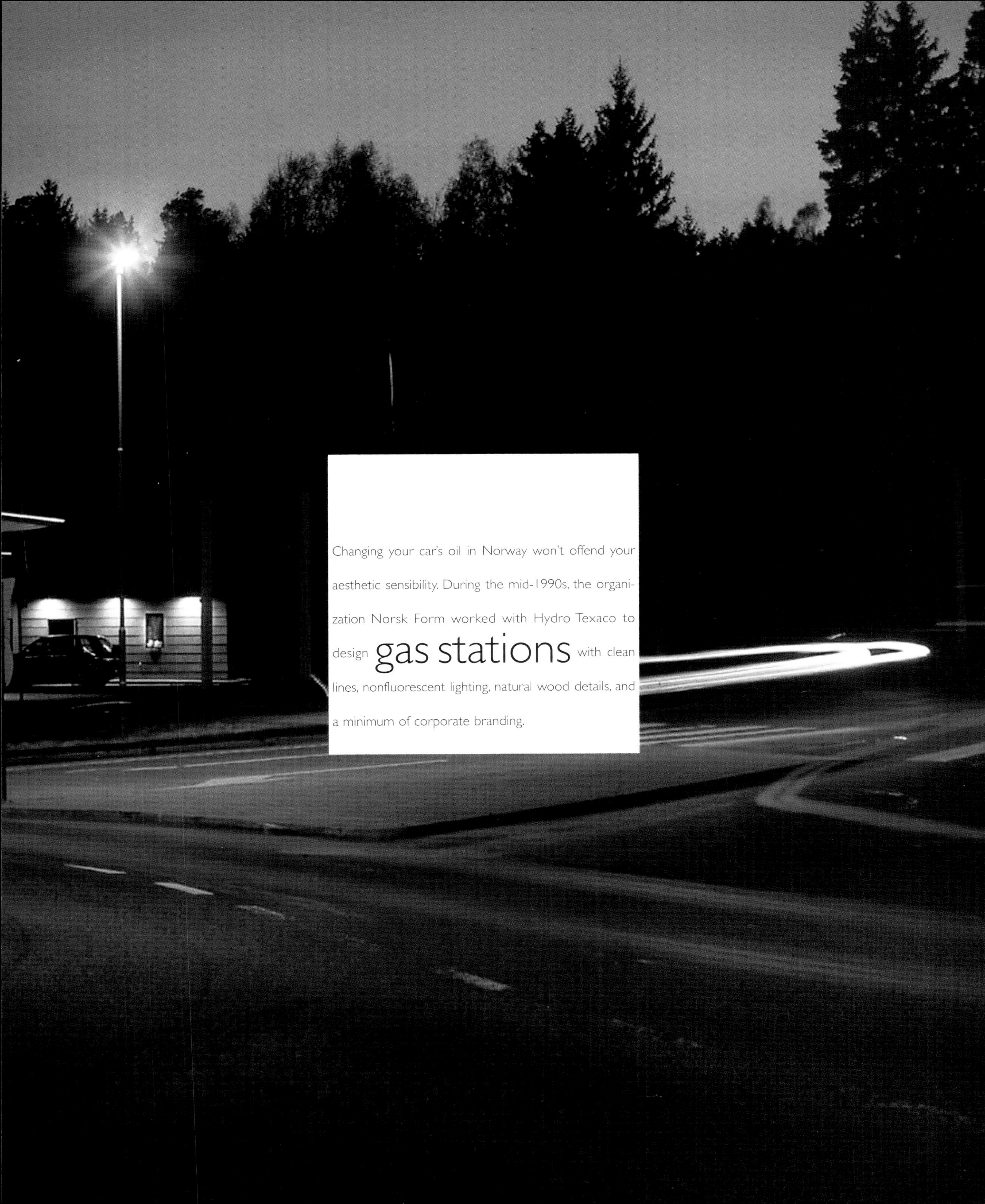

Changing your car's oil in Norway won't offend your aesthetic sensibility. During the mid-1990s, the organization Norsk Form worked with Hydro Texaco to design **gas stations** with clean lines, nonfluorescent lighting, natural wood details, and a minimum of corporate branding.

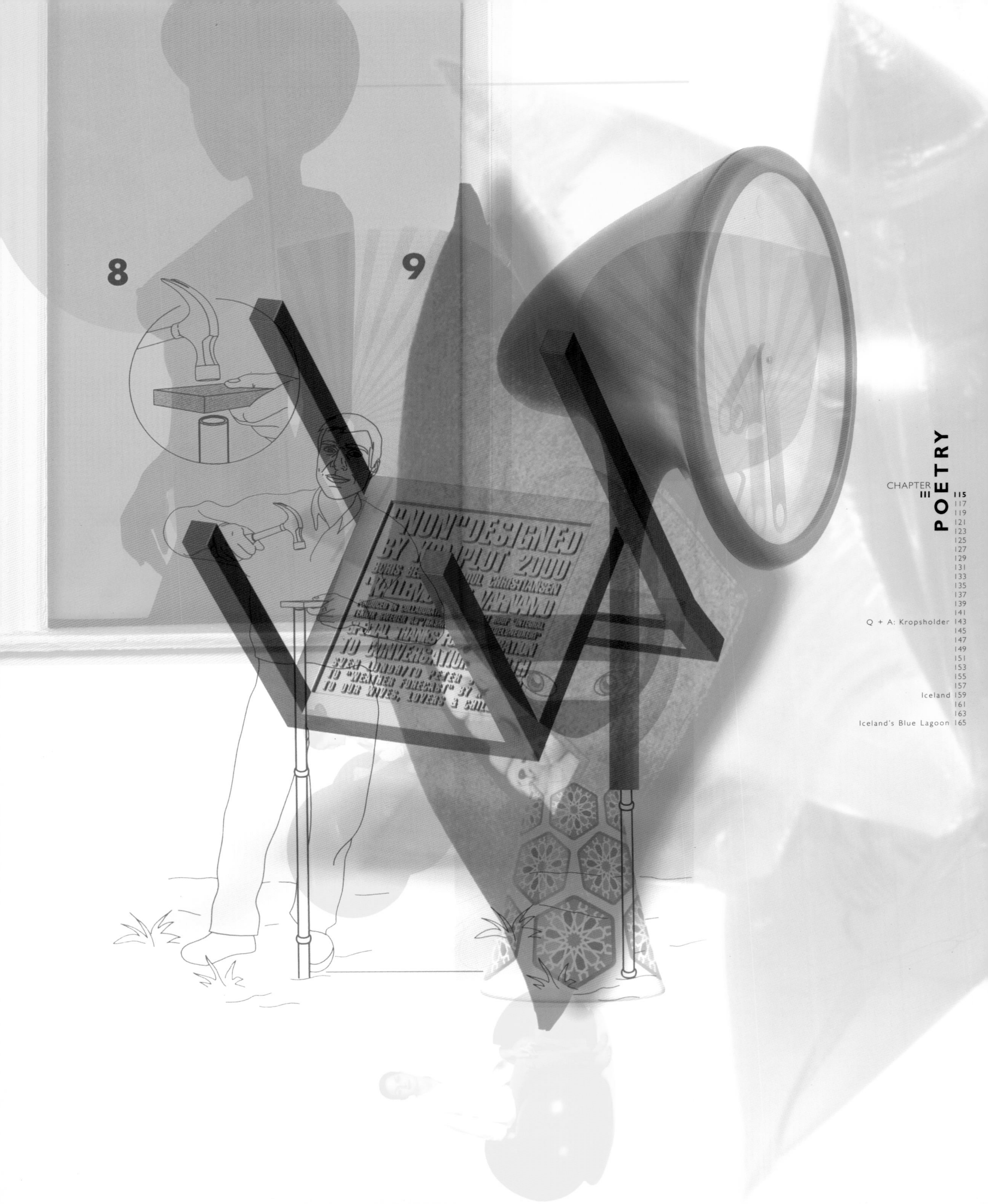

CHAPTER III

POETRY

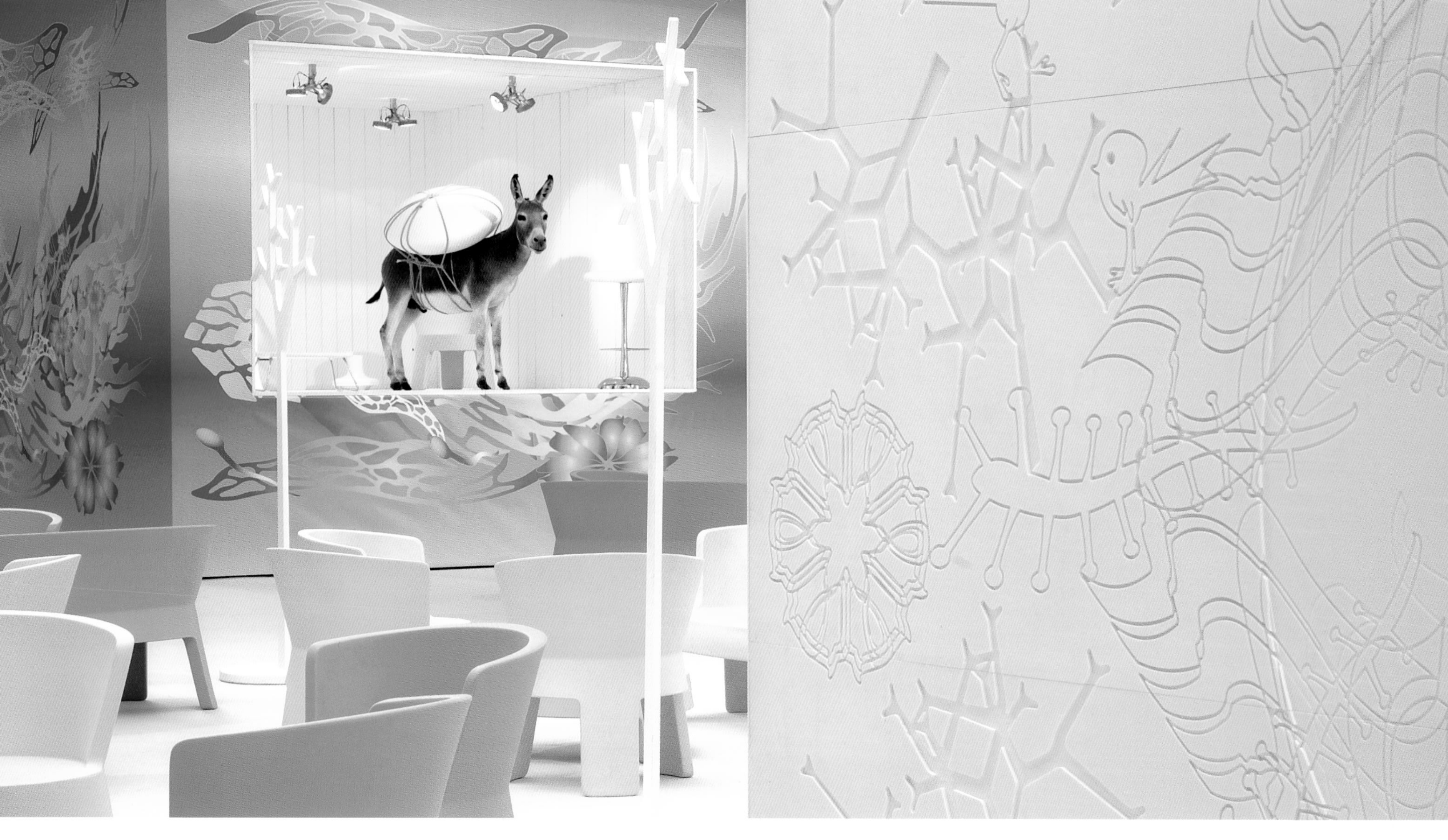

Rambler, a retrospective of the work of designer Michael Young
Michael Young, Katrín Pétursdóttir
ICELAND

POETRY

A visitor to the land of "Rambler" becomes easily disoriented, lost among swirling patterns of spermatozoa, snowflakes, birds, and centipedes. She wanders through a phantasmagoric forest of snow-white trees and sees three mysterious vitrines containing tableaus of a donkey, a bloody slab of whale meat, and Sony's hard-wired pet AIBO. Parched from the long walk, she passes by a refurbished 1950s Airstream trailer, the "Captain's Quarters," proceeding toward a food and beverage bar called "Young and Beautiful." After a heartening drink, she spies a path back to the real world—the showroom floor at the INTERIEUR International Biennial.

"Rambler," a 2002 design installation and retrospective of the work of British designer Michael Young, created in collaboration with his wife, Icelandic designer Katrín Pétursdóttir, revels in an extravagant synthesis of pop, retro, and fantasy. The Dionysian display—inspired a bit by the exotic reputation of Iceland, where the two make their home, but a lot more by Disneyland—holds romance in check with cheeky humor. It also points to the trend of the poetic in design from the Nordic countries.

The whimsical "Rambler" is a far cry from the practical Functionalism and essential forms that many associate with Scandinavian design. Yet elements of this installation—its excess, conceptual approach, and humor—are increasingly common on the Nordic scene. A growing group of practitioners, motivated less by practicality and more by personal expression, is reassessing the legacy of Modernism, the style that has dominated Scandinavian design for at least sixty years. These designers offer artistic statements to counter accepted wisdom regarding functionality and comfort. Their work doesn't necessarily reject Functionalism, but it often employs borderline usability to emphasize artful explorations. Envisioning an eclectic future, poetic designers perpetuate an expansive understanding of Scandinavian design.

Although solid functionality and popular appeal are values central to Scandinavian design, there are also historical precedents for limited edition, artistic solutions within this tradition. In fact, a dialogue between these two extremes—the democratic and the romantic—has informed many periods of Scandinavian design. In the 1920s, during the era of "Swedish Grace" (a term coined by British critic Morton Shand, after viewing the Swedish Pavilion at the 1925 "Exposition Internationale des Arts Décoratifs et Industriels Modernes" in Paris), luxury art glass by such designers as Simon Gate and Edward Hald offered a sumptuous, neoclassical alternative to the utility-focused designs of the previous decade. Even during the mid-twentieth century, at the very height of Scandinavian democratic design, designers produced artful pieces. It is often noted that the 1951 laminated birch platter by Finnish designer Tapio Wirkkala and the 1953 Orkidea ("Orchid") vase by fellow Finn Timo Sarpaneva—two objects that have come to epitomize Scandinavian style—are far more sculptural than functional. In 1955, the Swede Folke Jansson produced an early Scandinavian example of contemporary "art

The work of poetic designers doesn't necessarily reject Functionalism, but it often employs borderline usability to emphasize artful explorations. Envisioning an eclectic future, these designers perpetuate an expansive understanding of Scandinavian design.

SWEDEN
The Gardener's Sofa for Design House Stockholm
Eva Schildt
Lacquered steel

furniture," a concept central to the Postmodern movement of the 1980s. Jansson's jubilant Arabesk chair—asymmetrical, funky, and upholstered in a chaotic swarm of yellow and black—bordered on what Scandinavians viewed as "bad taste." Celebrated on its release, the extroverted Arabesk fell from favor afterward, but it has since regained appreciation in Scandinavian museums for its expressive qualities. Other influential twentieth-century Scandinavian designers who eschewed democratic dogma include Austrian-born Joseph Frank (1885–1967) and Dane Verner Panton (1926–98). Frank, who lived in Sweden, preferred individual taste to strict Functionalism. Frank noted, "The home must not be a mere effective machine...There are no puritan principles in good interior decoration." Panton, a radical designer who initially worked under the great Danish architect Arne Jacobsen, had difficulty gaining acceptance of his ideas within Scandinavia. His bold, colorful forms reflect his interest in fashion and an abstract relationship to furniture. Their two very different voices upheld many Scandinavian values, such as high quality and durability, but always paired tradition with personal expression.

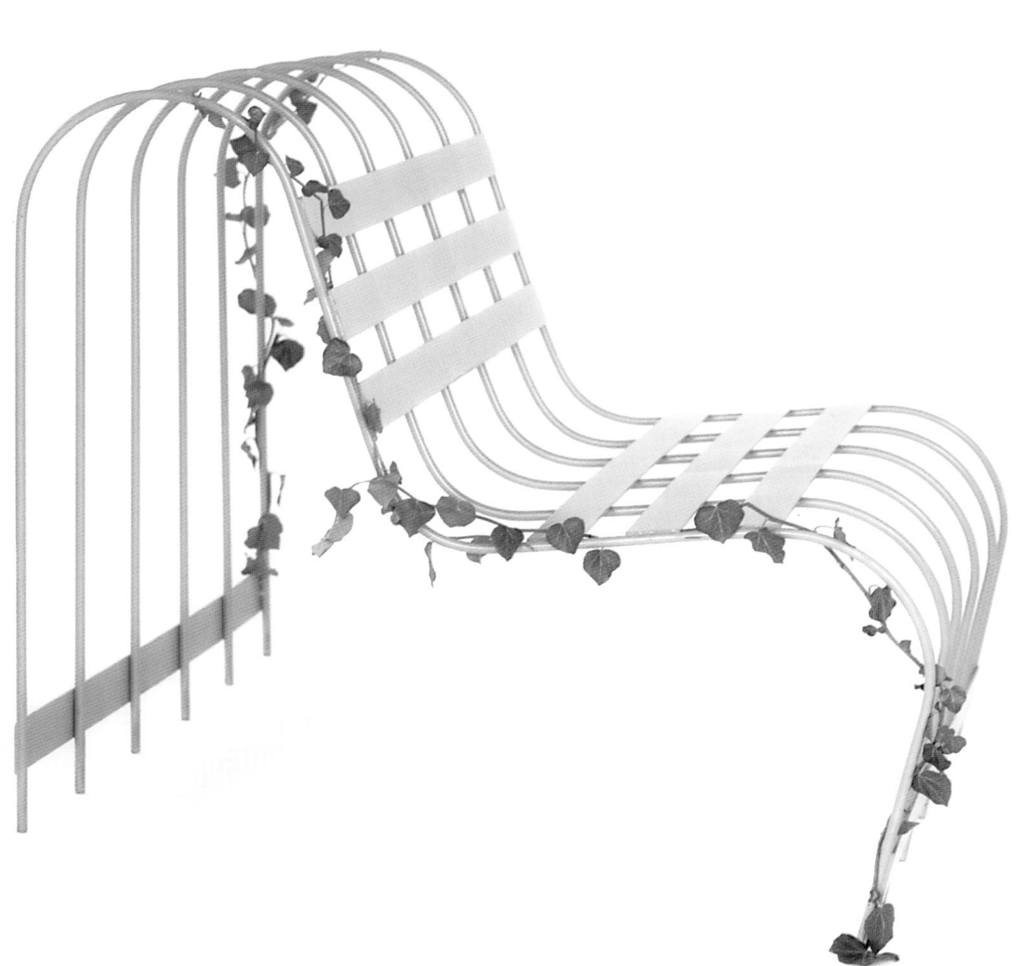

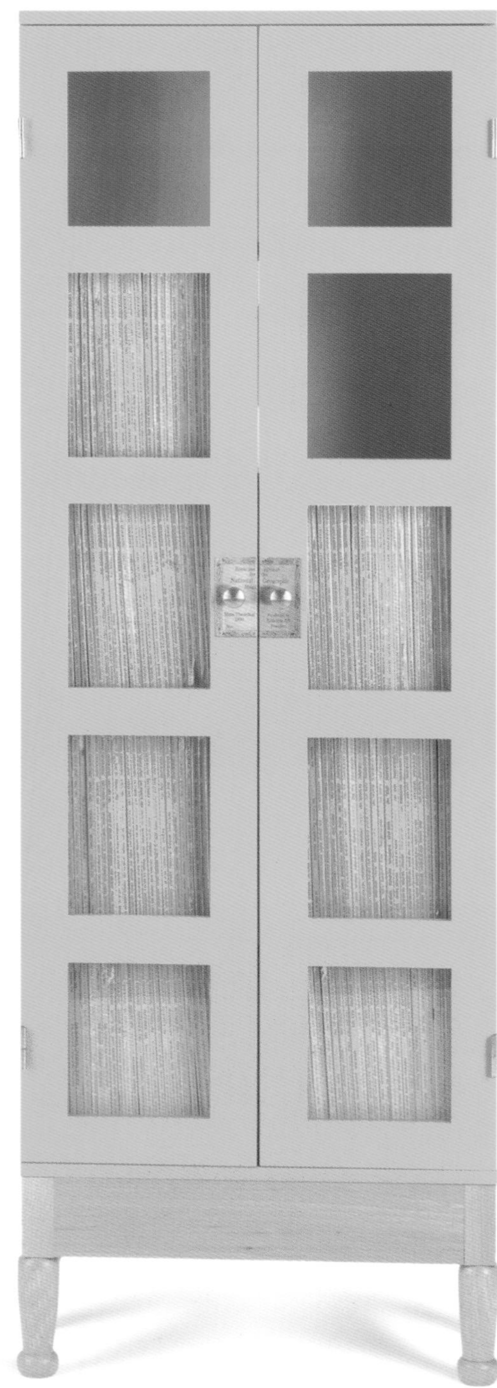

National Geographic cabinet for Källemo (A)
Mats Theselius
Glass, brass, beech
SWEDEN

DENMARK
Butterfly chairs (B)
Nanna Ditzel
Silk-screened fiberboard, metal frame

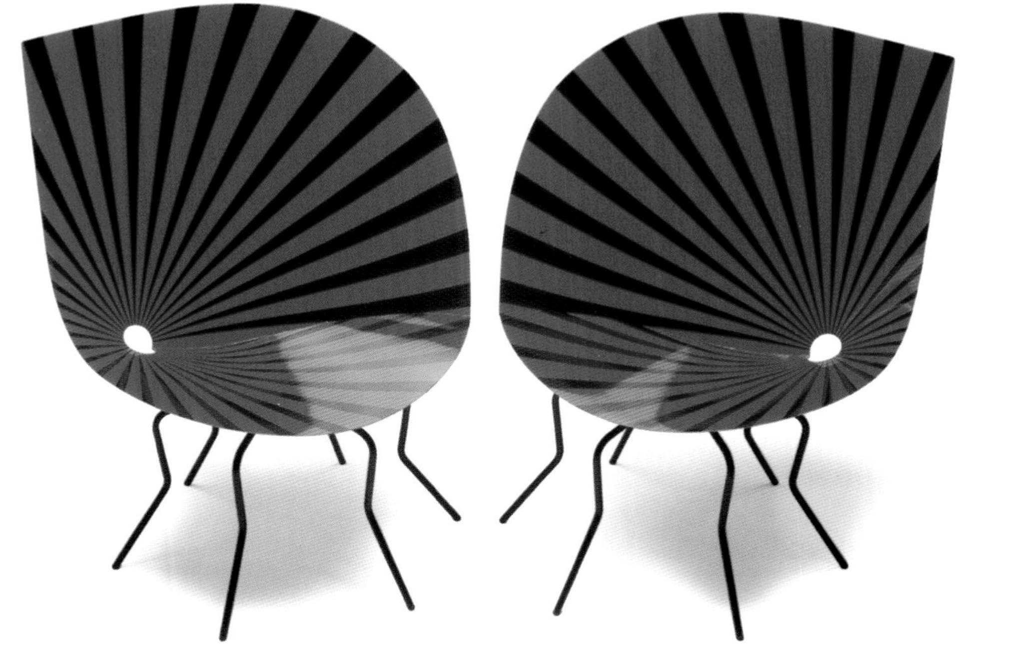

B

◄ **A**

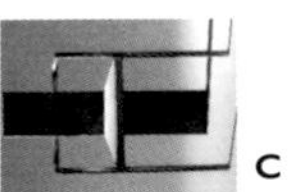

C

The renaissance of Functionalism has dominated Scandinavian design for the past two decades, but a handful of designers have sought more artistic solutions. By refusing to make their furniture accessible, or by crafting works of personal—not universal—interest, these designers refuse to bow to democratic tradition. In 1981, the Swedish designer Jonas Bohlin exhibited his iconoclastic Concrete chair **(C)** see **p 130**. Made from concrete and tubular steel, this sculptural, brooding chair flouts ergonomics, usability, and practicality; it is difficult to manufacture and uncomfortable to sit in. The company Källemo produced the art-inspired Concrete in a limited edition numbered one to one hundred. Bohlin's colleague, the quirky Swedish designer Mats Theselius, also blurred the boundary between art and design with his National Geographic cabinet (1990) **(A)**, which contains shelves just tall enough to accommodate issues of that magazine. Part homage and part personal symbol, the cabinet is a result of Theselius's effort to quit smoking: whenever the designer craved a cigarette, he would lose himself in an issue of the magazine. Needing a place to store his growing collection, he crafted this cabinet and painted it *National Geographic's* trademark yellow. A third response to Nordic Functionalism, and a foreshadowing of conceptual design, is the dancing Butterfly chair (1990) **(B)** by the grand dame of Danish furniture design, Nanna Ditzel. As fantastic as Bohlin's Concrete is austere, the bright-colored plywood chair captures the energy of the fluttering insect. Imagination, not usability, is Butterfly's guiding principle.

Today, young creatives take their lead from the art-inspired work of Bohlin, Theselius, and Ditzel by crafting idea-driven designs. Their methodology rejects strict Functionalism in favor of expressive forms, humor, and variety in materials. The work of Icelandic designer Hrafnkell Birgisson exemplifies this approach. Birgisson begins first with an idea and then builds his treatment by drawing on media ranging from found objects to computer renderings. One theme that intrigues him is nomadic living, particularly in the urban environment, and he addresses this in his low-tech Hab **(D)** series. Each design in the series features a life-size image of old-fashioned furniture, such as a Victorian bookcase and a Baroque chest of drawers, imprinted on polyurethane. After the sheet is hung on the wall, plates, saucers, and other utensils can be put away by sliding them under straps. The "heirloom" rolls up easily for the next move. A more traditional solution is Homobile **(E)**, a hollow seat with wheels that acts as an open storage unit. Birgisson's most ambitious design is architectural: a futuristic hotel pod concept called Sleep and Go **(F)**, which can be implemented as a low-cost shelter but also captures the quirkiness of Birgisson's vision with organic forms and heart-shaped architectural details.

Hab portable cabinet (D)
Hrafnkell Birgisson
Polyurethane sheet
ICELAND

Homobile furniture (E)
Hrafnkell Birgisson
Various materials
ICELAND

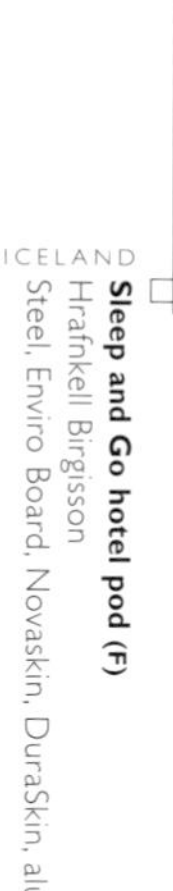

Sleep and Go hotel pod (F)
Hrafnkell Birgisson
Steel, Enviro Board, Novaskin, DuraSkin, aluminum
ICELAND

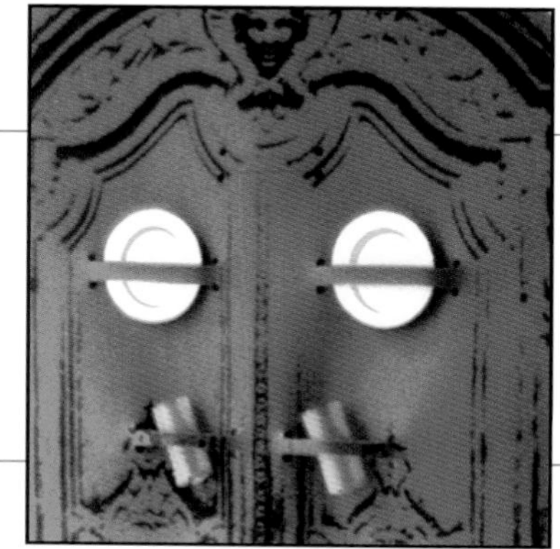

D

F ➤

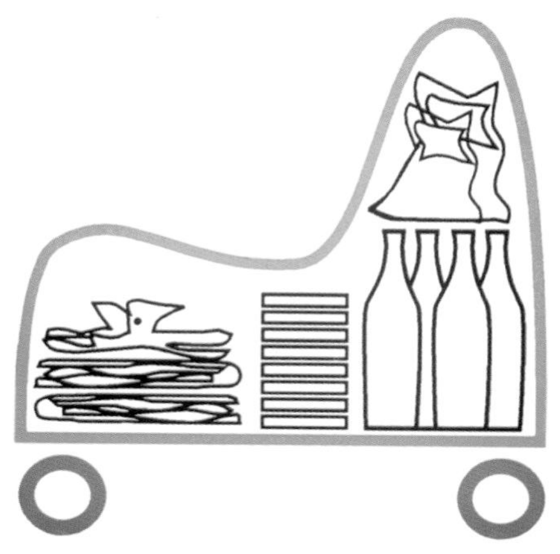

E

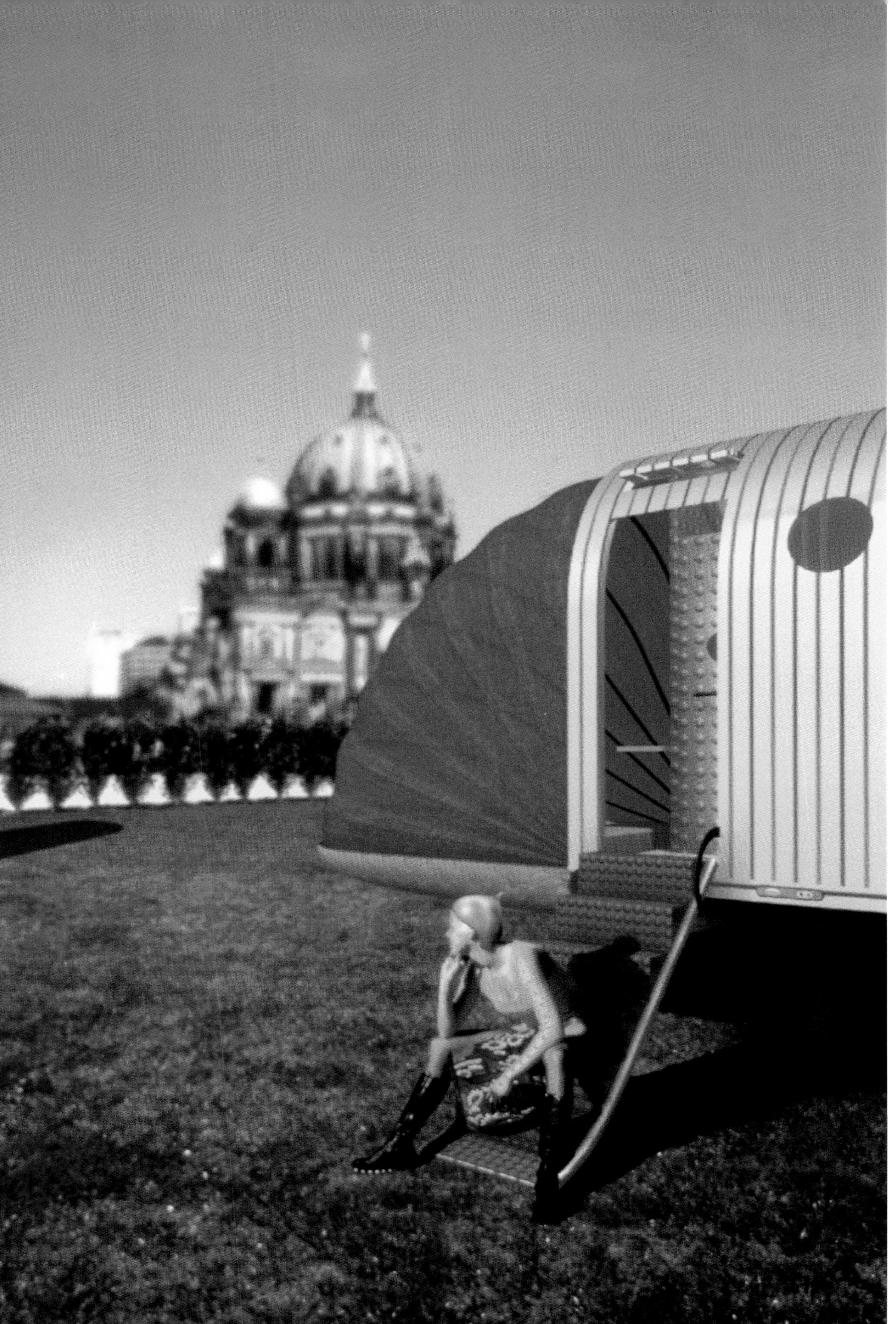

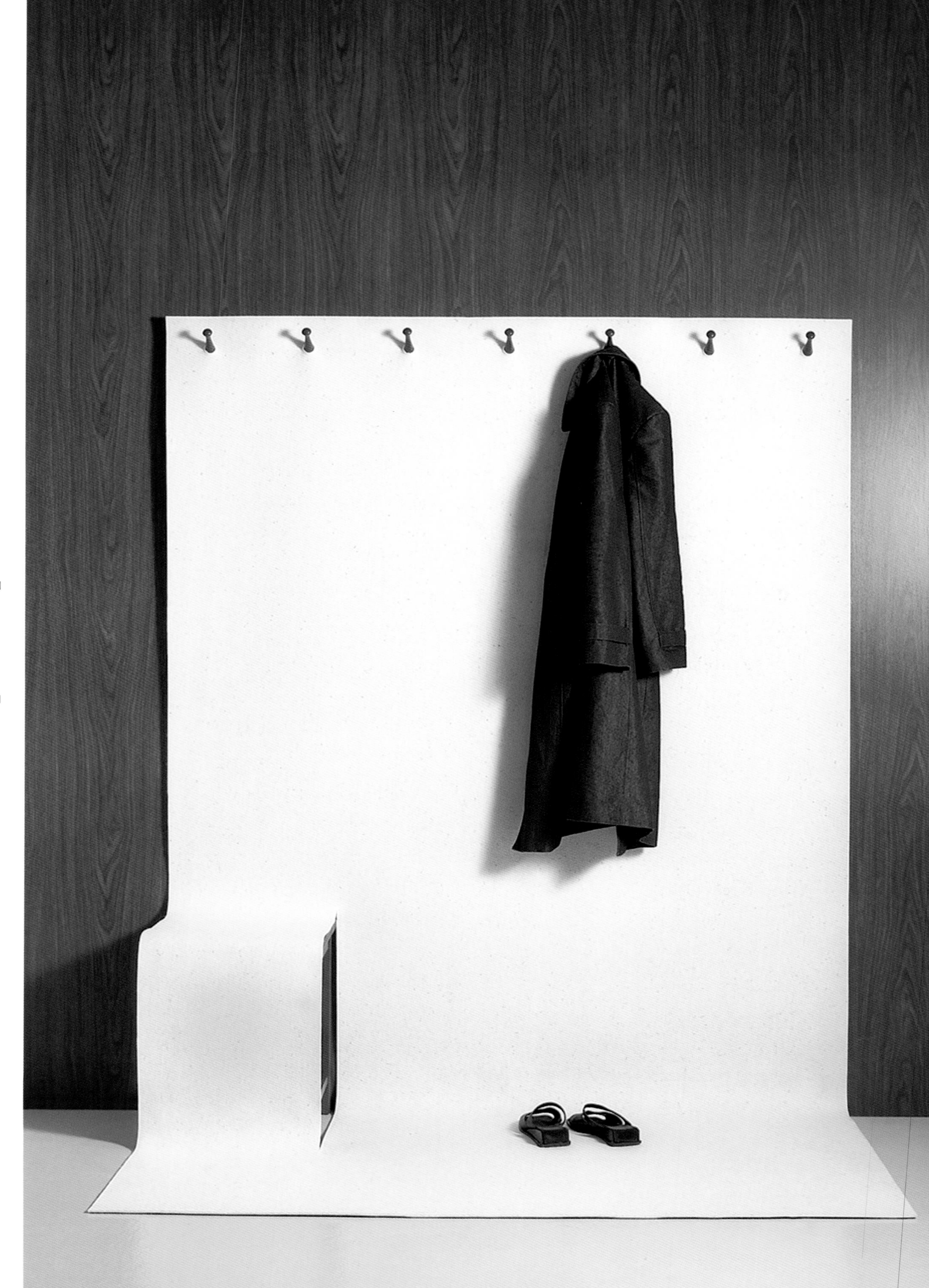

Hang Out (G)
Ditte Hammerstrøm
Felt, wood
DENMARK

DENMARK
Casual Cupboard for Bahnsen Collection (I)
Louise Campbell
Ash veneer

The recent emphasis on conceptual design doesn't mean creatives have a superficial grasp of the use of materials. Rather, their understanding is defined by flexibility. They often employ incongruous materials to surprise and occasionally jar us. Ukrainian-born designer Aleksej Iskos, who lives in Denmark, fashions works of ethereal beauty by juxtaposing unrelated "everyday objects" to question notions of safety and comfort. A halogen light surrounded by clear bags of colored water comprises his Waterfall chandelier **(J)** see p 138; the glittering Waterfall also disconcerts: water bags dangle directly overhead, with the liquid uncomfortably close to electricity. Iskos crafted the unnerving Night Ghost lamp **(H)** see p 150 with two elements: a hanger-shaped neon light and an oxford shirt. When placed on the hanger the shirt glows softly, evoking an eerie human presence. With subtle irony, the design reverses the calming effect of having someone watch over you and light your way.

This willingness to confound expectations turns Scandinavian rationalism on its head. Designers embrace the unpredictable, even the untidy; indeed, Danish designer Ditte Hammerstrøm welcomes clutter. Hang Out **(G)**, a prime example of artful functionality, is a versatile blend of architecture and textile that enfolds

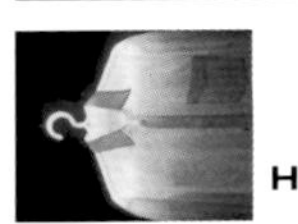

H

◄ G

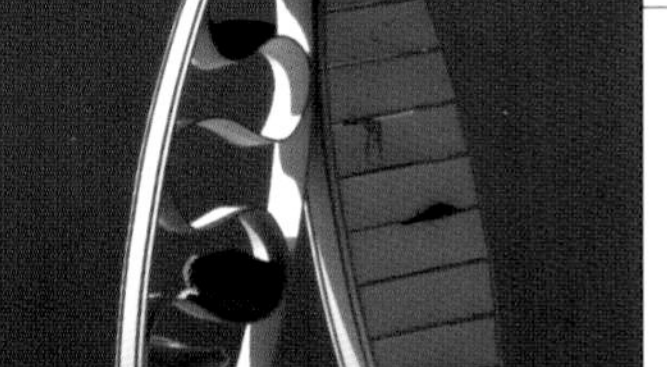

I

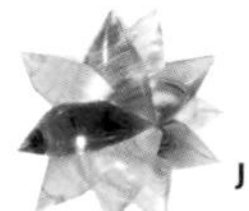

J

messiness in the front hallway. Most Scandinavian living spaces have racks near the entrance for coats and shoes, which are removed even in the home of a new acquaintance. This space, often the victim of hurried moments and crowded dinner parties, tends toward disarray rather than harmony. Hang Out, a single piece of wool hung behind the coat and shoe racks and draped down the wall to the floor, seeks to frame the chaos rather than reorganize or conceal it. The result is a comforting, welcoming space that Hammerstrøm describes as "an open hiding place." Hang Out doesn't reject the traditional Scandinavian notion of better domestic living through design, but it allows mess rather than enforcing purity.

Other designers also embrace the happenstance of real life, finding inspiration in the uncertainty of human relationships. Danish designers Louise Campbell and Malene Reitzel founded the influential all-female collective Kropsholder—meaning "body holder"—in 1997. While Campbell and Reitzel employ different visual languages, both push usability to the breaking point to underline emotional tension. Reitzel's unstable Airblock containers, which barely balance together, "tell a story about the fragility of life," she says. "They are deeply receptive to external and internal influences." The leaning shelving units of Campbell's Casual Cupboard **(I)** maintain equilibrium tentatively, requiring a wall or each other for support.

While Scandinavian designers explore uncharted territory with poetic design, they are not wholly captivated by the romance of personal expression. Humor holds their work in check, also offering a departure from an often serious and weighty tradition. Designs such as Theselius's National Geographic cabinet, a product of the designer's obsessive-compulsive tendencies, and Young and Pétursdóttir's "Rambler" a decadent feast of pop and imagination, share with us a self-conscious wink-and-nudge. Ironic humor also drives the poetic critique. To question the concept of consumption, Danish designer Annette Meyer assumes the trappings of consumer culture—she creates three-piece suits **(M)** see **p 137** from snack-food packaging. In shape and tailoring, each article of clothing is identical; the palette of each product's package, be it for Fig Newton cookies or Herr's potato chips, distinguishes one outfit from another, giving new meaning to the phrase "you are what you eat."

Engaging the images of popular culture opens the door to kitsch—a signifier of the ostentatious, sentimental, and nostalgic. In Scandinavia, designers engage kitsch not as much as a critique of

Flash chaise lounge (L)
Cathrine Torhaug
Fiberglass, stainless steel, leather
NORWAY

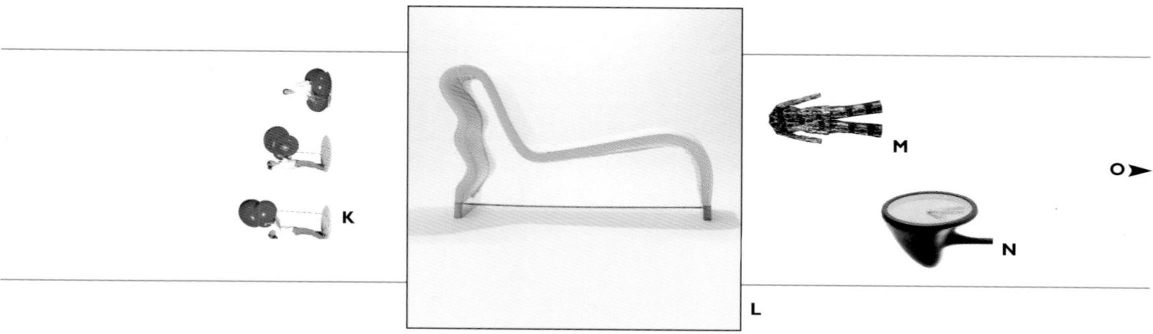

SWEDEN
Northern Enlightenment lamp (O)
Ludvig Löfgren
Wood, glass

consumer society, as is often the case in American design, but as a reaction to the dominance of honest design and, in their view, the moralistic notion of "good taste." The Swede Ludvig Löfgren calls his goofy tree-shaped lamp, Northern Enlightenment **(O)**, "a struggle against conformity." Northern Enlightenment is basically a functioning lamp, though it also makes an artistic statement. Crafted from traditional Scandinavian materials—hand-blown glass for the base, wood for the shade—the lamp subverts the "Northern" ideal of practical beauty; its decorative, cartoonlike qualities, awkward stance, and what Scandinavian's might view as tasteless design contradict the modest, essential forms and straightforward function typical of Scandinavian style. The lamp's quirky character underscores its designer's philosophy, beauty is not an ethical ideal but is in the eye of the beholder.

The new poeticism suggests a loosening of the airtight architectural language of Scandinavian design. From Icelandic designer Hlynur Vagn Atlason's bulbous Tunö clock **(N)** see **p 163** to Norwegian Cathrine Torhaug's curving, hot-pink lounger Flash **(L)**, freewheeling shapes are increasingly common. Henriette Melchiorsen's fantastical Flying Chair **(K)** see **p 128** may address a routine predicament—where to store an extra chair in a small apartment—but the solution, a floating, rubbery red cushion that can be pulled down by a string, is hardly

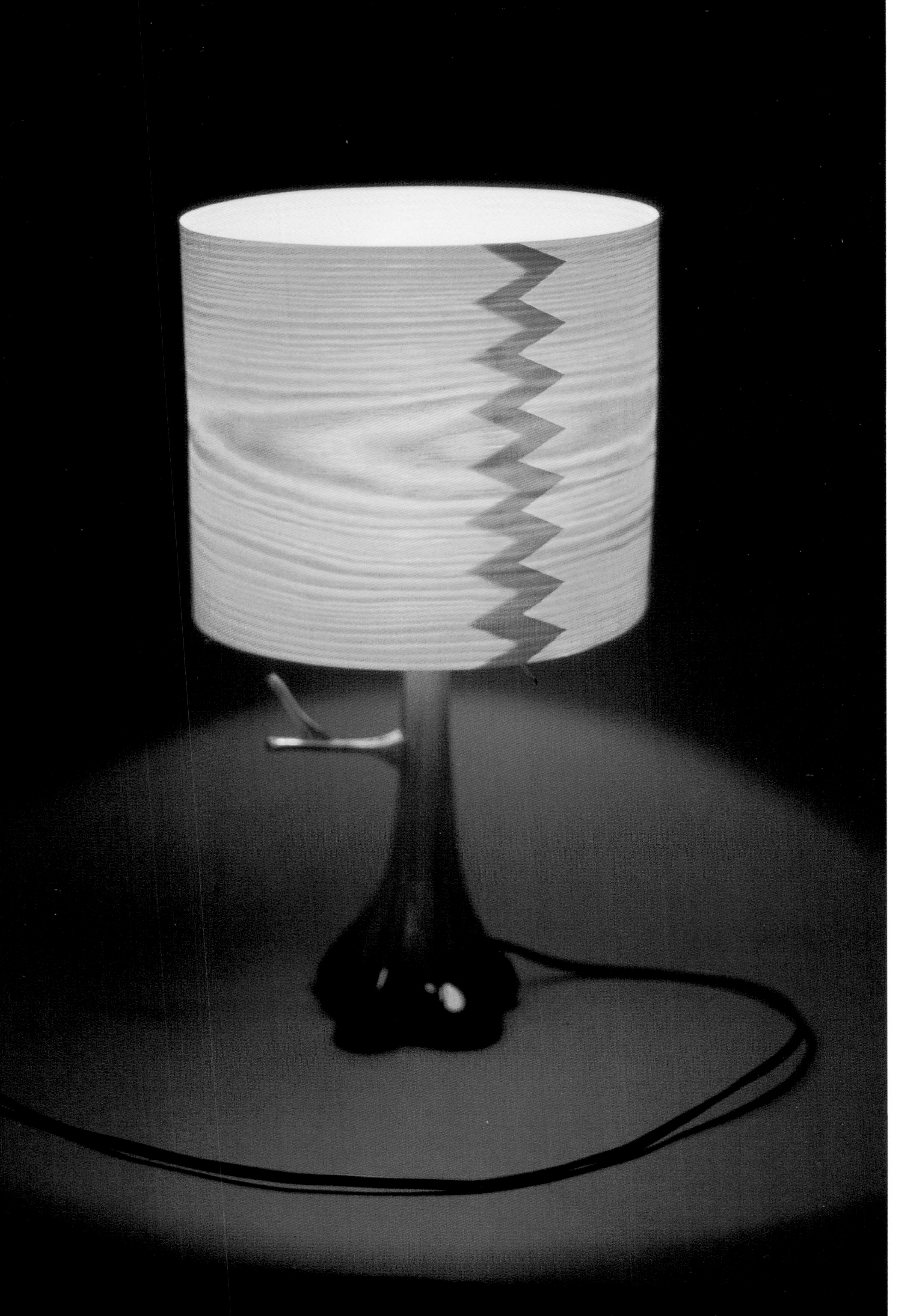

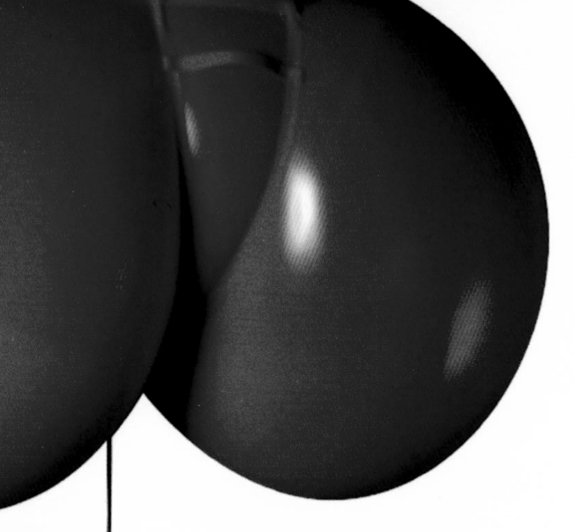

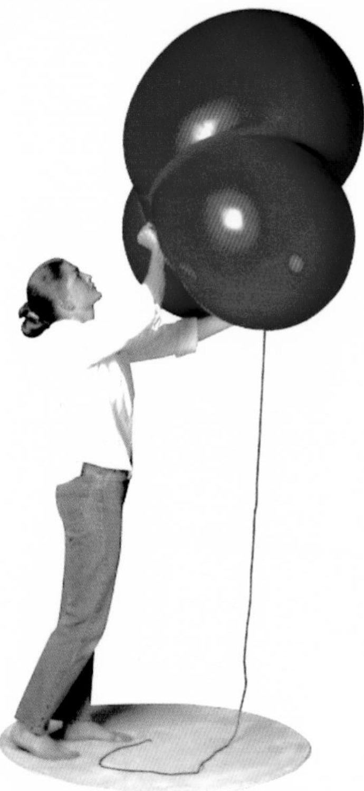

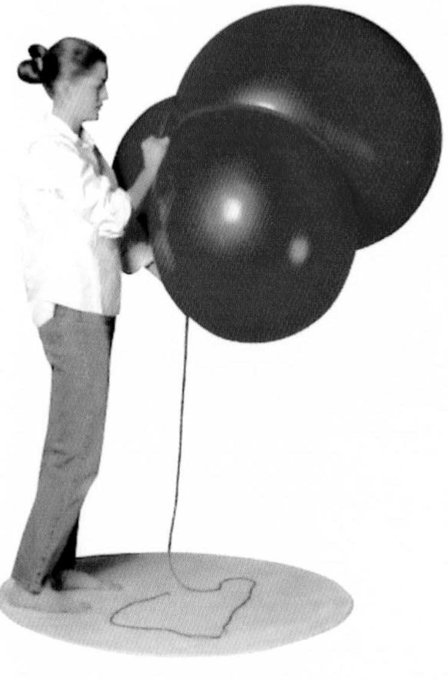

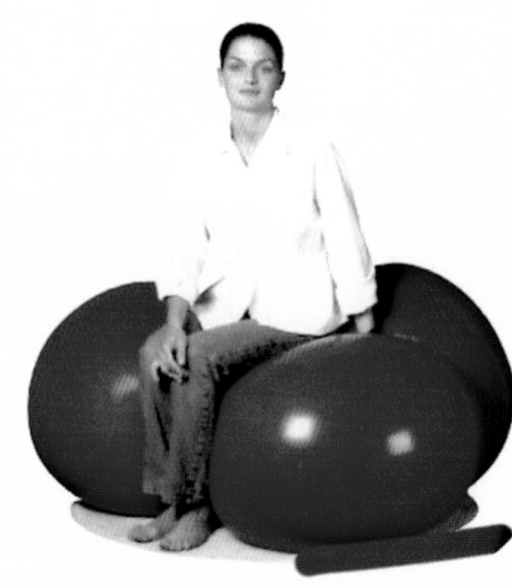

The Flying Chair (P)
Henriette Melchiorsen
Latex rubber, nylon, wool-carpet "launching pad"
DENMARK

DENMARK
Between Two Chairs for Bahnsen Collection (R)
Louise Campbell
Laser-cut metal, water-cut neoprene rubber, cotton, steel

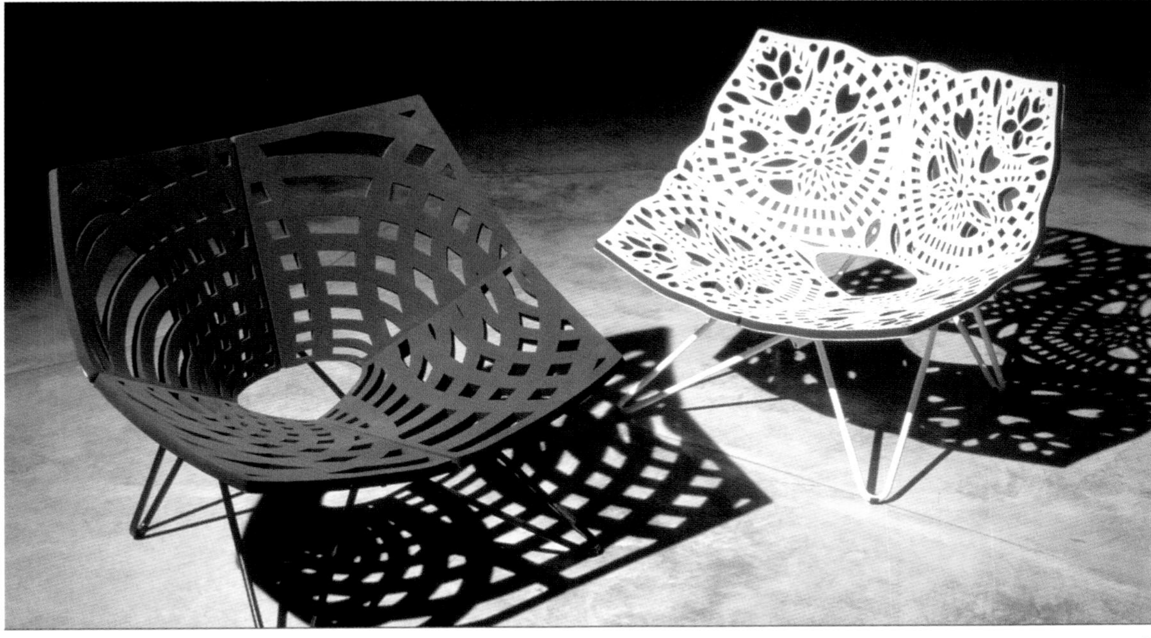

R

◄ P

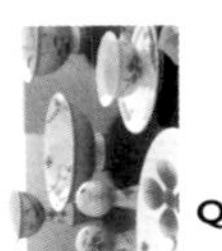

Q

predictable. And gradually, after the rigorous minimalism of the 1990s, Scandinavians are inching toward ornamentation, as evidenced by Louise Campbell, in her intricate Between Two Chairs **(R)**, and Katrín Pétursdóttir, with her fanciful Fudge finger-food dish set **(Q)** see **p 134** for Rosenthal.

The poetic is a formidable strain of new Scandinavian design and offers a strong reply to Scandinavia's history of Functionalism. Hardly a fringe movement, poeticism has now entered the mainstream. Recently, several major design schools, including Konstfack, University College of Arts, Crafts and Design in Stockholm, Sweden, the University of Art and Design in Helsinki, Finland, and the Denmark Design School in Copenhagen, Denmark, have all undertaken extensive revisions to their curricula to offer more solid training in conceptual thinking. (Yrjö Sotamaa, rector of the University of Art and Design, calls the reorganization at his institution a move away from becoming a "craft monastery.") What students will take away from their new coursework will bridge the practical with the fanciful. This doesn't mean young designers will stray too far from their roots—the work of Louise Campbell, for example, may be idea driven, yet her designs express the unique Danish concept of *hygge*, a word uniting the ideas of coziness and charm. Traditional values will remain a part of the creative repertoire, and a continuing cross-fertilization of these ideas with the poetic points to an exciting and unpredictable future for Scandinavian design.

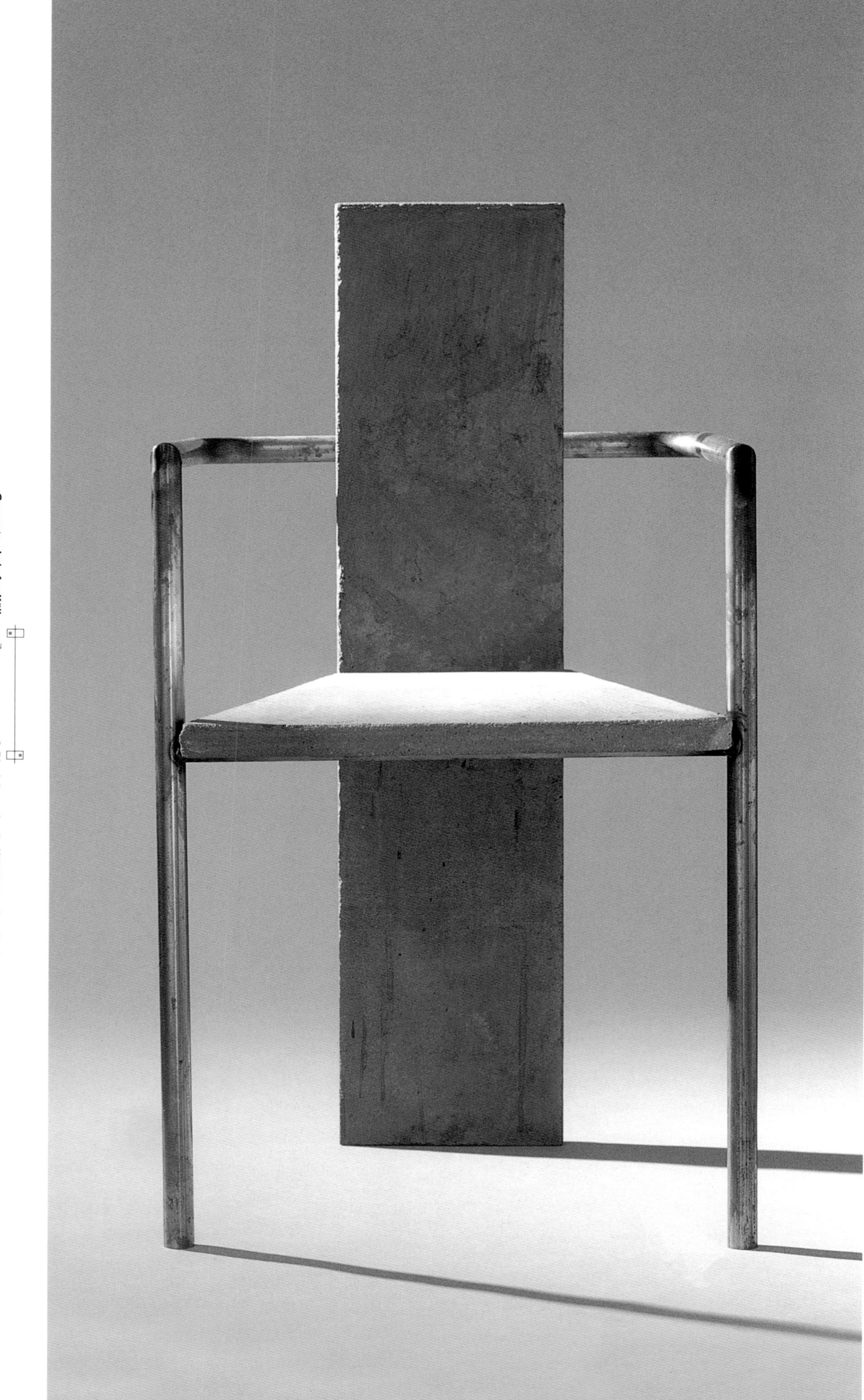

Concrete chair for Källemo
Jonas Bohlin
Conrete, steel
SWEDEN

FINLAND
Block lamp for Design House Stockholm
Harri Koskinen
Glass

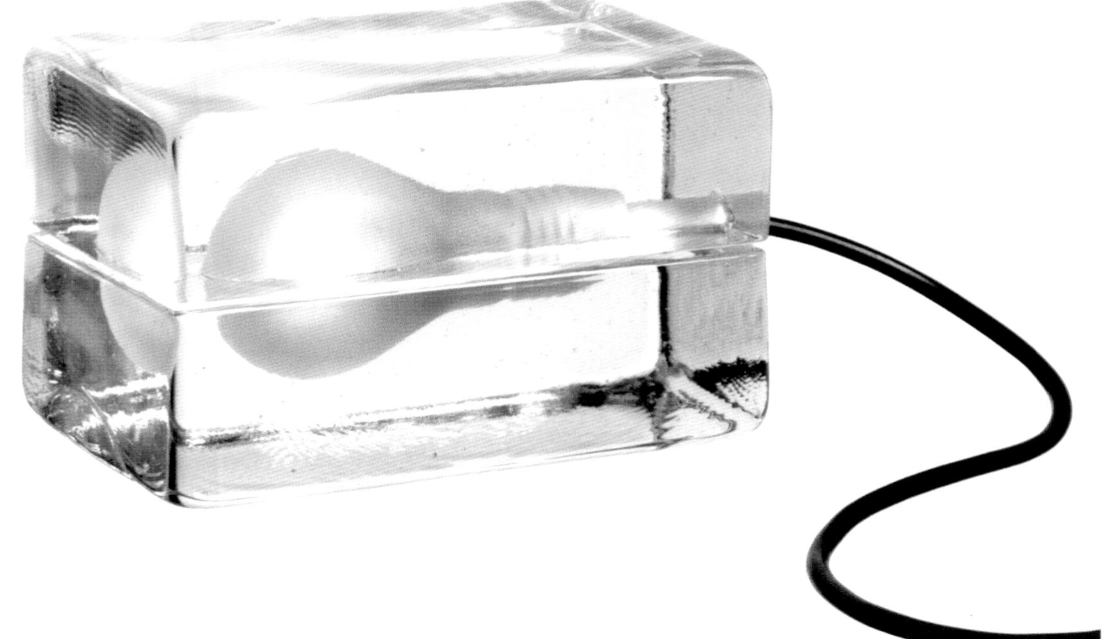

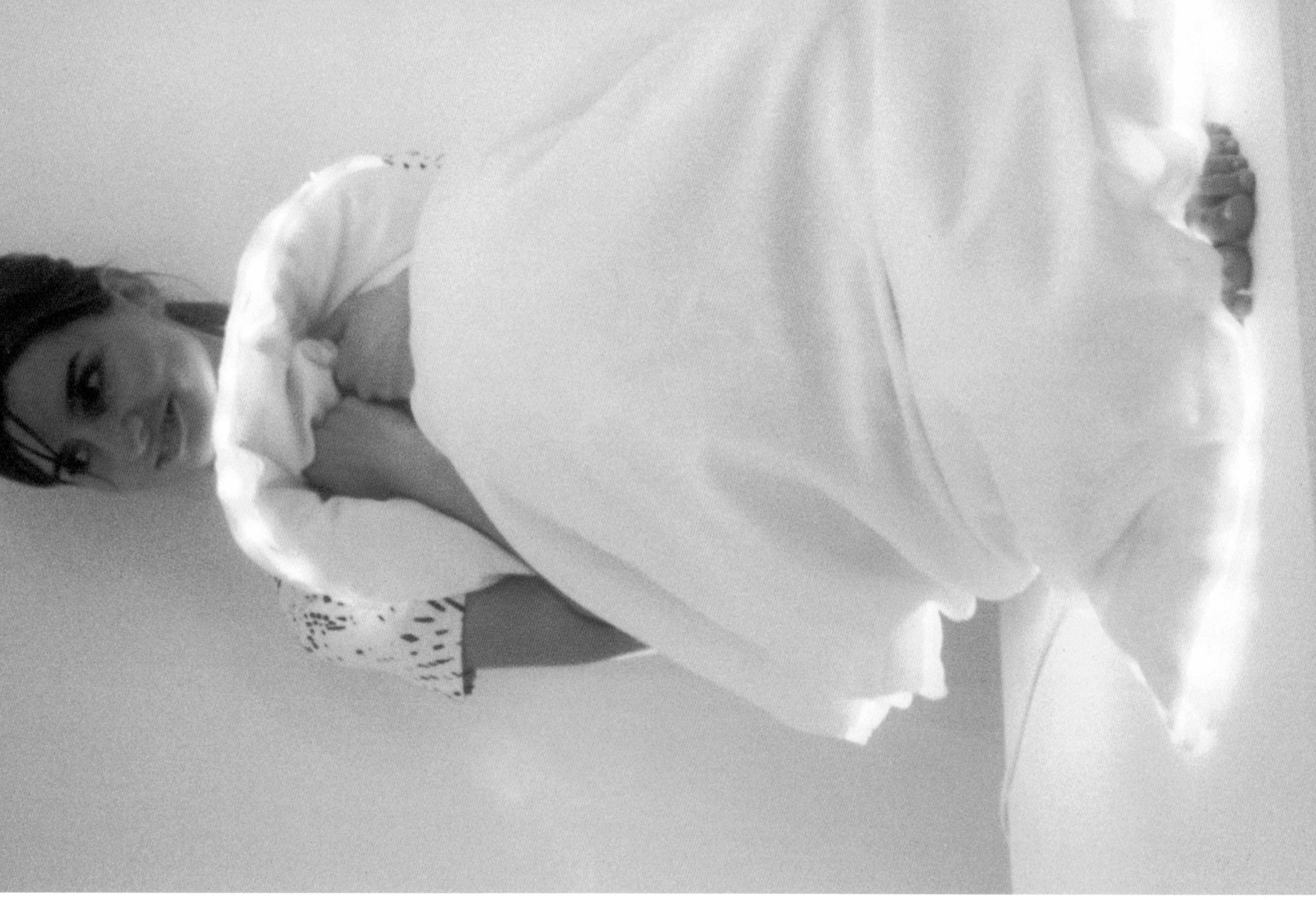

Blanket
Ditte Hammerstrøm
Wool, silk, cotton, lightbulbs
DENMARK

Trajektiv lamp
Hrafnkell Birgisson, Martin Seck
Glass bulbs
ICELAND

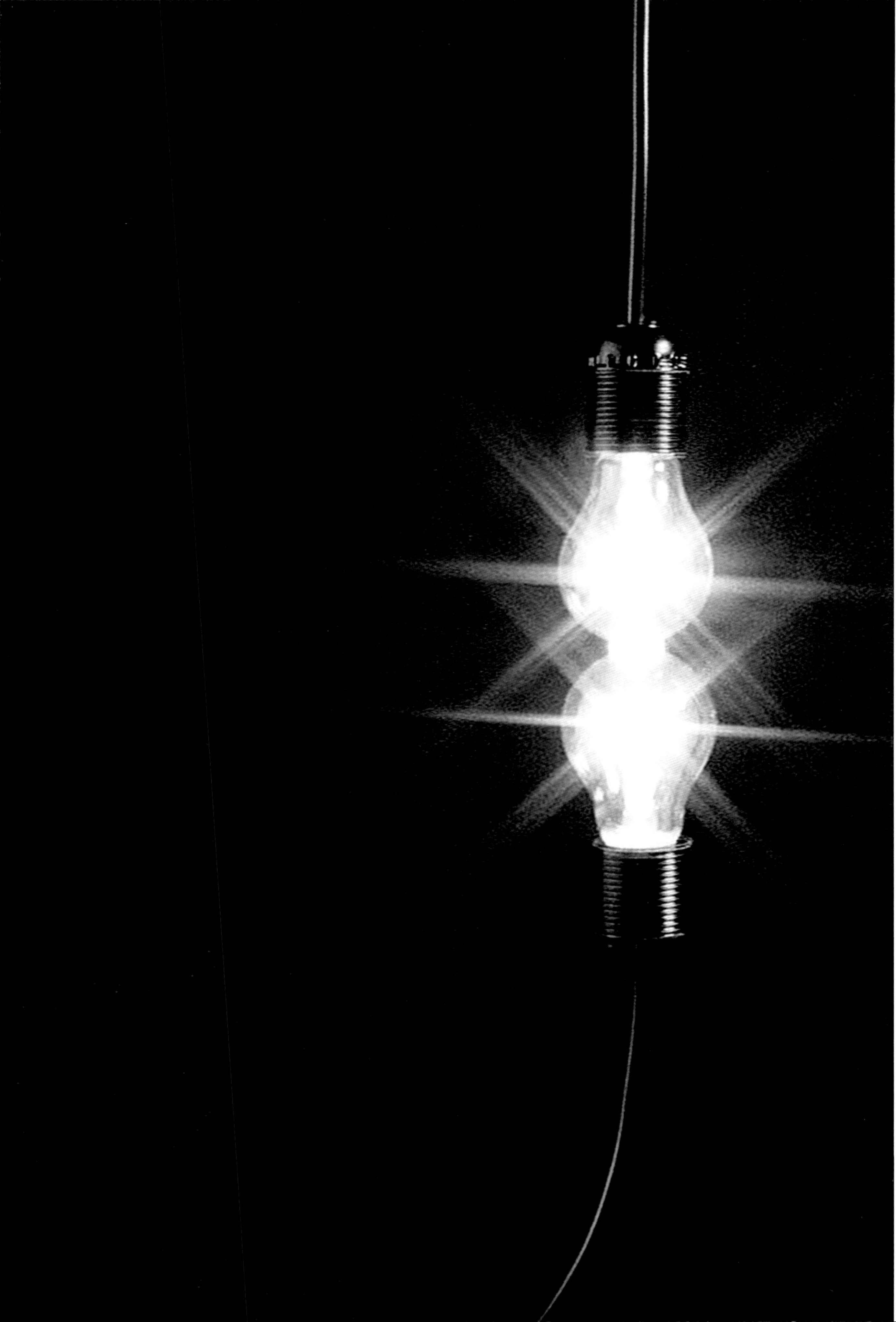

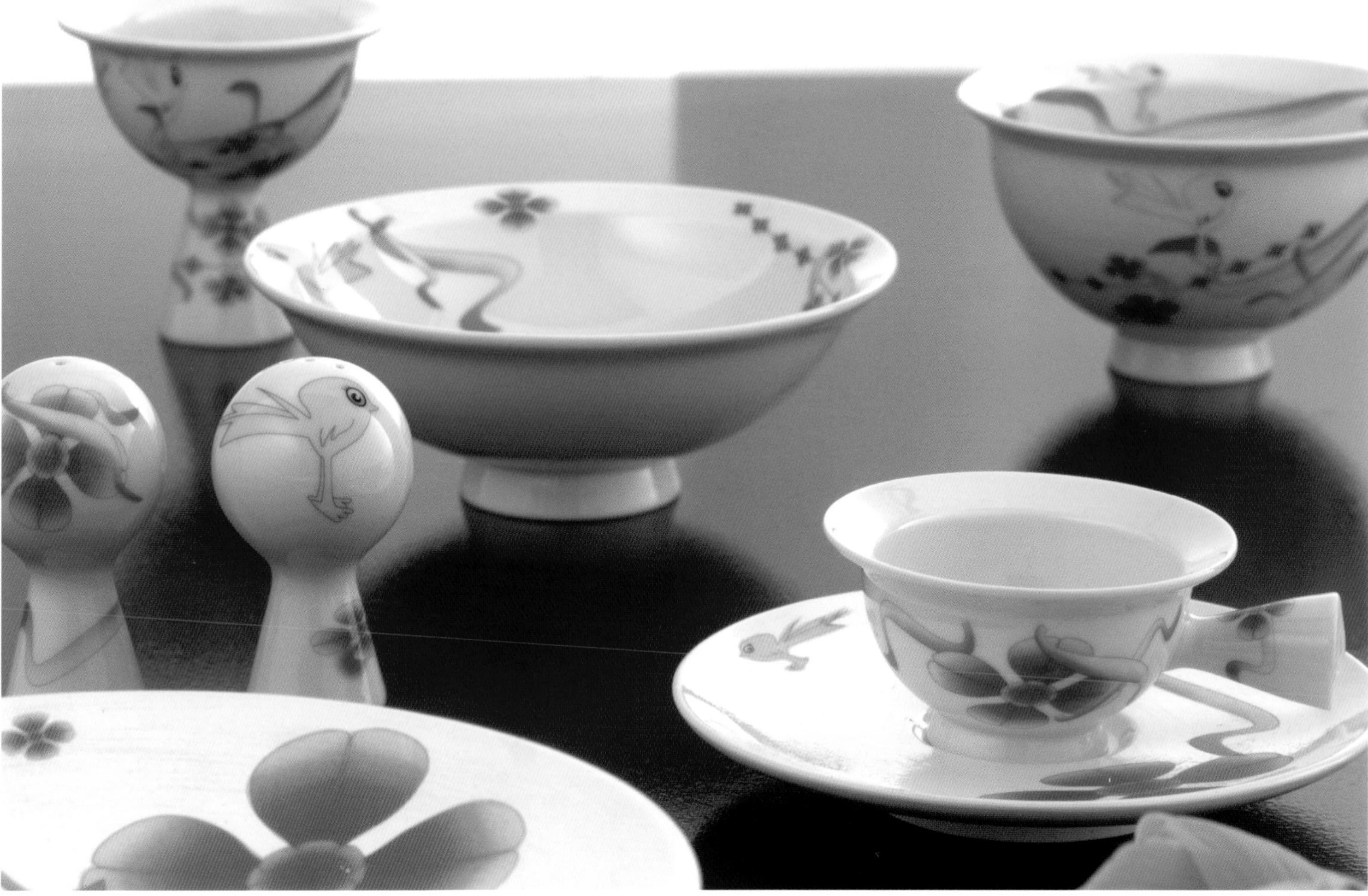

Fudge tableware for Rosenthal
Katrín Pétursdóttir
Porcelain
ICELAND

Sound Object
Anna von Schewen
Foam, foam-coated felt, loudspeakers
SWEDEN

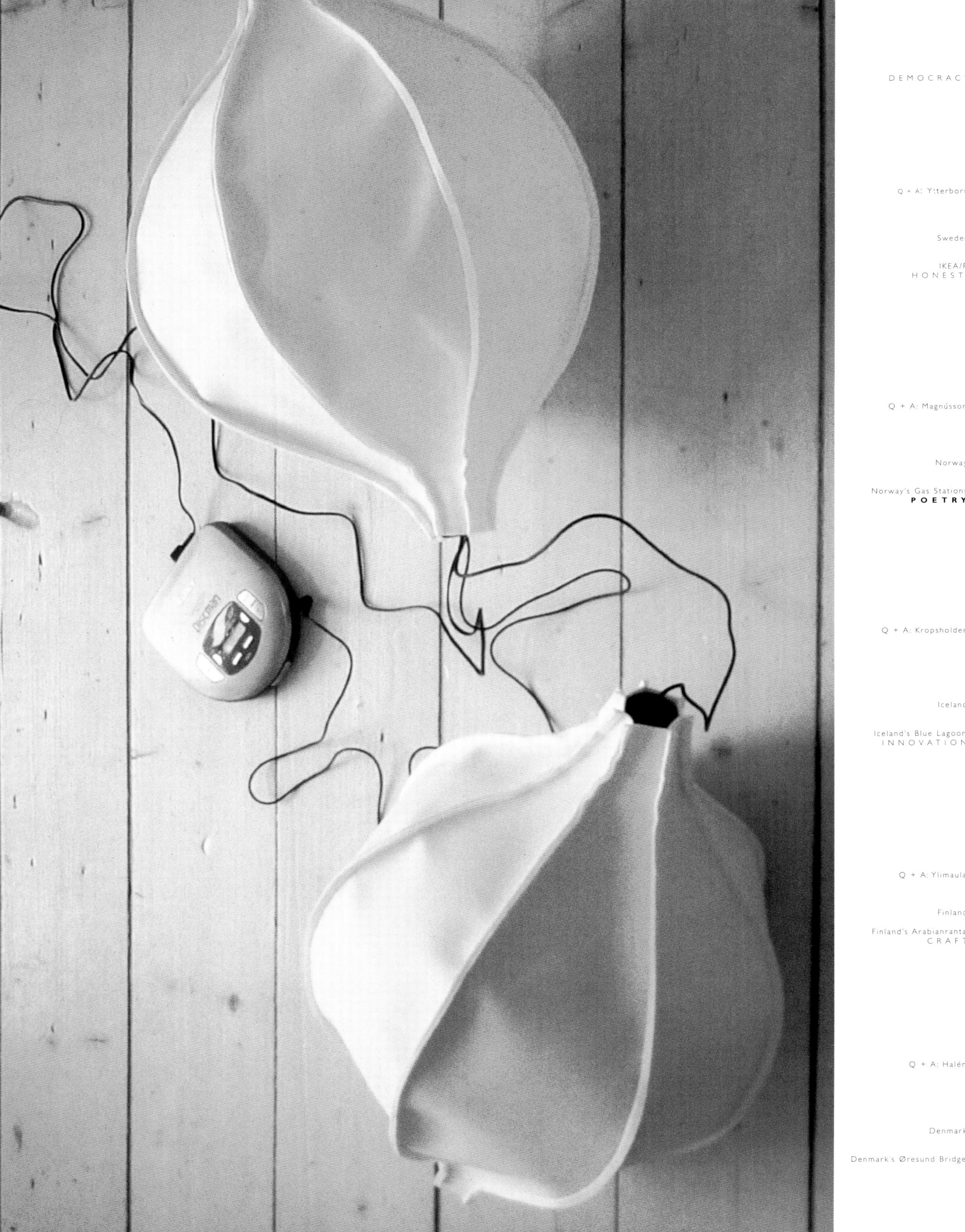
Discman

Friends eggcup for Ritzenhoff
Katrín Pétursdóttir
Ceramics
ICELAND

DENMARK
BODYWRAPPInc.NY three-piece suit
Annette Meyer
Disposable plastic wrappings

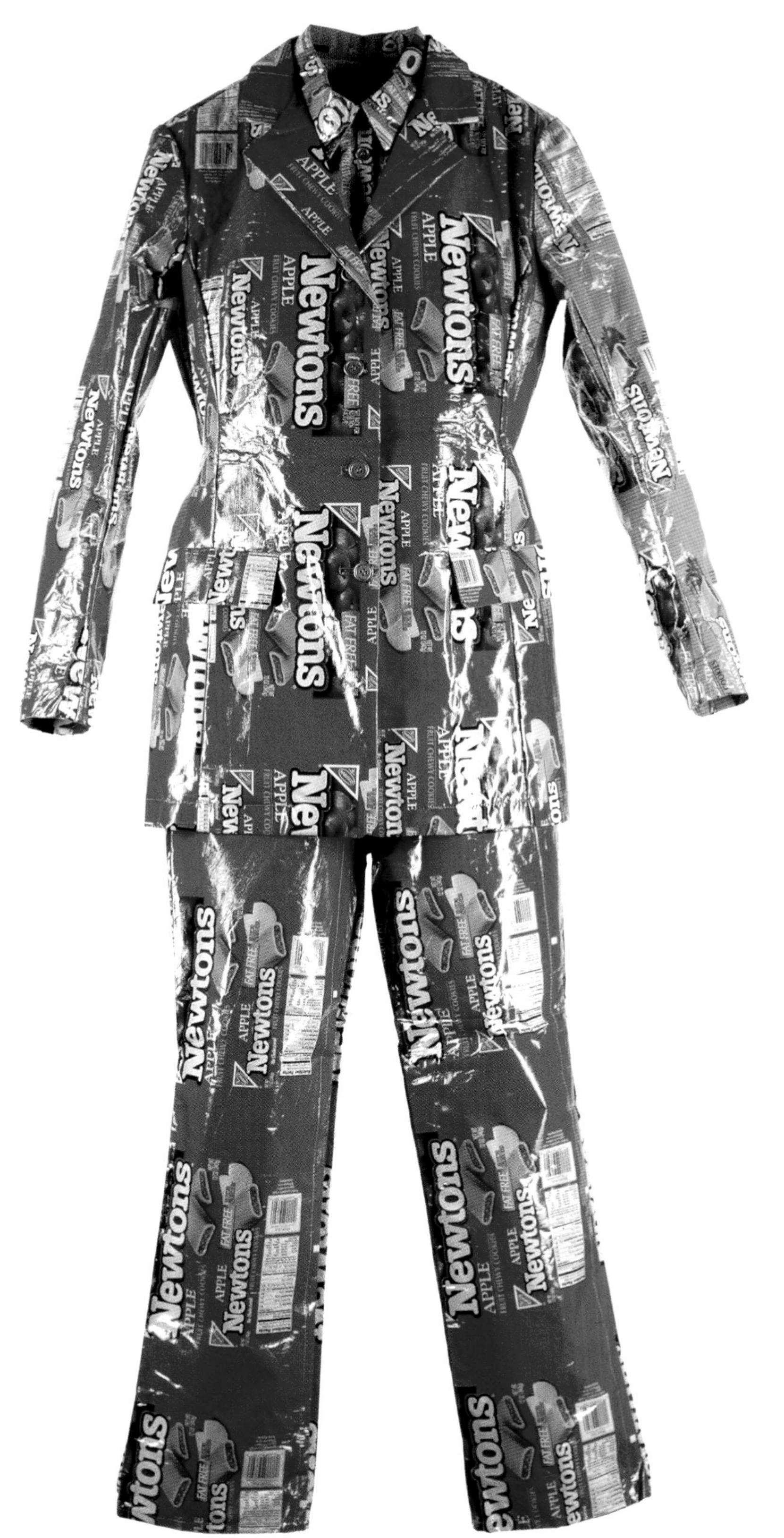
Newtons
APPLE
FRUIT CHEWY COOKIES
FAT FREE

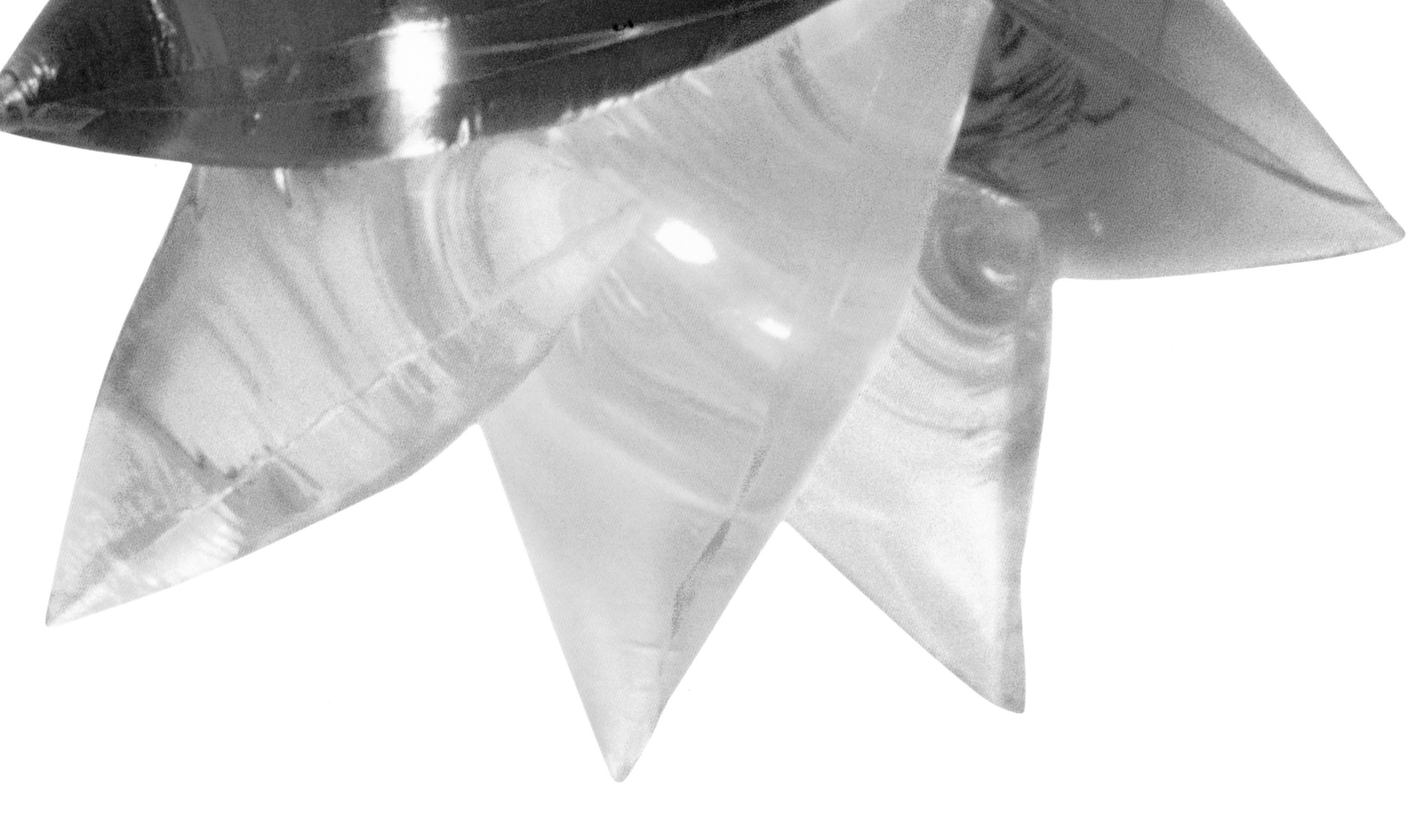

Waterfall chandelier
Aleksej Iskos
Plastic bags, halogen bulbs, colored water
DENMARK

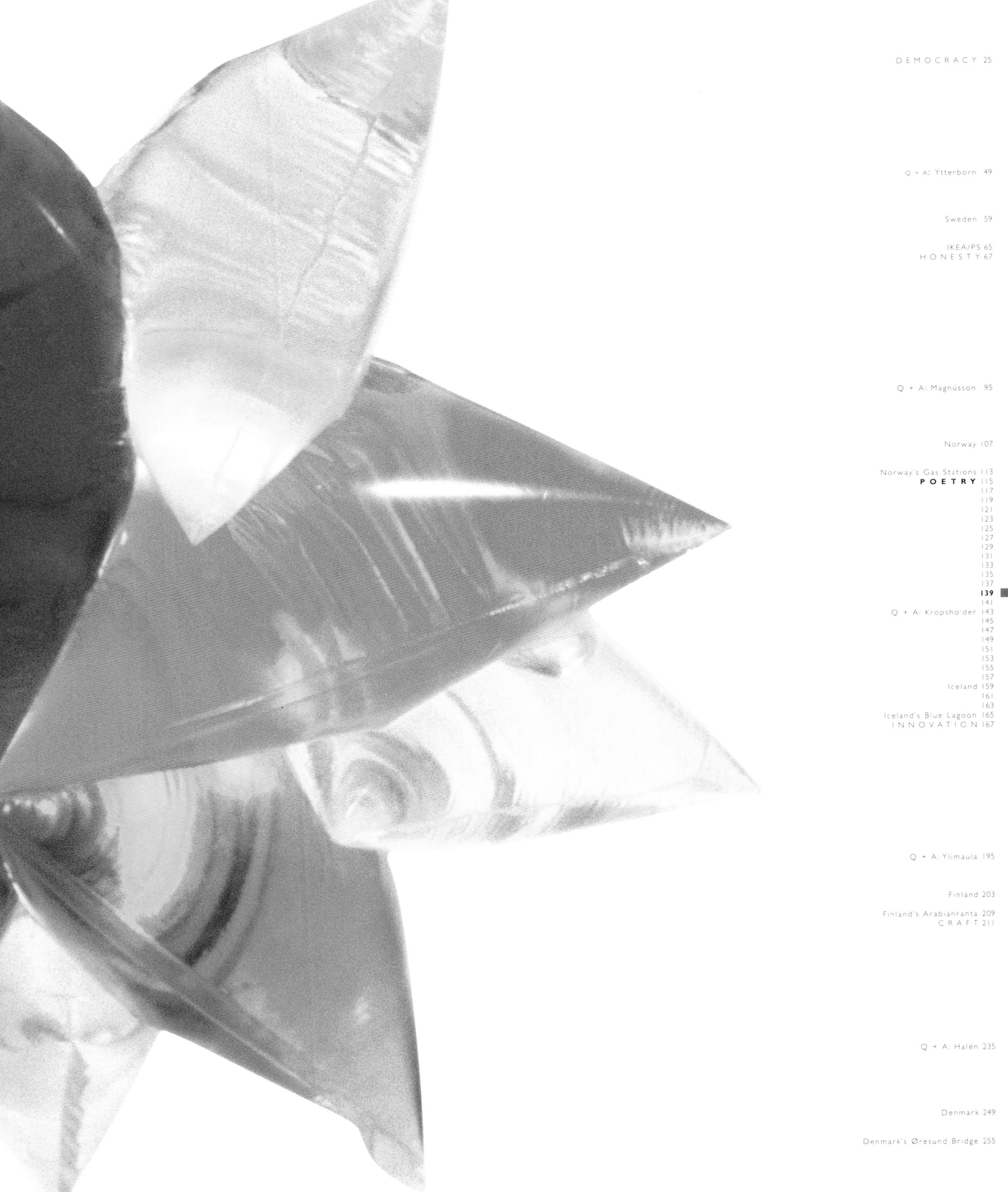

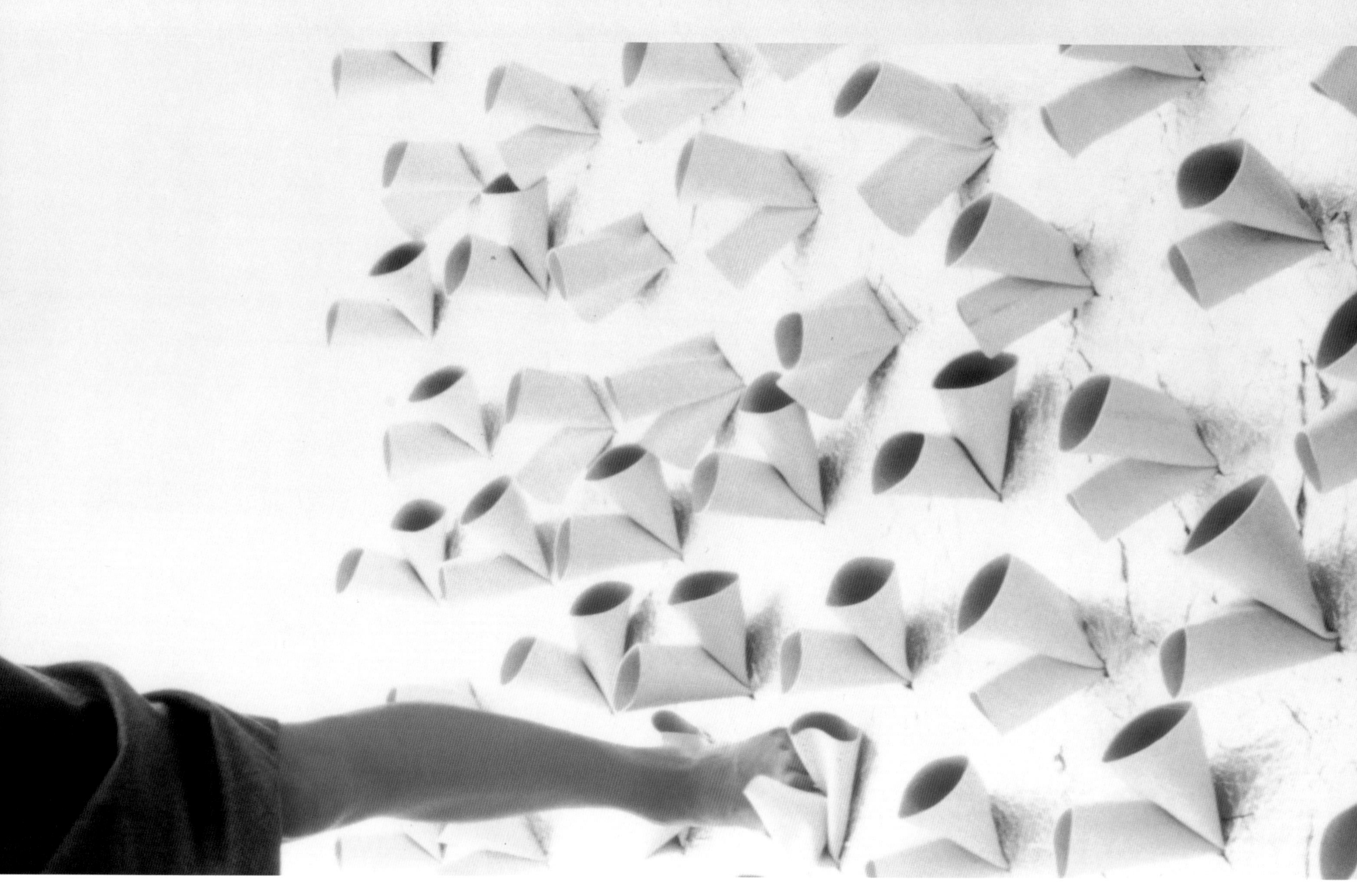

The Eye of the Hurricane, an exhibition of six "fondle mats" that visitors were invited to touch
Malene Reitzel, Louise Campbell, Pernille Vea
DENMARK

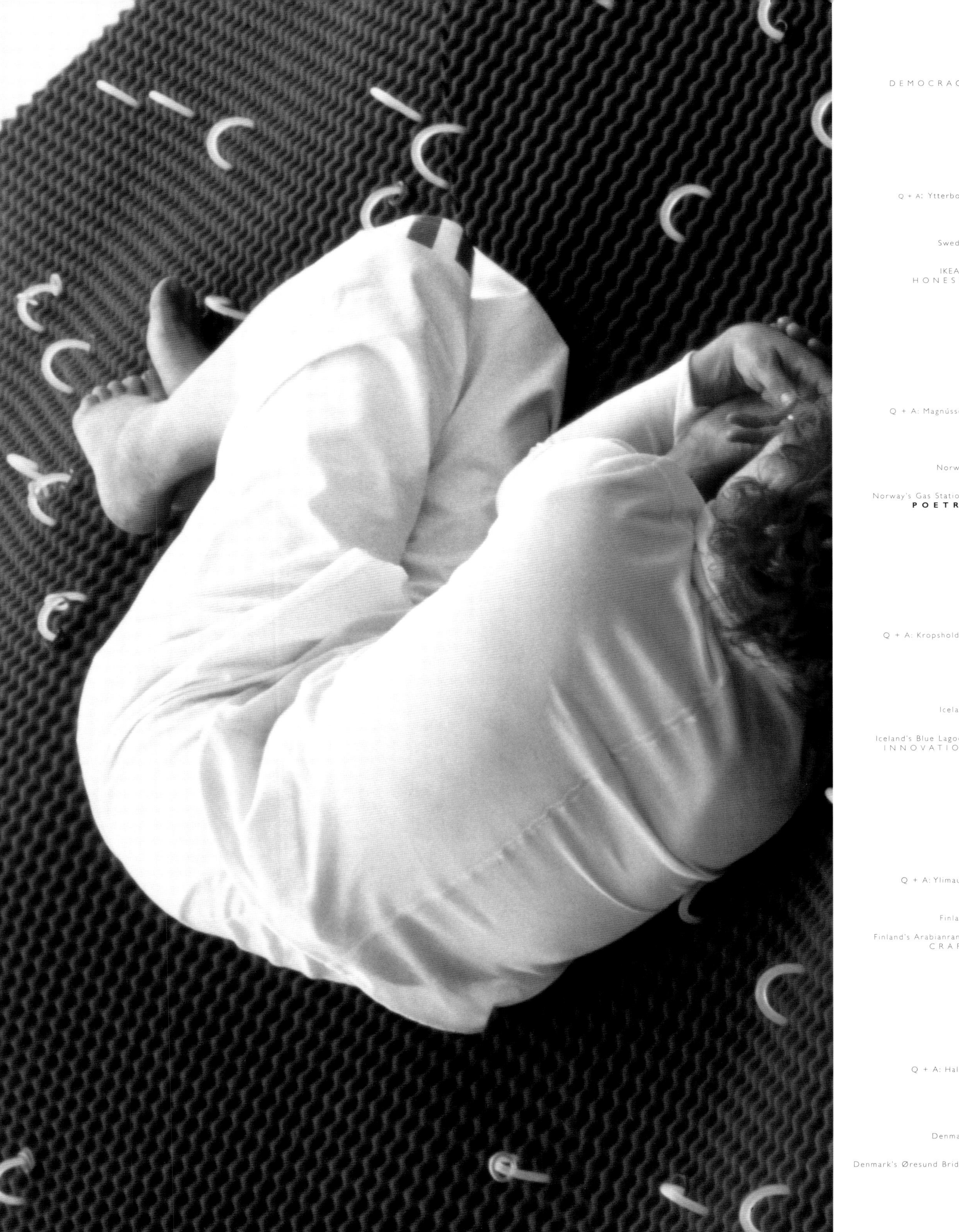

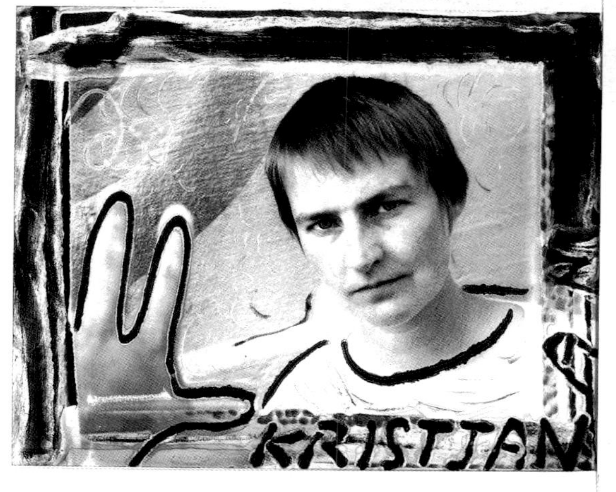

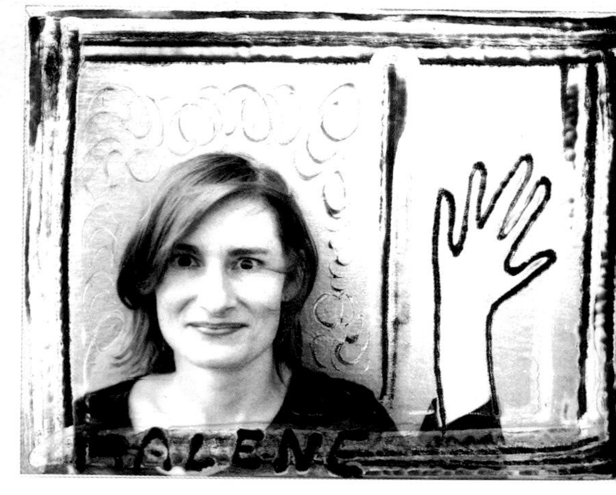

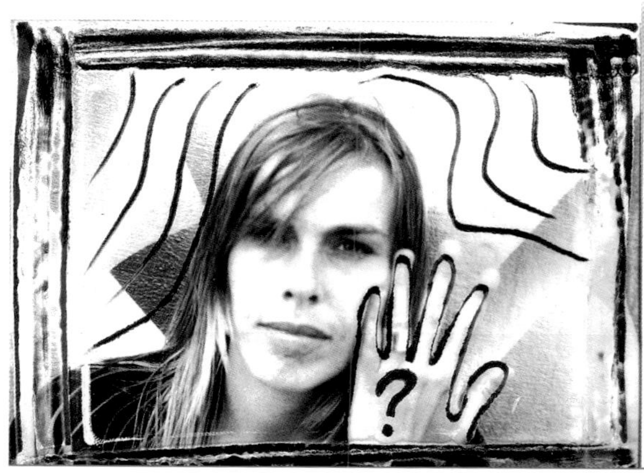

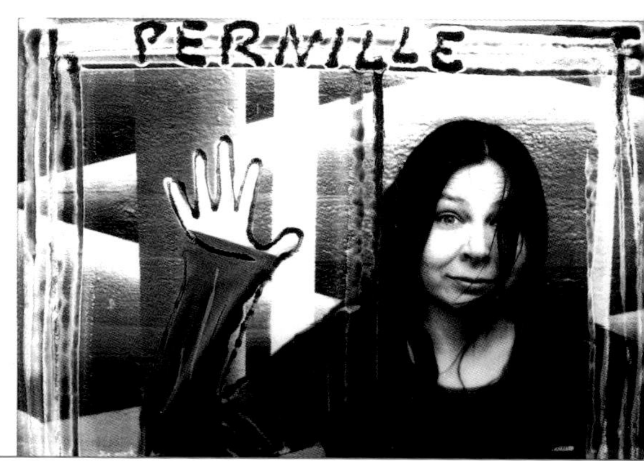

Kropsholder:
Gender and Tradition

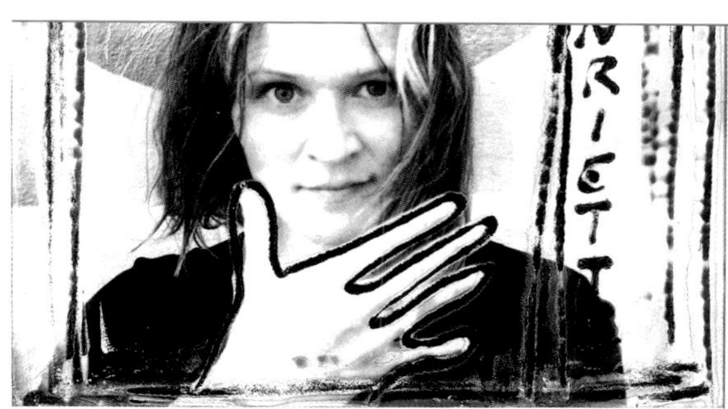

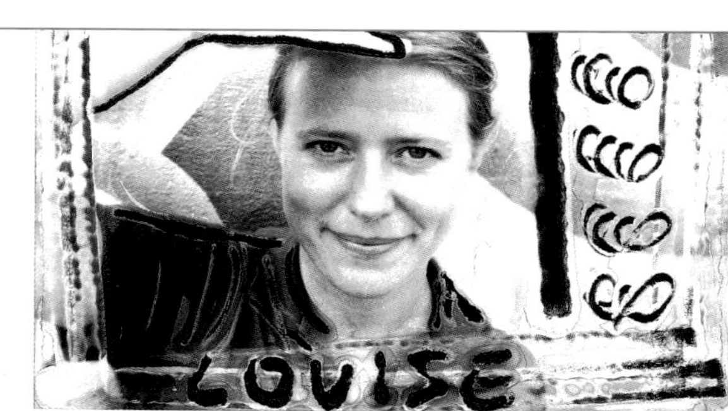

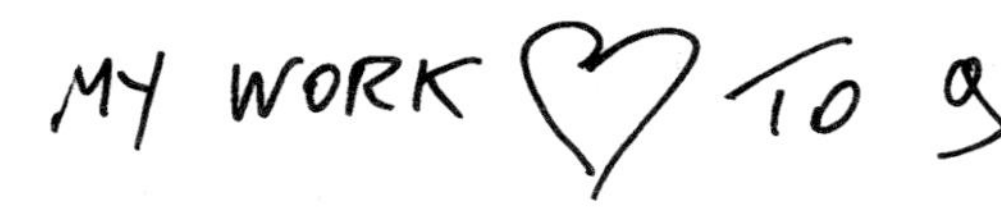

DESIGNERS"
KROPSHOLDER

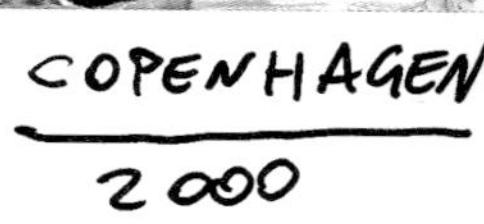

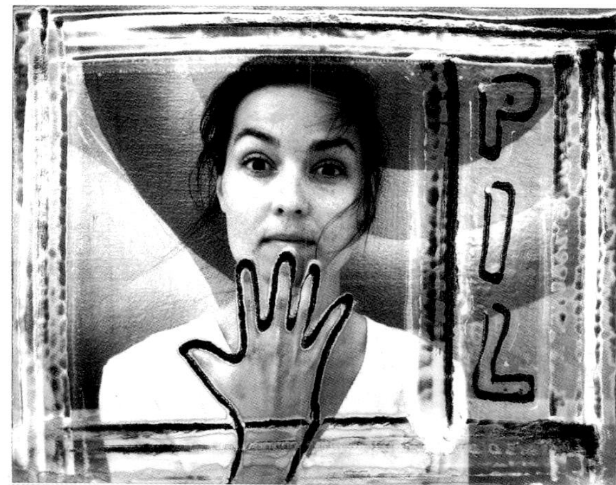

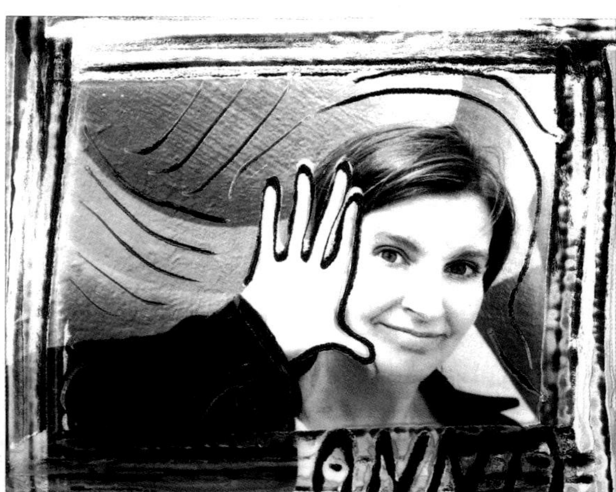

E KROPSHOLDER (WHICH MEANS "BODY CONTAINER" OR
FOUNDED IN 1997. TO DATE, THE GROUP HAS CREATED
BACKWARD), "RUMFANG"(A PLAY ON WORDS MEANING
NTERNATIONALLY TO FAIRS SUCH AS DESIGNER'S BLOCK IN
EMPLOYING UNEXPECTED MATERIALS, INNOVATIVE UPHOL-
MODEL FOR MANY YOUNG DANISH DESIGNERS—MEN AND
TS. AS FOR KROPSHOLDER'S LONG-TERM IMPACT, THIS IS THE
ED AN EQUAL RATIO OF MALE TO FEMALE PRACTITIONERS—
HAS TEN MEMBERS, INCLUDING HENRIETTE MELCHIORSEN,
RODUCT MANAGER FOR THE GERMAN COMPANY MENU.

KROPSHOLDER FORMED?
ıp's co-founders,] Louise Campbell and Malene
anything in common. We were all very excited.
any things we wanted to do. Q: WHAT
UP FOUND PARTICULARLY
on as we sat down. There were so many issues
ed a newspaper and saw an article about new
nds, or colleagues. A (Pil Bredahl): In Europe,
ducated are women, and we wondered where
hear about or see in the press at that time.
IT HAD A UNIQUE DESIGN
ginning we didn't know. We were taught only by
r own language. We were picked on a little bit
ce if we didn't know the measurements of dif-
rested to see if we would have another way of
trict in the design process as the men were—
up of women worked together, we were free-
t through to the end. You didn't always have to
idea that somebody else could make work. It
ESCRIBE YOUR WORKING

METHODS? A (PB): To be a member of Kropsholder, you have to be able to work in a group and like it. When you work in such a big group without a leader, you are forced to be very democratic. In the beginning, the meetings sometimes lasted late into the night. The women in our group have a lot to say, and everybody has to be heard. I also understand that there are women who don't like to work this way. It can be inspiring, but it can also be tiring. A (HM): Many decisions simply develop on their own. In a meeting, we sit there and discuss what to do. But if the answer isn't clear then we know we aren't ready to make a decision. A good example of our working method is how we found a name. In the beginning, we didn't want to have a name. We wanted to be a group without a name. But we were planning to have a name for each exhibition. The first exhibition was called "Kropsholder." Then everyone started talking about the group and calling us "Kropsholder." People kept phoning [our offices] and saying, "I need to talk to somebody from Kropsholder." And we just laughed; we thought it was really funny. But we realized that if we wanted to continue the group, and continue working together, we had to choose. It didn't seem to work to try to change the name. So in the end we gave up and accepted that we were called Kropsholder. Q: THE PRESS RESPONDED IMMEDIATELY TO YOUR WORK. CAN YOU DISCUSS THEIR REACTION? A (PB): I don't think the press reaction would have been the same if we had been a group of ten male designers. It would just be a new design group. But because we were women, that became an issue in itself. Some male journalists were actually provoked by the fact that we were all women. They said, "How can you do this? Wouldn't I be able to join the group?" And we said, "Well, no, actually." This was unexpected somehow. They also expected us to be much more feminist. But we are not the feminist generation that our mothers were. We were just working with the fantasy, the poetry, and the creativity, and not so much the political angle. The press reaction was difficult because we were all raised to think that being a woman itself shouldn't be [the only factor taken into consideration when evaluating someone's work]. I'm sure that all of us, in different degrees and at different times, felt a little bit embarrassed by the issue being so much in focus. At the same time, it was necessary to just say, "Well, we're here and we are a group of female designers, and you guys are making all the fuss about us—not us." Q: CAN YOU SPEAK ABOUT THE VISUAL LANGUAGE THAT KROPSHOLDER DEVELOPED? IS THE WORK PARTICULARLY "FEMININE"? A (HM): I am not done analyzing this, but I do think there is a traditional tendency for the male designer to go for technical things, to make industrial equipment, for example, and women are often into clothes, textiles, and furniture. It's fun to see that there is a tendency for female furniture designers to do more poetic things than men. Why? I think that generally it is in a woman's nature. But it's funny that I should say this because, as a designer and as a woman, I'm actually very interested in the technical aspects of design. A (PB): I think, first of all, there is a poetic aspect to the Kropsholder language since we work with storytelling from day one in the project. We make up a whole little world [with its own rules] where the project lives. There's a lot of poetry and a lot of humor and not taking ourselves and the whole thing so seriously. In Scandinavia, it can be tough working as a designer because what is good taste and good quality and good design is very defined. It's all about clear lines, less is more, and all those things. It's a relief to do something that is perhaps more emotional, comes straight from the heart, and not so much from the head. That's also characteristic of the work. Q: HOW HAS KROPSHOLDER HAD AN IMPACT ON THE DANISH DESIGN COMMUNITY? A (HM): Kropsholder is an inspiration to many young students and this makes me very proud. In general, in Danish design today, there is more poetry and more of a conceptual influence on the work. It's so much about storytelling today. Q: WHERE DO YOU THINK THE INDUSTRY IS HEADED? A (HM): I think that the Danish furniture industry has been very lucky that the Danish tradition has been so popular. And that is its golden egg. But we need new things, too. The old stuff is not going to go away, but I still see a space between the past and what will happen in the future. And it will be a problem if the Danish manufacturers don't experiment more.

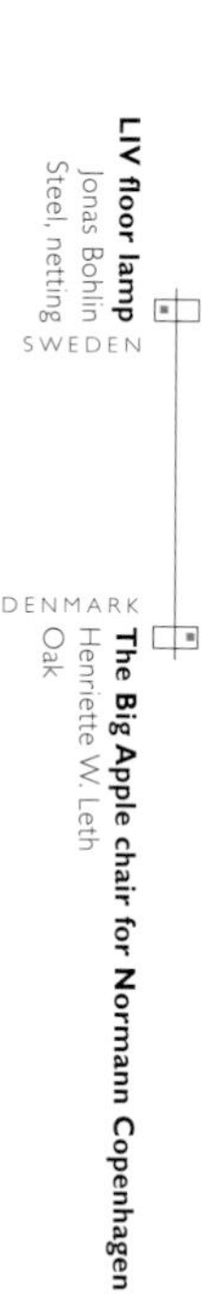
LIV floor lamp
Jonas Bohlin
Steel, netting
SWEDEN
DENMARK
The Big Apple chair for Normann Copenhagen
Henriette W. Leth
Oak

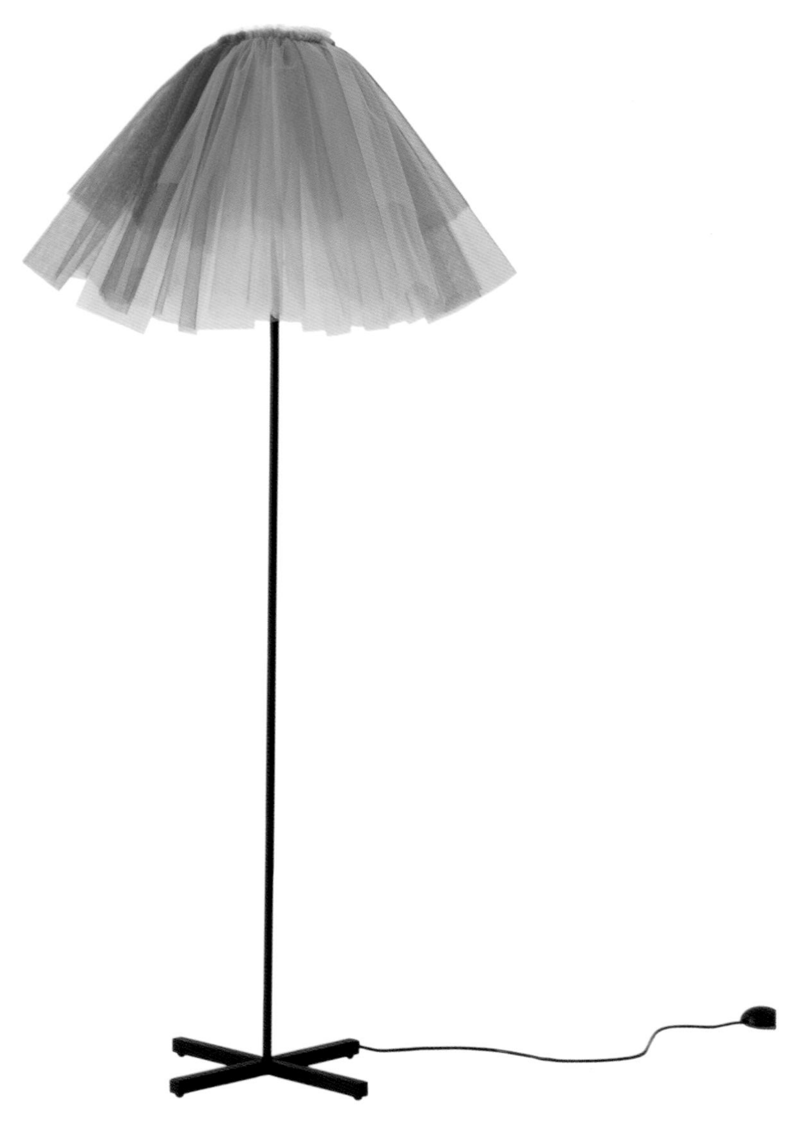

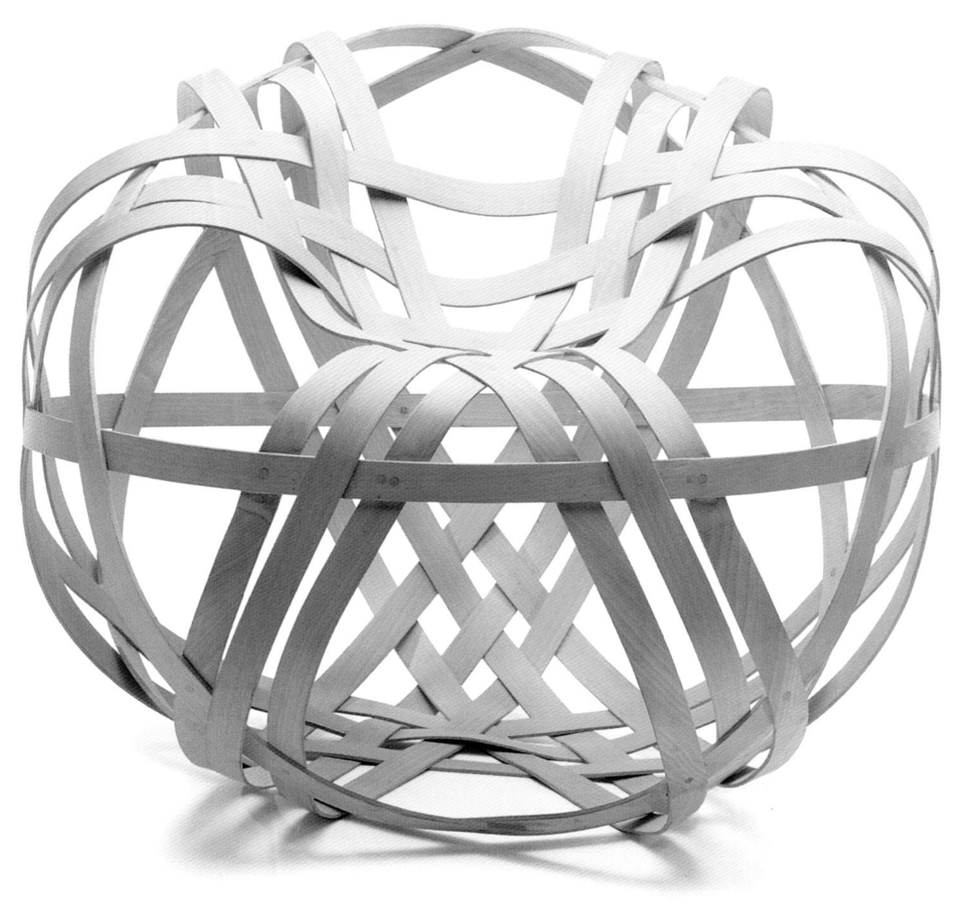

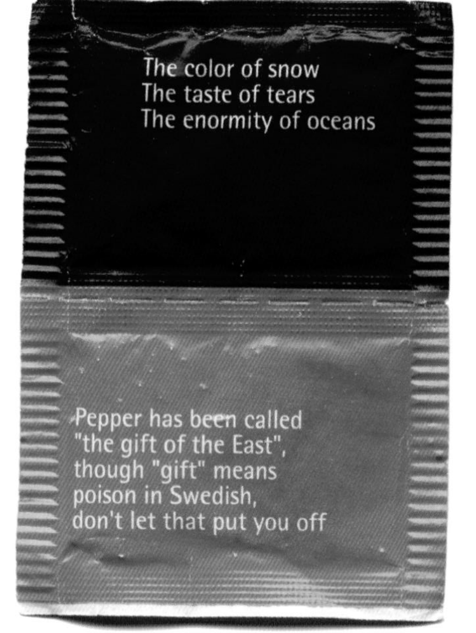

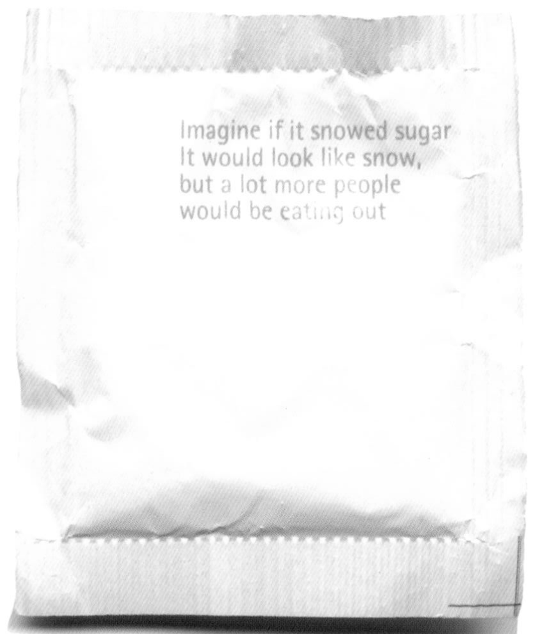

Salt, pepper and sugar packets for SAS
Stockholm Design Lab
Plastic silver foil
SWEDEN

Room with a View pillow
Permafrost
Recycled wool felt, PVC plastic foil
NORWAY

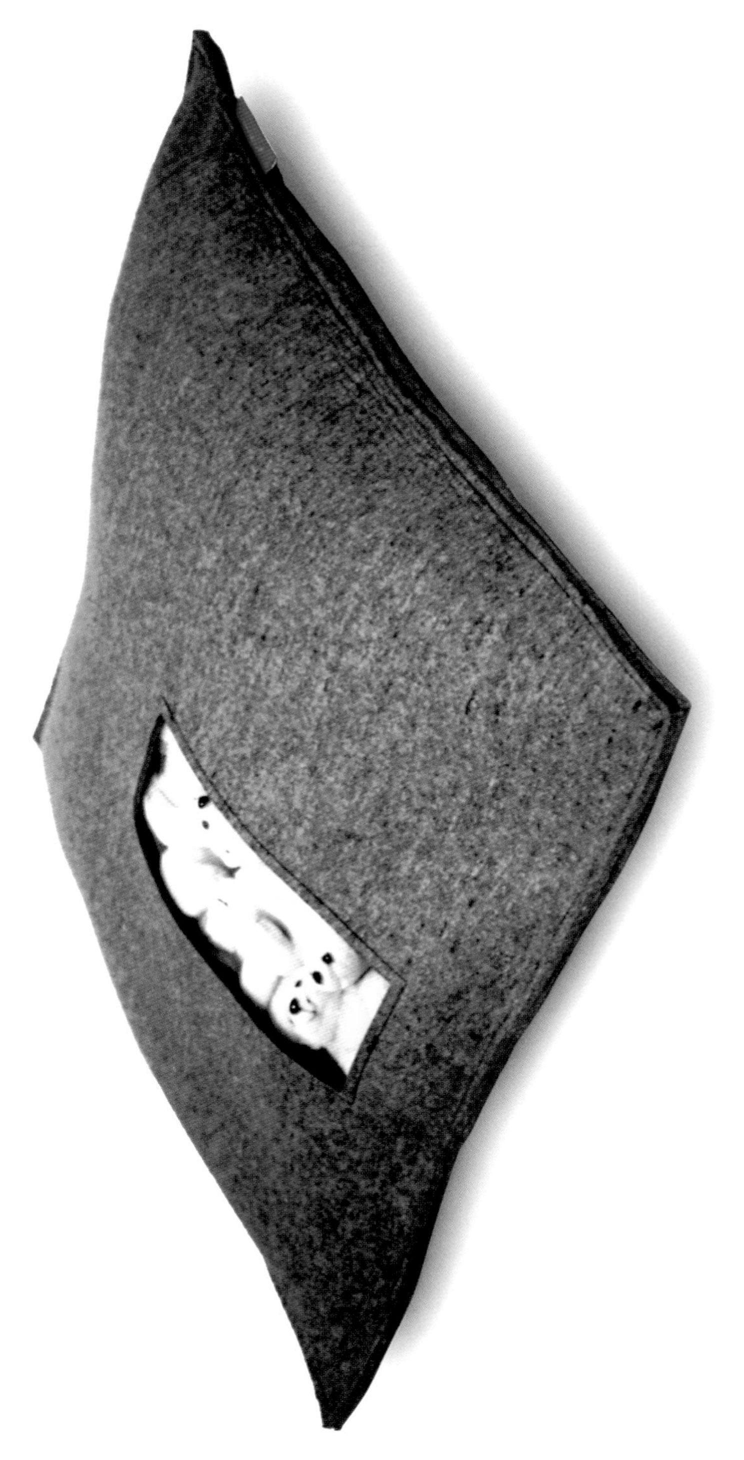

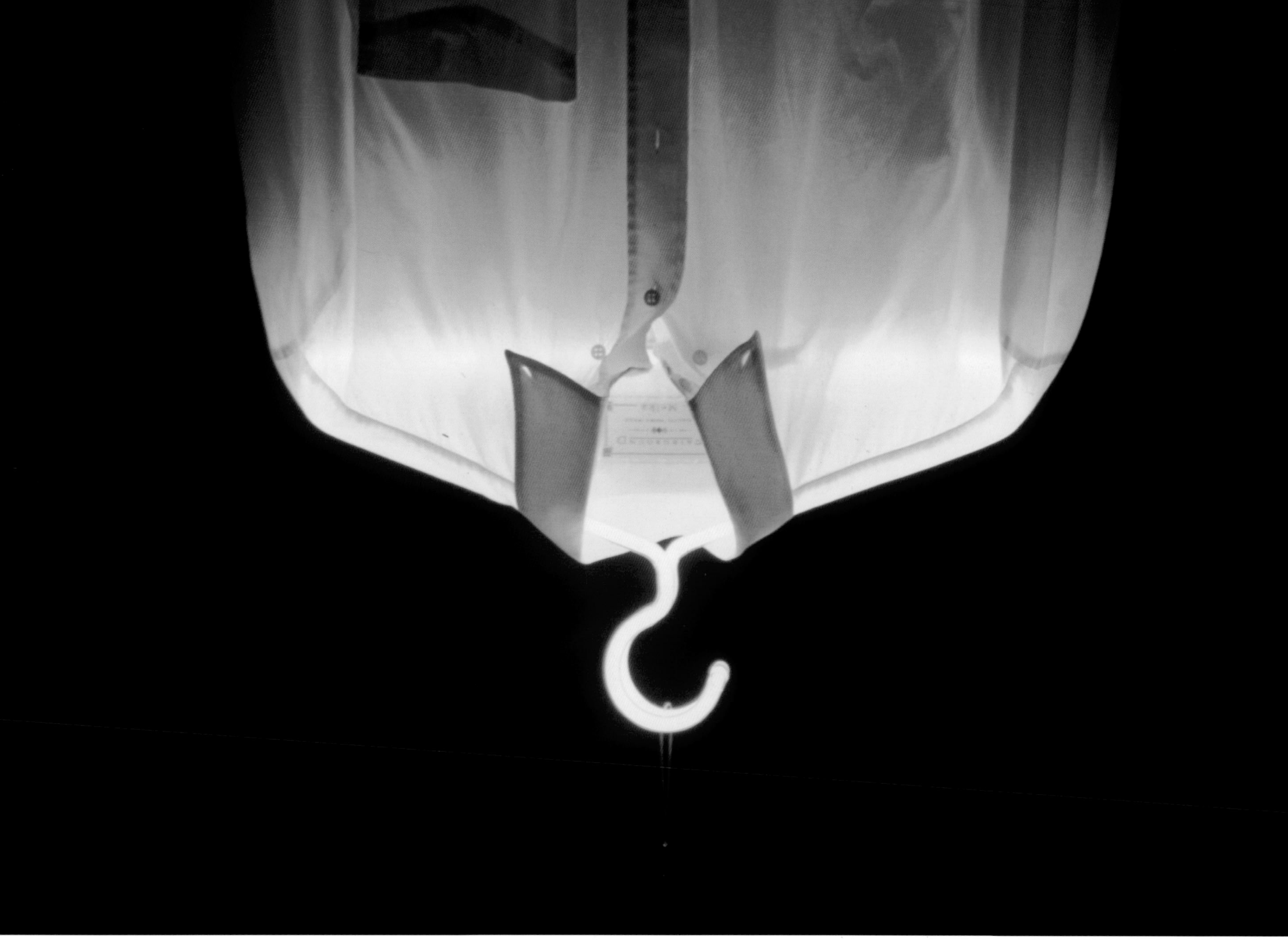

Night Ghost lamp for Miscellaneous Design
Aleksej Iskos
Neon tube
DENMARK

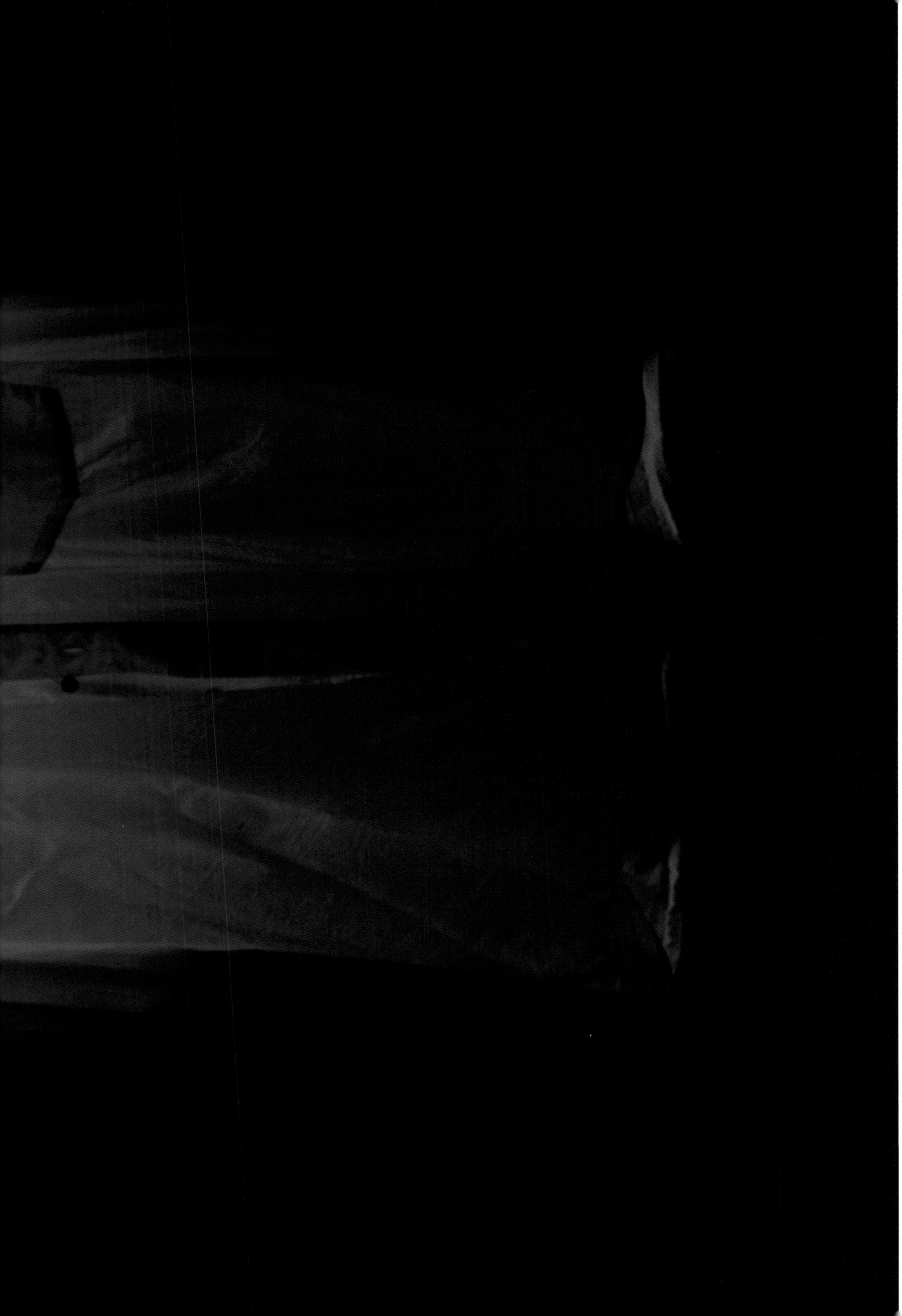

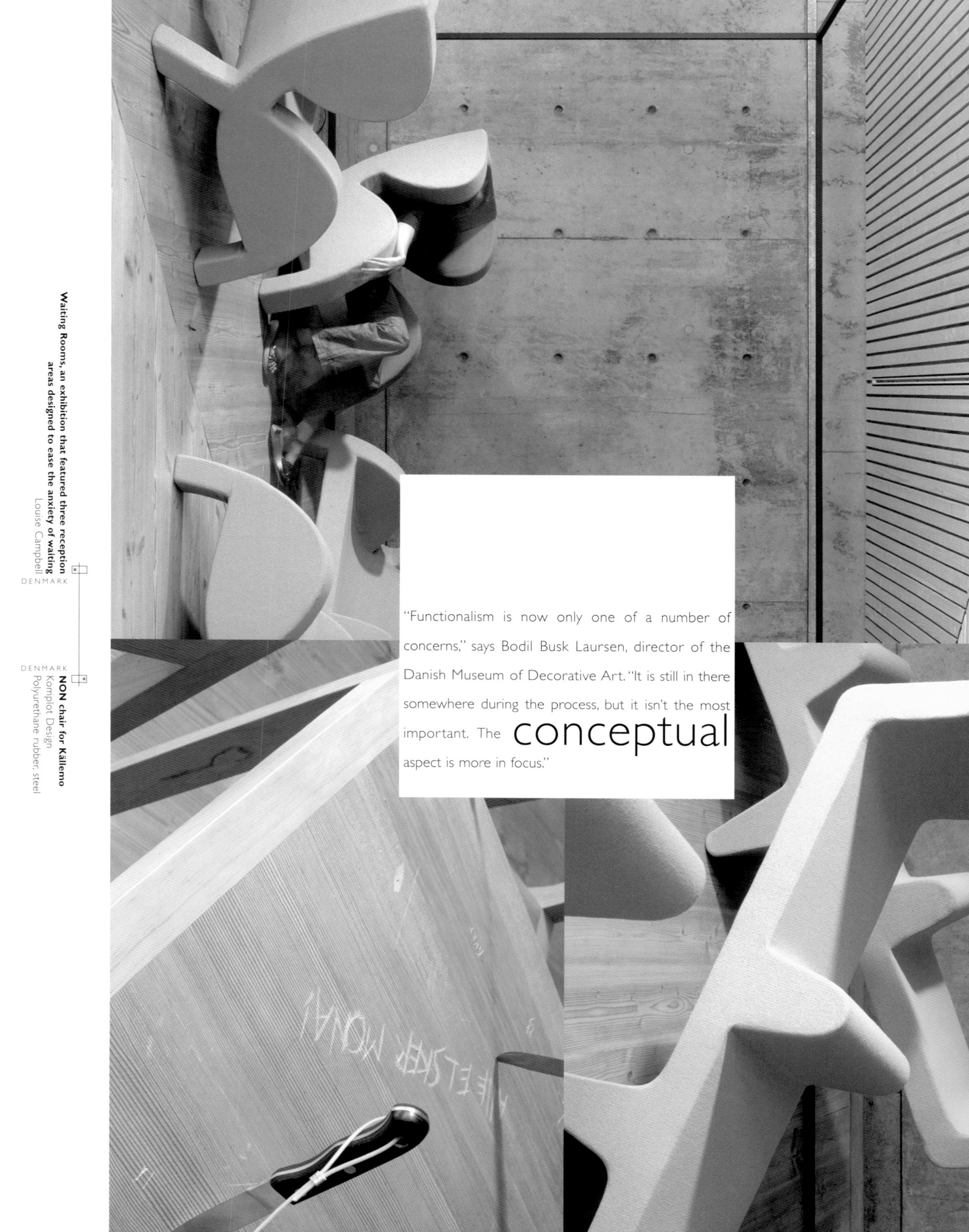

"Functionalism is now only one of a number of concerns," says Bodil Busk Laursen, director of the Danish Museum of Decorative Art. "It is still in there somewhere during the process, but it isn't the most important. The conceptual aspect is more in focus."

Waiting Rooms, an exhibition that featured three reception areas designed to ease the anxiety of waiting
Louise Campbell
DENMARK

DENMARK
NON chair for Källemo
Komplot Design
Polyurethane rubber, steel

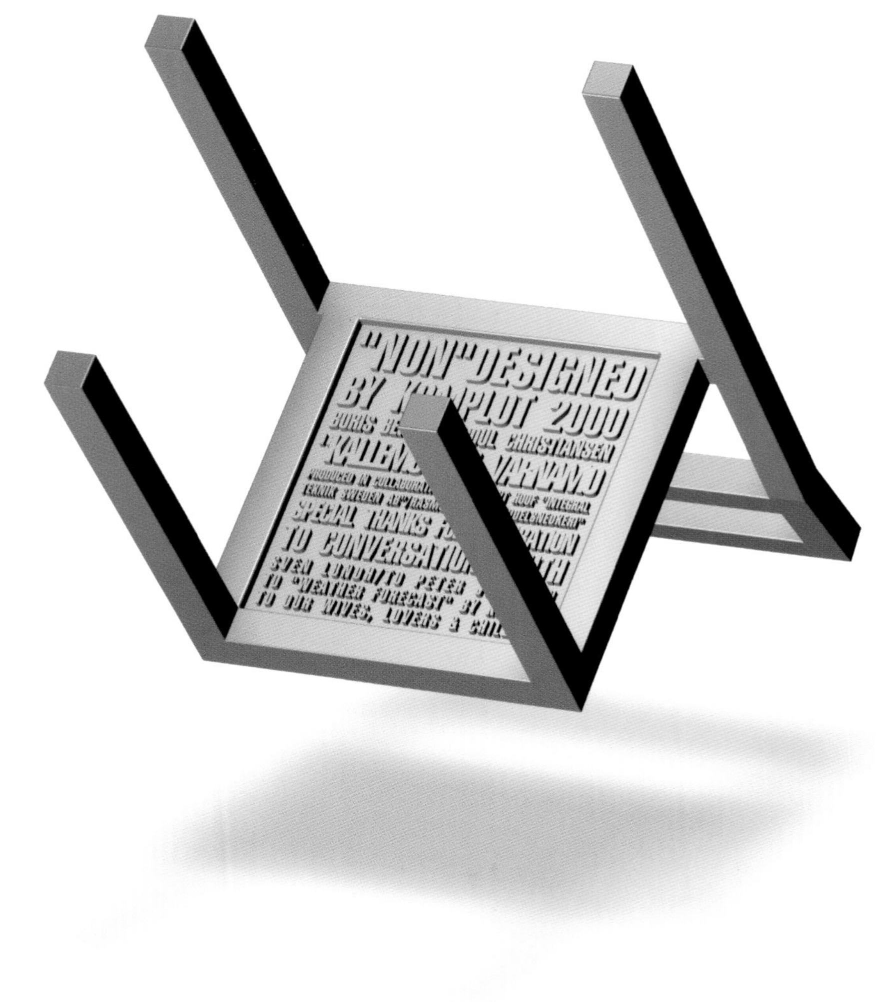

"NON" DESIGNED
BY K
PLOT 2000
BORIS
CHRISTIANSEN
"KALLEM
VAR-NAMO
PRODUCED IN COLLABORAT
TEKNIK SWEDEN AB" RASM
"INTEGRAL
SPECIAL THANKS FO
RATION
TO CONVERSATIO
TH
SVEN LUNDH/TO PETER
TO "WEATHER FORECAST" BY
TO OUR WIVES, LOVERS & CHIL

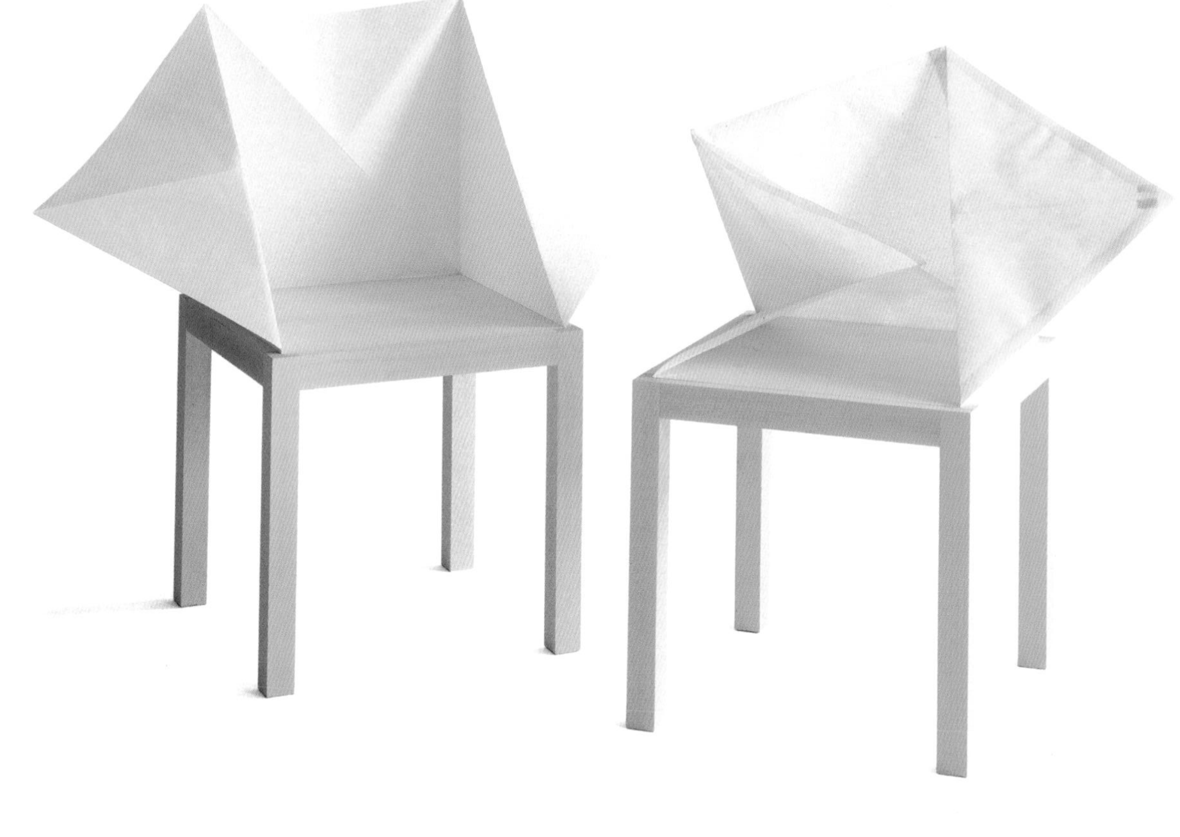

Homage chair
Cecilie Manz
Maple, parchment
DENMARK

Fold-A sofa
Louise Campbell
Felt, plywood, foam, steel frame
DENMARK

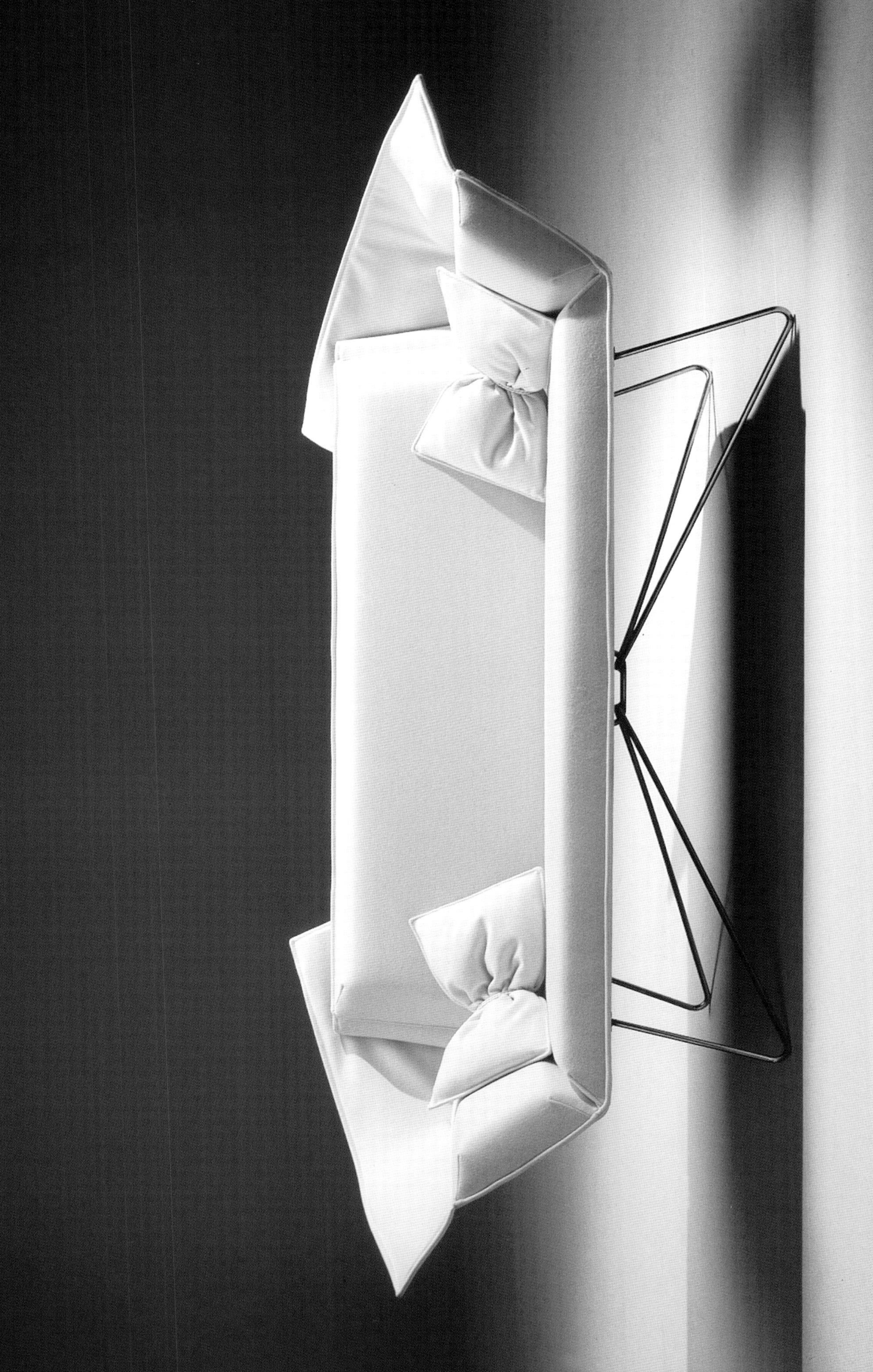

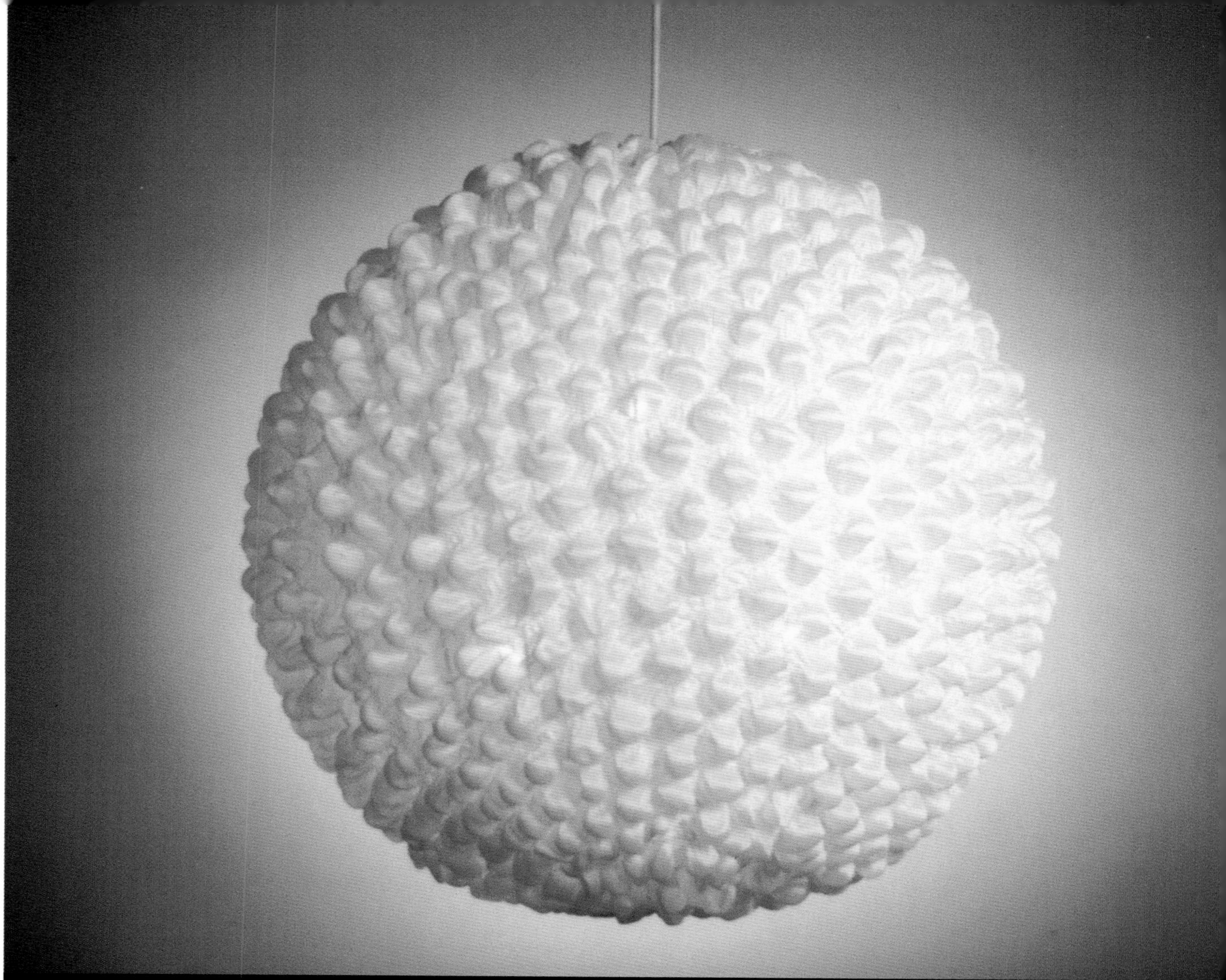

Bubble lamp BPL for Annell Ljus & Form
Camilla Diedrich
Diaphanous polyester
SWEDEN

Woman window shade
Hlynur Vagn Atlason
Nylon print
ICELAND

The poetic is a formidable strain in new Scandinavian design and a strong reply to Scandinavia's history of Functionalism.

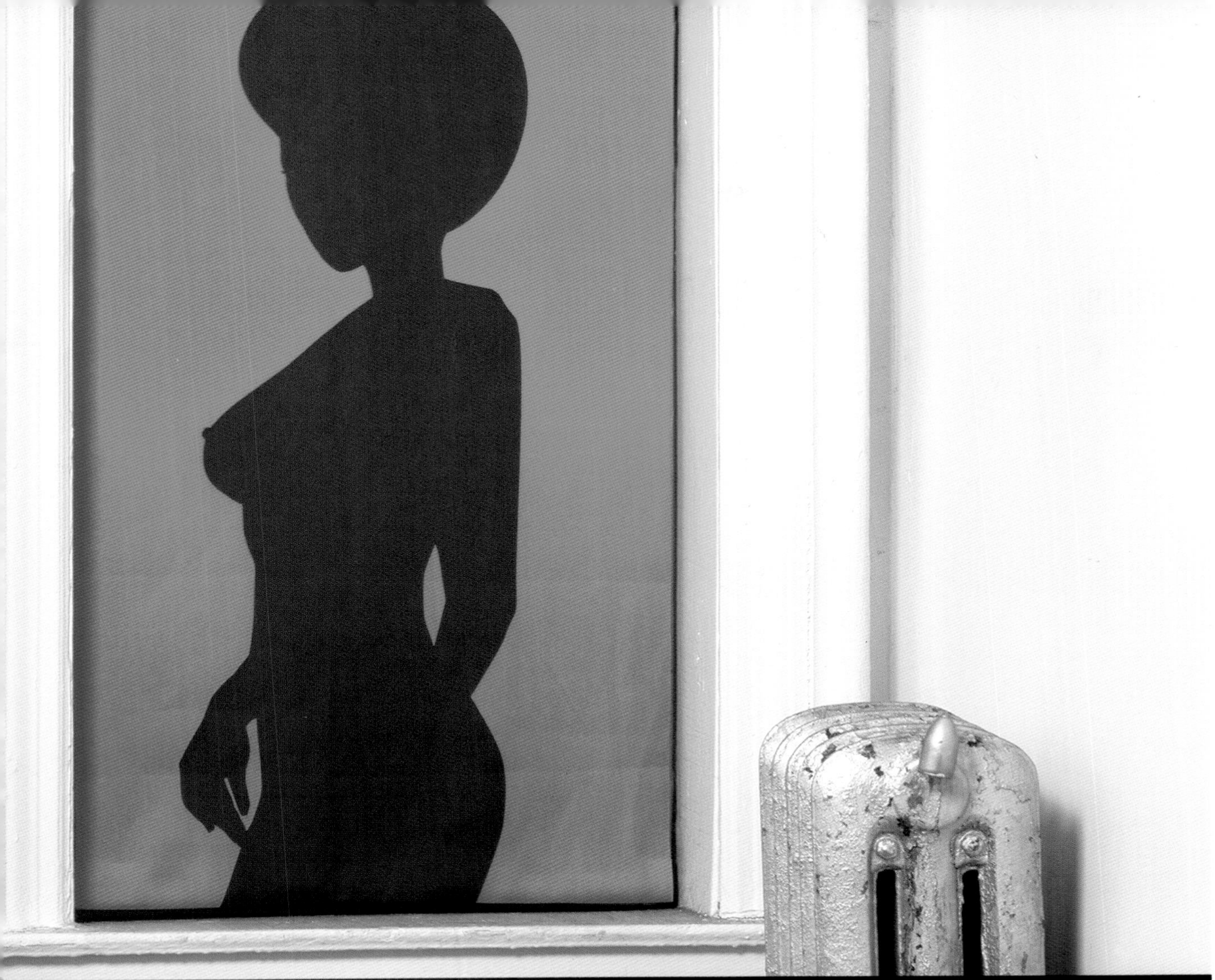

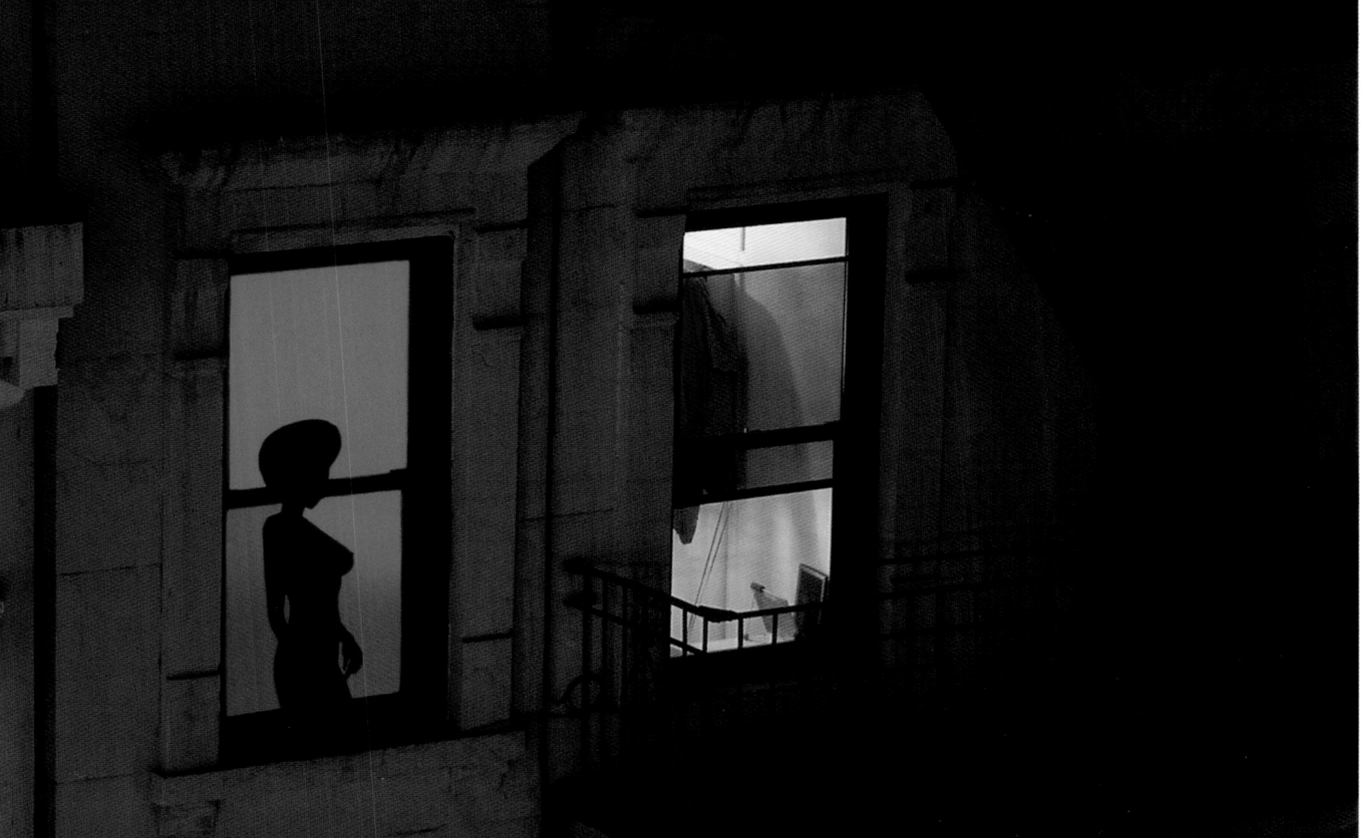

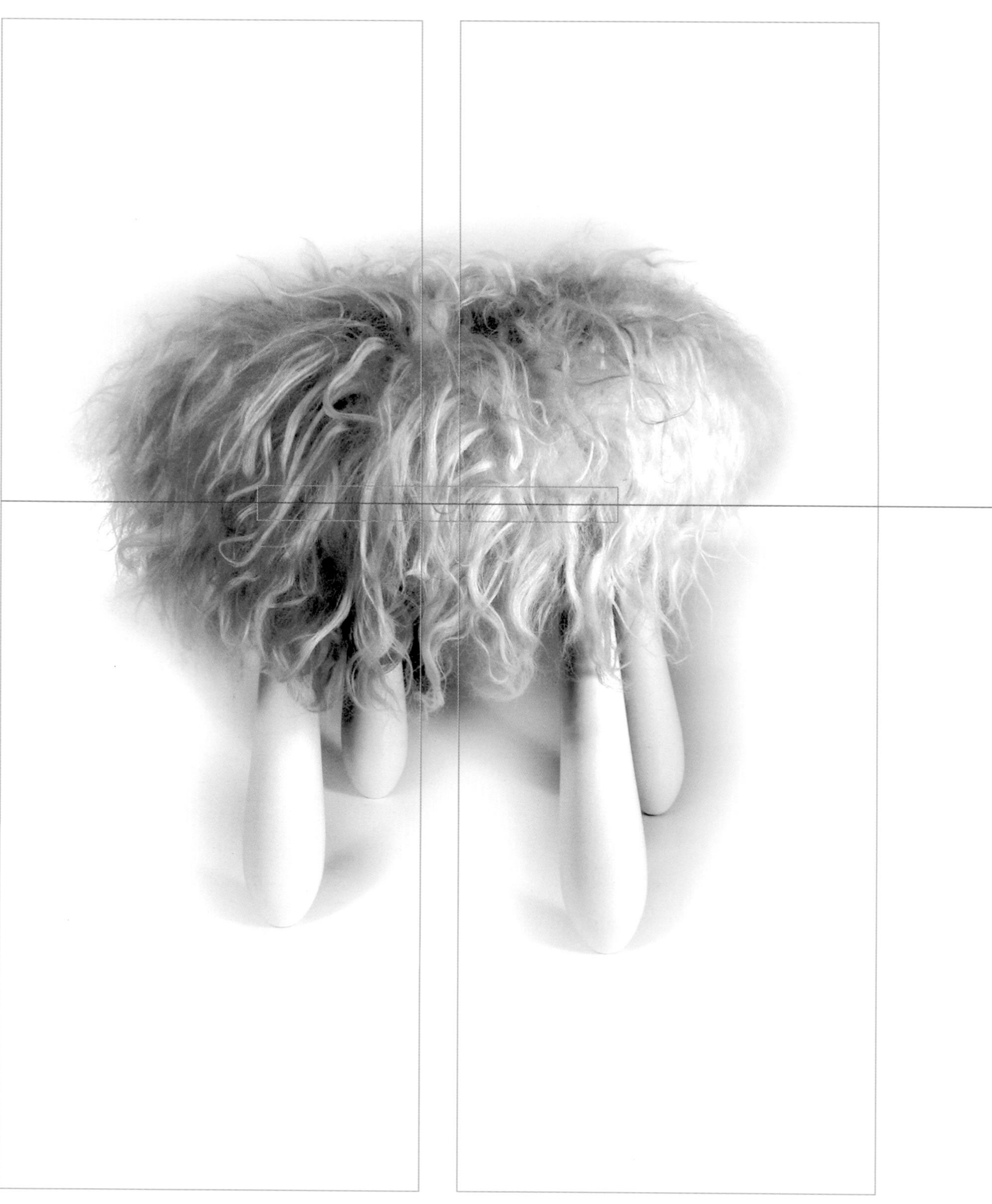

REYKJAVIK

Iceland

In 1974, Sigurdur Már Helgason created Fuzzy, a charming footstool with stubby screw-on legs and a long-haired wool seat that evokes a traditional mainstay of the Icelandic economy, sheep. Helgason lobbied to sell Fuzzy, which fit snugly into a portable hot-pink box, at the duty-free shop at Keflavík International Airport, his logic being that visitors taking home a bottle of Icelandic *brennivín*, a local schnapps, might add Fuzzy to their collection of souvenirs. Fuzzy never made it to the duty-free shelf, becoming instead a popular local gift for confirmations and graduations. The story of this whimsical creation exemplifies a trait typical of contemporary Icelandic design: its pioneering spirit.

Perhaps because remote Iceland was once a nation of scattered farmers—as portrayed by Nobel Prize laureate Halldór Laxness in his 1934–35 novel *Independent People*—Icelanders have little fear of striking out on their own. As late as the mid-twentieth century Iceland was a traditional agricultural society, but it has become one of the most educated, literate, and wired places in the world. Pétur H. Ármannsson, head of the architecture department at Reykjavík Art Museum, views the proximity of Iceland's pre-industrial past as the most important influence in shaping Icelandic culture today. "The transition from agricultural to industrial society happened very late in Iceland," says Ármannsson. "The country's infrastructure had to be built from scratch very rapidly, and Iceland is still working through the consequences of that rapid transformation. A lot of things that other nations have known for a long time are new in Iceland. In this sense, Iceland is a frontier country." (Iceland achieved its independence in 1944, after centuries of rule by the Norwegian and Danish crowns.)

A large part of Iceland's cultural revolution has taken place since the 1980s, in con-

Official name: The Republic of Iceland • Year Iceland gained independence from Denmark: 1944 • Population: Approximately 288,000 • Area: 39,000 square

junction with a 1990s explosion in tourism and telecommunications that led to an economic and cultural boom. Almost overnight, the capital, Reykjavík, morphed from a sleepy Scandinavian port into a small cosmopolitan center of one hundred and fifty thousand people (over half of the national populace) that fosters a celebrated nightlife and music scene. Design has played a part in this cultural awakening, and the field has seen lots of activity since 1998. A new Museum of Design and Applied Arts, founded in that year, makes its home in the Reykjavík suburb of Gardabaer; the Ministry of Industry and Commerce is currently hammering out the details of a new design center to promote Icelandic design; and in 2001, for the first time in Icelandic history, university-level design and architecture education was offered within the country, at the new Iceland Academy of the Arts in Reykjavík.

Fuzzy (previous spread)
Sigurdur Már Helgason
sheep pelt, wood
ICELAND

The very idea of a design field itself is a recent development in Iceland. "Icelanders lived on hard labor until the 1950s," says Frída Björk Ingvarsdóttir, a cultural critic for the newspaper *Morgunbladid*. "We're only about two generations beyond that." The development of the arts in Iceland reflects this traditional emphasis on farm life and the home. The country's most renowned cultural contributions are the tales, or Sagas, of the early Norse settlers, who colonized Iceland during the era of the Vikings. These Sagas spin epic stories of the everyday; they record the histories and genealogies, not of gods and goddesses, but of the actual settlers themselves. Likewise, traditional Icelandic architecture exists on a human scale, influenced by the history of agricultural living.

What there is of Icelandic design sometimes touches on craft, while still retaining the idiosyncrasies of individual expression. Mid-twentieth-century Icelandic furniture makers, far removed from design capitals like Copenhagen, brazenly appropriated the styles of imported designs with a finesse all their own. "What is interesting about this somewhat dubious practice is that Icelandic master carpenters very often improvised on the originals rather than copying them, so they are, in fact, part authors of the furniture," says curator Adalsteinn Ingólfsson, who is assembling a collection of twentieth-century Icelandic furniture for the new Museum of Design and Applied Arts.

The lack of a steadfast design tradition in Iceland, which has often been considered a hindrance for designers hoping to establish international careers, today proves to be an advantage. "Only over the last fifteen years or so is this freedom bearing fruit in a kind of creative anarchy coupled with stubborn individualism," says Ingólfsson. Iceland's strong craft community also offers interesting possibilities for Icelandic design, according to Ármannsson. Because of its small population, "standardization does not pay off in Iceland," he says. "It also goes against the Icelandic mentality. So I see huge potential to develop a design culture where the artist and craftsman work side by side creating custom-made items with a distance from big industry."

Some of the strongest evidence of the new enthusiasm for design can be found at the Iceland Academy of the Arts, which opened its doors in 2001 after ten years in development. The academy

miles (103,000 square kilometers) • Percentage of land covered by glaciers: 11 • Capital: Reykjavík • Longest annual period of daylight in Reykjavík: 21 hours • Shortest annual period

comprises departments of visual arts, drama, music, and design and architecture, awarding degrees in fields such as architecture and fashion for the first time within Iceland's borders. Roughly 90 percent of the design department instructors are practitioners themselves, so the academy serves as the focal point of the design community for professionals as well as students.

The roots of design education in Iceland lie in Western Europe and Scandinavia. The lack of university-level education forced the first generation of design students to study abroad in the 1980s and early '90s. Many studied in Scandinavia, but others traveled to Italy, France, central Europe, and North America. "All of our teachers were foreigners, and we were always studying and working somewhere outside of Iceland," says Halldór Gíslason, dean of the department of design and architecture. (One of the first generation of creatives to obtain a degree abroad, Gíslason left Iceland for Italy in 1979 to study architecture.) "Our tradition is actually European rather than Icelandic. Personally, I know much more about the Italian Renaissance than I do about Icelandic farmhouses. Studying the seventeenth century in Iceland is archaeology—it's for someone else, not for us, not for designers." This international connection continues today, with a large percentage of foreign instructors at the academy (seventeen at last count).

However, while the Iceland Academy of the Arts claims a direct European heritage, there is also an echo of the Wild West around the place. The absence of any long-standing design heritage in Iceland gives students and instructors a creative freedom unavailable in other countries. "Established Scandinavian institutions all have the problem of a long legacy of Scandinavian culture," says Gíslason. "That's what makes Icelandic design different from Scandinavian design. We aren't stuck with any local tradition."

With their fearless sensibility, Icelandic product designers take full advantage of the room for experimentation. Katrín Pétursdóttir blends imagery from pop culture, digital illustration, and fine art to create fantasied motifs. An anime-inspired pattern of fluttering birds and bright twisting flowers ornaments her porcelain collection, called Fudge, for Rosenthal. The design is "logical in its own illogical way," she says. Another designer, Hrafnkell Birgisson, juxtaposes disparate materials in quirky, intellectual statements. He adds wineglass stems to flowery, mismatched teacups for a playful take on the cocktail hour. A storage system called Rolling Stones, created by Tinna Gunnarsdóttir with Israeli designer Karen Chekerdjian, comprises globular units split into two hemispheres. The versatility of the capricious rolling objects means a top isn't always a top, and a bottom isn't always a bottom.

Even with the ambitious new focus on design, furniture and product designers hoping to reach a large audience with their work, or at least to move beyond prototypes and one-offs, still face challenges. "Product design is a young phenomenon in this country. Very few people have realized what it is about," says Gunnarsdóttir. "Many designers are still forced abroad in search of producers, and many of the most successful leave Iceland or live abroad for part of the year."

of daylight in Reykjavík: 4 hours • Official language: Icelandic (Minority languages include English, German, Norwegian, Danish, and Swedish.) • Largest export: Marine products

While little heavy manufacturing exists in Iceland, the country has pockets of innovation in industrial design. The company Össur, founded in 1971, sells high-quality, solidly designed prosthetics to clients around the world. The company's founder, Össur Kristinsson (an amputee himself), started his company by designing his own prosthetics. Today, the company bases its reputation on the pursuit of new technologies and materials, particularly carbon fiber and silicone, and it allocates a huge portion of its budget to research and development.

Balancing manufacturing capacity with the realistic product needs of a small nation remains key to promoting design within Icelandic industry. "This is a land with a small population and very few companies that produce objects providing more than just basic functionality," says Egill Egilsson, industrial designer and technical lead at Össur. "Also, there are very few companies big enough to employ an industrial designer full-time." Still, Egilsson remains hopeful about the future of Icelandic industrial design. "Iceland has the clean and low-price energy that is needed for all kinds of production. Labor and shipping costs are also getting more compatible with other countries. This is the reason that this little country has been able to come slowly up to market."

ICELAND
Tunö indoor/outdoor clock for IKEA/PS
Hlynur Vagn Atlason
Plastic, steel

With the last decade's focus on new technology, the world of virtual and conceptual design beckons Icelanders, who have one of the highest rates of Internet access per capita on the planet. Due in part to this computer savvy, digital and graphic design are thriving. Also, while product design and most other design fields are new to Iceland, graphic design has been taught at the university level for several years, giving the field time to mature.

While the paucity of manufacturing in Iceland makes it difficult for designers to get work produced, it also allows Icelandic designers the liberty to nurture unique visions. With their international focus and independent spirit, Icelanders often display a flair for art and experimentation more pronounced than that of their Nordic neighbors. "Apart from some breathtaking areas, the Icelandic countryside is very barren, flat, hostile, cold, and desolate," says Pétursdóttir. "It leaves you with a feeling of emptiness. I believe Icelanders have always had to imagine things to fill up that emptiness. Maybe because of the lack of everything, they thrive on the thought that there is something more than just reality."

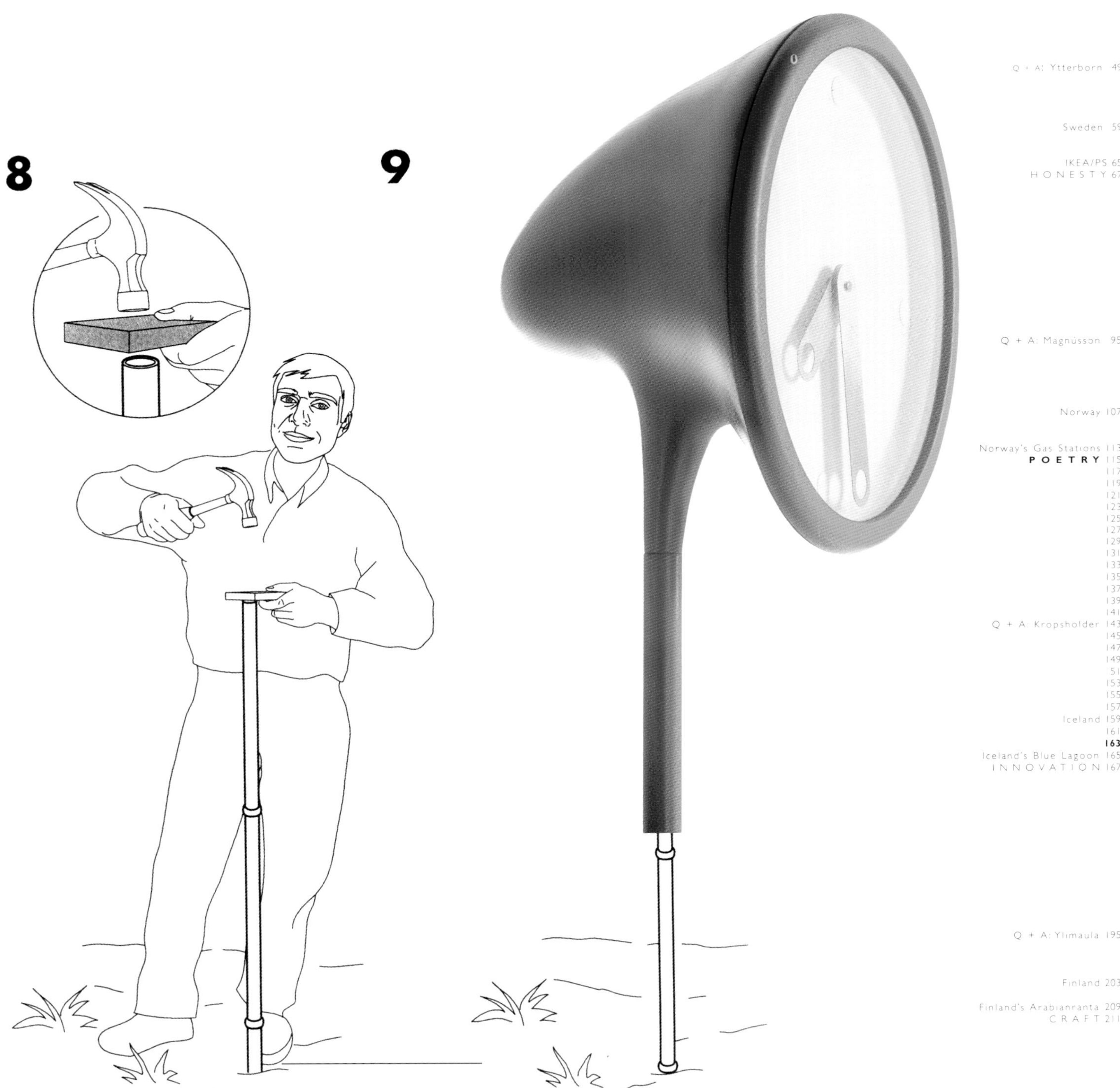
8
9

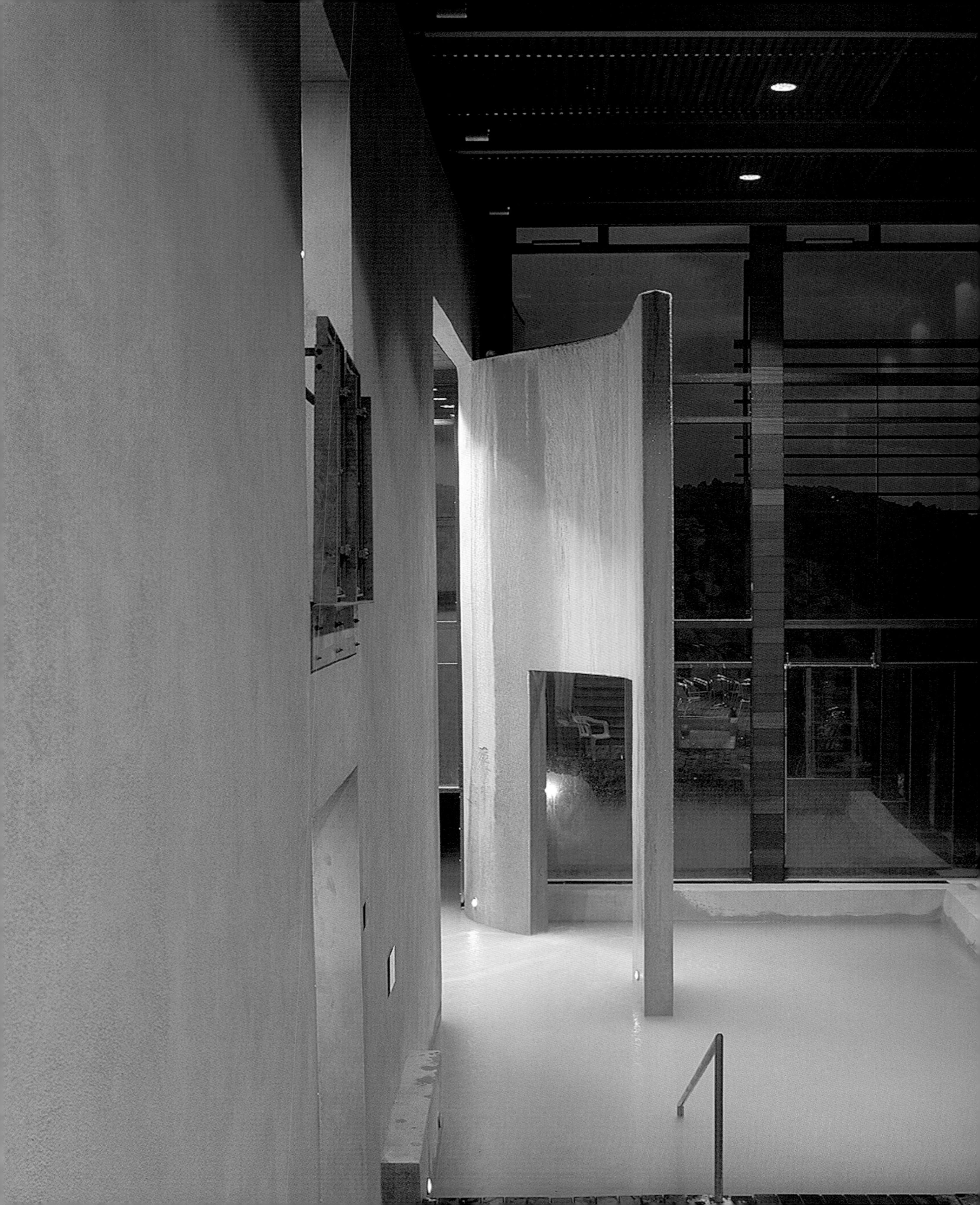

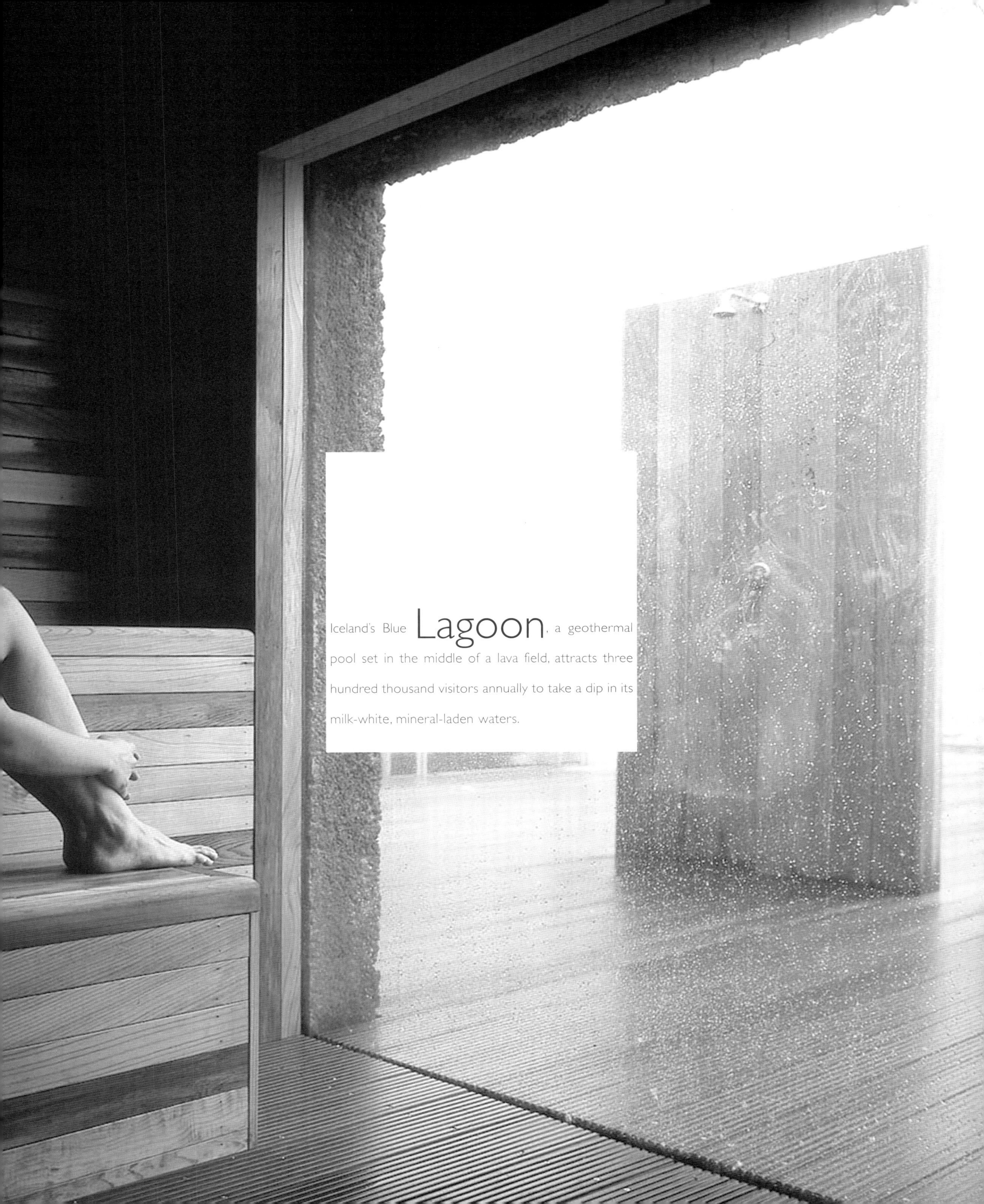

Iceland's Blue Lagoon, a geothermal pool set in the middle of a lava field, attracts three hundred thousand visitors annually to take a dip in its milk-white, mineral-laden waters.

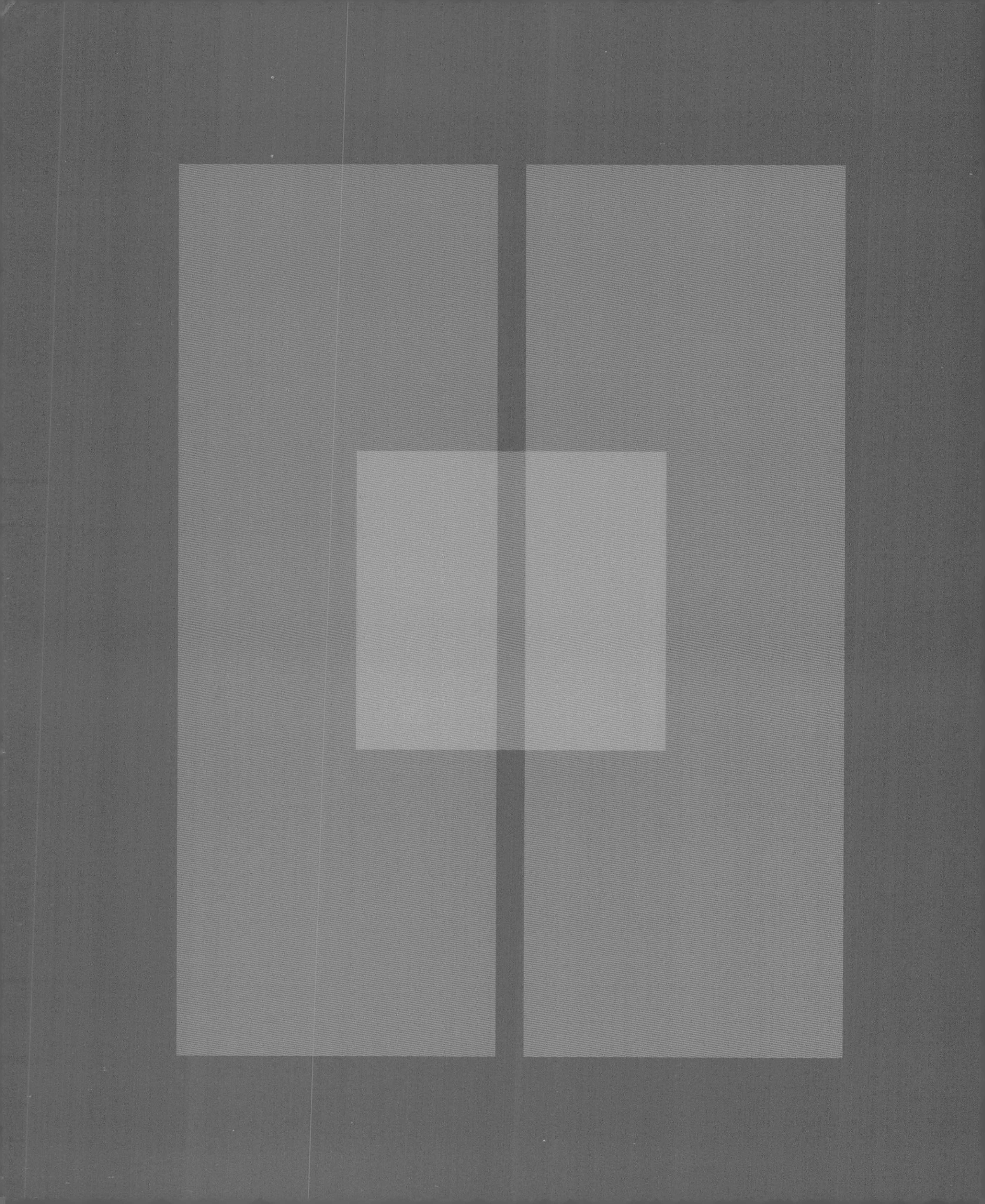

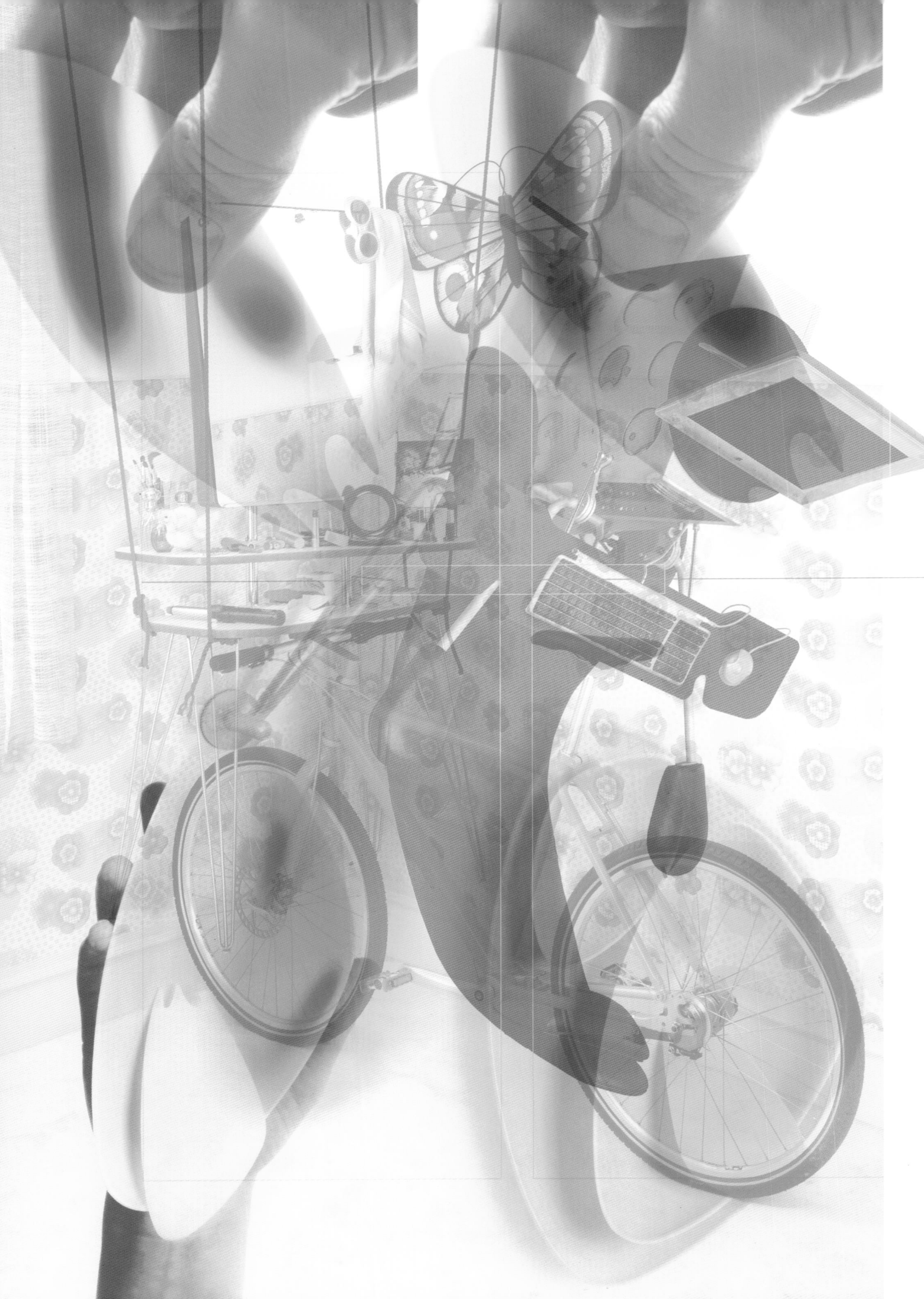

CHAPTER IV

INNVOATION

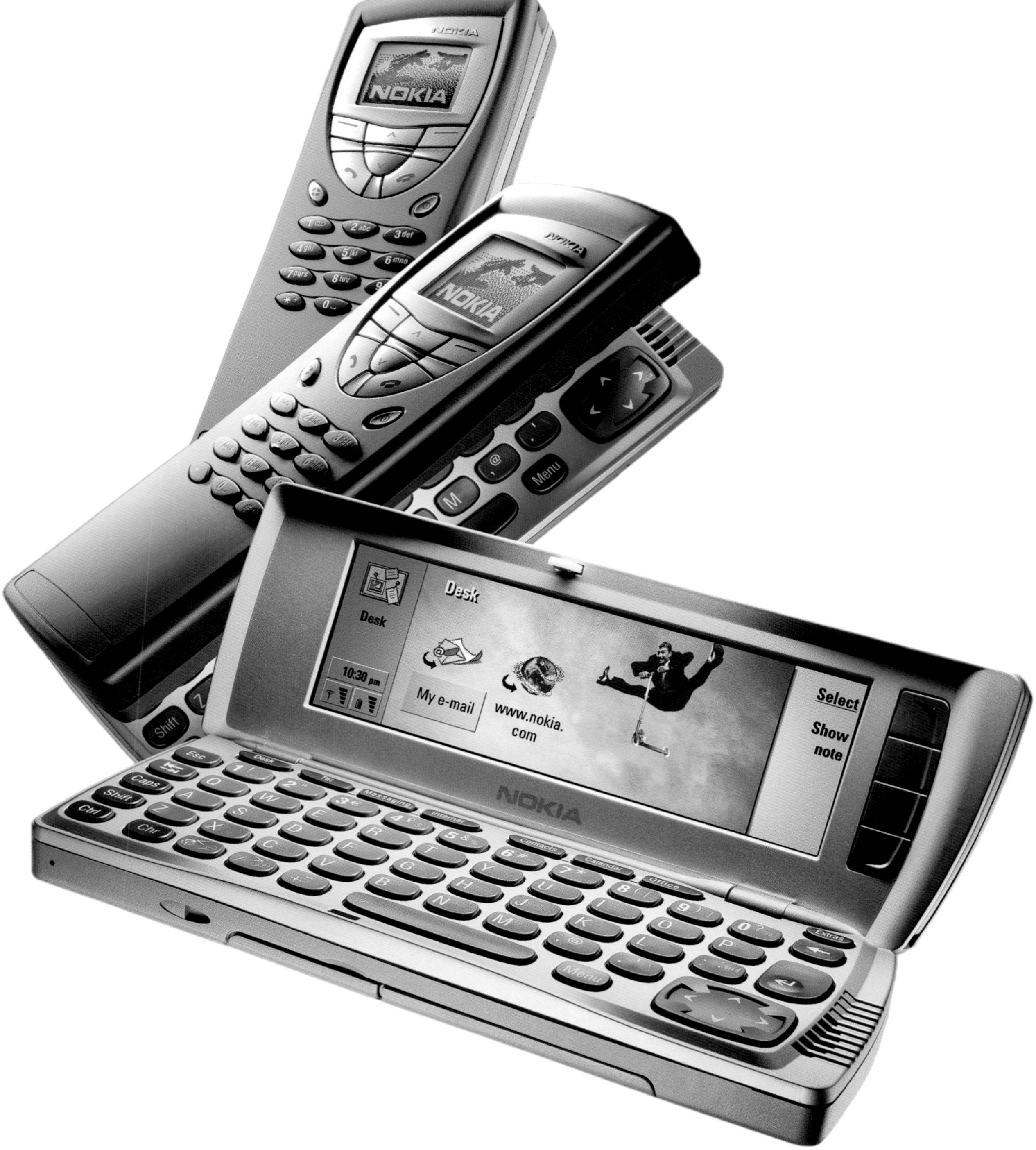

Communicator 9210i for Nokia
Nokia Design
Plastic, aluminum, painted plastic
FINLAND

INNOVATION

Each year, entrepreneurs, economic planners, and academics make a pilgrimage to Nokia, Finland. They come to visit the world's leading mobile phone supplier, named for its hometown, and the company largely responsible for the "Finnish Miracle." In little more than a decade, Finland has morphed from a struggling country into a high-tech powerhouse and economic model for small nations around the world. There are many forces—political, historic, geographic—that brought this country back from the brink of bankruptcy, but one of the most important is a sanguine belief in technological possibility.

As early as the 1910s Scandinavian leaders used the power of technology to overcome hardship, embracing mass production to improve living standards. Modern designers perfected these techniques, crafting "more beautiful everyday goods" that perpetuated their human-centric worldview. Today, new technology may be replacing old-time industry, but an optimistic view of innovation still characterizes Scandinavian design. Engaging new forms, materials, and working methods, Scandinavian designers draw from a well of time-honored values to realize technology's potential.

The digital revolution radically transformed Scandinavia, today one of the most wired regions in the world. (Finland, for example, has the most Internet nodes and mobile phones per capita of any country.) Remote geography may be partly responsible: from their vantage point at the top of Europe, Scandinavians readily appreciate the closer connection to the rest of the world that new communication technology provides. (Tyler Brûlé, former editor of the design and lifestyle magazine *Wallpaper**, once described Stockholm, capital of Sweden, as "an urban hub that has long functioned on the fringe and thrived on the margins" of other European capitals such as London and Paris.) Key players in the high-tech transformation of Scandinavia, such as Nokia and Sweden's Sony Ericsson, grasped the democratic potential of mobile technology. In the mid-1990s Nokia won over consumers with accessible design, pioneering the use of enticing graphic displays, fun ring tones, and swappable color faceplates in mobile phones. Although the devices could be tailored to the individual, their ubiquity emphasized interconnectivity and—a core theme of the Scandinavian welfare state—community. (Nokia's company slogan is "Connecting People.")

Designers at Nokia and Sony Ericsson, assuming a level of technological saturation and public acceptance, are free to finesse the details of product design. While mobile technology may be pervasive, innovative solutions are hardly generic. Nokia's handheld Communicator 9210 i **(C)** see **p 168** places the individual at the center of a powerful, convergent communications system that features Internet and fax services, e-mail short messaging, phone capabilities, and other functions. Sony Ericsson, on the other hand, offers a streamlined

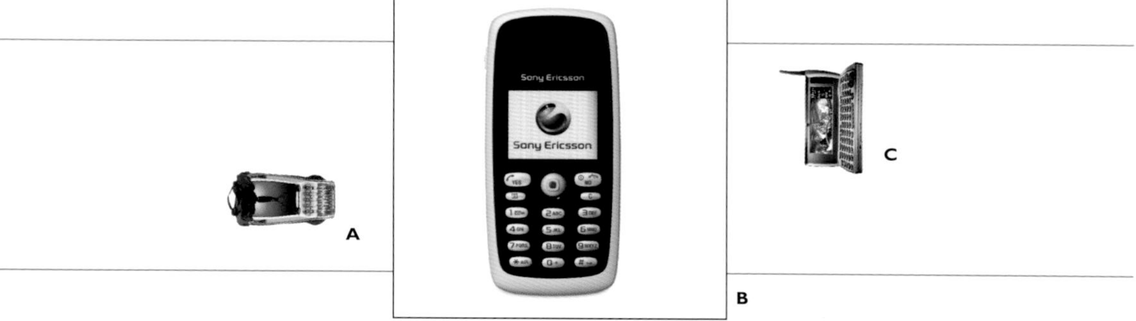

T300 mobile phone for Sony Ericsson (B)
Sony Ericsson Design
Plastic
SWEDEN

FINLAND
Nils Master Big Mouth fishing lure for Finlandia-Uistin
Pentagon Design
Injection-molded plastic, stainless steel

product: the geometric lines and straightforward keypad of the new T300 **(B)** bring to mind the essential forms of Scandinavian heritage.

The new mobility made possible by digital communications inspires some designers, who tailor their creations to "urban nomads," since people are no longer welded to their desks, stuck in their offices, or even confined to a building. The Swedish designer Jonas Blanking became frustrated by the damage his laptop sustained as he carted it around Copenhagen in a canvas backpack. In an ingenious marriage of industrial design and ergonomics, Blanking created Megalopolis **(A)** see **p 184**—a hard-shelled backpack that protects sensitive electronics. Boblbee's novel design blends durability with comfort: a "second skin," adapted from an injection-molded casing used in the air-cargo industry, lies next to the wearer's body. Today, Boblbee encompasses an entire "nomadic" product including cargo bags, backpacks, briefcases, and purses.

Mobility in work life has led to greater mobility in personal life. For those who want to pick up and go, the Finnish furniture design collective Snowcrash, whose name merges a vision of the

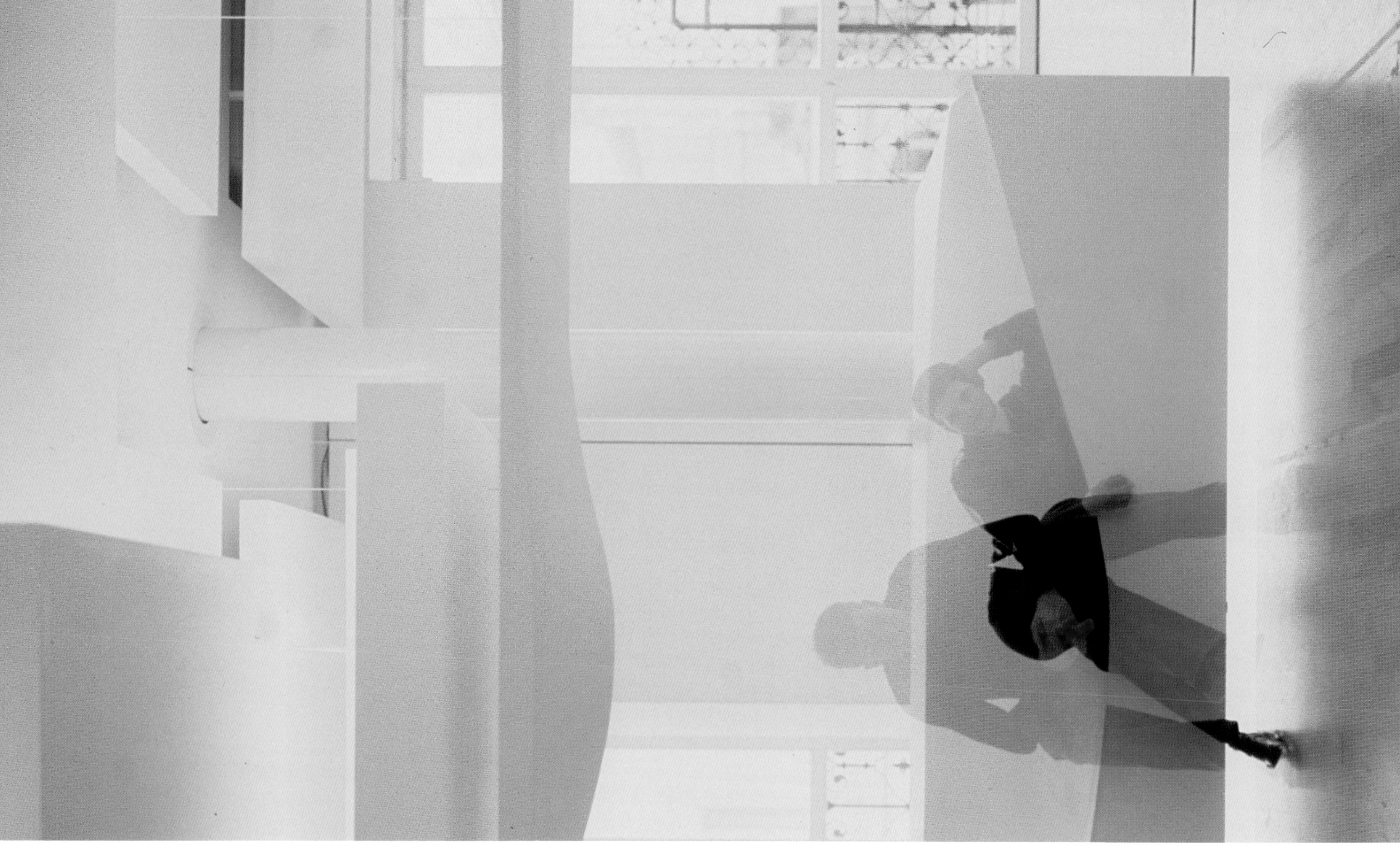

Formations, an architectural installation that explored the interplay among people, spaces, and objects
Tuuli Sotamaa, Kivi Sotamaa
FINLAND

FINLAND
Globlow lamp for David Design (H)
Valvomo
Steel, ripstop nylon

frozen North with the speed of contemporary living, has a solution. Snowcrash's first collection, launched at the Milan Furniture Fair in 1997, featured light-weight, easy-to-assemble pieces, such as Ilkka Suppanen's Flying Carpet sofa **(D)** see **p 188** and Timo Salli's Tramp chair **(E)** see **p 207**. Inspired by the new digital lifestyle, the group reconciled labor with leisure time in designs such as Netsurfer **(F)** see **p 202**, a computer work station with a reclining seat that encourages "kicking back," by Teppo Asikainen and Ilkka Terho. The group's designs were always dynamic; for example, the Globlow lamp **(H)** by Vesa Hinkola, Markus Nevalainen, and Rane Vaskivuori deflates, like a disappointed child, when turned off. At their core, Snowcrash designs demonstrate a belief in the power of new technology to perpetuate easy living—the only requirements for entering the digital age are a sense of humor and a light load.

While the transient lifestyle inspires some Scandinavian designers, others draw on their Modernist heritage to give permanence to the digital. The flawless forms of the Danish consumer electronics company Bang & Olufsen epitomize a classic Scandinavian look. (Current design head David Lewis, a Briton, initially assisted designer Jacob Jensen, who initiated the company's *über* minimalist design approach during the 1960s.) B&O TVs, stereos, and telephones **(G)** see **p 175** provide state-of-the-art technology (the company has one

D

E

F

G

H

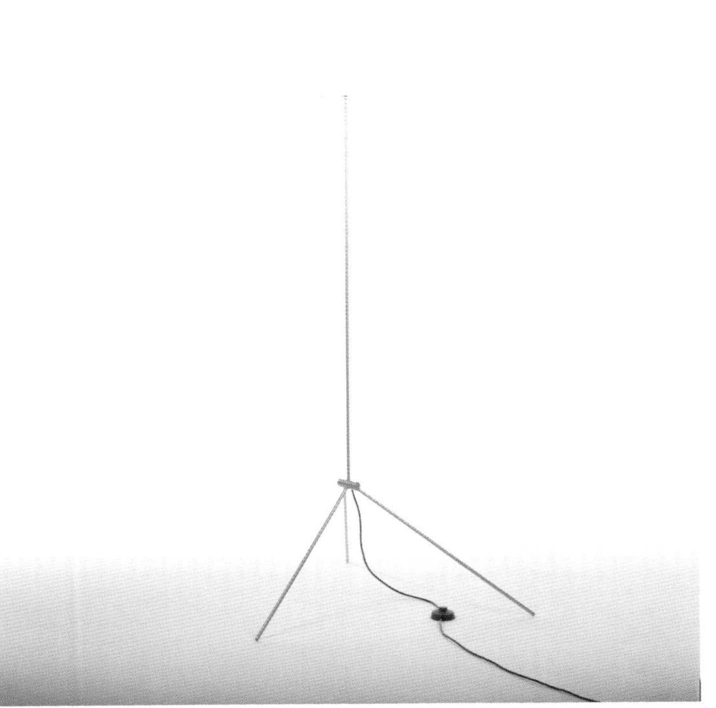

of the most elaborate sound-testing studios in the world). Even though their high price tags lend B&O products an air of exclusivity, their pristine shapes and technical precision encapsulate Scandinavian understated elegance.

Creating everything from mobile phones to furniture to consumer products, innovative designers in all fields have little fear of using synthetic materials and often seek new developments outside their discipline, as Blanking did with his Megalopolis backpack. Ilkka Suppanen, who like the other founders of Snowcrash now tackles projects with his own firm, has developed a vast library of new material samples including 3-D textiles and liquid wood (which he describes, disappointedly, as "feeling just like plastic"). "I use new technology a lot," says Suppanen, who is devoted to building his firm's database: "Whenever there is extra time and a materials fair is happening, I go there to collect samples."

Innovative designers don't hesitate to usurp the ultimate emblem of Scandinavian furniture design—bentwood. The Finnish designer Petri Vainio uses digital technology to expand the possibilities of the bentwood process, a method of molding wood veneer and a hallmark of Scandinavian furniture design. Vainio's computer-aided plywood experiments have resulted in accessories such as the Uni and Tuisku

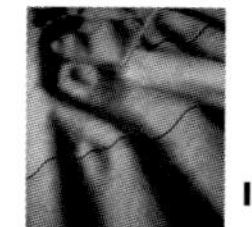

I

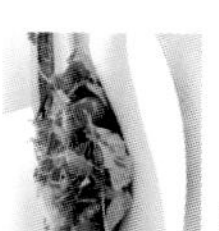

J

DENMARK
BeoCom 2 telephone for Bang & Olufsen
David Lewis
color - anodized aluminum

wooden bowls that—though two to three millimeters thick—undulate with surprisingly fluid form. The Finnish design Jouko Kärkkäinen achieves a similar effect with his own patented plywood molding method. Using this method, Kärkkäinen devises one continuous rolling wooden surface called PLY **(I)** see **p 198**, a massive mural of modular birch sound panels.

Due to the high level of education and extensive wiring in Scandinavia, innovative designers hardly think twice about employing the computer in the design process, though many temper technology with a hint of the handmade. Both the Finnish collective Ocean North and the Danish furniture designer Mathias Bengtsson process information from handmade models in the computer, but with two very different results. With its theoretical approach, Ocean North uses the computer to "generate a certain number of options within set constraints," says member Kivi Sotamaa. Working from these renderings, the group alternates between manual modeling and computer screen, applying this process to a vast range of scale, from tableware **(J)** see **p 207** to skyscrapers. A consistent architectural language—white, pristine, sensual—permeates the design. With his artistic bent, Bengtsson balances what he calls "the power of the free hand" with that of the computer. Bengtsson draws full-scale

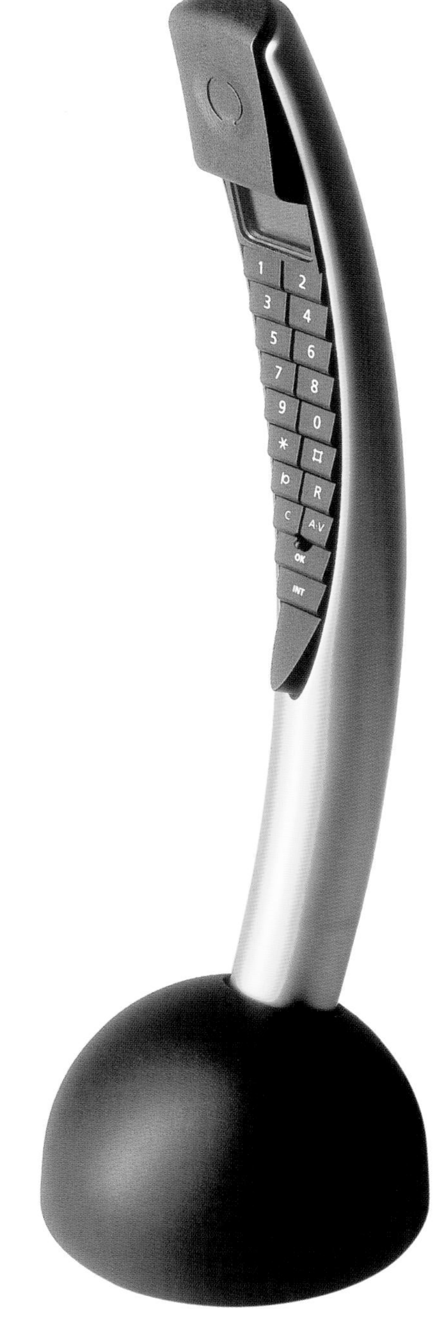

sketches and shapes clay models before moving to the computer for additional manipulation. Bengtsson's acclaimed chair Slice **(K)** see **p 193**, which melds digital process and poetic gesture, is assembled from 254 layers of laser-cut wood. "I have a sculptural background and interest in romantic furniture, but at the same time I am fascinated by evil heartless machines," says Bengtsson.

The computer has changed not only the creative process but Scandinavian manufacturing as well. Designers, such as Dane Kasper Salto, work within an increasingly mechanized production environment but retain a sense of craft. Initially trained as a cabinetmaker, Salto took five years to develop his Ice chair **(L)** for the manufacturer Fritz Hansen. Made from brushed aluminum and high-quality plastic, the components of Ice are completely molded and tooled by machines. The only time human hands touch the chair is during assembly of the manufactured parts. To give the chair a sense of value and history, Salto paid special attention to every aspect of construction, as in the almost-invisible water channels that allow rainwater runoff. "This chair is made by robots," says Salto. "So I think it is even more important not to overlook fine detailing."

Ice chair for Fritz Hansen (L)
Kasper Salto
Plastic, extruded and cast aluminum
DENMARK

NORWAY
THINK City electric vehicle for Think Nordic (M)
Stig Olav Skeie, Katinka von der Lippe
Thermoplastic body, aluminum space frame

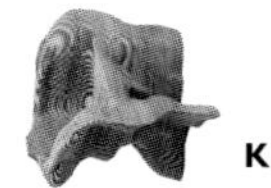

K

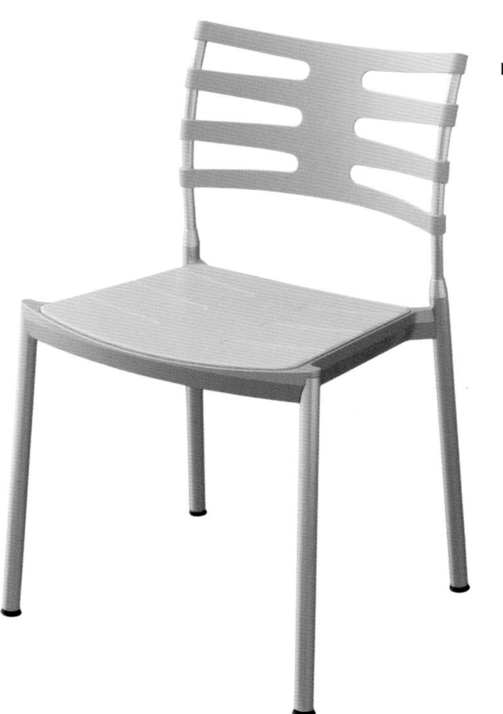

L

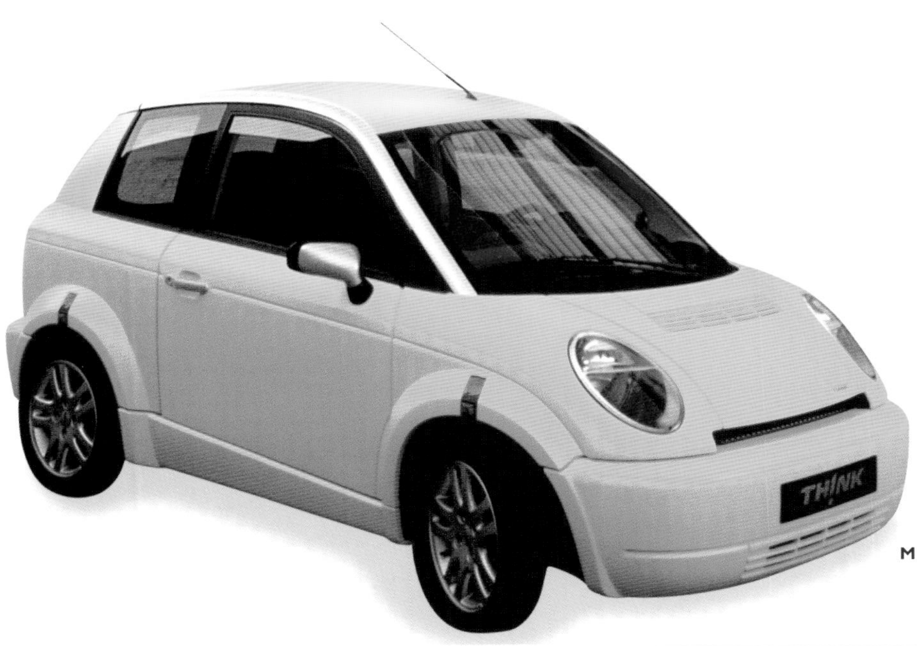

Scandinavian designers do not view technology and industry as antithetical to sustaining the natural world. Indeed, new technology is often a Scandinavian designer's most prized asset when creating sustainable products.

Scandinavian designers do not view technology and industry as antithetical to sustaining the natural world. Indeed, new technology is often a Scandinavian designer's most prized asset when creating sustainable products. And eco-product development allows Scandinavian designers to evolve their traditional kinship with the environment. With a growing body of pan-European legislation and standardized tools for life-cycle assessment, the field of eco-design in Scandinavia has reached new levels of sophistication. "There was a period when designers were developing [eco-]products that were kind of naïve and impractical," says Marianne Aav, director of the Finnish Museum of Art and Design. "This romantic period seems to be over, and now designers are quite serious about developing sustainable solutions." In the current culture, perspective-altering innovations are being made in fields as diverse as vehicle design, consumer products, and waste management. One of the world's most promising electric cars **(M)** called TH!NK City, is produced in the town of Aurskog, Norway. Primed for tooling around town rather than cruising the interstate, TH!NK City has limited battery life, like all electric cars. Its breakthrough design comes from its featherweight aluminum and steel frame and thermoplastic paneling, which, while complying with all European Union safety standards, makes battery usage more efficient. In addition, the car requires only 425 parts as opposed to the thousands in conventional cars, facilitating disassembly and recycling.

As is the case with TH!NK City, the most successful green products subtly alter established behavioral patterns. Two Danish eco-designers, Anne Bannick and Lene Vad Jensen rethink casual dining with their dinnerware set PAPCoRN **(N)** see **p 189**, which employs biodegradable plastics made from renewable resources such as wheat, maize, and lactic acid. The PAPCoRN set includes colorful, asymmetrical dishes, handy takeout boxes, and stylish "sporks," demonstrating everyday elegance in concert with energy efficiency.

Educational institutions across Scandinavia are also tackling the challenges of sustainable design. For instance, graduate students at the Future Home Institute at the University of Art and Design in Helsinki, Finland, work with a variety of corporate sponsors to create sustainable options. One noteworthy venture at the Institute, a brick and tile project **(O)** by ceramic artist Desiree Sevelius, explores waste management—literally. Conducting technical material studies, Sevelius developed a method of purifying sewage sludge for use in

Handmade bricks and tiles (O)
Desiree Sevelius
Fly ash, sewage sludge, recycled glass and clay
FINLAND

Copenhagen bicycle for Biomega
Jens Martin Skibsted
Aluminum
DENMARK

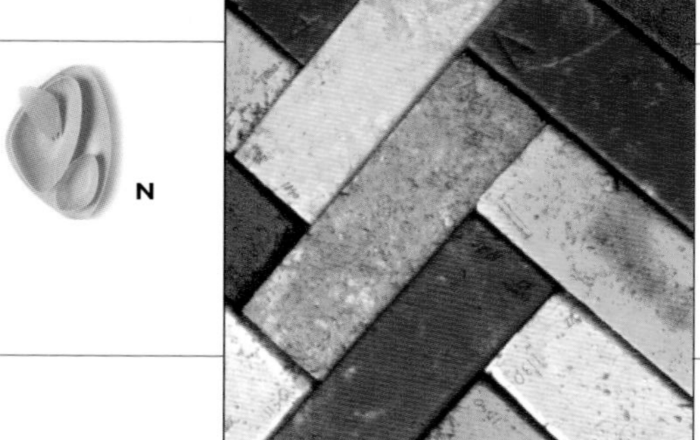

N

O

bricks and tiles in new housing projects. The surprisingly appealing results run the gamut of textures and earth tones. "It is an underestimation of human creativity and ethically indefensible to pass the bill . . . of pollution to future generations," Sevelius writes in a project catalog for the Future Home Institute.

Critics claim that the ubiquity of new technology perpetuates a generic global style, but crafting truly revolutionary products, such as Nokia's mobile phones or many of the sustainable designs mentioned above, always requires a pioneering vision. Throughout Scandinavia, interpretations of technological form and function vary greatly; from Bang & Olufsen's pristine geometries to Snowcrash's poetic predictions of future living, innovative design nurtures many Scandinavian virtues. The Scandinavian commitment to innovation, not simply an effort at crafting new consumables, reveals a genuine attempt to further better living. The drive to innovate, so deeply intrinsic to Scandinavia, will continue to enliven the field of design, making it as pertinent and relevant as ever. Given the achievements of innovative Scandinavian designers, the challenge for the rest of the world is to avoid falling behind.

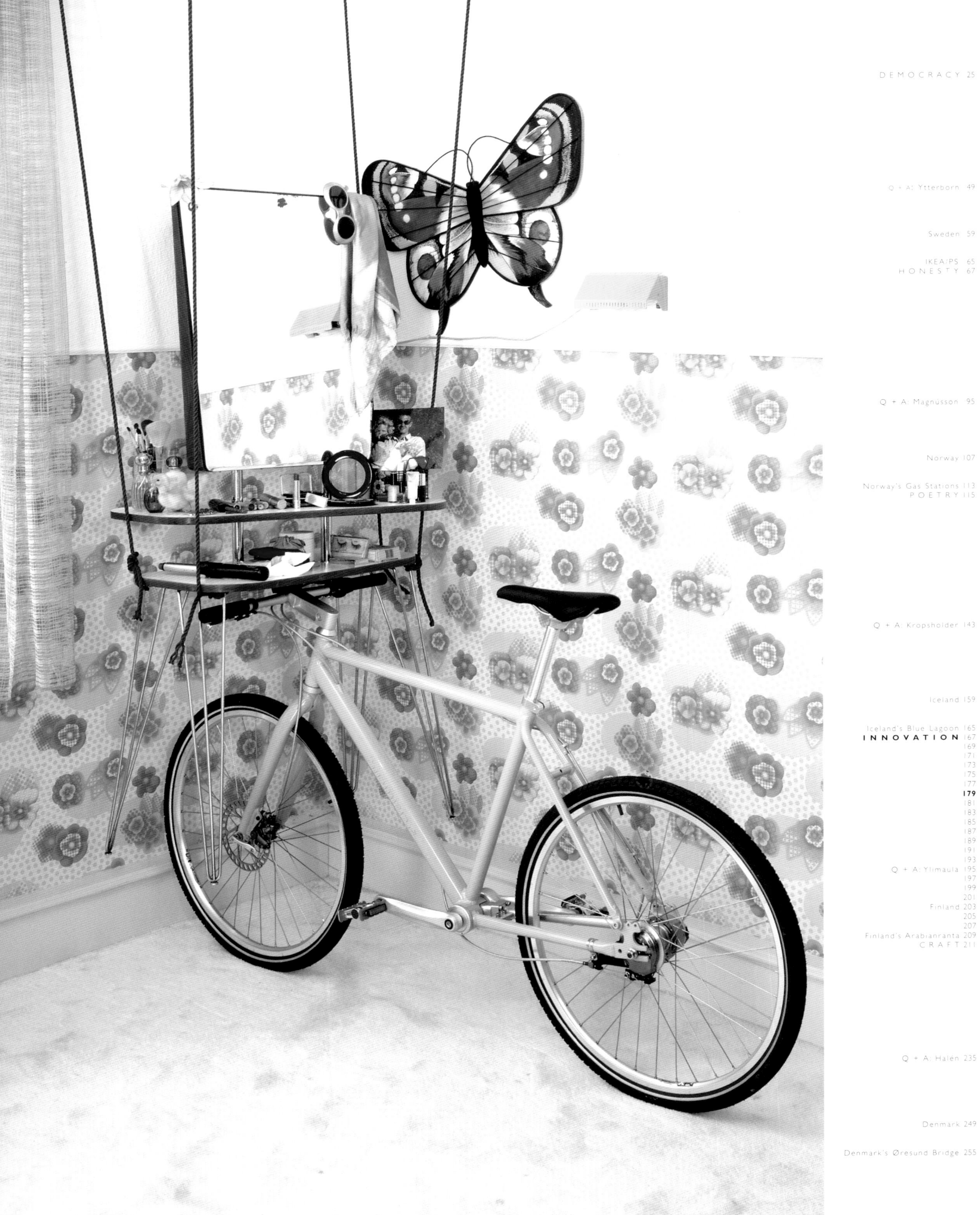

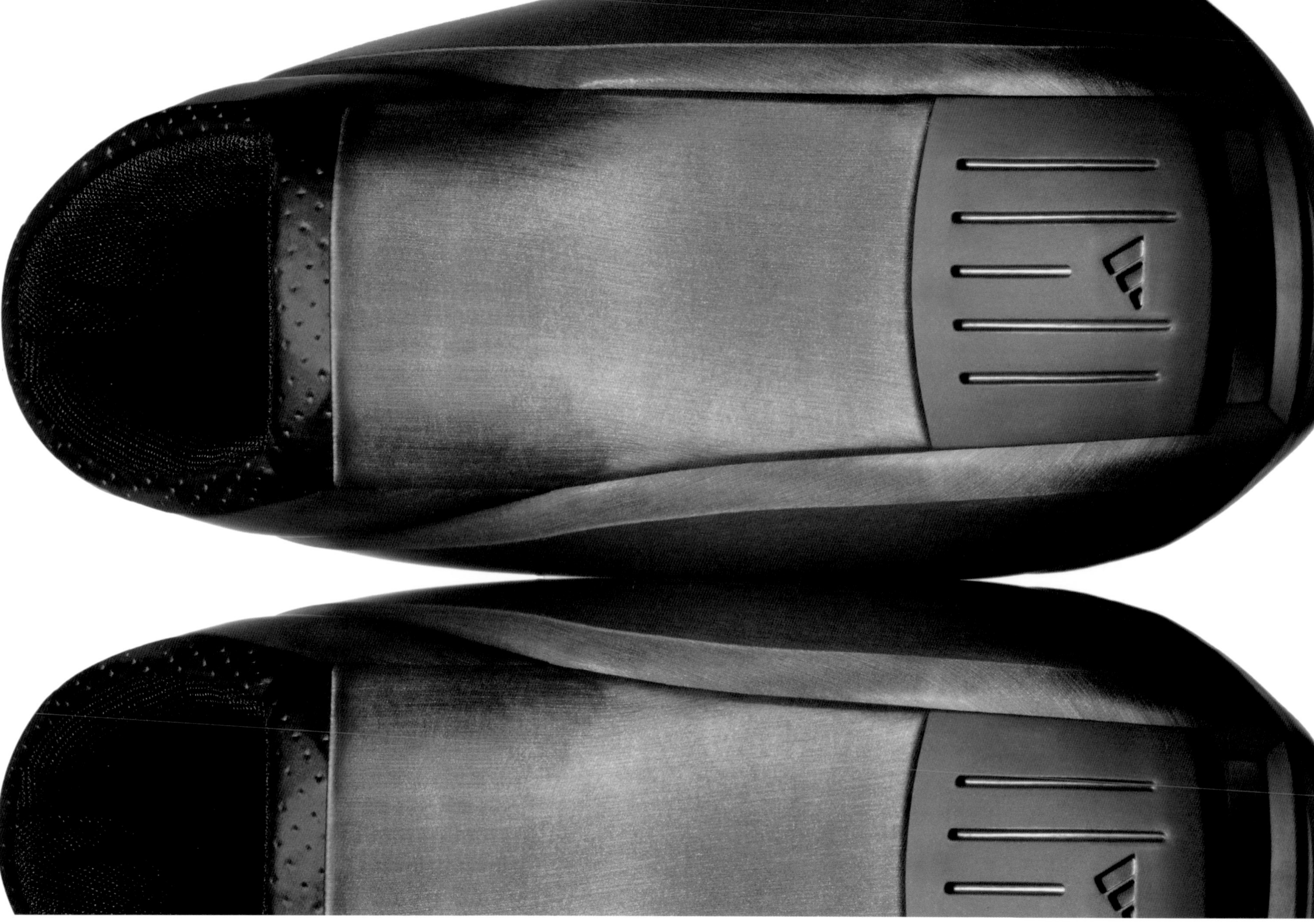

Kobe Two for Adidas International
Eirik Lund Nielsen
Carbon rubber, EVA synthetic leather, foam, plastics
NORWAY

AutoSock, a tire cover that improves traction
Hareide Designmill
Kevlar reinforced polyester
NORWAY

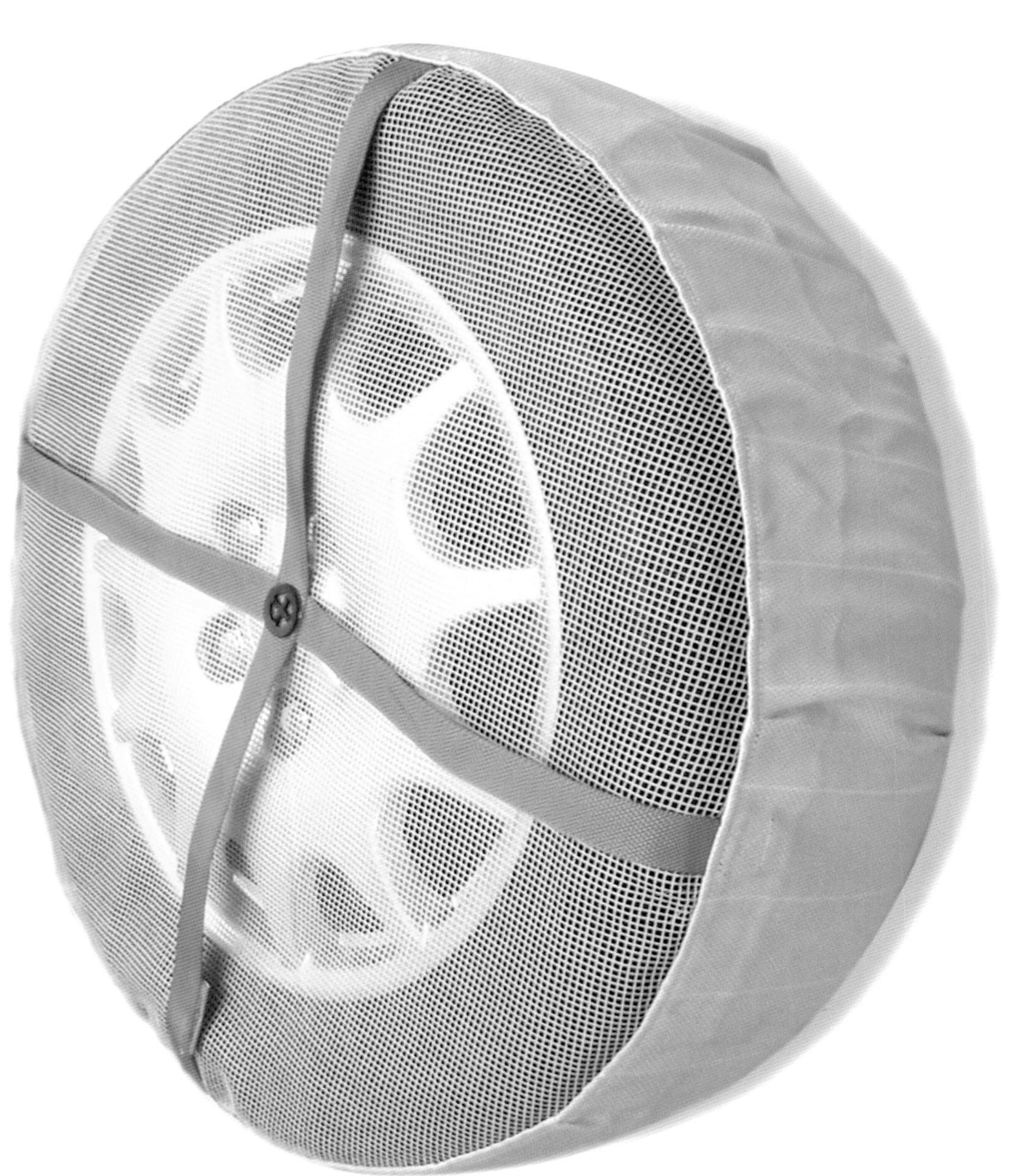

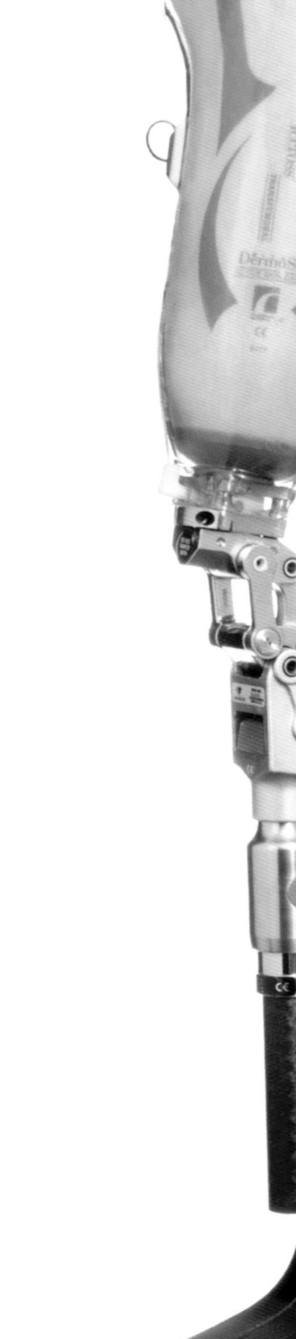

ICELAND
Prosthetic leg for Össur
Össur Research and Development Division

DENMARK
Laptop table for Paustian
Knud Holscher Industriel Design
Aluminum profiles, aluminum honeycomb plate

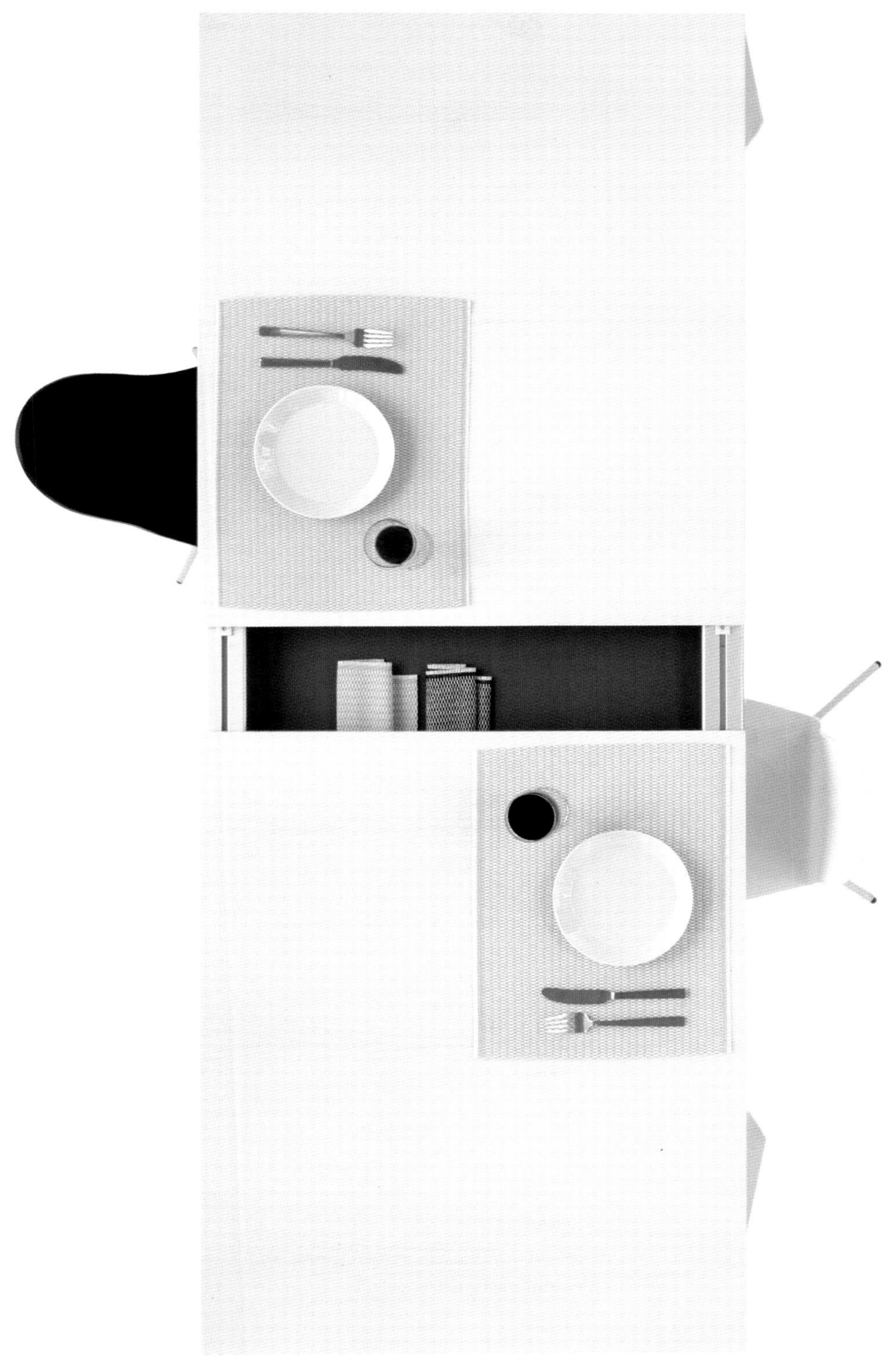

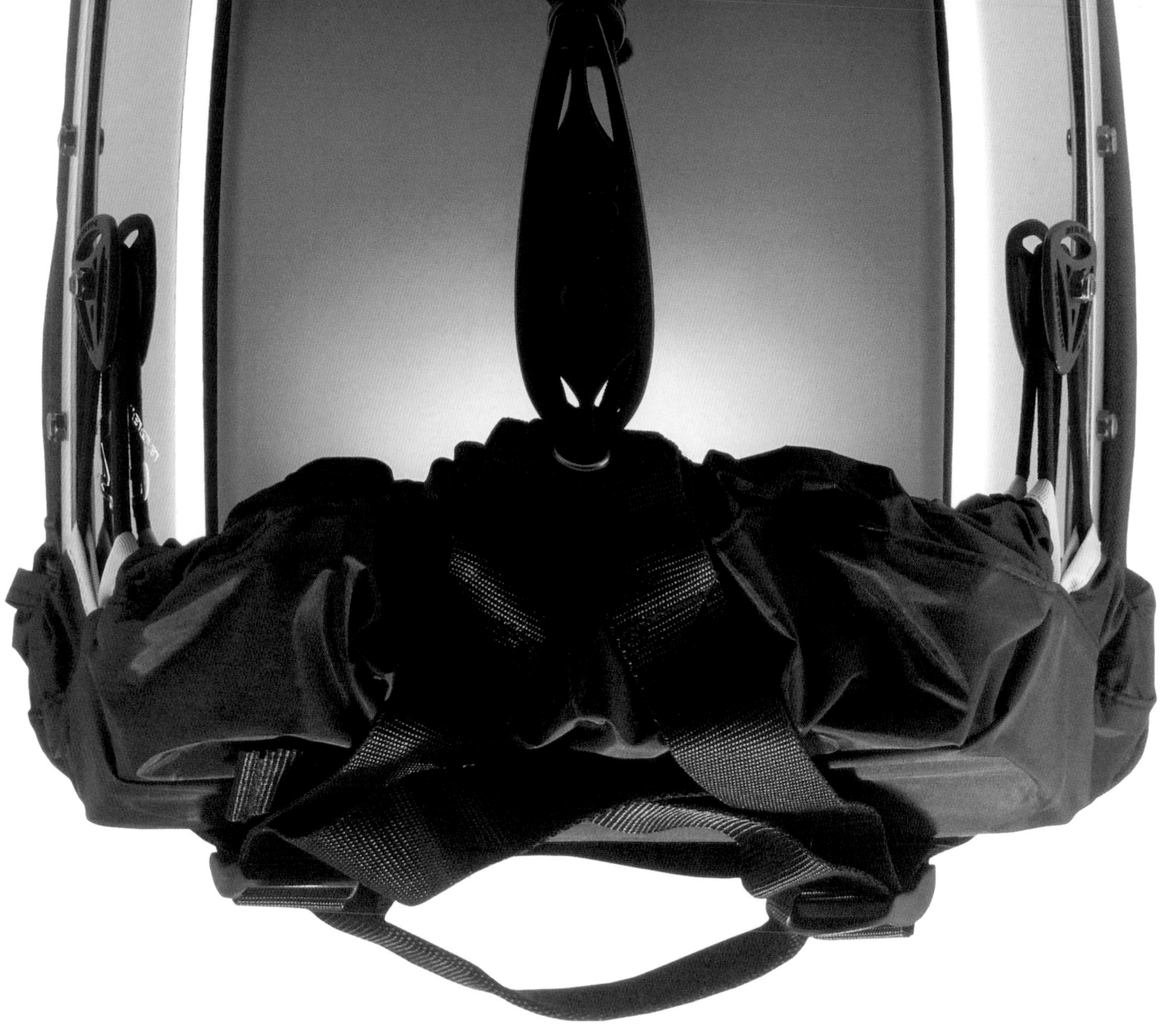

Megalopolis backpack for Boblbee
Jonas Blanking
Lacquered ABS, cross nylon fabric, EVA foam
SWEDEN

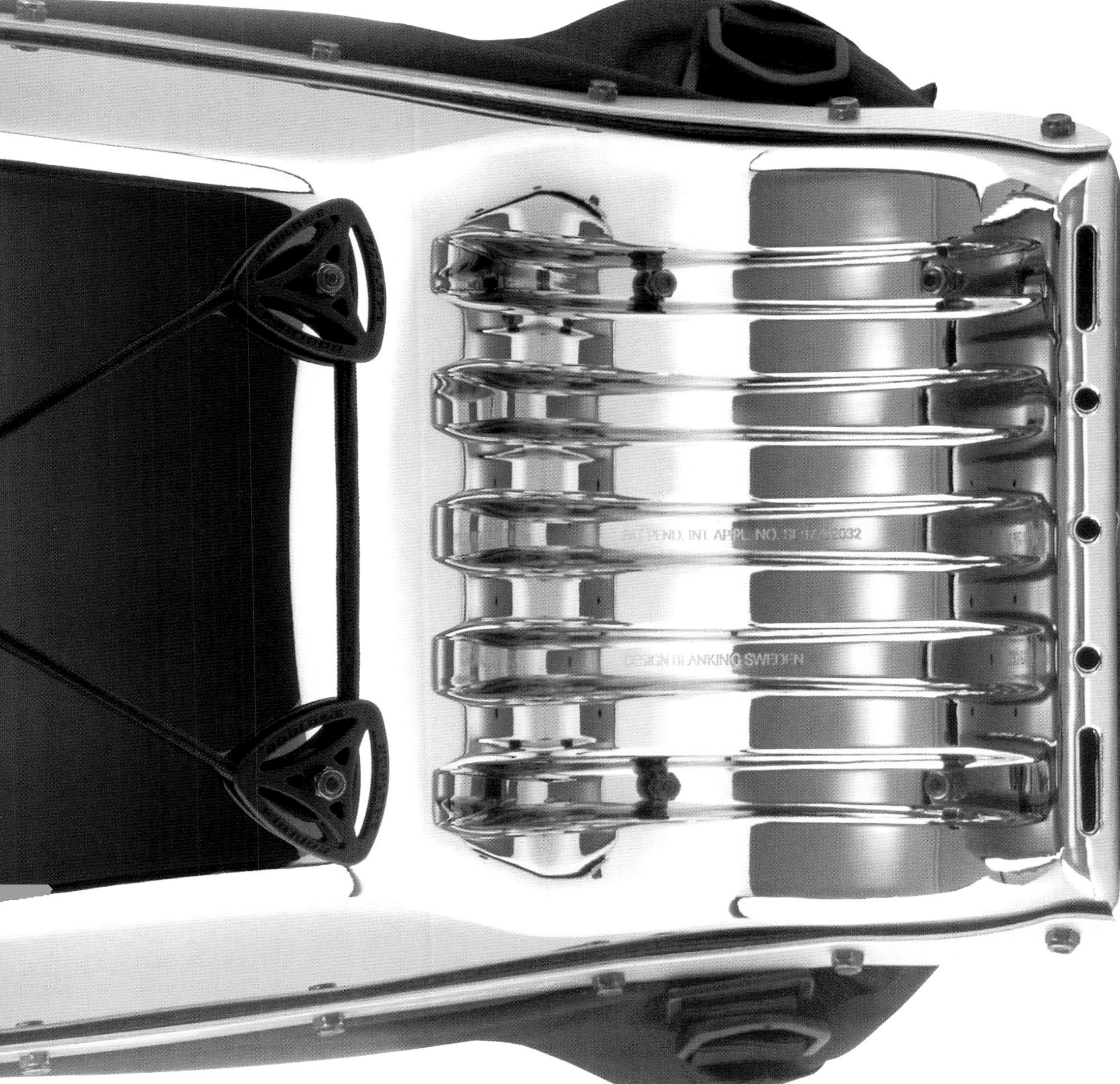
DESIGN BLANKING SWEDEN

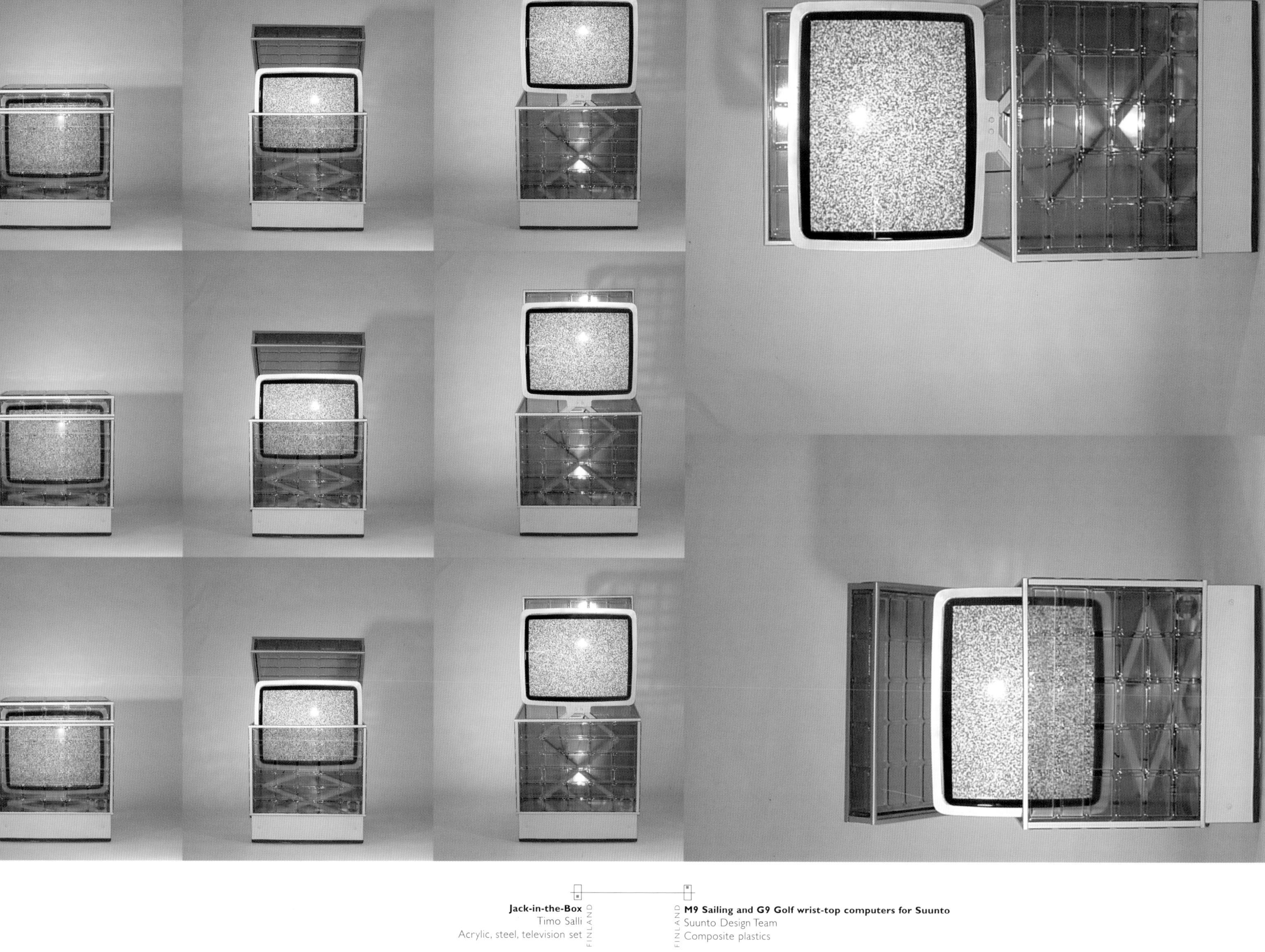

Jack-in-the-Box
Timo Salli
Acrylic, steel, television set
FINLAND

FINLAND
M9 Sailing and G9 Golf wrist-top computers for Suunto
Suunto Design Team
Composite plastics

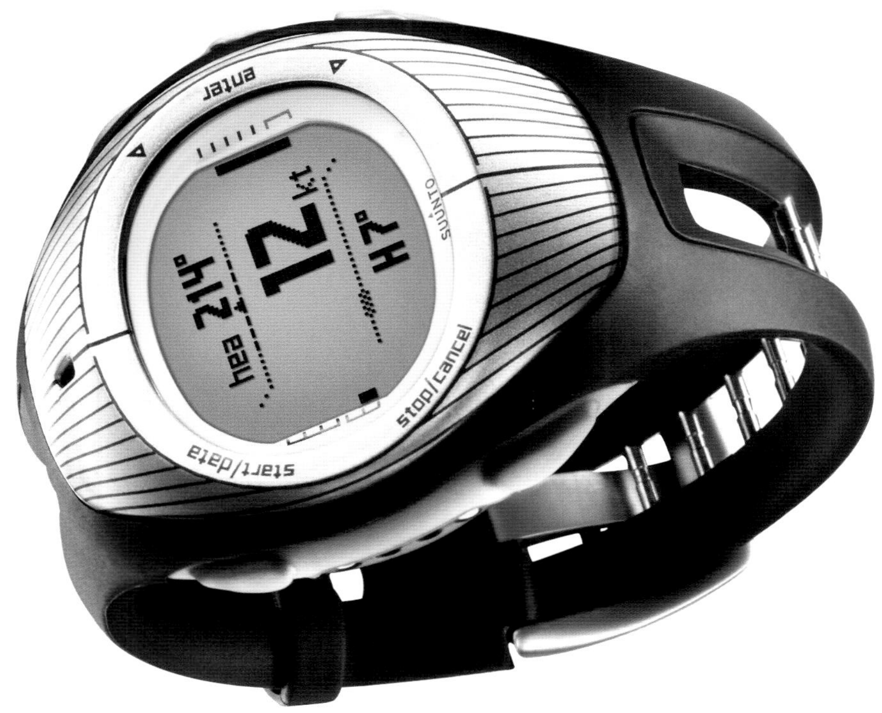
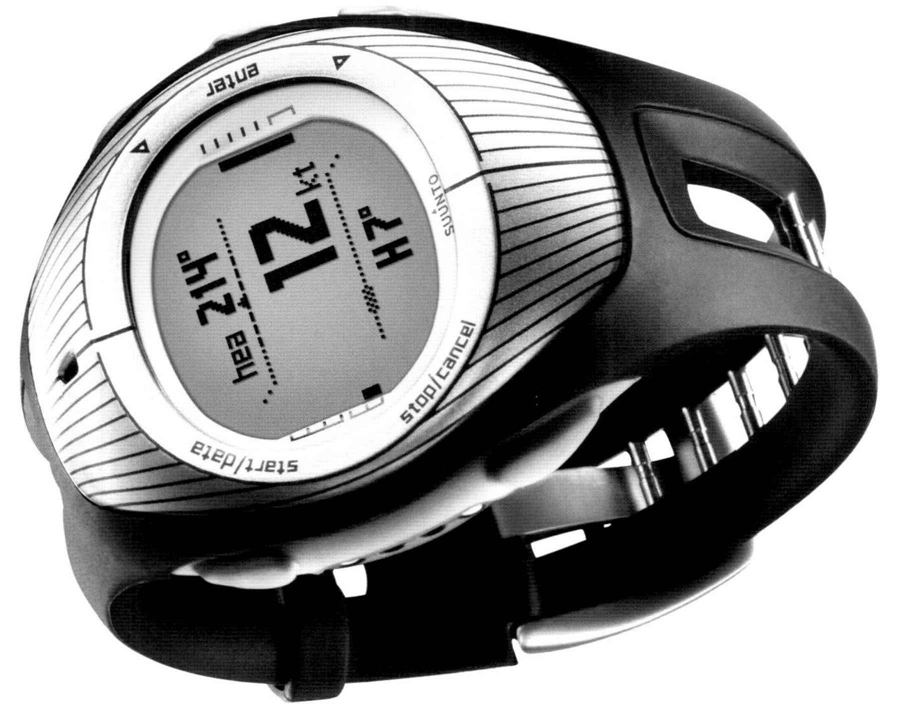
enter
hea 214°
12 kt
H7°
SUUNTO
stop/cancel
start/data

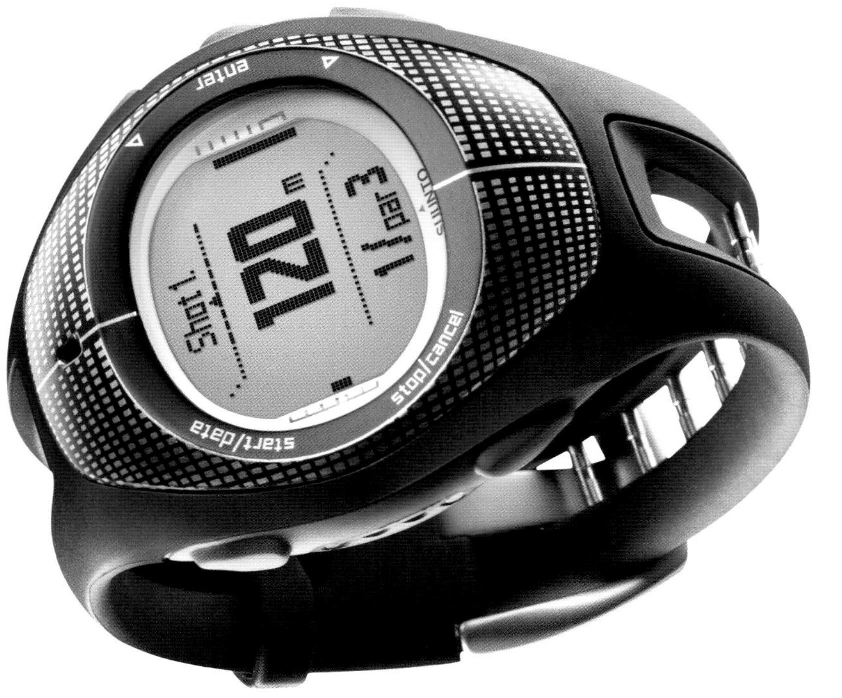
enter
Shot 1.
120 m
1/3
SUUNTO
stop/cancel
start/data

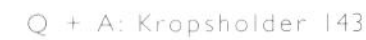

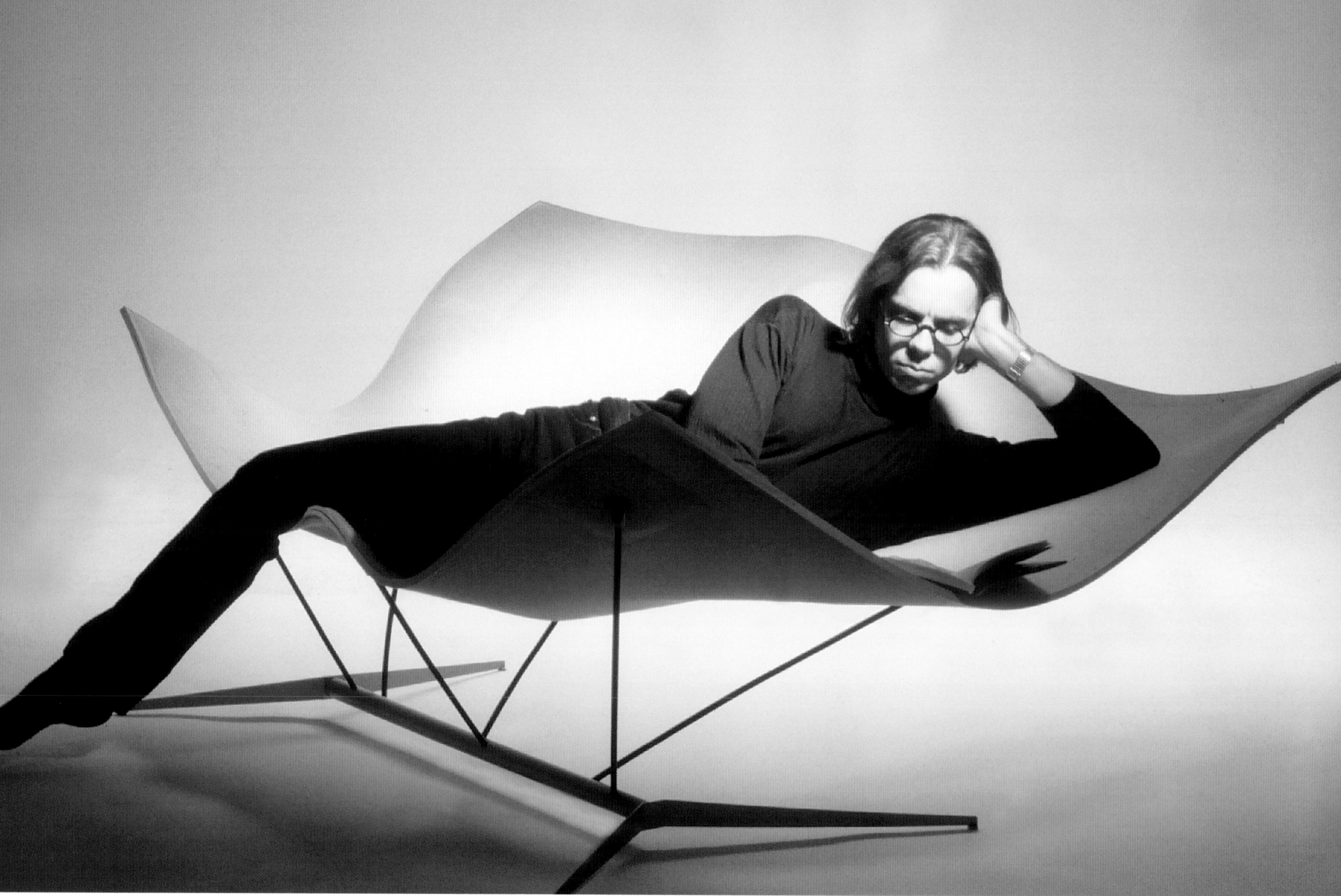

Flying Carpet sofa for Cappellini Spa
Ilkka Suppanen
Steel, felt
FINLAND

DENMARK
Biodegradable spork, bowl, and dinner set for PAPCoRN,
Lene Vad Jensen, Anne Bannick
Bioplastic

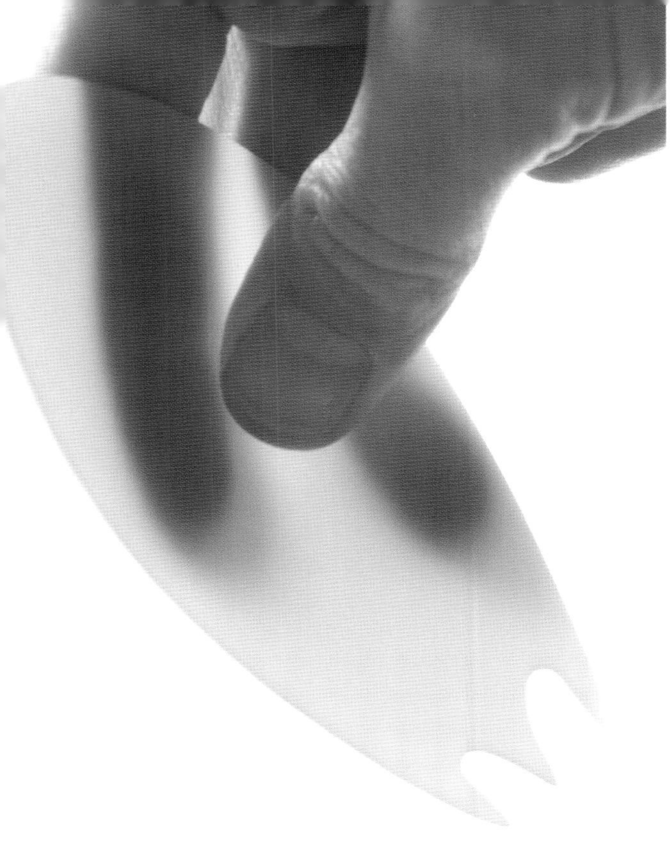

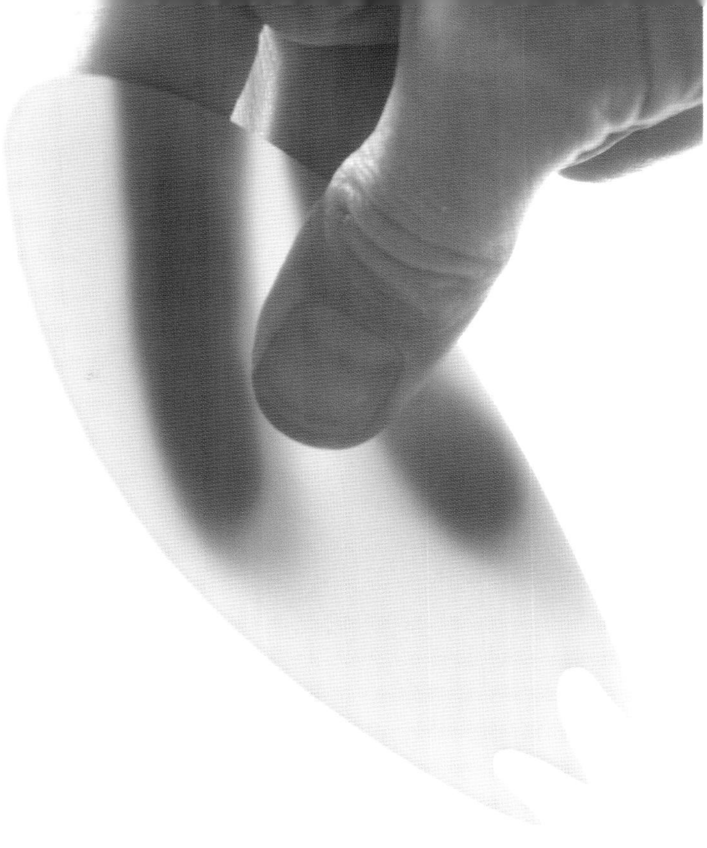

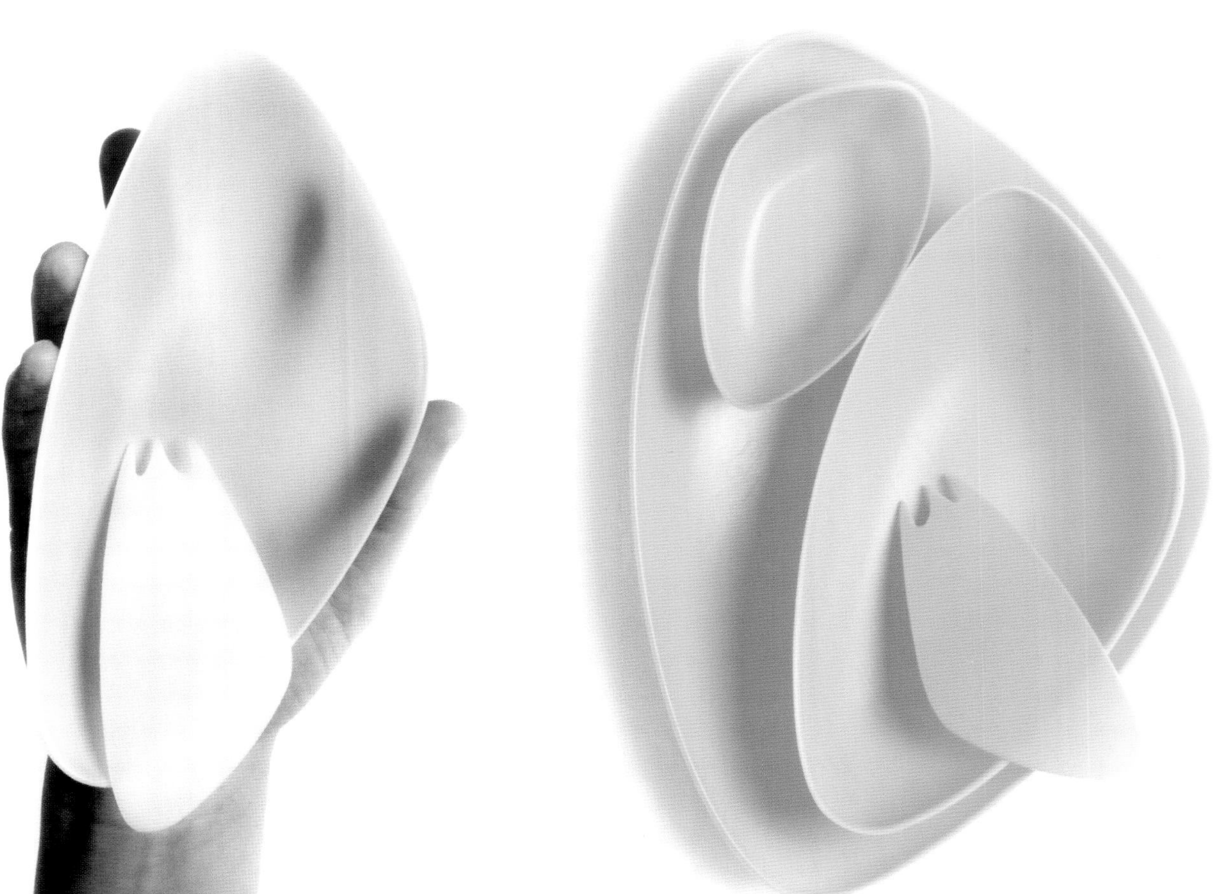

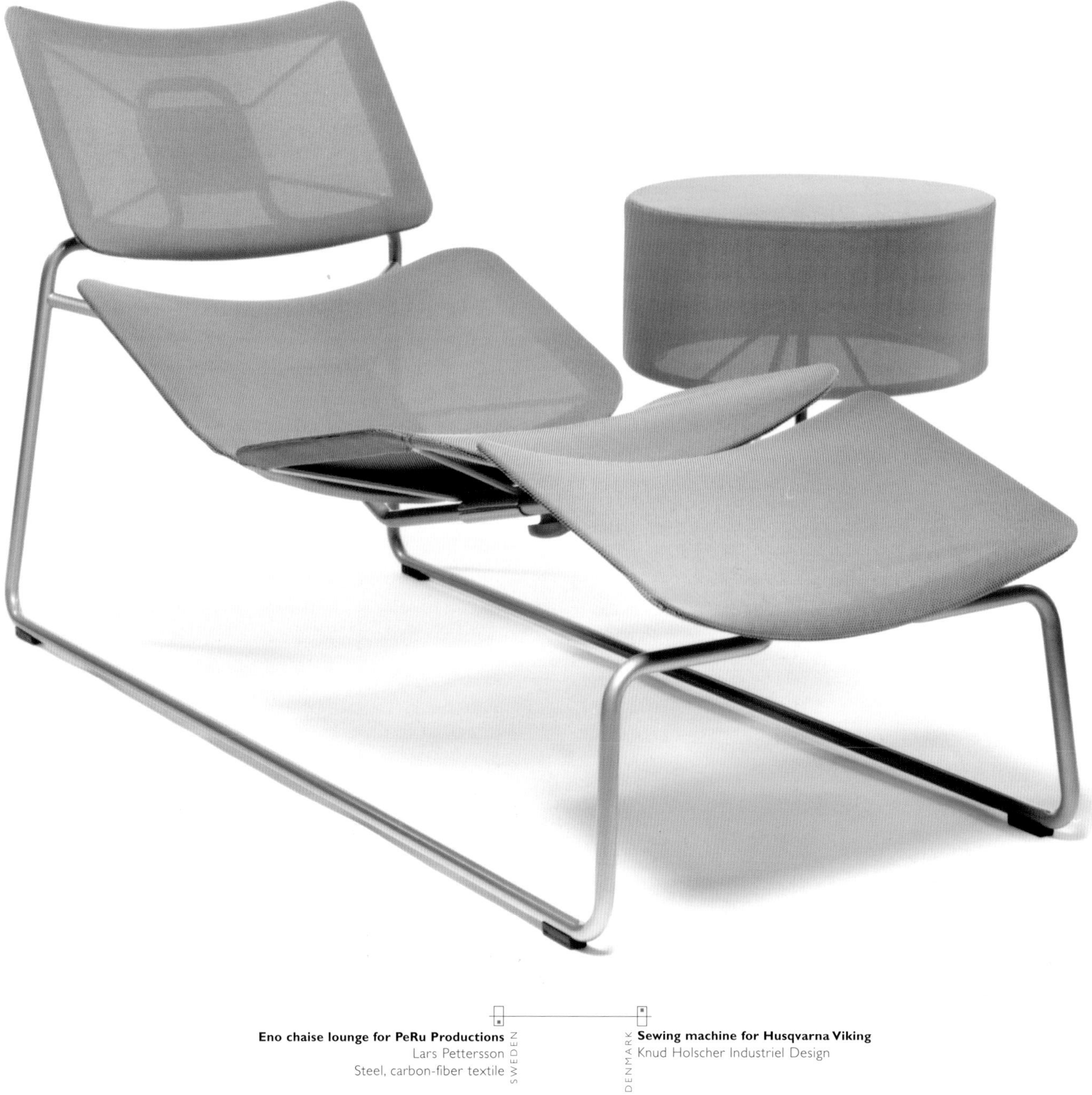

Eno chaise lounge for PeRu Productions
Lars Pettersson
Steel, carbon-fiber textile
SWEDEN

DENMARK
Sewing machine for Husqvarna Viking
Knud Holscher Industriel Design

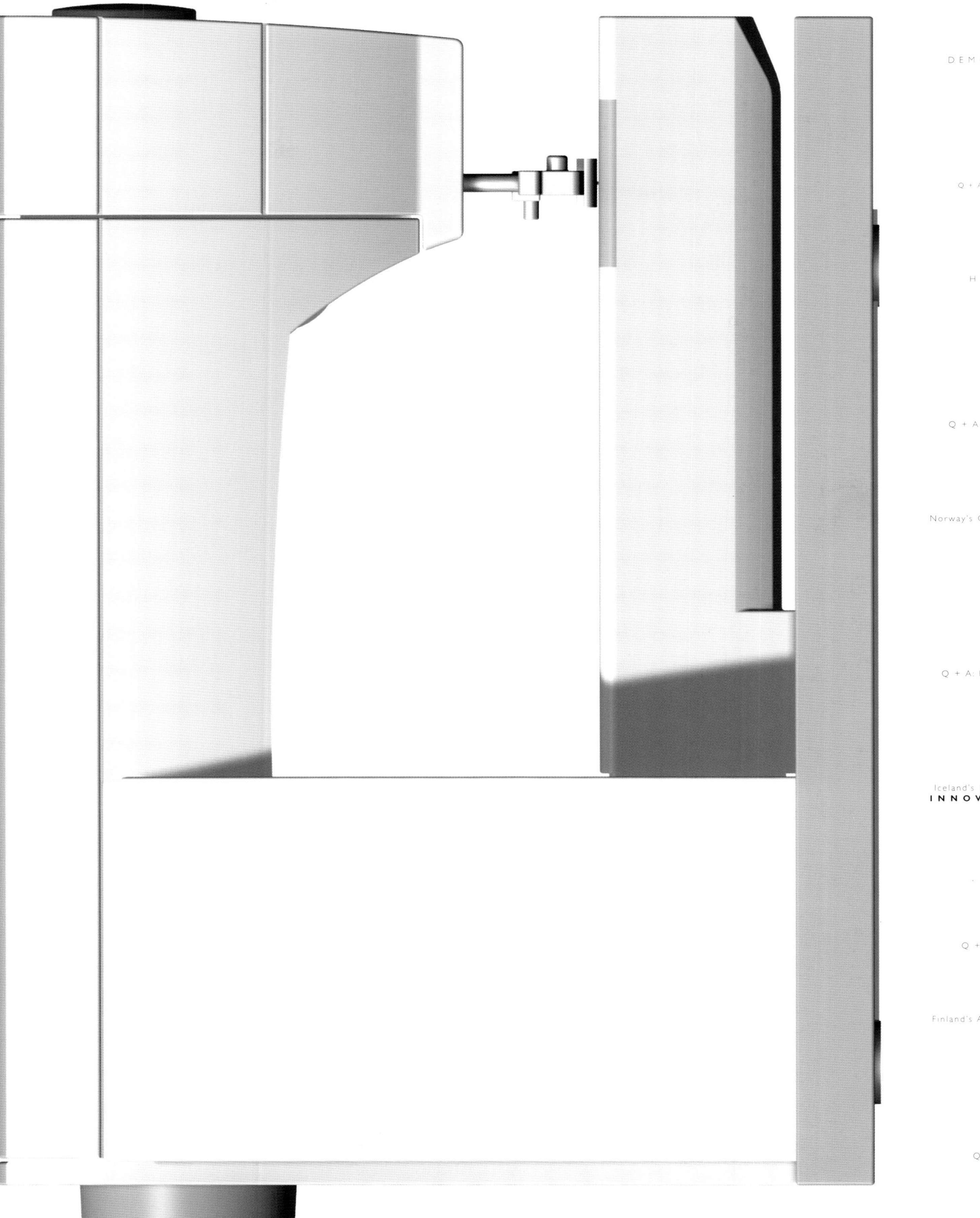

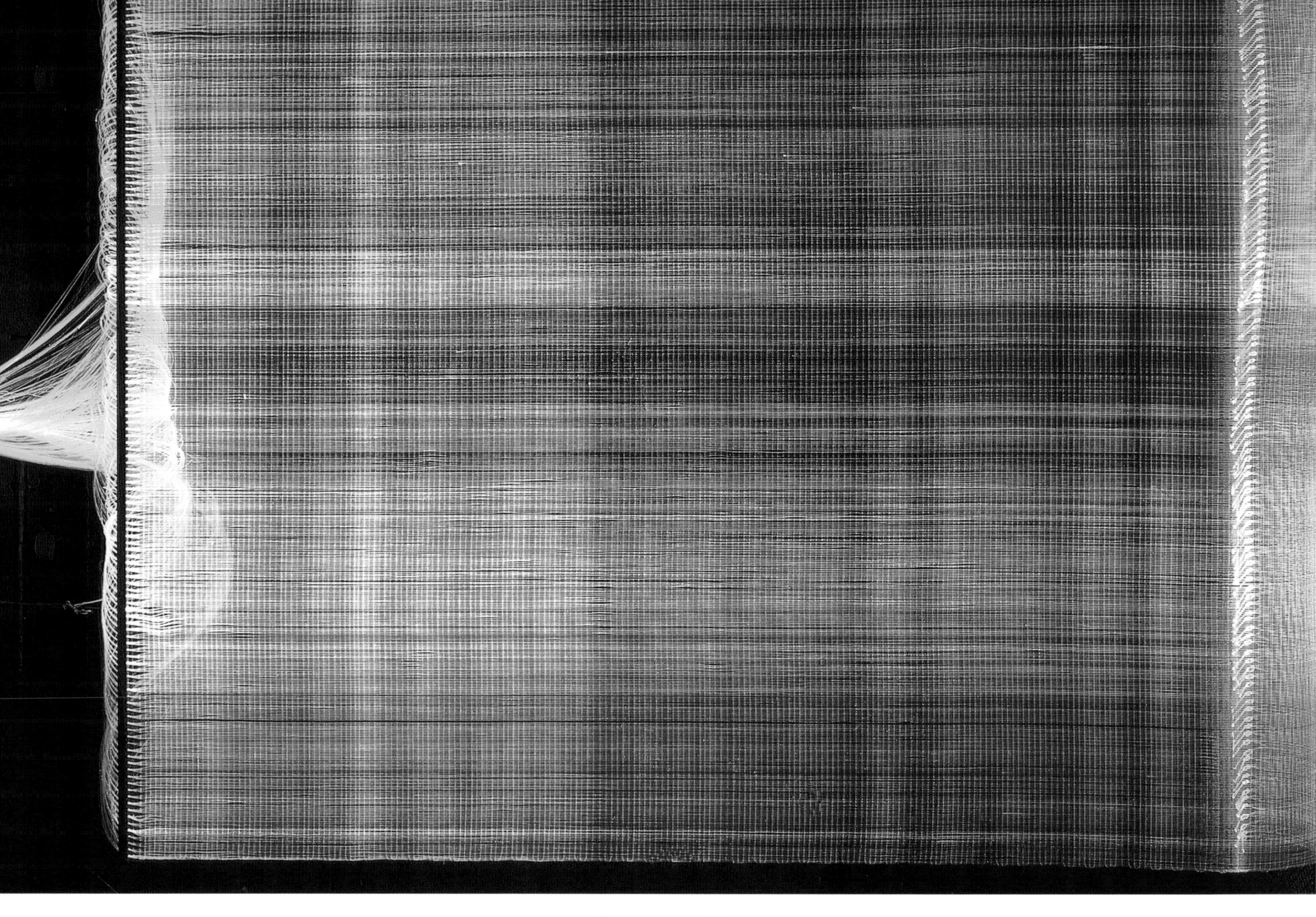

Blue luminescent textile
Astrid Krogh
Woven optical fibers
DENMARK

◄ Slice chair
Mathias Bengtsson
Laser-cut, glued plywood (254 layers)
DENMARK

► Points textile reliefs for Woodnotes
Ritva Puotila
Paper yarn, stainless steel
FINLAND

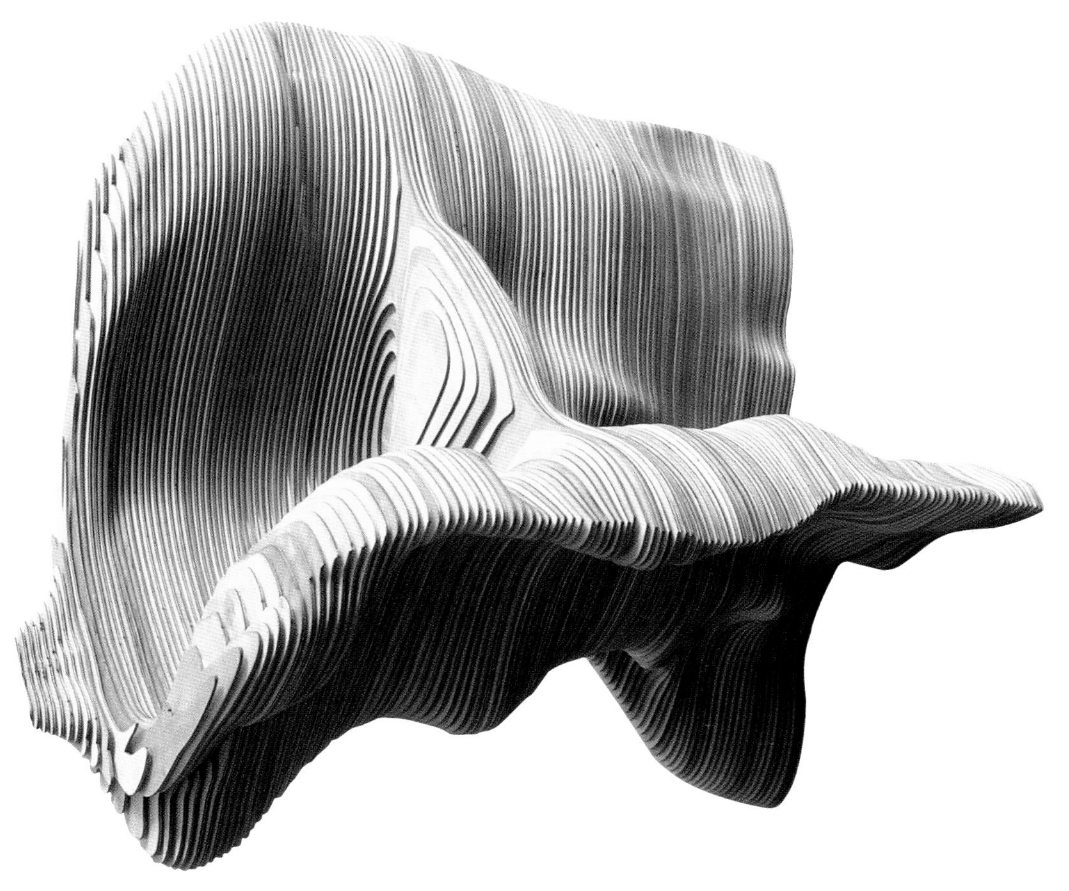

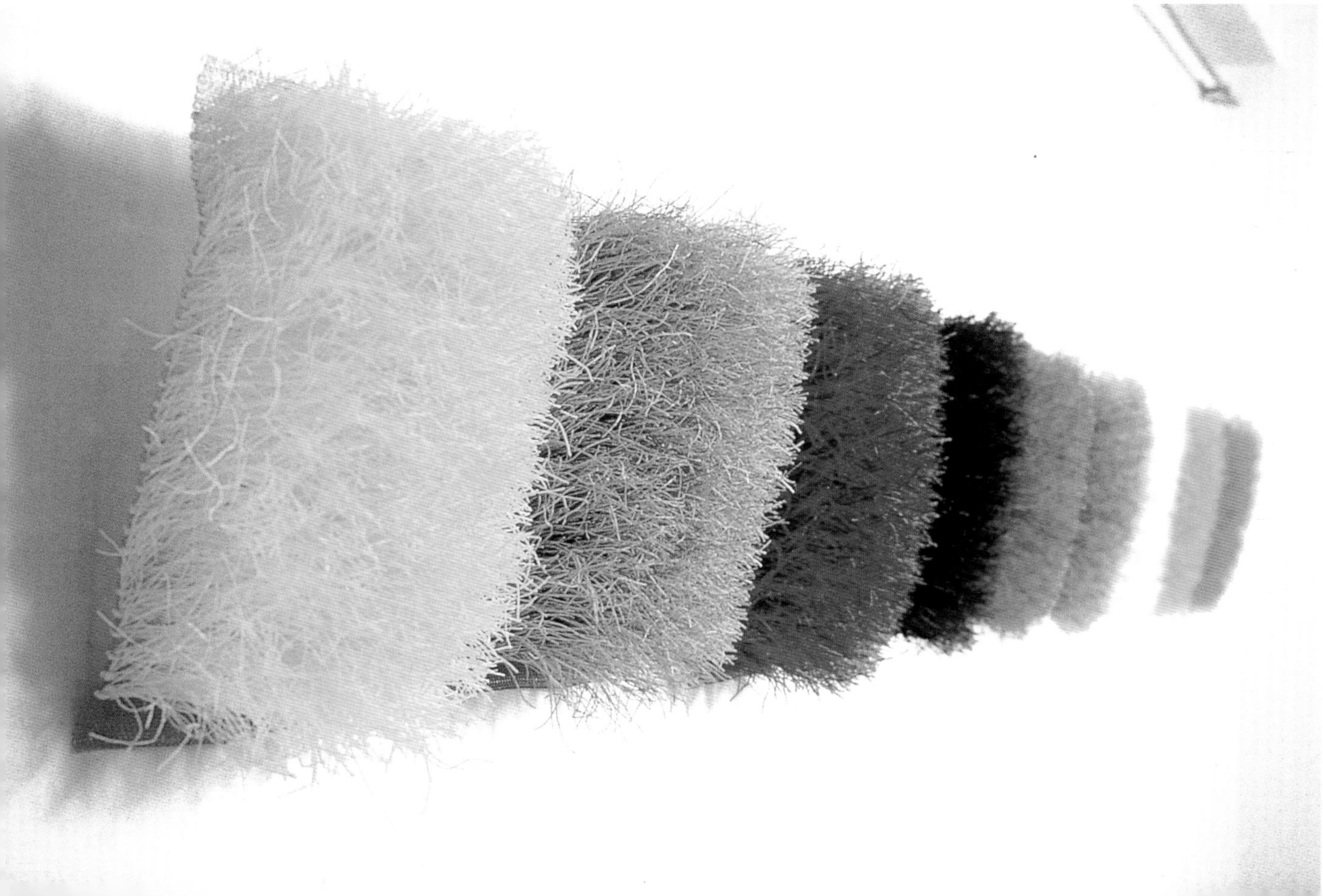

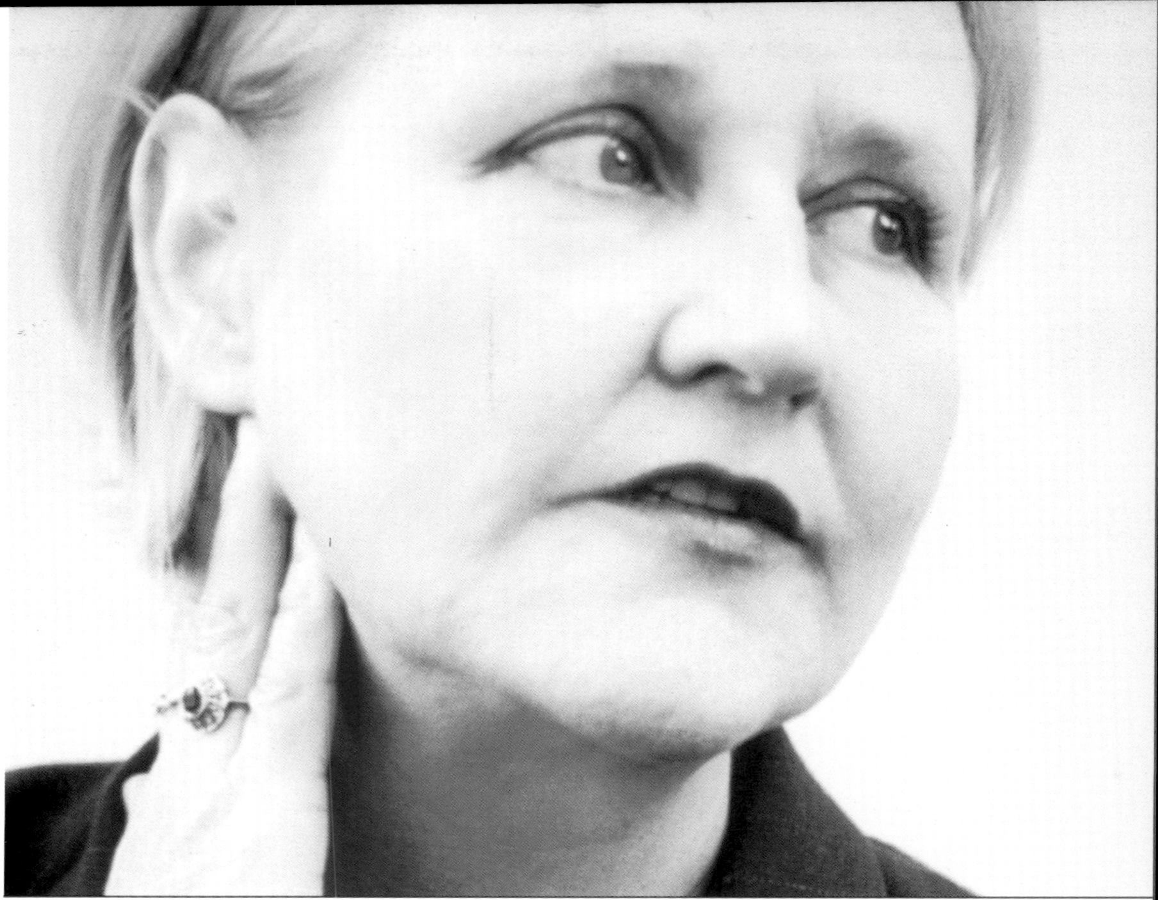

Anna-Maija Ylimaula

Technology and Democracy

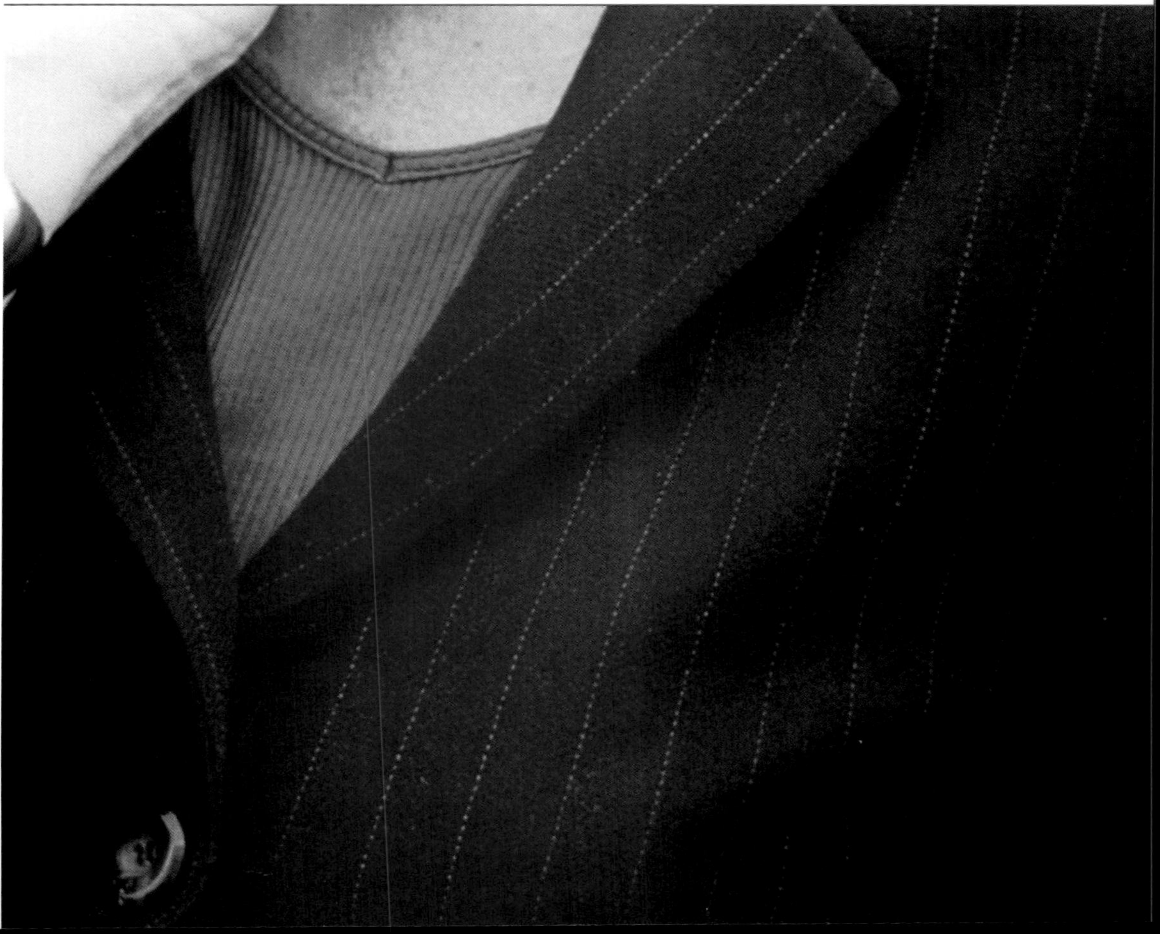

Anna-Maija Ylimaula is an educator, writer, lecturer, and practicing architect. From 998 to 2003, she was director of the Future Home Institute, a doctorate research facility that explores the use of new echnology to improve living conditions. Established in 1996, the Future Home Institute, located in Helsinki at the University f Art and Design, participates in the urban renewal of Arabianranta (the "Arabia Shore" district), an experimental residential nd commercial development neighboring the University. Slated for completion for 2010, Arabianranta serves as a testing round for many of the Future Home Institute's students, who have contributed extensive research and design prototypes o the development. The Institute also works with the City of Helsinki to approve the designs of individual contractors.

Ylimaula, who has often emphasized the value of design in humanizing new tech-ologies, received her master's degree in architecture at the University of Oulu and her doctorate at the Royal Institute of echnology in Stockholm. In addition to her work in design and architecture, she has published seven novels, three plays, nd several short stories in Finland.

Q: TO WHAT FACTORS DO YOU ATTRIBUTE THE BOOM IN INFORMATION TECHNOLOGY (IT) IN FINLAND DURING THE 1990S? **A:** Finland is a remote country; it is far from every place. Technology pre-ented a chance to get out of the periphery and to get connected to the rest of the world. And, for four hundred ears, there has been a good education system in Finland. We have free matriculation at the university level—all ou need is the talent to carry on your studies. So we have one of the most educated populations in the world. lso, since the Soviet export market collapsed in the late '80s, the Finns have had to come up with something of heir own because there was real financial trouble and a very high unemployment rate.

But today, because of technology, we haven't been able to get rid of the high nemployment rate. The more we make things automatic, the fewer jobs there are and the less you need people ehind the counter. It has become a self-serve society. So the technology coin has two sides. **Q: WHAT IS THE ROLE OF THE UNIVERSITY OF ART AND DESIGN'S FUTURE HOME INSTITUTE IN ARABIANRANTA, THE LANDMARK COM-MERCIAL AND RESIDENTIAL DEVELOPMENT THAT INCORPORATES NNOVATIVE TECHNOLOGY?** **A:** The Future Home Institute guarantees a certain quality of rchitecture and design in Arabianranta. For example, the institute has been able to employ around seventy artists, tudents, and professionals, to create environmental artworks. When the contractors are awarded a site, they must levote between 1 and 2 percent of their budget to artistic development. The institute decides what is done with his money—and it is a lot of money. The contractors can't say, "I want a fountain here or a sculpture there." It isn't ust decoration, like hanging a painting. The works must take the historical and natural aspects of the area into account. The piece might address the different seasons, for example. Some artworks can be seen through the show on winter evenings or only in summer during the midnight sun. It is installed so delicately that it may take a while before you notice you are standing in the middle of an artwork. The approach is based on human experience. Many of the artworks are interactive so that the people who live at Arabianranta can make their own final tweaks. For example, within certain parameters, inhabitants could actually alter the look of the glass facade of their flats with a remote control or computer. Q: WHAT ARE THE MAJOR ISSUES THAT CONCERN THE STUDENTS AT THE FUTURE HOME INSTITUTE? A: Many of the Future Home students worry about the future of the planet—clean air, clean water, and so on. For homes, technology can offer so much help with the logistics of how to take care of waste. For example, an item you want to recycle is both glass and metal; you don't know how to sort it. So you simply throw it into a smart box that scans it and puts it in the right place. We need sustainable development. We have to face up to the amount of garbage we produce. Actually, I think every individual should be personally responsible for the amount of waste that they produce. This is the only way that we can solve the problem in the long run.

The logistics of recycling are rather well developed in Scandinavia. And I was surprised by the attitude of the young students of design. They are quite without prejudice when it comes to deciding on what materials to employ in their work. They are eager to use any material available, even if it might seem disgusting to some people. We have one student who has developed a way to make beautiful ceramic tiles from sewage sludge, for example. And the students are eager to understand how waste materials can be treated so that they can be used. Q: FINNISH COMMUNICATIONS COMPANY NOKIA IS INVOLVED IN SEVERAL FUTURE HOME PROJECTS AND WORKS CLOSELY WITH STUDENTS. WHAT ROLE HAS NOKIA PLAYED IN TECHNOLOGY IN FINLAND? A: I think Nokia has had a great influence on Finland and has taught us that companies aren't just competing with each other but can benefit from cooperation with universities and research institutions. Nokia encourages transparency among experts. Traditionally, technology companies have guarded their secrets closely. They now realize they are not losing but gaining expertise by sharing. Q: IN FINLAND, TECHNOLOGY SEEMS TO BE VERY DEMOCRATIC. CAN YOU EXPLAIN WHAT FACTORS COME INTO PLAY IN THIS KIND OF ENVIRONMENT? A: There is a great risk that technology will widen the gap between poor and rich, men and women, unless we do something about it. I don't think the development of new technology should be left only to engineers. Professionals in the human sciences should also play a part in this development. Around the world, there has been this attitude that, in general, technology is for boys and not for girls. Girls take cooking and boys take computer science. But if the children would learn the basics of both we would have more fathers who could cook and wives who could program.

In Finland, there is almost a 50 percent split between the number of men and women working in technology. It is really important even in kindergarten that the teachers don't act as if math were more difficult for girls than it is for boys. That is a taught attitude. We have equal chances to learn. I think girls can bring different qualities to technology, more imagination, and more of a human touch. It would be really sad if only men developed new technology. Q: WHAT IS THE PROPER ATTITUDE FOR DESIGNERS TO HAVE TOWARD NEW TECHNOLOGY? A: I think it would be a missed opportunity not to take advantage of technology. But in design and architecture in particular it has to be aesthetic issues, not technological ones, that remain the most important. Technology has to be the slave, not the master, and it has to remain the slave. We decide what it is used for. Q: IS THERE ANY DOWNSIDE TO THE PROLIFERATION OF DIGITAL TECHNOLOGY? A: One of the disadvantages of technology is that it is combined closely with economics. People pay enormous amounts of money for some technologies. Take mobile phones, for instance. Actually, the sky is quite free. It doesn't cost anything, but there are still these companies that charge you for using it. You could talk, not only for a certain number of minutes, but all day, and it still wouldn't cost anything. Technology is like fresh air—it should be considered a basic human right. It shouldn't be available to only a few people who can afford it. That's why I support open source for computers [a nonproprietary software system]—because people are getting rich on something that belongs to everybody. Q: SOME MIGHT ARGUE THAT THOSE COMPANIES NEED TO COVER THE LARGE COSTS OF DEVELOPING THESE NEW TECHNOLOGIES. A: Their expenses are about 3 percent of what they are charging. The real costs are small. It is just copying a program and selling the rights to the copies. They just managed to establish these pricing systems at a time when people didn't quite understand what was happening. Q: WHAT IS THE ULTIMATE RESPONSIBILITY OF THE DESIGNER WHO WORKS WITH TECHNOLOGY? A: Design without any human dimension allows the creation of many unnecessary things. And there is this great danger of too many things in our lives. I know that people have a desire for totally unnecessary objects that give pleasure simply by their existence. We don't always have to make a concrete or functional object, but people need to be able to mentally or spiritually enjoy what we make. Designers have to work according to their own philosophies and be true to their own understanding of what is good, bad, wrong, or beautiful. It is the designer's individual choice that counts.

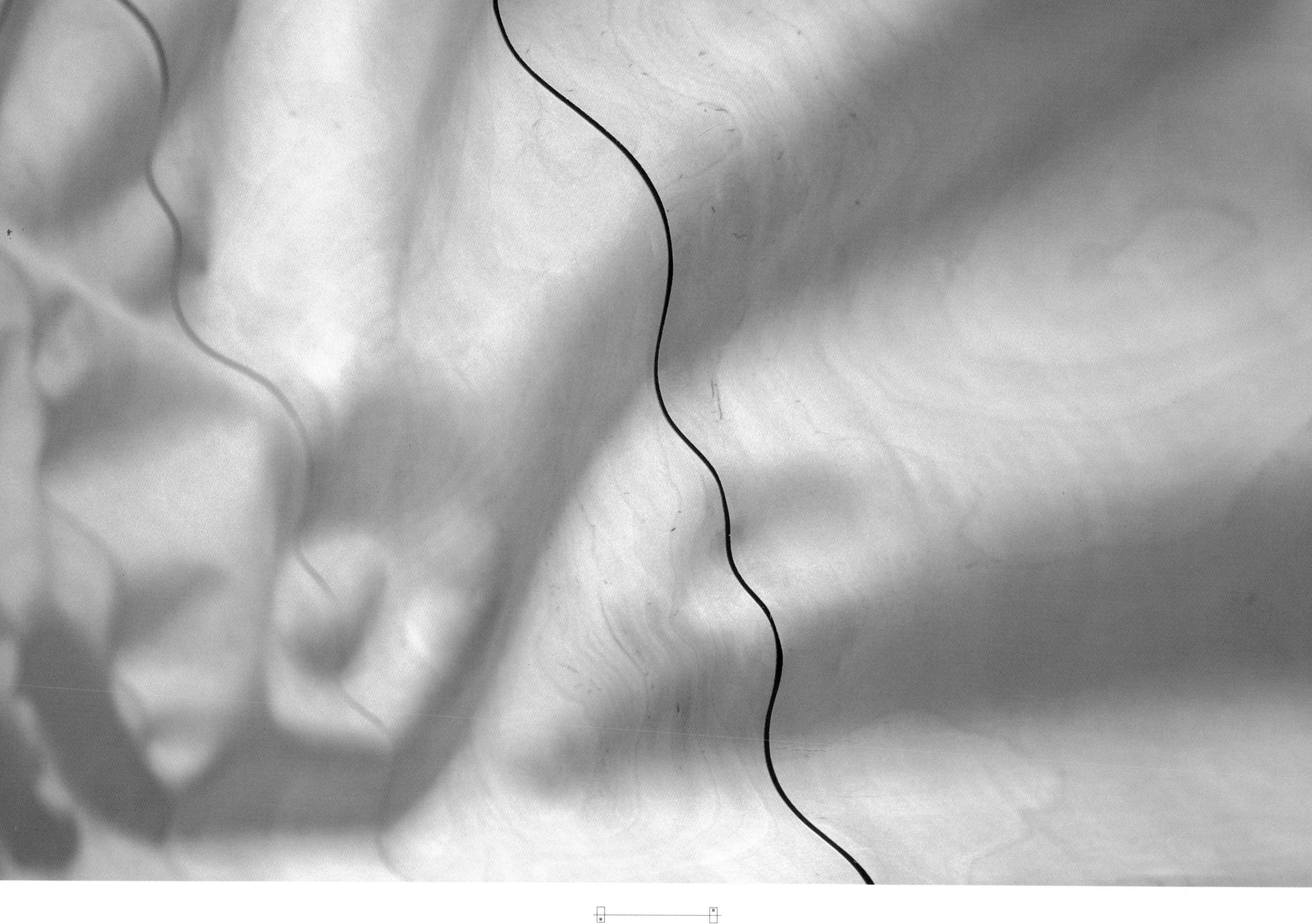

PLY wall surfacing for Showroom Finland
Jouko Kärkkäinen
Birch plywood, solid wood frame
FINLAND

DENMARK
Bionic Smart Jacket
Alex Soza
Laminated microfiber blended with nylon, computer chip

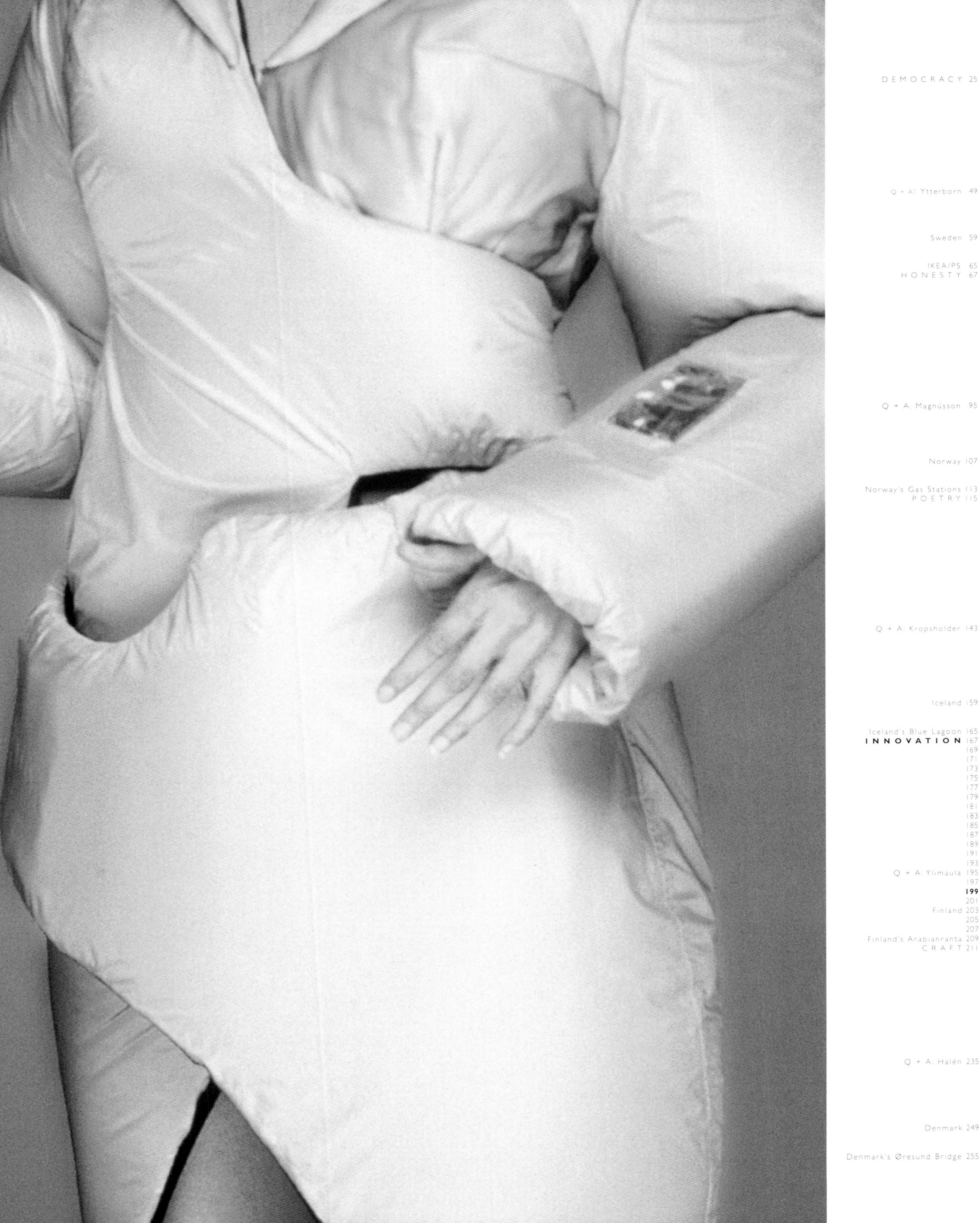

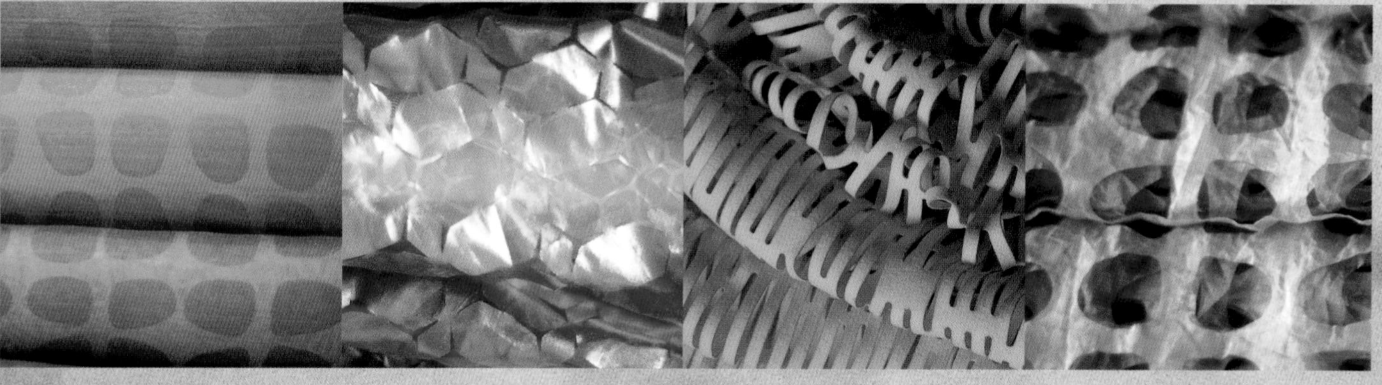

ICELAND
Laser-cut, layered, and laminated textiles
Margrét Adolfsdóttir, Leo Santos-Shaw
Polyester-polyamide, silk, and PVC

DENMARK
Glory light blanket
Anette Hermann
Silicone rubber, fiber optics

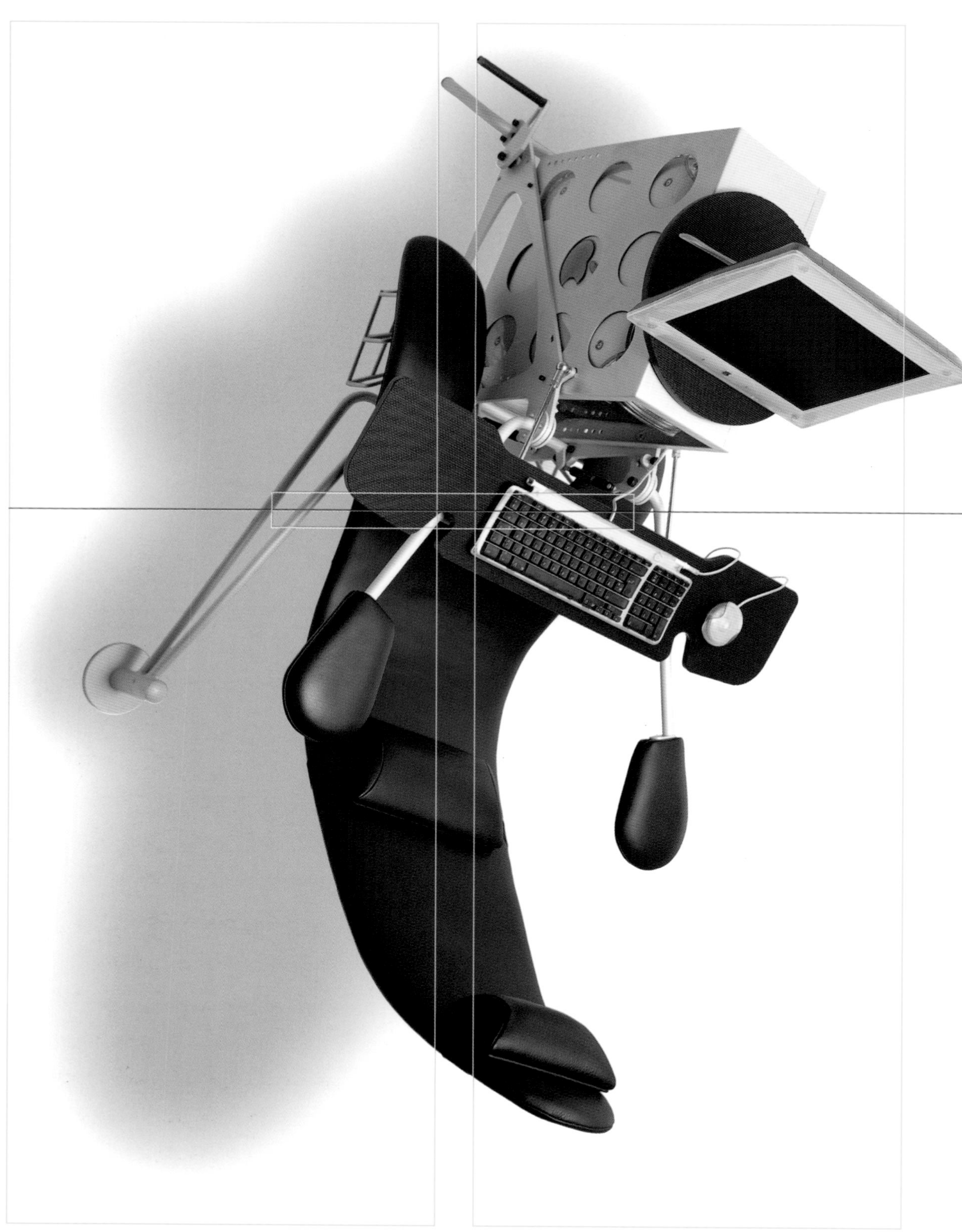

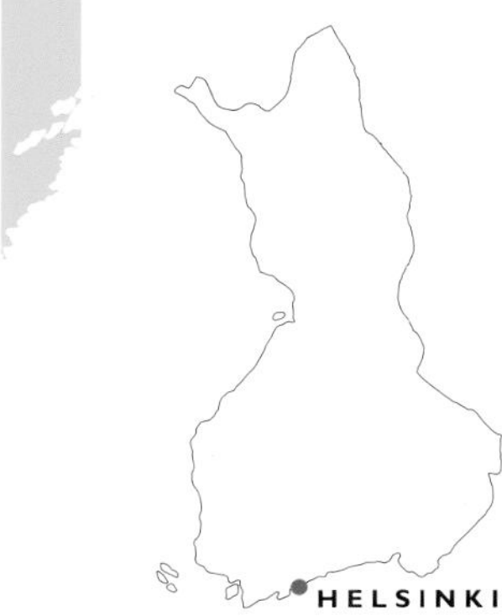

Finland

Smoke no longer billows from the chimney of the Arabia ceramics factory, located in an industrial neighborhood of Helsinki, Finland's capital city. This towering smokestack has long symbolized the heights of Finnish achievement in Modern design. Founded in 1932, the Arabia factory's famous art division embraced mass production to create beautiful everyday goods that—for many around the world—epitomized Scandinavian style. But today, with intense international competition, production has been moved elsewhere, and the old factory buildings have been converted to offices, an outlet store, and classrooms for Helsinki's University of Art and Design.

The most dramatic transformation, however, is still to come. The dilapidated waterfront district that surrounds the old factory is now a bustling construction site. In the shadow of the landmark smokestack grows a new symbol for Finnish design in the twenty-first century—a model town called Arabianranta ("Arabia Shore"), where Finnish design meets information technology. In development for more than a decade, Arabianranta is a massive residential and commercial project that employs the latest innovations in broadband and wireless connectivity, open architecture, and mass customization.

The project, intended to create thousands of new jobs, homes, and workplaces, is a response to the recent devastating economic recession in Finland that began in the late 1980s with the fall of the Soviet Union, a crucial trading partner. The slump was intensified by the worldwide economic slowdown; by the mid-1990s, unemployment in Finland reached nearly 20 percent, and the country itself teetered on the edge of bankruptcy. The Finnish government, educational institutions, and industries banded together, seizing on digital technology as a way to rejuvenate an

Official Name: The Republic of Finland • Year Finland gained independence from Russia: 1917 • Population: Over 5 million • Area: 130,093.6 square miles

outmoded industrial infrastructure that overemphasized raw materials.

Like the Arabia ceramics designers, who looked optimistically to mass production to spark post-war economic recovery, the architects and designers of Arabianranta combine design and technical innovation to provide better living and economic stability. "Design has been used in Finnish history in a very skillful way," says Yrjö Sotamaa, rector of the nearby University of Art and Design and a consultant on Arabianranta development company, "and it is being used again now as Finland is being branded the world's leading information society. Design is the tool for building this new image."

Clearly, the most important player in Finland's economic recovery, often called "the Finnish Miracle," is Nokia: once a struggling conglomerate, Nokia is today one of the world's most successful mobile phone manufacturers, employing an international workforce of more than fifty thousand. "Even after independence a century ago, the Finns seemed destined to supply raw materials to a more dynamic continental Europe. Nokia changed all that," writes G. Pascal Zachary in *Worldlink,* the magazine of the World Economic Forum. A strong emphasis on research and development (Nokia's budget in this area was about $3 billion in 2002) and a savvy understanding of design are two factors critical to the company's success. In the mid-1990s, Nokia broke away from its competition by developing mobile phones whose looks, usability, and technology appealed to consumers. Engaging the long-standing Scandinavian ideal of humanizing technology to meet people's needs, Nokia's phones gave personality to the colorless, unfriendly trappings of mobile communication, featuring enticing graphic displays, individual ring tones, and swappable faceplates.

Nokia's formula for success—a blend of global reach and design preeminence—has set the bar high for Finnish designers. Kari Korkman, who as producer at the company Luovi Productions Ltd. works with designers to develop new marketing ideas and products, says, "Nokia is a hero to the Finns. Through its example, it has encouraged a lot of young Finnish designers to look for innovations."

In particular, Nokia's success energized industrial design, which is now one of the easiest fields for designers to find work. "Our whole industry is a proportionally large part of the Finnish economy right now," says Anna Valtonen, a senior design manager at Nokia. "Not only is there Nokia, which hires a tremendous number of designers, but there are all of our subcontractors and so on." In this vigorous environment, some of the biggest industrial design agencies in Scandinavia, such as Creadesign and E&D Design, rub shoulders with small dynamic firms such as Pentagon, founded in 1996. Employing colorful plastics and a joyful design sensibility, Pentagon tackles projects from breadboxes to high-tech bath and home concepts. Tempering new technology with social responsibility, many of these Finnish firms engage sustainable design, even in the development of heavy machinery and forestry equipment. A "walking" harvester (a machine used by loggers to fell trees) made by a company called Timberjack pads lightly through woodlands on me-

Netsurfer computer divan for Snowcrash (previous spread)
Valvomo
Steel, black leather
FINLAND

(337,030 square kilometers) • Capital: Helsinki • Longest annual period of daylight in northernmost Finland: 73 days • Longest annual period without daylight in northern-

chanical legs, limiting the damage typically caused by wheeled vehicles to the forest floor and wildlife.

The possibilities of new technology have had a dramatic impact on the look and feel of Finnish design in almost every field. One of the most influential furniture design groups of the decade, Snowcrash, made its debut at the Milan Furniture Fair in 1997. Snowcrash's designs, inspired by the speed and flexibility of contemporary living, spoke to a group of young, Internet-savvy, global citizens; one chair, called Netsurfer—a laid-back chaise-longue-meets-computer-work-station—epitomized this vision. "Nomadic" furniture such as Ilkka Suppanen's Flying Carpet sofa and Timo Salli's transparent Tramp chair emphasized portability and lightweight construction. The group rejected wood, the mainstay of traditional Scandinavian design, opting instead for materials with an industrial sensibility such as nylon and steel. After years of trailing the lethargic Soviet market, the Finnish furniture field realized a major international breakthrough with the Milan exhibition, which brought the Snowcrash members prestigious international projects from companies such as Italy's Cappellini.

In the mid-1990s, the success of Snowcrash and high-tech Finnish brands including Nokia, Linux, Suunto, and Polar Electro caught the attention of Finnish policy makers, who now viewed new technology as the way out of the agonizing recession. In June 1999, Finland established Design 2005!, a comprehensive national design policy intended to promote innovation, increase exports, and encourage dialogue among industry, education, and business. Tekes, the National Technology Agency, has underwritten some of the policy's most concrete results, funding hundreds of diverse industrial design projects.

Another part of the Design 2005! initiative is the ARMI project (an acronym from the Finnish terms for architecture, construction, design, and information), a high-profile architectural showcase and public information center in downtown Helsinki under development with the Finnish group JKMM Architects. ARMI, located next to an office building by the famed Finnish architect Alvar Aalto, will bring the major players in the design community under one roof, including the Museum of Finnish Architecture, Design Forum Finland, and the City of Helsinki's Planning Department, all currently scattered across the city.

Alongside business and government, Finnish educational institutions have turned their attention to research, pursuing creative solutions using methods inspired by science. The Future Home Institute, a doctoral research facility at the University of Art and Design, contributed several projects to the Arabianranta development, such as innovative bath and kitchen concepts, new waste management techniques, and sustainable product designs. Graduate students conduct detailed material research even in traditional categories such as furniture and handicraft. For example, under the auspices of the Future Home Institute, Sari Anttonen explored the properties of recycled plastic, a material often criticized for its inconsistency, in furniture design. Other Future Home projects include Petri Vainio's artful application of digital technology to plywood compression and Mirja Niemelä's glittering ceramic sinks, bowls, and tiles made from industrial waste products. Occasionally, this research even results

most Finland: 51 days • Official languages: Finnish and Swedish (Minority languages include Russian and the Lapp language Sami.) • Number of islands: 179,584 • Number of lakes:

in new business ventures, such as a factory that produces architectural tiles from recycled glass. "In some countries, students work in companies to learn how they are managed and how they operate," says the university's Sotamaa. "We have a different idea. We encourage students to produce new knowledge through research that can have an impact on how companies are developed and what they do."

The massive restructuring of Finnish industry in the 1990s has inspired the design community, and a clutch of design groups and small businesses have opened since 1998. "The long period of bilateral trade with the Soviet Union did not favor small innovative companies," says Korkman, who founded his own venture, Design Partners, a design industry networking organization, in 1999. "It was all about mass production and long production lines. Now we need to build up new markets by founding companies that can develop and market [innovative and international] products and concepts." Two such groups are attracting attention: the collective Ocean North, whose cool, theory-driven designs range from serving dishes to sports stadiums, and the furniture design group IMU, founded in 2002, which goes by the self-appointed moniker of "Finland's National Design Team." New design-driven small businesses include the fashion company Ivana Helsinki, founded in 1999 by the brother-sister team of Pirjo and Paola Ivana Suhonen. The Ivana Helsinki clothing line adorned with humorous Eastern-Bloc inspired patterns and nostalgic 1970s touches, celebrates Finland's Russian past. Also opened in 1999, the ceramics company Tonfisk crafts sumptuous yet functional tableware more in the vein of traditional Scandinavian design using cork, wood, and other natural materials.

For its part, the University of Art and Design has supported, with its expertise and with funding, recent graduates attempting to start small businesses. In 2003, the school also sponsored its first-ever student field trip to the Milan Furniture Fair led by professor, and ex-Snowcrasher, Timo Salli. Dubbing the venture "Operation Saunabus," eight students converted an old bus into a sauna and drove to the fair. The students exhibited the bus, along with several of their own design items—a portable grill, fold-out chairs, electroluminescent towels, beer glasses, and pothole-proof vodka cups—making for a creative, if untraditional, sauna experience. The aim of the trip, according to Salli, was to encourage the students to look outside of Finland for inspiration and even to consider working abroad. "Everybody in Finland is big on this idea now—internationalization—but I do think we need it," says Salli. "If we get more young Finnish designers out there, after a while they will come back with new ideas and the courage to build up new companies." Even with his international focus, Salli views contemporary Finnish design as a bridge between two worlds. "It wasn't so long ago that Finland was quite isolated," he notes. "Today, we have one leg in globalization and the other leg still back there somewhere in the forest."

FINLAND
MoRay dining dish
Tuuli Sotamaa, Kivi Sotamaa
Composite ceramics

FINLAND
Tramp easy chair for Cappellini
Timo Salli
Steel, nylon net

187,888 • Percentage of land covered in forest: 70 (the highest percentage in the world) • Average number of Finnish films produced annually: 12

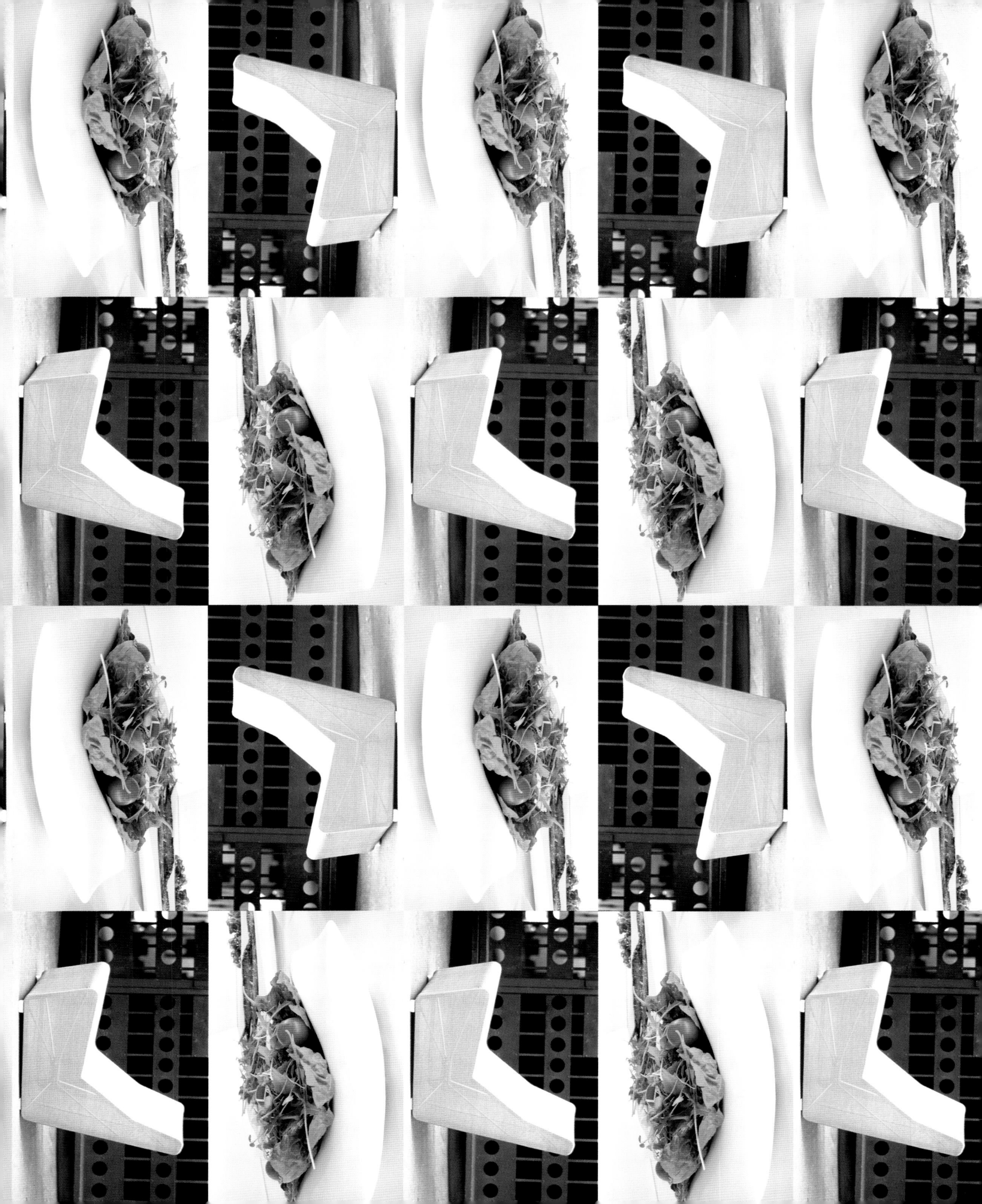

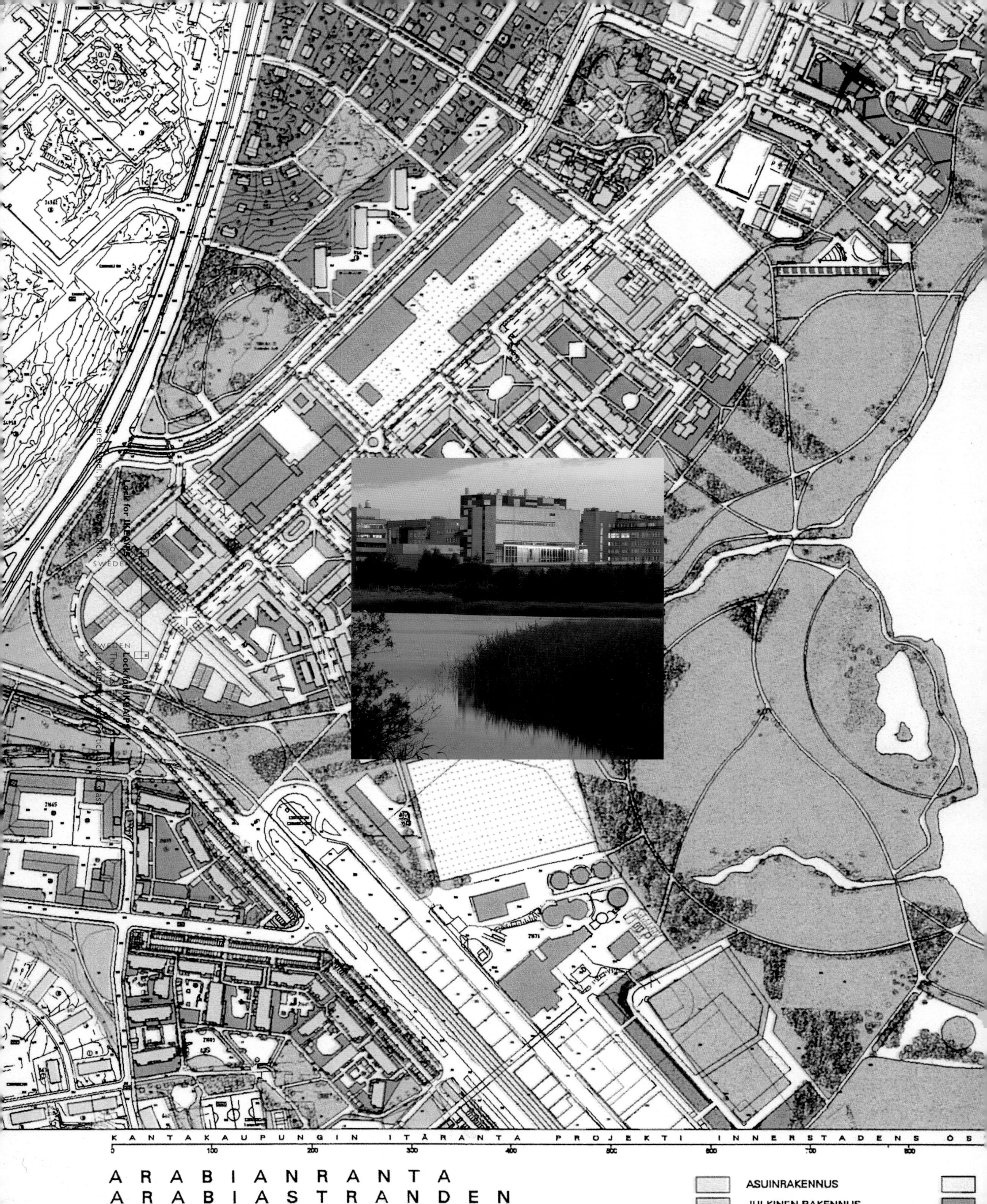
KANTAKAUPUNGIN ITÄRANTA PROJEKTI INNERSTADENS ÖS
0
100
200
300
400
500
600
700
800
ARABIANRANTA
ARABIASTRANDEN
ASUINRAKENNUS
JULKINEN RAKENNUS

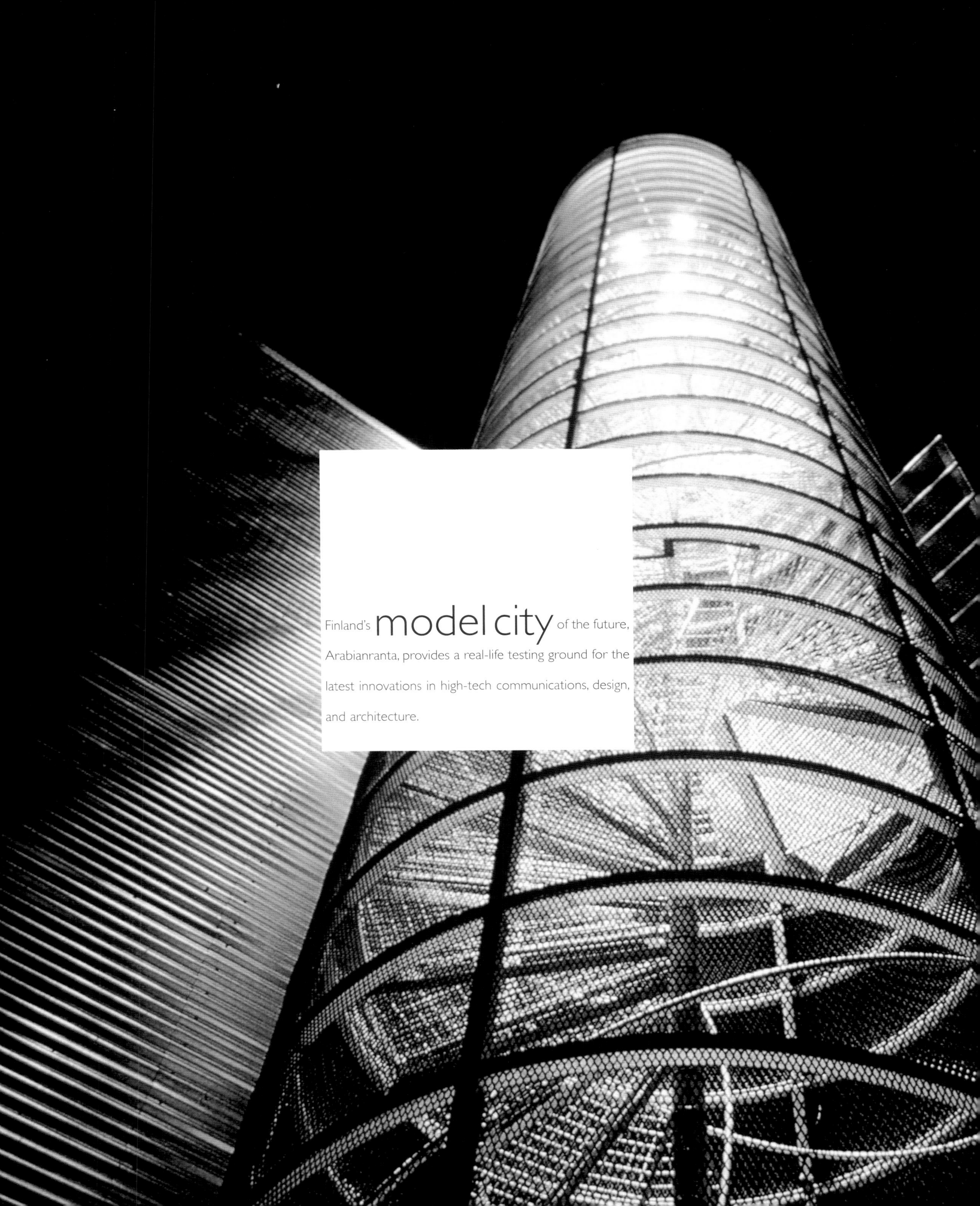

Finland's **model city** of the future, Arabianranta, provides a real-life testing ground for the latest innovations in high-tech communications, design, and architecture.

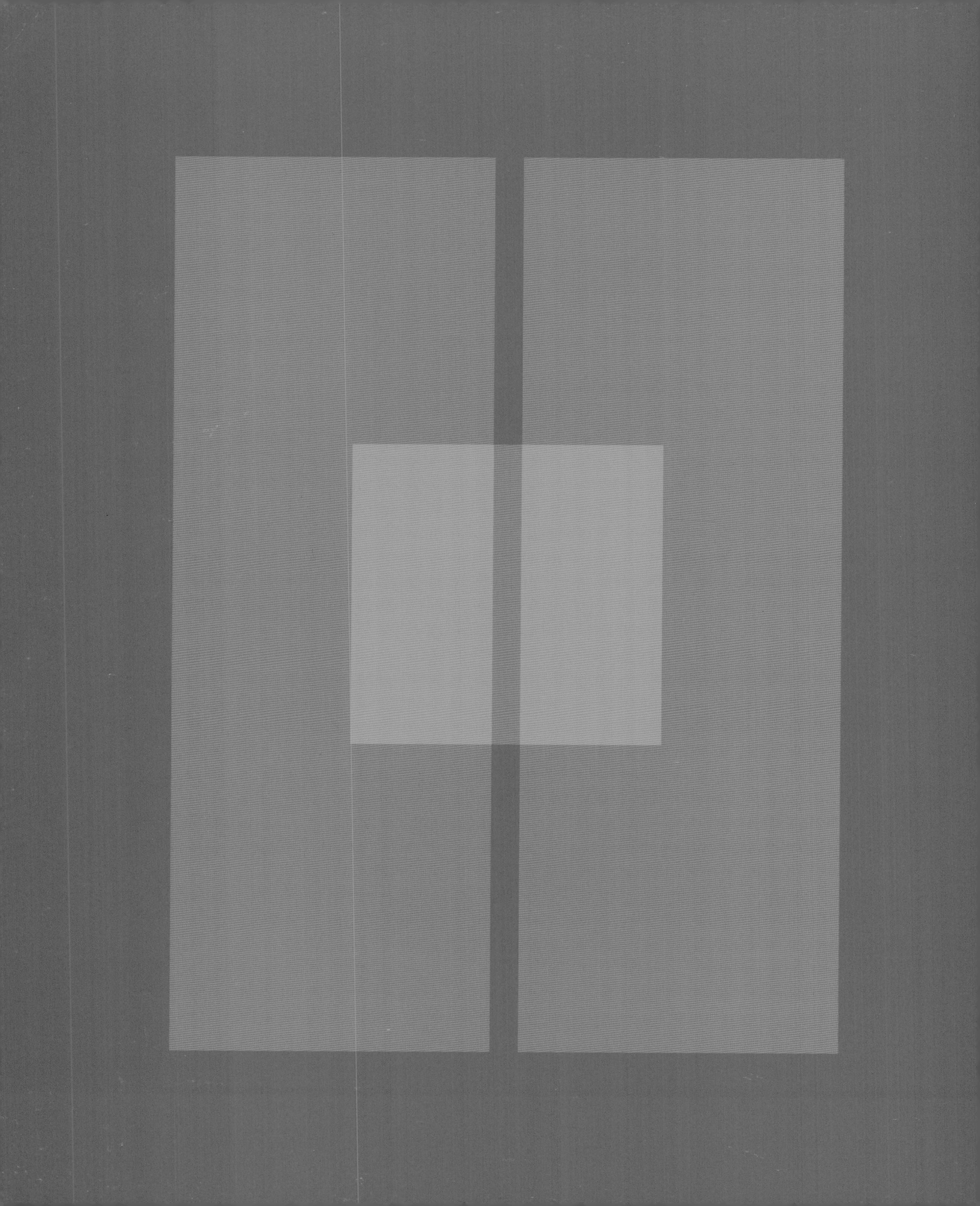

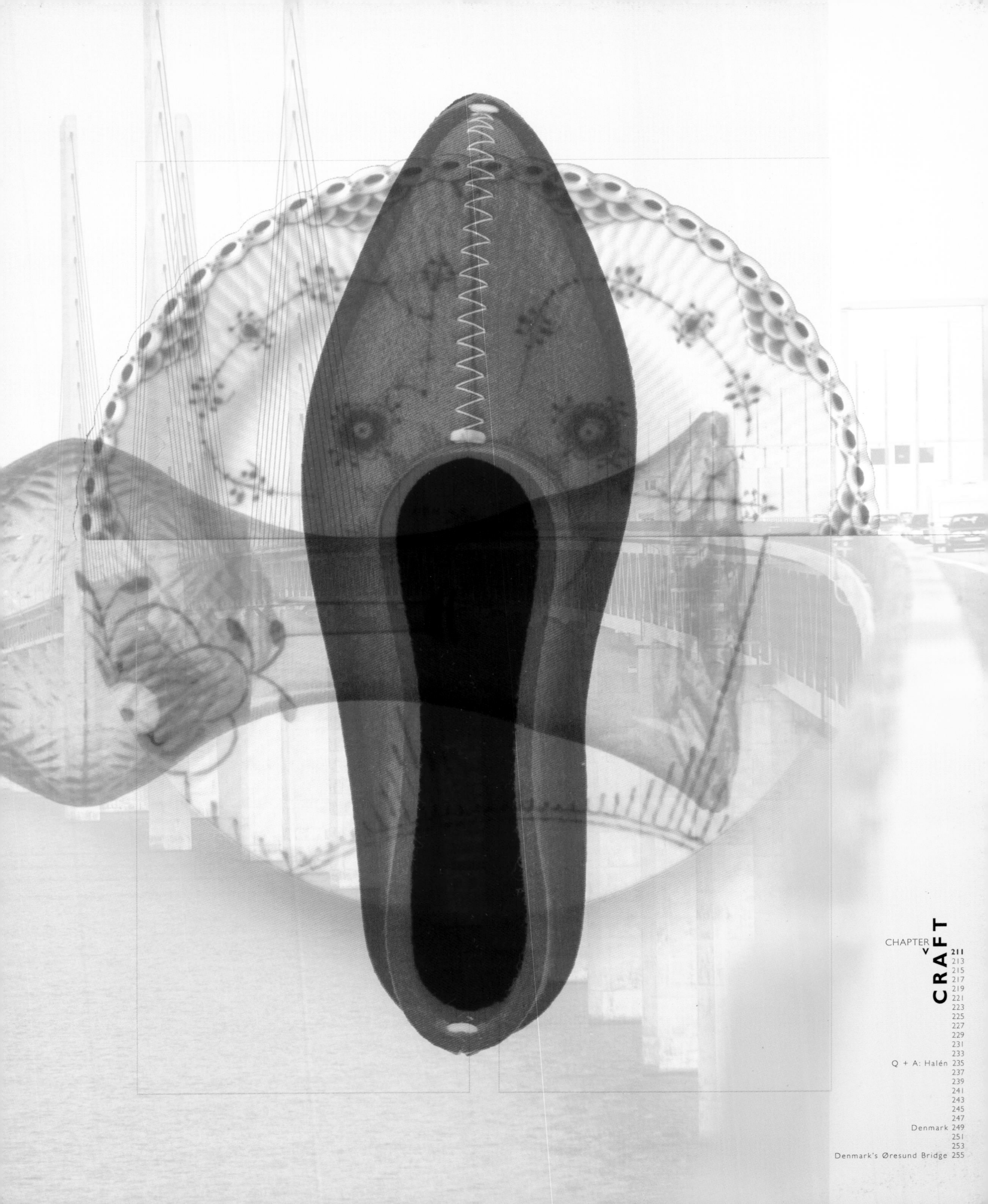

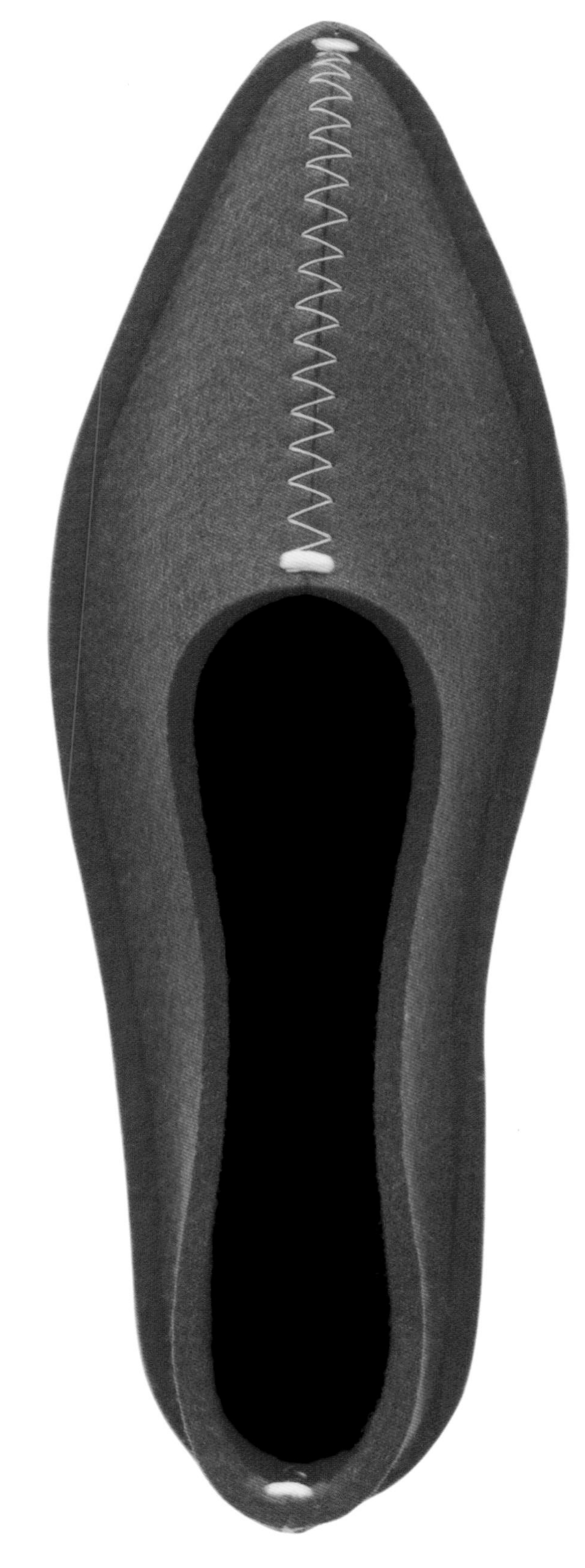

Unisex slipper
Pia Wallén
Felted wool, rubber-dot sole
SWEDEN

CRAFT

"Italian design is highly intellectual, being about this measurement or that radius. However, almost all the great Scandinavian designers were craftsmen. They sanded wood with a file and worked their way through the material until it felt just about right."

—Danish designer Erik Magnussen (from *Fokus* magazine)

The feel of a material resonates deeply with Scandinavian designers. This resonance also sets them apart, for Scandinavian design has long been defined by its close association to craft—a method of production based on manual labor and material knowledge. Industrialization came later to Scandinavia than to other parts of the Western world, and so local craft traditions were preserved well into the twentieth century. Although early Scandinavian reformers heralded the capability of new technology to mass-produce affordable, functional objects, they also viewed craft technique as essential to retaining high quality within the manufacturing environment. However, since the 1960s, international competition, mergers and acquisitions, and the outsourcing of local labor have eroded the traditional Scandinavian bond between art and industry. In response to the impersonal nature of globalization, contemporary Scandinavian designers are now renewing craft conventions such as making objects by hand and doing limited production runs. New approaches hardly mimic old techniques, but they reaffirm an intimate connection to the past.

In Scandinavia, the separation of craft and design has always been blurry; during the mid-twentieth century, this overlap gave Scandinavian products their unique character. "Classic Modern Scandinavian furniture designers like Hans Wegner were actually craftsmen," says Birgitte Jahn, head of the design organization Danish Crafts. "They made their furniture with their hands, and they knew how to treat and finish wood themselves." Many of these Danish masters also maintained close relationships to local woodworkers, and prominent pairings of designers and craftsmen—Finn Juhl and Niels Vodder, Ole Wanscher and A. J. Iversen—shaped many now-classic Modern pieces. Today, though hard hit by international competition, traditional Scandinavian industries such as furniture, glass, porcelain, and textiles preserve the careful balance of craft technique and industrial production. Glass concerns such as Finland's Iittala and Sweden's Orrefors have blowing rooms essentially identical to what they were a hundred years ago. Manual expertise such as cutting, engraving, and mold making is passed down from master to apprentice; this knowledge informs a new glass piece as much as its design does. While in-house designers at these glass-manufacturing companies create stemware for mass production, they just as easily put their talents toward limited-edition pieces, such as those featured in Iittala's Pro Arabia Art **(B)** see **p 224** collection. At the Danish company Royal Copenhagen, the art of hand painting the Blue Fluted service, the company's original porcelain pattern, has remained virtually unchanged since the pattern was introduced more than two hundred years

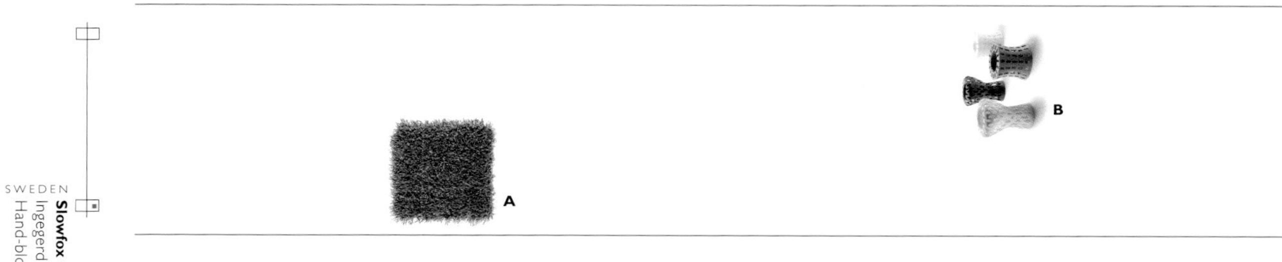

SWEDEN
Slowfox vase for Orrefors
Ingegerd Råman
Hand-blown glass

ago. A modest plate requires more than one thousand brush strokes. The same craftperson begins and completes each piece and signs his or her initials next to the Royal Copenhagen factory mark.

Designers who gain distinction within these fields employ craft techniques to deliver contemporary messages. Gunilla Lagerhem Ullberg meets this challenge as head designer of Kasthall, a high-end Swedish textile manufacturer founded in 1889. Today, Kasthall owns fourteen looms that all date back to the 1960s. Working within the constraints of these old looms, Lagerhem Ullberg draws on her knowledge of wool as well as the weavers' expertise to produce fresh pieces. Her Häggå series, an abstract play of color and composition, seamlessly unites craft technique with contemporary design. Lagerhem Ullberg also pushes production capabilities by looking beyond pattern to texture. In Moss **(A)** see **p 242** a series of hand-tufted rugs, yarns of different lengths and colors add glimmers of depth and vibrancy. The Monroe series takes a step further by incorporating sparkling polyester fibers that dazzle much like their namesake Marilyn Monroe.

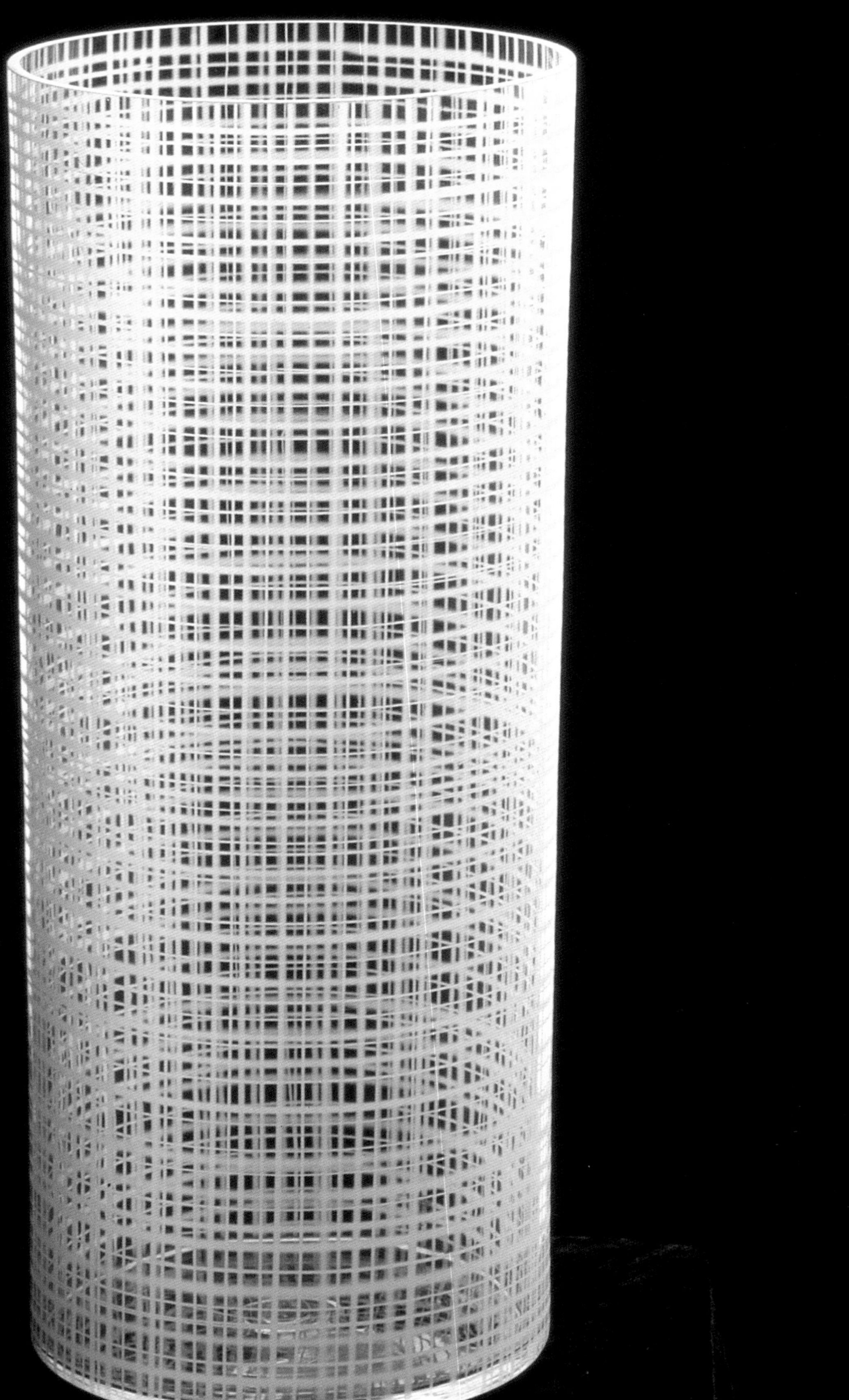

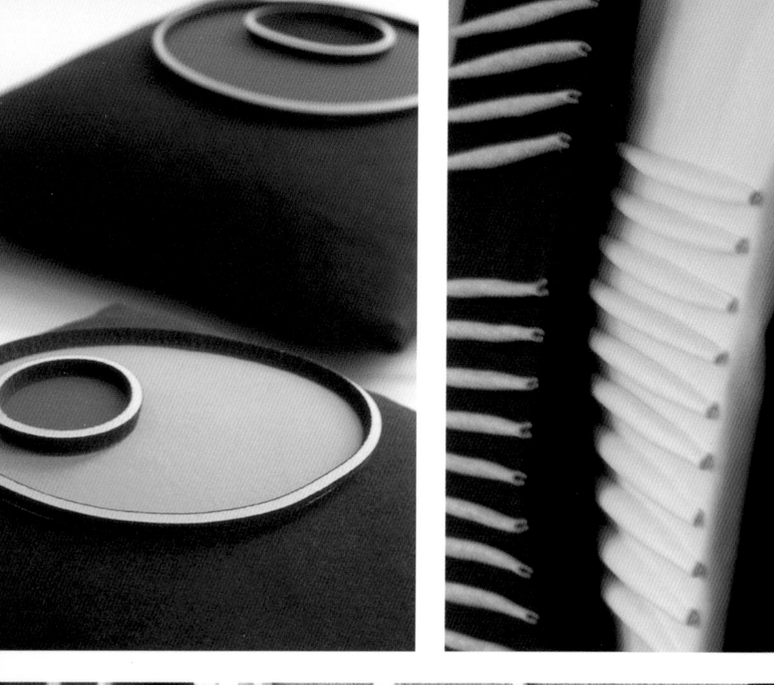

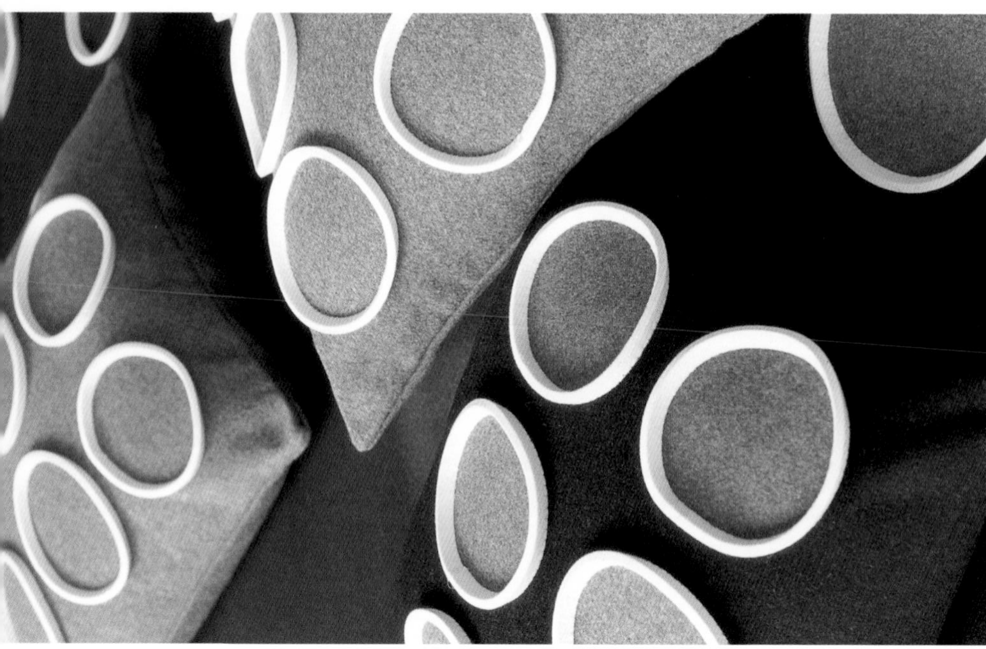

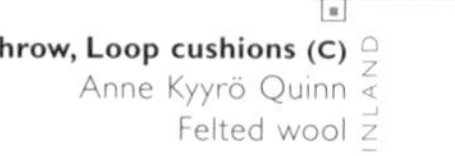

Bold and Target cushions, Linea throw, Loop cushions (C)
Anne Kyyrö Quinn
Felted wool
FINLAND

FINLAND
Polku carpets (E)
Verso Design
Felted wool

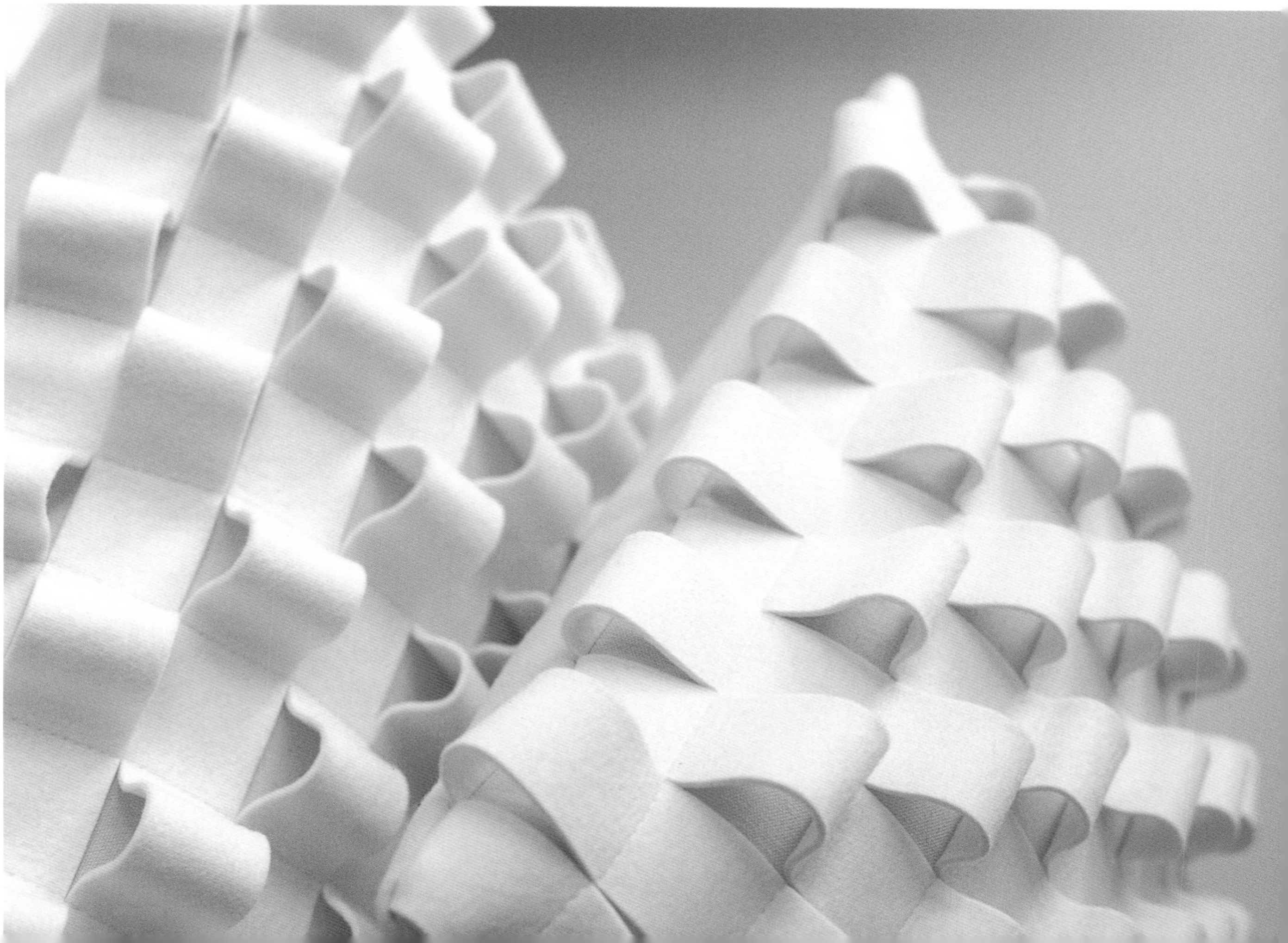

It is not such a big jump from using new materials in an old way to using old materials in a new way. The world's oldest textile fabric, felt, inspires many Scandinavians including the designer Anne Kyyrö Quinn **(C)** and the group Verso Design **(E)**, both from Finland. This insulating, cozy textile, a long-time folk favorite, is hand sewn to make traditional costumes and a wide range of clothing and footwear. While researching folk traditions in design school in the early 1980s, Sweden's Pia Wallén took note of the ancient fabric, which would become her life-long obsession. With an architect's instinct for space and color, Wallén shapes delightful felt creations as disparate as slippers **(D)** see **p 212** bowls, cat toys, dresses, and jewelry. Despite the history of her chosen material, Wallén's designs, like Lagerhem Ullberg's carpets for Kasthall, capture a completely contemporary sensibility. "Working with felt the way I do combines old techniques with modern designs," says Wallén.

Today's Scandinavian designers shake off the musty reputation of the term *craft* by reaffirming its conventions rather than imitating its techniques. ("The problem with the word *craft* isn't that it suggests funky leatherwork and fringed chenille but that it has lost its association with the world of ideas," Akiko Busch wrote in *Metropolis* magazine in October 2003.) In particular, the idea of the handmade, a core feature of

◄ **C**

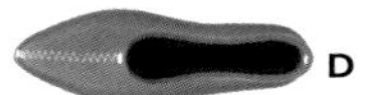

D

E

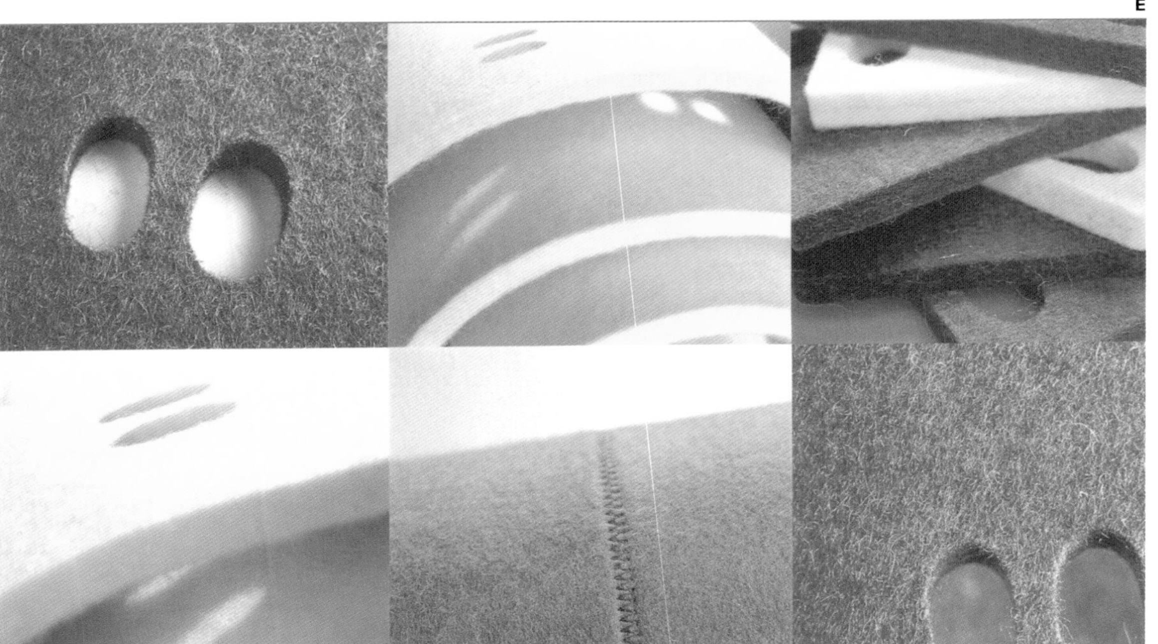

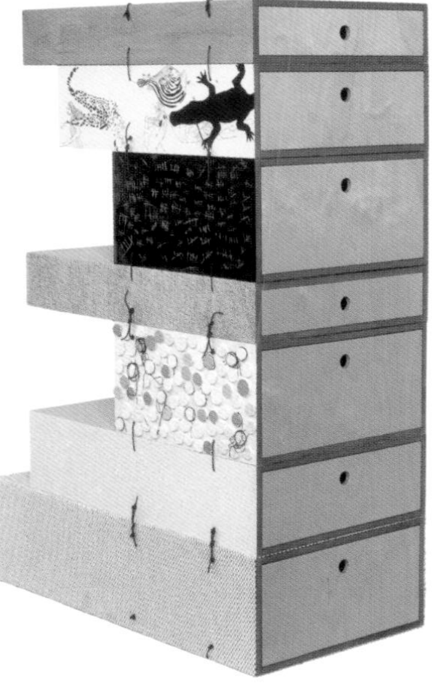

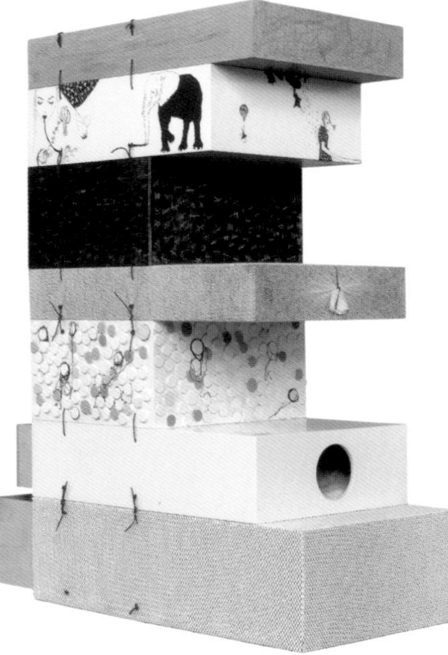

F

Zen-Sation cupboard (F)
Pil Bredahl
Painted wood, rubber, leather
DENMARK

"We didn't just make drawings and then have a factory make a prototype for us," says Kropsholder member Pil Bredahl. "We made each object with our own hands."

SWEDEN
Inner-Outer textile panel crafted by HV Ateljé (G)
Ulrika Mårtensson
Polyester, rubber

G ➤

craft, takes on new relevance for Scandinavians, who see it as a riposte to the anonymity of mass production. Revisiting the handmade in furniture design, the Danish collective Kropsholder assembled an exhibition called "Moment" that was shown at the Designer's Block, London, in 2002. "We didn't just make drawings and then have a factory make a prototype for us," says Kropsholder member Pil Bredahl. "We made each object with our own hands." Bredahl's contribution was a one-off cabinet, called Zen-Sation **(F)**, composed of hand-decorated boxes of various sizes sewn together with leather strings. Drawers were decorated with painterly figures, declarations of love etched in silver, and secret messages. One compartment, lined with rabbit fur, offered a hiding place for fragile, personal objects.

While Bredahl's Zen-Sation engages the handmade as a vehicle for personal expression, the Swedish designer Ulrika Mårtensson explores this convention by employing traditional craft techniques. Mårtensson works with seamstresses at the textile production studio HV Ateljé (Föreningen Handarbetets Vänner), founded in 1874, to produce unique fabric panels **(G)** for architectural environments. The textiles meld the two-dimensional and three-dimensional—balancing Eva Hess–like fluidity with Asian-inspired structure and repetition—achieving depth with age-old manual skills such as embroidery, folding, and pleating. To keep costs down, the textiles (which are washable, fire retardant, and sound absorbent) are ready-made, but then sewn by hand. "I enjoy blending the handmade and high-tech," says Mårtensson.

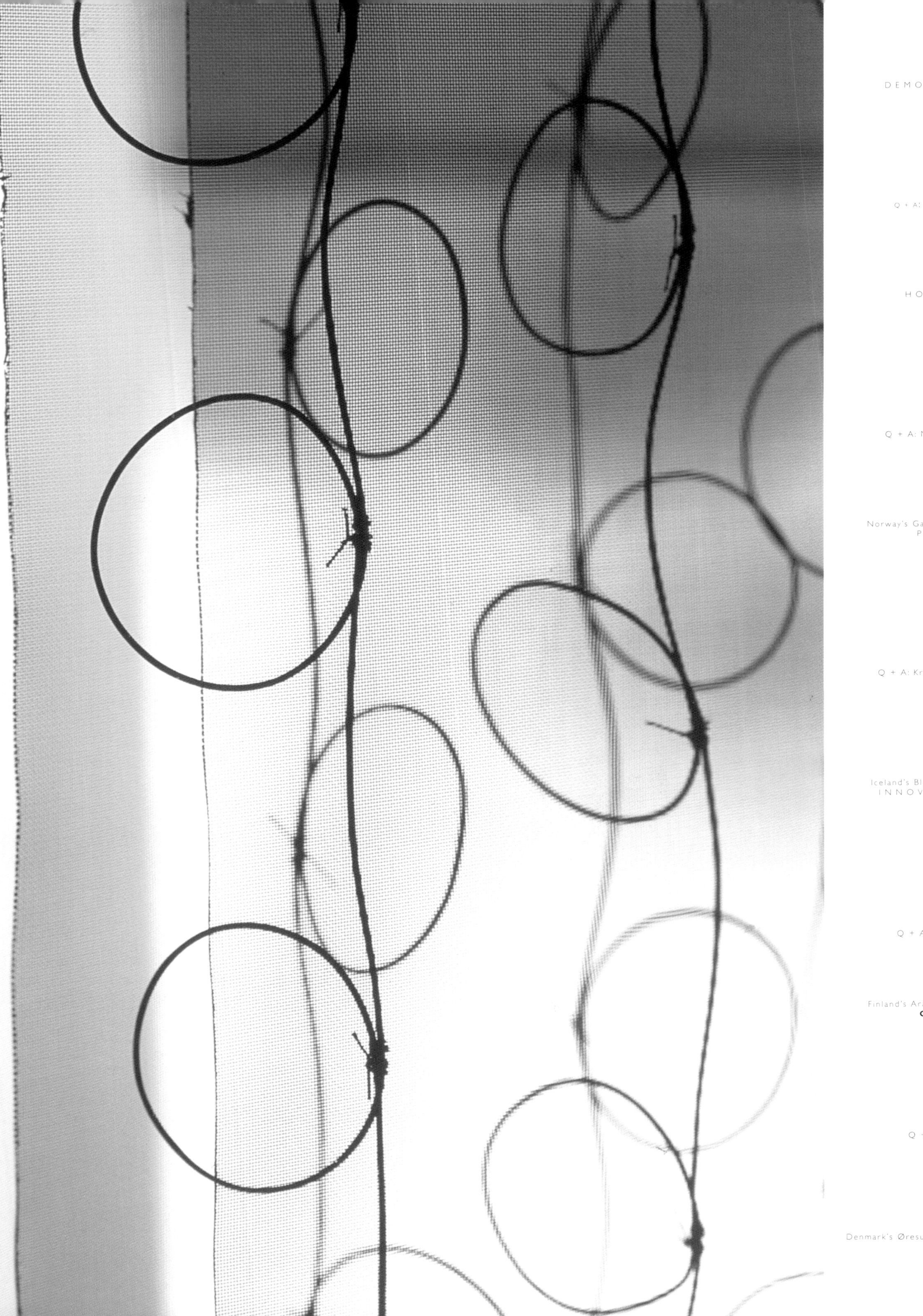

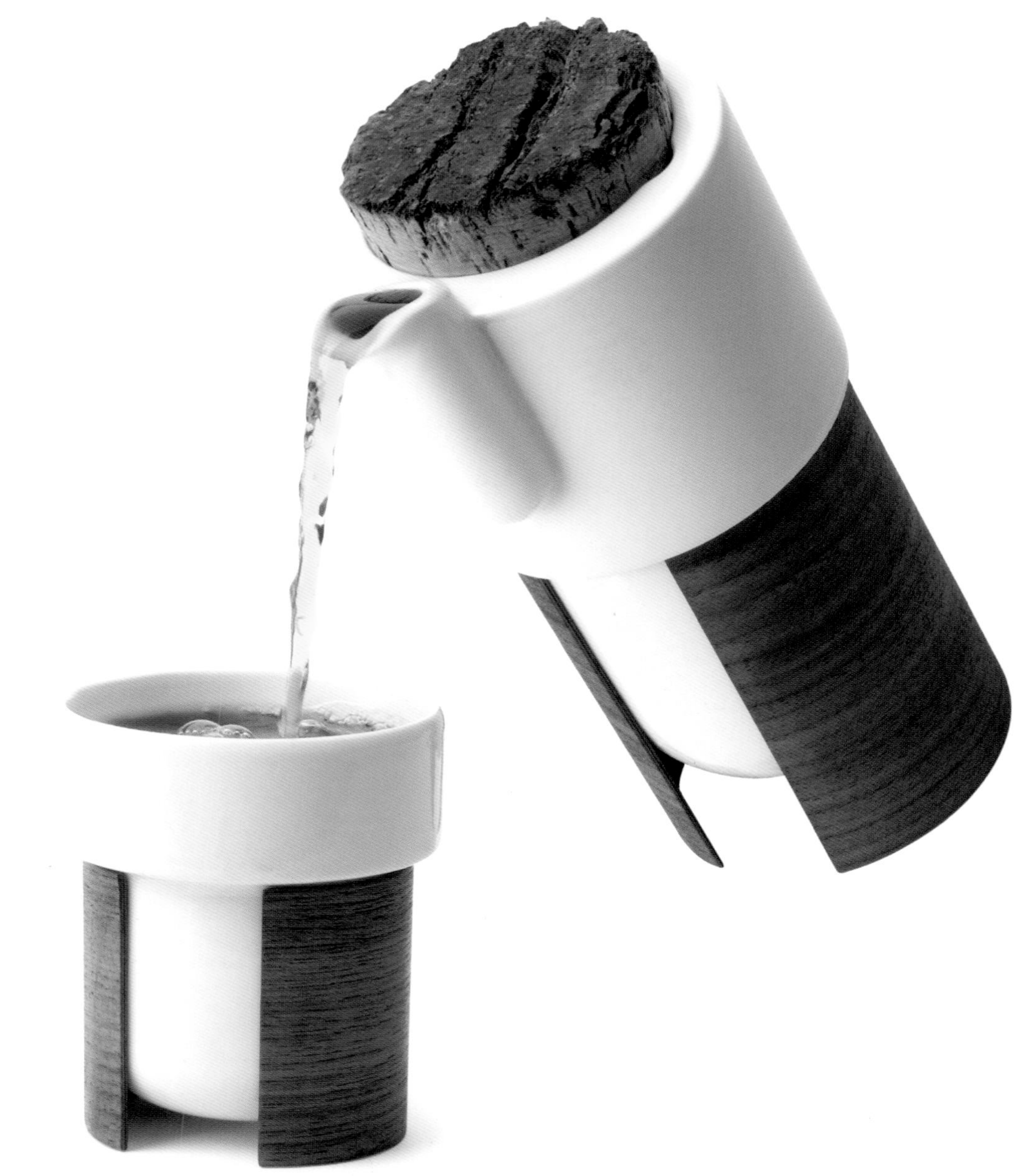

Warm teapot and teacup for Tonfisk Design
Brian Keaney, Tony Alfström
China, wood, cork
FINLAND

DENMARK
Yesterday's News chair (K)
Niels Hvass
Glued newspapers

During the Modernist period, Scandinavian designers used crafts to experiment with new techniques, materials, and colors in a way that was not possible on the production line. This tradition continues today as designers repurpose found materials in unique and limited-edition designs. The Icelandic fashion label Aftur makes new outfits from vintage clothing **(I)** see **p 244** appropriating discarded materials while retaining ties to the materials' former incarnations. The Danish furniture designer Niels Hvass used a similar technique when gluing a stack of old newspapers together for the chair Yesterday's News **(K)**. The newspapers' tabloid shape defines the furniture's blocky silhouette. Neither Aftur nor Hvass copies craft technique, yet both update craft values.

Scandinavian designers may salvage old materials in new designs, but they hardly wax nostalgic. They often rescue old-fashioned items from flea markets—flowery teacups, frayed needlepoint pillows, engraved wine glasses—and play them against industrial materials to produce unsentimental designs. For the lighting collection Old News, made for the "Moment" exhibition, Danish designer Liselotte Risell encased ruffled 1940s lampshades **(H)** see **p 253**. in cones of clear Plexiglas, renewing the shades' anachronistic shape. For another project

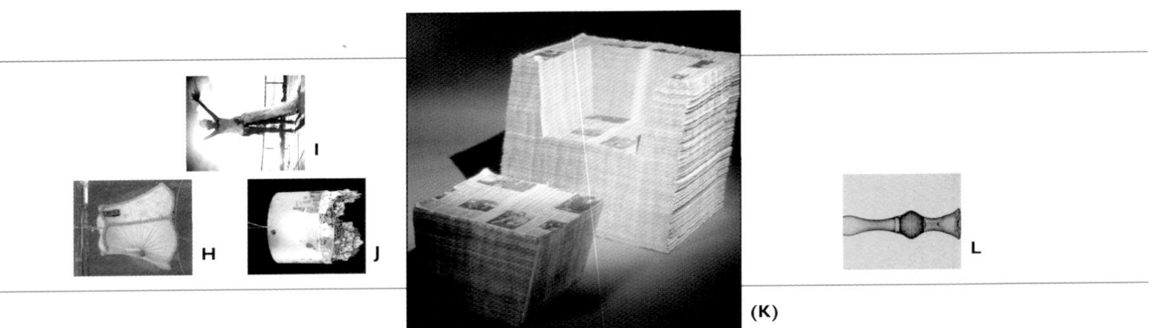

(K)

in "Moment," the Swedish designer Anna von Schewen crafted a family of curious flower vases **(L)** see **p 232** by stacking together tabletop towers of second-hand wine and water glasses and sheathing them in nylon. Another remarkable project that updates old-fashioned materials is the Anemone lamp **(J)** see **p 245**. which is crafted from hand-blown glass and handmade bobbin lace, by the Finnish collective IMU. The lamp's asymmetrical pattern and sleek shape add a youthful touch (say the designers) to "things from grandma's house."

With these mix-and-match creations, designers look to the familiarity and personality of the popular for inspiration. The Swedish company Pyra produces a collection inspired by the English Windsor chair—so ubiquitous in Sweden, Pyra's managing director Ivar Björkman says that Swedes often mistake it for their own invention. "The Windsor chair is considered more folk furniture than a high-design chair," he says. "You find it in homes of all kinds, owned by young and old alike." The form begged for reinterpretation, he says, and the collection's established to up-and-coming designers were given free rein to reconceive the chair's construction and meaning. Kristina Jonasson's Imprint chair **(M)** see **p 222**. in which a plastic backrest sits on a geometric base of traditional

SWEDEN

Windsor chair series for Pyra
Kristina Jonasson (top left),
Mårten Cyrén (top right, bottom right),
Per Sundstedt (bottom left)

FINLAND

Butterfly lamp for Microsoft Finland (Q)
Susan Elo, Nene Tsuboi
Cotton canvas, embroidery thread, steel frame

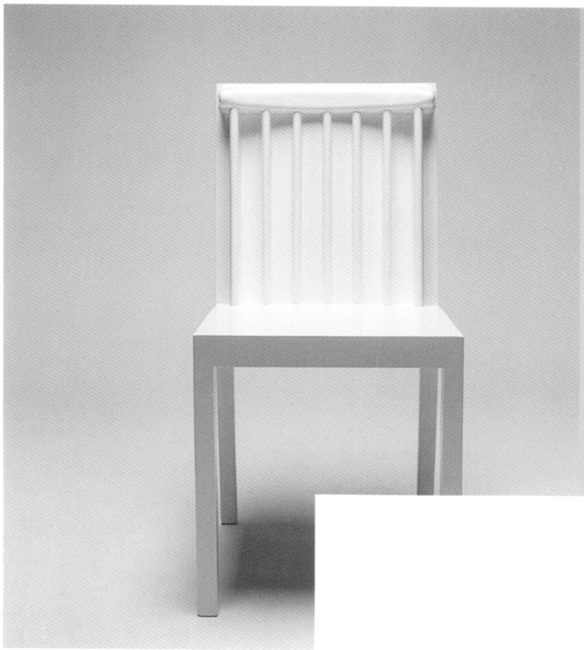

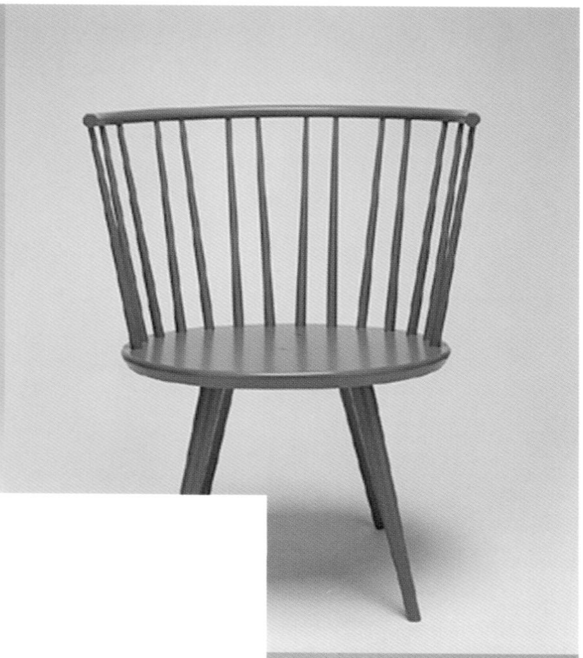

The Swedish company Pyra produces a collection **inspired** by the English Windsor chair—so ubiquitous in Sweden that Swedes often mistake it for their own invention.

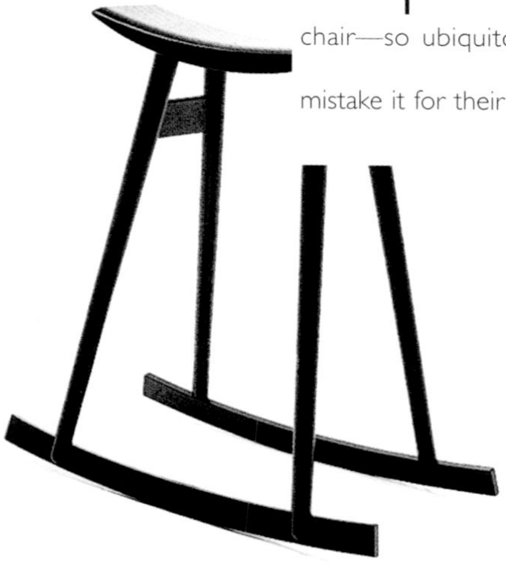

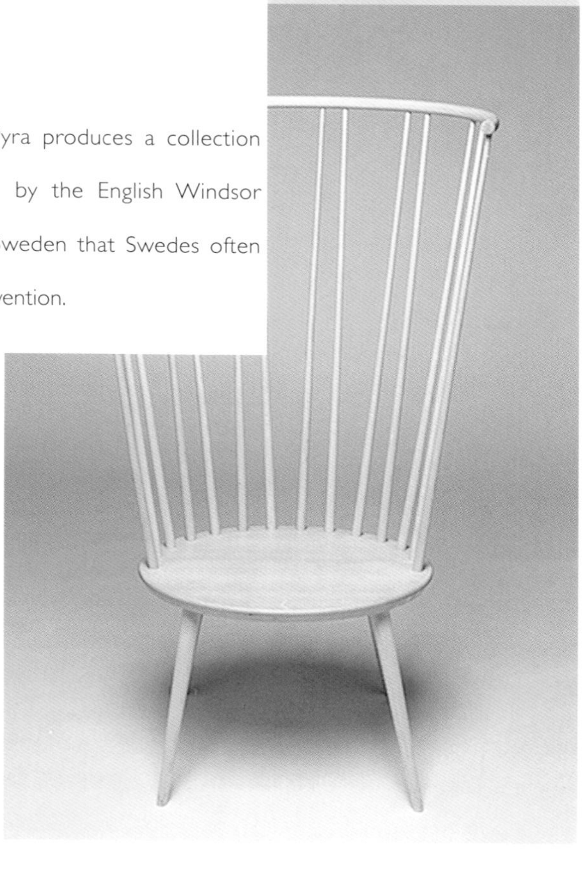

birch, shows new and old to be discrete components. Rather than recreating the Windsor, her chair evokes its memory: the plastic backrest retains a concave, ghostlike impression of the original. Other designs rearranged the chair from top to bottom, as in Per Sundstedt's Ving chair **(O)**, a quirky upside-down rocker, and Mårten Cyrén's Alice-in-Wonderland pair, the shrunken Lillängen **(N)** and elongated Storängen **(P)**, which literally pushes the Windsor to its limits.

Consistent among these inspirations and techniques is the need to reposition and renew craft ideas, especially in relation to the high-tech craze of the 1990s. "Society today is so high speed that you now find a need for simple, beautiful, sensual things in everyday life," says Jahn, whose organization, Danish Crafts, has perpetuated a contemporary view of the field by sponsoring exhibitions and promoting craft at international trade fairs. "I think the recent renewal of craft is related to a need for honesty, intimacy, and fundamental knowledge." Finnish designer Susan Elo would agree. Her softly glowing Butterfly lamp **(Q)** for Microsoft Finland featured an embroidered butterfly on a cotton canvas shade that complemented the company's "Butterfly" campaign.

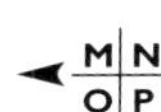

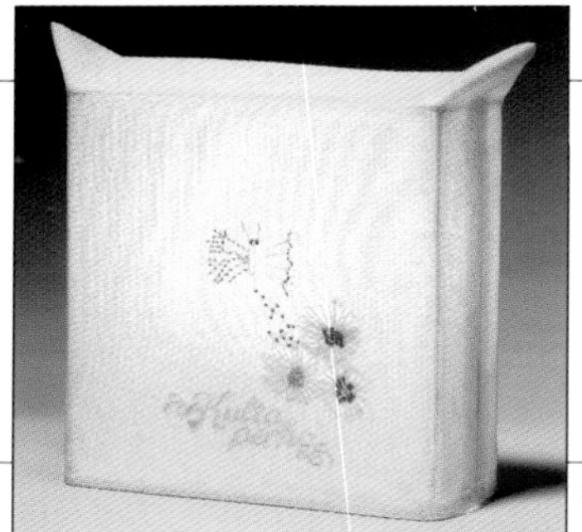

Q

"We wanted to do a design for the Microsoft people that was handmade, warm, and small—the opposite of what people expect from Microsoft—big, clean, and cold," says Elo.

Many contemporary designers long for a connection to the past. As material knowledge and local labor are disappearing, the traditional Scandinavian relationship to craft holds new relevance for young designers. It offers a way to ground conceptual thinking and reintroduces notions like veracity and intimacy into the dialogue surrounding design. The traditional balance of aesthetic and industrial concerns demonstrates that new technology isn't necessarily antithetical to craft and can even aid in the limited production of customized, high-quality objects. The current activity in the craft field proves that, while globalization may encourage a pan-European design style, many designers prefer their work to come from somewhere specific rather than a no-man's-land. "Craft is one of the oldest ways of expressing the cultural identity of human beings," says Jahn. "Craft tells us about human experience around the world; it is the witness to how life is lived."

Basket vase for Arabia (Pro Arabia Art Finland collection)
Kristina Riska
Ceramics
FINLAND

SWEDEN
Superstructure easy chair for cbi
Björn Dahlström
Oak

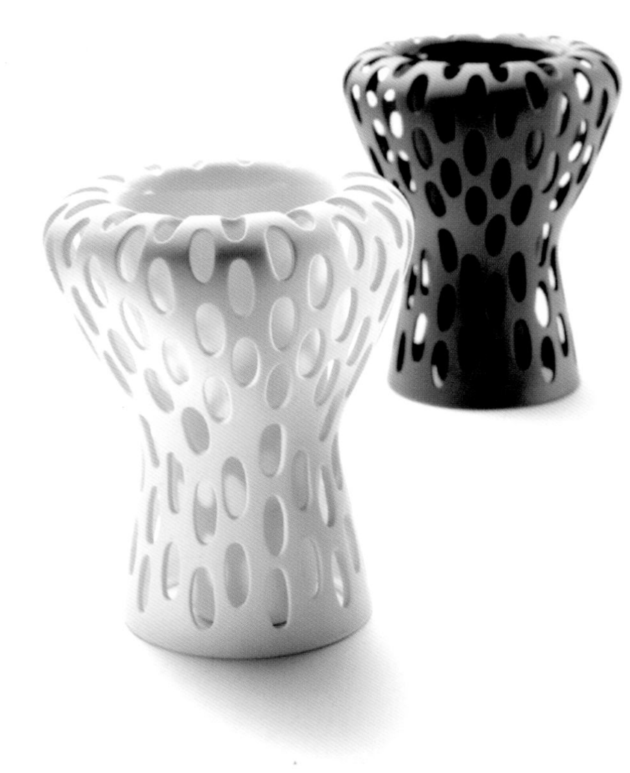

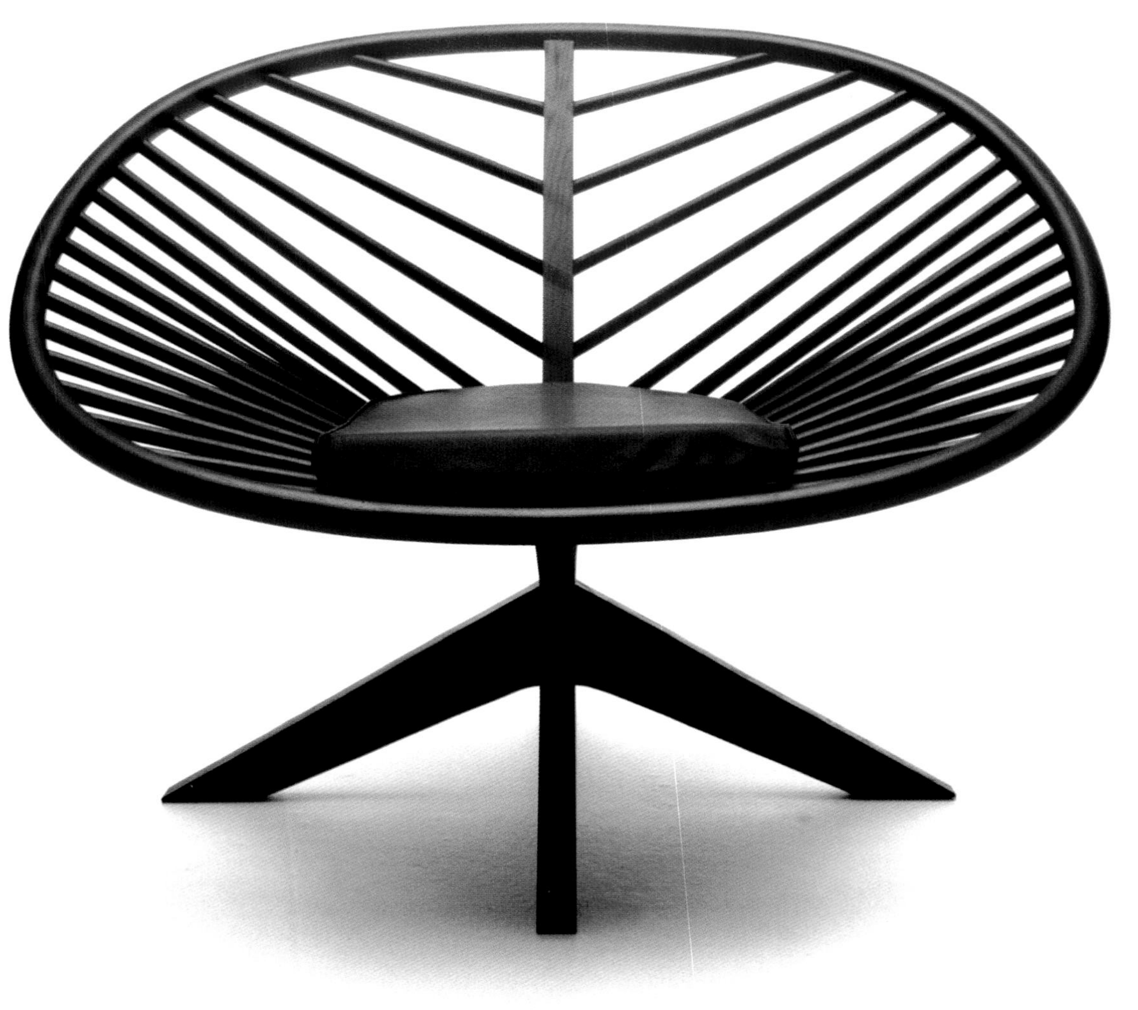

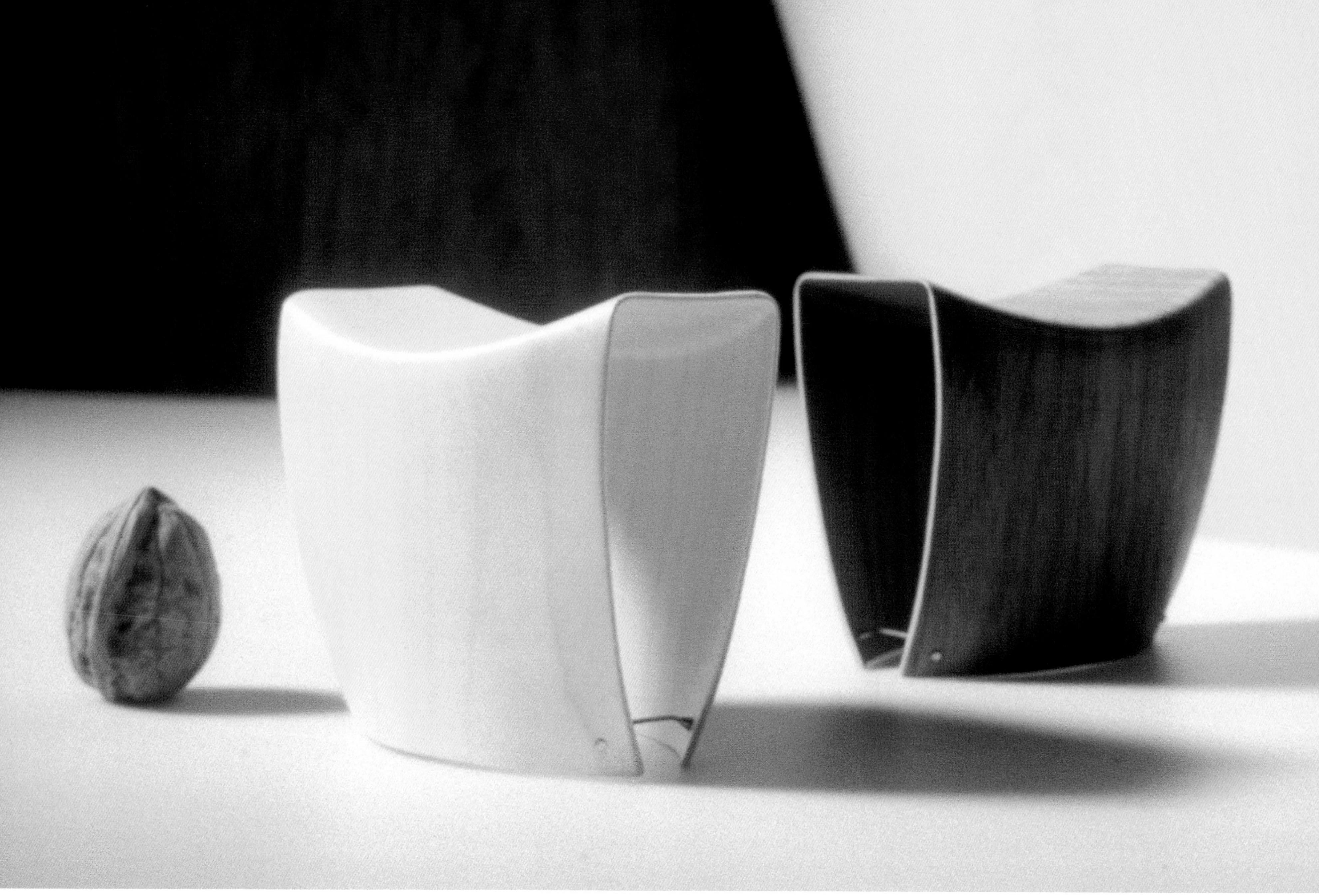

Gallery stool (scale model) for 1:6 DESIGN
Hans Sandgren Jakobsen
Wood veneer
DENMARK

NORWAY
Papermaster magazine rack for Swedese
Norway Says
Laminated wood

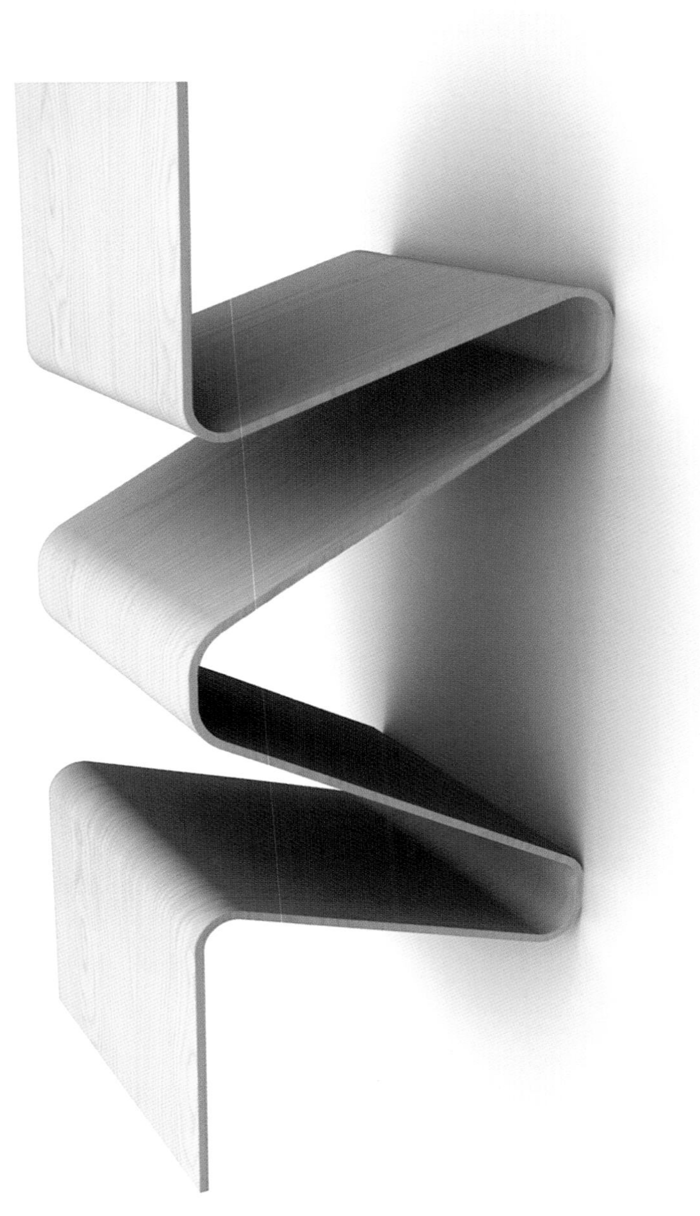

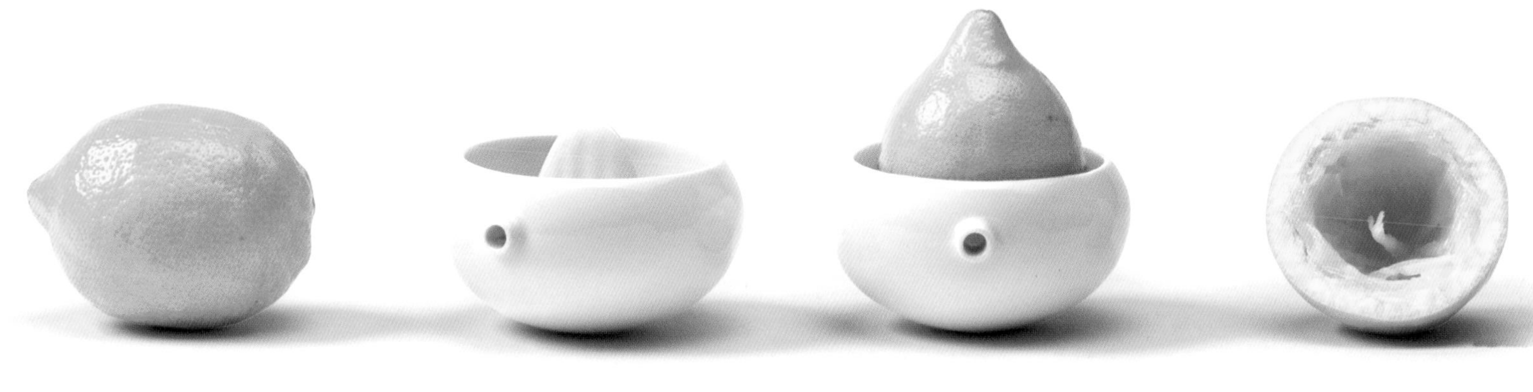

OMA lemon squeezer for Tonfisk Design
Susanna Hoikkala, Jenni Ojala
China
FINLAND

Vera chair for Korhonen
Teemu Järvi
Laminated plywood, steel rod, chrome plate
FINLAND

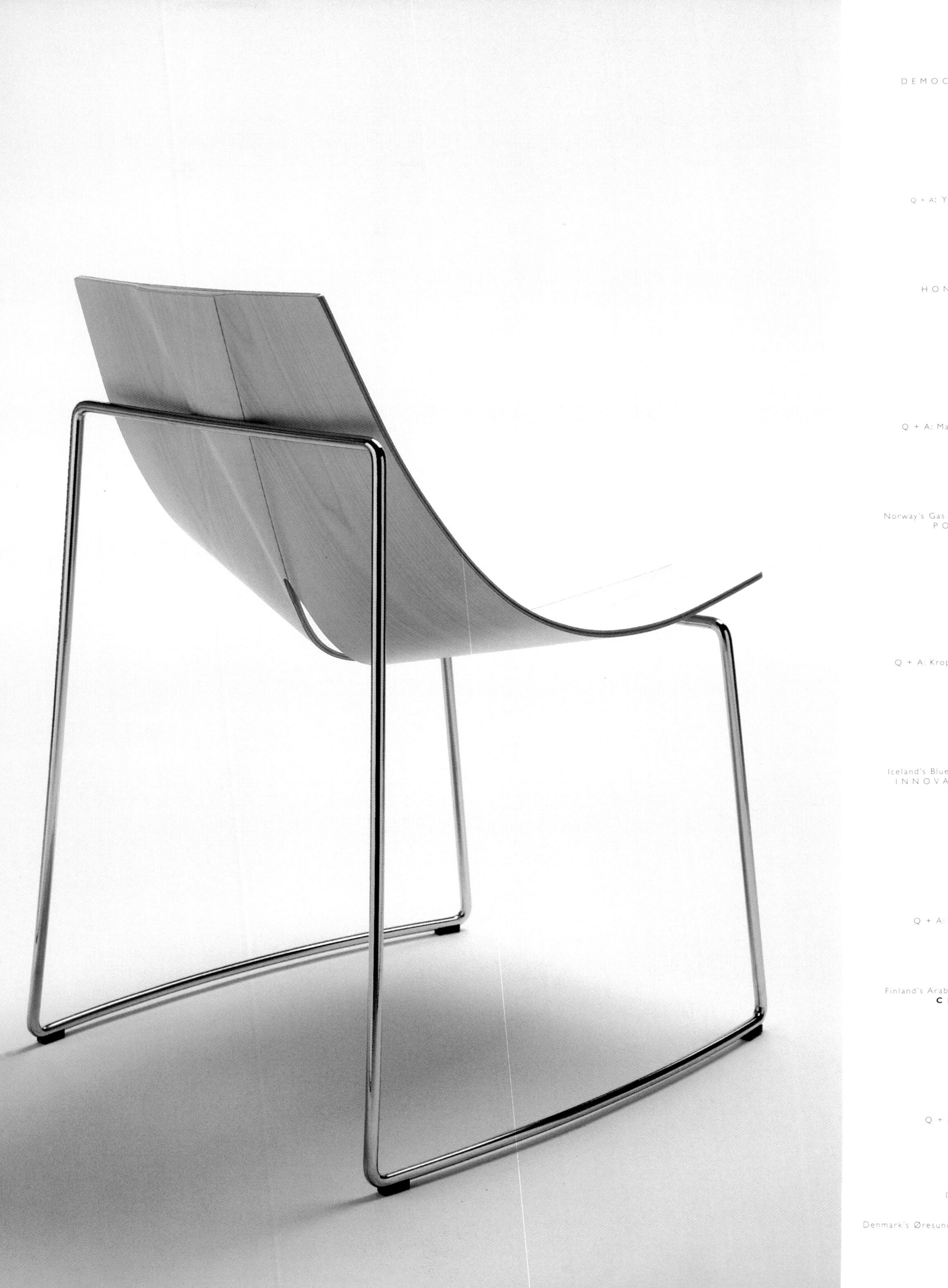

"The combination of cabinetmaking and design in **wood** was Denmark's strength, but very few designers have an interest in working that way now," says Louise Campbell. "We decided to get them to rise to the challenge."

Walk the Plank, an exhibition that featured wood furniture jointly created by designers and cabinetmakers
Various designers
DENMARK

Line chair for Fyns Facon Spaend
Mathias Bengtsson, Frank V. Holgersen
Molded plywood
DENMARK

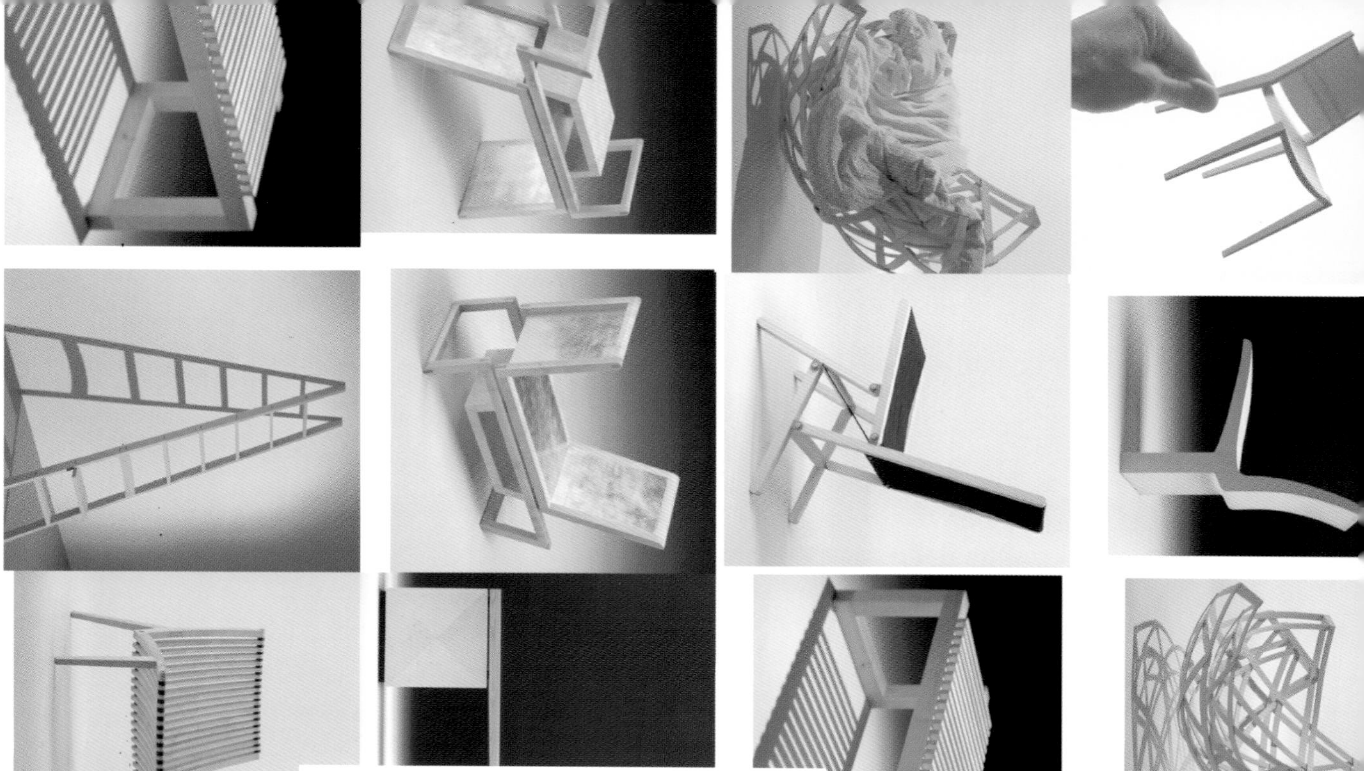

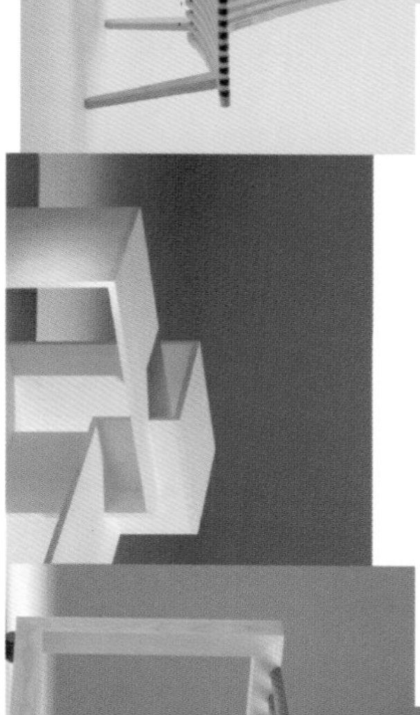

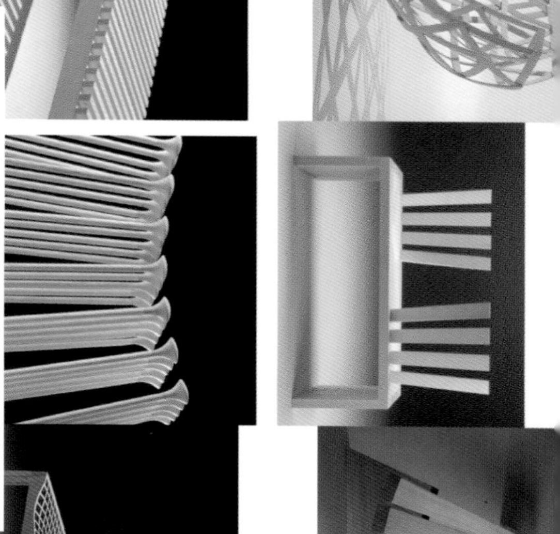

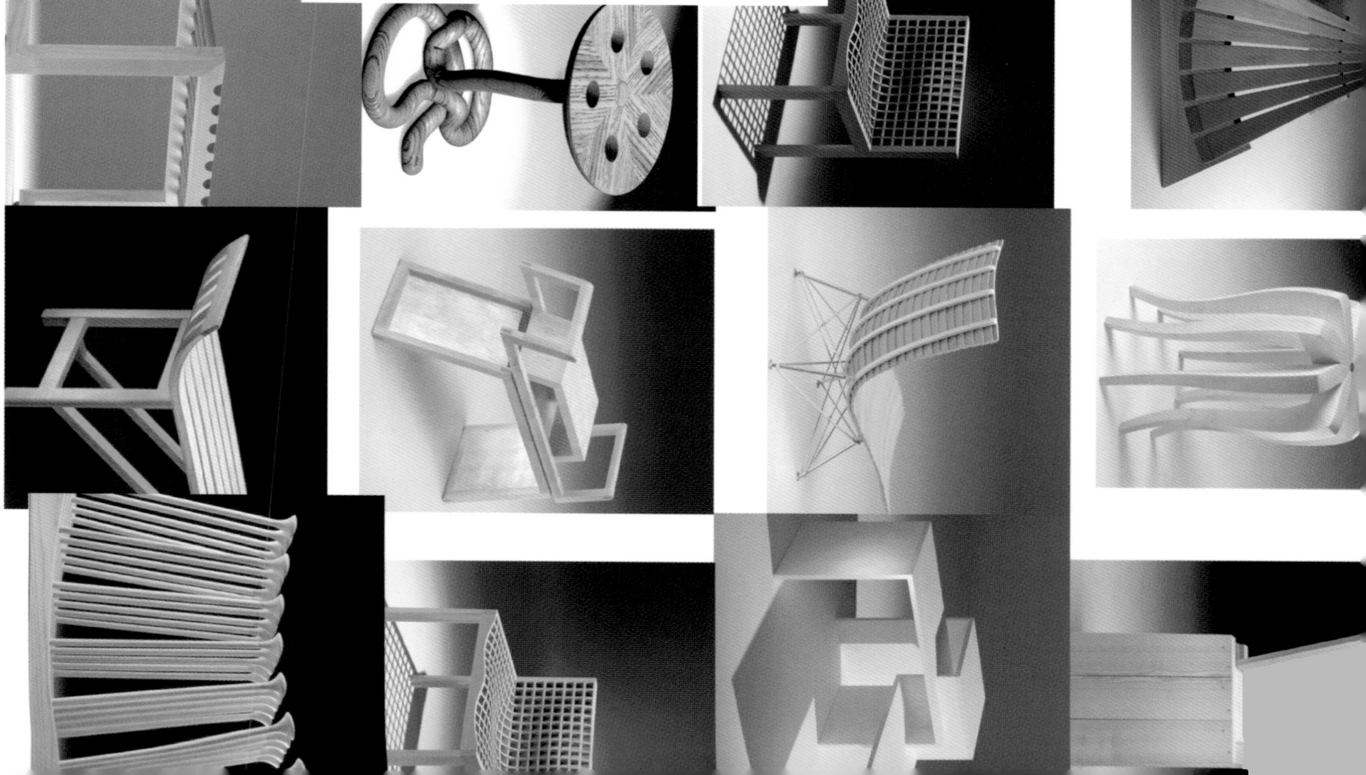

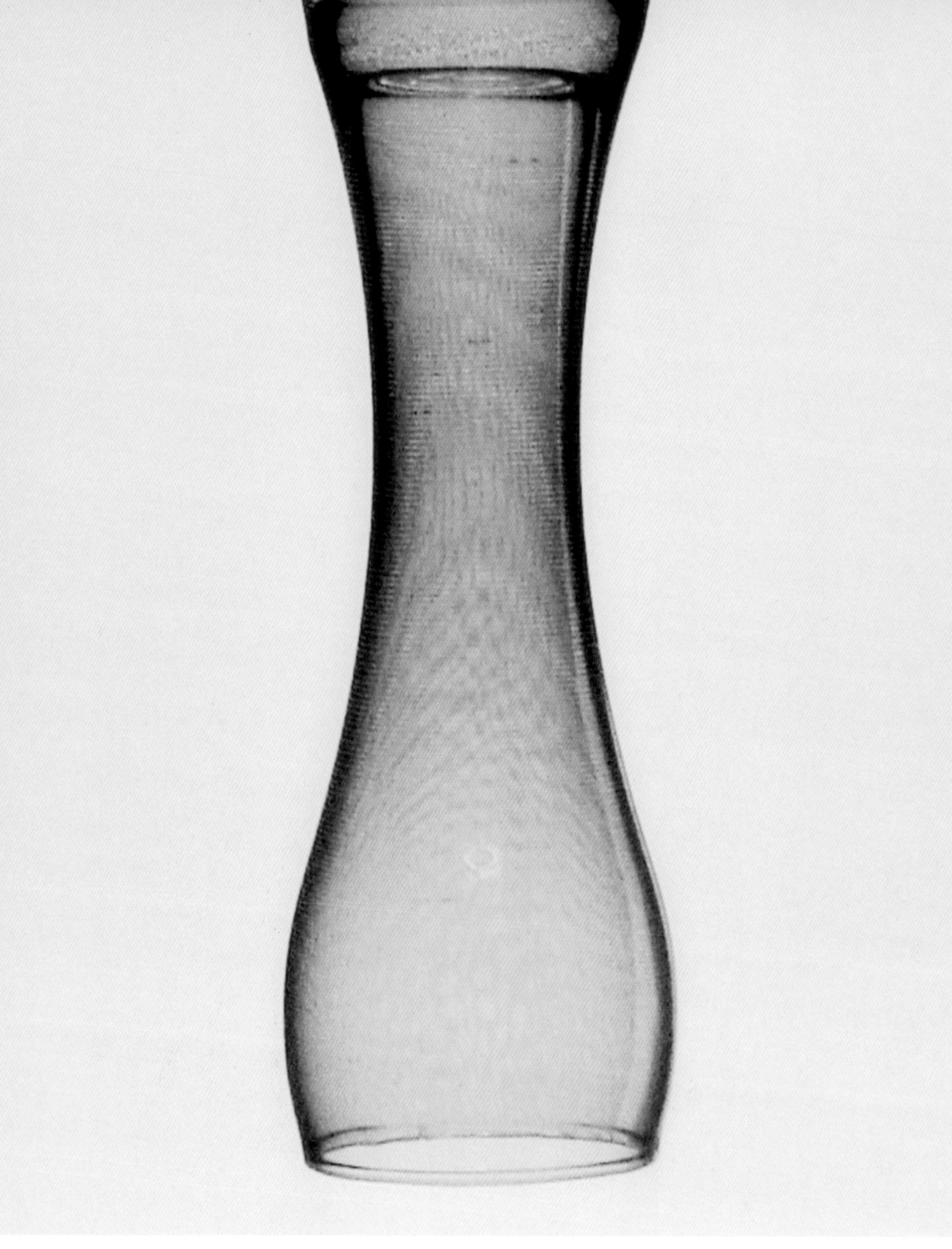

What's New vase
Anna von Schewen
Glass, polyamide/elastane
SWEDEN

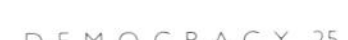

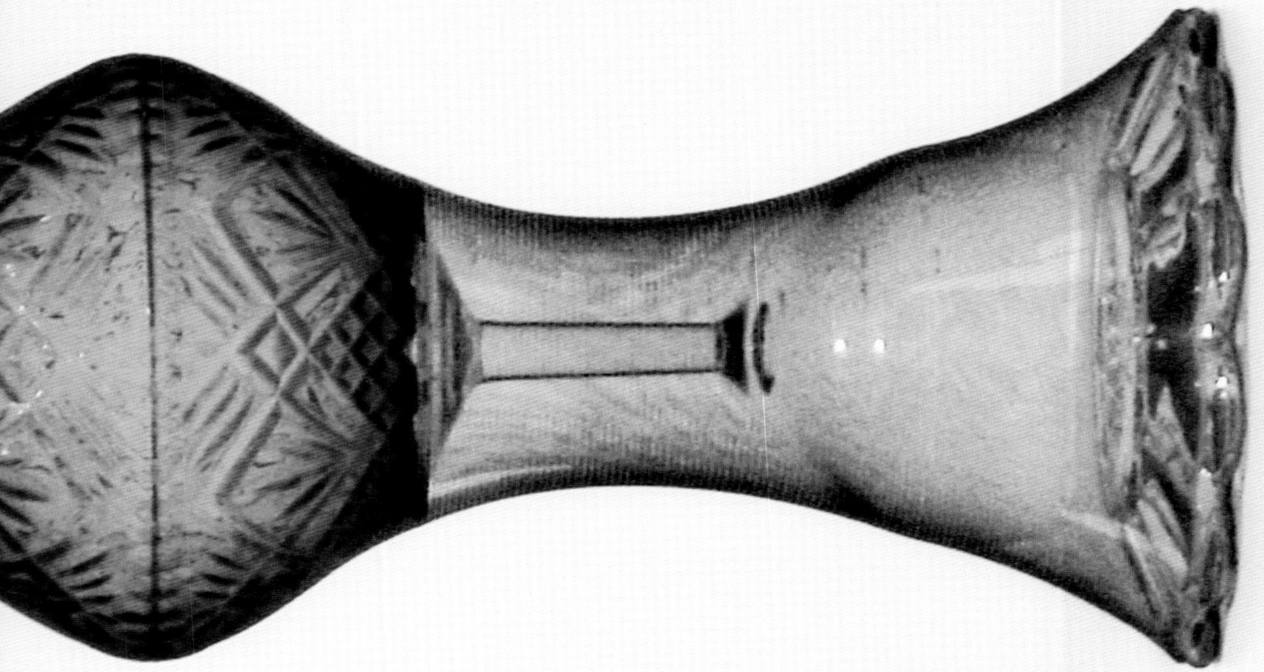

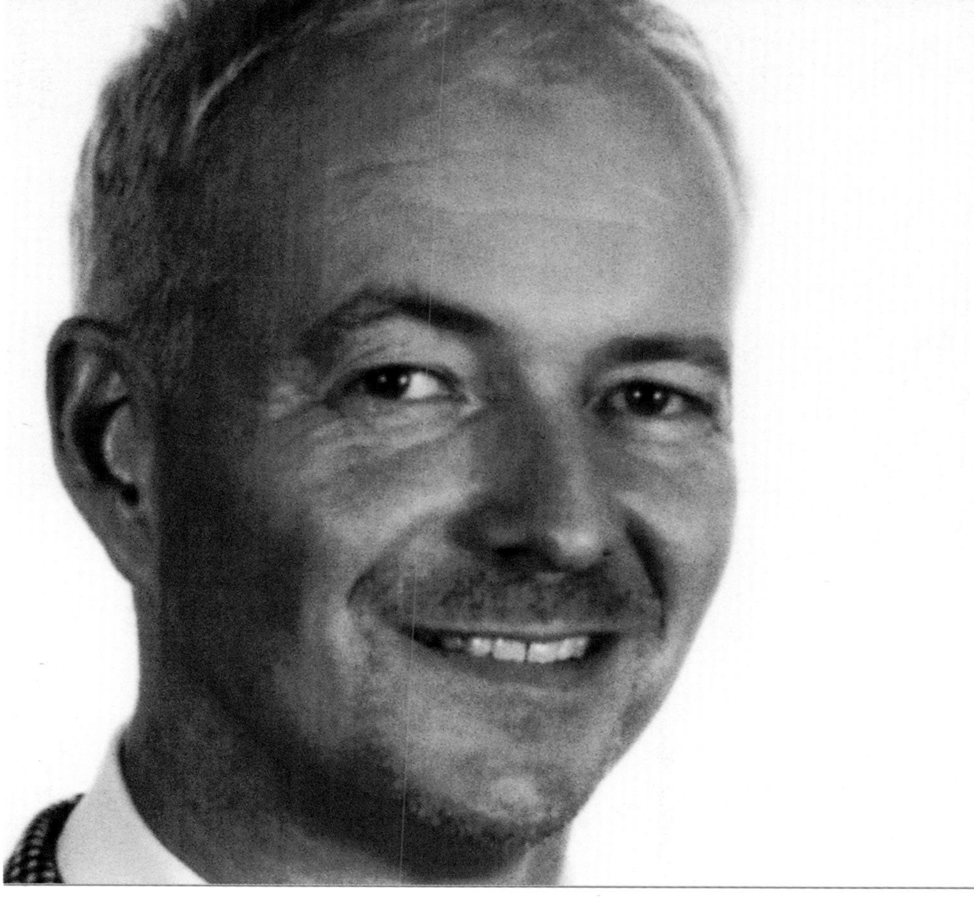

WIDAR HALÉN

The Myths of Scandinavian Design

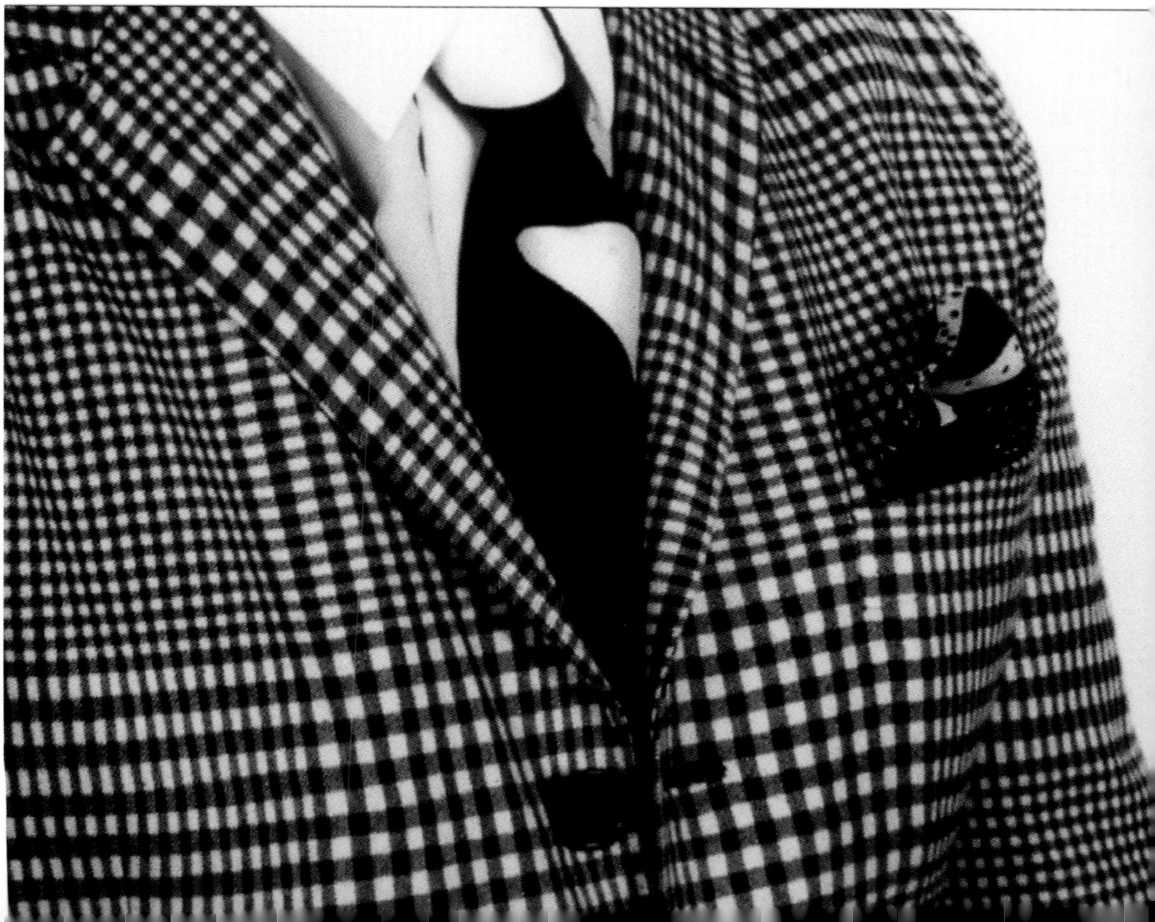

Widar Halén, a vital, critical voice in the field of Scandinavian design history, is chief curator of the Museum of Decorative Arts and Design in Oslo, Norway. Educated at Oxford University, Halén earned his doctorate in 1988 and later worked at Sotheby's in London. He authored the award-winning book Christopher Dresser: A Pioneer of Modern Design (1993) and has been instrumental in establishing a permanent design collection at The Museum of Decorative Arts and Design. He lectures around the world and recently curated the exhibition "Scandinavian Design Beyond the Myth," which opened at the Kunstgewerbemuseum in Berlin in 2003.

Q: IN THE DISCUSSION SURROUNDING SCANDINAVIAN DESIGN, WHAT ARE THE TYPICAL ASSUMPTIONS MADE BY CRITICS ABOUT THE SUBJECT? A: Probably the most repeated and unquestioned assumptions about Scandinavian design are its closeness to nature, its Protestant Puritanism, and its simplicity. Unfortunately, these descriptions are put forward without really analyzing how the simplicity or Puritanism inherent in the design differs from that which you might see in work from Japan or Holland or Germany. There are often descriptions of national temperament that are prevalent as well. It is said that the Danes are jovial, the Swedes are formal, the Finns are quiet, the Icelanders are poetic, and the Norwegians are naive.

There is often a comparison made between contemporary Scandinavian design and the achievements of the original Viking culture. It's pretty far-fetched, when you think about it, twelve hundred years after the fact, to introduce this notion into critical discussion. Things have progressed in Scandinavia a little bit since then. From the Anglo-Saxon point of view, Scandinavian culture is often viewed as slightly primitive. Anglo-Saxons often view Scandinavia the way they looked to the Orient in the 1880s. That is, the Anglo-Saxon approach, in criticism and in the press, often looks at Scandinavian culture as if it was something very different from the Anglo-Saxon culture. But in fact it isn't. Traditionally, the connections between Scandinavia and the British Isles have been very tight. We belong to the Anglo-Saxon culture, especially here in Norway, where half of the Kingdom of Norway was Anglo-Saxon in the old days. Many Norwegians are educated in England, and there are many familial connections. So I would say there is actually a very close connection in character and in taste. **Q: ARE YOU SAYING THAT SCANDINAVIAN DESIGNERS AREN'T, FOR EXAMPLE, INFLUENCED BY NATURE? A:** I'm saying that these notions have been overemphasized. They are repeated ad nauseum with no one questioning their verity by analyzing them in new ways. They are clichés, and even myths. The Quakers are another example of this kind of plight. Obviously they had a very close connection to nature, but so have many other designers around the world. In Scandinavia, the countryside is very close to the cities, which are not so large. But you will find the same thing all over Russia, for example, and in a large part of Eastern Europe. There, they also have a very strong attachment to nature. **Q: DID SCANDINAVIAN**

Q + A: Ytterborn 49
Sweden 59
IKEA/PS 65
HONESTY 67
Q + A: Magnússon 95
Norway 107
Norway's Gas Stations 113
POETRY 115
Q + A: Kropsholder 143
Iceland 159
Iceland's Blue Lagoon 165
INNOVATION 167
Q + A: Ylimaula 195
Finland 203
Finland's Arabianranta 209
CRAFT 211
213
215
217
219
221
223
225
227
229
231
233
Q + A: Halén 235
237
239
241
243
245
247
Denmark 249
251
253
Denmark's Øresund Bridge 255

DESIGNERS CONTRIBUTE TO BUILDING MYTHS AROUND THEMSELVES AND THEIR WORK? A: Figures such as Tapio Wirkkala, the Finnish glass designer, were very much into that. He went up to Lapland and sat in the mountains drawing pictures of the Lapps. He said that he fled from journalists, but in fact, there were a couple of very important magazines that managed to get up there and conduct interviews with him. So he definitely had a connection to the outside world as well as to nature.

Arne Jacobsen, the famous Danish Modernist architect and designer, is another person who built a romantic mythology around himself. He gave organic names to his designs, which hadn't really been done before. He emphasized nature in their titles—Egg, Swan, etc.—even though his designs are based on shells of polystyrene, a newly invented foam material. In that respect, they are as far away from nature as you can get. Q: WHEN WERE THESE NOTIONS OF SCANDINAVIAN DESIGN FIRST INTRODUCED? A: I think that the exhibition that toured America in 1954, "Design in Scandinavia," was very important. It was one of the first instances when the phrase "Scandinavian design" entered into the consciousness of a larger international public. It was a huge initiative put forward by all the Nordic countries together. It was a great marketing program, really. A year before the exhibition, a design directory was published listing all the different designers and manufacturers in the exhibition so that American department stores could order and display the merchandise. Hence, people could access the work on a very broad scale, much more so than if they had just read about it in the newspaper. They could actually see it in shop windows, try it out, and buy it directly. Q: IT IS OFTEN SAID THAT THE "DESIGN IN SCANDINAVIA" EXHIBITION GLAZED OVER MANY OF THE DIFFERENCES AMONG THE SCANDINAVIAN COUNTRIES, SUCH AS POLITICS AND ECONOMICS, IN ORDER TO PRESENT A UNIFIED VISION OF SCANDINAVIA. IN WHOSE INTEREST WAS IT TO PRESENT THIS UNIFIED VISION? A: Discrepancies in wealth and development among the Nordic countries were quite large at the time. It was important for Finland and Norway to participate because they were struggling during this period. Norwegian and Finnish industries were far behind those which had developed in Sweden and Denmark. And Norway and Finland had been hit hard by World War II. Sweden had remained neutral during the war, and Denmark was not so badly hit. Plus Sweden and Denmark had a longer history of design than either Finland or Norway. It was great for Finns and Norwegians to be able to associate themselves with this exhibition, and for them to learn how to develop themselves in the pattern of these two other countries that had actually managed to get a bit further.

Finland, which had only recently been liberated from Russia in 1917, had a relatively new design policy, as did Norway. Finland used design deliberately to demonstrate a connection to Western culture and show its independence from the communists. And, of course, this was the great concern for Americans at the time. When the show finally opened in 1954, the Americans who brought it to the United States were relieved: everything went well, and they didn't see any communist associations. Q: AFTER WORLD WAR II, WHY WAS THE AMERICAN PRESS SO INTERESTED IN THE IMAGE OF SCANDINAVIAN DESIGN AND HOW DID IT CONTRIBUTE TO OR EVOLVE THE IDEA? A: America's connection to another developing democratic society after World War II was very important. And from the American point of view, quite a few European regimes could be looked on as being not democratic: the Italians, the Germans, and, in many ways, even the French weren't terribly democratic. It was very important for the Americans to associate themselves with a part of the world that they saw as developing in the same way they were themselves, upholding the same ideals. And there was a commercial aspect, which has always been very important to Americans, and which the Scandinavians have learned to indulge in and take advantage of. The "Design in Scandinavia" directory is an example of this. There was a commercial interest from the Scandinavian side and from the American side Q: BESIDES "DESIGN IN SCANDINAVIA," WERE THERE OTHER EXHIBITIONS AROUND THE WORLD THAT CONTRIBUTED TO THE DISSEMINATION OF THE NOTION OF SCANDINAVIAN DESIGN? A: There was one important exhibition in France, "Formes Scandinave," in 1958 at the Louvre. It featured all the Nordic countries, including Iceland for the first time. It was also significant for the French who, like the Americans, saw Scandinavian design as an example of democratic expression. With the '68 revolt in Paris, everything Scandinavian became very popular.

There was also a "Design in Scandinavia" show in 1968 in Australia. At that point Australians hadn't seen Scandinavian design on a large scale, and they also wanted to be connected to the democratic society of Scandinavia. Then you have "Scandinavian Modern Design" in 1982 at the Cooper-Hewitt, National Design Museum in New York, and "Scandinavian Design: A Way of Life" in Japan in 1987–88. And then a very interesting exhibition, just after the Baltic countries got their freedom, was organized by the Nordic Council of Ministers in 1993 and called "From Dreams to Reality." It had an impact in the development of free expression and the establishment of industry in the Baltic countries.

Q: HAS THE NEW GENERATION OF SCANDINAVIAN DESIGNERS CONTINUED TO LEVERAGE THE NOTION OF SCANDINAVIAN DESIGN? A: They have continued to use these notions.

You see this especially in the minimal retro design that looks back to the Golden Age of the '50s. A lot of ide from that period have been taken up again, but then again, young designers have visited these ideas with renewe direction. They have a much broader worldview now than [their predecessors did] fifty years ago. And many these designers have been educated abroad and have worked all over the world. They don't consider themselv specifically Scandinavian anymore. You find that a lot of them use these traditional notions of Scandinavian desi in ironic and humorous ways, which is quite fun, really. **Q: IS THE NOTION OF SCANDINAVIAN DESIGN STILL RELEVANT TODAY? HOW DO YOU SEE I' EVOLVING? A:** I think it is relevant. Many people are talking about a renaissance of Scandinavian desig especially in the new minimalism that we have witnessed since the 1990s. Today, designers can open themselves u to the whole world to take and recreate ideas from many different cultures. You see that, for example, in IKE Although there is a lot of so-called "typical Scandinavian design" there, you also see influences from India, Nor Africa, and a variety of other cultures.

I also think it is interesting to look at the new united Europe. Even thoug Norway is still out of it, we probably will join sooner or later. The idea of a united Scandinavia is an old notio Now we see it materialized in the European Union. But a lot of us have thought that we should have created Scandinavian union long before the European Union was created, and that we could have done very well on o own. Together, a united Scandinavia can compete with great nations like Germany or France. So this momentu toward a united Europe has also given new life to that old idea of Scandinavianism, which was debated very heavi in the mid-to-late nineteenth century.

SWEDEN
Shelf
Uglycute
Chipboard, vinyl rope

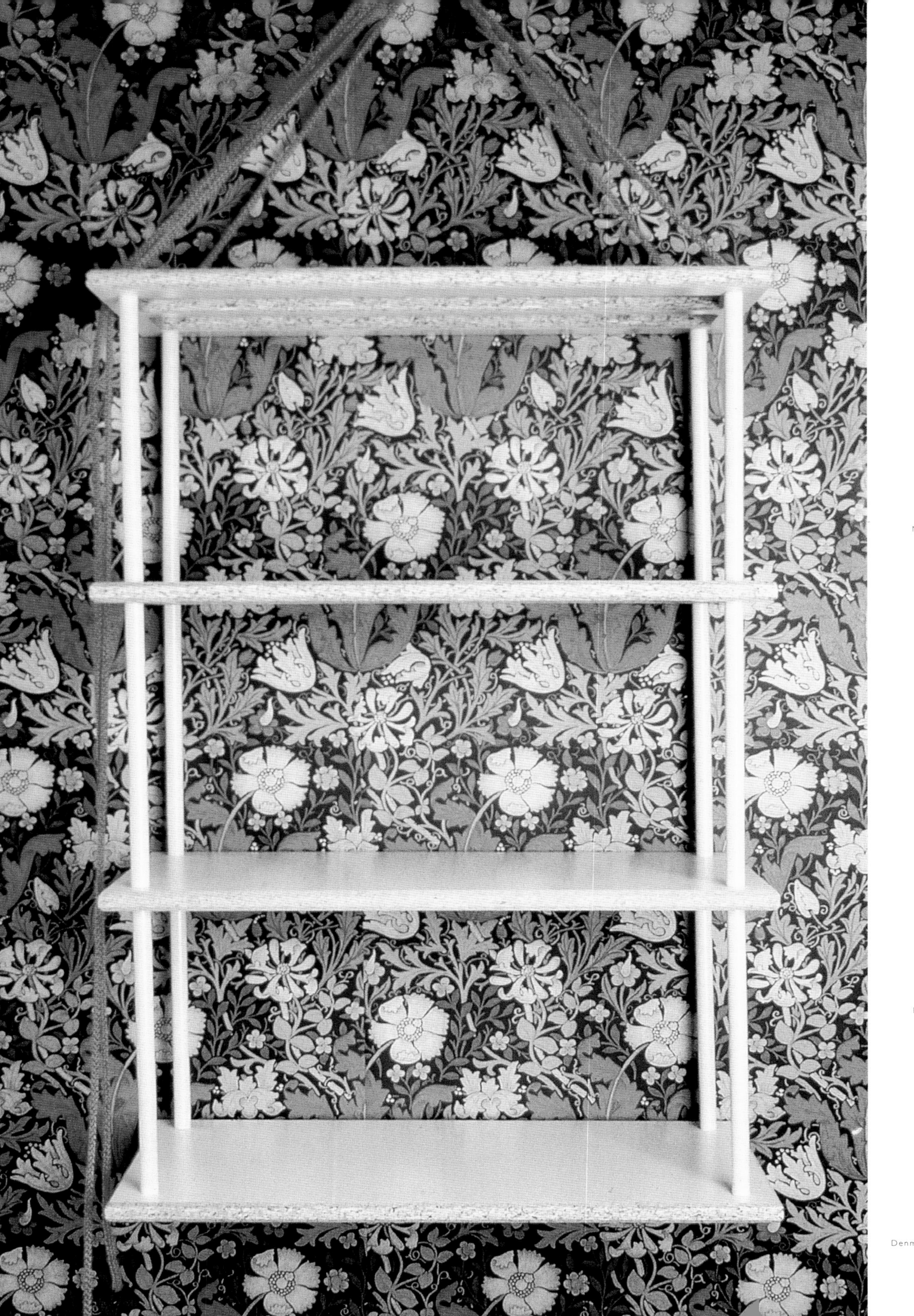

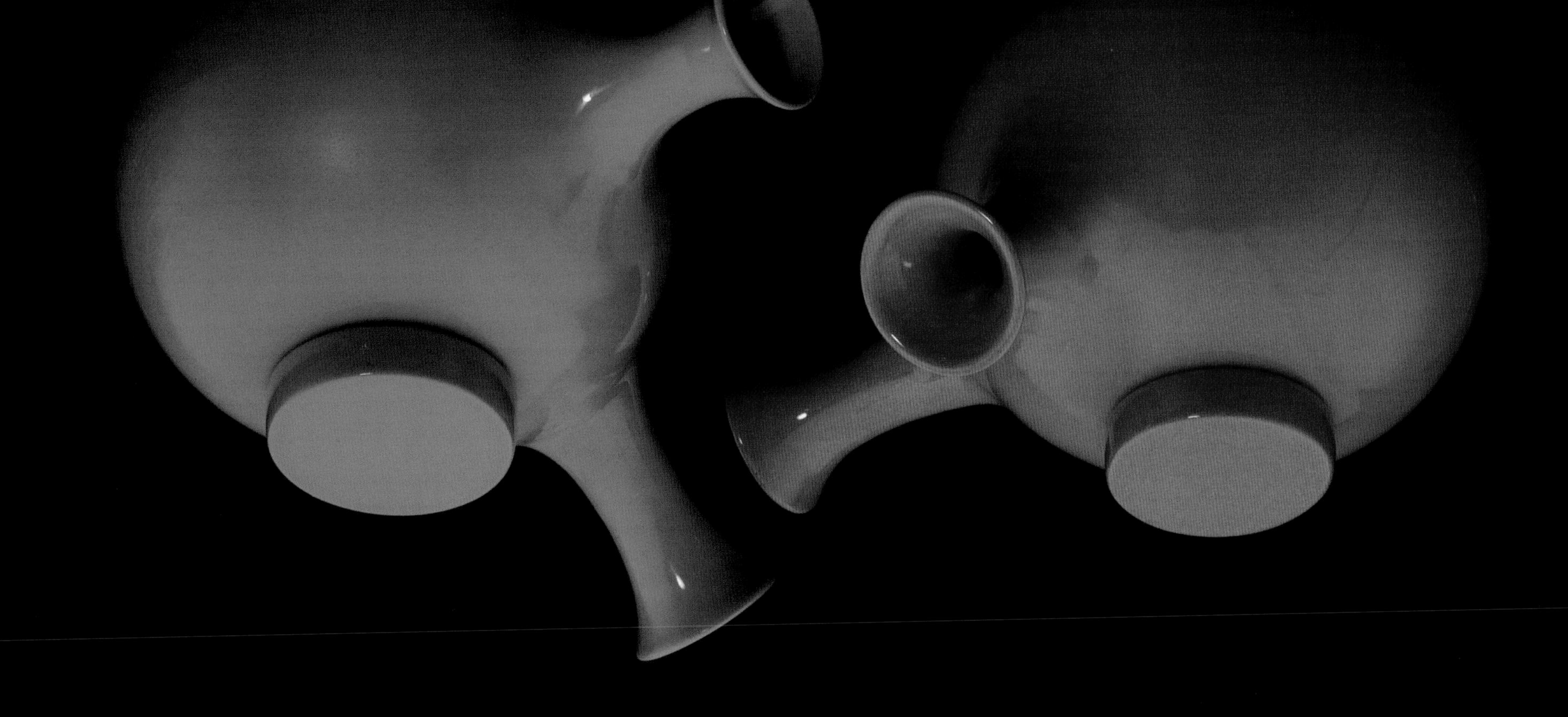

The Spout and Martian teapots
Michael Geertsen
Pottery with pink and green glazes
DENMARK

FINLAND
Omakuva ("Self-Portrait"), a Finnish ryijy rug, for Helmi Vuorelma
Harri Helorinne
Wool, linen

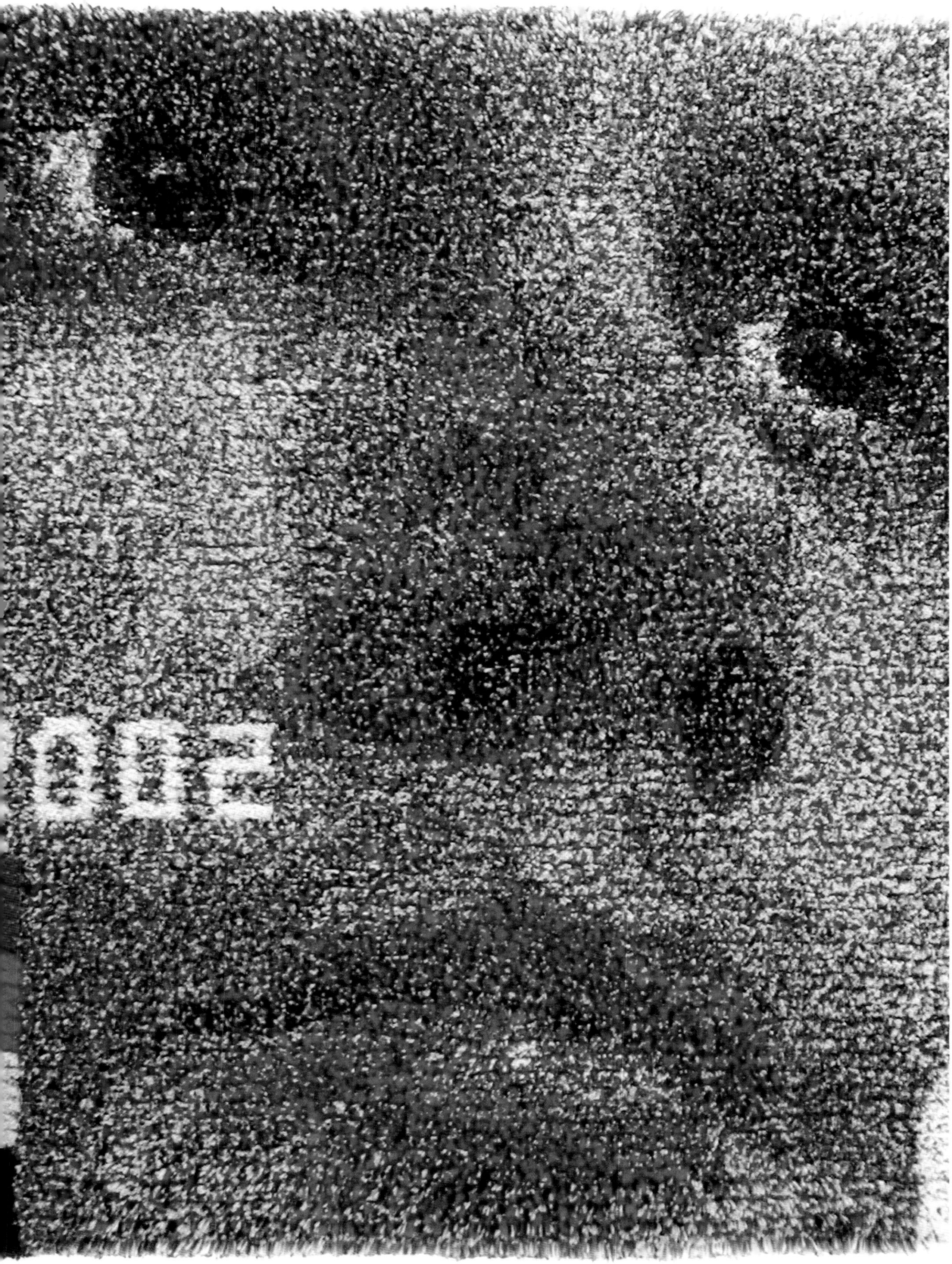

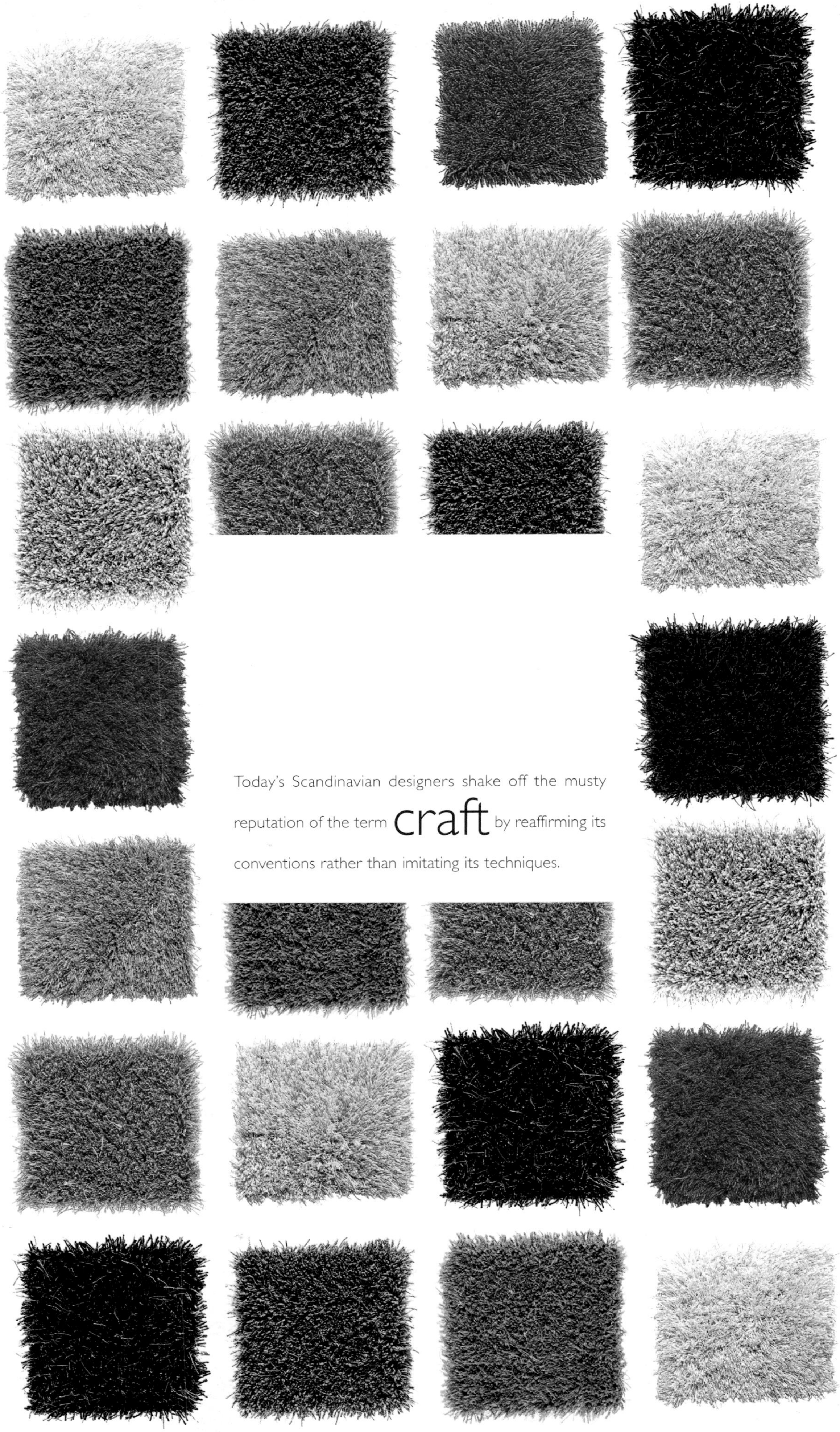

Moss carpet for Kasthall
Gunilla Lagerhem Ullberg
Hand-tufted wool and flax yarn
SWEDEN

FINLAND
TV2, a Finnish ryijy rug, crafted by Suomen Käsityön Ystävät
Pannu Puolakka
Cotton, linen

Today's Scandinavian designers shake off the musty reputation of the term craft by reaffirming its conventions rather than imitating its techniques.

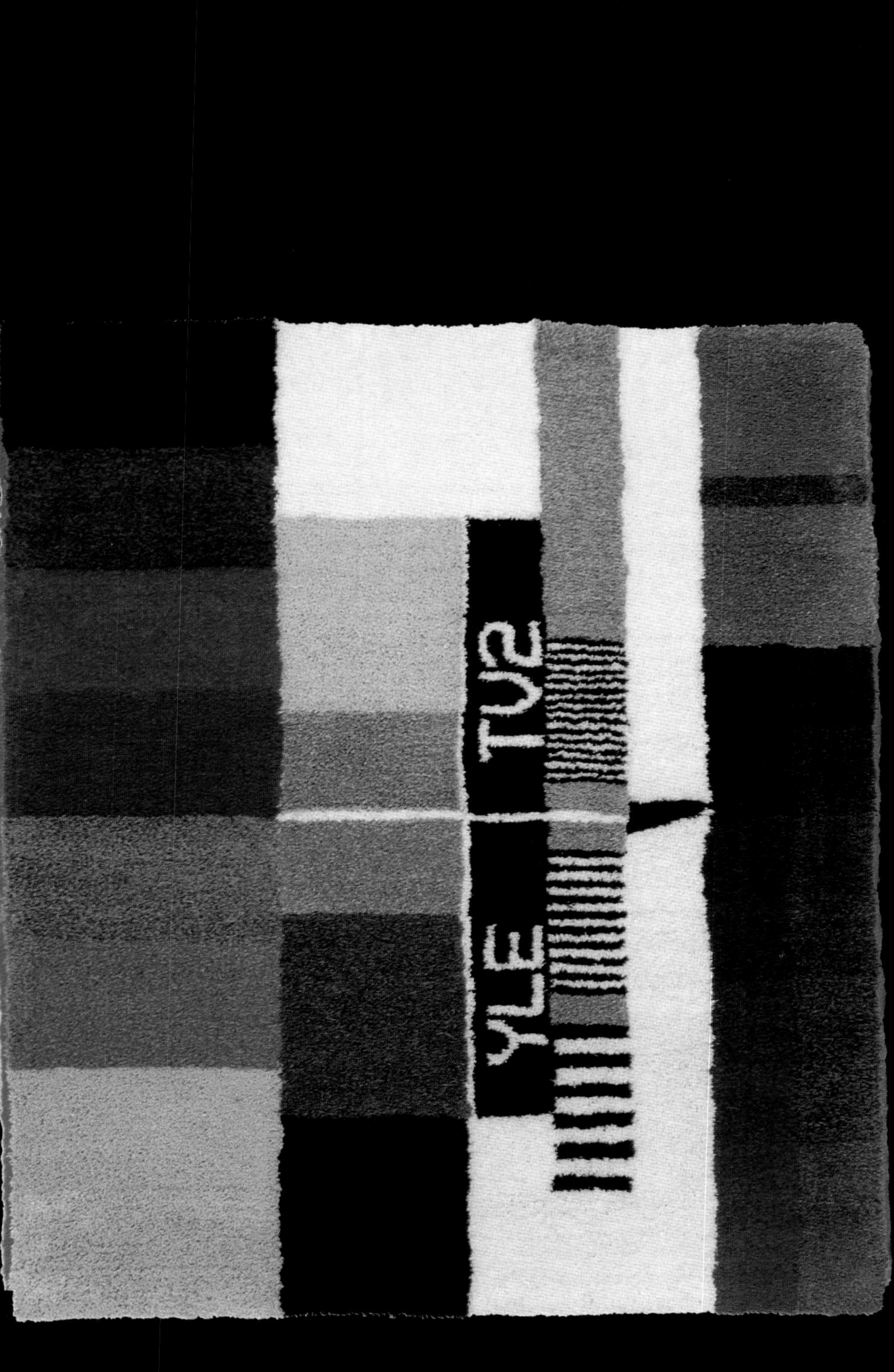
YLE
TV2

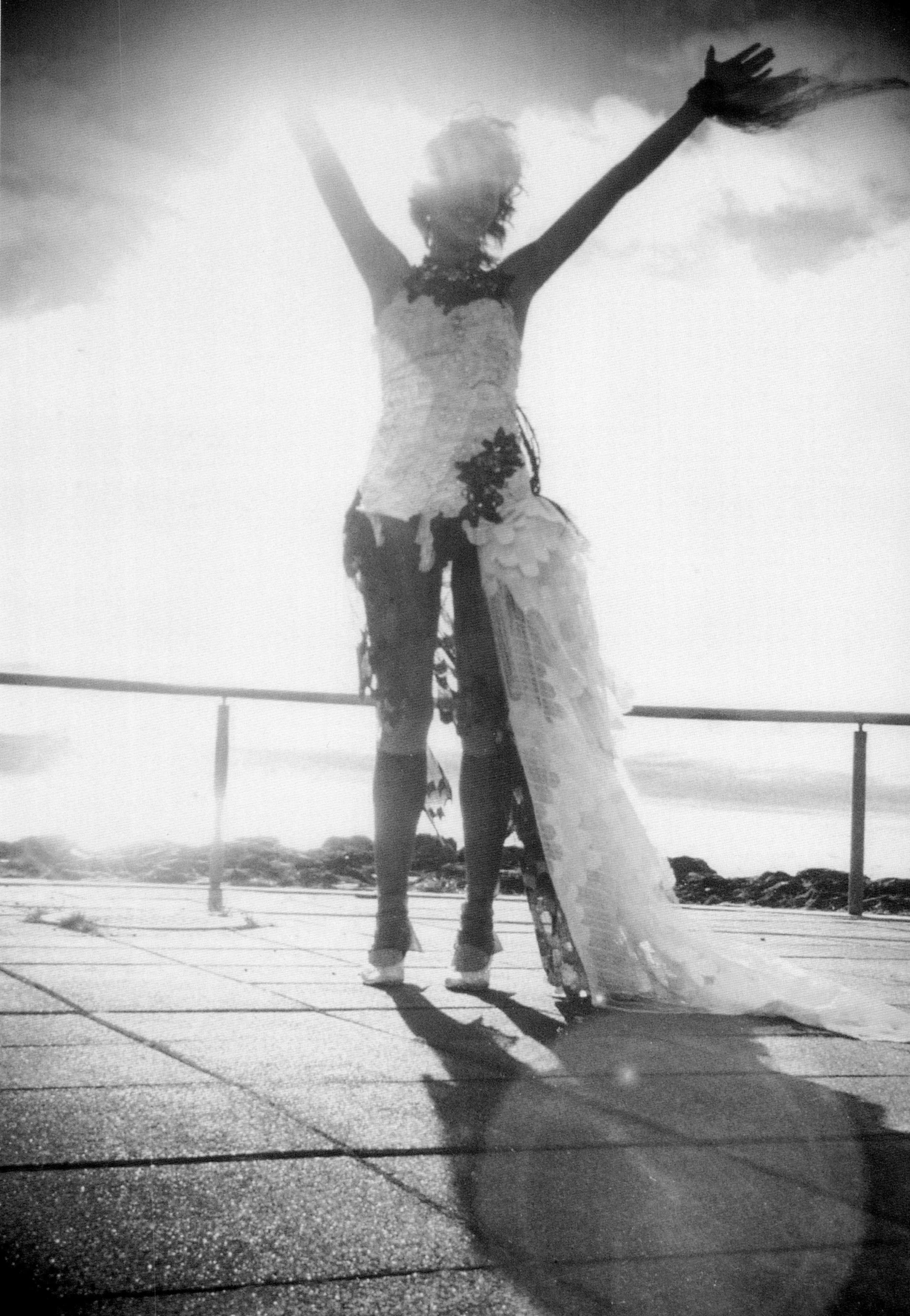

ICELAND
Dress
Aftur
Men's cotton busines shirts, lace curtains

FINLAND
Anemone lamp and table
Anna Katriina Tilli, Mari Relander
Hand-blown glass, handmade bobbin lace, silk-printed glass

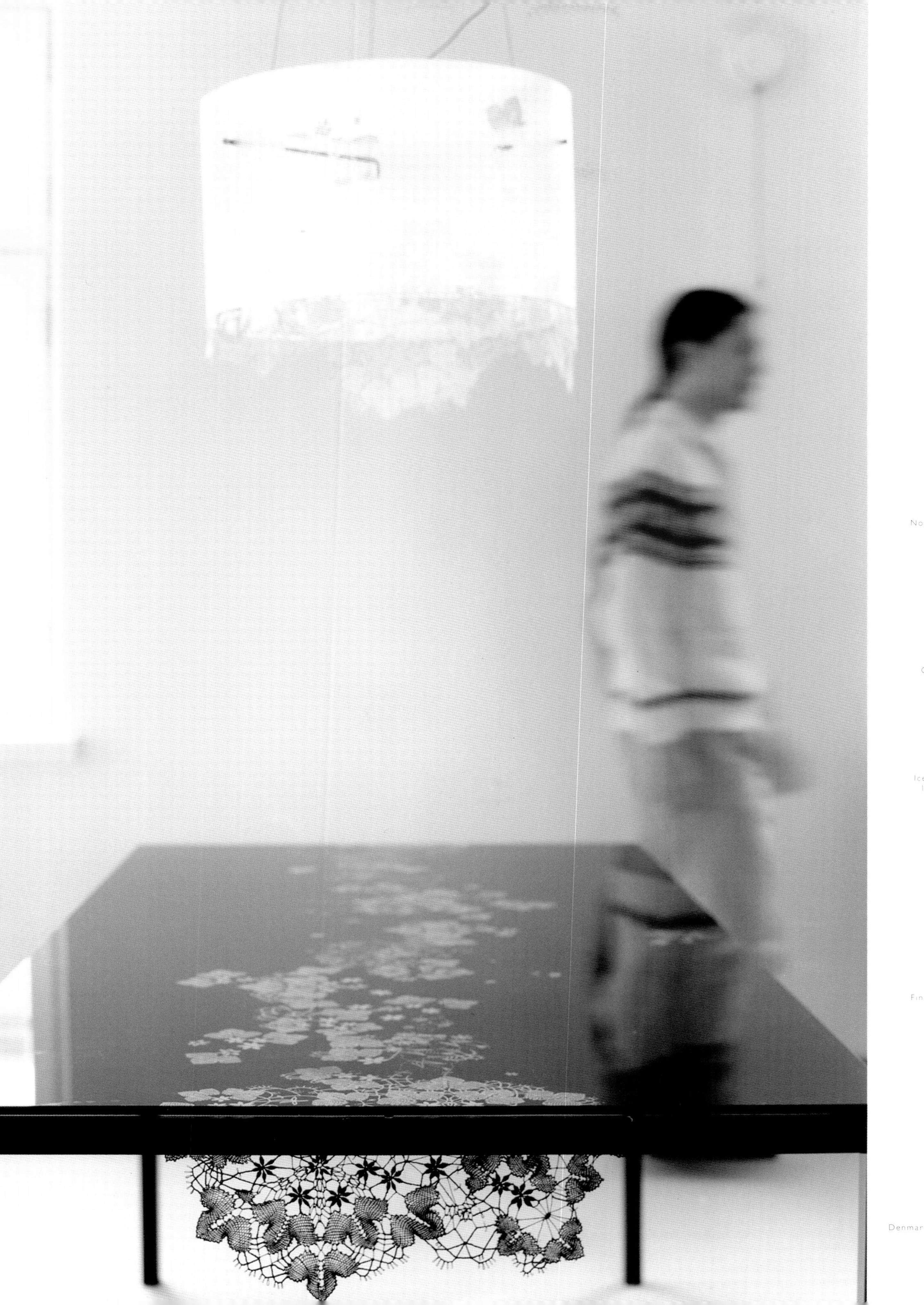

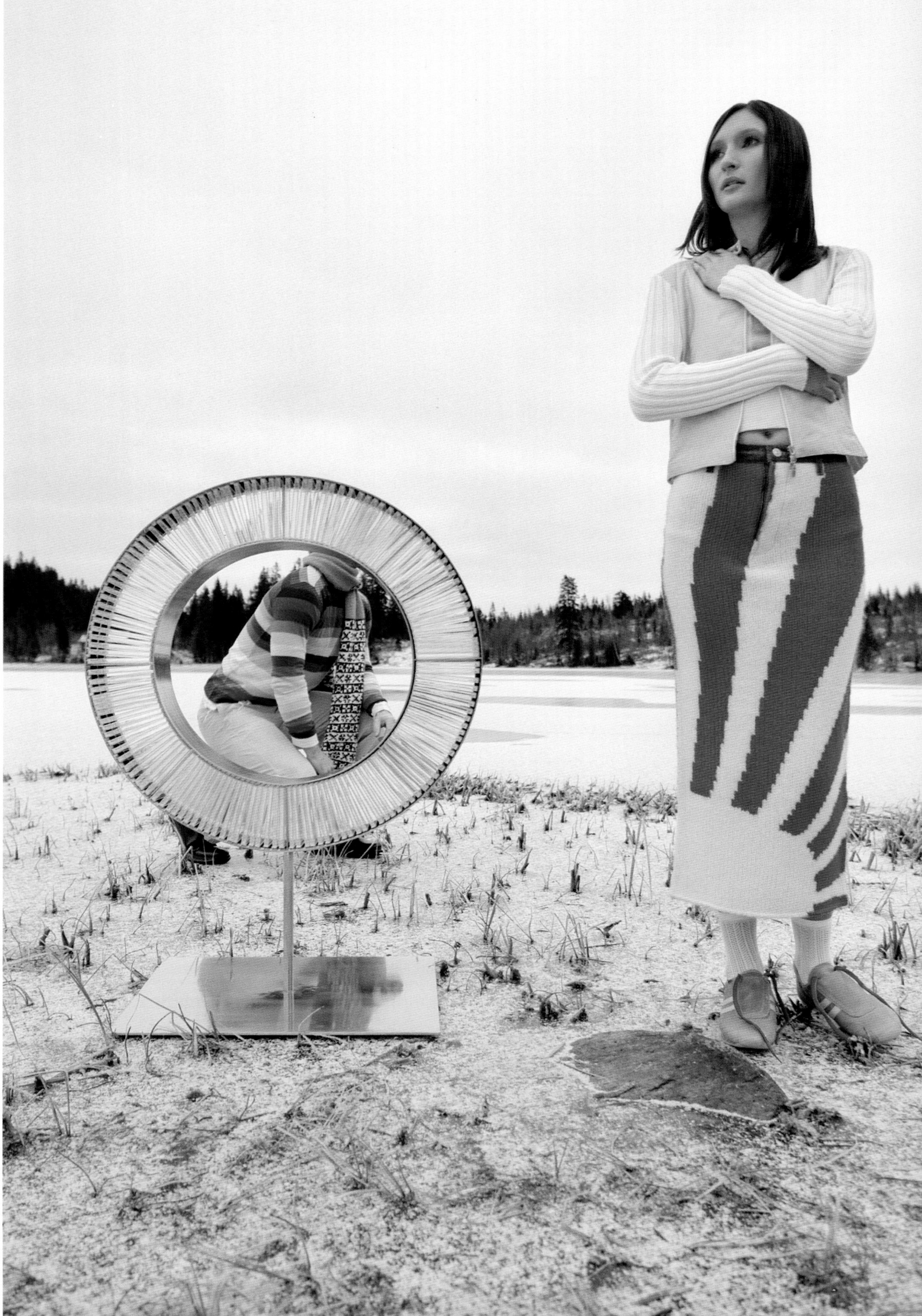

CD-Rundell
Lars Ernst Hole
Stainless steel
NORWAY

ICELAND
High Heel cups for Details-Produkte
Hrafnkell Birgisson
Porcelain, glass

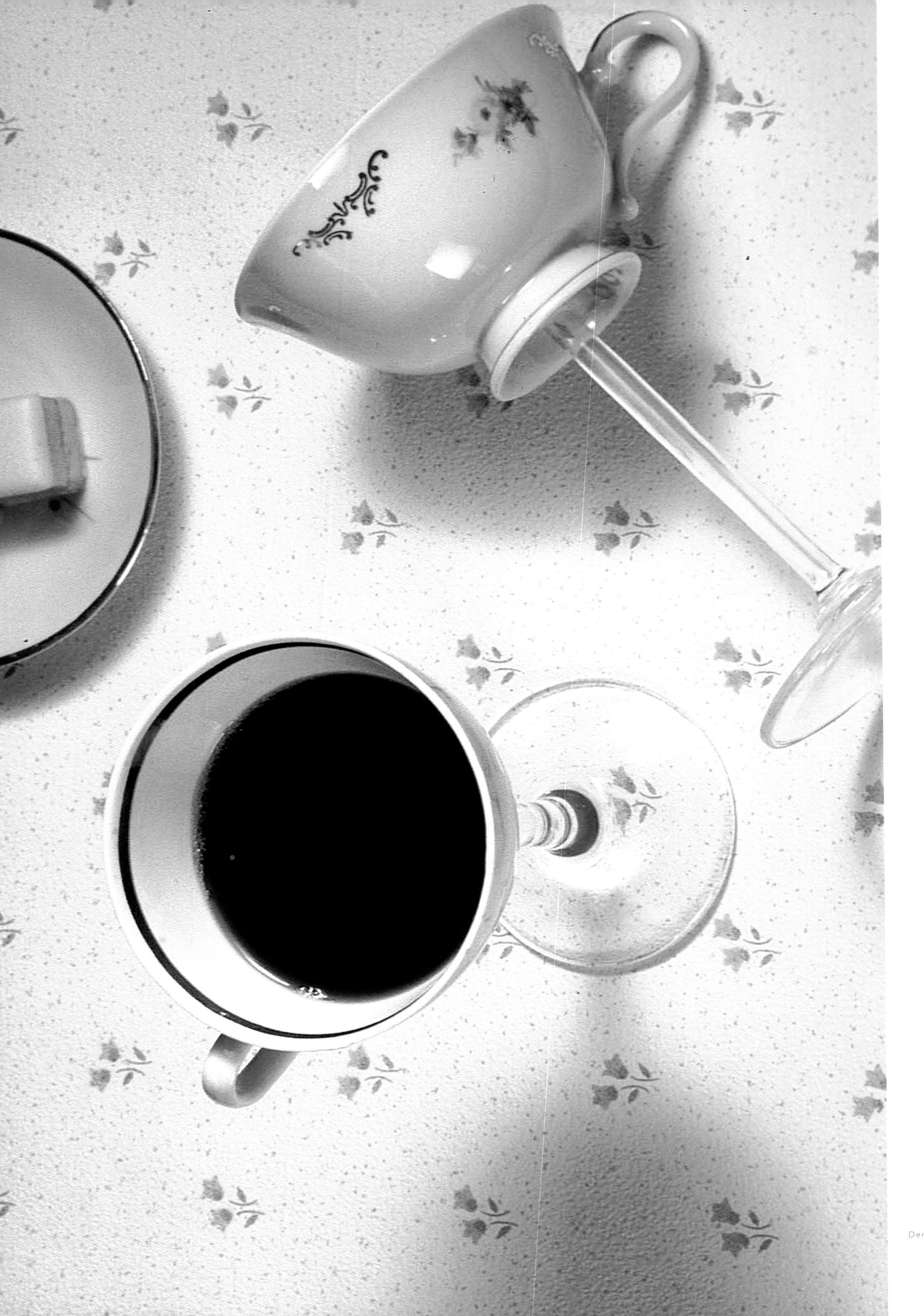

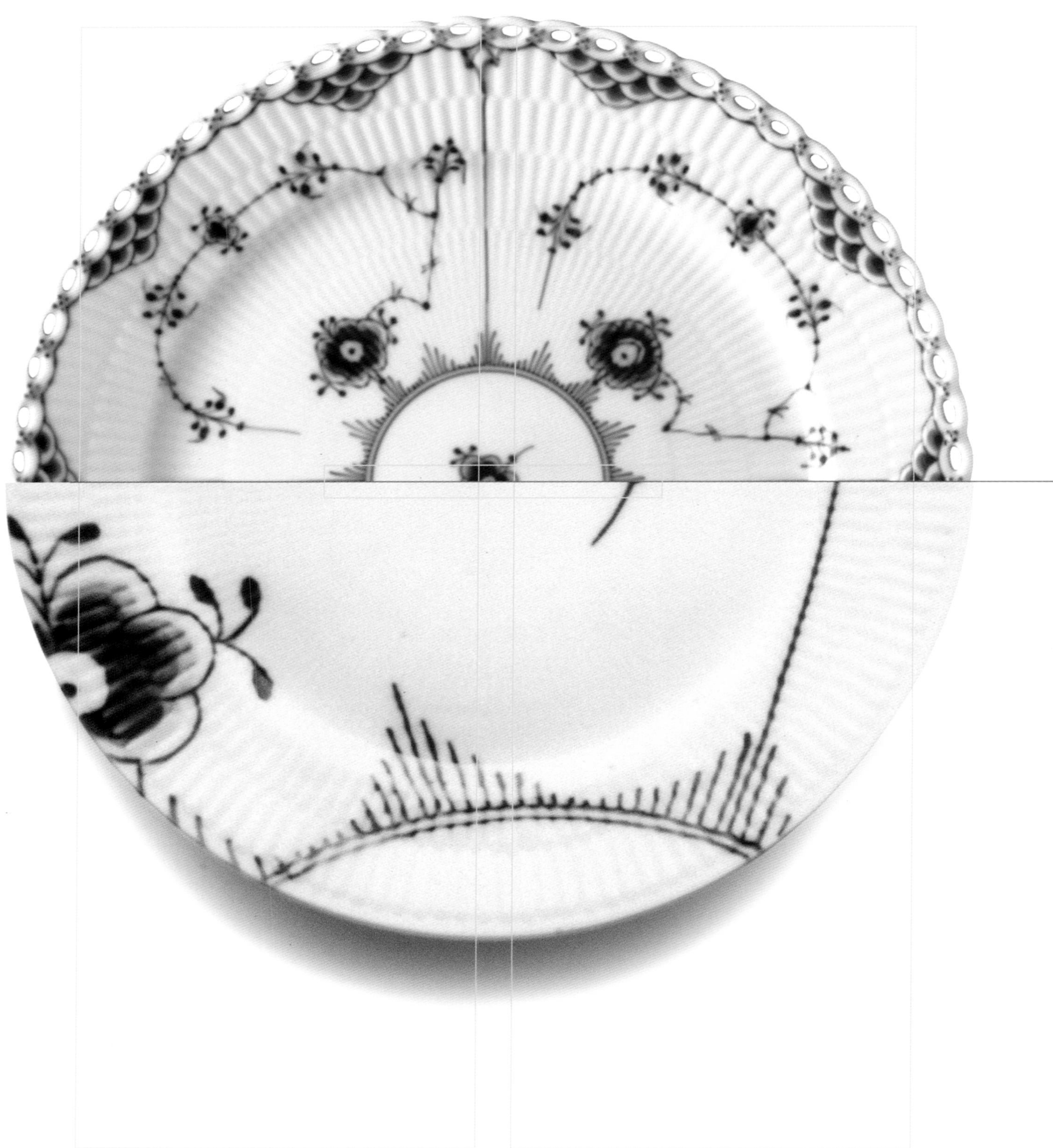

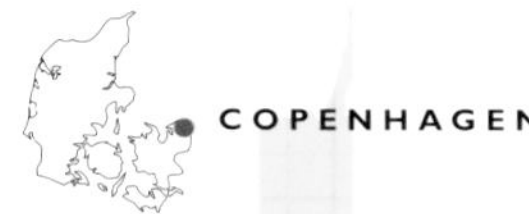

Denmark

In Denmark, Arne Jacobsen's 1952 Ant chair is as hard to miss as the swarms of bicyclists at mid-day intersections in downtown Copenhagen. The great Modernist's furniture populates not only cafés, libraries, and other public sites but also nearly every Danish home. With the enormous international recognition Danish Modern masters like Jacobsen have received over the years, it has been difficult for young designers to forge new territory in this design-saturated society. However, during the 1990s, three intrepid design groups—Octo, Panic, and Kropsholder—made headway, evolving an expressionistic design language. Inspired by these groups, the current crop of Danish designers is more diverse and dynamic than it has been for decades.

While the other Scandinavian countries also boast great Modern traditions, the sheer number of internationally recognized Danish designers from the mid-twentieth century period is unparalleled. "It's only during the 1990s that designers have been able to cope with what, in many ways, is an intimidating, even frightening, tradition," says Bodil Busk Laursen, director of the Danish Museum of Decorative Art. "What broke the ice was the fact that during the mid-1990s it became a common feature for the most experimental designers to form groups." The first of these groups, founded in 1989, was Octo, an eight-member multidisciplinary collective. In 1995, one of Octo's cofounders, Niels Hvass, designed an armchair and footstool set titled Yesterday's News, a hand-crafted, limited-edition piece that acts more as an artistic gesture than furniture-production prototype. With a sly nod to the Danish wood chair tradition, Hvass made Yesterday's News by gluing a thick stack of tabloid newspapers together and carving out a single square block to create both a seat (in the hollow left by the cut-out) and a footstool (the cut-out itself). Yesterday's News and other designs by Hvass, such as

Official name: The Kingdom of Denmark • Population: Over 5 million • Area: 16,639 square miles (43,094 square kilometers) • Capital: Copenhagen •

Royal Copenhagen's Blue Fluted MEGA
inspired by 1775 Blue Fluted pattern (previous spread)
Karen Kjældgård-Larsen
Hand-painted porcelain
DENMARK

his Willow chair, shaped from a chunky pile of willow branches, fashion found materials into sculptural designs and offer early examples of the conceptual approach so popular among young Danish designers today.

Also in 1995, five other young designers banded together, taking the name Panic. The members of the collective, still undergraduates at the time, reacted against what they viewed as a creative malaise in the Danish design community. "Design had become such a fine art that you couldn't execute it any more," says founding member Mathias Bengtsson. Like Finland's upstart Snowcrash, Panic eschewed the traditional Scandinavian medium, wood, and instead embraced synthetics such as carbon fiber and thermoplastic. "We wanted to move Danish design in a more international direction and not just follow the path of the old masters," says another cofounder, Sebastian Holmbäck. The group found props in junkyards and broke glass on showroom floors in staged events, but behind the punk attitude was a freewheeling experimentation with forms and materials, exemplified by Bengtsson's prickly wire easy chair, made from more than 1500 wire bits randomly welded together, and Holmbäck's twisted Viscous Tree table, comprised of a goopy mass of polyethylene plastic and an acrylic tabletop. "We did not consider production or economy," says Holmbäck. "It was all about shape, looks, and statements. We tried to be the opposite of what we saw at the furniture fairs: all the 'right stuff.'"

Founded in 1997, Kropsholder emerged as the third influential group on the Danish design scene. Kropsholder (Danish for "body container" or "body keeper") became the first all-female design group in Danish history. "When we began Kropsholder, we discovered that there were a large number of individual female furniture designers in Denmark," says Louise Campbell, who cofounded the group with Malene Reitzel. "It was also clear that the men of our generation seemed to have sharper elbows and easier access to the industry and the media." The group developed limited-edition, art-inspired designs as well as functional furniture that playfully engaged users' emotions. Both Pernille Vea's Non Reclining mirror and Pil Bredahl's Zen-Sation cabinet offer enticing features such as hidden compartments and mysterious, secret inscriptions.

The conceptual language and unconventional approach first introduced by Octo, Panic, and Kropsholder during the 1990s informs much of Danish design today. Progressive thinkers on the scene: Astrid Krogh, creator of glowing fiber-optic textiles; Alex Soza, a designer of futuristic "smart" clothing; and Cecilie Manz, who builds meticulous, delicate furniture. New design groups are also on the rise, one standout being Culture Corporation—whose members include Ditte Hammerstrøm, Claus Bjerre, and Jeremy Walton—which takes a quirky, narrative approach to design. The group exhibited its Bænken er Din ("Growing Bench") project in downtown Copenhagen, assembling a snaking seat of driftwood and discarded lumber in a public park called Glentehaven. The designers relinquished control of the project's outcome as passersby were encouraged to add their own building materials to the expanding construction. "Functionalism is now only one of a number of concerns," says the Museum of Decorative Art's Laursen. "It is still in there somewhere during the process, but it isn't the most important. The conceptual aspect is more in focus now."

Longest annual period of daylight in Copenhagen: 17.5 hours • Shortest annual period of daylight in Copenhagen: 7 hours • Official language: Danish (Minority languages

It is also notable that, for the first time in Danish design history—indeed, in design history, period—the ratio of female to male designers is fairly equal. The large number of women actively contributing to the field may have had an impact on the current design vocabulary, with sensuality, lush textures, and less rigorous architectural solutions becoming more pervasive. "Perhaps Kropsholder can take a little of the credit [for the number of women designers working today]; perhaps it's just about a global change in habits," says Campbell.

While Danish designers are open to new ideas, they balance this receptivity with a great respect for their design tradition. In general, Danish design remains a humanistic practice focused on users' needs; this quality has been important in the field since the early twentieth century when the architect and scholar Kaare Klint, the father of Modern Danish furniture design, pioneered a revolutionary new method using human measurements in the design process, which he called "anthropometrics." This humane sensibility has surfaced once again in a concern for quality of life and personal well-being in work by young groups such as Kropsholder, Culture Corporation, and others.

Another key Danish value, high-quality craftsmanship, has not diminished. This concern springs from the influential collaborations between mid-twentieth-century Danish Modern designers and highly skilled cabinetmakers. These famous pairings—Finn Juhl and Niels Vodder, Ole Wanscher and A. J. Iversen—shaped many now-classic Modern pieces. Young designers such as Hans Sandgren Jakobsen and Kasper Salto, who both began their careers as woodworkers, continue the tradition of fine detailing while pushing new technology in pursuit of timeless solutions. Jakobsen, who got his start assisting Danish furniture designer Nanna Ditzel, created an Asian-inspired molded-wood masterpiece with his Gallery stool for the art museum Kunstforeningen in Copenhagen. Salto, who works closely with Fritz Hansen, the manufacturer of several landmark Arne Jacobsen chairs, enhances his patient exploration of material with a sharp eye for detail, particularly in Ice, his indoor/outdoor chair. "The consideration of the materials and the finish is very important today," says Laursen. "That is part of the heritage from craft, and it still dominates Danish design."

While today's momentum in Danish design is due in part to the groundbreaking work of many practitioners, the government has also actively supported the field. Its national design policy, created in 1998 under the auspices of the Ministry of Industry, was the first of its kind in the world, according to Birgitta Capetillo, deputy manager of the Danish Design Center, an organization founded in 1977 to increase awareness of design in both the private and the public sectors. With legislation and government funding, the national design program aimed to improve design education and to encourage the use of design in business in areas such as product development, strategy, marketing, and advertising. The policy also served indirectly, says Capetillo, as a model for similar programs in Sweden and Finland. (Although the recently elected Danish government decided not to renew its funding for the policy in 2001, talks are underway for new legislation to be presented in the next few years.) Calling the national policy "quite effective," Capetillo says she has noticed a higher level of design saturation in business over the last several years. "When the Danish Design Center was established

include Faroese, Greenlandic [an Inuit dialect], and German.) • Number of islands: 406 • Number of wind turbines: 6,300 • Percentage of electricity supplied by wind

in the 1970s, it was a fight to get industry to understand what design was about," she says. "It is still tough but, at the moment, *design* is a buzzword in Denmark, and globally too."

The government's commitment to design includes a particularly forward-looking agenda for craft. Although the expertise of Danish craftsmen has traditionally had a huge influence on design, the knowledge is in danger of disappearing as companies cut costs by hiring workers abroad. Danish Crafts, an organization founded in 1999 under the Ministry of Culture, has worked to invigorate the field by training craftsmen to become entrepreneurs and aiding them in establishing business contacts in sectors such as retail, marketing, and the media. Significantly, Danish Crafts initiated an annual guest-curated collection of high-quality goods that it promotes at lifestyle fairs around the world. Emphasizing veracity, authenticity, intimacy, and the human touch, Danish Crafts collection projects—including a flexible rubber cleaning basin by Ole Jensen, biodegradable dinnerware by PAPCoRN, and jewelry made from 1950s lace undergarments by Kasia Gasparski—update craft conventions rather than imitate old-fashioned techniques.

While there is renewed energy in the design community and positive momentum in government and industry, the specific influences that came together during the Golden Age of Scandinavian Modern are gone for good. "At the time, there just wasn't much international competition," says Capetillo. "That's why it worked so well, and the Danish designers became so famous. Today, all the Western world is doing design. It is difficult for national design to be brilliant today." And the amazing success of past achievements often means consumers have fixed expectations about Danish design. "A huge challenge for young designers is the enormous popularity of Arne Jacobsen and the mid-twentieth-century classics," says Capetillo. "Here in Copenhagen, young people save up to buy Jacobsen's Egg chair. This creates a problem for young designers because people of their generation aren't saving up to buy their work."

Yet Danish designers today seem more on target than in previous years. Instead of being burdened by their tradition, they find inspiration in it. In 2003, an exhibition called "Walk the Plank" at the Danish Museum of Decorative Art in Copenhagen revisited Danish design history by pairing expert woodworkers with a range of up-and-coming and established designers. "The combination of cabinetmaking and design in wood was Denmark's strength, but very few designers have an interest in working that way now," says Louise Campbell, who was one of the exhibition's organizers. "We decided to get them to rise to the challenge."

Today, designers make a conscious choice to engage—or not to engage—a national style. "Of course designers have roots," says Capetillo. "But how much emphasis they put on these roots is up to them."

DENMARK
Old News lamp
Liselotte Risell
Acrylic, lace

power: 15 • Percentage of paper products produced from recycled waste: Over 80 • Percentage of GNP given to foreign aid: 1 (the highest in the EU)

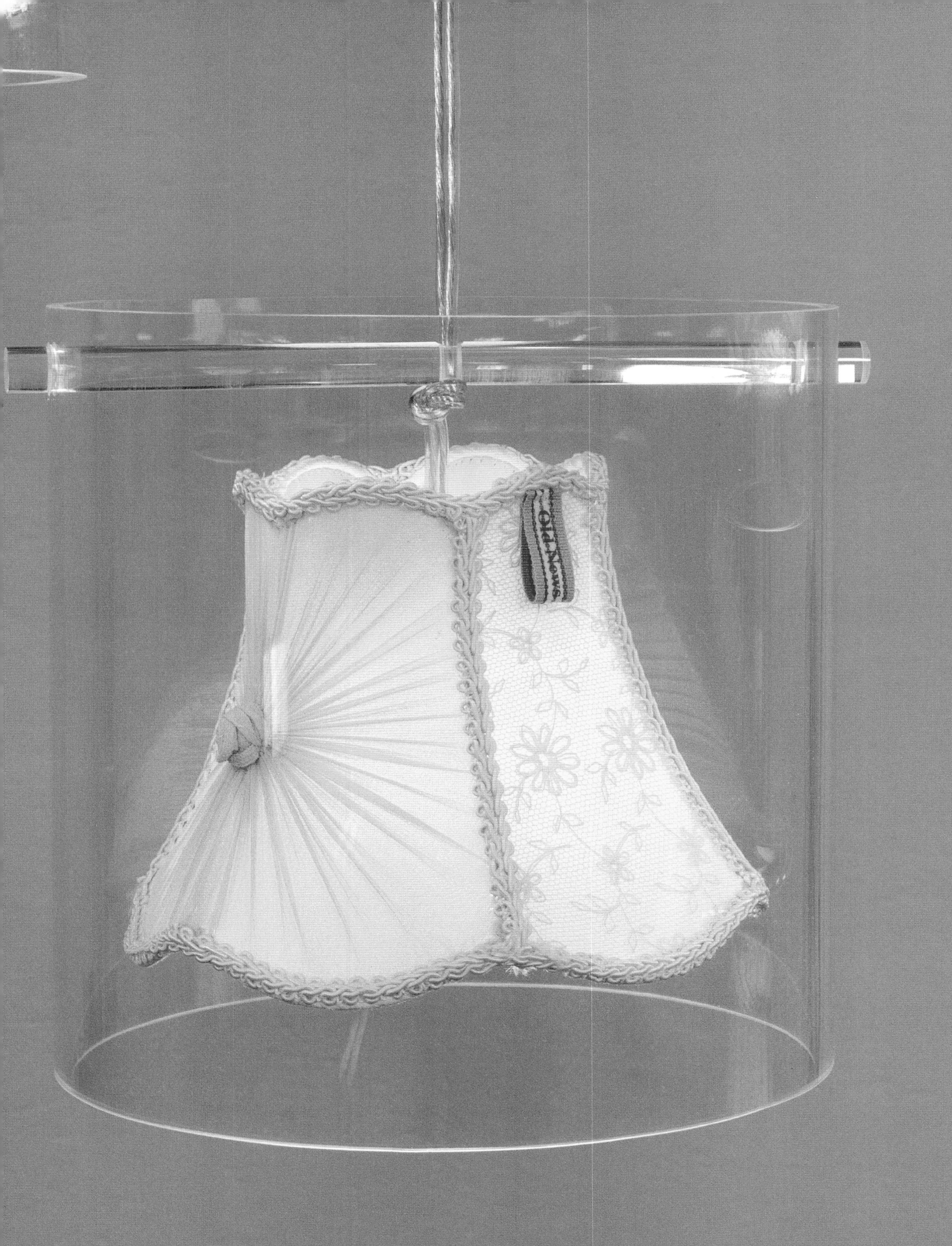
OldNews

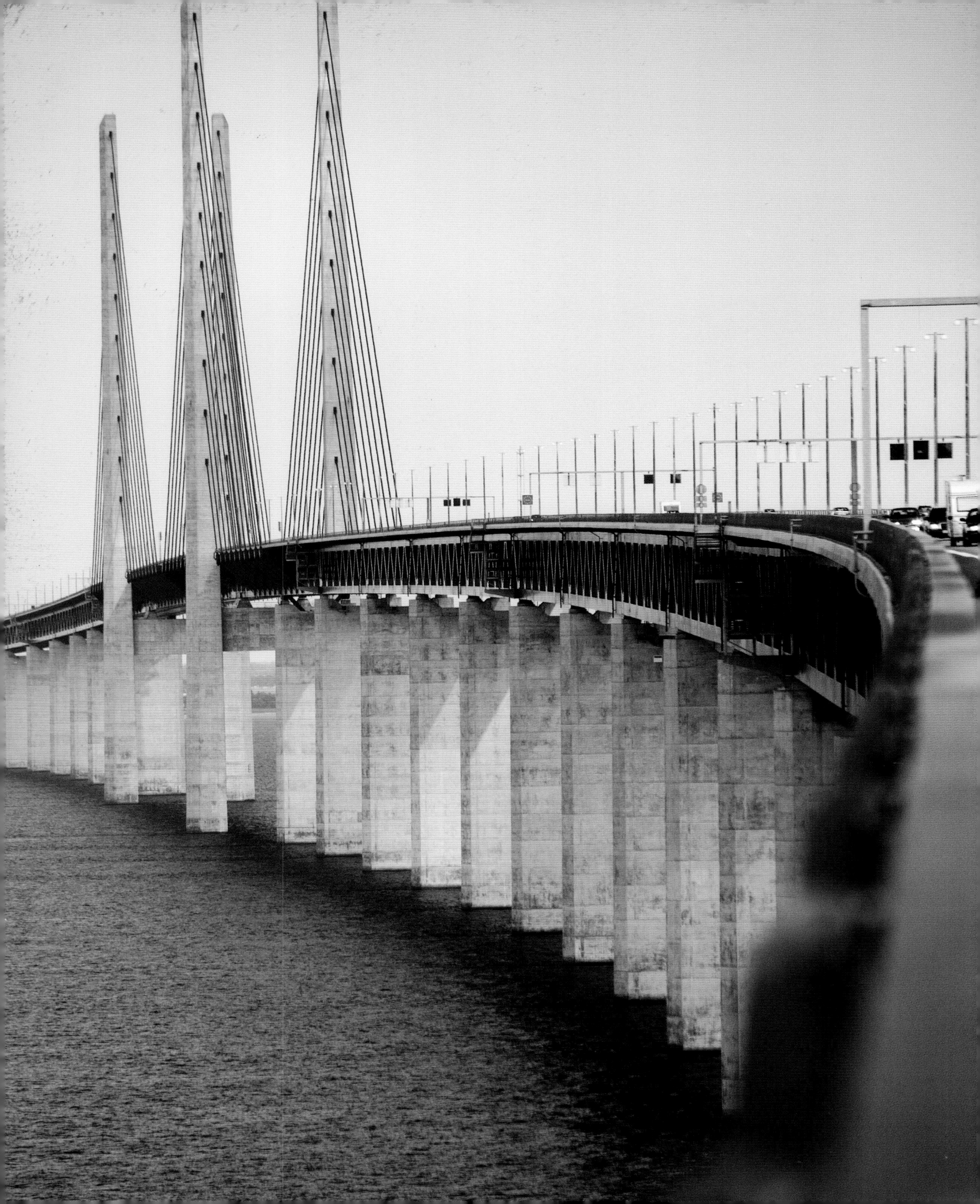

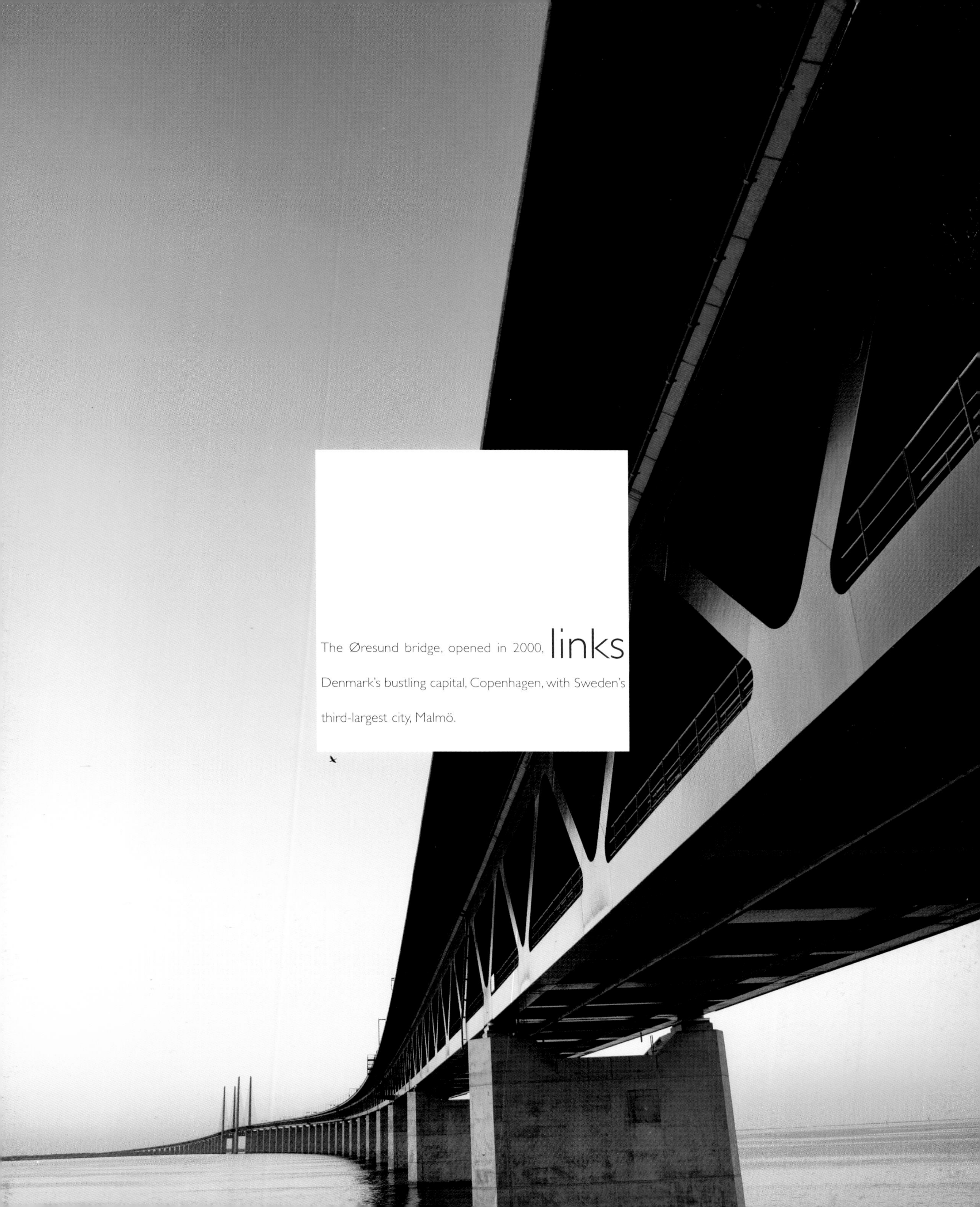

The Øresund bridge, opened in 2000, links Denmark's bustling capital, Copenhagen, with Sweden's third-largest city, Malmö.

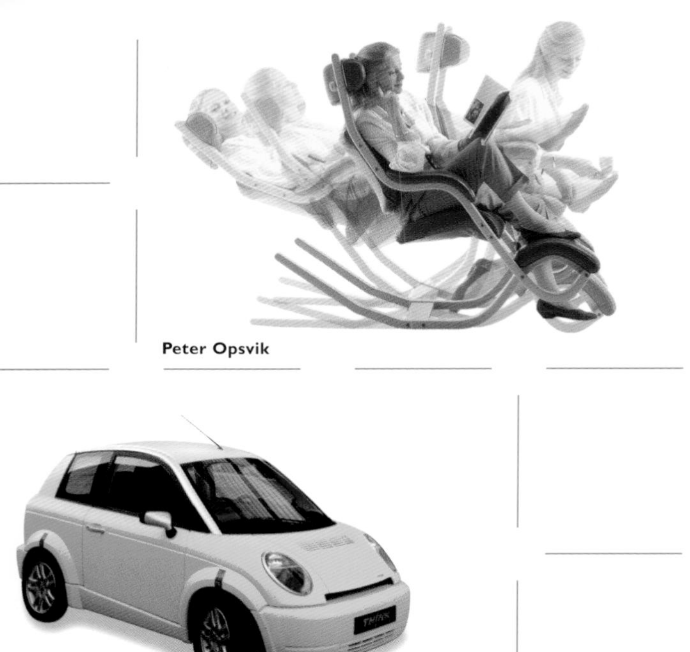
Peter Opsvik

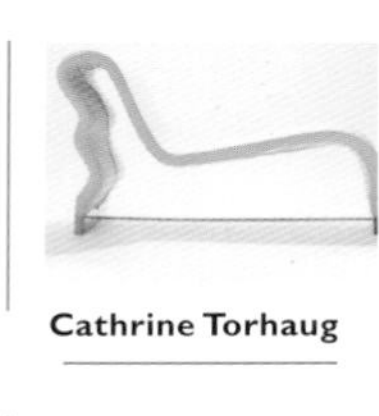
Cathrine Torhaug

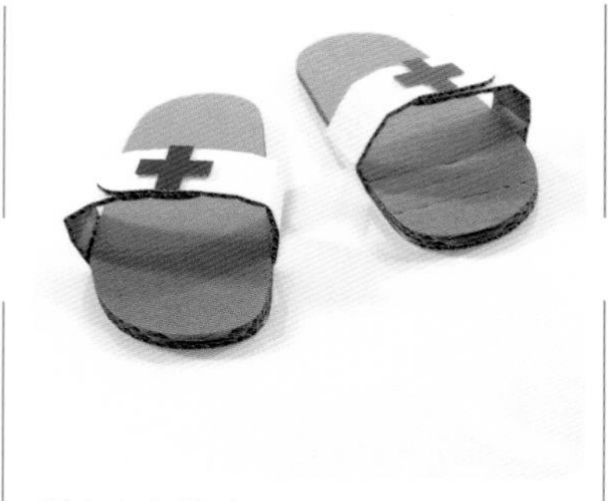
K8 Industridesign

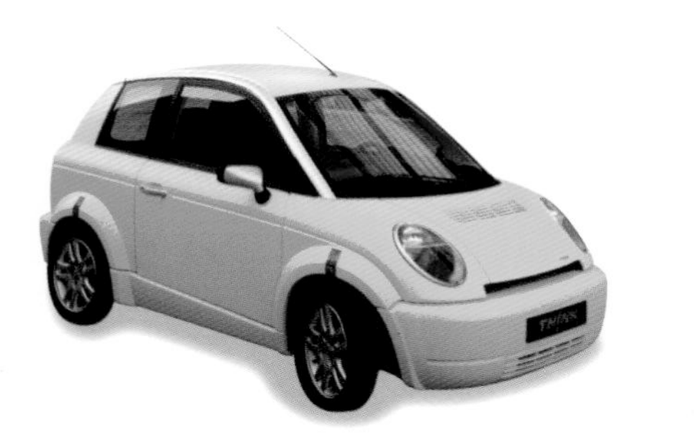
TH!NK Nordic

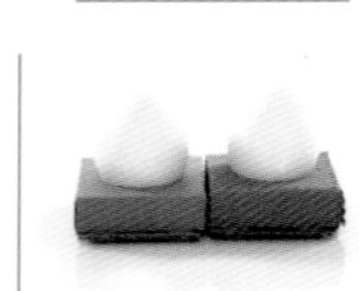
K8 Industridesign

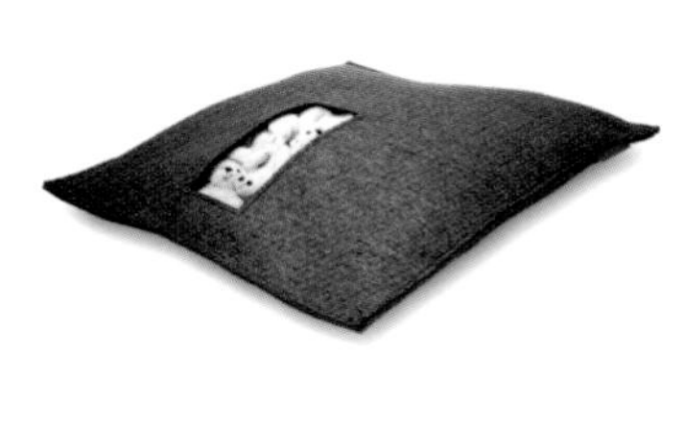
Permafrost

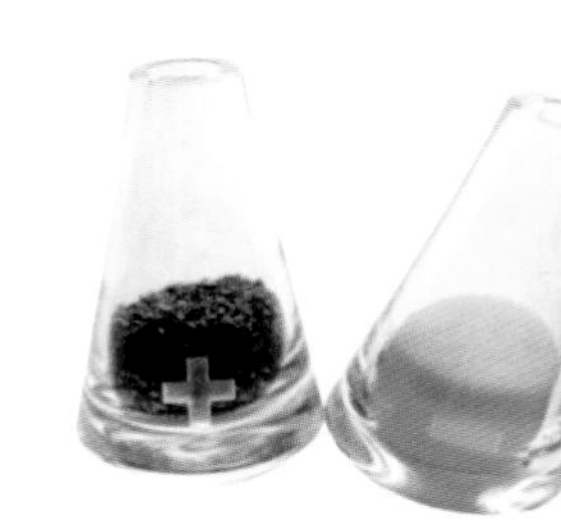
Cathrine Maske

Johan Verde

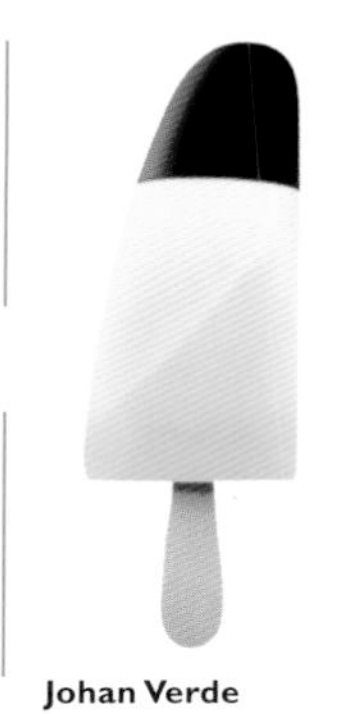
Johan Verde

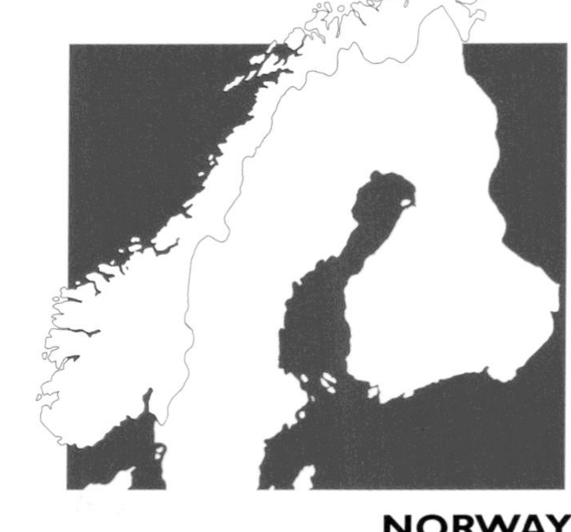
NORWAY

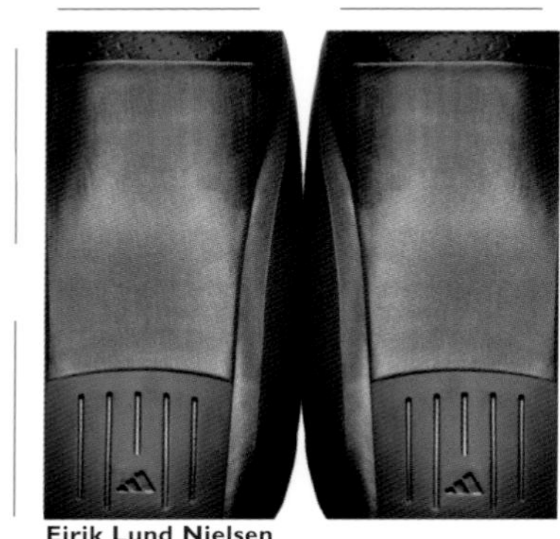
Eirik Lund Nielsen

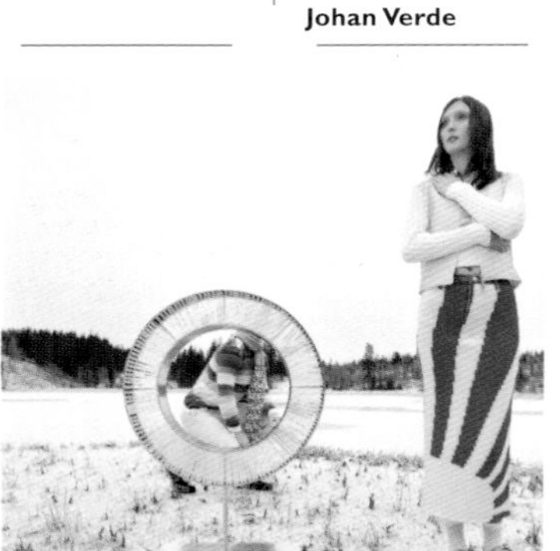
Lars Ernst Hole

Norway Says

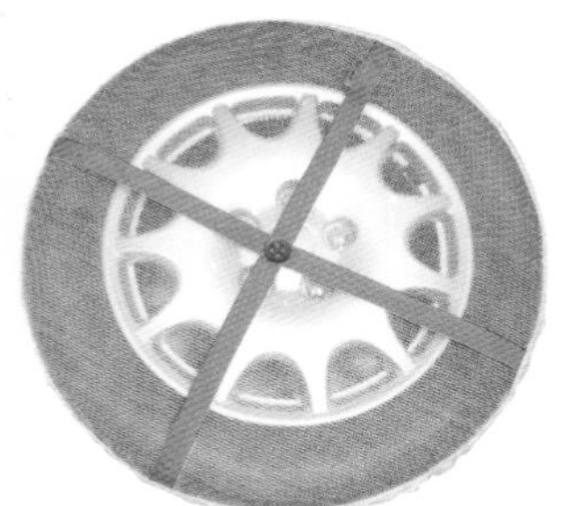
Hareide Designmill

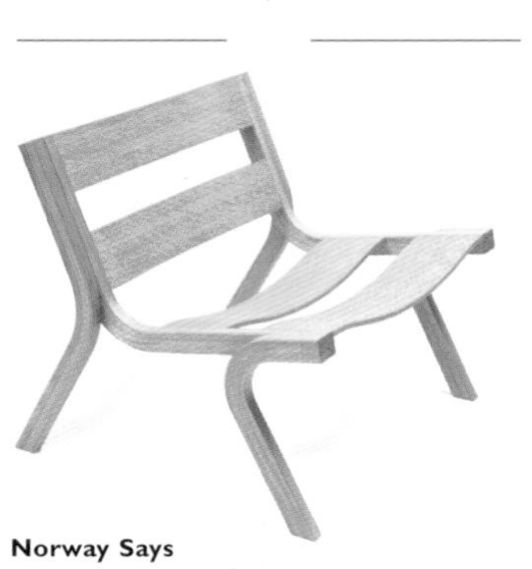
Norway Says

Olav Joa

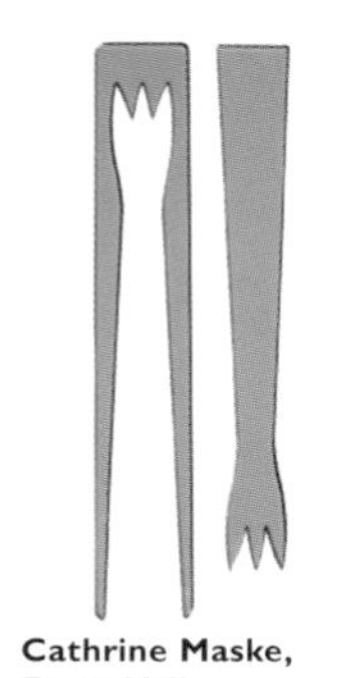
Cathrine Maske, Espen Voll

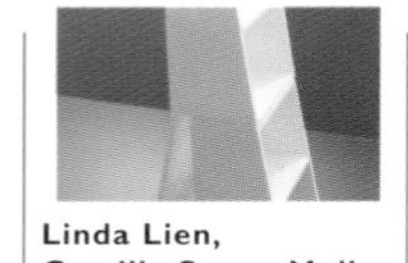
Linda Lien, Camilla Songe-Møller

Norway Says

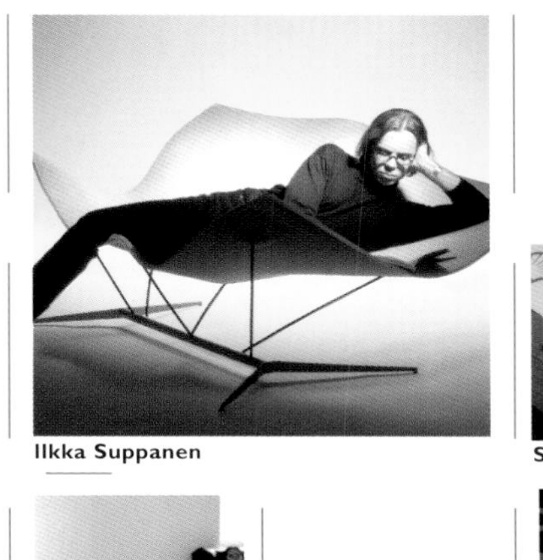
Ilkka Suppanen

Stefan Lindfors

Timo Salli

Tonfisk Design

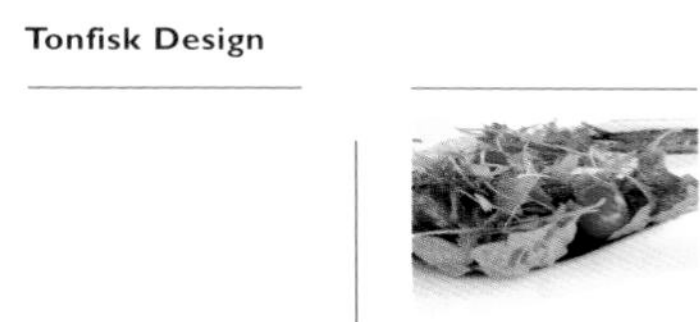
Ocean North

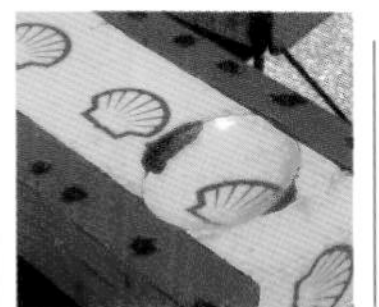
Sari Anttonen

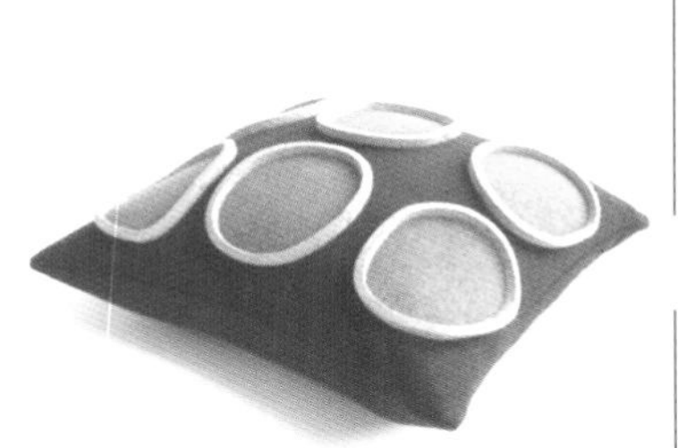
Anne Kyyrö Quinn

Perhonen

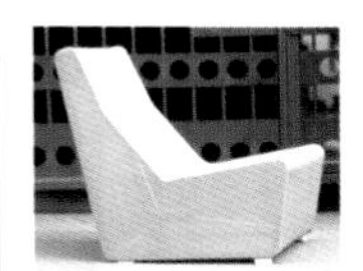
Timo Salli

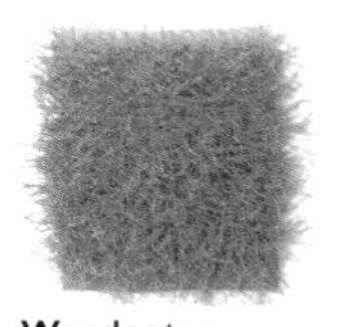
Woodnotes

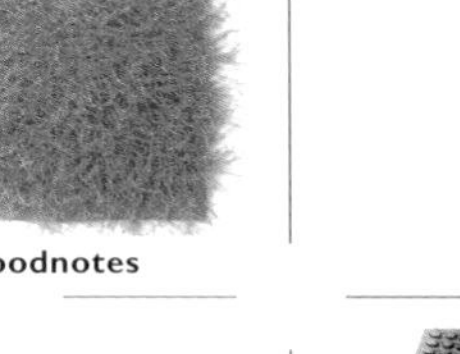
Nokia

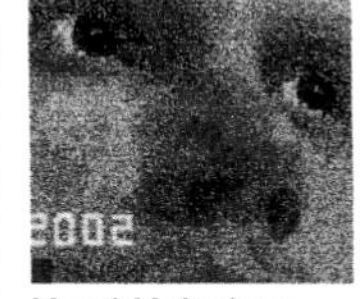

Harri Helorinne

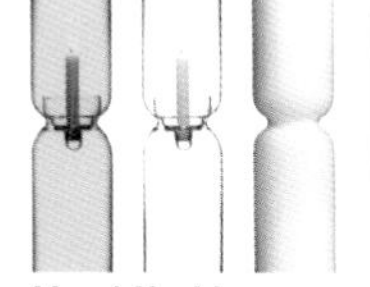
Harri Koskinen

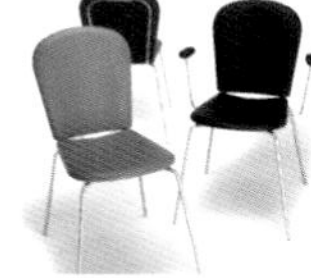
Sari Anttonen

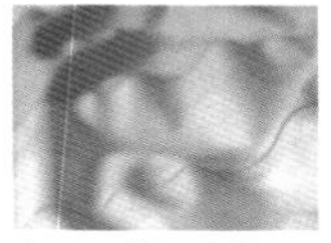
Jouko Kärkkäinen

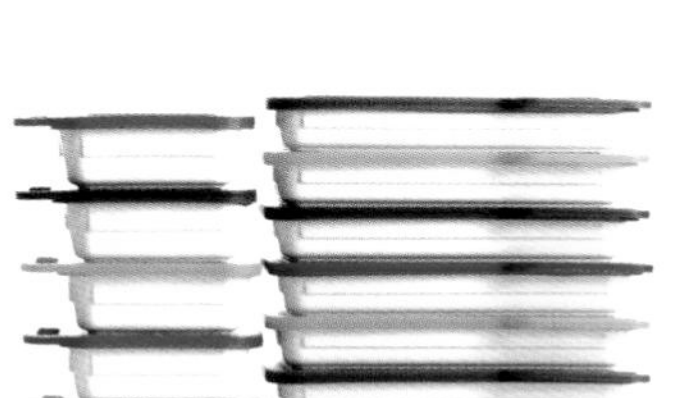
Harri Koskinen

Pannu Poulakka

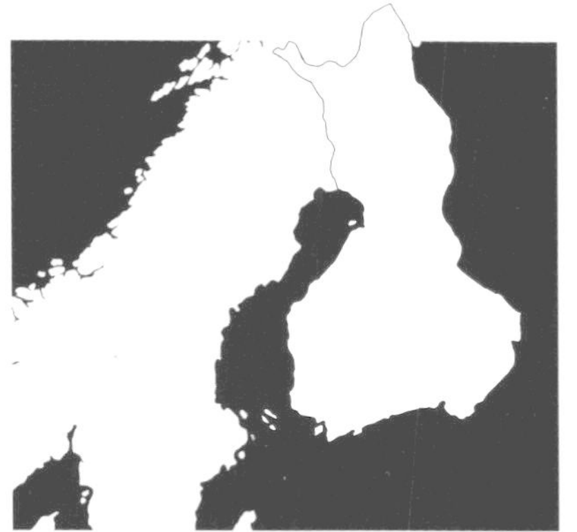
FINLAND

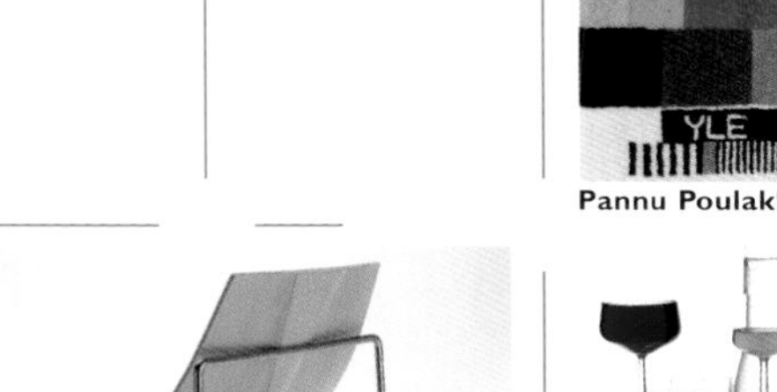
emu Järvi

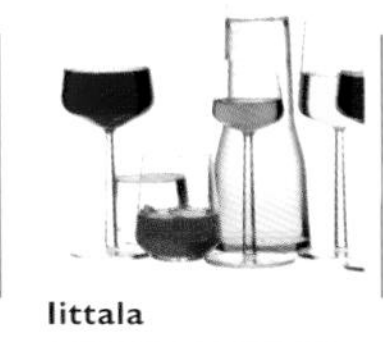
Iittala

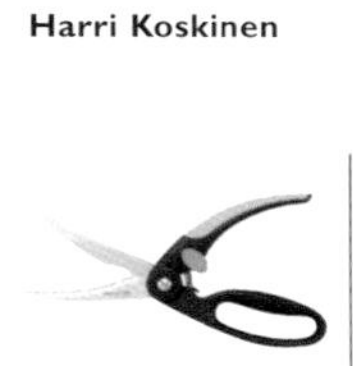
Olavi Lindén

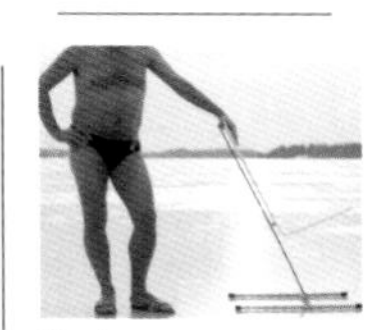
Perhonen

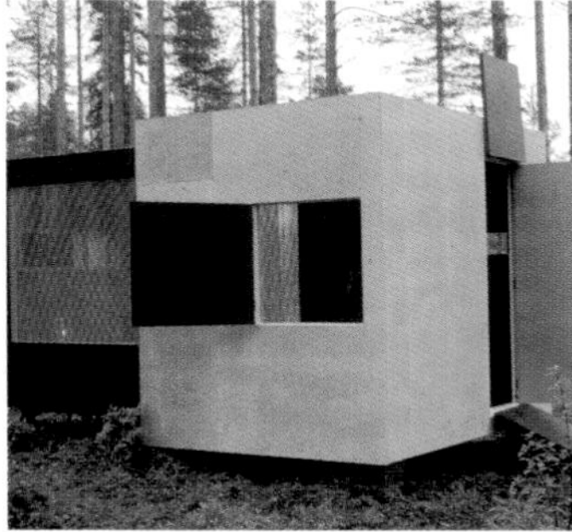
Markku Hedman

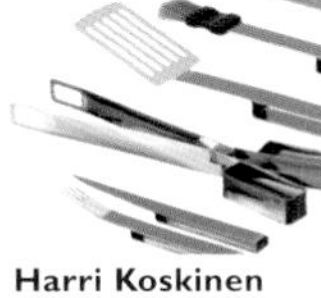
Harri Koskinen

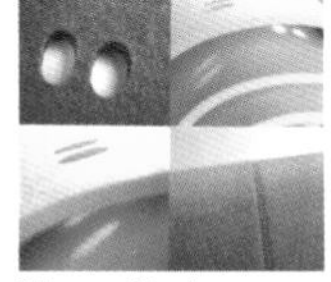
Verso Design

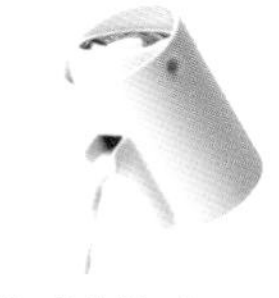
Tonfisk Design

Arihiro Miyake

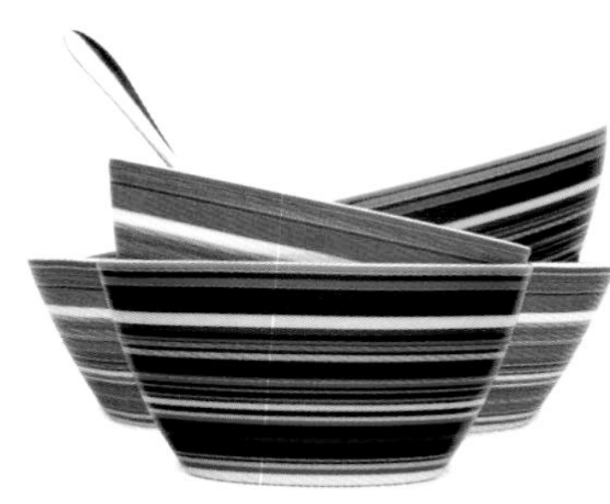
Iittala

Valvomo

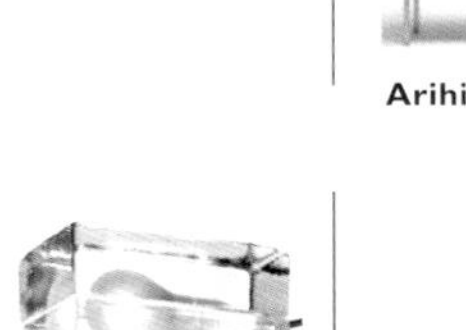
Harri Koskinen

Marimekko

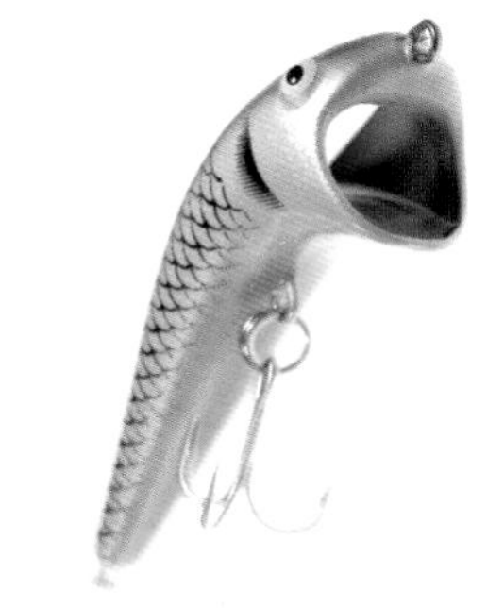
Pentagon Design

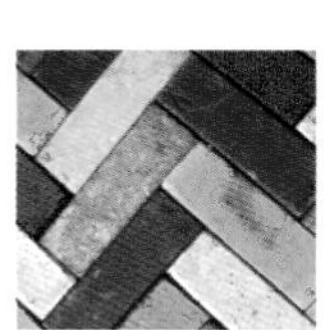
Desiree Sevelius

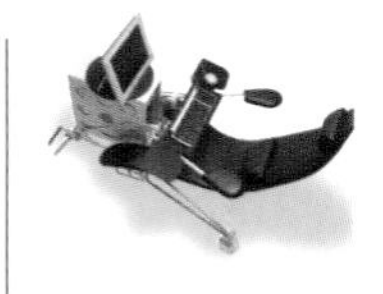
Valvomo

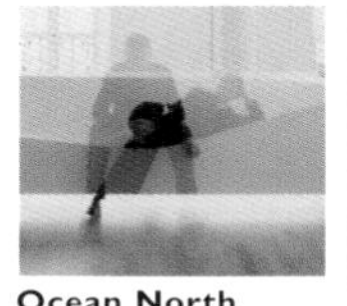
Ocean North

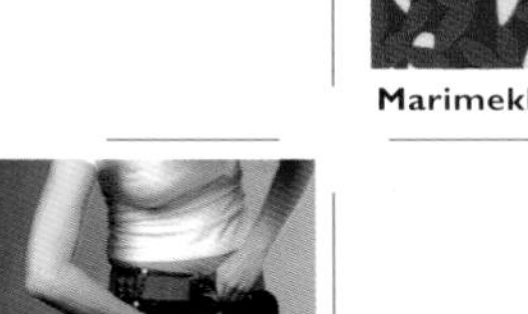
Mikko Paakkanen

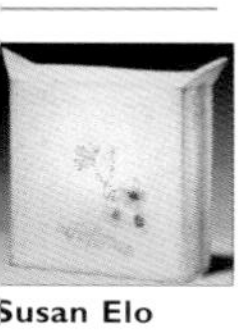
Susan Elo

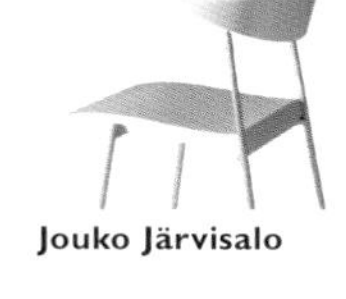
Jouko Järvisalo

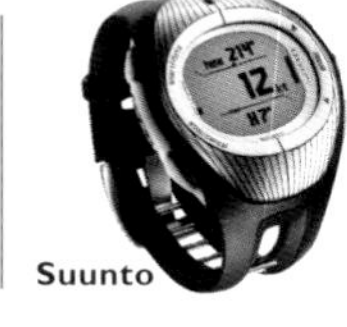
Suunto

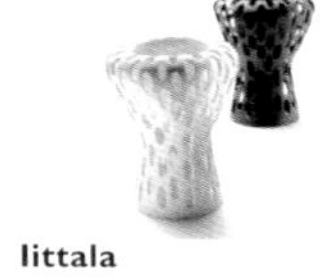
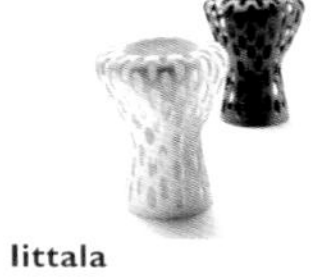
Iittala

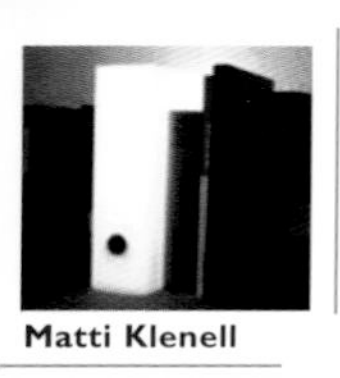
Matti Klenell

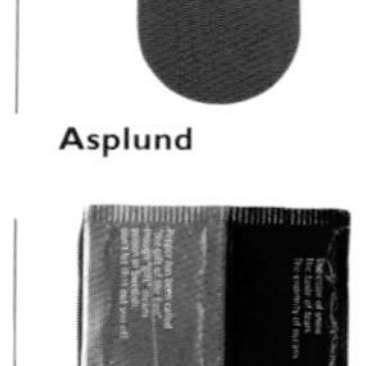
Asplund

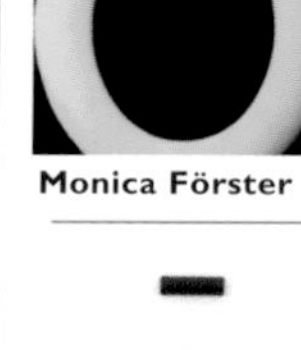
Monica Förster

Thomas Eriksson

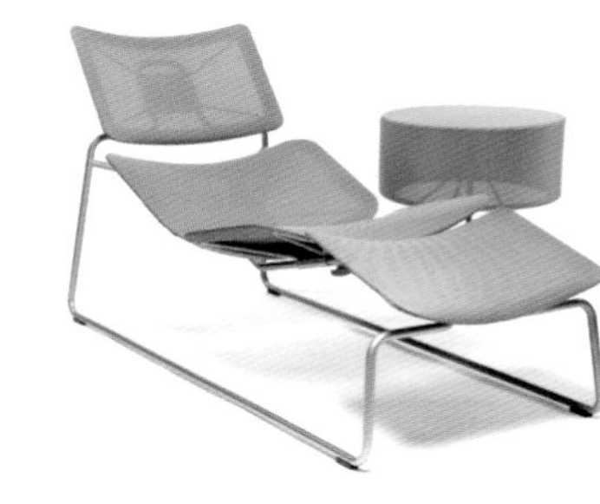
Lars Pettersson

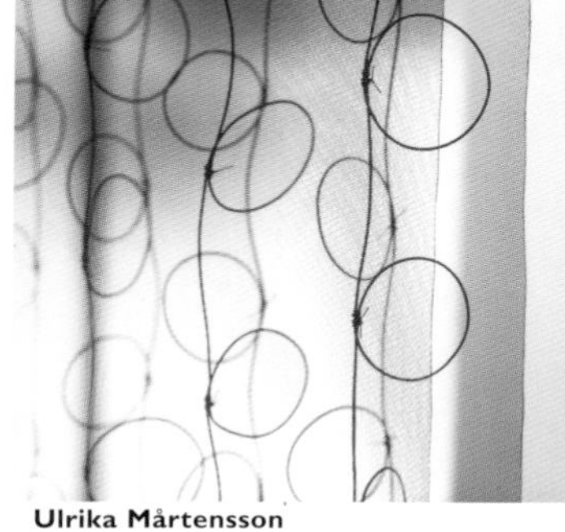
Ulrika Mårtensson

Stockholm Design Lab

Gunilla Allard

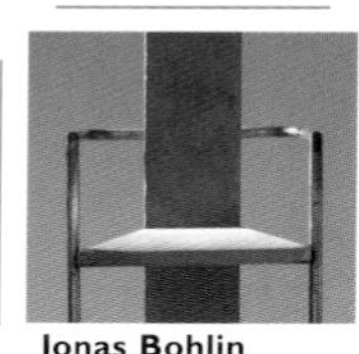
Jonas Bohlin

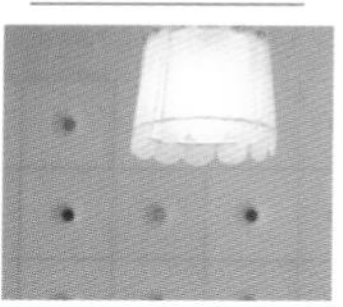
Pia Törnell

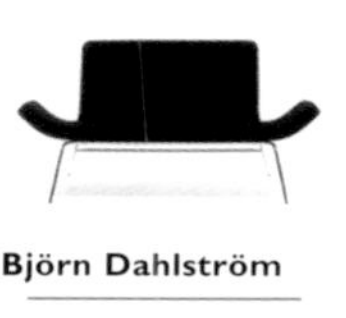
Björn Dahlström

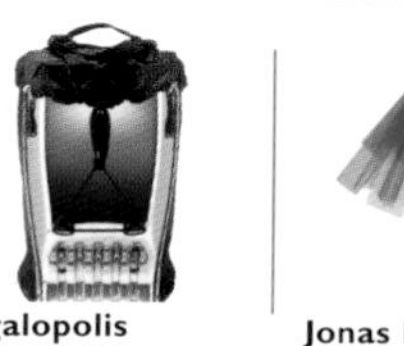
Megalopolis

Jonas Bohlin

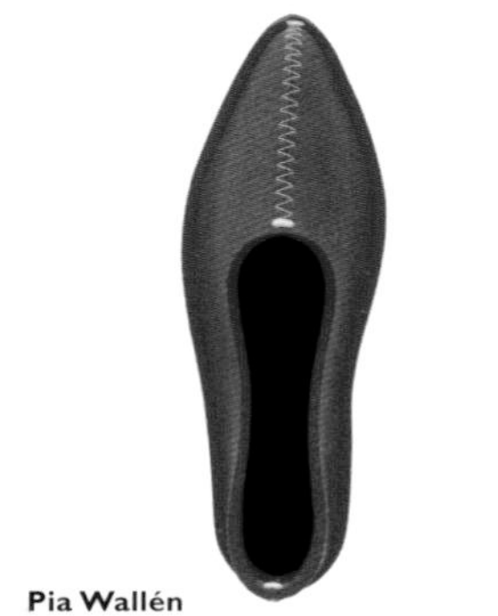
Pia Wallén

Åke Axelsson

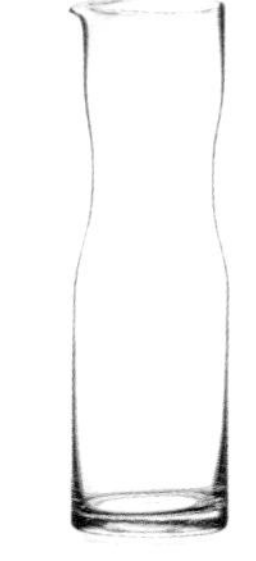
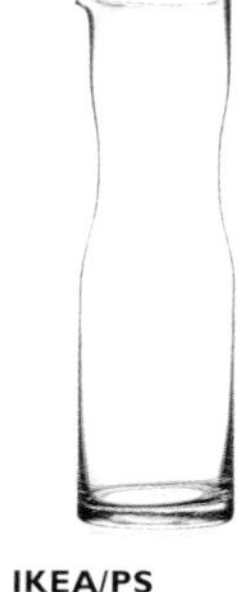
IKEA/PS

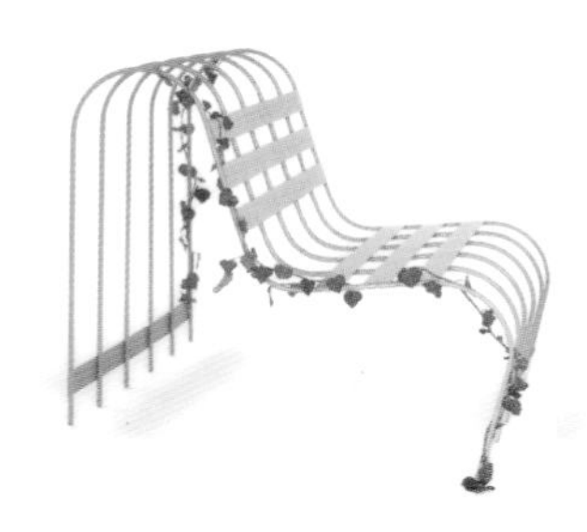
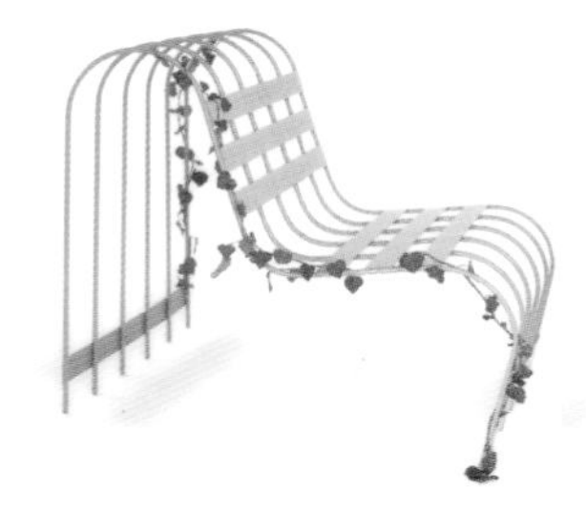
Eva Schildt

Claesson Koivisto Rune

Thomas Eriksson

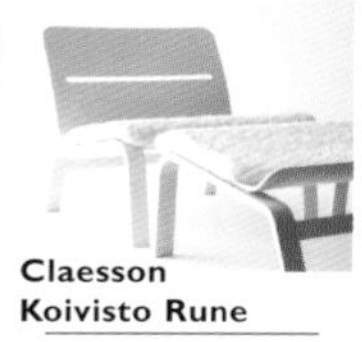
Claesson Koivisto Rune

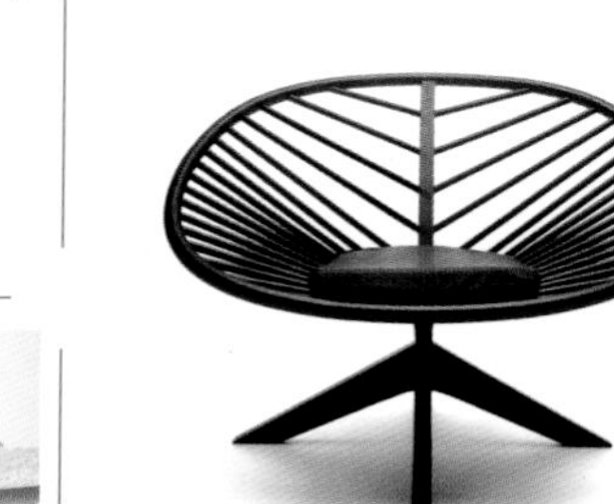
Björn Dahlström

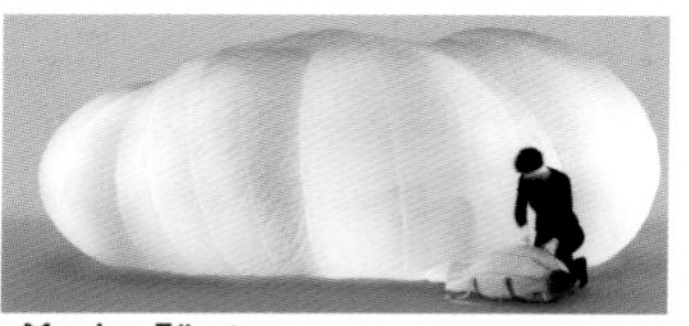
Monica Förster

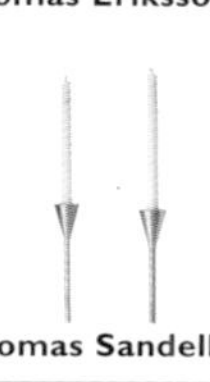
Thomas Sandell

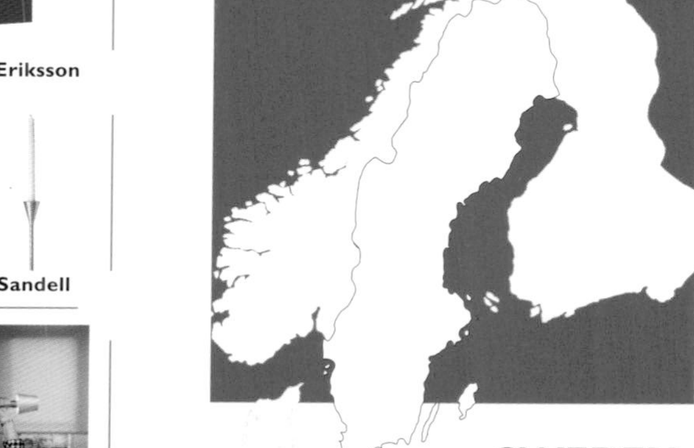

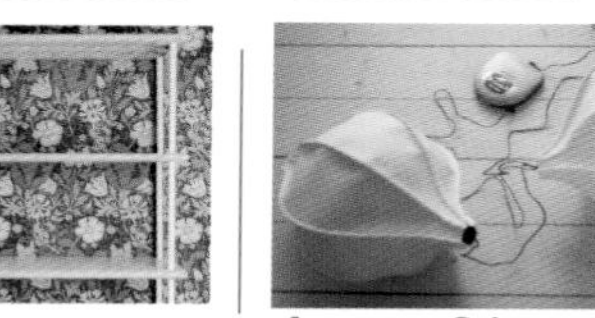
Uglycute

Anna von Schewen

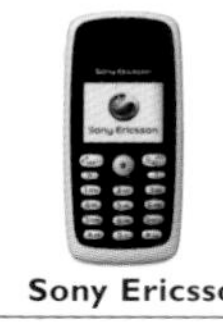
Sony Ericsson

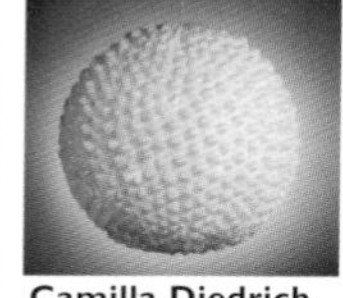
Camilla Diedrich

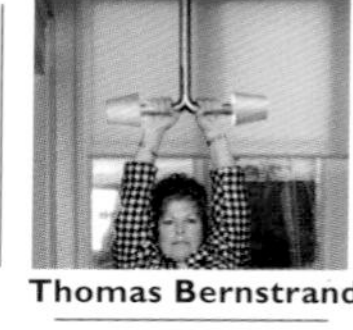
Thomas Bernstrand

Erika Mörn

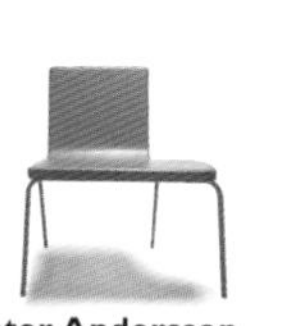
Peter Andersson

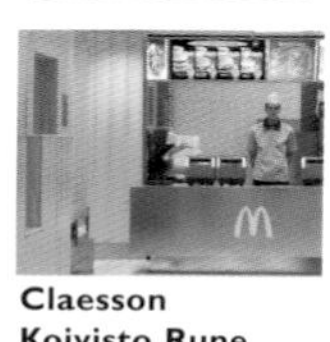
Claesson Koivisto Rune

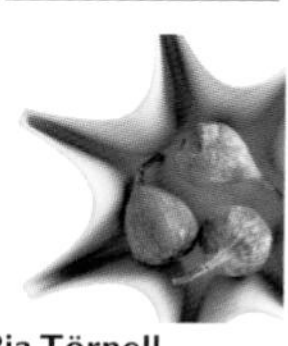
Pia Törnell

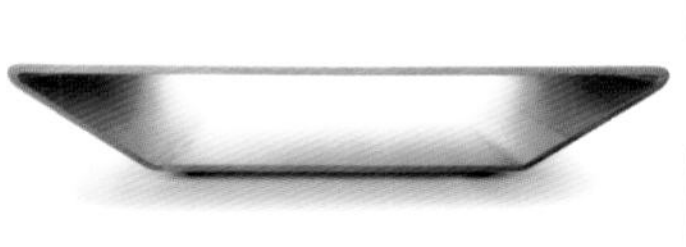
Claesson Koivisto Rune

Jessica Signell

Ergonomidesign

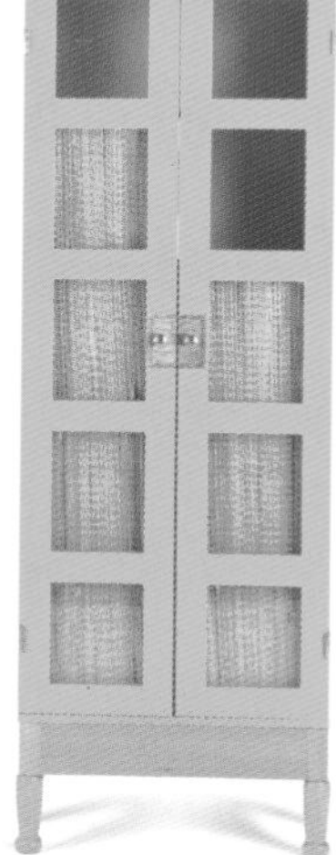
Mats Theselius

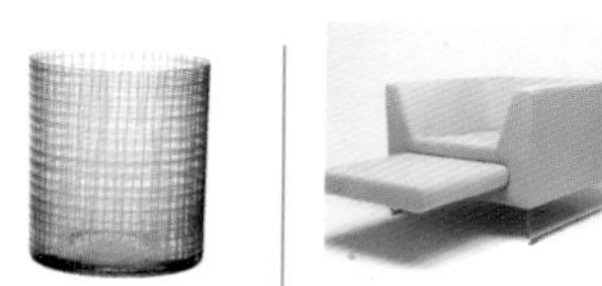
Ingegerd Råman

Thomas Bernstrand

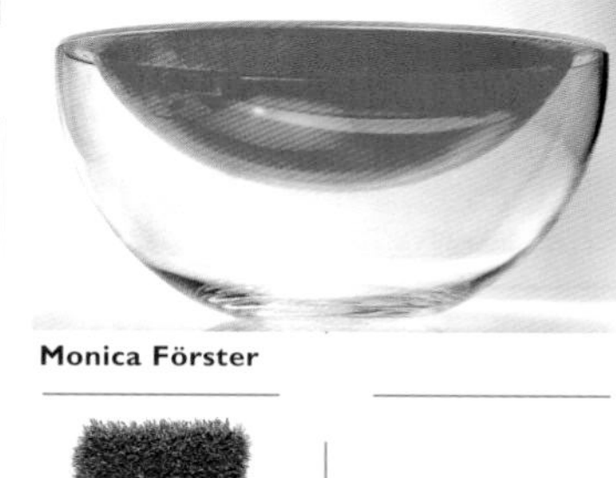
Monica Förster

Claesson Koivisto Rune

Pyra

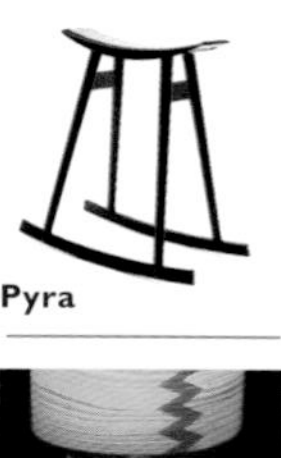
Claesson Koivisto Rune

IKEA/PS

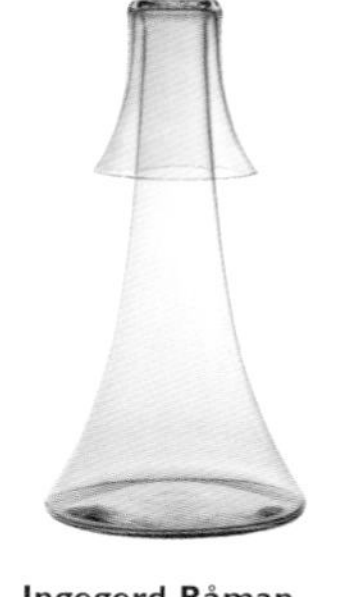
Ingegerd Råman

Gunilla Lagerhem Ullberg

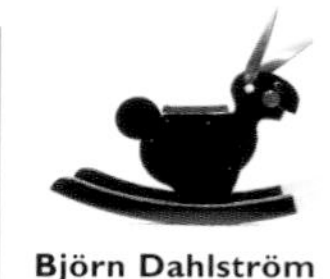
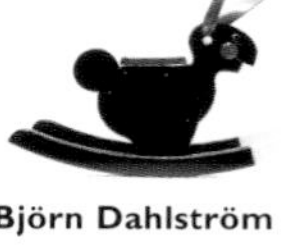
Björn Dahlström

Anna von Schewen

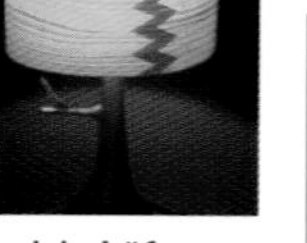
Ludvig Löfgren

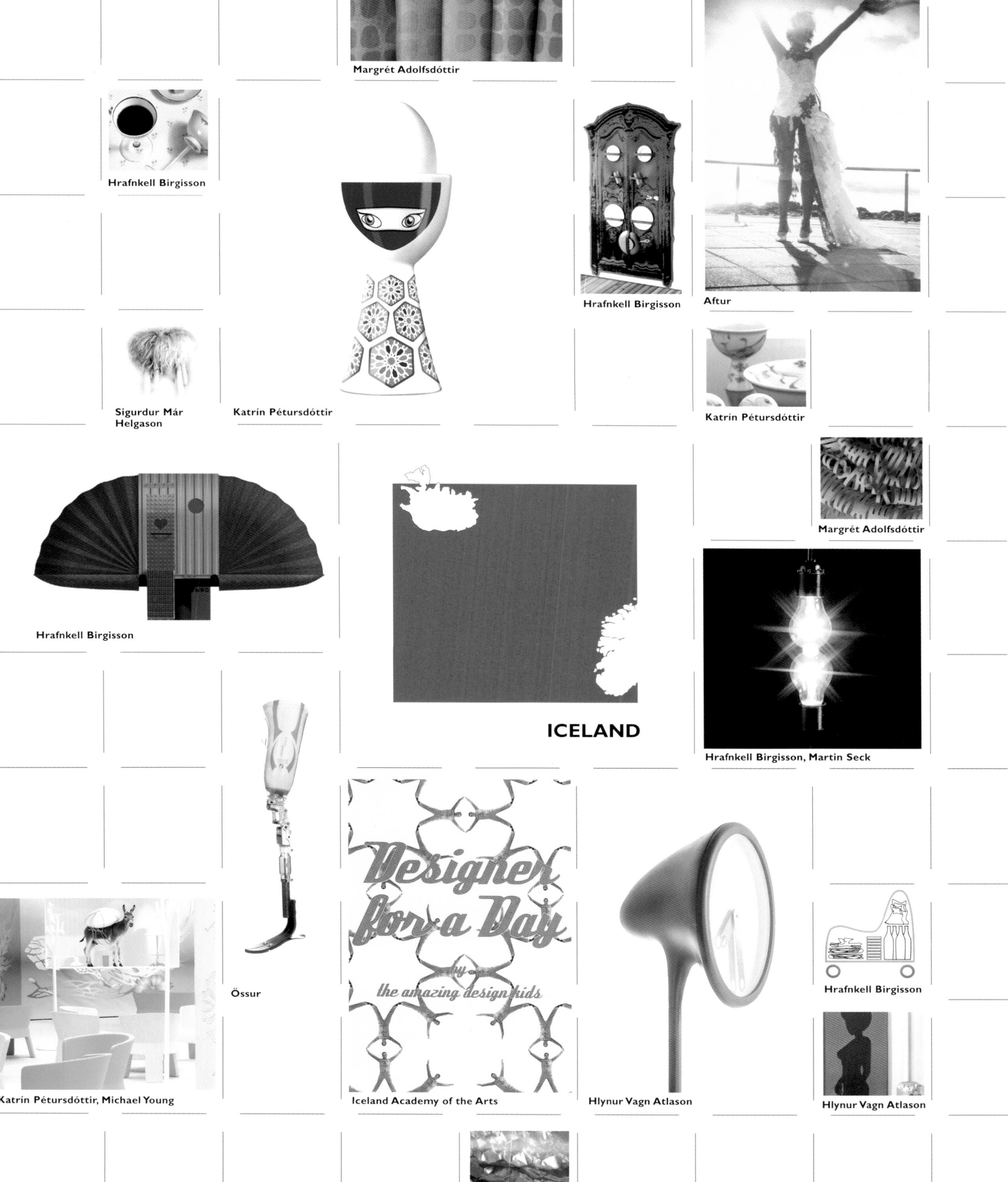

ICELAND

Margrét Adolfsdóttir

Hrafnkell Birgisson

Katrín Pétursdóttir

Hrafnkell Birgisson

Aftur

Sigurdur Már Helgason

Katrín Pétursdóttir

Margrét Adolfsdóttir

Hrafnkell Birgisson

Hrafnkell Birgisson, Martin Seck

Össur

Katrín Pétursdóttir, Michael Young

Iceland Academy of the Arts

Hlynur Vagn Atlason

Hrafnkell Birgisson

Hlynur Vagn Atlason

Margrét Adolfsdóttir

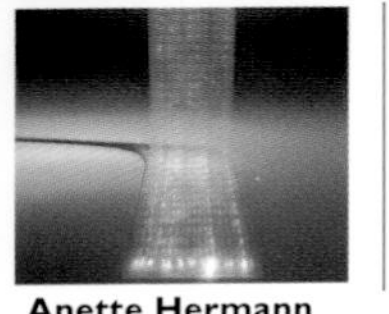
Anette Hermann

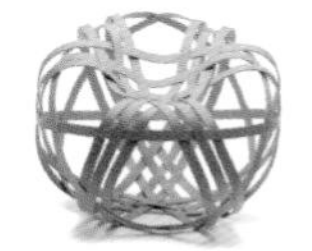
Henriette W. Leth

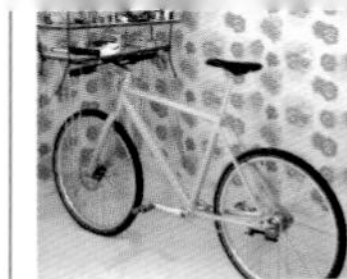
Biomega

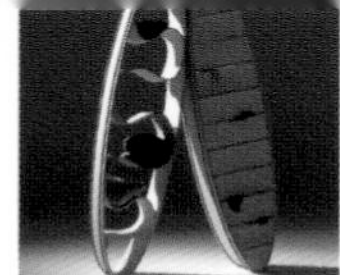
Louise Campbell

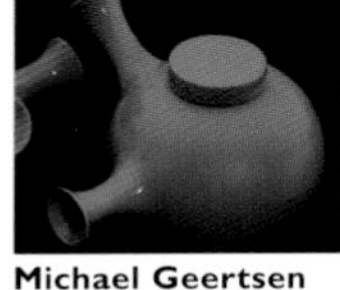
Michael Geertsen

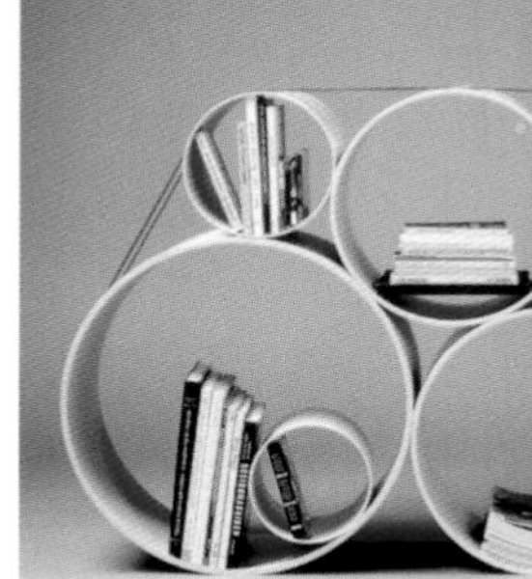
Pil Bredahl

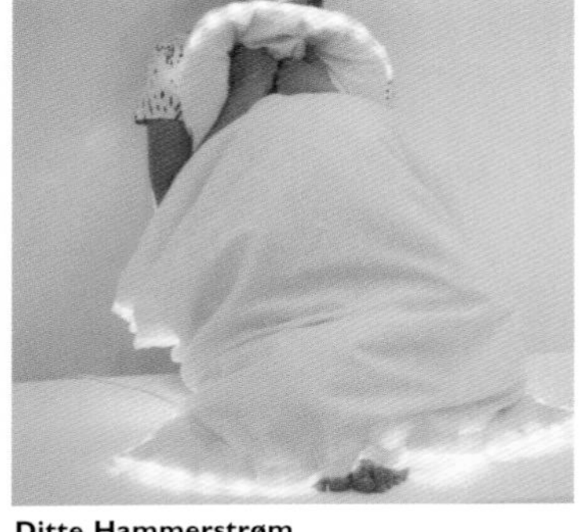
Ditte Hammerstrøm

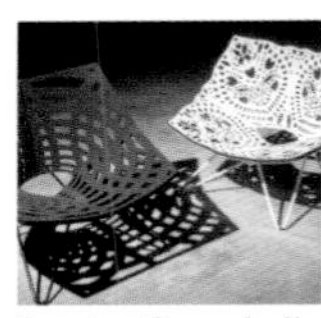
Louise Campbell

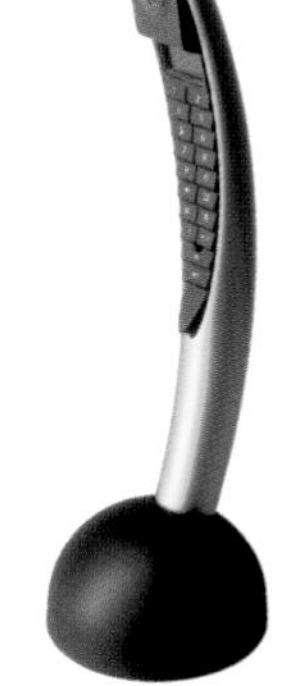
Bang & Olufsen

Pil Bredahl

Nanna Ditzel

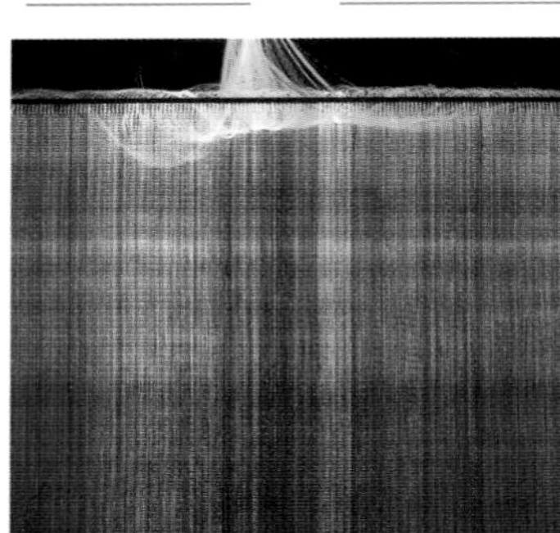
Astrid Krogh

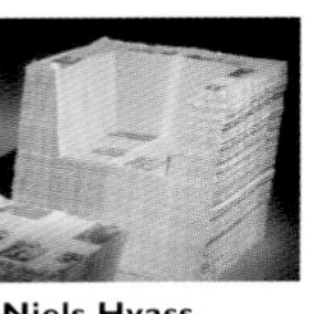
Niels Hvass

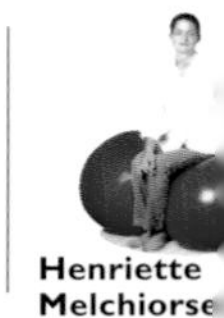
Henriette Melchiorse

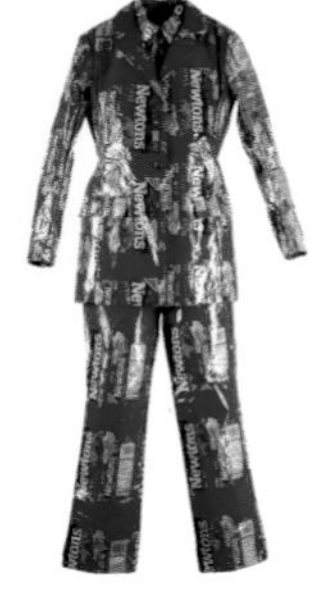
Annette Meyer

Knud Holscher Industriel Design

Hans Sandgren Jakobsen

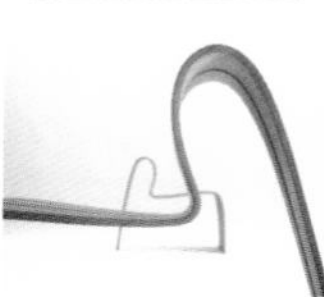
Mathias Bengtsson

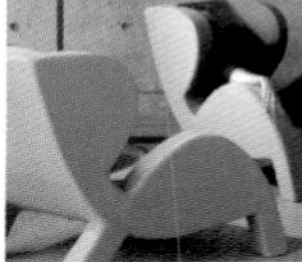
Louise Campbell

Cecilie Manz

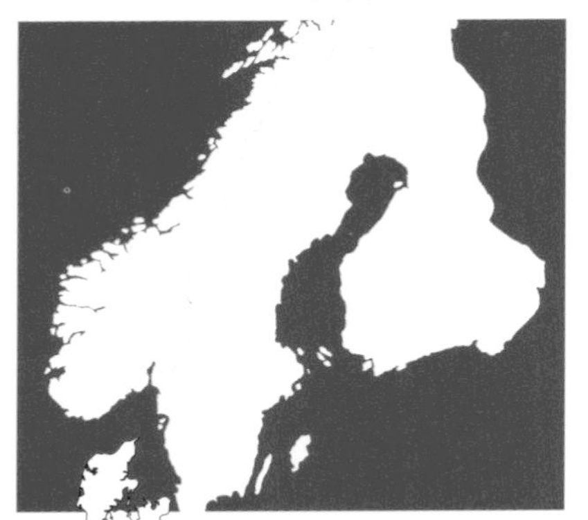
DENMARK

Louise Campbell

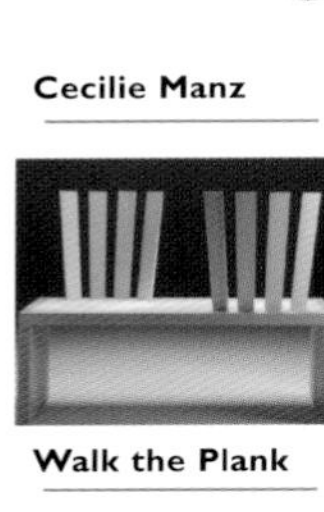
Walk the Plank

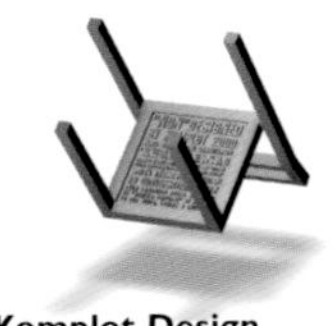
Komplot Design

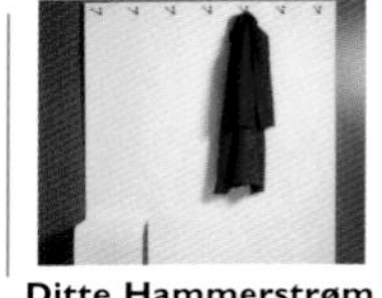
Ditte Hammerstrøm

PAPCoRN

Erik Magnusse

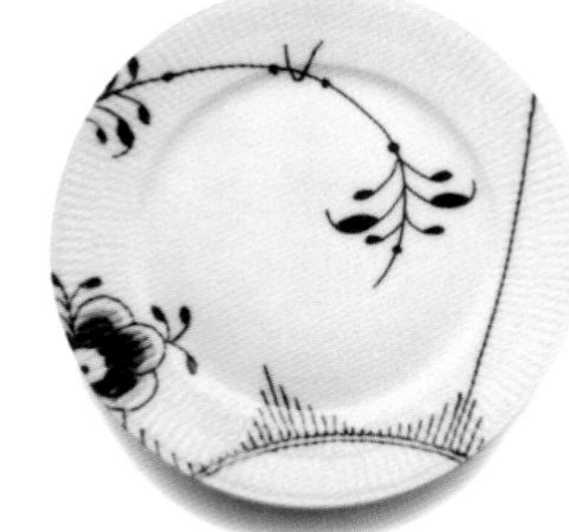
Karen Kjaeldgård-Larsen

Mathias Bengtsson

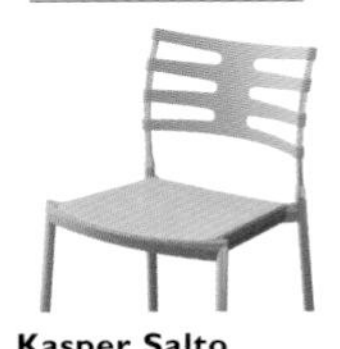
Kasper Salto

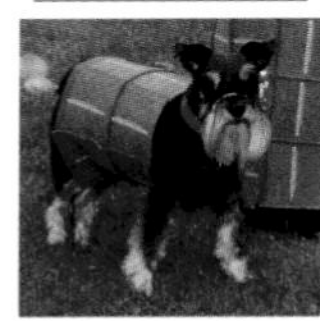
Fortunecookies

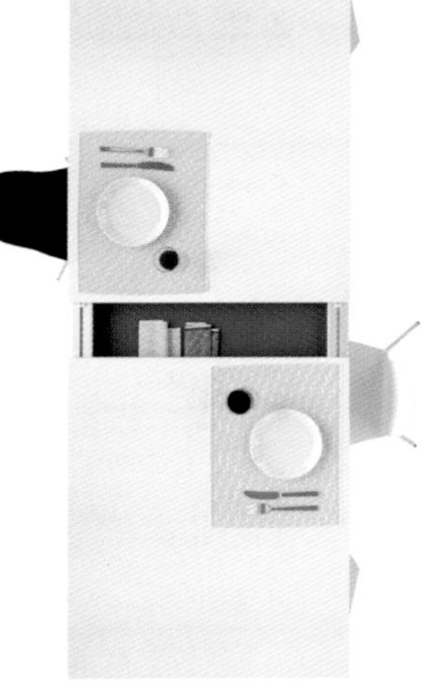
Knud Holscher Industriel Design

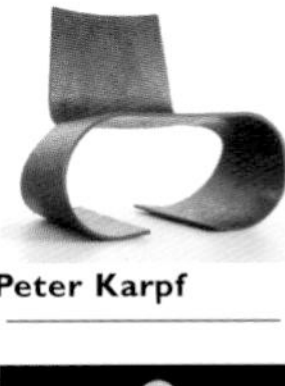
Peter Karpf

Malene Reitzel, Louise Campbell, Pernille Vea

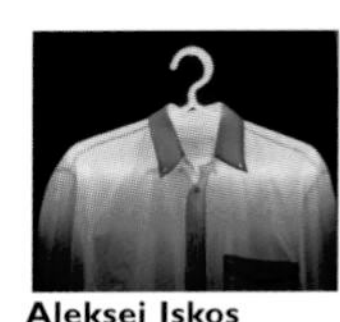
Aleksej Iskos

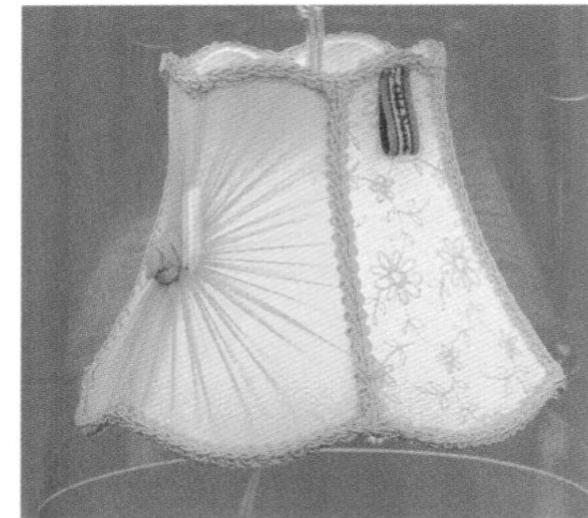
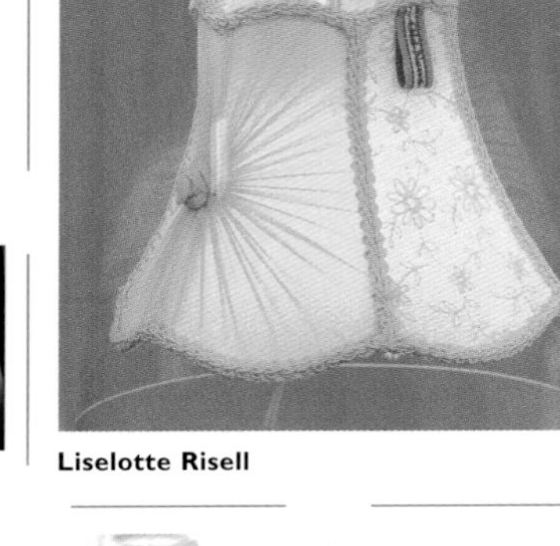
Liselotte Risell

Aleksej Iskos

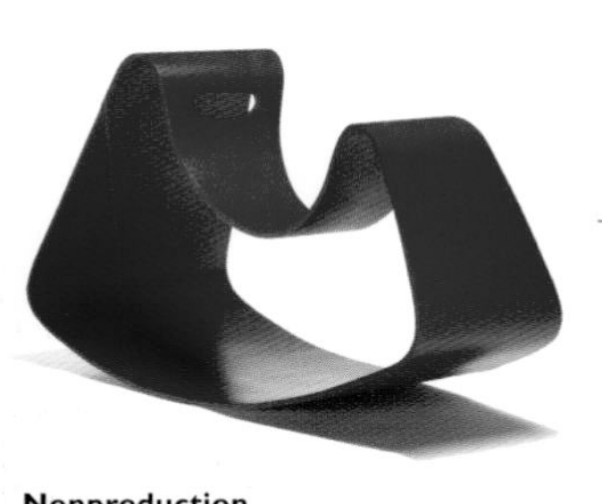
Nonproduction

Pelikan Copenhagen

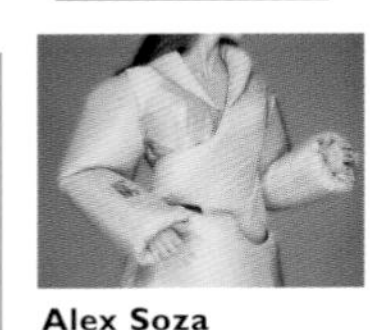
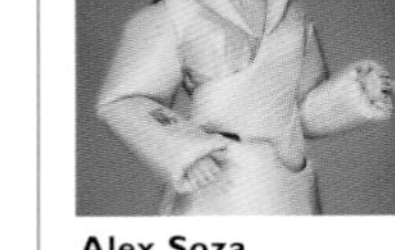
Alex Soza

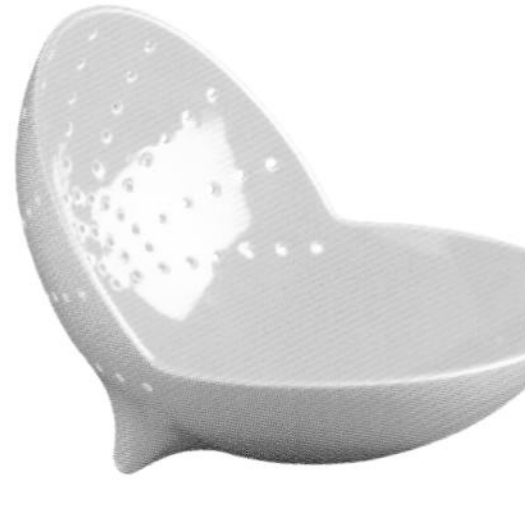
Ole Jensen

Index of Designers

by country

DENMARK

MATHIAS BENGTSSON

www.bengtssondesign.com

Line chair
(p. 231)
W 890, D 680, H 750 mm
Design: with Frank V. Holgersen

Slice chair
(p. 193)
W 890, D 680, H 750 mm

BIOMEGA

www.biomega.dk

Copenhagen bicycle
(p. 179)
Design: Jens Martin Skibsted
Photo: Tue Schiorring

PIL BREDAHL

pilbredahl@get2net.dk

1 to 100 shelf system
(p. 45)
H 90, W 150, D 35 cm
Photo: Kim Ahm

Zen-Sation cupboard
(p. 218)
H 120, W 40, D 70 cm
Photo: Dorthe Krog

LOUISE CAMPBELL

www.louisecampbell.com

Between Two Chairs
(p. 129)
W 1000, H 800, D 800 mm

Casual Cupboard
(p. 125)
W 40, H 180, D 30

The Eye of the Hurricane exhibition
(pp. 140–141)
H 12, L 200, W 200 cm (left)
H 7, L 200, W 200 cm (right)
Photos: Christian Stæhr

Fold-A sofa
(p. 155)
W 200, H 70, D 80 cm

Waiting Rooms exhibition
(p. 152)
Entertainment (chairs with built-in speakers): 39.4 x 39.4 x 35.5 in; Seesaw (rocking chair): 94.5 x 15.6 x 30 in; Leave Your Mark: 25.6 x 20 x 31.5 in. (chairs), 35.4 x 35.4 x 29.5 in (table)
All photos (with the exception of The Eye of the Hurricane): Erik Brahl

NANNA DITZEL

www.nanna-ditzel-design.dk

Butterfly chairs
(p. 121)
H 94, W 74, D 65 cm
Photo: Erik Brahl

FORTUNECOOKIES

www.fortunecookies.dk

Fortunecookies modular clothing
(p. 44)
12 x 12 cm
Design: Jacob Ravn Jürgensen, Christina Widholm, Jonas Larsen, Stine Andersen
Photo: Gabriella Dahlman

MICHAEL GEERTSEN

www.galleri-noerby.dk

The Spout and Martian teapots
(p. 240)
H 16, W 23, L 21 cm
Photo: Ole Akhøj

DITTE HAMMERSTRØM

www.hammerstroem.dk

Blanket
(p. 132)
90 x 155 cm

Hang Out
(p. 124)
190 x 159 x 86 cm
Photo: Peter M. Madsen

ANETTE HERMANN

www.plana.nu

Glory light blanket
(p. 201)
H 218, W 42, D 0.8 cm
Photo: Erik Brahl

KNUD HOLSCHER INDUSTRIEL DESIGN

www.knudholscher.dk

Laptop table
(p. 183)
W 75, L 180–240,
H 70–85 cm

Sewing machine
(p. 191)

NIELS HVASS

www.strand-hvass.com

Yesterday's News chair
(p. 221)
W 800, D 700, H 750 mm

ALEKSEJ ISKOS

aleksej@e-box.dk

Night Ghost lamp
(pp. 150–151)
H 60, W 45 cm
Photo: Planet Foto

Waterfall chandelier
(pp. 138–139)
H 90, B 60, W 60 cm
Photo: Sofie Helsted

HANS SANDGREN JAKOBSEN

www.hans-sandgren-jakobsen.com

Gallery stool (scale model)
(p. 226)
W 87, H 78, D 58 mm
Photo: Graae & Bangsboe Fotograf

OLE JENSEN

www.royalcopenhagen.com

Ole colander
(p. 57)
80 cl

PETER KARPF

www.iform.net

VOXIA series
(p. 86)
XUS (far left): W 65, D 70, H 110; seat height 37 cm
OTO (center left): W 78, D 61, H 71; seat height 38 cm
VUW(center right):46 x 46; seat height 37 cm
ECO (far right): W 45, D 48, H 81; seat height 45 cm
All photos: Johan Kalén

KAREN KJAELDGÅRD-LARSEN
www.royalcopenhagen.com
Blue Fluted MEGA pattern
(p. 248)
Various sizes
Photo: Mads Morgan

KOMPLOT DESIGN
www.komplot.dk
NON chair
(p. 153)
H 77, W 44, D 41.5; seat depth 39 cm
Design: Boris Berlin, Poul Christiansen

ASTRID KROGH
www.astridkrogh.com
Blue luminescent textile
(p. 192)
W 2.5, H 3 m
Photo: Bent Ryberg

HENRIETTE W. LETH
www.thechair.dk
The Big Apple chair
(p. 147)
Diameter 85 cm
Photo: Stewart Mc Intyre

DAVID LEWIS
www.bang-olufsen.com
BeoCom 2 telephone
(p. 175)
H 272; diameter 28 mm
Photo: Ib Sørensen

ERIK MAGNUSSEN
www.stelton.com
Spaghetti spoon
(p. 53)
H 3, W 4, L 29 cm

CECILIE MANZ
www.manzlab.dk
Homage chair
(p. 154)
46 x 46 x 45/88 cm
Crafted by Ernst Rasmussen and Soeren Risvang
Photo: Peter Krasilnikoff

HENRIETTE MELCHIORSEN
designhm@get2net.dk
The Flying Chair
(p. 128)
W 120, D 100, H 80 cm
Photo: Bjarne Birger

ANNETTE MEYER
www.annettemeyer.com
BODYWRAPPInc.NY three-piece suit
(p. 137)
150 x 55 cm
Photo: Erik Molberg Hansen

NONPRODUCTION
www.nonproduction.dk
Fabel I
(p. 103)
L 1000, W 460, H 640 mm
Design: Rikke Rützou Arnved
Photo: Martin Soelyst

PAPCORN
www.papcorn.dk
Biodegradable tableware
(p. 189)
28 x 18 x 3 cm
Design: Lene Vad Jensen, Anne Bannick
Photographer: Claus Christensen

PELIKAN COPENHAGEN
www.pelikan.dk
IKEA/PS Tea Light
(p. 57)
H 45, W 70 mm; diameter 50 mm
Design: Ehlén Johansson

MALENE REITZEL
http://malenereitzel.homepage.dk
The Eye of the Hurricane exhibition
(pp. 140–141)
H 12, L 200, W 200 cm (left)
H 7, L 200, W 200 cm (right)
Photos: Christian Stæhr

LISELOTTE RISELL
liselotte.risell@teliamail.dk
Old News lamp
(p. 253)
18 x 13 cm
Photo: Dorte Krogh

KASPER SALTO
www.kaspersalto.com
Ice chair
(pp. 12, 176)
H 79, W 50, D 48; seat height 45 cm

ALEX SOZA
www.alexsoza.com
Bionic Smart Jacket
(p. 199)
Photo: Peter Svendsen

PERNILLE VEA
vea@oncable.dk
The Eye of the Hurricane exhibition
(pp. 140–141)
H 12, L 200, W 200 cm (left)
H 7, L 200, W 200 cm (right)
Photos: Christian Stæhr

WALK THE PLANK
www.walktheplank.dk
(p. 230)
Design: Various

FINLAND

SARI ANTTONEN
www.reflexdesign.net
Kiss chair
(p. 34)
48 x 53 x 83 cm
Photo: Marja Helander
Nen table (from the Tubab series)
(p. 40)
46/80 x 95 x 77 cm; 60/95 x 60 x 77 cm

SUSAN ELO
susan.elo@saunalahti.fi
Butterfly lamp
(p. 223)
H 240, W 240, D 90 mm

MARKKU HEDMAN
markku.hedman@hut.fi
Summer Container
(p. 47)
2800 x 3500 x 2400 mm

HARRI HELORINNE
www.hydestudiot.com
Omakuva ryijy rug
(p. 241)
115 x 115 cm

IITTALA
www.iittala.com
Basket vase
(p. 224)
H 19 cm
Design: Kristina Riska
Essence glassware
(p. 102)
Various sizes
Design: Alfredo Häberli
Orgio mugs and bowls
(p. 105)
Various sizes
Design: Alfredo Häberli

IVANA HELSINKI
www.ivanahelsinki.com
Telttatakki ("Tent Jacket")
(p. 1)
Various sizes
Design: Paola Ivana Suhonen
Photo: Maria Miklas

TEEMU JÄRVI
www.hkt-korhonen.fi
Vera chair
(p. 229)
H 77, W 50, D 56 cm
Photo: Marja Helander

JOUKO JÄRVISALO
www.mobel.net
Mokka chair
(p. 79)
H 725, W 500, D 525; seat height 450 mm
Photo: Jussi Tiainen

HARRI KOSKINEN
www.harrikoskinen.com
Air service
(p. 46)
Various sizes
Block lamp
(p. 131)
16 x 10 x 10 cm
Hackman barbecue utensils
(p. 31)
Varied from 35 x 9 x 5 to 19 x 2 x 1.5 cm
Lantern
(p. 81)
H 60, W 15 cm

OLAVI LINDÉN
www.fiskars.com
Poultry shear
(p. 30)
260 x 86 mm

STEFAN LINDFORS
www.lindfors.net
Neste motor oil canisters for Neste
(p. 31)
Photo: Marco Melander

MARIMEKKO
www.marimekko.fi
Kaktus pattern
(p. 30)
Various sizes
Design: Erja Hirvi

ARIHIRO MIYAKE
arihiro@hotmail.com
1789/Cupboard
(p. 80)
H 1350, W 1190, D 435 mm (small); H 1350, W 1770, D 435 mm (big)
Photo: Benjamin Rinner

NOKIA
www.nokia.com
Communicator 9210i
(p. 168)
158 x 56 x 27 mm
Design: Panu Johansson

OCEAN NORTH
www.ocean-north.net
Formations architectural installation
(p. 172)
Design: Tuuli Sotamaa, Kivi Sotamaa
Photo: Carlo Lavatori
MoRay dining dish (from the Manta Ray series)
(p. 207)
22 x 22 x 6 cm
Design: Tuuli Sotamaa, Kivi Sotamaa

MIKKO PAAKKANEN
www.studiohelsinki.com
Belt
(p. 56)
1230 mm

PENTAGON DESIGN
www.pentagondesign.fi
Nils Master Big Mouth fishing lure
(p. 171)
75 x 17 mm;
swimming depth 0–2 m
Design: Tani Muhonen
Photo: Pekka Kiirala

PERHONEN
www.perhonen.com
Anemone lamp and table
(p. 245)
Diameter 30–40 cm (lamp);
various sizes (table)
Design: Anna Katriina Tilli, Mari Relander
Photo: Liisa Valonen
Rocking Chair
(p. 88–89)
Design: Anna Katriina Tilli
W 500, D 650, H 850 mm
Photo: Manu Rantanen

PANNU PUOLAKKA
ppuolakka@hotmail.com
TV2 ryijy rug
(p. 243)
146 x 176 cm
Photo: Jani Mahkonen

ANNE KYYRÖ QUINN
www.annekyyroquinn.com
Bold, Target, and Loop cushions
(p. 216)
various sizes
Linea throw
(p. 216)
145 x 160 cm

TIMO SALLI
salli@timosalli.com
Jack-in-the-Box television cabinet
(p. 186)
H 600, W 550, D 500 mm

Tramp easy chair
(p. 207)
H 880, W 670, D 900 mm

DESIREE SEVELIUS
http://futurehome.uiah.fi
Handmade bricks and tiles
(p. 178)
30 x 30 cm maximum

SHOWROOM FINLAND
www.showroomfinland.fi
PLY wall surfacing
(p. 198)
60 x 60 cm
Design: Jouko Kärkkäinen
Photo: Marja Helander

ILKKA SUPPANEN
www.suppanen.com
Flying Carpet sofa
(p. 188)
1600 x 800 x 950 cm
Photo: Ninna Kuismanen

SUUNTO
www.suunto.com
M9 Sailing and G9 Golf wrist-top computers
(p. 187)
53 mm (case);
18 mm (thickness)
Design: Kimmo Pernu, Topi Lintukangas, Mikko Ahlström
Photo: Studio Opte

TONFISK DESIGN
www.tonfisk-design.fi
OMA lemon squeezer
(p. 228)
H 7; diameter 10 cm
Design: Susanna Hoikkala, Jenni Ojala
Warm teapot and teacup
(p. 220)
0.6 or 1.1 liter (teapots), 0.24 or 0.4 liter (cups)
Design: Brian Keaney, Tony Alfström
All photos Jefunne Gimpel

VALVOMO
www.valvomo.com
Globlow lamp
(p. 173)
H 1780; diameter 800 mm
Design: Vesa Hinkola, Markus Nevalainen, Rane Vaskivuori
Netsurfer computer divan
(p. 202)
W 1610, D 780, H 980 mm
Design: Teppo Asikainen, Ilkka Terho
All photos: Urban Hedlund

VERSO DESIGN
www.versodesign.fi
Polku carpets
(p. 217)
150 x 220 cm (Polku 1);
diameter 160 cm (Polku 2)
Design: Elina Keltto, Tuttu Sillanpää

WOODNOTES
www.woodnotes.fi
Points textile reliefs
(p. 193)
30 x 40 cm each
Design: Ritva Puotila
Photo: Sameli Rantanen

ICELAND

MARGRÉT ADOLFSDÓTTIR
sa-tex@dircon.co.uk
Laser-cut, layered, and laminated textiles
(p. 200)
Various sizes
Design: with Leo Santos-Shaw

AFTUR
www.aftur.com
Dress
(p. 244)

HRAFNKELL BIRGISSON
www.hrafnkell.com
Hab portable cabinet
(p. 122)
Various sizes
High Heel Cups
(p. 247)
Diameter approx. 10 cm
Homobile furniture
(p. 122)
70 x 70–140, x 76 cm
Sleep and Go hotel pod
(p. 123)
240 x 200 x 350 cm (closed),
670 x 200 x 350 cm (open)
Trajektiv lamp
(p. 133)
21 x 6 cm
Photo: Martin Seck

SIGURDUR MÁR HELGASON
Fuzzy stool
(p. 158)
H 16; diameter 14.5 in
(assembled)

ICELAND ACADEMY OF THE ARTS
www.lhi.is
Designer for a Day brochure
(pp. 38–39)
H 33, W 24 cm
Design: Högni Jónsson, Ísak Winther, Ódinn Bolli Björgvinsson, Phoebe Jenkins, Gudrún Edda Einarsdóttir, Gudfinna Mjöll Magnúsdóttir, Lóa Audunsdóttir, Brynhildur Pálsdóttir, Páll Einarsson, Sighvatur Ómar Kristinsson, Ragnheidur Tryggvadóttir, Sigrídur Ævarsdóttir

ÖSSUR
www.ossur.com
Prosthetic leg
(p. 182)
Various sizes

KATRÍN PÉTURSDÓTTIR
katrin@lhi.is
Friends eggcup
(p. 136)
Approx. 120 x 50 mm
Fudge tableware
(p. 134)
Various sizes
Rambler exhibition
(p. 116)
From 400 x 400 to
500 x 600 cm
Design: a collaboration with Michael Young

HLYNUR VAGN ATLASON
www.atlason.com
Woman window shade
(p. 157)
24 x 60 in
Photo: Ioulex
IKEA/PS Tunö clock
(p. 163)
H 31 1/8–47 5/8;
diameter 14 1/8 in

NORWAY

HAREIDE DESIGNMILL
www.hareide-designmill.no
AutoSock
(p. 181)
Various sizes
Design: Anders Hansen
Photo: Bård Løtveit

LARS ERNST HOLE
www.holedesign.com
CD-Rundell
(pp. 11, 246)
H 120, W 15 cm;
diameter 90 cm
Photo: Bård Ek

OLAV JOA

www.figgjo.com

Figgjo Boat form
(p. 111)
12 x 8 x 2.5 cm

K8 INDUSTRIDESIGN

www.k8.no

Papp Fiction design exhibition
(p. 54)
W 6, H 2, D 6 cm (egg cup);
W 11, L 28, H 7 cm (slippers)
Design: with Hanna Design and Kystgaz
Photo: Trine Vallevik Håbjørg

LINDA LIEN

linda.lien@kritt.no

ReachUp Chair
(p. 83)
H 92, D 45, W 40 cm
Design: with Camilla Songe-Møller
Photo: Espen Strand Pedersen/Kallen Fotostudio

CATHRINE MASKE

www.artoslo.com

Chopsticks
(p. 71)
28 x 4 cm
Design: with Espen Voll

PlussMinus salt and peppershakers
(p. 92)
8 x 3 cm
All photos: Bjørn Olaf Johannessen

EIRIK LUND NIELSEN

www.adidas.com

Kobe Two shoes
(p. 180)
Various sizes

NORWAY SAYS

www.norwaysays.com

Konrad chair
(p. 91)
Design: Torbjørn Anderssen
W 70, H 65, D 70 cm
Photo: Eirik Brekke

Papermaster magazine rack
(p. 227)
H 30, W 32, L 73 cm
Design: Torbjørn Anderssen
Photo: Mir Visuals

Seza sofa
(p. 76)
W 120 x L 120 cm
Design: Frode Myhr
Photo: Mir Visuals

PETER OPSVIK

www.opsvik.no

Balans Gravity rocker
(p. 106)
W 0.65, H 1.20, D 1.30 m
Photo: Odd Steinar Tøllefsen

PERMAFROST

www.permafrost.no

Room with a View pillow
(p. 149)
90 x 90 x 20 cm
Design: Tore Vinje Brustad, Eivind Halseth, Oskar Johansen, Andreas Murray

THINK NORDIC

www.thinkev.com

TH!NK City electric vehicle
(p. 177)
L 3.14, W 1.64, H 1.56 m
Design: Stig Olav Skeie, Katinka von der Lippe
Photo: Knut Bry/TinAgent

CATHRINE TORHAUG

www.torh.no

Flash chaise lounge
(p. 126)
H 83, W 146, D 53 cm
Photo: Anders Corneliussen

JOHAN VERDE

www.verde.no

Spir teapot
(p. 100)
120, 70, 40 cl
Photo: Egon Gade

Sunrise ice cream bar
(p. 35)
H 15 cm

SWEDEN

GUNILLA ALLARD

www.lammhults.se

Cooper easy chair
(p. 99)
H 111, W 71;
seat height 43 cm
Photo: Pelle Wahlgren

PETER ANDERSSON

www.peterandersson.com

Solidarity chair
(p. 37)
W 55, H 78, D 56 cm
Photo: Fredrik Sandin Carlsson

ASPLUND

www.asplund.org

Egg carpet
(p. 104)
W 1200, L 1800 mm
Design: Mats Bigert, Lars Bergström
Photo: Patrick Engqvist

ÅKE AXELSSON

www.galleristolen.se

Anselm chair
(p. 76)
W 41.5, D 49, H 85 cm
Photo Lennart Durehed

THOMAS BERNSTRAND

www.bernstrand.com

Boxer armchair
(p. 82)
600 x 800 x 800 mm
Photo: Fredrik Sandin Carlsson

Do Swing chandelier
(p. 36)
500 x 460 x 80 mm
Photo: Bianca Pillet

JONAS BLANKING

www.boblbee.com

Megalopolis backpack
(pp. 184–185)
56 x 30 x 20 cm
Photo: Emil Larsson

Delite backpack
(p. 21)
49 x 29 x 15 cm
Photo: Jonas Ingerstedt

JONAS BOHLIN

www.scandinaviandesign.com/jonasbohlin

Concrete chair
(p. 130)
H 490 cm

LIV floor lamp
(p. 146)
H 188 cm
All photos: Lennart Kaltea

CLAESSON KOIVISTO RUNE

www.claesson-koivisto-rune.se

Beckham coatrack
(p. 84)
W 155, D 50 , H 164 cm
Photo: Anna & Petra

Bowie chair and footstool
(p. 78)
W 70, D 72, H 70 cm
Photo: Anna & Petra

Brasilia table
(p. 68)
W 120, D 120, H 28 cm
Design: Eero Koivisto, Ola Rune

Omni chair and footstool
(p. 85)
W 70, D 80, H 97
Design: Mårten Claesson, Eero Koivisto

PO 0018 vase
(p. 77)
W 30, D 30, H 28 cm
Design: Ola Rune
Photo: Louise Billgert

McDonald's restaurant interior
(p. 58)
360 sq m
Photo: Åke E:son Lindman

BJÖRN DAHLSTRÖM

www.dahlstromdesign.se

BD 5 Easy Chair
(p. 93)
43 x 51 x D 39.5 inches
Photo: Jonas Linell

Rocking Rabbit
(p. 42)
H 390, W 270, D 740 mm

Superstructure easy chair
(p. 225)
H 888, W 1080, D 1080 mm
Photo: Jonas Linell

CAMILLA DIEDRICH

www.diedrich.se

Bubble lamp BPL
(p. 156)
Diameter 390 and 650 mm
Photo: Bengt Wanselius

THOMAS ERIKSSON

www.teark.se

IKEA/PS Clock
(p. 26)
H 470, W 280 mm

Red Cross cabinet
(p. 73)
H 435, W 435, D 150 mm

ERGONOMIDESIGN

www.ergonomidesign.com

Mushroom knife for K J Eriksson AB, Mora
(p. 63)
160 x 70 x 30 mm
Design: Maria Benktzon, John Grieves
Photo: Camilla Sjödin

MONICA FÖRSTER

monica.forster@swipnet.se

Cloud, an inflatable meeting room
(pp. 32–33)
4 x 5m

Glow-in-the dark toilet seat
(p. 41)
410 x 320 mm

Bowl (from the Mix series)
(p. 52)
314 x 131 mm
Photo: Stefan Nilsson

IKEA

www.ikea.com

IKEA/PS Carafe
(p. 29)
1 liter
Design: Sofia Uddén

IKEA/PS Lömsk swivel chair
(p. 2)
W 59, D 62, H 75;
seat height 17 cm
Design: Monika Mulder

IKEA/PS Hoppig trampoline
(p. 65)
H 30, W 94 cm
Design: Carina Bengs, Eva Lilja Löwenhielm

IKEA/PS Virrig balance cushions
(p. 64)
H 24; diameter 72 cm
Design: Eva Lilja Löwenhielm

MATTI KLENELL
www.mattiklenell.com

Enlightenment lamp
(p. 90)
H 22, W 7, D 16 cm

GUNILLA LAGERHEM ULLBERG
www.kasthall.com

Moss carpet
(p. 242)
Customized in any size and shape; pile depth approx. 40 mm

LUDVIG LÖFGREN
www.weworkinafragilematerial.com

Northern Enlightenment lamp
(p. 127)
H 400, W 200, D 200 mm

ULRIKA MÅRTENSSON
www.hv-atelje.com

Inner-Outer textile panel
(p. 219)
230 x 50 cm
Photo: Nisse Petersson

ERIKA MÖRN
www.david.se

Wool wine cooler
(p. 43)
H 270 mm; diameter 90 mm
Photo: Anna & Petra

LARS PETTERSSON
www.larsdesign.se

Eno chaise lounge
(p. 190)
625 x 1650 x 780 mm
Photo: Fredrik Sandin Carlsson

PYRA
www.pyra.se

Imprint
(p. 222) (top left)
H 84 (45), D 49, W 40 cm
Design: Kristina Jonasson

Lillängen
(p. 222) (top right)
H 85, F 52, W 71 cm
Design: Mårten Cyrén

Ving
(p. 222) (bottom left)
H 58.5, D 28.5, W 56 cm
design: Per Sundstedt

Storängen
(p. 222) (bottom right)
H 133, D 56, W 78 cm
Design: Mårten Cyrén

INGEGERD RÅMAN
www.orrefors.se

Slowfox vase
(p. 215)
H 330, W100 mm
Photo: Rolf Lind

Tanteralla decanter
(p. 74)
H 220, W 110 mm
Photo: Per Larsson

THOMAS SANDELL
www.sandellsandberg.se

Lucia candlestick
(p. 100)
H 28 cm
Photo: Patrick Engqvist

EVA SCHILDT
www.evaschildt.se

The Gardener's Sofa
(p. 119)
90 x 76 x 85 cm
Photo: Åsa Kristenson

JESSICA SIGNELL
www.jessicasignell.com

Omtanke bowl
(p. 55)
H 16, W 24 cm
Photo: August Eriksson

SONY ERICSSON
www.sonyericsson.com

T300 mobile phone
(p. 170)
106 x 42 x 22 mm
Design: Henrik Jensfelt, Rodolfo DeLeon

STOCKHOLM DESIGN LAB
www.stockholmdesignlab.se

SAS corporate-identity and airport-lounge design program
(p. 98)
Photos: Jens Mårtensen, Stellan Herner, Peter Lederling, Åke E:son Lindman

SAS salt, pepper and sugar packets
(p. 148)
10.5 x 6 cm
Design: Björn Kusoffsky
Photo: Jens Mårtensen

MATS THESELIUS
www.theselius.com

National Geographic cabinet
(p. 120)
H 171, W 74, D 65

PIA TÖRNELL
http://home.swipnet.se/pia_tornell

Asteria bowl
(p. 87)
H 5.5, diameter 30 cm

Swedish Museum of Architecture tiles
(p. 101)
25 x 25 cm
Photo Åke E:son Lindman

UGLYCUTE
www.uglycute.com

Shelf
(p. 239)
H 120, W 60, D 30 cm
Design: Markus Degerman, Jonas Nobel, Andreas Nobel, Fredrik Stenberg

ANNA VON SCHEWEN
www.annavonschewen.com

Sound Object
(p. 135)
Diameter 30 cm

Vase (from the What's New series)
(pp. 232–233)
H 48 cm

PIA WALLÉN
www.piawallen.se

Unisex slipper
(p. 212)
Various sizes
Photo: Fredrik Lierberath

Subject Index

Selected Bibliography

Aav, Marianne and Stritzler-Levine, Nina. *Finnish Modern Design.* New Haven and London: The Bard Graduate Center for Studies in the Decorative Arts/Yale University Press, 1998.

Ellison, Michael and Piña, Leslie. *Designed for Life: Scandinavian Modern Furnishings 1930-1970.* Atglen, PA: Schiffer Publishing, 2002.

Fiell, Charlotte and Fiell, Peter. *Scandinavian Design.* Köln: Taschen, 2002.

Hägströmer, Denise. *Swedish Design.* Stockholm: The Swedish Institute, 2001.

Helgesson, Susanne and Nyberg, Kent. *Swedish Design: The Best in Swedish Design Today.* London: Mitchell Beazley, 2002.

Hiort, Esbjørn. *Finn Juhl: A Biography.* Copenhagen: The Danish Architectural Press, 1990.

Klanten, Robert and Hellige, Hendrik. *North by North: Scandinavian Graphic Design.* Berlin: Die Gestalten Verlag, 2002.

McFadden, David Revere, Ed. *Scandinavian Modern Design 1880-1980.* New York: Cooper-Hewitt and Harry N. Abrams, 1983.

Mount, Christopher (Bartolucci, Marisa and Cabra, Raul, eds.). *Arne Jacobsen: Compact Design Portfolio.* San Francisco: Chronicle Books, 2004.

Oda, Noritsugu. *Danish Chairs.* San Francisco: Chronicle Books, 1999.

Polster, Bernd. *Design Directory Scandinavia.* London: Pavilion Books Limited, 1999.

Thau, Carsten and Vindum, Kjeld. *Arne Jacobsen,* Copenhagen: Danish Architectural Press, 2001.

Tuukkanen, Pirkko, ed. *Alvar Aalto Designer.* Jyväskylä: Aalvar Aalto Foundation/Alvar Aalto Museum, 2002.

Wickman, Kerstin. *Orrefors: A Century of Swedish Glassmaking.* Stockholm: Byggforlaget, 1998.

Photography and Design Credits

SAS Royal Hotel lobby, Copenhagen
(p. 2)
Design: Arne Jacobsen

Country images
(pp. 3–7)
Jokulsarlon, Iceland (p. 3), The Blue Lagoon, Iceland (p. 4), Rune Wikstrom, Sweden (p. 5), Grinda Wardshus historic hotel, Sweden (p. 6), Kjell Karlsson, Sweden (p. 7)
Photos: Catherine Karnow

Nordic Embassy Complex
(pp. 22–23)
Photos: Christian Richters
Design: Nielsen, Nielsen & Nielsen (Danish Embassy), Wingårdh Arkitektkontor (Swedish Embassy), VIIVA Arkkitehtuuri (Finnish Embassy), SNØHETTA (Norwegian Embassy), Arkitekt Palmar Kristmundsson (Icelandic Embassy), Berger + Parkkinen architekten (common building and master plan)

Hydro Texaco Vinterbro gas station
(pp. 113–114)
Photo: Lasse Hedberg; design: Andisdahl Sand and Partnere, Odd Thorsen Design & Arkitektur

Blue Lagoon
(pp.165–166)
Photos: Björn Th. Sigurdsson
Design: VA Architects

Arabianranta
(pp. 209–210)
Photos: Jefunne Gimpel (inset), Voitto Niemela (Media Centre Lume tower)
Map: Helsinki City Planning Office
Design: Mikko Heikkinen and Markku Komonen (Media Centre Lume)

Øresund bridge
(pp.255–256)
Photos: Miklos Szabo
Design: ASO Group, ISC, Georg Rotne

Acknowledgments

We are extremely grateful to numerous individuals and institutions whose encouragement and support made this book possible. We offer special thanks to Amelie Heinsjö, Claes Jernaeus, and Elisabeth Halvarsson-Stapen of the Consulate General of Sweden in New York; Charlotte Juul of the Swedish Institute in Stockholm; Irene Krarup and Ane Mandrup Pedersen of the Royal Danish Consulate General in New York; Eva Moksnes Vincent of the Royal Norwegian Consulate General in New York; Kristine Hauer Århus of the Royal Norwegian Ministry of Foreign Affairs in Oslo; Ilkka Kalliomaa of the Consulate General of Finland in New York; Pétur Óskarsson of the Consulate General of Iceland in New York; and Pétur Ómar Ágústsson of Icelandic Tourist Board in New York.

Special thanks are also extended to Mait Juhlin; Yrjö Sotamaa and Outi Raatikainen of the University of Art and Design, Helsinki; Anna-Maija Ylimaula; Sari Anttonen; Marja Korkeela and Riika Finni of Marimekko; Leena Venho of Fiskars; Päivi Jantunen and Lisa Sounio of Designor Oy; Anne Stenros of Design Forum Finland; Birgitta Capetillo of the Danish Design Center; Kent Martinussen of the Danish Center for Architecture; Peter Husted of Stelton; Birgitte Jahn and Dorthe Rud Michaelsen of Danish Crafts; Peter S. Meyer and Mette Strømgaard Dalby of Trapholt Museum of Modern Danish Art, Applied Art, and Furniture Design; Hans Sandgren Jakobsen; Eigil Thomsen, Dorrit Nielsen, and Claus Bundgaard of Bang & Olufsen; Ulla Riemer of Louis Poulsen; Kropsholder; Gunnel Hasselbalch of IKEA; Christina Grossmann and Claus-Christian Eckhardt of Lund University; Karin Lindahl of Orrefors-Kosta Boda. Peter Bodor of Sony Ericsson; Stefan Ytterborn of Ytterborn & Fuentes; Cilla Robach of the National Museum of Fine Arts in Stockholm; Clara Skoog Åhlvik and Annika Enqvist of the Swedish Society of Crafts and Design; Susanne Lorenz-Brynolfsson and Dag Klockby of Galleri Stolen; Widar Halén of Museum of Decorative Arts and Design, Oslo; Peter Opsvik and Anita Iversen; Per Farstad; Jan R. Stavik and Eline Strøm-Gundersen of the Norwegian Design Council; Ole Rikard Høisæther; Margrét Ólafsdóttir and Gudn ý Magnúsdóttir of Form Island; Gudmundur Oddur Magnússon and Halldór Gíslason of Iceland Academy of the Arts; Adalsteinn Ingólfsson of the Museum of Design and Applied Art. Thanks are extended to the numerous Nordic designers who provided us with their time and photographic material.

We would also like to thank our editor, Alan Rapp, for his insight and steadfast support, Karen O'Donnell Stein for her deft copyediting, and Piper Grimsrud and Jillian Moffett for their vital art, permissions, and administrative assistance.

Katherine E. Nelson extends her thanks to Ariana Donalds and Carrie Chase Reynolds for their invaluable editorial suggestions; also Martin Fox; Todd Pruzan; Christopher Mount; Carl Liungman; Vanessa Druschel Guida; Thomas Juncher Jensen; Carl Dieker and Paula von Seth; Maud and Thorsten Lunderquist; Thomas Lunderquist, Linda Gustavsson, and Ester Lunderquist; Brit and Finn Kavli; Annika Wester; Per and Maj Britt Bjellerup and family; Robert and Julie Dickson; Robert and Margaret Green; Paul Sanford Toney and Chris Marchese; Keith and Paddy Nelson; and Jane Wallace. I dedicate this book to Eric Wolske.

Raul Cabra also extends thanks to Katherine Karnow, Anna-Li Carlson, Tintin Blackwell, Wesley Ito, Hotel Birger Jarl in Stockholm, Betty Ho, Michael Sledge, and as always, Walter.

HLOOW 745
.2094
8
N427

NELSON, KATHERINE E.
NEW SCANDINAVIAN
DESIGN
LOOSCAN
03/07